AUTHORITY
to birth
REVIVAL

AUTHORITY
to birth
REVIVAL

POWER OF GOD IS FOUND IN
THE
SECRET PLACE

VOLUME 4.

Ric Steininger

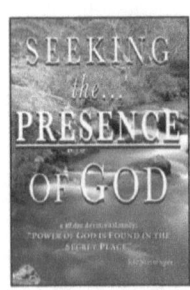   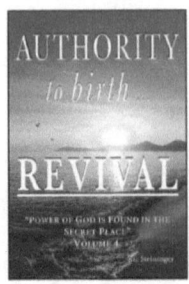

POWER OF GOD IS FOUND IN THE SECRET PLACE

Volume 1. *"Seeking the Presence of God"*
Volume 2. *"A Study on Spiritual Warfare"*
Volume 3. *"Planting Heaven on Earth"*
Volume 4. *"Authority to Birth Revival"*

Copyright © 2024 Ric Steininger
Text, photography, and design by Ric Steininger
Published by Ric J Steininger Publications Pty Ltd
Release date: 3 September 2024
ISBN: 978-0-9581633-8-5 *SB*, 978-0-9581633-9-2 *HB*, 978-1-7637385-0-8 *eBook*
Email: BirthingRevivalMinistries@gmail.com
Facebook: Birthing Revival Ministries
X @BirthRevivalMin

Wholesale orders please email: BirthingRevivalMinistries@gmail.com

All rights reserved. No part of this book may be reproduced or transmitted in any form or by any means, electronic or mechanical, including photocopying, recording, or by any information storage and retrieval system, without permission in writing from the copyright owner.
Scripture quotations marked NKJV are taken from the New King James Version. Copyright © 1982 by Thomas Nelson, Inc. Used by permission. All rights reserved.
Scripture quotations marked NIV are taken from the Holy Bible, New International Version®. NIV®. Copyright © 1973, 1978, 1984 by International Bible Society. Used by permission of Zondervan. All rights reserved. [Biblica]
Scripture quotations marked AMP are from The Amplified Bible, Old Testament copyright © 1965, 1987 by the Zondervan Corporation. The Amplified Bible, New Testament copyright © 1954, 1958, 1987 by The Lockman Foundation. Used by permission. All rights reserved.
Scripture quotations marked TPT are taken from The Passion Translation®. Copyright © 2017, 2018 by Passion & Fire Ministries, Inc. Used by permission. All rights reserved. ThePassionTranslation.com.

Intimacy
in the Father,
in closest of relationship,
abiding in the Bosom
of the Almighty,
one can truly
make Him **known**.

John 1:18

THE BIRTHING OF SPIRITUAL MOVES

This book is centred around the incredible prospect that as born again believers we have capacity to initiate Moves of God. Initiate Outpourings of the Spirit and Revivals of God. That you and I have the capacity inherent, through the Blood and gifted Holy Spirit; to *release* the Salvation of the Lord.

Over the generations, Christian culture has held the vision of only looking up to God in times of need. When it has been God, all this time, who has been longing to *relocate* you. Reposition and restore you back in realms of Dominion, where you release the Power of God.

For just as Elijah left a 'double' anointing for his disciple Elisha to pick up, so has Jesus to those who love and follow Him; to do even *greater* works than He. Not only to speak or prophesy but walk in the Resurrected Power of the Son.

Jesus came to *"Pour out Fire on the earth"*. And what is that ... this *Fire?* But to walk in the Glory of God where you make change, where you move Heaven and earth ... where you *trigger* moves of God.

I pray that you are most blessed with the thoughts contained in this book. And though it might start off a little slow, you soon will have to strap in for a ride that will radically change your life.

This book is the fourth in a series titled, *"The Power of God is Found in the Secret Place"*. And though I really value the journey the Lord has had me on leading to this publication; what is contained in this book will open you to Heavenly Wonders … *far* beyond human comprehension.

Today, when looking around the world, there is so much grief and sorrow. So much evil spreading across the land. But you and I, we are not alone … we are not orphans*!* Hence, I so deeply encourage you, now is the time to rise up in your true identity; rise up in your sonship 'revealed' — as *Child* of the Living God. As is said:

> *"Creation waits in eager expectation for the children of God to be revealed."*
>
> *Romans 8:19*

Each one of us are called into something vastly bigger than just believing in Jesus. We are called to *become* Him. For truly, all creation is yearning in earnest for us to step into who we truly are in Christ Jesus. And then what is said shall come to pass, *"The earth shall be filled with the* **knowledge** *of the Glory of the Lord, as the waters cover the sea."*

Bless you, in Jesus Name.

Ric

In gratitude to:

David Hogan,
who powerfully introduced me
to the Fire of God.

My pastors,
Danielle and Massey Dixon
who greatly welcomed and supported
and made a home for me.

And pastors,
Rodney and Bev Wallis
who stood by me
in dark hours.

To my Mum and Dad,
whose faith never wavered.

THE BREAKING OF THE STRONGMAN

*Encounters with God,
in the Fire of His Holy Presence,
breaks the strongman, and
ushers forth great Moves of God.*

Moses,
*and the burning bush
before Pharaoh.*

Daniel,
*fasting and praying,
and Archangel Michael
sent to confront the
'Prince of Persia'.*

Jesus,
*sent by the Holy Spirit,
dealt with Satan in the Desert.
And returned full of the
Power of the Holy Spirit.
And His fame
spread across the nation.*

Ps. Jimmy Njino

CONTENTS:

i.	Communion in God	2

LIVING IN A STATE OF PERPETUAL ENCOUNTER

1.	Ascension	8
2.	Perpetual Encounter	11
3.	Sea of Sapphire	14
4.	Ancient Gates	21
5.	Zion	29
6.	Passing Through the Door	40

THE JOY SET BEFORE HIM

7.	The Joy Set Before Him	54
8.	The Outpouring of the Spirit	63
9.	Heaven Empowered	69
10.	Co-Habitation	80
11.	It's Not About Me!	93
12.	Presence is a Weapon	103

UNION IN HIM

13.	Come up in Me (part 1)	111
14.	Come up in Me (part 2)	120

AARON'S STAFF

15.	Faith Wrought Through Encounter	130
16.	Aaron's Staff	142
17.	Dominion Over the Birds (part 1)	153
18.	Dominion Over the Birds (part 2)	168

COMMAND A HARVEST
19.	*Roar of a Lion*	*183*
20.	*Command a Harvest (part 1)*	*202*
21.	*Command a Harvest (part 2)*	*214*
22.	*Waiting Upon the Lord*	*228*
23.	*Revivals and the Glory Come*	*250*

MOUNT SINAI, THE WAY OF THE ANOINTED
24.	*Mount Sinai, the Way of the Anointed*	*267*
25.	*Training for Kingship*	*275*
26.	*Realms of Dominion and Anointing*	*286*
27.	*Meet with God*	*294*
28.	*Way Maker*	*308*
29.	*Banqueting Table (part 1)*	*326*
30.	*Banqueting Table (part 2)*	*344*
31.	*Banqueting Table (part 3)*	*349*
32.	*Banqueting Table (part 4)*	*358*
33.	*Relationship: 'Born to Rule'*	*371*

THE PERSON OF GOD WITH US
34.	*Evolutional Leap*	*397*
35.	*Blueprints from Heaven*	*417*
36.	*Shekinah Glory*	*439*

AUTHORITY TO BIRTH REVIVAL
37.	*Authority to Birth Revival*	*463*
38.	*Manifesting Sonship (part 1)*	*477*
39.	*Manifesting Sonship (part 2)*	*485*
40.	*Manifesting Sonship (part 3)*	*504*

AN INTRODUCTION

An Introduction (#83)
COMMUNION IN GOD

Opening Scripture:
Therefore, believers, since we have confidence and full freedom to enter the Holy Place [the place where God dwells] by [means of] the Blood of Jesus, by this new and living way which He initiated and opened for us through the Veil [as in the Holy of Holies], that is, through His flesh [His broken Body], and since we have a great and wonderful Priest [who rules] over the house of God, let us **approach** [God] with a true and sincere heart in unqualified assurance of faith, having had our hearts sprinkled clean from an evil conscience and our bodies washed with pure water. Let us seize and hold tightly the confession of our hope without wavering, for He who promised is reliable and trustworthy and faithful [to His word]. *(Hebrews 10:19-23 AMP)*

What is the purpose of Communion? Like the Passover Meal, it reminds us of what God has done. But also, it reminds us of what God as **yet** desires to do. For like in the Exodus story, the Salvation of the Lord is not the end, but only the beginning of what God desires for each one of us. It is a birth ... a doorway of openings to the vastness of the Dreams of God revealed.

The word 'Communion', what does it mean to you? Communication ... meaning, personal **dialogue** in the Person of God. It can also mean 'Commune', the joining and being made part of the Community of Heaven.

But most importantly, the reality of Communion is this: the **Dining** with the very Person of Jesus [a]. For as you dine in Him, so too are you also continually fed and given of from Heaven. Built up in the spiritual 'bones' of your inner-man in great Strength, Hope, and Power.

A number of Scriptures talk about this. In the Book of Revelation [b], it speaks of how Jesus constantly is knocking at your door. And if you would honestly 'listen to His Voice' and open your heart to Him, so would He come in and 'dine' together with you.

In the Gospel of Luke [c], Jesus talks about how He desires to 'prepare you a Meal', whereby He has you 'recline', and in 'dressing Himself to serve' … **waits** upon you. In the Gospel of John [d], Jesus speaks of how from your innermost being 'Rivers of Living Water' shall flow. And in the book of Isaiah [m], here in the realms of the Presence of God, He will 'prepare a rich feast' for all the people, 'a banquet of aged wine … the best of meats and the finest of wines'.

My testimony of this is expressed in a previous chapter titled *(Vol. 2 [e])*, *"My Jesus Loves to Cook me Pancakes"*. This chapter is about how, as a dear and most close trusted Friend … Jesus likes to surprise me. And in coming to my home, new and fresh each day … shares yet another 'morsel' of Wonder.

I was speaking of this to a lady recently, who told me she had been suffering greatly from anxieties, fears, and worries. Her daughters as well … suffering the same, even with thoughts of suicide. And I shared with her how one can make a 'date' with Jesus, and how important and valuable it is each day. And how the Person of Jesus deeply desires to come, and have you personally *recline* in His Presence, and Minister personally richly into your life.

I said to her, that if she would open herself up and make a regular and purposed *date* with Jesus, to meet with Him … He would come. Pray about your needs, yes … but more importantly, pray for Encounter. Seek and ask for personal close meetings with the Lord of Glory … and when He is ready, He will come.

You know what? The very next day she came and told me that she did what I said and had made *4pm* her time in the Lord. She said that such a Peace came over her, something that she had not experienced before. And as we know … this is but the 'residue' of the Presence of God [f]. He has so much more in store.

Scripture:
For by the one offering He has perfected forever and completely cleansed those who are being sanctified [bringing each believer to spiritual completion and maturity]. And the Holy Spirit also adds His testimony to us [in confirmation of this]; for after having said,

"This is the covenant that I will make with them after those days, says the Lord: I will imprint my laws upon their heart, and on their mind I will inscribe them [producing an inward change]," He then says, "And their sins and their lawless acts I will remember no more [no longer holding their sins against them]." Now where there is [absolute] forgiveness and complete cancellation of the penalty of these things, there is no longer any offering [to be made to atone] for sin. *(Hebrews 10:14-18 AMP)*

We can go to God with our needs and problems, and that is good and that is right. But God has greater Desire and Promises *(ie; 'Promised Land')* for each one of us than we know. So let Him become greater than your needs, your issues, and your problems.

You can live under problems, going from one problem to another. However, raise your sights higher than problems and issues — and seek the Face of God. For Jesus Himself is the '**Door**' — and as you pass through in Him so are you given Grace and Capacity that surpass understanding. [g]

Keep your sights set High on Him and it will be He who raises your sights higher and higher [h]. Even being continually 'taken' in fresh Visions and Dreams, with ideas and doors continually opened [i]. Keep raising your sights High in Him and you'll find yourself replaced by Him. His Presence will come upon you in very real ways … *inexpressible*.

The continual *heart-chatter* of the Lord will speak in your soul and thought-life; these same 'Whispers' of the Lord that are laced with the burning Joy and Love of God. And when you think that your sights are high in Him, they are only taken higher and higher [j]. So now, when looking at problems and needs, they appear so small; even the mountains of impossibilities … *inconsequential*. And when you speak you see great change. [k]

Before, you were always under problems and needs, going from one problem to another. But now God has raised you up over them; something has been given you from Above. And in the course of time, you see impossible problems just fade away as 'chaff in the Wind' [l]. For you are abiding in the 'Community' of the

Kingdom of God. Walking among the Hosts of Heaven … and being taken Places man cannot go.

So now one can better understand the word 'Blessings' a bit more; for this is when Jesus and His angels scheme together for your good. But now also is the word 'Anointing' better understood; for this is where you together scheme with Jesus and His angels … releasing good.

Such is the Power of the Blood and the Body broken of the Lord, the Wine and the Bread. For as you dine with Him — in the grand Banqueting Halls of Heaven [m] — it is Jesus who lifts you out from the 'miry mud' [n] and sets you in high Honour. It is He who takes you out of the 'gutter and alleyways' [o] and sets you within the Company of God. This being not for the self-sufficient or the righteous, but for the broken … and the hungry.

———————

"Adam walked with God in the cool of the evening.
So too, as '**my child**' are you to the praise of His Glory." [p]

"Call to me, and I will answer you,
and will tell [and show] you
great and hidden things,
which you do not know
[mighty, mysterious, and unsearchable]." [r]
(Jeremiah 33:3)

… in Memory of Mum and Dad. [q]

Appendix:

a. John 6:56-57, ***b.*** Revelation 3:20, ***c.*** Luke 12:37, ***d.*** John 7:38, ***e.*** chapter #56, *"My Jesus Loves to Cook me Pancakes"*, ***f.*** Galatians 5:22-23, ***g.*** Philippians 4:7, ***h.*** Colossians 3:2-3, ***i.*** Acts 2:17, ***j.*** 1 Corinthians 2:9-10, Exodus 24:9-10, ***k.*** Matthew 17:20, 18:3, ***l.*** Isaiah 41:14-16, John 3:8, ***m.*** Isaiah 25:6, 55:1-2, Song of Solomon 2:3-4, ***n.*** Psalm 40:2, ***o.*** Luke 14:21, ***p.*** Ephesians 1:12, ***q.*** *My Mum was touched by a word given her from the Lord. As a young girl, she came out of great brokenness. And one day the word of the Lord came to her and said, "As 'my child' are **you** to the praise of 'His Glory.'" It was a very personal word to her. God speaking about her through the vision of His eyes.* ***r.*** *This Scripture verse was my dad's personal favourite. Even the Places God wants to take His people that so surpass imagination.*

Dated: 17/1/19

LIVING IN A STATE OF PERPETUAL ENCOUNTER

1. Living in a State of Perpetual Encounter (#84)
ASCENSION

Scripture:
No man has ascended up to heaven, but he that came down from Heaven, even the Son of man who is **in** Heaven. *(John 3:13 NKJV)*

Until the time of the Christ, one could not ascend into Heaven except He who came down from Heaven. In the past, prior to Jesus, people who were called were brought up. However today — 'in Him' — you can be anywhere 'in spirit' for you are **one** in Him. Jesus co-abided 'in Heaven' as He walked this earth; therefore, where you choose to position yourself is most important [a]. Today you can ascend into Heaven as you hold the Lord in your heart, or as Paul says, as you *"Set your affections"* in Him. [b]

Some are taken up in spirit, but again, as Paul says, *"Whether in the body or not in the body I do not know"*[c]. Jesus lived in a state of perpetual Encounter in God; and in holding this dear in your heart, even ascension, do you open yourself to the same. For where your treasure is so too is your spirit also. The Lord plants a Seed; and as this Seed is treasured does it come into fruition. And sometimes many Seeds are needed, even to build a framework. A sturdy structure of Truth forming realities of increasing manifestations of Heaven.

Scripture:
Then Jesus told him, "Because you have seen me, you have believed; blessed are those who have not seen and yet have believed." *(John 20:29 NIV)*

Jesus said to Thomas, *"Blessed is the man who believes without seeing."* And why is this? ... but because of their response unto the Spirit. Their response unto the continual tugging of the Father in their heart. It is the calling of the Lord, the desire and question placed in your heart retained, that is most valuable. For as David 'strengthened himself in the Lord' ... so can you and I [d]. Such is the Power found in the Secret Place. The 'perpetual' seeking of the

Presence of God; opening you up to a life of perpetual Encounter. Seeking not gifts alone but the **Giver of gifts**.

As the Seed is nurtured and you find strength in the Word; the precedent of these accounts recorded make a **pathway** opened to you as well [e]. And as you hold the Lord close to heart so too are you lifted up: some in spirit and soul … but some also in their physical bodies as well.

Like the elders in the Exodus story, who were taken up in their bodies and ate and drank in Heaven on the Sea of Sapphire [f]. But now, even the 'least' in the Kingdom [f] have far greater opportunity than they. Encounters in the Lord are always precious and change a person's life forever. But perpetual Encounters is a *lifestyle;* the very same of which Jesus Himself lived in. And as Jesus lived in a state of perpetual Encounter — to one who walks as He — does **also** as He.

*"The Lord shall send the rod of **your** strength out of Zion."* [g]

Upon the Mountain of the Lord, come experience transfiguration. The Lord says, *"Not by might, nor by power, but by my Spirit"* [h]. The emphasis then, is always the Spirit. And as you personally draw near to God and hold these things most dear, even *ascension;* so too are you 'captured' up in Him. And this to the measure of your own heart's desire. Your ability limited only to that of your capacity to believe [i]. And as you Encounter and experience God, so too is the measure of your faith — and the extent of your vision — ever increased. And here, in Him, are you trained and tutored how to go deeper in Him — deeper into the More. And just as the depths and width and breadth of God are beyond comprehension; so too are you taken into Places that are Above the High Places.

THOUGHT-LIFE, THE RENEWED MIND

In seeking the Presence of the Lord so too are you lifted and raised up in Him. These very ascensions sanctifying your soul and thought life. The — being clothed — in garments of Praise and **garments of Light** [j]. In all things, the Grace of God is sufficient [k]. For what qualifies you is the Blood of Jesus and the Blood alone. Repentance is simply a looking up, a 'returning' back to your true origins *l*. The Kingdom of Heaven is 'at hand' and so too is your capacity of perpetual and unceasing interaction. To such walk in the full Inheritance of the Promise.

Appendix:

a. John 15:4, 9, *b.* Colossians 3:1-3, Revelation 2:4-5, *c.* 2 Corinthians 12:2, *d.* 1 Samuel 30:6, *e.* 2 Corinthians 1:20, *e.* Exodus 24:10, *f.* Matthew 11:11, *g.* Psalm 110:2, *h.* Zechariah 4:6, *i.* Matthew 9:29, 2 Kings 13:17-19, *j.* Zechariah 3:5, Psalm 40:3, *k.* 2 Corinthians 12:9, *l.* Isaiah 44:22

Dated: 7/2/19

2. Living in a State of Perpetual Encounter (#85)
PERPETUAL ENCOUNTER

*"Lord, **I seek ascension**. I ascend my affections in you. I ascend my thoughts and my soul. I leave all my cares and needs in you that I might come up. As a little child, I lift up my arms that my Father may pick me up. I seek ascension, I seek again to be taken up in you. Blessed be the Name of the Lord."*

Jesus lived in a perpetual state of Encounter. He never experienced a moment without the active Presence of God. And these Encounters only expanding and increasing in great Signs and Wonders. Jesus lived in continual dialogue with the angelic realm, as a 'ladder' ascending and descending upon the Son of Man [a]. He lived with great interaction with the Spirit of Understanding and Knowledge [b], even from a young age. And He openly saw His Heavenly Father and heard His Voice as He went about regular daily life. So, in stating most clearly: that Jesus has made the way for us to walk in the **exact** and very same.

Opening Scripture:
Then Moses went up, also Aaron, Nadab, and Abihu, and seventy of the elders of Israel, and they saw the God of Israel. And there was under His feet as it were a paved work of sapphire stone, and it was like the very heavens in its clarity. But on the nobles of the children of Israel He did not lay His hand. So they saw God, and they ate and drank. *(Exodus 24:9-11 NKJV)*

Where your *treasure* is so too your heart is also: In Christ Jesus, you have it within yourself capacity of unlimited interaction in Heavenly realms. And this to the measure of your own heart's desire. Your ability only to that of your capacity to believe. But as you allow yourself to Encounter God, so too is the measure of your faith, and the extent of your vision, ever increased. And as you seek the Lord, so too are you lifted up in Him. These very 'ascensions' sanctifying your soul's thought-life [c] and clothing you in garments of Light. [d]

As the depths of God are far beyond comprehension, so too is your ability to expand in Him. And as you lift your eyes so too are you lifted up to see all the more; higher into the High Places that are above the High Places. No man can comprehend the depths, the breadth, or the width of God. But in the Spirit are you captured up in Him; and when you thought you were lifted up high you are only lifted up all the more.

To *humble* yourself before the Lord, so too are you lifted up. To choose the chair of the least are you seated in high honour[e]. To say to the Lord that you know nothing, that you are nothing outside of Him[f], this opens you able to continually Receive. For the cup that is *empty* before the Lord is filled.

To have had an experience in the Lord a few years ago is not enough. Even an Encounter with an angel or a Heavenly ascension; one's vision still remains insufficient. The dream of the believer needs become the same as the Father's; that you live in a continual and increasing state of perpetual Encounter; dialogue, vision, and experience in Him *(ie; your ability to 'hear' and 'see')*. The basic Dream and Call of the Father is to be **fashioned** into the Likeness and Image of the Son. To walk as He, live as He — become as He — to this the stage has been set.

Jesus was born of both woman and Spirit. This, then, clearly makes you a **bridge** between two distinct 'dimensions' … two distinct realms. The earthly realm and the Heavenly realms. Truly, you are a New Creation; genetically, of origins, blood and birth — a totally New Being. A 'Gateway-being' of Heavenly origins.

Scripture:
I pray that the eyes of your heart may be [opened] enlightened in order that you may **know the hope** to which He has called you, the riches of His glorious Inheritance in His holy people, and His **incomparably** great Power for us who believe. *(Ephesians 1:18-19 NIV)*

I pray that the eyes of your heart may be opened. No longer with only the vision of mere mortal man; with eyes set unto the visions of this earth. But that you may be 'enlightened' … lifting your eyes up in Him. Hungering for Encounter more than your *daily bread*[g]. Dreaming for the Lord and His Dreams opening before your eyes.

Even the constant and perpetual pouring into your soul of His very Thoughts and Being.

Why ... and how ... can anyone live content in a way less than the full Dreams of God? I pray that *His* Living Word becomes 'flesh' in you [h]. Being no longer one satisfied with only a 'knowledge' about Him, but constantly **Dining** with the Author of Life with His Life beating in your veins. For truly, this is the Place where Christ's Resurrection Power comes from. [i]

Appendix:

a. John 1:51, ***b.*** Isaiah 11:2, ***c.*** Romans 8:5-6, 1 Corinthians 2:10-16, ***d.*** Psalm 104:2, Revelation 3:18 *(Luke 14:28-33)*, Zechariah 3:4, ***e.*** Luke 14:10, ***f.*** John 5:19 -20, ***g.*** Matthew 4:4, ***h.*** John 1:14, ***i.*** Psalm 27:4, 110:1-2, Philippians 3:10

Dated: 19/2/19

3. *Living in a State of Perpetual Encounter (#86)*
SEA OF SAPPHIRE

Scripture:
Because of his great love for us, God, who is rich in mercy, made us alive with Christ even when we were dead in transgressions; it is by grace you have been saved. And God raised us up with Christ and seated us with him in the Heavenly realms in Christ Jesus, in order that in the coming ages he might show the incomparable riches of his grace, expressed in his kindness to us in Christ Jesus. *(Ephesians 2:4-7 NIV)*

The picture of this word 'ascension' has been foreign to me, but now has come as a **huge open door** with massive and broad implications. With endless possibilities and wonders presented. Phrases like, *"Who are the Warriors?"* now come to mind. They of whom function on high and most powerful levels; in tune and under direct Instruction and Tuition of King Jesus and His angels [a]. This, for the greatest and the least alike. For Jesus has opened the Door for each and all who might believe.

There are so many new flavours that the Lord is leading me into that are most precious. Many times, the precedent of such things open the way for both you and I. *"Is it possible for me?"* … one might ask. And yes, it is [b]. I then think of the Sword coming out of the mouth of Jesus and moving swiftly against the *Enemy* [c]. Such new awarenesses; words given you of the Lord that open incredible doors of possibilities.

These things have always been there. But today, we can all the more freely step into. And words like 'ascension' being like sharp arrows, that direct and catapult you specifically where focused. Even right up upon the 'Sea of Sapphire' [d] … this same Place where Moses spent a lot of time. Even in Places where he said, *"I am terrified and my body shakes"* [e]. In such I delight and long to abide, for the 'Fear' of the Lord is the **beginning** of Wisdom. The very same Place where Jesus Himself delighted in. [f]

This shooting of the 'arrow', this earnest seeking of the Presence of God — even the very Face of God — is the retained preference and purpose of my soul. Do you recall the time when Elisha said to the king, *"Open the east window, and shoot the Lord's arrow of victory?"* But he only struck the ground three times. Then in frustration, Elisha said to him, *"You should have kept striking the ground"*[g]. I tell you, that in the earnest seeking of the Lord — so shall you find Him — and so shall you be *found* by Him. [h]

Scripture:
"You will seek me and find me when you seek me with all your heart. **I will be <u>found</u> by you**," declares the LORD … and will bring you back [into the 'Place of Promise']" *(Jeremiah 29:13-14)*

Man thinks in terms of factories of production and workers, but God thinks of saving a nation in a day [i]. Man's way is endless instruction and teaching about God … but God's way is about showing up[j]. Man's way thinks about becoming ready; about being perfect before the Lord. But Jesus' way is that you are already accepted; His Blood spilt is the finished work of the Cross. The first is the Blood, the first is the Grace of God; now you can go meet with God to the measure of your own heart's desire … even in Ascension. And here, it will be, by the Spirit of the Lord, so shall He bring continual and **<u>catalystic</u> change** in your life.

The Power of God is in one's mouth, held in one's ability to believe. And if the Lord says 'yes', then where is your limitation? Everything in the Lord is 'yes' and 'amen' [k] … even laid as precedent for you to walk in also. Man was built for Encounter. Fallen man lost this, but Risen man has unfathomable and incredible capacity and access of both realms inherent.

Therefore, if you have been risen in Christ Jesus then you are a New Creation. The Old has gone and the New has come. You are a 'Super' … a supernatural being of supernatural Origins. Of unlimited potential and unlimited Resources. The vision of fallen man has obscured your eyes, even Religion has blinded and *binded*. But as you Encounter the Lord, so too is the vision of your eyes continually opened in Him.

Within you is inherent capacity of infinite growth. Infinite growth into the Image and Likeness of God ... for the shift in your DNA is Christ Jesus. Therefore, avoid responding like John the Baptist's dad, of whom said, *"What proof is there for this?"* [l] But be like Mary, who said, *"I am the Lord's servant, let everything you've said happen to me."* [m]

As Jesus says to you this day, *"Let it be done **just as you believed** it would"* [n]. Or in another place, *"According to your faith let it be done to you"* [o]. Even unto the man who cried out to Jesus, *"Please help me in my unbelief"* [p]. Be no longer plateaued in your understanding. There is a right way going about things if you truly wish to walk in Abundant Life.

The Gospel speaks of itself as the 'hidden' mysteries of God **revealed** [q]. And these things that are now being revealed to you open yet other Doors of Vision and Wonder. Jesus speaks of how He has things of Heaven to show, reveal, and impart ... but you **must be willing** [r]. The Power is in your ability to believe. For each of us are motivated and driven by what we fundamentally believe. And to the measure use: so too is it measured unto you also [s]. In this, your faith links arms with the Amen.

If you would simply believe and accept the Gospel message; these of the 'earthly teachings' of Christ Jesus. Then you would open yourself unto 'heavenly things' [t]. Otherwise, by your own choice of *indifference,* do you close yourself off to the More.

The Gospel message itself is the **keys** to the Hidden Mysteries of God revealed. These very things hidden and lost since the beginning of time. So fundamentally then, believe in the Gospel even though you may not yet be able to walk in it. For as keys, they open incredible doors of Opportunity. And if you can believe, so too are **you made able** to walk in the fullness of them.

Theme Scripture:
Then Moses went up, also Aaron, Nadab, and Abihu, and seventy of the elders of Israel, and they saw the God of Israel. And there was under His feet as it were a paved work of sapphire stone, and it was like the very heavens in its clarity. But on the nobles of the

children of Israel He did not lay His hand. So they saw God, and they ate and drank. Then the LORD said to Moses, "Come up to Me on the mountain and be there; and I will give you tablets of stone, and the law and commandments which I have written, that you may teach them. *(Exodus 24:9-12 NKJV)*

In the Exodus, when Moses ascended the Mountain of the Lord [u], he was given the Laws of God written on tablets of stone. And now for us today in Christ Jesus, as you too 'ascend', does God write on the tablets of your heart; [v] **Living Words of wonder** proceeding from the mouth of God right into your heart. And these Words will 'mark' you; they will mark your life forever [w]. And they will become like scrolls and books of God's Word written in your heart. Like Paul, who received the Gospel by Divine revelation [x], so too shall God's Living Word [y] continually speak Alive in your soul. Hence therefore, your own heart of *affection* is key; ever set upon the **manifest** Presence of God. [z]

Later in this time, as we read, Moses and the Seventy Elders went up upon the Pavement of Sapphire. And ate and drank in the Presence of God. Let not your heart remain hard and closed, but in humility ever open yourself to what God **desires to give**.

What does it mean to be tutored, do you know? You have a classroom setting, but to be tutored is to have King Jesus in Person come as a Friend ... and personally **show** and teach you of Heavenly things. There are many prayers you can have, but in truth ... **only one is needed**.

The Lord comes to me continually, for my heart perpetually yearns for Him to do so. The last chapter written *(#85)* was written in a hardware store, as I held onto the shelves trying to keep myself steady. All the wonders of God are yours ... therefore, as you honour Him so does He come. Come then and perpetually **seek** the Lord so that the Lord may perpetually come. And He will send Tutors and Scribes from Heaven to teach and open your eyes all the more.

Who am I but a wretched man, a sinner of the lowest of lows. But it was God's Dream to pick me up from the gutter, even from the pigpen of worthless thinking and deeds. Setting me in such High Honour in Him. Therefore, if He would pick me up, then surely, He would pick you up as well!

Many times, I have had to pull over in the car overwhelmed by the Presence of God. Or when washing the dishes, have to just stop what I am doing and bow down on the floor in praise and honour, as the Presence of the Lord comes. I deeply honour the Lord, and when He comes so shall I bow my knees. For my attentiveness is always in the Lord, and in Him my heart is overwhelmed with Praise. Even as the God of Heaven and earth says, *"My Presence will go with you, and I will give you rest (peace and victory)."* [1]

Seek Encounter, even perpetual encounter; and this as the root culture and inherent nature and purpose of your soul. Just delight in Encounters, Visitations, and Revelation … and it will be the Lord who will come and speak into your soul like sweet chatter, like melody and sweet music in your heart. Then so too shall you begin to perpetually walk in such things.

For what you honour you magnify. And what you honour you draw unto yourself. And to He of whom you set your heart is in Him of whom you function and abide. And He of whom you honour speaks continually, and comes and visits continuously night and day. We all have access but who honours; who longs for and who loves? Who draws, who dreams, and who dares to dream with God?

God's is like a deep deep ocean. And you can just sit on the surface if you wish, on the 'boat' of your own control and vision. But in Christ Jesus, you have unlimited access and unlimited ability to go deeper and deeper in Him. And be taken Places that man cannot comprehend. Places where words do not suffice, not even books and books of words written.

Within the capacity of the *Risen* is the inherent ability to be lifted up in Him, even the very capacity of Ascension. However, love is key … not law but love.

God is Love, hence how you engage with Him is always through a heart of endearment and affection. Learn to approach your Heavenly Father as a fully redeemed child *(even without nappies)*. Fully redeemed by the Blood of the Lamb … just as you are. For your heart is the gateway.

Within the Risen is unlimited resources. Unlimited finances, unlimited capacity and capabilities, and unlimited wonders and surprise. The human mind simply cannot comprehend all that God has kept and made ready for each one of us who believe [2]. So the answer is not about you … but about Him.

In our bodies we walk this earth, but in our spirit we can **walk in the Heavenly realms** at will. For Heaven itself *is* our inheritance and rightful possession. And as Paul says, *"In my body or in my spirit I do not know"* [3] … for it becomes seamless. And as Jesus said, *"The Father is **pleased** to give you the Kingdom of Heaven"* … for it was God's Dream before it became yours. And it was Jesus' Dream as He willingly (and in joy) laid down His own life upon the Cross. To such cause Satan to fall like lightning unto the ground of utter defeat. [5]

So even in these last two chapters; chapter 85 came to me whilst I was in a hardware store … as I was overwhelmed by the Presence of God. And having to hold onto rails, onto the shelves, finding a quiet place in the BBQ section. And here, I did my best to quickly write down these precious words. These precious words of 'impartation'; **plantings of the Spirit** that are taking me places. New doors of openings, possibilities, and wonders that I never knew existed. These are just beginning; just stepping stones; just introductions. And the Lord, by His Living Word … His Rhema Word; prepares you able to receive all the More. 'Constructing' and preparing you able to further step into all the More that is in Him.

The *revealed* Word of God is as like prophecy speaking of your life. This given of the Lord. Though others may make you aware, as you take these precious things deeply to heart … so too are they made *flesh* in you. Our 'focus' being not in the accrual of knowledge, but the manifestation of what Truth declares. The transitioning between the unseen and the seen; the intangible to the manifestation thereof.

I call this Place, the "Sea of Sapphire", in reference to the Book of Revelations where it is referred to as the Sea of Glass [6]. But in Moses' time it is referred to it as a Pavement of Sapphire; being as like 'the very heavens in its clarity' [7]. This is where God has fixed my eyes. So too, where awareness has now opened; your 'focus' will catapult you ... will shoot you like an arrow.

Appendix:

a. Acts 10:30-33, Acts 8:39, Luke 1:13, Matthew 4:11, Daniel 10:12, 8:15-18, Revelation 1:17-18, 2 Kings 6:17, Exodus 3:2, *b.* 2 Corinthians 1:20, *c.* Revelation 19:15, *d.* Exodus 24:10, Revelation 15:2, *e.* Hebrews 12:21, *f.* Isaiah 11:3, *g.* 2 Kings 13:17-19, *h.* Jeremiah 29:13-14, *i.* Isaiah 66:8, *j.* 1 Corinthians 2:4, *k.* 2 Corinthians 1:20, *l.* Luke 1:5, *m.* Luke 1:38, *n.* Matthew 8:13, *o.* Matthew 9:29, *p.* Mark 9:24, *q.* Colossians 1:26, *r.* Matthew 23:37, John 16:15, John 14:21, *s.* Mark 4:24, *t.* John 3:12, *u.* Exodus 24:12, *v.* Jeremiah 31:33, Isaiah 2:2-3, Psalm 24:3-8, *w.* Revelation 2:12, *x.* Galatians 1:11-12, *y.* Matthew 4:4, *z.* Colossians 3:2-3, *1.* Exodus 33:14, 2. 1 Corinthians 2:9, *3.* 2 Corinthians 12:2-4, *4.* Luke 12:32, *5.* Luke 10:18, Matthew 16:18, *6.* Revelation 4:6 *7.* Exodus 24:10

Dated: 26/2/19

4. Living in a State of Perpetual Encounter (#87)
ANCIENT GATES

Opening Scripture:
The LORD replied, "My **Presence** will go with you, and I will give you **Rest** [peace and victory]." *(Exodus 33:14 NIV, CEV, GNT)*

The Presence of God that you seek, even Encounters and Ascensions, cause you able to enter the desired realm of **God's Rest**. This, the very Place of Peace, of Dining, and of Victory [1]. Ever 'Abiding' [2] in the Counsels and Power of God [3]. And as a Pillar of Fire at night and a Pillar of Cloud by day, so shall He lead you and so shall you be continually provided. And so shall His Presence upon you [4] **release the 'Angel Armies'** [5]. Therefore, *"Lift up your heads, you gates; lift them up you ancient doors, that the King of Glory may come in."* [6]

God refers to you as an 'ancient door'. There are many mysteries that are hard for the linear *(two-dimensional ... flat)* mind to comprehend. But *since* before the founding of the earth, you were known in Him and called into greatness [7]. It is Satan who has only sought to diminish, but it is God who seeks only to restore [8] — 'reclothing' you in His Glory [9]. Christ Jesus was slain for our sins, but He was also raised again for 'our' Glory ... that His **Radiance** may be ever upon us [10]. This is the miracle of the 'Third Day'.

God sees you as a '**gate**'. Therefore, as you 'lift up your head' unto the Lord, so too do you allow the King of Glory to come in. And by His Grace, openly and actively be engaged you in your life; lifting you up able to see His Face and sit with Him in His Glory. [11]

Such is the Power of the Blood. And such is a heart set not upon the world but ever upon His Glory [12]. Therefore, as you also 'ascend' *(ie; lift up your heart)* the Mountain of the Lord like Moses [13], then in Him will He Tutor; and in Him so too re-raise you in that of which was forgotten, in that of which was lost [14]. Even that the Radiance of the Lord may **shine upon your face** [15] and upon your person. For in Christ Jesus, you are no longer born of 'flesh and blood' but born of Eternity — of Eternal Divine Origin.

Theme Scripture:
Who may ascend the mountain of the Lord? Who may **stand in his holy place**? The one who has clean hands and a pure heart, who does not trust in an idol or swear by a false god. They will receive blessing from the Lord and vindication from God their Savior. Such is the generation of those who seek him, who **seek your face**, God of Jacob.
Lift up your heads, you gates; be lifted up, you ancient doors, that the King of glory may come in. Who is this King of glory? The Lord strong and mighty, the Lord **mighty** in battle. Lift up your heads, you gates; lift them up, you ancient doors, that the King of glory may come in. Who is he, this King of glory? The Lord Almighty — he is the **King of glory**. *(Psalm 24:3-10 NIV)*

As one in Christ Jesus — in Him — so too are you now able to freely 'ascend' the Mountain of the Lord ... as you please. You are a gate, even ancient and of ancient lineage. You are a People of the Promise ... **called unto the Seated realms** [16]. Therefore, lift up your heads you 'ancient doors', that the Glory of your King may come in.

To ascend the Mountain of the Lord is to 'touch', it is to connect and to **make** connection. And it is to 'Remain' ... it is to 'Abide'; [17] ever surrounded by His Counsels and Might through **tight bonds** of love. Your heart and your thoughts can be anywhere, but 'in Him' do you engage in His Glory all the more.

As a people who release the Angel Armies; so are you also one who ceases the groans and tribulations in your world. [18]

In Christ Jesus, you have entered through the **Gate of Righteousness** [19]. Through He of whom shed His Blood and has given you perfect license. With open passage to enter and engage with God, and the Divine Heavenly realms, to the measure of your own heart's desire *(that is your own limitation)*. Therefore, lift up your head right where you are. Lift up your heart unto the Lord and ascend your affections in Him. Rise up, rise up, and ascend in the

Lord and allow Him to continually lift you up. Such is the Word of the Lord concerning you this very day. [20]

Come, and remain then, no longer a people confined and constrained by mental human intelligence [21] but a people who gain hold of 'Spirit Intelligence' [22]. For who knows the Thoughts of God but by the Spirit of the Lord [23]. And as is said, *"We all have received, not the spirit of the world, but the Spirit who is from God, that we might **know** the things that have been freely given to us by God"* [24]. For the 'tree' of our own knowledge is death, but partaking of the Tree of Life ... is Life evermore: body, mind, soul, and spirit.

Scripture:
Thus says Yahweh of Armies [God-of-the-Angel-Armies]: "If you will walk in my ways, and if you will follow my instructions, then **you also shall judge** my house, and shall also keep my courts, and I will give you a place of access among these who stand by [all my attendants standing here will be at your service]." *(Zechariah 3:7 WEB, MSG)*

The Heart of the Father, and the precedent and pattern laid here, is that if you would choose it in your heart to walk in God's Ways *(according to 'Spirit-Knowledge')*. Then you would be given access to the Angel Armies. And these that are 'standing here' shall be 'at your service' to consult, tutor, and engage with you perpetually ... and subsequently, ride upon your words. You are a *"Chosen people, a royal priesthood ... God's special treasured possession"* [25]. Given Divine calling and place of access to 'oversee' the House of God; to judge and to keep His Courts. Therefore, though in the past, you have only been schooled on this limited earthly plane. Now, as one in Christ Jesus, allow yourself ever to be one schooled in the Heavenly plane ... unto exceedingly great Glory.

By the Blood of Jesus are you here, through the finished work of the Cross. But until now, you have neither had vision or sight to **know who you truly are in Him** [26]. To 'hear' and to 'see' that is the Way of the Christ [27]. The Seven Spirits of the Lord are before the Throne of God [28]. Therefore, through your continual engagement in the Spirits of the Lord, and being led through, do you sit in position to release the Seven Spirits of the Lord.

Train yourself to look up in Him. Practice, for Power and Knowledge is of God. And here in Him, in the Presence of the Lord, allow yourself to be one continually snatched up again into Heavenly Places and Heavenly Sight. Such is the power of praise and of worship; of simple prayer and fasting; here, setting your heart in 'wait' upon the Lord [29]. For so are you magnifying Him in your heart's eye.

Be captured up again in Him, even enraptured right into His ministering and instructional Presence. Here, in the very Place of Impartation, the Place of the receiving of Gifts. For you are called to enter His Rest, not your rest — but His. And so it shall be, that in Him, shall His Rest and His Strength come upon you. And shall you ever be raised in Victory! For the world needs something more than a knowledge about God, they **need God showing up**.

Many fast for answer to prayer, but so few fast for God's Prayer answered and fulfilled in them.

Scripture:
I pray that the eyes of your heart may be Enlightened [opened] in order that you may know the hope to which He has called you, the riches of His glorious Inheritance in His holy people, and His incomparably great Power for us who believe. *(Ephesians 1:18-19 NIV)*

The Kingdom of Heaven is in you, it is right at hand. His *incomparably* great Power is in you to cause you able to **win!** Such is the Grace of God concerning you.

Do you yet realise that this Power is greater than the power in stars? Greater than weapons of war, and greater than sickness and death? This incomparably great Power within you is without compare; and this for each and every single one who believes. And what qualifies you is the Blood of the Lamb and the Blood alone. The very same Grace of God that tore and parted the Veil. It is Jesus who desires to tutor you and lead you deeper into your 'Glorious Inheritance'. For you to openly walk in His 'incomparably Great Power'. This, through the equally 'incomparable richness of His Grace'. [30]

I was recently listening to a passage in John, where the Pharisees were talking to Jesus and thought, 'you do not realise that you are talking to the Great I AM" [31]. Standing right before them was the very Word made flesh. This same Word in which spoke all Creation into existence. He was right there ... in the flesh!

Think of this: In Christ Jesus, you have incomparable Power to have the Word made flesh in you, The great 'I AM' functioning dynamic and alive. And you have incomparable capacity to have the Kingdom of Heaven manifest and incomparable Grace in Him to do so. In appearance, you may look like just a regular person, just like Jesus who was in 'disguise'. But you have the great I AM in you; made *one* in Him and He in you [32]. And in speaking about angels, do you remember the importance of showing hospitality? For one never really knows who they have invited over for dinner. [33]

You may appear like just a regular person ... however, people do not know the vastness of your reach, nor who you are in the Lord. So regardless of your earthly appearance; your station in Heavenly realms is vast and wide. Realise, that the Pharisees of old; the spiritual and intellectual leaders in the day of Jesus, did not recognise Him. They didn't recognise Him at all. But He was God incarnate standing right before them. Taught by man, and set only unto the vision of man, they fully missed Him. And so too is much missed in our current Age. Such as it was that Nicodemus said to Jesus, *"How can this be?"*

So I encourage you, continue to transition from one who only has knowledge of God, to one who walks in open and living experience. That is the desired transition. No longer as like an astronomer who only looks up into 'Heaven', but as like an astronaut that traverses the 'stars'.

Intelligence is good *('IQ')*, but like Nicodemus one can be still held and restricted in the confines of one's own mind: even through books and books of the understanding of man. However, the desired transition is to gain Spirit-Intelligence; the same of which transcends space, time, and mortality *('SQ')*. And from here, you can bring forth **all answers** to the needs of man. Creativity and

Discovery, Inventiveness and Healing, and Power and Restoration. To such are true sons and daughters of the Living God; bringing forth the 'revealed' God on earth. [34]

It is easy to speak of God … even as an authority in a subject, but who has met with Him and stands in His Counsels? This is the desired transition. For where you orientate yourself, so too do you draw. And where you build your house, so too are you established.

A testimony of David Hogan's that I heard a while ago, spoke of how, as a ministry, they have a near 100% healing rate for cholera. But being exposed so much, one of his pastors came down with symptoms and was hospitalised. And there, in a different part of the hospital, was a lady who gave birth to a stillborn baby. The treating nurse, knowing that this man of God was only just down the hallway, called for him to be wheeled up in his bed. And upon laying his hand on the dead baby, the little thing immediately came back to life. And this while he was still under the effects of cholera.

"Oh Lord, may we be the More that you have made us!"

You may well be currently under 'symptoms' of this world, in a season … however, where you choose to abide in the Lord **makes you most powerful**. This always needs remain your choice and retained central vision of your soul. And as you are fed so too are you filled.

It is here, in the desired ministering Presence of the Lord, that you are continually built up and made aware. One can remain only on the 'surface' … or otherwise, retain it treasured deeply in your heart: the desire to go deeper into the vast ocean of the very Person of God.

This pastor knew the Power of God and was totally unwavering in his faith *(due to his own personal Encounters and experiences)*. As Jesus says, *"The Kingdom of Heaven is like a little mustard seed that you plant in the ground, and it becomes the greatest of trees"* [35]. Hence your growth in the Kingdom of Heaven is without limit. Therefore, as one choosing to look past this life right unto the Glory Cloud — has you always been 'taken' [36] — Enraptured up in Him, and this right where you are.

As Promised, you have been 'seated in *Heavenly Places*' [37]. And by His Blood and His Grace are you here. Hence as you keep ascending the Mountain of the Lord, so too are your eyes made open to all that is already yours.

Therefore now, in cherished union in Him, allow yourself to be one seated upon the Throne with Him; the Throne of the Judge, the Throne of the King and Ruling Authority. To set your eyes on earthly concern trains you in earthly confined thinking. But to set your eyes unto Heaven's Glory, are you lifted up and **shown all** that's rightfully yours; the Place of Origins, the pre-fallen state. Now from here in Him — by Him — are you raised Victorious.

The Seven Spirits of the Lord are before the Throne of God, and through engaging with them, are you raised to be seated upon the Throne with Him [38]. And here, when you speak, do you release the Spirits of the Lord. And how is it that you can engage? ... but through your 'first love' [39]. Your first drive unto beholding God.

It is through your first love that the '**Lampstand**' is set in your midst. Through the enduring Love of God, that resides in you — that is set wholly upon the Lord. And here in Him, by the Seven Spirits of the Lord, so too are you raised Triumphant in Him. And just as the Son, when you speak, does Life and Spirit ride on your words. [40]

Is there an any greater university that one can attend than the University of Heaven? The coming under the very schooling of the Spirits of the Lord. You can surround yourself with the counsels of men, seeking their honour and approval — but that is linear, a boat on the surface. What is desired, is to surround yourself with the Spirits of the Lord. Delving ever deeper into the Eternal Goodness and Joy of God ... as one 'standing' in His Counsel. Where you are personally given Words to 'save a nation'. As is said, *"If they had **stood** in My counsel then they would have turned them from their evil ways."* [41]

When real problems come … like this fellow with cholera, you can choose to come under the difficulties or hardship, or otherwise choose to strengthen yourself in the Lord [42]. And here in the Joy of the Lord, **so shall you be <u>made</u> Victorious** in Him; such is the Power of the treasured Presence of God. Even to walk in His Rest, His Peace, and His Victory. To such sit on the Throne of the Judge and pass judgement … setting to task the Power of God [43]. Blessed be the Name of the Lord.

Closing Scripture:
O LORD, I love the house where You dwell, the place where Your glory resides. *(Psalm 26:8 NIV)*

Appendix:

1. Hebrews 4:11, Psalm 23:5, 110:2, Revelation 3:21, **2.** John 15:7, **3.** Isaiah 11:1-2, **4.** Exodus 33:14-16, Isaiah 11:3-4, 2 Kings 2:13, **5.** Zechariah 3:7, **6.** Psalm 24:9, **7.** Ephesians 1:4, Jeremiah 1:5, **8.** Isaiah 44:22, **9.** Genesis 3:10, Revelation 3:17-18, **10.** 1 Corinthians 4:20, **11.** Revelation 5:9-10, Exodus 33:18-23, **12.** John 5:44, Colossians 3:1-2, John 17:20-24, **13.** Matthew 14:23, Psalm 24, Isaiah 2:2-5, Exodus 24:15, **14.** Genesis 1:26, 1 Corinthians 15:45-49, 2:16, **15.** Exodus 33:18, 34:35, **16.** Psalm 2:7-8, 110:1, 2 Kings 2:9, **17.** John 15:7, **18.** Romans 8:22-23, **19.** Psalm 118:20, **20.** Revelation 3:22, **21.** Genesis 2:17, **22.** Genesis 3:22, **23.** 1 Corinthians 2:11, **24.** 1 Corinthians 2:12, **25.** 1 Peter 2:9, **26.** Galatians 4:7, 1 Corinthians 2:12, Romans 8:14, 19, **27.** John 5:19, Revelation 3:18, **28.** Revelation 1:4, **29.** Isaiah 64:1-4, **30.** Ephesians 2:7, **31.** John 8:58, **32.** John 17:21, **33.** Hebrews 13:2, **34.** Romans 8:19, **35.** Matthew 13:31-32, **36.** Genesis 5:24, **37.** Ephesians 2:6, **38.**..Isaiah 11:1-4, Revelation 3:19-22, **39.** Revelation 2:4-5, Psalm 27:4, **40.** John 6:63, **41.** Jeremiah 23:22, **42.** 1 Samuel 30:6, **43.** Isaiah 11:3-4

Dated: 10/3/19

5. Living in a State of Perpetual Encounter (#88)
ZION

Opening Scripture:
No one has ever seen God, but the one and only Son, who is himself God and is in **closest** relationship with the Father [the 'Bosom' of the Father], has made him known. *(John 1:18 NIV)*

The way of ascension is to seek the Presence of God. The laying down of one's life in Him and passing through the Veil [1]. And here in the 'quiet still voice' being ever surrounded by the Counsels and Powers of Heaven. Setting yourself aside as one Tutored and Instructed and continuously lifted up. We all can come to the Lord for specific needs, but the greatest wonder is your ability to abide in Zion — the Heavenly Jerusalem. [2]

Initially, it is in spirit, for where your **treasure** is so your heart is also [3]. Such is the mystery of the Presence of God. And here in His Presence do you encounter 'revelation'; the Sevenfold Spirits of the Lord enveloping you in Wisdom and Understanding, in Counsel and Power and Might; **entering** deep into the Knowledge and Glory of God [4]. And through a heart of praise and honour, so are you also covered and enveloped in Praise and Honour [5]. The Lord assigning ministering angels to work and speak into your life. And as you continue to seek His Presence, so does your soul ascend.

Such is the mystery of ascension, of dynamic Experience and Encounters in the Lord. For simply you find yourself bonding and drawing ever deeper of the Vine. Deeper of the 'sap' of the Branch ... with Life of the Spirit 'welling up' in ways unceasing [6]. The Bible simply refers to this as: the Place of Strength. [7]

*A side note; spirit, soul, mind, and body: Presence Encounters is a very broad subject. But by faith, your **spirit**-man (your 'angel') sees the Face of God as soon as you turn your heart towards Him. And '**soul**' Encounters is where your <u>mind</u> is inspired with new vision and revelation; your <u>will</u> shifted and your motives moved, and your <u>emotions</u> overwhelmed with a deep sense of Peace, of Love, with tears of Joy. And '**mind**' Encounters is where Knowledge and Understanding; a 'knowing' enters your heart; a faith, a strength that is not* *from this world. And '**body**' Encounters, is the physically being captured up in your whole person, and in bodily form 'seeing' God just as Moses and Elijah. And if this can be where your heart truly lies then you open unto yourself vast doors.*

Scripture:
Father, I [pray] desire that they also whom You gave Me may be **with me** where I am [in Heaven], and that they may **behold** [see and experience and carry] my Glory. *(John 17:24a (John 3:13 NKJV))*

Jesus is the Door, and one of the greatest gifts bought to you by the Blood is your ability to 'see' the Face of God [8]. The passing through the Veil and being taken by hand into the great Mysteries and Wonders of Heaven [9]. One can come to God with their own agenda, and that's fine. But in choosing to humble yourself [10] and 'wait' in His Holy Presence [11], do you increasingly enter and participate in His Dreams.

At one time, when Jesus was speaking to Bible scholars, He said to them, *"You have never heard His voice, or seen His form, nor does His Word dwell in you"* [12]. These men read and studied the Word of God as a life pursuit, but in Jesus' opinion … God's Word did not dwell in them.

I so encourage you, there is something so much more important for you and your life, and that is the very Word that proceeds Alive — ever-present and flowing — from the mouth of God. This is what you want, this is what you needs ask for. For to such as these, the Gates of Hades cannot prevail, *ie;* no spiritual forces, realities, or opposition [14]. The Gospel is very specific about this, and it's called are '**daily bread**'. It's called the 'bread' that man cannot live without. [13]

Remain one who no longer operates only out of an earthly vision or standpoint. But centralise and purpose yourself in this: and become a people who operate out of your Divine position in Him. As a citizen of Heaven, born child of the Living God, do you **enter an open Heaven**. Therefore, a heart that perpetually seeks the Presence of God, so too shall you be perpetually 'captured up'.

Enraptured in spirit; in soul and mind; ... and for some, in their bodies. [15]

In the opening Scripture, John states, *"No one has seen God but the Son"*. Then going further, he says, that through own Jesus' closest of relationship with the Father ... did He made God known on earth. Again, I so encourage you today: **this is key** for anyone who truly loves the Lord and truly wishes to see the world saved.

To they who truly desire to see the Kingdom come, for they who dearly wish to see the Spirit outpoured; through your own personal 'closest of relationship', *ie;* your secret and true honest heart set unto the Secret Place of God, it is God Himself who makes Himself **known**. First, showing and revealing to you personally the 'incomparable riches of His Grace' [16]. Then through this; your closely held relationship in the 'Bosom of the Father', He steps through your life ... made **manifest** on earth.

God first revealing Himself real and alive to you personally ... and who you are in Him. Then He comes and reveals your sonship on earth, as one who ceases the 'groans of creation' [17]. As is said, *"People brought the sick into the streets and laid them on beds and mats so that at least Peter's shadow might fall on some of them as he passed by."* [18]

Hence, as you also come behold the Glory of God, like Peter, and like Moses and others; so shall you carry. For such as these 'see' the Face of God. First in spirit ... as Jesus says, *"The angels ('spirit') of the little children always see the Face of my Father in Heaven"* [19]. So a question would be, is Jesus only talking about the young, *ie;* the little children? Or is He not talking about those who truly humble themselves as a little child? For truly, it is those who approach the Father in honesty — in *carefree* innocence — whose spirit always see the Face of God. [20]

Have you ever asked yourself why, that all throughout Scripture, the Bible speaks about 'seeking the Face of God' if it is not possible to see His Face? Is this wording only a metaphor, simply a figure of speech, or just a phrase? No, God is never one to deceive or mislead. Therefore, if it is a calling in Scripture to seek the Face of God, then it is the Face of God that you shall see. First in spirit ...

then in soul and mind ... and for some, in their flesh. And if you think that this is impossible for you, then remember, for God all things are possible [21]. And so it is, to the **measure** you use so shall it be measured to you also; pressed down, shaken, and poured out to overflowing. [22]

There are accounts recorded in Scripture of people seeing the Face of God. Like Moses who sat face to face with the Lord 'as a friend' [23]. And Adam who walked in the Garden with God in the cool of the day. The question would be then, did God wear a veil? If so, it would be His Radiance ... His Glory that covers Him.

The moral of the story, then, is this: As you also personally choose to humble yourself naked and ever bare before Him, and step into His Glory ... passing through the 'veil', then so too are you one who shall behold Him in His Glory [24]. And as you truly respond to His Calling and allow yourself to sit upon the Throne of God *(enter the Sabbath-day of Rest)*, then there is no veil between you ... for you are **one** in Him. The Old has passed and the New has come; even as one who walks in Likeness of the Resurrected Christ on earth.

A side note: These things we are talking of here, are never about a unique calling or a special position amongst men ... but about who you are in Him. For even "The least of the Kingdom of God are greater than they" [25]. *Greater than who? But all who walked before. And even if you have no apparent scroll written, and are of little or no notice, not even known in Heavenly places at all; seek to come up upon the Sea of Sapphire and 'dine' like Moses* [26]. *For **God is about <u>raising</u> His little children** ... even 'the least' ... unto Divine and Glorious Purpose.*

Scripture:
But He said, "You cannot see My face; for no man shall see Me, and live." *(Exodus 33:20 NKJV)*

God can come in many ways, but if in His Glory one may not survive. I have heard of accounts where the Presence of the Person of God came upon a conference in such intensity that everyone had to leave; and in great awe and reverence, only able to look into the auditorium from outside. I have also heard of accounts where the Glory of God came so mightily upon a church service, that as the nearby village people ran, the Presence of God came upon both believers and unbelievers alike. Even nursing babies, held in their mother's arms, were slain under the Glory of His Presence. And I have heard of the Glory of the Lord coming into a service where some were able to enter, but others were not permitted … like a wall of Power, a physical wall of Glory.

I have also heard of a man who saw God in His Person; passing through the same 'dark cloud' that was presented Moses. And with tears in His eyes, God said to him, *"It has been a long time since someone came here."* The Glory of the 'Face of God' is a mysterious thing. Perhaps this is the Fear that Jesus delighted in? Or that of which caused Moses to exclaim, *"I am terrified and my body shakes."* This very same Glory that made his face glow; the very same that made his 'eyes not to dim'. So, I encourage you, *"To he who has an ear let him listen **intently** to what the Spirit is saying to the Churches."*

What a wonder it is, that God would honour a person so much as to 'humble' Himself; and taking on a 'lowly' physical form to where a man could see Him in Person. Such is the Love of God for each one of us. As a beloved and cherished child of the Living God, His Love for you is **unfathomable** and beyond comprehension. Even to this, is the very reason why Satan became so jealous and vengeful, because He saw God's vulnerability towards this creature called 'Man'. And in this, you cannot fully comprehend … who you truly are in Him.

In God's Glory, a person could not survive, lest you are covered in the 'cleft of His Hand' and called by Him to enter [27]. And until the time of the Cross, it was Jesus alone who was able to go into God's Glory and see His Face upon will. But now, it is the gifted Holy Spirit who has opened realities incomprehensible.

You are clothed in white by the Blood of the Lamb. And through ascending your heart and affections in the Lord, so are you enraptured. As you take it upon yourself to wait upon the Lord *(as Jesus always did)*, then so shall you **see**. And through 'spirit' ascensions so shall you ever engage the Spirits of the Lord who are before the Throne; and through your Divine interactions and engagements; your thought-life shall ever be renewed and sanctified from a fallen state to the Risen. And as your spirit, soul, mind, and flesh are sanctified in His Holy Presence *(the All-Consuming Fire)*, does He cause you able to sit upon the Judgement Throne, the Ruling Throne, the Throne of the King. And this by the very same Spirit of the Lord.

Scripture:
John, to the seven churches which are in Asia: Grace to you and peace from Him who is, and who was, and who is to come, and from the seven Spirits who are before His throne. *(Revelation 1:4 NJKV)*

How is it that the Seven Spirits of God are before the Throne? For their own reasons, but for us, it is they who prepare you able to *re-*sit upon the Throne. Can it ever be thought, that in human capacity, or in human reasoning alone, that one can issue judgements, rulings, and commands from the Throne of the King; the Throne of the Judge ... the Throne of Absolute Authority and Power; without first coming under the Tuition and Counsel of the Spirits of the Lord? Do you think that through one's own boldness and zealousness for God, that a person could truly function here? No, not ever*!*

God is about Family; He is about Union, He is about Oneness; spirit, soul, mind, and flesh. Therefore, in the deepest of honour and gratitude, greet the Spirit of the Lord, the Father and the Son. And enter in to be with Jesus where He is — in His Glory — in Heaven. [42]

Scripture:
You have come to Mount Zion, to the city of the living God, the Heavenly Jerusalem. You have come to thousands upon thousands of angels in joyful assembly, to the church of the firstborn [Jesus our Brother, Friend, King, and Forerunner], whose names are written in Heaven [registered citizens]. You have come to God, the Judge of all, to the spirits of the righteous made perfect [saints who have gone before us], to Jesus the mediator of a new covenant [go-between and guide], and to the sprinkled blood that speaks a better word than the blood of Abel. *(Hebrews 12:22-24 NIV)*

It is the dream of many to travel to Israel ... as would I. But the greatest wonder and adventure is to see Zion. To be one who regularly traverses into the Heavenly Jerusalem, the City of the King ... and this upon will.

One of the most incredible gifts presented the believer today, is your ability to pass through the 'Curtain' right into the dimension of the Kingdom of Heaven. And in reflection of this, do you think that the Holy of Holies was the smallest room in the Temple? *No!* ... for as one passes through the Veil, do you enter through a 'dimensional gateway' right into the fullness of God *(ie; the Sabbath-day 'Rest', enjoying the full fruits of all His labour and the finished work of the Cross [28])*. This is the power of your hope set upon Him [29]. No longer unto earthly concern or desire [30] ... but this Heavenly Divine Place of Honour.

Through the Blood and gifted Spirit of God; the Kingdom of Heaven is now seamless to your world ... no separation. And so too your ability to enter and engage. This by the Spirit of the Lord.

Do you recall in the Parable of the Mustard Seed, where Jesus said, *"Although it is the least of your seeds it grows into the mightiest and greatest of trees?"* [31] Oh the wondrous treasure set before you. This of your inherent and natural ability to have the Glory of God growing in you — in incomprehensible measure — in measure upon measure [32]. And just as the depths and breadths of God are unfathomable; and just as Eternity is deep and wide, so too is your inherent ability of growth in Him. The Glory of God in you expanding incomprehensibly and unimaginably ... and this without ceasing. Such is the birthing of the Spirit of God alive in you. The manifold wonder of the 'Mustard Seed' planted in the heart of each believer.

There is no greater treasure ... no greater value imaginable; even in the streets of Zion, gold is just pavement stone, and gems are like gravel and sand. For **the treasure of Heaven is the Glory of God** ... the very same of which is planted in you. Even expanding from Glory to Glory, and from Glory to exceedingly great Glory. And such is the Presence of the Lord, even that you truly may live *as* the Son. Walking and talking and seeing the Face of God — in His Glory — and this upon will.

There is a man who was known to have traversed into Heaven several times a day *('in body or in spirit I do not know')*. He would be seen surrounded by angels issuing instructions and tasks. This man used to be an alcoholic until he was forty years old. But then by the Grace of God and the Grace alone, he was raised and set in such high honour *(Grace being the Empowerment to win)*. He was a struggling sinner, just like you and I, picked up from the alleyways and byways. But in the treasured Presence of God, he was renewed.

Come then, and set your heart unto the Living and Dynamic Presence of God *(ie; the Equipping Zone)*. And in Him shall you also be lifted up. Lifted up from the miry mud of which you have known and **set** upon the Rock [33]. And so shall you be healed and made whole, and in the Presence of God … ever surrounded by Him. The name of this man is Bob Jones.

By the Blood and the Spirit have you been gifted eyes that see and ears that hear. Therefore, from here within the treasured Presence of God, so shall you see with your 'eyes' and shall hear with your 'ears'.

How can one traverse into Zion, the Heavenly Jerusalem … upon will? But through the simple realisation that the Kingdom of Heaven is 'at hand'. [34]

Those born of God are citizens of Zion, with their names written in the Lamb's Book of Life. Therefore, as you also chose to 'ascend' your heart in Him so too are you taken. Snapped up and captured in Him through a heart of submission and honour.

Dreams and prayers are most powerful. But have them raise up ever higher in Him. If your prayer and dreams are for the salvation of souls, then **go** to the God who saves souls. And if your prayer and dream is to heal, then unite and bond yourself closer to He who Heals. For where the core root of your 'prayer' remains then so too do you abide and construct your dwelling. And if it is in the Lord, then that is where your spirit abides; and that is where your spirit, soul, mind, and flesh is actively engaged.

Manifest first in the spirits of the people. Burning in their souls and consuming their thoughts. And their flesh touched by the Finger of God.

To travel one doesn't just stay home but goes out their front door. So too is it the same in Christ Jesus … He, as the Son of Man, is the 'front' Door. And through Him, do you step out into the vastness of the Kingdom of Heaven. And as a bird set free from a cage, do you traverse in Him deep into the Heavenly realms; bringing back 'souvenirs' of what you have seen [5], and to that of which you have collected and have experienced … to the world.

Your birth into the Kingdom of Heaven is simply like the arrival at the 'airport' [36]. Here, with the whole country and its rich treasures laying before you; to explore and **take** 'possession'. [37]

If one wishes, you can enter into depravity and despair. But in the same way, even from the depths of despair, can one ascend their heart up unto the Lord and be led out upon the **Sea of Glass** [38]. The answer is not in religion or philosophy, nor the depravity of man, but through the right of *perpetual* Encounters in the Person of Jesus. A people no longer living life based on human IQ … but Spirit IQ. And this given freely of the Lord to any and to all whom might ask! [39]

Jesus is the open Doorway, and just as Mary didn't fully comprehend who she was birthing into the world, neither do you. But how proud, and how she has realised utter joy, as she sees her Son in Glory. Hence in Him, <u>**are** you **known**</u>, and in Him so <u>**shall you know**</u>. You shall see, and so shall your eyes be opened to see all the more.

To ascend the Mountain of the Lord … even Mount Zion, are you continually captured up in Him into Places that cannot be described. Nor can fit into the comprehension or vision of man [40]. When Jesus was Transfigured, He demonstrated that the flesh is the **lowest form** of *us*. That truly we are people of Light [41] — Eternal Creatures of Glory. So where you personally choose to position yourself is up to you. And in this there is no condemnation. But in Christ Jesus, you can set your heart unto realms whereby you stand before Jesus in His Glory [42]. And now when He appears so shall you also appear with Him in His Glory. [43]

Two Closing Scriptures:
1. And when he had sent the multitudes away, he went up into a mountain apart to pray: and when the evening was come, he was there *alone. (Matthew 14:23 NKJV)*
2. And it came to pass in those days, that He went out into a mountain to pray, and continued *all night* in prayer to God. *(Luke 6:12 NKJV)*

A closing thought: When Jesus went into the lonely place to pray, did He go there with lists and lists of needs and requests that took all night to pour out? No, of course not.

Now words like 'worship', 'ascension', 'wait upon the Lord', and 'seek the Face of God' take on a whole other meaning. Words like 'stand in His Counsel', the 'Sea of Sapphire', 'Jacob's ladder', and an 'open Heaven' ... take on an even greater relevance. The truth is, that as you seek the Presence of God so **shall** you see the Face of God. And so shall your face come to glow and your eyes not go dim. [44]

There is the 'Old Wineskin' of laws, self-reliance, and one's own labour and vision. And then there is the 'New Wineskin' of Ascension, Divine Encounters, and Impartation ... and perpetual Interaction in the New Jerusalem. To this is the way that Jesus — the 'pioneer' lived — Jesus, our very 'precedent' and 'forerunner' — who worked to demonstrate and lay the way before us — actively exampled for each one of us.

The truth is, that the New Wine just can't function in the Old ... they are simply not compatible. The New just can't function *nor* can be contained in the Old. [45]

Today, it's just a matter of coming to truly recognise the complete and finished work of the Cross. And to all that of which Christ Jesus has already laid opened for you — and step further in.

Appendix:

1. Matthew 27:51, Hebrews 6:19, John 12:24, Luke 9:23, *2.* Hebrews 12:22-24, 1 Kings 19:11-13, John 15:4-11, *3.* Matthew 6:21, Luke 17:21, *4.* Revelation 1:4, *5.* John 5:44, *6.* Philippians 3:8, Isaiah 11:1-9, Revelation 5:6, Psalm 36:8, John 7:38, 4:14, Galatians 5:22-23, *7.* John 15:7, 5:19, Psalm 110:2, *8.* Matthew 18:10, John 17:24, Exodus 33:18-23, Revelation 3:18, *9.* 1 Corinthians 2:9-10, *10.* Matthew 18:3, 10, *11.* Isaiah 64:1-4, Exodus 33:18-23, Revelation 4:1, *12.* John 5:37-38, Matthew 4:4, 6:11, 13:15, 16:17-19, *13.* Matthew 6:11, 4:4, *14.* Proverbs 6:31, Deuteronomy 28:7, 7:20, Isaiah 54:13-17, *15.* 2 Corinthians 12:2, *16.* Ephesians 2:4-7, *17.* Romans 8:19, *18.* Acts 5:15, *19.* Matthew 18:10, *20.* *In Scripture, 'spirit' and 'angel' are sometimes interchanged. For example, when the people thought that Peter's 'angel' was standing at the door* — Acts 12:13-15, *21.* Matthew 19:26, *22.* Mark 4:24, Luke 6:38, *23.* Exodus 33:11, *24.* John 17:24, Genesis 3:10, Revelation 3:17-18, 21, *25.* Matthew 11:11, *26.* Exodus 24:9-11, *27.* Exodus 33:17-23, 24:11, 1 Kings 19:11, *28.* Genesis 2:1-3, Hebrews 4:1-11, *29.* Hebrews 6:19, *30.* Matthew 13:22-23, *31.* Matthew 13:32, *32.* 2 Corinthians 3:18, *33.* Psalm 40:1-3, *34.* Luke 17:21, Matthew 4:17, *35.* John 3:11, *36.* Matthew 23:13, *37.* Deuteronomy 1:8, *38.* Isaiah 44:22b, *39.* James 1:5, Matthew 7:7, Psalm 2:7-8, *40.* 2 Corinthians 12:4, 1 Corinthians 2:9-10, *41.* 1 Thessalonians 5:5, Ephesians 5:8, *42.* John 17:24, *43.* Colossians 3:4, 1 John 3:2, *44.* Deuteronomy 34:7, 2 Timothy 1:10, Mark 16:18, *45.* *The New is like the wind, you do not know where they come from nor where they are going* — John 3:8

Dated: 24/3/19

6. *Living in a State of Perpetual Encounter (#89)*
PASSING THROUGH THE DOOR

Let's start this chapter with a question: If Jesus is the 'Door' … what is He the *door* to? And if Jesus is the Door to Heaven, is death your only key or point of access, or do you not already have the Keys of Heaven? So, in realising that the Keys are in your hands, and Jesus was sent as the Door opened you, let your faith arise. And as your faith begins to rise … let it rise all the more.

Jesus was crucified and raised again to bring you to your Heavenly Father … so go to Him. At the Fall, Heaven and earth was wrenched apart. But however now, through the precious Blood and gifted Spirit of God, has the Cross brought about the 'Restoration'. The re-connection, the re-joining, and the re-positioning you back in Glory [1]. And like a 'thread' of hope [2] forming into tight bonds; roots forming into a great tree; [3] does your continual seeking of the Presence of God *(behind the Veil)* re-establish you in all that was lost. As is said, *"We, who with **unveiled** faces contemplate (look Intently into) the Lord's Glory, are being **Transformed into His image** with ever-increasing Glory."* [4]

The Kingdom of Heaven is like a 'Seed' [5]. And as you draw this Seed dearly to heart [6] do you open yourself to the fullness of Heaven. And like a Spring 'welling up' into Everlasting Life; do you open yourself to dynamic and experiential Realities of God. [7]

"The Kingdom of God is not a matter of talk but of Power." [8]

Right now, through faith, your spirit-man is standing before God right now [9]. And if Jesus says, *"Your flesh counts for nothing"* but it is the *"Spirit that **gives Life**"* [10], then why not set your heart wholly unto these realms of the Spirit? [11] It is through love that you unite yourself with He who is Love. There are many things that you can concern yourself with. But in God, are you lifted up and can interact and engage in Heaven … and this, in ever increasing measure.

Space is an empty place, but Heaven is full of the burning Joy and Love of God. Space is a cold dark vacuum, whilst Heaven is full of companionship and Light. Our life on earth can be much the same, but the answer to the human condition is **perpetual** and open interaction with the Person of God [12]. This, the very same that Jesus Himself walked in — and of whom, Himself opened up the way for us all this very day. Even this, the very same that was lost man in the Beginning, *ie;* the Restoration.

At the time of the Fall, the Angel of the Lord was commanded to bar the way to Eden and to that of the Tree of Life [13]. However now it is, that through the New Adam [14], access has been fully restored. With these very realms of the Kingdom of Heaven now — fully right 'at hand' [15]. Therefore, in coming to embrace this fully gifted access — and stepping through He who is the Door [16] — shall pathways form. Well-trodden trails becoming as like a 'Highway' of broadening interaction [17]. Ever expanding truths and living realities pouring richly into your life [18]. With angels ascending and descending upon the sons and daughters of God. [19]

Scripture:
He then added, "Very truly I tell you, you will see 'heaven open, and the angels of God ascending and descending on' the Son of Man [upon the sons and daughters of God]." *(John 1:51 NIV)*

In Christian circles, believers have only thought of miracles as to the healing of the sick. But what about the miracle of your Salvation? And what about the miracle that the Kingdom of Heaven is now at hand? What about the miracle of your ability in Christ Jesus to hear and see God; and walk in realms of the Spirit just as the Son? And what about the miracle of your ability to now live as one raised and tutored in the Glory and Might of God? I tell you; **this is the basis of a miracle-filled life**. A life full of the Love, Peace, and Joy in the Power of God. [20]

The demon has acted as a fog obscuring, and the spiritual forces of the air like a great heaviness upon your life. But like a knife does the Blood of Jesus cut right through into an open Heaven. Not because of your good deeds, nor anything that you can do of yourself … but by the Blood of Jesus and the Blood alone. And without any understanding of how you got here, it is the Spirit of the Lord that shoots you up into the realms of Holiness and Power, even then as the Prince of Peace comes and stands in your midst.

Scripture:
The water that I will give him shall become a spring of water welling up [continually] within him unto eternal life [giving him]. *(John 4:14b AMPC/KJV)*

Heaven is your **Home**, with Divine access your fundamental Birthright. As Jesus said, *"You are not of the world even as I am not of the world"* [21]. And here, abiding in the realms of Presence, are you ever strengthened and ever built up in the Lord [22]. With vision in your eyes and the sights and sounds of Heaven ever before you — as one being 'Clothed' in Glory [23]. Your engagements and interactions only ever increasing; as too the open manifestation of the Kingdom of Heaven in your midst [24]. For the core Prayer of our Saviour still remains the same, *"Your Kingdom come, your Will be* **done on earth** *just as it is in Heaven."* [25]

The purpose and underlying motive of Jesus is to **make you Like Him**. And just as Jesus engaged with God and the realms of Heaven; this very same reality has been laid open for you as well. Therefore, as you also choose to pass through He who is the Way, does the Kingdom of Heaven pass through you. Like a Doorway, a 'ladder' or a portal; God stepping through His children all across the nations.

Recently, I happened to pick up a book of Smith Wigglesworth's life's teachings. And I stumbled upon a paragraph that happened to read in line with the thoughts of this chapter. And it goes like this, *"God, who is from everlasting to everlasting, has always had people who He could trust, people that He could '***illuminate***', that He could enlarge. Until there is nothing in them that could hinder the Power of God."* [26]

I so encourage you, that as you come also to stand **before** the Glory of the Most High God, like Moses of Old [27], so too shall your *being* begin to emanate and radiate the very same Glory [28]. And regardless of your station in life, or seasons that you might find yourself in, you have full right of passage to enter through the 'Door' whenever you desire.

I tell you a secret: Jesus didn't go into the secret place [29] just to read out lists and lists of prayers and requests. But He stepped right into an open Heaven. This is why He spoke only what He *heard* His Father saying and did only what He *saw* His Father doing [30]. And in the same way, when the three disciples saw Jesus Transfigured into light; it was simply in witness of something Jesus always did. I so encourage you, this very same right of passage, has been given all who love the Lord.

Let's begin ...

TO BE CLOTHED IN GLORY

As a people, what we want to learn about is how to receive from Heaven. And if anything, learn how to go deeper in and receive all the more liberally for our life and the world around us [31]. God is not about religion; He is about relationship. God is not about arguing doctrine but pouring out the Holy Spirit's Fire. As Jesus said, *"I have come to bring fire on the earth, and how I wish it were already kindled."* [32]

As we notice here, it is 'kindling' that prepares you for the Fire of the Holy Ghost. Meaning, your delighted in and welcomed revelations [33] and experiences in the Lord, lays ground for the Glory of God to pour into your life. And just as purposed, you are an open Heaven; each one of us have unique opportunity to go into the Presence of God and engage; and this to the measure of our own heart's desire *(this being our only limitation)*. Hence this subject is about **decisively** choosing to pass through He who is the Door ... to be 'Clothed in Power'. As Jesus again says, *"Wait in the city until you have been clothed with Power from on High."* [34]

Two Scripture verses:
1. Without faith it is impossible to please God, because anyone who comes to Him must believe that He exists and that He rewards those who **earnestly** seek Him. *(Hebrews 11:6 NIV)*

2. Make every effort to live in peace with everyone and to be holy; for without holiness no one will **see** the Lord. *(Hebrews 12:14 NIV)*

The Church has not known about the Glory of God, nor their place in it.

There are many places that one can abide. But if — in your spirit, soul, mind, and flesh — you can *abide* in God, then so shall you deeply 'delight' Him. Meaning, deeply stir and move His Heart whereby He deeply responds to you [35]. And here, shall you enter into a lifestyle of perpetually experiencing the Lord. And through your own personal Interactions, Experiences, and Encounters with God, be 'rewarded' in all your pursuits. This is the basis of faith: [36] that you might *first* believe that God exists — **and also** — that He personally **responds** to your seeking.

To such as these God 'rends the heavens'. He tears away the opposition and obstructions — and in most **significant** ways — responds to you [37]. Doing crazy, unexpected, and wonderful things. And this ancient truth may have been expressed in the Old Testament, but how **much more is it real** and purposed today for all born of the Spirit.

As a people, what we want is to be known in Him — known by the Lord [38]. In Christ Jesus, each one of us have the unbelievable privilege to perpetually seek His Face [39] … regardless of seasons, or what we might be going through. For in the exact same manner He comes … perpetually. As a person being continuously engaged and continuously lifted up in the Lord. First in spirit, then in soul and mind, and so too in your flesh. [40]

It is said that Enoch walked in close fellowship with God. Then one day he was not found because God took him [42]. I tell you, the greatest blessing you can ever be for your people is to walk close with God. Even as one 'taken' … as one 'captured up in Him'. Today, in the New Covenant, this is not about a departing the earth, but about richly engaging with God — where He is — and bringing His Glory and Goodness to earth.

AS 'LIGHTNING' DOES THE GLORY COME

God is not drawn to problems; He is drawn to faith. But now, as a people of faith, when you speak: problems are fully exposed to the Glory of God. For where your treasure is, so your heart is also. And if your treasure is in the Lord; does your spirit rise up as one who stands in His Glory [40] ... as one 'found' in Him. Now, when you speak, does your spirit join with your prayers, and as '**lightning**' the Glory of God strikes the earth. [43]

As is said, *"When Jesus **appears** so shall you appear with Him in Glory"* [44]. And why is this? But simply, as a lifestyle, your spirit-man is actively and continuously engaged with Him in Glory. Not in other places, but with Him behind the Veil. Such is the Presence of God. And such is the Power of Encounter and God showing up; the strongman destroyed, and the Glory of God revealed. The Power of God released and the many coming into the knowledge of God. [45]

A side note: Did you know that lightning starts from earth? Like your hands lifted up in praise unto the 'rumbling' Heavens and connecting — drawing down the Power of God. The 'Glory Cloud' of Heaven excited and attracted by your heart set upon Him [46]. *And when you speak, you draw down 'flashes' of Glory bring healing and the spontaneous moves of God. Just as Jesus exclaimed, "Someone touched me, for I felt Power going out from me."* [47]

The problem with miracles is always the same: you have to have a problem in the first place. But so too is the answer always the same: seek the Presence of God. For through a heart of simple honour [48] and thankfulness, do you rise up from under the 'weather' to function 'Above' in Him. Not only as one who approaches the Counsels and Throne of God in times of need. But one who resides — **part** of His Counsel — where Heaven listens intently to the words of your mouth.

> *The Throne is your underlying Calling. And the Spirit your Guardian and Tutor* [49]. *And to such as these, ever walk in the Glory and Power of God.*

Many Christians pray and attempt to do the 'work' of the Kingdom whilst still residing on *earth*. Calling out to 'our Father who is in Heaven' [50]. But the *(post-Cross)* Gospel is fundamentally about 'Ascension' ... being Risen, the coming up in Him. The co-abiding, co-reigning and co-seated with Him in the Glory realms. Jesus is about you abiding and functioning — where He is now — just as He [51]. This is why He declared, *"It's better that I go"* [52]. So that each one of us might walk in 'Like' as He, as true sons and daughters of the Living God. [53]

Problems tend to remain because believers don't come here. Though they still believe in Jesus, their hearts are always set on other cares and desires [54], and not in where they are supposed to be going ... nor unto the Glory of God purposed them. Subsequently, believers tend to always come 'under' circumstances rather than coming up Above. Even as one who walks the earth with the full backing of Heaven.

The more open you are to welcoming the Holy Spirit to align your heart; the more able you are to **live** as one raised in Glory. Personally taken by hand — in the Spirit — into the great Mysteries of God's Wonders. Ever dwelling in His Abiding Word [55], in the very Living Word that sanctifies and speaks Alive in your soul. And as you continue to hold the Lord most dear, so too do you open your heart for Him to engage with you. And as one 'dining' with Him and He with you; are you continuously 'served' to of and by the Lord [56]. For through honour and praise so are you also lifted up in Honour and Praise.

*On a side note: Did you realise that there are two layers of sanctification? The sanctifying Power of the Blood that has gained you **perfect access** unto the Father. And then the sanctifying Power of the Spirit that Instructs and Trains; **maturing you able** to sit upon the Throne (ie; 'nothing in you that hinders the Power of God'). For though, through the Blood and the rending of the Veil, have you been 'birthed' child of God; it is only through the humbling of oneself as like a little child* [57], *that truly makes you truly able to participate in the Power of His Resurrection.*

Scripture *(two translations):*
1. If you remain in me and my words [that 'proceed from my mouth'] remain in you, ask whatever you wish, and it will be done for you. *(John 15:7 NIV)*

2. If you live in life-union with me and if my words live powerfully within you — then you can ask whatever you desire and it will be done. *(John 15:7 TPT)*

Throughout the Gospels, Jesus spoke primarily of 'earthly things', earthly teachings according to righteous living and the ways of the Kingdom. However, His dream and the purpose of His heart is always about teaching and showing you ... 'Heavenly things' [58]. Hence therefore, as one who deeply loves the Lord, ever resign yourself to this wonderful prospect.

The Gospel message, as the 'moral of the story', always points to the Spirit and unto the manifest Kingdom of Heaven on earth. Therefore, the 'earthly' teachings of Christ Jesus can be likened to soil, whilst the 'Heavenly' teachings are the very Plantings ... *ie;* the very Purpose and Heart of God. That here and today, you truly might come to function, as one bringing Heaven and the Will of God to the world.

For what is sought after is the **manifestation** of the Kingdom of Heaven on earth. The written Word made *flesh* and walking amongst us; the Promises of God made manifest and real before our very eyes. This is the very 'Lord's Prayer' for us today: the manifestation of the "Will of God done on earth" [59]. Not only as a people who know the Kingdom of Heaven exists. But a people who perpetually enter in and actively engage bringing Heaven to earth. And as Creatures of Light [60], continuously transiting into the realms of Light; making way for God to reveal and make plain: that of which was hidden beyond the concepts and imaginations of man. [61]

> *'You were once darkness, but now you are Light in the Lord.*
> *Come then and **walk** as children of Light'.* [62]

The natural motive of the demon is to degrade man. And the natural inclination of man is degradation. However, irrespective, the Heart of the Father is always directed unto man. And the Lord, as He continues to lead us forward, so does He make way for His own Goodness to be poured out. Hence, I so treasure the Dreams of God fulfilled. Come Holy Spirit, be outpoured upon the nations, and make you Name known upon the earth. This, for the honour of the Son and the healing of the souls of man.

Scripture:
Christ's resurrection is **your** resurrection too. This is why we are to **yearn** for all that is above, for that's where Christ sits enthroned at the place of all power, honor, and authority! Yes, **feast** on all the treasures of the heavenly realm and **fill your thoughts** with heavenly realities, and not with the distractions of the natural realm. Your **crucifixion** with Christ has severed the tie to this life, and now your true life is **hidden away** in God in Christ [Jesus]. And as Christ himself is seen for who he really is, who you really are **will also be revealed**, for you are now **on**e with him in his glory! *(Colossians 3:1-4 TPT)*

The Resurrection of Jesus *is* your ability to rise up with Him in Glory *(such is the Fire of God)*. Christ Jesus died in place of you — so that you need not die in order to enter Heaven. There are many places where a person can go and function from. But in Christ Jesus, one can pass through the Veil and function in Heaven — in His Eternal Glory — and this right where you stand.

For 'death' is not your hope ... Life is. As Jesus is referred to as the Door, the question is, what is He the door to? On earth, there are many things that keep the people tethered. But as one who chooses to seek the real and most manifest Presence of the Person of God, then so too do you liberally pass through.

Scripture:
Woe to you, teachers of the law and Pharisees, you hypocrites! You **shut** the door of the kingdom of heaven in people's faces. You yourselves do not enter, nor will you let those enter who are trying to. *(Matthew 23:13 NIV)*

The Purpose of the Christ has always been to the *passing* through and functioning from right within the realms of Heaven. And this reality ... only ever increasing. And only made more manifest and real on earth. And just the same as Christ Jesus; He who is our Precedent ... Christ Jesus our Forerunner and King; so are we also called to **follow Him in His Footsteps**, and on the 'pavement' of His example. Living and functioning just as He; even unto greater works and deeds. *63*

The spirit of Religion only seeks to restrict and create walls against that of which the Spirit has freely given. But to those who truly embrace the work of the Spirit, and **harken earnestly** with the ears that have been given *64*, does the Spirit of the Lord continuously lead each one of us forward. And when the *Enemy* does rise up like a flood ... so does the Spirit of the Lord raise a standard against him. Destroying all his works and plans and purposes. *65*

People like Smith Wigglesworth understood these things. And spent more time in Heaven — in the Glory of God's Presence — than they did on earth. But in this, he influenced and affected millions upon millions. And to this very day, his mark still impacts lives. Religion assigns people like Smith Wigglesworth as 'special' called and gifted ones. Hence relegating the Anointing that he carried to the realms of the unreachable and unattainable. Even with Heaven itself being accessible only upon death. But as is clear, death is not your saviour — Jesus is! Therefore, the Glory Smith Wigglesworth carried upon his life is available to us all, for each and every one in Christ Jesus are one in Him ... *if* this is truly your heart's desire.

Scripture:
[I pray] that they all may be **one**, as You, Father, are in Me, and I in You; that they also **may be <u>one</u> in Us**, that the world may believe that You sent Me. And the glory which You gave Me I **have given them**, that they may be one just as We are one: I in them, and You in Me; that they may be made perfect in one [brought to complete unity in Us], and that the world **may <u>know</u> that You have sent Me**, and have loved them as You have loved Me. Father, I desire that they also whom You gave Me **may be <u>with</u> me where I am** [in Heaven], and that they may **behold** [see and experience] **my Glory** which You have given Me; for You loved Me before the foundation of the world. *(John 17:20-24 NKJV/NIV (John 3:13 NKJV))*

God loves you, in the exact same way as He loves the Son. And the exact same capacity that was in Jesus as He walked this earth — is now available in you [66]. Anointed people, like Smith Wigglesworth, are believers who simply passed through the opened Door right into the Kingdom of Heaven. Right into the Divine Wonders of the Holy Presence of God. They are people who personally **set their own dream** upon the very Person of Christ Jesus. And in affection and love, continually **sought** the Face of God [67]. So how then, can one of whom beholds the Glory of God, of whom stands in His Glory, not also come to hold and carry the very same Glory?

Some have a Divine fragrance, a perfume of Heaven coming all over them. Some have gold dust and gems. And some, when they lift their arms, half the church falls under the Presence of God. And why is this? For their soul and their flesh has simply been phasing in and out of Heaven. They have been **passing in and out** of the Heavenly realms as is their daily norm. Entering through, via He who is the open 'Door', via He who is the 'Way'. Such is the Power of faith: the setting of your heart *(your desires and affections)* on things Above. [68]

Scripture:
I am the door: by me if any man enter in, he shall be saved, and shall go in and out [of Heaven], and find pasture. *(John 10:9 NKJV)*

There are accounts where Smith Wigglesworth would step onto a bus, and the Glory of which he carried brought everyone to fall to their knees. And in repentance gave their life to God. I so encourage you, let your spirit and soul come stand before the Glory of God; that your flesh and your thoughts may emanate and radiate the very same Glory. The **answer is the Presence of God** — this, the very same right of passage given you by the Cross. Preparing the way … *kindling* you … unto the Outpouring of the Fire of God.

> *"All creation is in eager waiting for the sons and daughters of God to be revealed."* [69]

To close ...

As was mentioned in the opening of this chapter: God doesn't respond to problems, but He responds to faith. The subject of this book is always the same: the **manifestation** of the Power and Presence of God on earth. So that we no longer remain a people who only beat against the air, but a people capable of **moving** the Hand of God. A people who **know** who they are in Him and how to **liberally receive** from Heaven … moving mountains [70]. Such is the Power found in the Secret Place; the very same that Jesus spent such a lot of time, and King David's soul longed for. [71]

"Held in the hearts of the little children; mustard-sized Seeds of Faith planted of the Lord. The very same that moves mountains; and removes all hindrances and all obstructions in the land. Wiping away the tears of many, replacing grief and sorrow with tears of Joy." [72]

Appendix:

1. Romans 3:23-24, Revelation 5:9-10 *NKJV*, *2.* Hebrews 6:19-20, *3.* Isaiah 61:3b, Psalm 1:3, Revelation 2:7, *4.* 2 Corinthians 3:18, Genesis 1:26, *5.* Mark 4:26-32, Matthew 13:18-23, *6.* Psalm 27:4, *7.* John 4:14, 3:11, Acts 4:20, *8.* 1 Corinthians 4:20, *9.* Matthew 18:10, *10.* John 6:63, Luke 12:37, Revelation 3:20, Matthew 4:4, 6:11, 16:17-19, 13:15, John 5:37-37, *11.* Colossians 3:1-2, *12.* Exodus 33:15-17, Exodus 24:9-11, *13.* Genesis 3:24, *14.* 1 Corinthians 15:21-23, 45-47, *15.* Matthew 4:17, *16.* Psalm 27:4, 37:4, *17.* John 1:51, Genesis 28:12, *18.* Matthew 3:2-3, 4:17, Luke 12:49, *19.* John 1:51, Genesis 28:12, Luke 3:21, *20.* In parallel: Matthew 16:17-18 / Mark 16:17-18, *21.* John 17:16, *22.* Psalm 110:1-2, 23:5, 27:4, 2:7-8, *23.* 2 Kings 6:17, 1 Corinthians 15:53-54, Revelation 3:17-18 *(Luke 14:28-33)*, Psalm 2:7-8, 82:6-8, 110:1-2, Luke 24:49, Genesis 3:10, Exodus 33:14-18, *24.* Romans 8:19, *25.* Matthew 6:10, *26.* Smith Wigglesworth: The Complete Collection of His Life Teachings page #151, *27.* Exodus 19:20, *28.* Exodus 34:29, *29.* Matthew 6:5, 6, 16, Luke 5:16, Luke 6:12, *30.* John 5:19, 8:28, *31.* Mark 11:24, John 15:7, *32.* Luke 12:49, *33.* Luke 24:32, *34.* Luke 24:49, *35.* Daniel 10:12, *36.* Hebrews 11:6, *37.* Isaiah 64:1-4, *38.* Matthew 7:21-23, John 15:4-7, 17:3, Exodus 33:14-18, *39.* Psalm 37:4, John 15:7, *40.* John 1:14, *41.* Genesis 5:24, *42.* Zechariah 3:7, *43.* Revelation 2:26-27, Psalm 110:1-2, *44.* Colossians 3:4, *45.* Luke 4:1-15, Mark 1:21-28, *46.* Exodus 20:21, *47.* Luke 8:46, *48.* John 3:14-15, *49.* Zechariah 3:7, Ephesians 3:14-19, John 14:26, 16:14, Galatians 4:1-2, *50.* Matthew 6:9, *51.* NKJV; John 17:20-24, 5:19, 3:13, 1 John 4:17, John 15:4, 7, Revelation 1:5-6, Matthew 8:26, Mark 3:14-15, *52.* John 16:7, *53.* John 1:12, *54.* Mark 4:18-20, *55.* John 15:7, 1 John 2:27, Matthew 4:4, *56.* Luke 12:37, Revelation 3:20, *57.* Matthew 18:3, *58.* John 3:12, *59.* Matthew 6:10, *60.* 2 Corinthians 5:17, 1 Thessalonians 5:5, Ephesians 5:8, *61.* 1 Corinthians 2:9-10 AMPC, *62.* Ephesians 5:8, *63.* John 14:12, *64.* Matthew 11:15, Revelation 2:29, *65.* Isaiah 59:19, *66.* Luke 4:14, Luke 5:17b, *67.* Philippians 3:8, *68.* Colossians 3:2-3, *69.* Romans 8:19, *70.* Isaiah 41:15, *71.* Psalm 27:4, *72.* Matthew 17:20

Dated: 24/4/19

THE JOY SET BEFORE HIM

7. *The Joy Set Before Him (#90)*
THE JOY SET BEFORE HIM

Scripture:
I am the Door: by me if any man enter in, he shall be saved, and shall go in and out and *find* pasture. *(John 10:9 NKJV)*

A QUESTION
Christ Jesus is referred to as the Door. But what is He the Door to? So if Jesus is the Door to Heaven, why would you want to wait until death before you access? Before you 'go in and out?' When death is not your Saviour ... Jesus is.

THE JOY SET BEFORE THE LORD
When thinking of Communion, and the meaning of Easter, people usually only focus on the Crucifixion and the Resurrection. But what I'd like to focus on: is the 'Joy' that was the Lord's as He faced the horrors of the Cross. [1]

IMAGE AND LIKENESS OF THE SON
In Scripture, it speaks about being conformed to the 'Image and Likeness' of the Son [2]. And when discussing, Christians typically focus only on Jesus' character and nature. But again, what I'd like to focus on here, is the *Joy* that is the Lord's, whereby through the finished work of the Cross: **you have been made Like Him** '**in Glory**'. In Likeness of the very Person of Christ Jesus ... in ever-increasing Glory. [3]

Even as it says in Scripture, *"As Christ Jesus **is** so are we in the world"*. And elsewhere, that we might *"Be **with** Him where He is"* [4]. And where is that? ... **in Glory**. Abiding where He is in Glory, **unified one** in the very same Glory of God. The Radiance of His Person; the Wonder of Him ever resting upon you; the Light of light ... the Joy, the Hope, and the Life of God. And the ever-increasing 'Revealing' of your sonship made manifest on earth. [35]

THE TRANSFIGURATION
When reading about the Transfiguration, [5] or let's say, when the Disciples witnessed Jesus Transfigured into Light; [6] was this the first

time for Jesus ... or was it His norm? Perhaps now it can be better understood when Jesus would say, *"I only do that which I see my Father doing"* [7]. For where did He go? ... and where did He see?

Here, what is said shall come true, *"The rod of **your strength** [Iron Sceptre] shall come out of Zion saying, 'Rule in the midst of your enemies!'"* [8]

ANOINTED AUTHORITY IS GIVEN OF GOD

This Scripture verse speaks of the basis of one who walks in the Glory of God. For as one in Christ Jesus so are we called to Rule. We are called to Rule in the midst of all that comes against. Not to be a people weak or frail, nor continuously coming under. But by the Grace of God: a people Empowered of Heaven.

"The Joy of the Lord is my Strength."

Jesus openly declared that He could do nothing of Himself [9]. Therefore, in His Likeness — so too are you 'Strengthened' in the Presence of God [10] — in 'Zion'. For Power is not in what you see, nor in human understanding or that of the flesh, but the 'Rod' of **your Strength** *(ie; the Anointed Authority given of God ... the 'Iron Sceptre'* [11]*)* — that comes out of Zion — releases the Sovereignty of God on the earth.

Everything is about Presence. Everything is about you 'returning' [12] ... returning back into the pre-fallen state. These Heavenly realms of Dominion, Life, and Liberty. The very same of which Adam fell, or better still ... in Christ, the upgraded version. It was Satan who dislodged man, he didn't replace but dislodged; hence today, the Place of the Son of Man awaits you.

In the New Testament, Jesus is referred to as the Morning Star [13]. And it is the same that He is offering you [14]. In the Old Testament it was Satan [15] ... but as Jesus said, *"I saw Satan fall like lightning from Heaven"* [16] ... or otherwise said, *"I saw Satan fall like a shooting star"*. However today, Jesus speaks to the born renewed, *"Behold, I have given you Authority to trample on serpents and scorpions, and over all the power of the Enemy, and nothing shall by any means hurt you."* [17]

Satan came in place of the Son ... *ie;* the *Position*. He is the lawless one trying to operate in the realms 'in-between' ... you and the Glory of God. As in the Exodus story, Satan has occupied your Promises, but it is through *engaging* of the Spirit of God *(ie; 'Presence')* that causes you able to take possession of that of which is already yours.

There is the 'first heaven', which is the earth. Then, there is the 'second heaven' of which is — in between — that of the 'Third Heaven', of which is God's Abiding Place. It is the Calling of God to come back, not to remain in the place you were before, but **breakthrough** into where you are going. These, the 'forgotten' realms that you have not known; but so shall the Spirit of the Lord continue to reveal to you as you are 'found in Him'. [18]

Satan shall be moved, and the Lion of Judah released by the word of your mouth! So rebuke the works of death [19], and in place of death; release Spirit, Life, and the Fire of God. Release the Vengeance of God — and the Hornets [20] — against the Devourer, for the battle is not yours [21]. The focus is unto Presence, it is unto the Fire and Glory of God ... the 'returning'. Ever to dwell in the Place Christ died to bring. And more! ... was raised again that you be Raised as He.

Not problems, it is Presence that releases Power.

Scripture:
Yet the news about him spread all the more, so that crowds of people came to hear him and to be healed of their sicknesses. **But** Jesus often withdrew into lonely places and prayed. *(Luke 5:15-16 NIV)*

THE POWER OF THE SECRET PLACE
This Scripture is a favourite of mine, and it makes me smile as I picture the scene. It starts like this, *"Fame about Jesus spread all the more, so that crowds of people came to hear Him and to be healed of their sicknesses."* However, there then is a full stop and the word 'but'. And the next sentence starts of, *"**But** Jesus often withdrew into lonely places where He prayed."* In other places it says, *"He prayed all night"*. So, a question would be, did Jesus have lists and lists of needs and

requests that took Him all night to pray? Or does 'prayer', in this instance, mean something else? … does it mean something more?

Does it not mean: The Secret Place, the Abiding Place, Ascension … the being captured up into Zion, where you are given 'Hidden Manna' [22]. Isn't your privately going into the 'cupboard' to meet with the God, a place of Invitation? [23] A place of personal Visitation as one **engaging** Heaven? Where you are continually strengthened and built up in the Presence of the Lord. And are you not the Temple of God? And is not the Holy of Holies within you? Therefore, inherently; your innermost place is a Gateway!

*Jesus' vision is **union**.*
And until you make it
— your vision —
then you will always
— feel lost.—

UNION

In Christ Jesus, you are called to be one with Him [24]. Therefore, in responding, all the Promises that are the Lord's, are now yours as well. For you are in Him — **if** that truly is where your heart lies.

This next Scripture verse is oftentimes overlooked, for it is addressed to the 'King'. But I so encourage you, what is the Lord's is now **yours** as well [25] … they belong to the Church, they belong to the People of God. And as you come into understanding of this, then so shall you be ever Strengthened in the Lord. Not only Strengthened but made Powerful and Anointed. And this is what your world needs, not more of you … but the Glory of God that is in you. The Power of the Kingdom of Heaven, the Power of the Presence of the Person of the Living God, of whose you are and who you belong.

Two Scripture verses:
1. I will proclaim the LORD's decree: He said to me, "You are my son; <u>**today**</u> **I have become your Father**. Ask me, and I will make the nations your inheritance, the ends of the earth your possession. *(Psalm 2:7-8 NIV)*

2. The LORD says to my lord: "**Sit at my right hand** until I make your enemies a footstool for your feet." *(Psalm 110:1 NIV)*

Oftentimes, our prayers are misaligned, for our 'prayer' is supposed to start *here*. The root of our heart set upon beholding the Glory of God [26]. The same Place where Jesus Shines, where Jesus Fights, and where Jesus Heals and Restores. This is the summation of the Word of God: the Glory of the Living God with you and going out before you unto the honour of the Son. [27]

In the book of Genesis, it speaks of our pre-fallen and lost 'Dominion' *(ie; our Rule)* over all creation [28]. Then in the Psalms, it speaks of an 'Invitation to sit at the right hand of God' [29]. In Hebrews it speaks of *"Diligently enter the Sabbath-day of Rest"* … meaning, the full finished work that God has achieved for you. And then in the Book of Revelations, it speaks of 'open door' to come sit as a king [30]. A pathway, a method … a means; to open your heart and let the Christ come in and sit with you and you with Him *(in and though all things)*. And He will raise you Victorious and Triumphant; shaping and forming and **making** you able to Rule.

All these Scriptures referred to here, they are all **re-positional** Scriptures. For it is the fundamental Purpose and Calling of God to **return back** [31] into the Glory of the Son. To be re-raised and restored; repositioned over creation. Over all issues of life, over all that comes against, and all that tries to kill, steal, and destroy, *ie;* the *Ruling* position.

Jesus lived in a state of perpetual Encounter [32]. And not only is He the Door, but He is our Living Example and Precedent to follow. Jesus Himself is the decided step forward. He smashed the **way** clear and opened for us all — that we might become **Like Him** in Glory. Before we were fallen, but now we are Risen in Him. Purposed to Rule in 'Dominion' over all creation; over all powers, authorities, and realities [33]. And as we allow God to continually reveal Himself to us and make Himself known; [34] so is our 'sonship' made manifest in the world. To a world that suffers and travails under the grip of the Curse. [35]

Choose then the right thing, not to be busy 'serving' in ministry ... but to **sit** at Jesus' feet [36]. Your answer in life is to hear and see the Lord personally. An Anointed life stems from this Place, lest you waste decades and decades and suffer great loss.

Creation is under the Curse; it is under the Demon. The answer is an outstretched hand unto Christ ... that He might life you up.

Scripture:
Behold, I stand at the door and knock. If anyone hears My voice and opens the door, I will come in to him and dine with him, and he with Me. To him who overcomes I will grant to sit with Me on My throne, as I also overcame and sat down with My Father on His throne. *(Revelation 3:20-21 NKJV)*

TUTORED OF THE SON IN VICTORY

This Invitation of the Lord is His cry; that you might open your heart. And as you truly allow Him to minister into the realities of your life [37], so are you strengthened and ever built up. And here, in the Strength given you of the Lord, does He **make** you Victorious — as one truly breaking free of the trappings of the world. For as He gives you Grace to Triumph and Win ... so are you also given Authority over all things. Even as one seated over and Above all the high places; over all powers and authorities ... and over all the schemes and works of the *Enemy*.

SHOW YOU HEAVEN

The Gospel message is what Jesus refers to as 'earthly' teachings. But how He deeply yearns and desires to show and lead you into 'Heavenly' things [38]. The Pharisees and Sadducees, *ie;* the law-focused believers in the day of Jesus, completely failed to recognise the Christ. For **revelation** only comes from the Father to whom you turn. [39]

Crucial to walking in the Power of God, is a heart bent upon the free flowing 'Spoken Word' pouring into your soul. Even valuing this Word that '**proceeds from the mouth**' of God more dearly and more purposed sought after than your daily needs or cares. For Life comes not by eating bread, *"**But** by every Word that proceeds from the mouth of God."* [40]

The 'industry' of the Pharisees was unto the study of the biblical text. And if this truly is where faith comes from, then they would have been most powerful. And truly, they would have clearly recognised the Christ. No, faith is given from the mouth of God. And don't get spooky; the Imparted Word, the Knowing; the kind of Faith that moves mountains ... is more than words. They are Seeds planted in good soil.

Much then can be spoken of regards **humility** and submission ... a yearning heart that is bent unto the Glory of God. Not arrogance or the seeking of the honour of man; but that of an honest, true, and humble inquiry before the Most High. Faith comes from here, it is given of God [41]. The very kind that moves mountains [42] ... the kind where the Gates of Hades cannot prevail [43]. And here, and only here, does the Glory of Heaven open wide before your eyes. [44]

HONOUR THE PRESENCE OF GOD

Honour God with **your** 'presence' — and God will Honour you with **His**. To come under the Shadow of the Almighty, so shall your own life bear forth the very same Glory. [45]

For as God '**clothes Himself in Light**' and stretches out the heavens; [46] so too do you also. For in clothing yourself in 'His Holy Presence', so shall your garments radiate His Glory, and shall **you** stretch forth the Power of God in your world. [47]

To ***Clothe***
Yourself in Glory
So shall you Stretch forth
the Glory of God.

Scripture:
The LORD wraps himself in light as with a garment; he stretches out the heavens like a tent. *(Psalm 104:2 NIV)*

Be not dismayed, and be not discouraged, it is God who **fights** your battles. It is God who goes out far and wide before you ... with His Presence occupying and standing firmly in your destiny.

THE LORD'S PRAYER

I personally need Heaven. I personally need Heaven richly upon my life and the continual expanding wonder of it. My family needs Heaven, and as I look about the world, I quickly see that the world needs Heaven.

But isn't that the Lord's own very Prayer? Isn't it the very heart of the Gospel message? And how does it go, *"May the Kingdom of Heaven come, and may the Will of God be done ... just as liberally, and just as freely and abundantly ... as it is in Heaven"* [48]. Now, as we also choose to join our hearts unto these things, so too do we join ourselves with the Heart of the Father. Heaven interlocked arm-in-arm, with angels ascending and descending upon the sons and daughters of God. [49]

The 'Presence of God' is experiencing God visiting your house. But 'Ascension' is when you visit God's House. And 'Glory' is when God clothes you with His very Person.

Scripture:
Father, I [pray] desire that they also whom You gave Me may be with me **where I am** [in Heaven], and that they may **behold** [see and experience] my Glory which You have given Me; for You loved Me before the foundation of the world. *(John 17:24 (John 3:13 NKJV))*

This particular Lord's Prayer is mostly unknown in the modern-day Church. But is something most precious to draw deeply to heart. And in closing, I would like us to pray ... I would like us to make this Prayer of the Lord's personal. So I have paraphrased this Scripture, and if you are willing, let's pray it together.

"Thank you, Lord Jesus, for the finished work of the Cross. That now I am called one of your own. Lord, I thank you, that through the Blood I now have perfect access unto the Father — just as the Son. And I pray that I might be with you where you are, even with you in Heaven. And that I might see you in your Glory. And I pray that I may also come to radiate this same Glory, to the joy of the Lord and the setting free of the people. This I pray in Jesus Name, amen."

Bless you ...

Appendix:

1. Hebrews 12:2, ***2.*** Romans 8:29, ***3.*** 2 Corinthians 3:18, ***4.*** 1 John 4:17, John 17:19-24, ***5.*** Mark 9:2-3, ***6.*** Matthew 17:2, ***7.*** John 5:19, ***8.*** Psalm 110:2 *NKJV,* Revelation 2:25-29, ***9.*** John 5:19, ***10.*** Psalm 27:4, 37:4, ***11.*** Revelation 2:26-27, 19:15, ***12.*** Isaiah 44:22, ***13.*** Revelation 22:16, ***14.*** Revelation 2:28, ***15.*** Isaiah 14:12-15, ***16.*** Luke 10:18, ***17.*** Luke 10:19, ***18.*** Philippians 3:8-9, ***19.*** 1 John 3:8, ***20.*** Exodus 23:28, Joshua 24:12, ***21.*** Exodus 14:14, 33:14, ***22.*** Revelation 2:17, ***23.*** Psalm 2:7-8, James 4:8a, 2 Kings 2:9, ***24.*** John 17:21, ***25.*** Romans 8:17, ***26.*** Psalm 27:4, John 17:24, Exodus 20:21, 33:18, ***27.*** Exodus 33:14-18, John 15:8, ***28.*** Genesis 1:26, ***29.*** Psalm 110:1-2, ***30.*** Hebrews 4:1-2, Revelation 3:20-21, 5:9-10, ***31.*** Isaiah 44:22, ***32.*** Matthew 27:46, ***33.*** Genesis 1:26, Psalm 110:1-2, Revelation 3:20-21, ***34.*** Matthew 4:4, ***35.*** Romans 8:19, ***36.*** Luke 10:38-42, ***37.*** Luke 12:37, ***38.*** John 3:12, John 14:21, ***39.*** John 6:45, 15:7, Matthew 4:4, 6:11, 16:17-19, 18:3, 23:13, Romans 10:17, ***40.*** Matthew 4:4, ***41.*** Matthew 11:27, Hebrews 12:2, 1 Corinthians 12:9, ***42.*** Matthew 17:20, ***43.*** Matthew 16:17-19, 23:13, ***44.*** John 5:44, Zechariah 3:7, ***45.*** Psalm 91:1, Acts 5:15, ***46.*** Psalm 104:2, ***47.*** Genesis 3:10-11, Luke 24:49, 1 Corinthians 15:53-54, Revelation 3:17-18 *(Luke 14:28-33),* 2 Kings 2:14, Genesis 1:26, ***48.*** John 10:9, *49.* John 1:51

Dated: 19/5/19

8. *The Joy Set Before Him (#91)*
THE OUTPOURING OF THE SPIRIT

Opening Scripture:
You will show me the path of Life; in your Presence is fullness of Joy; at your right hand are pleasures forevermore. *(Psalm 16:11 NKJV)*

This is the truth, isn't it? If anyone has a heart for the Father, then you are **taken** Places that man cannot go. But if you have a heart only for what you want and can now understand ... then where are you taken?

To be one humbled before the Presence of God — as one who seeks Him — are you led into the circle of God's Counsel. Not only as one who is built up and strengthened; but one where God listens to the 'counsel' of your mouth. Not that He needs or requires your counsel, but as a *child* of God, He honours you so much as to **listen intently to what you have to say**. And the angels that standby are released according to the words spoken here [a]. Such is the Anointing of God. [b]

Matthew 6:33 *(paraphrased)*:
Seek first and earnestly pursue after Heaven and the Righteousness of God, and all these other things shall be added and given you as well.

In reflection of Easter just past, there is the memory of the Crucifixion and then there is the memory of the Resurrection. But perhaps there can be another? ... and that is the Joy that was before the Lord as He faced the Cross [c]. And what was this joy, and what did it signify? That for each one of us now, for all who love the Lord, we can liberally access the Father and **Transit**; entering in and openly engage Heaven just as the Son. And subsequently — in Him — thwart the works of Satan and that of death [d]. As a people *transfigured* into Light: entering into Glory and coming out radiating the very same Glory on earth. [e]

The pain of the Cross was insignificant compared to the Joy of this Eternal gain. Both for man, who now has regained God, and for God who has now **regained** man. And as one who Transits into Heaven, are we led out of the frailty of the flesh *(ie; the limitations and the 'cage' of humanity)* and taken up into the realms of the supernatural.*f*. With Life and Spirit perpetually pouring into you as like Springs of Living Water. Even then as one stepping in ... wading in the River of Life. *g*

I have a question for you, 'The Tree of Life that is in the Garden of Eden, was it in Heaven or was it on earth? *h* So if it was in Heaven, then where was Eden? And if the Angel of the Lord *(the Cherubim)*, that was commanded to guard the way, to what was he guarding? Was it a physical place on earth, or was it not free and liberal access to the centremost point of Heaven?'

The truth is, that the Tree of Life has not ever been transplanted — but has always been in Heaven. So what was it that Adam lost? But free and liberal access to Heaven and the very Heart of the Father; open Interaction with God, the Angels, the Resources, the Abundance ... and the Joy. At the Fall, Adam himself became just a man. A man fully dependent upon the flesh and that of his own earthly understanding and capacities; *i* such is the legacy of the Fall and that of the Curse. However, in Christ Jesus, what is now the legacy of the Risen?

Have you ever considered the frailty of man? The physical weakness and being prone to sickness, disease, and death? **Humanity is of the earth**, crushed under the effects of the Fall — and outside of a 'God-likeness'. Purely of the flesh and of one's own understanding — and not of the **Divine state**. But this has now changed for us in Christ Jesus, for we are a New Creation; as a people coming back into a knowledge of what that means.

One more question, if King David longed for the Courts of God *j*, did his heart long for the Judicial Courts of Heaven, for Justice and the Vindication of God? Or was it not otherwise, that his heart only ever sought and longed to see the Face of God and to gaze upon His beauty? *k* So the 'Courts of God' are not legal courts ... but the Garden realms. Also, David refers to 'seeking God in His

Temple'. But in David's time there was no temple, for it was Solomon who built the Temple of God [l]. So which Temple was David referring to? But the very Temple that is in Heaven. Even the very same of which the Tabernacle was made after; as but a mere 'shadow' and 'copy'. [m]

So the point of emphasis in all this is: Divine Prosperity and Protection. The Protection, Provision, and Abundance that is demonstrated and **represented** in Adam ... *prior* to the Fall [n]. And this is so much bigger than you can comprehend [o]. But so it is, that as one who walks according to the Spirit of God, shall you truly begin to walk in and engage; taken by hand into the Rich Wonders of the Unfathomable. For this right of access, this Divine Provision of God has been regained you through the finished work of the Cross. Therefore, let the Lord reveal to you — ever through the **humbling** of your own soul — who you truly are in Him. For revelation only comes to a heart that is willing and eager to hear. [p]

A side note: Adam was given Dominion over the fish of the sea and birds of the air. But these creatures live fully in realms to which man has no real physical access. So how would have Adam exercised his 'dominion' ... with a fishing line? Ah, but of course; from realms of which he was **seated**. *Now it can be better understood when Paul says, "All creation is longing for the sons of God to be revealed"* [q]. *For in Chris Jesus, you fundamentally have capacity to be positioned in a Place over all creation; both the physical and the spiritual.*

The Word precedes the Move of the Spirit. The Word *always* precedes the Move of the Spirit of God and that of Divine Encounters and the Outpouring of Heaven. Just as Jesus — He of whom came as the Word made flesh — came also to usher forth the Spirit and the Outpouring of the Kingdom of Heaven on earth. Therefore, in speaking and introducing these things to you in this book: it is God of whom is **preparing** you in the manifestation of these very realities.

In the Old Testament, the Word spoke of the Christ to come. Then Christ Jesus came in — **manifestation** — of the very same Word. Then, as the very Word made flesh, He came and walked amongst us, and what was the purpose of His coming? To usher forth the Spirit and that of the Kingdom of Heaven. Even that you also may walk in 'God-likeness' as the Son. In perfect union — as is the Dream of the Father — and the way of the Christ.

*God is about manifestation.
Not about doctrine or beliefs.
But real and **manifest** God in our midst.*

So, for the *Enemy* to target the Word in you, is to try to come against the very **source** of the outpouring of the Spirit of God and that of Heaven. Even as Jesus says *(paraphrased), "You are still stuck in truly coming to believe the Gospel message, how then can I then even begin to show and reveal to you Heavenly things?"*[r] Hence to warmly receive the Word to heart — to they — the same Word multiplies thirty, sixty, and even a hundredfold.

The Word points to the Spirit, and the Spirit to the Fire.

Closing Scripture:
Then Jesus answered and said unto them, Verily, verily, [honestly and truly] I say unto you, The Son can do nothing of himself but [only] what he sees the Father do; for all that he does, this also the Son **does <u>together</u> with him**. *(John 5:19 JUB)*

Do you remember when Jesus came, after His Resurrection, and walked with two of His Disciples but they didn't recognise Him? And what was it that they said afterwards, *"Didn't our hearts **burn** as He opened the Scriptures to us"*[s]. Ah, now you have a picture of what it means when Jesus says, *"Man does not live on bread alone but by every Word that proceeds from the mouth of God."*[t]

Bless you, in Jesus Name!

A CLOSING THOUGHT

Have you ever just gone into a hidden place and said to the Lord, *"I want to meet with you?"* Have you ever sought to make this 'seeking the Presence of God' the most **central** prayer of your soul? For this very same heart's pursuit was central to Jesus own personal life.

Luke 5:15-16 *(paraphrased):*
Then multitudes came out to hear Jesus and to be healed of their diseases — **BUT** — Jesus often went aside into places where He could not be found and was captured up again in the Father. To the rest of the world, it was just hours, but to Him, it was days and days of ministering rejuvenation in the Presence of God. Being lifted up and strengthened and renewed in Him. And He delighted in the Lord, walking with His Father in the 'cool of the day'. And with Him, He came — and the Power of the Spirit — was upon Him to heal.

Psalm 110:2
"The Rod of your Strength shall come out of Zion saying, 'Rule in the midst of your enemies.'"

Psalm 84:2
"My soul yearns, even faints, for the courts of the LORD, my heart and my flesh cry out for the living God."

To me the Courts of the Lord were *never* the Legal Courts ... but the Garden realms. The very same that David longed for. David was not one to long for the Justice of God, but ever to abide in His Person, and to have these precious moments walking with Him. Even in the cool of the day.

Eden was never on earth ... it was always in Heaven. For prior to the Fall, Heaven was perfectly intertwined and one with earth.

Adam was given dominion over the birds of the air and the fish of the sea; neither of which were in his hand's reach. The Heavenly realms of — Dominion — was where he abided, to which he spoke in Governance.

The same now is for the Renewed — for they who walk Risen in Christ Jesus. Therefore, to **gain a heart** as like David; **seeds** both the 'Christ' *(ie; Glory of Heaven)* ... and the 'Solomon' *(ie; Abundance on earth)*.

Psalm 84:1, 28:4

"How lovely is your dwelling place, Lord Almighty" ... "Oh, to gaze on the beauty of the Lord and to seek him in his Temple."

Appendix:

a. Zechariah 3:6-7, Psalm 40:1, *b.* Luke 10:39, John 11:32-34, *c.* Hebrews 12:2, *d.* 1 John 3:8b, Matthew 16:18, Joshua 24:12, *e.* John 10:9, Luke 5:16-17, *f.* Mark 16:17-18, *g.* John 4:14, Revelation 22:1, *h.* Revelation 2:7, 22:1-2, Genesis 3:22-24, *i.* Genesis 3:17, *j.* Psalm 84:2, *k.* Psalm 27:4, *l.* 1 Chronicles 17:1, *m.* Hebrews 8:5, *n.* Exodus 14:14, 33:14-18, Psalm 110:1-2, Romans 8:32, *o.* 1 Corinthians 2:9-10, *p.* John 5:44, *q.* Romans 8:19, *r.* John 3:12, *s.* Luke 24:32, *t.* Matthew 4:4

Dated: 25/4/19

9. *The Joy Set Before Him (#92)*
HEAVEN EMPOWERED

A question: Why did Jesus need to go to the Cross, when Scripture clearly says that He was *"Slain from the foundation of the world."* [1] So why did He go then? ... but to give you something to visualise.

The things that we are going to go through in this chapter, really can confound the religious and legalistic. But that's ok, for these things are of the Spirit; of which our 'linear mind' can find difficult to grasp. Hence, this is why we need the Spirit of God, or better said: why we need to be **Holy Spirit <u>focused</u>** [2]. For these things regarding our Inheritance and our co-reigning in God are so far **beyond** human comprehension.

Everything in God is established and built upon something; from where we have come from to where God desires to take us. And though God dearly honours you, and loves you so deeply ... He is **always** about moving you forward. And like the Exodus and the Promised Land, Jesus is always teaching and is always at work to lead you, whereby you might be one **<u>increasingly</u> Empowered** of Heaven [3]. For our mortality is fragile and finite ... but our Eternal is without limit.

HEARING AND SEEING

God is about you hearing and seeing. Jesus came as the Word made flesh; He wasn't Glory, He wasn't Power ... He was the Word made flesh. Therefore, the Word is fundamentally interconnected with His Glory on earth. So for the Word of God not to remain central in our lives; even though Revivals or Outpourings may come ... they would be unsustainable. Revelatory Knowledge is crucial for each and every believer. The written Word, as well as the Rhema Word that the Bible points to: the Living Word that 'proceeds' out from the mouth of God.

Now part of the *hearing* and *seeing* God, means that you come out with Knowledge and Understanding. Not necessarily how the Streets of Heaven may look ... for in truth, they are but the 'surface'. But how the Inner Heart and Mind of the Glory realms look … and it is beautiful. For we are called to gain the Mind of Christ. [4]

Satan knows that his days are coming to an end. Therefore, the times and seasons that we are coming into now are really intense. And if we are going to be successful: we need to attain to a Higher vision. As Jesus said, *"Flesh counts for nothing … it is the Spirit that brings Life."* [5] Therefore, the underlying work of the Holy Spirit — what God is 'saying' and 'doing' [6] — is always about drawing His children back into the realms of Spirit and Life. These, the very realms of Glory, Power, and Grace. [7]

In the Exodus, many of the people of Israel were so annoyingly stubborn. Hence, God gave them over to their own devises [8]. And much is the same in our current generation. To this is why the Church doesn't openly walk in the Glory and Authority of God.

It is the Lord 'who *opposes* the proud … but gives Grace to the humble'. This means, that as you truly submit your heart to Him … He responds, *ie;* He leads the humble forward; giving the meek **possession** of all things [9]. Therefore, positioning is most very important. Always allowing and giving place for the God of Heaven and earth to reveal to you *who* you truly are in Him. For if the Israelites had truly known who they were — and who their God is — even the plan of God for their lives; then they would never have succumbed to the wiles of the *Enemy*. [10]

Scripture:
Create in me a pure heart, O God, and renew a steadfast spirit within me. *(Psalm 51:10 NIV)*

A HEART LIKE DAVID

Come, gain a heart like David. For to gain a heart like David, **seeds** both the manifest Christ *(ie; the Glory of Heaven)* and the manifest 'Solomon' *(ie; unlimited provision on earth)*. And in addition, forms and establishes you as one seated in the realms of 'kingly' Authority. [11]

The singular drive of David was always held in the yearning deep desire to gaze upon the beauty of the Lord — inquiring and seeking

Him in 'Heaven' [12]. And the outworking of this lifestyle deeply affected the realms of Heaven; with the Jesus being called the 'Son of David' for all Eternity. And it so marked this earth, with the wealth of Solomon being even more famous than he. But in addition to this; the kingly line of David, is of such that never ceases; this too is **our** legacy in Christ Jesus.

Fundamentally and most central, has God called you to **return back** into the Glory of God; into these realms that are so far Above Satan — the realms of Dominion. And the way this occurs is to remain Heaven focused ... like David; whereby you are also Heaven Instructed and Heaven Strengthened. The Temple of God ... to which David 'inquired', was not on earth but in Heaven. Hence so too, through the shed Blood of Jesus — just in the very same way — has Jesus opened the Door for you to learn and receive **directly** from God [13]. And by the Power of the Spirit, so shall you transcend in both thought and deed.

Now as Moses made a conscious decision to 'turn aside' to see the Burning Bush [14], as a child — chosen of God [15] — you have a choice to turn aside and 'see' as well. That is, to *humble* yourself, taking off your 'sandals', and listen to God **in** His Holy Presence. For all this time, His Hand has been outstretched to a stiff-necked and stubborn people [16]. For all man has known, and all they have ever had their hearts set upon, is either the lie or the lure of the 'god of this Age' [17]. Even in deception, where man forever remains beneath.

From God's perspective, the Glory of which man fell from — man has no idea or comprehension [18]. And this is the very reason why man was created: **to dwell with Him in Glory**. Therefore now remains the calling, in Christ Jesus, to keep seeking God of Heaven and earth — and the mystery found in Him — that you too may again rise up in Dominion. Meaning, the Ruling Position over Satan and the whole earth; [19] over sickness and disease; over hopelessness and despair; and over poverty, fear, and frailty. And over and Above all the works and cunning of Satan.

The Calling is to rediscover God, and your Place in Him.

To ask another question: What is the difference between you and Jesus? Other than being the Christ ... Jesus, from birth, was born Son of God. So, Heaven opened to Him from birth. And from birth, He lived in a state of perpetual Encounter and Engagement in the Person of God. And so, what is the difference between you and Jesus? **Nothing**! ... for through the Blood and the gifted Spirit, you have the exact same opportunity of unfathomable access in the Person of God, just as the Son.

Scripture:
By which are given unto us exceedingly great and precious promises: that by these you might be **partakers** of the divine nature, having escaped the corruption that is in the world through lust. *(2 Peter 1:4 NKJV)*

POSITIONING IS KEY

I so encourage you, God has so much more for you than simply dealing with what you are facing. You are a most **cherished** child of the Most High God — let that be your focus. And God's Love for you is unconditional and without compare ... regardless of your past. Therefore, in Christ Jesus, we all have the same 'starting' point. But it is what we do from here, that is what matters.

In Christ Jesus, you have the right to live *as* the Son of God on earth. With the Power of the Spirit in your hands [20]. And just as Moses willingly turned aside to see the burning bush; so too, as you also personally choose to turn aside, does God respond with Fire. [21]

Luke 5:15-17 *(paraphrased)*:
The fame of Jesus went far and wide, and multitudes came out to hear Him and to be healed of all their diseases. **But**! ... Jesus often was not found. For He often would go into places where He would allow Himself to be captured up again in God. To the world it was just hours, but to Jesus it was days and days of ministering rejuvenation in the Presence of the Most High. And He delighted to be here ... walking with God in the 'cool of the day'. Hence, regardless of the opposition or difficulties that came, the Glory of God was upon Him; and the Power of the Spirit was with Him to heal. [22]

This picture describes the Way of the Christ. The walking as one Strengthened and Anointed of God. For just as Jesus came and walked amongst us, so too did He also come to demonstrate to us the 'Way' of Glory. And here, as the very people to whom Jesus was sent — these people in need, as they came to Him — He was often not there. For He Himself was 'seeing' the Father. [23]

This 'action' is most very important. For though Jesus is the Christ to come to in need. His very Purpose is to **bring you to the Father**. To hear and see God yourself. For in this Jesus deeply celebrates you [24]. So here, as the people waited, they also had now the exact same opportunity to 'seek' God … just as the Son. For Power to move mountains is not found in just believing in Jesus, but personal connection with the Father: to this is why the Christ was sent.

The path to a winning lifestyle is found in the God to whom Jesus leads you to. Do you realise that the Bible has a purpose? The Word of God has an underlying purpose — and that is for you also — to personally meet and walk with the Person of God. Even to have His 'Shekinah' Glory resting upon you. [25]

If the study of the Word alone was the answer, then the Pharisees would have been a most Power-filled and Anointed people. But instead, they didn't even recognise the Christ. No, Power comes through Divine Access and personal intimate relationship with the Father. The Power of the Resurrected Christ is established deep from here within the Glory of God [26].

Therefore, the path to **winning** is found in the God to whom Jesus Himself points. Fair enough, when you find yourself struggling … call out for help. But fundamentally always remember: the **Purpose of the Christ** *(and sometimes it is the very reason for trials and testings)* is for you yourself to establish ever-more-deepening roots in the Person of God and these realms of Glory. For you are **heirs of God** … and God Himself **is your Inheritance** and your exceedingly great reward. [27]

So again, what is the Bible's underlying purpose? That you too might personally meet God, meet the God of the Bible. Hence, if the study of the Word alone is the answer, then the Pharisees would have been a most faithful and powerful people. No, Power and Anointing comes only by Divine Access to the Father ... but this takes a genuine and a most true heart.

COMPANIONSHIP

There is great companionship and a great sense of belonging in Heaven. And all throughout your days, as you sit at the feet of Jesus — here under His care and His Tuition — with the blazing fire in His eyes — there is great tenderness and strength in His Words [28]. And as you walk openly with your Heavenly Father, wrapped in the cloak of the Holy Ghost; [29] after walking the Streets with angels, and beholding the beauty of the Lord ... truly, all else pales. However, He of whom you walk with, also walks with you in His Glory — in His Covering, His Might, and His Provision — as you walk this earth. [30]

Three Scripture verses:
1. He who dwells in the Secret Place of the Most High shall remain stable and fixed under the shadow of the Almighty **[whose power no foe can withstand]**. *(Psalm 91:1 AMPC)*
2. I waited patiently [with expectation] for the LORD; and He inclined [His ear] to me [**stepping down and drew close**], and heard my cry. *(Psalm 40:1)*
3. God's Angel then charged Joshua, "Orders from God-of-the-Angel-Armies: 'If you live the way I tell you and remain obedient in my service, then **you'll make the decisions** around here and oversee my affairs. And all my attendants standing here will be at your service. *(Zechariah 3:6-7 MSG)*

THE THIRD HEAVEN

Satan is not the enemy of God. For he is by no means on any level nor on any par with our Heavenly Father. However, when it comes to liberating the hearts and minds of man from Satan's grip; from his enticements and influence — this is the *challenge*. For the availability and function of the Spirit of the Lord, and these of the realms of the Kingdom of Heaven — are subject to the will and choices of man.

When watching movies like Star Wars, Harry Potter, and the stories of superheroes; the classic battle between 'good and evil'. They do not represent truth accurately at all.

Picture the three realms: The *earth* is referred to as the 'first heaven' [31]. Then there is the 'second heaven', of which is the spiritual realm of the god of this age ... and his *angels* [32]. Then there is the 'Third Heaven', [33] as we know is the Kingdom of Heaven, *ie;* the abiding place of the Lord God Almighty.

The point is that these three realms are very much three distinct and different realms. But as we know, a person is able to draw from, or be influenced by ... any one of these realms.

Hence, all throughout history of man there has been the 'spiritualist', of whom engages the 'second heaven' *(either good or bad, black or white, yin or yang)*. However, then there is the Christian faith; they who have capacity to go 'in and out' of Heaven whenever they please. Then drawing out from the Realities of the Kingdom realms and the Will of God upon the earth.

Now part of the Fall is that man *fell* out of Glory, *ie;* has fallen out of the Third Heaven [34]. To then become now a people 'underneath' the second heaven. With the realms of Heaven and the realms of earth fully separated — the way guarded by Cherubim with flashing flaming swords [35]. Now, as we know, in the Beginning, man was formed from the dust of the earth, however, his spirit was made Alive in God. This is why, when God warned Adam that he would 'surely die' [36] — he **died to the realms of Everlasting Life**. And when before Satan was under his foot; man came underneath the influence and powers of the demonic realms, *ie;* the 'birds of the air'. Hence today, these same spiritual realities speak continually into the hearts and minds of man, trying to bear their influence.

So, the default now, is man is destined, and has only ever known, the toiling 'by the sweat of his brow' to scratch a living on earth [37]. Whereby before God provided, now all mankind is held under the capacity of his own strength and understanding; and through the vision of his own eyes makes reference of his reality — without any

Higher connection — without any higher Vision or Perspective or Power.

In the Beginning, man ate of the Tree of Knowledge of Good and Evil. So what did this release, and what did it open? Many things … however, man did not gain great knowledge or understanding; for the truth remains, that many cannot even distinguish between man or woman. So what did Adam really release upon the earth? But the 'powers' of both good and evil. That is, the desires and forces of good and evil; and if anything, the open reality of experience of living with them both.

So then, here after the Fall, man is left to his own devices. Making his own choices and decisions of what is good and evil … right and wrong … but this fully independent of God.

HARRY POTTER; BLACK AND WHITE MAGIC

My son is eleven years old, and recently he wanted to watch Harry Potter, so I let him. It is true, that if you ever want to do a study about **witchcraft**, then go to the kid's section of the library. So in this, I cannot stop him, for he is going to be exposed to it anyway. I do, however, need to be able to guide him through that he might understand. And after watching all eight of them *(I didn't realise that there were that many)* he asked me to please watch them with him … so I did.

Scripture:
And no wonder, for Satan himself **masquerades** as an angel of light. *(2 Corinthians 11:14 NIV)*

It is important to realise that part of the Fall are the powers of 'good and evil', 'yin and yang', and both 'black and white' magic. And they were given right and dominion on earth through the erroneous choice of Adam. And as we read Scripture, we know, that there can still be the presentation of 'good' from the demonic realm — but it is just **not of God**. The fallen spirits are fallen; and all that they know was that of the Heavenly realms from whence they fell. Therefore, everything they do is in counterfeit of the Kingdom of Heaven.

"You are from below; I am from Above." [38]

A few years ago, my family and I were travelling in the north part of Bali and happened upon a large temple area. And in walking around for an hour or so, I noticed an area to the back there was a circle of statues. And when looking closer, I saw that half of these statues had faces of angelic nature, and the other half had faces of demonic and foul nature. So in asking the guide who was with us, what they represented, he told me that they represented white and black magic.

In Balinese spiritual culture, before learning the art of white magic, one must first learn the **black magic arts** in order to know how to combat it *(sounds like Hogwarts)*. Now this same reality of black and white magic is everywhere, throughout the whole world; it can be seen in every culture and in every nation. For all throughout the ages, there has been the white and black magic arts. But both are *demonic,* or let's say; both are fallen angels and they are not of God.

There are all kinds of names for them, and they are in all cultures: the British Isles, Continental Europe, the Americas, Africa, and Asia. And though they come in many different forms, they all have the **<u>exact same root</u>**. And as we see, there rarely can be any union: only rivalry, hatred, and the seeking of power and dominance.

When Adam fell, he **released** upon the earth hordes of demonic forces and principalities, that have taken stronghold in areas all around the world. But again, it is most important to realise; that they are all of the second heaven — they are all fallen — **part of the Curse**. They are not of the Authority of Heaven nor are they on any par. And by the Name of Jesus, the moment that His foot touches the ground, all must bow; voluntarily or involuntarily. And who is He that dwells within you? ... but the Lord of Glory.

When you look at large and powerful religions like Buddhism or Hinduism; they are not based, nor are they rooted, in love at all. However, they all are rooted in mastery over the flesh, striving for inner peace, enlightenment, and the gaining of power. All the temples, upon all the high places, are for this purpose.

Love is unique to the God of Abraham, Isaac, and Jacob. This, the **singular** God of Heaven and earth ... **is one**. Where the 'gods' that the world has known ... are many. And principalities are simply demonic royalty; generals that form part of great religions.

KNOCKING ON HEAVEN'S DOOR

Now, as one who has opened the door of your heart unto our Lord and Saviour Christ Jesus. You have opened yourself to the realms of Life and Immortality [39]. Today, as one who seeks God, you have stepped into the realms that are **over and Above** sin, death, and the grave. And you have stepped into position where you hold the very Keys of the Kingdom of Heaven [40]. This, far Above, and fully outside the realm or influence of the powers of Satan and this world. However, it is up to you to step in, it is up to you to abide, and it is up to you to remain [41]. As one co-abiding — **co-habitating** — and co-walking in Heaven as you walk on this earth. This is most unique and real for all who seek to live 'Risen' lives in Christ Jesus. [42]

Scripture:
Behold, I stand at the door and knock. If anyone hears My voice and opens the door, I will come in to him and dine with him, and he with Me. *(Revelation 3:20 NKJV)*

On this earth, one can remain influenced by any one of these realms ... by choice and by will. However, as you personally decide to come knock on Heaven's door, shall you go 'in and out' — shall you engage and shall be raised an Overcomer.

In Christ Jesus, nothing can triumph over you ... nor can have any hold, but what you yourself allow. For the Power held within you far exceeds all realms under, on, or above the earth. And for those who truly **abide** in the Lord; abide in Him where He is now ... in the **Third Heaven** [43]. This, a realm far Above all principalities, and all powers, of both the first and the second. And such is unlocked through a heart of praise and through humble honest pursuit.

IN CLOSING

What you honour is what you draw unto yourself. And He you long for is ever drawn to your heart's cry. And to where you open your heart to so too do you go.

Heaven has permanently marked my life, and continually does so day by day. Hence, in choosing to **step into the River** … there is a constant filling and pouring in. I do apologise if some of the things I say come across strange or foreign. However we, as a people, who truly desire to see God **manifest** in this world — His Goodness and Grace — we all need to be willing to consider things that we don't already know. Being willing to put ourselves aside for a moment and allow the Living Word of God to wash over us fresh each day. This I pray in Jesus Name.

Appendix:

1. Revelation 13:8, *2.* Romans 8:9, John 3:6, *3.* Mark 16:17-18, 1 Corinthians 15:53-57, *4.* Romans 8:5-6, 12:2, 1 Corinthians 2:16, *5.* John 6:63, 5:30, *6.* John 5:19, *7.* Romans 3:23, Isaiah 44:22, Ephesians 2:6, *8.* Psalm 81:11-12, *9.* James 4:6, 2 Chronicles 7:14, Daniel 10:12, *10.* Ephesians 6:11, *11.* Deuteronomy 28:13, *12.* Psalm 27:4, *13.* Matthew 23:8-10, Isaiah 54:13, *14.* Luke 24:49, *15.* John 1:12-13, *16.* Romans 10:21, Psalm 81:11-12, 136:12, Isaiah 65:2, *17.* Genesis 3:1, *18.* Genesis 2:17, 1 Corinthians 2:9-10, *19.* Genesis 1:26, *20.* Matthew 14:16, *21.* Luke 24:49, *22.* Luke 5:17, 4:14, *23.* John 5:19, Matthew 6:6, *24.* Matthew 16:17-19, Luke 7:1-10, *25.* Exodus 33:9-11, 15-16, 34:35, 40:34-38, 2 Chronicles 7:1, Luke 12:49, Acts 2:1-4, *26.* Exodus 33:11, 34:35, John 1:18, *27.* Romans 8:17, Genesis 15:1, Ephesians 1:13-14, *28.* Revelation 1:14-17, Luke 24:32, *29.* Exodus 33:22, 1 Kings 19:13, 2 Kings 2:13, *30.* Exodus 33:14, *31.* Revelation 21:1, *32.* Ephesians 2:2, Genesis 1:26, *33.* 2 Corinthians 12:2, *34.* Romans 3:23, *35.* Genesis 3:24, *36.* Genesis 2:17, *37.* Genesis 3:19, *38.* John 8:23, *39.* Genesis 2:17, 3:10, 1 Corinthians 15:54, Revelation 3:18 *(Luke 14:28-33)*, Psalm 104:2, 110:1, *40.* Matthew 16:19, *41.* John 15:4, *42.* 2 Corinthians 5:17, John 1:12, *43.* John 3:13

Dated: 1/6/19

10. *The Joy Set Before Him (#93)*
CO-HABITATION

Opening Scripture:
Your faith and love rise within you **as you access** all the Treasures of your inheritance stored up in the Heavenly realm. For the revelation of the true Gospel is as real today ... [coming] to bear the fruit of Eternal Life as [you] experience the reality of God's Grace [and Love]. *(Colossians 1:5-6 TPT)*

When David's wives and children were taken, and his men were speaking of stoning him, it says in Scripture that 'David **strengthened** himself in the Lord' [1]. That is, David turned to the Lord — his Strength — and God gave him Strength [2]. There is, in God, a Place ... a Place exampled in the life of David that he regularly went into. A Place of Strength, a Place of Equipping and 'seeing' ... a Place of great Wonder and Joy. And here today, liberal and free access has been given all who love the Lord. [3]

It's most valuable to understand David's relationship with God, and the **incredible impact** it had. Not only on the Eternal Heavenly plane but so greatly here on earth. And this secret Place that he loved, his own deep yearning desire to enter the *abiding* Presence of God [4] — is key.

David's integrity and goodness of heart never left him, even through times of great injustice and the being chased down by a jealous king [5]. I so encourage you: **learn to turn and strengthen yourself in the Lord**. For so shall you find Strength far beyond human understanding; and Anointed capacity that greatly impacts your world. And so shall your heart be ever filled with unceasing Joy and energies that abound. [6]

David treasured 'seeing' God more than the throne that was his [7]. And for us also, this same Wonder is experienced as we too set our heart back unto our Divine Place-of-Origins [8]. For just as Adam fell, so are we now pushing back ... and stepping deeper into the **fullness** of our Restoration. [9]

Here, you have an unknown boy, the least of an unknown family ... who had Encounters with God as he tended sheep. And through this lifestyle of Encounters: he became a musician, a poet, and a great prophet. And though, from a family of simple sheep herders; he became a warrior, a leader of men, and a great king. And he so marked the Heart of the Father, for the Lord of Glory to be called the 'Son of David'. And his own son Solomon, gained such fame of wealth and wisdom that is known to this day.

David deeply **treasured Encounters** with God. And continually wrote of his desperate desire to go into Heavenly Places ... into the God-of-his-Strength. Such is the incredible treasure found in gaining a 'vertical' view to that of a linear one [10]. The coming to sit and dine [11] at the feet of the Author of Life [12] — in the Wonder of Him — co-abiding Heaven as you still walk this earth [13]. For such was the lifestyle of the Son [14], and to such as these; as exampled ... step into the very same kingly Anointing. Bearing great influence in the Heavenly realms as well as here on earth. [15]

Scripture:
They are abundantly satisfied with the fullness of Your house, and You give them drink from **the River of Your pleasures**. For with You is the fountain of life; in Your light we see Light. *(Psalm 36:8-9 NKJV)*

'**In your Light** ... **we see Light**'. This was not only a revelation, nor was it just a word in David's soul; this wording was written from physical experience in the Person of God! And this 'Source' [16] bore forth the very Glory of God in David's life. And laid foundation for the Christ to come, of whom walked in the very same [17]. Even in Kingly Divine Authority, that you too may bring — and in Authority — establish the Kingdom and the Will of God on earth.

Not by power, nor by might, but by my Spirit says the Lord.

In Christ, we are born of the same ancestral line of the King. Even from the very same 'priestly order of Melchizedek' [18]. That each one of us, who are rooted in Him ... unified one in Him [19], may also walk in the very same Image and Likeness of the Son ... unto the Glory of God.

This prophetic Word of David, regarding the Christ to come, *"The LORD said to my Lord, 'Sit at My right hand, till I make your enemies Your footstool'"* [20]. Was a Word visible and most evident in David's own personal life. And so it is also, for all in Christ Jesus; it is as an 'Invitation' presented to each one of us. That we all might truly come to sit in the realms of God's Presence — at His right hand [21] — where we are nourished and built up in the Lord. Instructed and personally Tutored by the Person of God; [22] as sons of God, as heirs to the Throne, heirs to the Kingdom of Heaven. Just as was purposed in the Beginning. [23]

NICODEMUS

The linear-minded man refuses to look up. In his intellectualism [24] he never looks outside his three-dimensional world; his understanding, his pride, nor his reputation. However, as one who chooses to truly **open** your heart unto the Lord [25], does the Spirit of the Lord come and speak of matters that far Transcend. And as you come and set it purposed in your heart to seek Heaven, seek the Presence of God like David ... and Jesus ... are you continuously lifted up in sight and vision.

Here, with Nicodemus, you have an intelligent but linear-minded man, who in honesty of heart chose to come to Jesus [26]. And though not having any imagination at all, but deeply stirred within, he personally sought out the Lord. *Ah, the beginnings of ascension ...* Heaven being right at hand for this greatly learned man. Not only coming to Jesus, who is the Doorway. But to the many Places where Jesus desires to give you Entrance.

It is true, that as one born again, the confines of the linear mind [27] can still plague the believer. But it's not right for one born of the Spirit to remain **bound** in the flesh. Therefore, going into Heaven and living in Encounter of the Father, shall you continually be renewed and given sight. Coming increasingly, to rise up in the fullness of your Birthright. For the Word speaks of God ... but now, as one in Him, does the Lord speak and show. [28]

Humility, the Blood, and not loving your life unto death.

What a believer thinks as a believer, and what Jesus thinks, can oftentimes be quite different. And what does Jesus express in the Gospels? *"And these signs will accompany those who **believe**: in my Name they will drive out demons; they will speak in new tongues; they will pick up snakes with their hands; and when they drink deadly poison, it will not hurt them at all; they will place their hands on sick people, and they will get well"* [29]. To me then, it appears, that God has something far more in store, for each one of us, than what we have currently known.

THE IMMORTAL INTEGRATING INTO MORTAL MAN

This incredible prospect that one can walk more immune to that of which is common to man. Not only so — but intervene and stand in the gap for others — releasing Life and change; such is the Kingdom of Heaven on earth. Do you realise that this is the very reason why Nicodemus came to Jesus in the first place? *"Rabbi, we know that you are a Teacher come from God; for no one can do these signs that you do unless God is with Him"* [30]. Therefore, this very same reality: Jesus is presenting to each and every believer to do the very same. And to such bring incredible Glory to God.

Maturity brings honour to God; immaturity brings dishonour.

In this life, things can get really complicated really quickly at times. And though we mean well, sometimes we can be more of a contributor to problems than a contributor of good. This is why we need to practice a more vertical view, not a linear one but a vertical one, just as Jesus ... that we might live out of dynamic and living Experience in the Goodness of God [31]. Not as orphans, independent and alone, but as cherished Children of Light. For though born of the Spirit, a believer can still live influenced by so many other things. And Satan — the 'Sower of Tares' — still plants thoughts and feelings in your heart and thought life that can run you totally contrary.

The believer, even though brought into Life and the Salvation of the Lord, some of the things we say and do can be cause of great regret. And as believers, we can still live and act more like unbelievers at times. Even as one who loves the Lord, we can still live and think resembling one who doesn't believe at all. And why is this? Because on this planet we are exposed to mixed sources of influence: receiving 'seeds' from the Truth as well as from the Lie. Therefore, to which Tree that we choose to come under; bears its fruit in us. Either the fruits of Death ... or the Fruits of Life.

Jesus would say, *"Man cannot live on bread alone, but by every word that proceeds from the mouth of God"* [32]. The encouragement is then, to develop in yourself a deep hunger, putting aside other things: and yearn for the abiding and spoken Word. For through this heart of 'invitation' God will shape and form very deep roots ... that will cause you able to draw effortlessly from the God-of-your-Strength. Living as one in symphony, with His Word and His Presence burning alive in your soul. As one freely going in and out of Heaven ... finding pasture [33]. And as David ascended in God, in Christ Jesus ... you will go Places man cannot go.

Scripture:
I was in the Spirit on the Lord's Day, and I heard behind me a loud voice, as of a trumpet. *(Revelation 1:10 NKJV)*

Jesus held and retained in Himself a **totally vertical view** ... regardless of what was going on. And though He was the Christ, and demonstrated the unfathomable Wonders of Heaven in Him, He still most clearly stated, *"I can do nothing of myself"* [34]. Hence — just like you and I — Christ Jesus always had a choice: to **open Himself to hunger and to eat** richly of the Tree of Life. And so it was also with John, who on the Lord's Day, was 'captured up in the Spirit'. Hence, this very same opportunity is presented us all who love the Lord. To walk in Glory, in these realms of God that **cause us to be Strengthened**, that cause us to Transcend. And a heart of simple humility and love is key.

'Tares' [35] vs. *'Seeds of Faith'* [36] ...
a heart ever set upon His Abiding Presence. [37]

Still Jesus, though the Christ and born Son of God; baptised and filled with the Holy Ghost ... He would clearly say, *"Why call me good, only God is Good"* [38]. Both King David and King Jesus established firm picture and pattern for us, through their own personal lives and the realities they faced. Their hearts — regardless — remained singularly set open: to **receive from Heaven** ... and liberally receive they did.

Christ Jesus, the Son of God — became 'Son of Man' — in order to **make way also**, for you and I to become sons of God. Hence in His picture and precedence, so too are you able to become just like Him. For within the Person of Jesus is this exact very same 'mould' of opportunity [39]. Therefore, just like Jesus also walked, come also humble yourself and lay your life down; in order also to walk in 'Like' as Him in Glory.

"Humble yourselves under God's mighty hand, that He may lift you up." [40]

Opening Scripture *(in continuation)*:
Your hearts can soar with joyful gratitude, when you think of how God made you worthy to receive the glorious inheritance; freely given to us by living in the Light. *(Colossians 1:12 TPT)*

Let us then come and set our hearts to co-abide in Heaven just as Jesus [41]. In real, dynamic, and undeniable living experience as dreamed of by the Son [42]. For to such who walk like this greatly mark this earth; bringing radical change. Even Heaven, for as you speak do you also release Life and Spirit [43]. Walking in your Divine Inheritance, brought about by **living** in the Light.

"In your light we see Light."

It is by choice and by will that you come to 'live in the Light' [44] ... even as one continuously **captured** up 'in the Spirit' [45]. Now, it is Satan who has only sought to divorce you of God and your rich Inheritance in Him. However, it is in Christ Jesus that you are made united one in Him ... even through living Engagement. And to where Jesus is now, so too are you also, if you believe. The restored Love and Goodness of God; overshadowing all brokenness and all corruption of sin.

It is true, that though we call ourselves believers, we can still be filled with so much unbelief. And though born again and filled with the Holy Spirit; words and deeds can come from us that are highly regrettable. And it is true, that what we desire and see in God we ourselves are not doing [46]. And though we wish to do good, we find ourselves seriously messing up. Therefore, what we need to recognise is, that we are not the saviour of the world — Jesus is. And though we know this, the Accuser still speaks, creating insecurity when otherwise our security needs to be in God. Therefore, this very same Place where Jesus always looked, and **sharply** set the thoughts of His soul — is the single source of Seed.

EMPOWERMENT THROUGH THE GRACE OF GOD

Though 'seated' in Heavenly Places [47], we can operate still out of a deeply carnal and deprived mentality. With a linear and carnal mindset, hemmed in by the god of this Age. So the answer always is, the coming to establish a greater and more firmer vertical view — and in this, being continuously lifted up in Him. And though the voice of *resistance* may still remain ... just as Jesus in the wilderness; as you break free do you begin to operate in planes far Above Satan's reach [48]. For even though the believer has the written Word in their hands, so too do you also have unique and special opportunity to **sit with the Author of Life**. The very Author of the Word and your Faith — and be renewed.

Therefore, who can save us from this wretched state? ... Jesus. And as one who turns your heart to the Lord, so shall the Grace of God pick up the slack [49]. And right where you are ... so shall His Grace cover and fill all the gaps in the soul of man. And this same Grace shall come and give Strength where there was none; with Life penetrating your very bones. And if you truly and honestly desire to step into these realms of Life, then honestly and truly lay down your life in Him. Ever abandoning yourself unto the Cross. And here, you will notice a subtle and **inconspicuous door** at the base of the Cross. A door suitable only for a little child. Which, then, you simply pass through and openly 'see' the Kingdom of Heaven.

The musician practices his music. An artist, his art and his technique. And in the same ... the born again believer practices the Presence of God.

Scripture:
I pray that they all may be one, as You, Father, are in Me, and I in You; that they also may be **one in us**, that the world may believe that You sent Me. *(John 17:21 NKJV/NLT)*

Oh, the impact that you have as the Glory of God comes upon your life. And here, the world truly coming to believe that God sent the Christ into the world. For it is through belief in 'witness' [50] that the many enter into Life; and decisively put aside all remnants and holds of Death. For such is the Heart and Dream of the Father. And the Joy that was set before the Lord as He faced the Cross: that you too might be one **united in the Father** … one in '**us**', and the Divine Wonder that it brings.

So, if you truly wish to press into the 'Divine Nature'; into the Divine Outpouring of the Spirit, and that of the very Kingdom of Heaven on earth. Then allow the Lord to establish your roots all the more deeper and whole in Him — in depths beyond depths. And here, your words shall carry such weight as to bring about such amazing moves of the Lord.

If your prayers are just for needs and problems, then this is a 'lower' form of prayer. However, if your prayer is for the Heart and the Dreams of God, then this is higher. But again, if your prayer is to *abide* in Him and to be with Him *where* He is … this is joining with His very own Prayer. [51]

Scripture:
I have not sent these prophets, yet they ran. I have not spoken to them, yet they prophesied. But if they had **Stood** in My counsel, and had caused My people to hear My words, then they would have turned them from their evil way and from the evil of their doings. *(Jeremiah 23:21-22 NKJV)*

You and I, in Christ Jesus, have Divine capacity and right to Stand in the Counsel of God. And here, as you choose to come under the 'Shadow of the Lord God Almighty' [52], so shall your own shadow begin to cast the very same Glory [53]. And God, so dearly valuing you as a person; as a 'member' of His Person — married in union with Christ Jesus, and one in Him — as you speak do release the

Goodness of God. For so it is, that the linear-minded man has only stood in the counsel of his own reasoning ... and that of others. But who honestly and truly has it in their heart to stand in the Counsel of God? ... even then as one who abides?

To honour God is to stand in His Counsel. To love the Lord is to abide in His Presence. To wait upon the Lord is to honour His Presence come upon you. And to retain faith in the Lord is to be deeply pleasing to Him. To praise the Lord is to elevate Him before your eyes. And to meditate upon His Word is to elevate Him in your soul. To seek Him and long for Him, even in the midst of great problems and despair, is to love Him and fervently lay hold of Him.

To pray and hunger for the Lord is to open your mouth wide to receive. To hold a firm vertical view, continually has you enraptured — as one continually lifted up in the Lord of Grace. To fix your heart upon the Heavenly realms is to enter in. And as your spirit is uplifted so too is your soul and thought life. To draw close to the Lord so shall He draw close to you. And to seek His Face so shall you see. To walk in the Garden with Him so shall you come to know Him. And to ascend your heart in Him so shall you be taken and enraptured up. Moments on earth can be days in equivalence in Him ... with deep impressions upon your life and His mark left. And as His Seed is retained, so does it ever continuously expand and expand.

> *Truth appears real, but there are Higher Truths that shift reality. Natural law overshadowed by a Higher Law; and death swallowed up by Life.*

As a believer, you can choose only to operate on this **earthly** plane. And as a believer, you can remain still operating from remnants of the **second heaven**; clinging onto fear and cherished sin. Or otherwise, you can choose it in your heart to rise up holy and pure before the Lord. With your heart 'wholly' fixed unto the **realms of the Spirit**. And here ride in planes of Power and Glory that blow your mind.

It is through death that many seeds come forth [54]. Jesus laid His life down and was Risen, so that you need not physically die in order to rise up also and enter Heaven; and this while you still walk this earth. For to such co-abide in the Heavenly plane of Glory; in His Counsel and Might just as the Son. Shifting from one who not only 'believes'; unto one who believes **as Christ Jesus believes**. Transitioning from our faith in Him — to His Faith in us [55]. Righteousness being the right of access; and Goodness being where God's Good comes upon you. Truly the Son of God became the Son of Man ... that you may truly become **sons of Light**!

All Scripture is precedent and license for you also to walk in the very same. All moves of God are yours — and all Promises and historical fact has been recorded ... in order for you to walk in today. That is the very purpose of the Word of God and the gifted Spirit of the Lord ... not only one who is able to quote Scripture but **walk in the reality** of what the Word speaks.

ON A PERSONAL NOTE

I was at the movies the other night with my little eleven-year-old boy, enjoying quality time with him. But so it happened that the people behind were so noisy and were continually bumping at the back of my seat. So after a while my flesh really began to rise up. But instead of saying something ... I moved. *OK,* so that was wise.

I have had issues in my business; money owed, injustice, and demands that have been especially taxing these last few days. And it's been going on for about a year now and I have had to start to draw a line. And again, my flesh had cause to be on edge.

Then this morning I went to a different Post Office and the ladies must have had a bad weekend, for their 'helpfulness' was not so helpful at all. And all I wanted to do is pick up my stuff and go back to my normal friendly Post Office. So again, my flesh was rising up ... and I did my best and stayed calm.

As believers, we always have the choice: to operate out of the flesh or operate out of the Spirit of God. And this option is presented to us all the time. But now, let us come and recognise the wondrous difference. I know that, in my flesh, I could get really nasty at times ... especially if the right buttons are pushed. But as a son of God

— in *alternative* — I can stop right there and say to the Holy Ghost, *"You **manage** my business, as for me I seek the Presence of the Lord."*

Do you see the difference, do you see the different abiding place? The firm choosing to abide in the Light. So I can either become consumed or overtaken by a thing ... or otherwise, **choose to stand** firm in the Presence and Authorities of God. I can easily stand in my own counsel and power, or otherwise rise up and come stand in God's. And here even change the atmosphere and the very realities presented. So this is what I did.

You can either be consumed by an environment, or in God ... shift and change reality by whose we are, and in Him of whom we belong.

It reminds me of a powerful testimony I heard of David Hogan *(a missionary in South America)*. On the way to church one day, up in the mountains of Mexico, he found himself surrounded by six hundred armed men who were sent to kill him. However, as he 'strengthened himself in the Lord' ... he shouted out, *"The Lord God rebuke you in Jesus Name!"* And suddenly, such confusion came over them all [56]. And as they fought amongst themselves ... as to who was going to kill him ... they just walked off arguing.

Another testimony he shared: In the jungles of South America, there are some very exotic and dangerous plagues that sometimes come through. And one time a whole village was dying, and because of the aggressive nature of this virus, was sealed off by both the Mexican army and the US Medical Corps. However, a couple of David's pastors went, and after days of pleading to gain access were finally allowed in. And upon laying hands on every dying soul ... **all were healed** and raised up!

I say to the Holy Ghost, *"You manage my finances; my family, my flesh, and my future ... as for me I seek the Presence of God."* Here, a sharp vertical line is drawn in the sand, given of the Holy Ghost. And like a Sword, I cut between joints and marrow, soul and spirit ... choosing to no longer come under that of which is before me. But here, fully relinquish and **release** all things exposed to the Powers and Glory of the Spirit.

In Christ Jesus I have a choice, I can carry of the Immortal realms of Heaven; and walk in the Eternal realms bringing angels everywhere I go. Otherwise, I can be like the *many* and be flesh-bound, retaining a linear mindset. And this whilst still being called a 'believer'. I can take matters into my own limited hands, or otherwise, I can release and set to action the very Spirit of the Lord. This, by whose I am and who I am in Him*!* And that is why I seek the **manifest Presence of God** continuously, because in this the Presence of God continuously comes. A door not closed but flung open to the Lord of Glory — and this I prefer — I greatly **prefer who I AM in Him**, rather than who I am outside of Him.

To bring Heaven to earth ... be one who *walks* in Heaven. To bring the Glory of God ... be one who *stands* in His Glory. To bring the Presence of God, go *abide* in His Presence. And now, as one who remains in His Counsel, so also do you *'give'* Counsel in Him. Such are the prayers of the saints heard before the Lord. And here the Hosts of angels respond to the words spoken here. For living in treasured union in the Lord, so too are you one with Him — in the Godhead — in perfect union: body, mind, soul, and spirit.

The Spirit is not the bottleneck; the Spirit is not the resistance ... the believer is. Or let's say 'was' ... for your heart, this very moment, is being renewed in Him and made alive. For where the Spirit of the Lord is there is Freedom; and the same is liberally outpoured upon the earth.

Bless you, in Jesus Name*!*

Jesus — the Spirit — and the Wilderness.
The Apostles — the Spirit breathed — and the Upper Room.
The Spirit-filled — the Secret Place — and the Fire come.

To be continued ...

Appendix:

1. 1 Samuel 30:6, *2.* Romans 10:17, Matthew 4:4, 16:17-18, 17:20, John 15:7, 5:44, Hebrews 11:6, *3.* John 3:16, Luke 3:16, 2 Corinthians 3:16, *4.* Psalm 27:4, John 15:4, *5.* 1 Samuel 24:9-10, *6.* Isaiah 40:30-31, 35:3-7, Psalm 84:6, Malachi 4:2, *7.* Psalm 84:10, 27:4, *8.* Genesis 1:26, Exodus 33:14, Psalm 110:1-2, Hebrews 4:1-11, Revelation 3:20-21, 5:10, Genesis 5:24, *9.* Genesis 3:22-24, Revelation 2:7, 22:2, *10.* Psalm 37:4, *11.* Revelation 3:20, Luke 12:37, Psalm 36:8-9, *12.* Luke 10:39, Mark 3:13-15, John 17:24, *13.* John 17:20-24, 13:33, 36, 5:19, *14.* John 3:13 *NKJV*, *15.* Hebrews 7:12-19, Revelation 1:5-6 *NKJV*, Zechariah 3:7-9, *16.* John 7:38, *17.* John 5:19, *18.* John 7:42, Matthew 22:42-45, Hebrews 7:17, Revelation 5:10 *NKJV*, *19.* John 17:21, 14:11-14, *20.* Psalm 110:1, *21.* Colossians 3:1-3, *22.* Isaiah 50:4, Hebrews 10:16, Matthew 23:9, *23.* Genesis 1:26, Revelation 3:21, 5:10 *NKJV*, *24.* Genesis 2:17, *25.* Revelation 3:20, *26.* John 3:1-2, *27.* Romans 8:6, *28.* John 3:12, *29.* Mark 16:17-18, *30.* John 3:2, *31.* Matthew 16:17, Luke 7:9, John 15:7, 5:44, Jeremiah 23:21-22, *32.* Matthew 4:4, *33.* John 10:9, *34.* John 5:19, *35.* Matthew 13:25, *36.* Matthew 17:20, *37.* John 5:44, 15:7, *38.* Luke 18:19, *39.* Romans 8:29, *40.* 1 Peter 5:6, *41.* John 3:13, *42.* John 17:20-24, *43.* John 6:63, *44.* Psalm 36:8-9, 1 John 1:7, John 1:4, Ephesians 5:8, *45.* Revelation 1:10, *46.* Romans 7:21-25, *47.* Ephesians 2:6, *48.* Luke 4:14, *49.* Romans 8:1 *NKJV*, *50.* Revelation 12:11, John 14:13, *51.* John 17:20-24, John 14:1-4, *52.* Psalm 91:1, *53.* Acts 5:15, *54.* John 12:24, *55.* Galatians 2:20 *KJV*, *56.* Exodus 14:25, Exodus 23:27

Dated: 16/6/19

11. *The Joy Set Before Him (#94)*
IT'S NOT ABOUT ME!

Theme Scripture:
I pray that they all may be one, as You, Father, are in Me, and I in You; that they **also may be <u>one in us</u>**, that the world may believe that You sent Me. *(John 17:21 NKJV/NLT)*

The power of choice that is held in the hands of the believer — the very Keys of Heaven that are in your very hands [1]. Through your choice you have incredible capacity to open Heaven phenomenally wide in your life ... or otherwise, keep it closed. This, by your will and by your choice. The Spirit of God is not in authority in this area ... you are! For it is the believer that has been made in Likeness of God on earth and **has** been given Dominion. [2]

Somewhere out there, there just might be a believer who is opening Heaven [3] and pouring out the Spirit of God. And in this, you have no resistance when the Spirit moves. No ability to stand or resist against the Presence of the Person of God ... all shall bow willingly or unwillingly. So in this, who is it that you wish to be, one who takes but just a thimble full ... or one who takes in deep deep drafts?

Moves of the Spirit come by opening doors for the Spirit to move. Outpourings of the Spirit are in the believer's own hands [4]. Opening Heaven with the Keys given [5] ... even striking the earth [6]. Such is the Power of a firm vertical view. For just as in the time of Jesus, the linear world of which you live shall be shaken — with the Life and Fire of God triumphing over sin and death [7]. In the Old Testament, God chose men and gave them special abilities to save the nation. But in the New Testament — **<u>all</u> are chosen**. Opportunity is in the believer's hands to step into the realms of Power [8] and set uto charge the Spirit of the Lord.

At one time, Jesus, in celebrating Peter, said to him, *"Blessed are you, Simon son of Jonah, for this was not revealed to you by flesh and blood, but by my Father in Heaven."* [9]

Jesus was marvelling at something most significant here — the fact that Peter *heard* from God. Did you know that there were only two times in Gospel that Jesus praised a person? I really encourage you in this; this is such a 'hidden' and understated message. [10]

Do you realise, that except for the lady at the well, there is not a single time that Jesus revealed that He was the Christ? Not one time! There is great mystery and importance in this. Jesus defines this as the 'Abiding Word' … *ie;* the Witness within that speaks. Even as He said, *"If you remain in me and my Words remain in you, ask whatever you wish, and it will be done for you."* [11]

In Christ, we are called to honour and hunger for the Word that **transcends** words. The Word that personally 'proceeds out from the mouth of God' into your soul impressing, *"I know that I know"*. It is a faith given you from Above, a strength that comes from outside of you; a knowledge that transcends what can be heard … *ie; "The Rod of your Strength that comes out of Zion."*

This is the underlying drive and purpose of the Father; the Heart-to-heart dialogue that causes you to *"Rule in the midst of your enemies"* [12]. And if you can ever truly get this; the honour to 'see' and 'hear' God; the desire to come up upon the Mountain … your life will be forever changed. And all that you have ever been believing for, will be fast-tracked. For your *first* prayer is Him, and in Him *everything* follows.

Then Jesus continued, *"Upon this rock I will build my Church, and the gates of Hades shall not prevail against it."* And going still further, *"I will give you the Keys of the Kingdom of Heaven … and whatever you bind on earth will be bound in Heaven, and whatever you loose on earth shall be loosed in Heaven."*

I so encourage you, as one purposed in soul to hear and see God, *ie;* one looking beyond the Veil into what He is saying and doing … and *listening* [13]. Then so shall your life be ever strengthened and built upon the Rock. As one entering into the realms of the 'Abiding Word' [9], where the Gates of Hades cannot prevail against you. For so it is, as one listens and learns … so are you gifted Authority to manage and 'direct' Heaven. [14]

As expressed in the opening Scripture verse, the 'Prayer' of your Saviour is that you might become one in Him; one in spirit, soul, mind, and body. This is the **orientation of <u>all</u> His efforts**, that you be unified one in the Godhead. Your heart and your thoughts can be anywhere. But in the Lord, you have phenomenal capacity to be in Him.

Therefore, it's not about 'me' ... but about Him. It's not about an ambition, an office, or a vision of mine; but firmly Abiding in the Vine [15]. And subsequently here, giving full right of *passage* for the Spirit of the Lord to move [16]. For just as the right has been given you to enter and engage Heaven [17] — just as the Son — in Like *as He*. So is the right of passage for the Spirit of God to move in the reality of your world — is it in *your* hands. [18]

Such is the treasure found in seeking the Presence of God — for in this His Presence comes [19]. For here, deep in the ministering Presence of the Lord — in the open Joy of Him [20] — do you gladly put aside all that hinders and has held you captive [21]. And by the Spirit of the Lord, are you positioned by Him under the continual Outpouring [22]. And this is what is most valuable, to be aligned *under* the Glory of God. Coming under the Shadow of the Lord God Almighty ... whereby your own shadow casts the very same Glory.

A side note: The other time that Jesus marvelled at a person was the Roman Centurion. This, a man who deeply loved the Jewish people and their faith in God. He was given of God, through his honour ... not that he paid for it, but his honour drew God [23] *... He was given deep revelation of the Christ. And this revelation caused Jesus to marvel at the depths of his insight ... and therefore respond to him.*

The greatest testimony that you can bring to the world is the manifestation of Heaven on earth. [24]

Recently, it was my little boy's birthday. And I was thinking, can you imagine him asking for some cake when we have already made and set his birthday cake on the table? And though we have told him over and over, he just kept asking as though he can't hear and can't see. So is it the same regarding the things of the Spirit. [25]

The Word and the Spirit bear continual Testimony of such things. Jesus, who is King and Priest unto God of Heaven and earth; earnestly seeks also to establish you as 'king' and 'priest' with Him, *ie;* co-heirs … co-reigning … and co-seated [26]. The wonder of this is detailed in the earlier chapters of Revelations *(chapters 1 - 5)*. But what is also most clear, is that this incomprehensible Glory of God, once given … can also be taken away [27]. And this is what we see today: the modern-day Western Church failing to walk in the Power of the Book of Acts.

However, this is changing … for so it is, that as one truly gives their life unto the Lord, *ie;* lays their life down in Him, that Life truly is found [28]. For it is Jesus Himself who personally stands with you and works to raise you Victorious and Triumphant. And as He raises you Triumphant, so does He also dress you able to operate in the Authorities and Powers of the Throne of God. [29]

Scripture:
He humbled you, allowed you to hunger, and fed you with manna which you did not know nor did your fathers know, that He might **make you know** that man shall not live by bread alone; but man lives by every word that proceeds from the mouth of the LORD. *(Deuteronomy 8:3 NKJV)*

Most of us have experienced hardship or times of difficulty. And it is true, that most are instigated by the *Thief* … for we live on a fallen world. But some trials and tribulations are also given, or let's say, allowed by the Lord for this one important reason: that your roots may draw deep and be ever more established in the Lord. This, to teach one important thing: to **hunger** for the Living Word that 'proceeds from the mouth of God'.

Our knowledge and understanding can oftentimes be linear. Meaning, something that has been passed on or given you of man. But then there is the Knowledge that is given of God. And **this is what you want**! Earthly knowledge and information is good … but is just a shadow; like grass that is here one day and gone the next. However, the Knowledge that is Imparted to you of God penetrates deep in your soul. And becomes as like deep roots that form into 'Oaks' of righteousness [30]. Seeds planted deep within from Above … Rivers of deep water [31] that Divinely move and motivate you.

Problems come upon all who walk the earth. However, as Jesus says, *"Take heart for I have Overcome the world"* [32]. Hence, we continually choose to **look** unto He the *"Author and Finisher of our faith"* [33]. In this life, we live on a fallen world; with fallen spirits and fallen mindsets. Therefore, how we truly come to win is to '**return back**' into the pre-fallen state [34]. The Bible teaches you about God … but the 'Abiding Word' [35] this is found as you personally step in and Dwell in Him. To such as these abide in a Place of continual and perpetual Impartation of Heaven: Spirit *(realms of Everlasting Life)*, Soul *(Joy and Peace)*, Mind *(the Mind of Christ)*, and Flesh *(made manifest)*.

Now, by the Blood have you been made the Righteousness of Christ. But the right to sit upon the Throne of God and 'wield' the Spirits of the Lord [36] — this takes **full submission** in Him. Even just as Moses said, *"If you are pleased with me, teach me your ways so I may know you and continue to find favour with you."* And so too will God respond to you also saying, *"My Presence will go with you, and I will give you Rest."* [37]

So then, in example for each one of us this very day, Moses goes on even further, *"If your Presence does not go with us, do not send us up from here. For what will distinguish me and your people from all the peoples of the earth?"* And so also shall God respond to you saying, *"I will do the very thing you have asked."* [38]

You see, God's fundamental and underlying desire is to fulfil His Promise and Purpose in you [39]. However, this is only made possible by He of whom you seek … so humble yourself and seek*!* Before, the Promised Land was but a physical destination. But now, the realms of Heaven … the very Glory of God, **is your very Purposed destination**. Jesus Himself *left* to go 'make' a Home for you, and so shall He then 'receive you unto Himself' [40] as you *yield* yourself to Him.

So for us too then: Moses continues and said to God, *"Show me your Glory."* I tell you something most precious, in Christ Jesus, these realms of Glory are your **purposed Dwelling Place**. This, as dreamed of by the Son [33]. As He said, *"May they be one in us"* ... and ... *"May they be with me where I am"* [41]. Hence, as you also personally respond and come to the Father asking Him to teach you ... so He shall. And these realms that He opens to you, far exceed all human comprehension. [42]

Picture for a moment the 'architecture' of Heaven. It is Jesus who sits upon the Throne at the right hand of God — *with* Him. So ... in this picture, where is the Spirit of the Lord? The Seven Spirits of God are before the Throne [43] ... not *on* the Throne, but before the Throne. Therefore, as you choose to engage personally and closely with the Spirit of God so are you also raised by Him. And as one made unified in the Lord [41], so are you made by Him able to pass through and sit upon the Throne. That is, upon the Judgement Chair, the Ruling Chair, the Chair of Absolute Authority and Power.

Scripture:
God is Spirit, and those who worship Him must worship in spirit and truth. *(John 4:24 NKJV)*

God is Absolute Power and Authority. However, as a Church, in Christ Jesus [44] we also called to sit upon the Throne — *with* Him [45]. The Invitation of the shed Blood is that you be *unified* one with Jesus; fundamentally called by Him to be with Him where He is. And so, in this picture, where is Jesus now? But seated at the right hand of God [46]. So the question is, where are you supposed to be? ... but seated here with Him.

There is no corruption [47], nor is there any contradiction in this Place. No mixed seed ... only *perfect* union; one with Him in spirit, soul, mind, and body. Therefore, the orientation of the believer needs always be unto union. Not needs or desires — but union. However now, when you speak, your desires and needs are fully met. [48]

Bob Jones was known as a man who would go into Heaven several times a day. And a man whose prophecies were so powerful and accurate. I tell you a trick: value not so much the prophetic words spoken, **compared** to that of going into and seeing God just as he. This is the Will of God concerning all who love the Lord — for Power to win only comes from Him.

This was the same for the likes of Smith Wigglesworth, Even Roberts, and TL Osborn. They chose and preferred to come up into the Presence of God and stand in the Place where His Living Word liberally flows. And this was the same for King David and Jesus — He our Living Precedent and Pattern. Therefore, to live and walk like Jesus — one needs first to do *just* as He. And go into the Place He always went and has Personally made the Way. [49]

Let me tell you another little trick: If you are suffering with a sin, or an addiction, or some other kind of deep grip that is upon your life ... then do this. Or if you are otherwise under financial strain, family or relationship difficulties, or any other form of hardship. Then bow upon the knees and in your heart pray, *"Holy Ghost you manage these things, you go out and fight my battles* [50]. *As for me I seek the Presence of God."*

Each and every believer — has the Spirit of the Lord. But what you want is to walk in fluency of the Seven Spirits of God [51]. For only by the Spirit of the Lord are you made Triumphant and Victorious in all things. No longer coming under the influences and powers of this Age, but one made able to rise up Above. Therefore now, as one in Him, when you speak do you release the very same Spirits of the Lord unto action [52]. For here upon the Throne — in perfect union with Him — are you Anointed to 'wield' the Spirit as like a sword in your hands.

To such have passed through the Cherubim — and dine liberally of the Tree of Life, bringing healing to the nations [53]. And the very same Glory of the Spirit, that was held in the Ark of the Covenant, is now in you! [54] And the very same is released according to the words of your mouth. This, your ultimate Destination — our Purpose and Destiny in Christ Jesus — but so few are coming. [55]

A side note: God says, "Let us form and make man into our Image and very Likeness. And let us give him Dominion over and above the earth" [56]. *In the Book of Genesis, Satan is referred to as but a snake on the ground 'under'*

Adam's feet (a worm). Then in the Book of Revelations, Satan is referred to as a dragon. Today, in Christ Jesus, everything is about re-positioning! And where is it that you wish to be? One remaining 'small' under the serpent and his works, or one restored Above in Christ Jesus towering over him?

This, fundamentally, is why Christ came: to reposition each one of us. That you too might be made in the Image of the Risen Man. Meaning, restored back into the realms of Dominion over and Above all things. So say this prayer with me, "Lord Jesus, please continue to raise me in the fullness of the 'why' you went on the Cross. That I too might walk in the fullness of you as I walk this earth. Even with an open Heaven [57], in the Power of the Spirit to bring Life and Hope. Bless you ... amen."

Come now, and choose to stand in the Counsels of God [58]. Being one ever eager to engage and be **raised** up in Him [14]. For a believer who remains unaware of such things, prays from earth as they call out to a faithful God. However, it is our very same God of Heaven and earth that has been calling and calling for you to come up in Him — **into union** — body, mind, soul, and spirit [41]. And this is why there can be unnecessary delay [59]. For by your *faith* shall you press in; and by your *roots* shall you be established in Him — deeper and deeper within His Abiding Presence [60]. Not in that of which is before you in this world — but in Him. And to the one who sits upon the Throne in God; sits also in Heavenly Places and prays from within Him — seeing change.

In Christ Jesus, you have been sanctified ... by the Blood and finished work of the Cross. But unto this aligning and moving under the 'Outpouring'; that is only achieved through the work of the welcomed Spirit of God. He of whom lives alive in you. This is why Jesus says, *"True worshipers will worship the Father in Spirit and in Truth, for these are the kind of worshipers the Father seeks"* [61]. For you cannot make yourself holy, as God has called you to be holy; [62] this is the active work, between the Person of the Spirit of God ... and the willing.

Such is the Treasure found in pursuing the Presence of God. For here, in the Heart of Him is your soul ever renewed and lifted up. Made soft and supple and true: **able to continuously receive** Good Seed to heart. And to they who are made holy in and by the

Lord ... so too do they always 'see' God. As is said, *"Without holiness no one will see the Lord."* ⁶³

IN CLOSING
*"May they **be in us** so that the world may believe you sent me."* ⁶⁴

Do you see now, the Dream and Prayer of your Saviour? For truly, to be — **in Him** — causes you also able to truly *behold* His Glory. And such who behold carry also the very same Glory as you walk this earth. And here, through the undeniable manifestation of His Glory upon your life; shall the world come to truly know that the Father truly did send the Son into the world. This to the Glory of the Son ... that all may put their faith in Him. And truly find Salvation for their souls.

The 1st Lord's Prayer: "Your Kingdom come, your Will be done, on earth as it is in Heaven *(manifestation on earth)*. And give us today our **daily bread** *(the Living Word that proceeds from the mouth of God into your soul)*."

The 2nd Lord's Prayer: "Father, I want those you have given me to be with me where I am, and to see my Glory *(relocation unto the realms of Power, even as one clothed)*."

The 3rd Lord's Prayer: "And may they be in us so that the world will believe you sent me *(salvation through the Blood and the 'bearing witness')*."

Bless you, in Jesus Name!

Appendix:

1. Matthew 16:19, *2.* Genesis 1:26, *3.* Isaiah 64:1-4, *4.* John 7:38, *5.* Psalm 84:6, *6.* 2 Kings 2:13-14, Psalm 110:1-2, Isaiah 11:1-4, Revelation 2:26-27, 19:15, *7.* 1 Corinthians 15:55, *8.* Luke 24:49, *9.* Matthew 16:17-19, *10.* Proverbs 25:2, Deuteronomy 29:29, Romans 11:33, John 14:21, Jeremiah 33:3, *11.* John 15:7, *12.* Psalm 110:1-2, *13.* John 5:44, Matthew 17:20, Revelation 1:10-18, 2:29, *14.* Zechariah 3:7-9, Revelation 3:18-22, Exodus 33:13-17, Isaiah 11:1-4, *15.* Isaiah 11:1-4, Zechariah 3:1-10, John 15:1-8, *16.* John 12:24, Galatians 2:20 *KJV*, *17.* John 10:9, *18.* John 5:19, *19.* Luke 5:16-17, Luke 4:14, Exodus 34:29-30, Revelation 1:10, *20.* Psalm 27:4, *21.* Psalm 84:10, *22.* Revelation 22:1-2, 12-17, 21:6, 2:7, John 4:14, *23.* Luke 7:5, Revelation 3:18, *24.* Matthew 6:10, *25.* Revelation 3:6, *26.* Romans 8:17, *27.* 2 Timothy 2:12, *28.* Matthew 10:39, *29.* Revelation 3:16-22, Zechariah 3:7-9, 1 Corinthians 6:3, *30.* Isaiah 61:1-4, *31.* John 7:38, *32.* John 16:33, *33.* Hebrews 12:2, *34.* 1 Corinthians 15:45, *35.* John 15:4, *36.* Isaiah 11:2, Revelation 19:15a, *37.* Exodus 33:13-14, *38.* Exodus 33:15-17, *39.* Exodus 33:1, *40.* John 14:3 *NKJV*, *41.* John 17:20-24, *42.* 1 Corinthians 2:9-10, *43.* Revelation 1:4, *44.* John 17:20-24, *45.* Revelation 1:5-6, 5:9-10, 3:21, Psalm 110:1-2, 2:7-8, Matthew 22:14, *46.* Hebrews 10:12, *47.* John 14:30, Hebrews 12:14b, *48.* Psalm 37:4, Matthew 6:33, John 15:7, *49.* John 14:6, *50.* Exodus 14:14, 33:14, 23:28, Matthew 6:33, *51.* Isaiah 11:1-4, *52.* Revelation 19:15, 2:26-27, Psalm 110:1-2, *53.* Genesis 3:24, Revelation 2:7, 22:2, *54.* Genesis 3:24, Exodus 3:2, 19:18, 1 Kings 18:37-39, Isaiah 11:3, 33:14b-15a, Matthew 3:11, Luke 12:49, 24:49, Acts 2:3, 5:9, Hebrews 12:21, 12:28-29, Revelation 1:10-14, *55.* Matthew 22:14, *56.* Genesis 1:26, Exodus 33:14, Psalm 110:1-2, Hebrews 4:1-11, Revelation 5:10 *KJV*, *57.* John 1:51, *58.* Jeremiah 23:22, *59.* Deuteronomy 8:3, *60.* John 15:7, 5:44, Matthew 16:17, Luke 7:9, Jeremiah 23:21-22, *61.* John 4:23-24, *62.* 1 Peter 1:15, *63.* Hebrews 12:14, Zechariah 3:1-5, *64.* John 17:21

Dated: 27/6/19

12. *The Joy Set Before Him (#95)*
PRESENCE IS A WEAPON

Three opening Scriptures:
1. The LORD will fight for you; you need only to **be still**. *(Exodus 14:14 NIV)*
2. The LORD replied, "My Presence will go with you, and I will **give you rest**." *(Exodus 33:14 NIV)*
3. And I will **send hornets ahead of you** so that they will drive out the Hivites, the Canaanites, and the Hittites from you. *(Exodus 23:28 NKJV)*

The Presence of God is a weapon. It is the means to win in every circumstance [1]. A preference for Presence of God over problems. A preference for the **manifest Presence** of God in your midst over the lures and temptations and the fears of this world. Even as one relocated … and dwelling [2] in Him, able to send forth the very same Presence of God.

> *Hornets: the Spirit of God can be shaped into any form. A conscious weapon directed unto any target or purpose or problem.*

The Presence of God is full of the Grace, the Joy, and the Love of God. And within is a **deep sense** of Belonging, of Companionship, and Wonder [3]. The world is full of pride, of lust, and a dread of loss. However, as you personally choose to draw yourself near to God [4] — in *every* circumstance — so does He Raise and Tutor you able to move Heaven. And as one who walks in the realms of Everlasting Life, do you also become a holder of Life and Spirit. To break down every stronghold and every obstruction pouring out the Fire of God.

Scripture:
I did not send these prophets, yet they have run with their message; I did not speak to them, yet they have prophesied. But if they had **stood** in my council, they would have **proclaimed my words** to my people and would have turned them from their evil ways and from their evil deeds. *(Jeremiah 23:21-22 NIV)*

The Presence of God is **full of the Counsel of God**. And in choosing to Abide and Remain here [5], so do you also welcome the Wisdom and Knowledge of God to speak ... and speak He will. To prefer the Dreams of God over that of your own dreams; not only is God a fulfiller of dreams [6], but He remains fully *active* in areas that you did not even ask. And in dwelling and remaining in this Place, so are you given capacity to 'Rule' [7] As one bringing about the manifestation of the Kingdom of God here on earth.

Scripture:
There remains therefore a Rest for the people of God. *(Hebrews 4:9)*

The Rest of the Lord is central to walking in the Power of God. The here being 'still' [8] and allowing the **Presence** of the Person of God **to fight for you** [9]. And this Rest is a Gift, it is not something you can conjure up in yourself but is given richly of God. As He said, *"I will give you Rest"* [10]. And this Rest of God is the very Promised Land to enter ... the Garden realms. The very Place of Authority and Grace. It is the Ruling Place where God works actively on your behalf [11] ... just as was in the Beginning.

The Presence of God is laced with the Joy of the Lord. His right hand — the very Place from where the River flows [12]. And out of Zion, shall the '**Rod of your Strength**' come — that you might truly Rule in the midst of all that comes against. [13]

Hence, retaining the mindset of the world, one can never truly live in **experience** of the Life and Freedom of God. To cling onto your life ... so shall you lose it. But to freely give it up unto the Lord ... so shall you find [14]. For in giving preference for the Presence of God ... it is He who will cause you able to walk in open wonder of Heavenly Delights.

Scripture:
v5-6 Your faith and love rise within you as you '**access**' all the treasures of your inheritance stored up in the Heavenly realm. For the revelation of the **true gospel is as real today** ... [coming] to bear the fruit of Eternal Life as [you] experience the reality of God's Grace [and Love].

v12 Your **heart can <u>soar</u>** with joyful gratitude, when you think of how God made you worthy to receive the glorious inheritance; freely given to us by **living** [Abiding] in the Light. *(Colossians 1:5-6, 12 TPT)*

1. **The Calling of the <u>Blood</u>:** The right of passage to liberally engage Heaven and walk close with your Heavenly Father — is Jesus' Gift concerning you. However, the right of passage for the Spirit to outpour this — is in *your* hands*!*

2. **The Calling of the finished work of the <u>Cross</u>**: Is that you have perfect right of access to engage your Heavenly Father and walk in these of the Heavenly planes — as much as you might desire. But to the outpouring of the Spirit, this — is something of **your** choice. For the Keys of the Kingdom of Heaven are in the hands of those who *hear* and *see* God. [15]

3. **The Calling of <u>Heaven</u>:** Irrespective of the entanglements of sin, or the brokenness in your life; you are free to approach your Heavenly Father as a son — just as you are [16]. And here … right here … you can pause. Right in the midst of wherever you are, you can be still and say to the Lord, *"I love you Lord … I need you … please continue to lead me in my life."* And in the Presence of God, you can go *even* further and say, *"Spirit of the Living God you manage these things: you go out before me. As for me I seek the Presence of God."* For your fundamental **Calling**: is the returning back into the Place from whence Adam fell. And Heaven's fundamental calling: is to go out on your behalf. [13]

The very word 'Anointing' means: the **Authority <u>of</u> God** to speak; Power and Authority given of God to move and shift reality. And these are simply *kingly* attributes, the nature of a son or daughter of God. They of whom are **heirs** of God Himself and co-hears with Jesus of the very Kingdom of Heaven [17]. Another word to describe this, is the being transformed into the very Likeness of the Son — gaining **His Mind** and perspective — even that of the New Adam. And another way to describe it is, the being 'reclothed' … transfigured back into *your* former Glory. As is said, *"Let us make man like one of us … and let us give him Dominion."* [18]

I so encourage you, let your approach in God be different. And let your approach to all things that you are dealing with in life … also be so very different.

Scripture:
John, to the seven churches which are in Asia: Grace to you and peace from Him who is and who was and who is to come, and from the Seven Spirits who are before His throne, and from Jesus Christ, the faithful witness, the firstborn from the dead, and the ruler over the kings of the earth. To Him who loved us and washed us from our sins in His own blood, and has **made us kings** and priests to His God and Father. *(Revelations 1:4-6 NKJV)*

Picture again the 'architecture' of Heaven. Here, you have Jesus sitting at the right hand of God … **with Him** upon the Throne. You have the Spirits of the Lord and the innumerable hosts of angels that are here before the Throne. So the question is then, in this picture … where are you supposed to be? What is your Purposed and fundamental Calling in God?

It is the **Dream** of your Heavenly Father, *since* the very Beginning, that you respond [19] and come sit upon the Throne. In deep and in closest of relationship with Him in His 'Bosom' [20]. And this always remains the 'struggle' … and is the diligent effort for all believers [21]. For just as the world always seeks to drag you down [22] — it is the Spirit of the Lord that always seeks to **lift you up**. [23]

The Heart of Father is always set upon you responding, as one **positioning** yourself in Him. Ever preferencing these realms of His Abiding Joy … these realms of Power and Grace. Not other things, not unto other places — but **in Him**, in ever-deepening union. This was the Way your Saviour walked; the very Pattern and Precedent He demonstrated and made clear for each one of us. And though before, we used to pray and operate from an earthly footing and perspective … and in our own humanity looking up to God saying, *"Please help me"* … *"Please bless me"* … *"Please empower me."* However now, as is the fundamental Heart's Desire and Purpose of the Father — we **come up** in Him and are seated. And now when you speak, do you **release** the Spirit of God to action … just as the Son.

Such then, is the purpose of trials and testings; to **train** you able to win [24]. And win you shall ... if *truly* it is God of whom you love [25]. On earth you will have trouble, for we live in a fallen world. **But!** ... Christ Jesus has overcome the world [26], do you yet see? Christ Jesus is the **Victory!** Therefore, as one who diligently listens and remains ever attentive to His Voice, so are you led in and out to find Pasture [27]. Entering right into the Provisions of the Lord ... even right in His Ministering Presence of His Divine Glory. And here, ever lifted up in Him; **lifted** up in Power and Authority over the whole earth. This is the Dream and Heart of the Father ... but who is responding?

You can either come *under* a thing or can choose to rise up Above. And right in the midst of all things you can say to the Lord, "*Spirit of the Living God, you look after these things ... you manage, you go out, you set straight. As for me, I choose to* **enter the Rest** *of God and* **sit here** *in His Holy Presence.*" For it is always the Holy Spirit's fundamental Purpose to fight for you. Just as it is your fundamental Purpose to enter the Rest of the Lord ... *ie;* the Ruling Place. [19]

To sit with God is to enter His Rest. The entering into the realms as one continually fed and lifted up. The very same realms where God goes out before you; the seated realms where you are raised in the attributes of a king.

It is the **Spirit's work** to raise and seat you with your Heavenly Father. Even so, that you may appropriate ... and operate ... more fully in that of your Divine Inheritance and Birthright. And now, as you speak, so do you release the Life and Spirit of the Lord. You as a child of God — **born to Rule**: the Spirit is your Counsellor; that in your hands you may come to hold the Resurrection Power of God.

When you look at the Sword of the Spirit, what do you see? There is the blade and the handle. So it is a question to ask, what is the purpose of the handle? But that you, as a child of the Living God, **may wield** the very Spirits of God to action. [28]

It is massive to think, but in your hands ... you are Purposed of God to **direct** the Spirit of the Living God. And as one submitted to the Christ ... following Him and He alone ... you are simply coming back into your pre-fallen Origins. This, the very Purpose of your creation: that you also might be fashioned into the Image and Likeness of Christ [29]. Even as one in Dominion over all powers and all authorities. Seated in Heavenly Places with the Lord God Almighty. And this is the purpose of the Resurrecting of the Son: that you also may walk in His Resurrection Power ... as one Risen in Him.

On this earth, we all have our challenges ... but where do you go? And to whom do you turn? If it is the Lord, then it will be He who will give you Grace. And if it is the Person of God, it will be **He who shall Empower you to win**. Ever filling your life with the Love and Joy of God. So in Him who do you serve ... is it God or is it man? If it is God, then in love ... so shall you serve man. Not ever to put your trust in 'princes' of man [30] ... but in God alone.

THE 'THIRD' LORD'S PRAYER

Closing Scripture:
I pray that they all may be one, as You, Father, are in Me, and I in You; that they also may be **one in us**, that the world may believe that You sent Me. *(John 17:21 NKJV/NLT)*

It is the Lord's Dream and deepest Desire that you live in a state of perpetual Encounter in God. Here in the Rhema Word, the Abiding Word ... in the Agape Love of the Most High God. For it is from this Place that you shall be raised: no longer frail or as a troubled people ... but Powerful in God. And this true and open reality comes from deeply treasured union in Him. This, the very 'wielding' of the Spirit ... and the Powers of God, is birthed out of deeply treasured union in Him. But it remains a choice, doesn't it? ... to remain a people ever built up in this of our Divine Origins. Not in separation to Him, but in ever-increasing union; body, mind, soul, and spirit.

It is the demon's way, for the believer to live under fear and hopelessness. But it is the Lord's Way, that you may live in the Power and Freedom of God.

Bless you, in Jesus Name.

Appendix:

1. Matthew 16:19, 17:20, ***2.*** John 17:20-24, John 15:7, Exodus 19:10-20, Psalm 27:4-5, Colossians 3:1-4, ***3.*** Zechariah 3:7, ***4.*** James 4:8, ***5.*** John 15:1-16, Isaiah 11:1-4, ***6.*** Psalm 37:4, ***7.*** 2 Chronicles 1:11-13, ***8.*** Psalm 46:10, Isaiah 28:12, ***9.*** Psalm 91, Exodus 14:14, Deuteronomy 32:35, Joshua 24:12, ***10.*** Exodus 33:14, Hebrews 4:6, ***11.*** Hebrews 4:8-11, Genesis 1:26, 2:17, 3:19, ***12.*** Revelation 22:1-2, ***13.*** Psalm 110:2, ***14.*** Matthew 10:39, Luke 18:22, Hebrews 4:1-3, ***15.*** Matthew 16:17-19, ***16.*** Isaiah 44:22, Zechariah 3:1-2, ***17.*** Romans 8:17, ***18.*** Genesis 1:26, 2:17, 3:19, 5:3, 1 Corinthians 15:45, Revelation 1:5-6, 3:17-22, 5:10, ***19.*** Psalm 110:1-2, 2:7-8, Revelation 1:5-6 *NKJV*, 3:19-21, 5:9-10, ***20.*** John 1:18, 17:21, Psalm 17:8, ***21.*** Hebrews 4:11, ***22.*** Genesis 3:1, 4:7, ***23.*** Genesis 1:26, Psalm 2:7-8, 110:1-2, Isaiah 11:1-4, 64:1-4, Revelation 1:5-6, 2:26-27, 3:17-22, 5:9-10, 19:15, 2 Kings 2:9, ***24.*** James 1:2-4, ***25.*** Revelation 3:15-16, ***26.*** John 16:33, ***27.*** John 10:9, Revelation 3:22, ***28.*** Isaiah 11:2, ***29.*** Romans 8:29, ***30.*** Psalm 118:8

Dated: 18/7/19

UNION IN HIM

13. Union in Him (#96)
COME UP IN ME *(Part 1)*

Opening Scripture:
Those who live according to the flesh have their minds set on what the flesh desires; but those who live in accordance with the Spirit have their minds set on what the Spirit desires. The mind governed by the flesh is death, but the mind governed by the Spirit is life and peace. *(Romans 8:5-6 NIV)*

The greatest key in life is your ability to come up in God. Regardless of how well things have been going, or how bad things may be … you have inherent capacity to be captured up in Him [1]. And to such, whatever you are now facing, now has to face the Glory of God. Before you were a people of mortality [2], but now you are a people born of the Immortal [3]. And before, you were a people of the dirt and dust [4], but now you are a people of the Spirit of God. [5]

To set it in your heart to 'transition' [6], *ie;* from the carnal mind unto the Mind of Christ [7], does one begin to experience much change. However, this process requires the Spirit … in order to truly be able to walk according to the Spirit [8]. We need the 'transport' system of the Holy Spirit of God to shift, the 'funnel' of impartation dynamic and active in our lives, in order to truly live and function effectively in Him. And this is a choice, isn't it? This 'right of passage', this welcomeness to be active, remains a choice in the hands of each and every Spirit-filled believer. To all who are called by His Name.

In the past, we did our best to reach out to God in *our* faith. However now, it is **His Faith** that is beginning to penetrate our souls [14]. And before we tried to honour God through the works of our hands. But now, it is God who is beginning to honour His Name through the Works of His [9]. And this free right to approach our Heavenly Father has been **freely gifted** us through the sending of the Christ. However, the right of passage for the Spirit of the Living God to be freely active in your life — this is in your hands. This is in *your* choice.

To truly come to honour the Lord your God ... with the **best** of you; [10] and actively pursue after His Abiding Presence active in your life, so too are you giving full right for the Spirit of Living God to engage with you. And to such gain an ever-deepening meaning of the word 'Faith' — the '**iron rod**' of Authority [11] that is wrought through your Divine engagements with Him. 'Authoritative' Faith that is ever built up in Him and strengthened, as you draw your heart to Him and He continues to reveal His Heart to you.

The Father's Heart and Dream is always unto union; [12] body, mind, soul, and spirit *(ie; the full truth of you)*. And though your Heavenly Father will always meet you where you are at and respond to that of which your *faith* seeks. It remains His singular Desire that you **come up in Him** — and from here, in union, speak and move and have your being. And as a believer, function more fully in that of your Inheritance and Birthright — even God Himself. Here, from the realms of the 'Abiding Place'; from the Throne of Power and Grace.

It is true, that our linear *(two-dimensional ... flat)* minds have little or no reference of such things. Hence, this is why the Father sent His Son: for in coming to *look* closely into the Person of Jesus, **we see our own 'Image and Likeness' in Him**. That is, Jesus Himself is our Precedent and Living Example ... so when I say, *"Our Image"*, I mean, He is the very Picture of God's Dream and Vision for each and every believer. Even this, **the New Adam embodied in us** [13]. Hence, as you also retain a root culture to *Abide* in His Holy Presence; so too are you continually lifted and built up in Him ... as the Faith **of** the Son [1] begins to 'invade' and penetrate your soul. [14]

Throughout this chapter, I would like to reflect on the following:

1. Jesus' desire for you to *practice* a non-orphaned lifestyle.
2. How to effectively *manage* all issues of life; including both ministerial success and strong opposition that comes.
3. *Avail* yourself to Encounters with God.
4. How the *Power* of the Spirit is with you.
5. Walk according to what the Spirit is *disclosing*.
6. Operating with the *Keys* of Heaven.

7. Shifting away from the holds of doubt and unbelief ... and *walking* in the Power of the Son.

Before we start, lets revisit my favourite 'but' Scripture verse. And this time with an additional layer.

Scripture:
- v15 Yet the news about him spread all the more, so that crowds of people [from every town and village] **came to hear him** and to be healed of their sicknesses.
- v16 **But** ... Jesus often withdrew to lonely places and prayed.
- v17a On another day Jesus was teaching, and Pharisees and teachers of the law were sitting there. They had come from every village of Galilee and from Judea and Jerusalem [**to confront Him**].
- v17b And the **Power** of the Lord was **with Jesus** to heal the sick [Power of the Spirit [15]]. *(Luke 5:15-17 NIV)*

What you find sandwiched here right in the middle of this passage, is this reality of '**Jesus often not being found**' [16]. He was often not found ... for He would withdraw into lonely places to pray. He, as the Son, often went into the secret place to Encounter and to be Ministered to personally of God [17]. And as mentioned before, the Word 'prayer' has dual meaning, but in this instance, it is about you sitting and dining in the Presence of God [18]. It's about availing yourself to Visitation ... the hearing and seeing ... **and receiving** just as the Son.

God already knows your needs. Hence 'prayer' isn't always about focusing on needs or desires ... ***but*** ... Divine Encounters with the Person of God *(relationship and union)* [19]. And in Him, as one continually lifted and built up in the Lord — just as the Son — coming into living experience of Heaven opening wide for you. Even the very reality '**rent**' open, where God Himself comes down and stands in your midst, doing powerful and amazing things. [20]

This 'lifestyle' is most powerful ... and highly impacting. Just as demonstrated in the life of a young shepherd boy who became a warrior. A young ruddy boy named David, who became a great **musician**, a great **prophet**, and a great **king**. And of whom *so* touched the Heart of God as to call Jesus … the 'Son of David', for all Eternity. And as well, so touching the nations of the world of whom came to give tribute to the wisdom of Solomon.

In this 'precedent' we see much; even as was the very same way that Jesus Himself sought the Father. Not through dead and lifeless religious practices … **but** … through deeply treasured relationship founded and rooted in Love and acceptance.

In this Scripture, the multitudes of people, who honestly sought out the Lord, were left to wait. Their Saviour Jesus *caused* them to wait. Now, this picture demonstrates two most important things: **1.** the genuine seeking of the Lord God by the Son, even right in the midst of genuine need. And **2.** it demonstrates how you and I also are not a Fatherless generation … **but** … can also seek God in the **very same manner**. And such as these who respond, they open themselves up to Encounter.

Then, when the multitudes did end up seeing Jesus, and sat here at His feet, it was Jesus' own messages that **always** talked about His Heavenly Father and the Kingdom come. These very things of whom He Himself — dynamically engaged.

The underlying drive and purpose of the Person of Jesus is always unto the leading of the believer in the exact and very same as He. For **we are not orphans**, but through the finished work of the Cross are born sons and daughters of the Most High God. Therefore, just as Jesus is the bridge … so too is He the Door. And in His Person: He always points to the Father and the Kingdom of Heaven that is 'right at hand' [21], that **you also** might live in the Power to win.

Now, when approaching the Disciples, the people would have been told that Jesus was often not found, *"He will come … He will be here. But for now, He is alone somewhere with His Heavenly Father."* And by this, Jesus demonstrated also by example: [22] not for example sake, for it was His own **personal** deep yearning and desire.

Here … right here in the midst of all the unfathomable responsibilities set upon His life, Jesus would enter deeply into the

Ministering Presence of the Lord. And Himself be continuously built up and renewed in Him. And just as Jesus would say of Himself, *"He could do nothing ... **but** ... only what He saw and heard His Father doing"* [23]. For it was here, in this secret *abiding* Place, that He was constantly captured up into the Heavenly realms. Crossing over from this three-dimensional world into the dimension of the Lord God Almighty. And though born the Son, born of the Spirit of God ... just like you and I ... He still needed, and deeply yearned and desired for, these 'behind closed doors' sessions with His Heavenly Father.

> *Everything is about meeting God.*
> *Everything is about hearing and seeing.*

And what we also find, is that though Jesus deeply honoured the people coming out to Him. The 'management' of all these issues was not in Him. But was released as He personally availed Himself to the Lord. This was always the priority for Jesus — ***Encounter***. That is, the hearing and seeing God [24]. And what's more, when powerful legal and spiritual opposition did come, even from 'every town and every village' to confront Jesus — the *"Power of the Spirit was (defiantly) with Him to heal."* [15]

So understand more how this works, as described in Isaiah 11 verse 3, that Jesus' eyes were not fixated on either the genuine need that was before Him, nor on the mountains of insurmountable problems ... **but** ... on the Presence of the Person of God — in **unceasing Delight in Him**. However, when He did make 'judgements', this very same honoured Presence and Power of the Spirit came and moved in all that He did. And all situations before Him ... all realities and issues ... became fully exposed to the Goodness and Glory of God.

A ROMAN CENTURION

Scripture:
When Jesus heard this, he was *amazed* and said to those following him, "Truly I tell you, I have not found anyone in Israel with such **great** faith." *(Luke 7:9 NIV)*

What needs to be understood and most treasured, is the importance of **hearing and seeing the Lord**. For revelatory Knowledge of the Lord is found only through one's own personal sessions in Him. Even beginning to live in a state of perpetual Encounter ... *just* as Jesus. He, our precedent and Living Example to follow. And not in all of Israel, nor even seen in His own Disciples, was there any faith found like this Roman centurion.

In this picture, we begin to see a higher vision of what the word 'faith' actually means. For there is *our* faith that reaches up to our most faithful God ... **but** ... then there is **His Faith** that begins to enter and flow into us that totally shift our vision and our reality.

You have *your* faith in the Lord, but what follows is **His Faith in you**. You have your faith, but then you have the Spirit of God coming upon you. So in reading through this account of the Roman centurion, you see how he greatly honoured and loved the God of Israel [25]. And in such, his love and 'good deeds' came up as a sweet offering. For so it is, that these things open you to the Rhema Word ... like *kindling* for the Fire. The preparing and making way for the Outpouring of the Spirit. And this treasured and sought after 'Abiding Word' — that speaks constantly and alive in your soul — continues to transforms you most Powerful and Unstoppable.

> *There is a great correlation between the word 'faith' and this 'hearing and seeing God'. Like mustard-sized seeds of faith planted by the Lord, through a heart of honour, integrity, and honest pursuit.*

Some people, I have heard, would be working in the field, and the Resurrected Christ would come down in a shroud of light, and they would sit together for hours speaking one-to-another. I so encourage you, be open to what is possible in your relationship with Jesus. For he who seeks — **finds** — and to what you truly honour, so shall you draw *close* to yourself. But if you scoff, then like those of old ... do you close the door. For the Spirit of God opposes the proud but **gives great Grace to the humble**. [26]

THE KEYS OF THE KINGDOM OF HEAVEN

Scripture:
Jesus replied, "Blessed are you, Simon son of Jonah, for this was not revealed to you by flesh and blood ... **but** ... by my Father in heaven. And I tell you that you are Peter, and on this Rock I will build my church, and the gates of Hades will not overcome it. I will **give you the <u>Keys</u> of the Kingdom** of Heaven; whatever you bind on earth will be bound in Heaven, and whatever you loose on earth will be loosed in Heaven." *(Matthew 16:17-19 NIV)*

So again, the Rhema Word — this desired and sought after — 'Word that proceeds from the mouth of God'. This very same Word that is needed in order to **truly be able to <u>Live</u>** [27]. This same Abiding Word that opened the mind of Peter to the reality of the Christ. As we read, we see that this Authority that is released is the exact same Power we read of in the Book of Acts.

Come and let us again open the Body of Christ to the Glory of God. For to such who live as the Son also walks as the Son. For through this very same **Abiding** Word — so too do you come to hold the Keys of the Kingdom of Heaven in your hands. And to such: **<u>nothing</u> can stand against**, not even the powers of Satan.

"If you have faith as a grain of mustard seed, so shall you say unto this mountain, 'go throw yourself into the sea' ... and it will be done for you" [28]. It is most clear in life, that one can remain taught only of man ... under the wisdom and schooling of others. However, is there anyone out there who is Taught and Schooled of God? All are from the dirt and dust; and return to the dirt and dust ... **but** ... by the Spirit of God are you raised of and from the Heavenly realms; speaking and moving as one who walks with God. For in this deep 'Abiding Union' shall you come to preside over all creation.

Scripture:
I counsel you to **buy** from Me gold refined in the fire, that you may be **rich** ... and anoint your eyes [and ears] with eye salve, that you may **see** [buy ear cleaner that you can hear]. *(Revelation 3:18 NKJV)*

Prior to this verse, Jesus rebuked the Church by saying, *"You think you are rich and have it all together — but you do not know how wretched, miserable, poor, blind, and naked you are".*

You can never buy the Glory of God — you cannot buy the Fire*!* However, your honour attracts. I so encourage you, to **buy** 'ear cleaner' so that you can **hear**. And 'eye salve' that might **see**. For singularly, the most powerful reality is the ability to hear and see God. And don't get *spooky*, expecting a lightning bolt from Heaven ... for though God may speak with audible words, the Abiding Word 'transcends' words. And what follows is Triumph and Victory as the Lord of Glory *leads* you to sit with Him.

A defiant and arrogant man cannot sit upon the Throne of Glory, but he who is contrite and humble of heart.

Two closing scripture verses:
1. Most assuredly, I say to you, the Son can do nothing of Himself, but what He **sees** the Father do; for whatever He does, the Son also does in like manner. *(John 5:19 NKJV)*
2. If you abide in Me, and My words abide in you, you will ask what you desire, and it shall be done for you. *(John 15:7 NKJV)*

It is honour, and humility, and sacrifice that draws the Abiding Word that does not come from flesh and blood. The very same Word that transcends definition and human understanding. A knowing within; a faith given from Above; doors opening, and great wonders revealed.

*A side note: I am who I am because God is in me. But if I was to put aside Him for what is before me ... then I would become just a regular human. As Jesus said, "Do you not believe that I am in the Father and the Father is in me? It is the Father who dwells in me who does the works. And **he who believes** in me will do even **greater works** for I go to the Father"* [29]. *If I would bow to 'princes of men' and listen to them, then I would become just a regular man ... **but** ... it is my Lord and Saviour who has called me a 'god' ... as one who is filled with Power and Grace.* [30]

Bless you, in Jesus Name.

Appendix:

1. Revelation 1:10, 12, *2.* Psalm 82:6-8, *3.* 1 Corinthians 15:53, 1 Peter 1:23, Romans 8:11, Revelation 3:18 *(Luke 14:28-33)*, Luke 24:49, *4.* Genesis 3:19, 1 Corinthians 15:49, *5.* Isaiah 60:8, Psalm 84:3, *6.* Matthew 17:2, Romans 8:29, *7.* Romans 12:2, *8.* Romans 8:1-17 *NKJV,* *9.* John 5:44, 15:7, 17:21, *10.* Proverbs 3:9, Psalm 27:4, Luke 5:16, 7:4, Romans 12:1, Revelation 1:10, *11.* Revelation 2:26-27, *12.* John 17:20-24, *13.* Romans 8:19, *14.* Galatians 2:20 *KJV,* *15. Only one other time was this wording used regarding Jesus, "The Power of the Spirit was on Him to heal". The other time was when Jesus came out of the 40 days in the desert* — Luke 4:14, *16.* Genesis 5:24, *17.* Matthew 4:11, *18.* Isaiah 28:12, Hebrews 4:11, Revelation 3:20, Isaiah 25:6, Exodus 24:9-11, Psalm 84:2, Deuteronomy 8:3, Matthew 6:11, John 7:38, *19.* Matthew 6:5-13, Exodus 20:21, John 17:20-24, *20.* Isaiah 64:1-4, *21.* Matthew 4:17, *22.* Isaiah 55:4, Zechariah 3:8, Romans 8:29, *23.* John 5:19, *24.* Revelation 3:18, Matthew 16:17, John 15:7, Luke 7:9, John 5:44, Matthew 6:9-11, Deuteronomy 8:3, Galatians 2:20 *KJV,* *25.* Luke 7:5, *26.* James 4:6, *27.* Deuteronomy 8:3, Matthew 4:4, Matthew 6:11, *28.* Matthew 17:20, Mark 11:23, *29.* John 14:10, 12, *30.* Psalm 118:8, 82:6-7

Dated: 31/7/19

14. *Union in Him (#97)*
COME UP IN ME *(Part 2)*

In continuation from the previous chapter ...

A TWO-LAYERED GOSPEL

Do you notice in Gospel how there are two layers? For example, *"If you do not forgive then you will not be forgiven"* [1]. But later, our triumphant Lord Jesus 'breathed' upon His Disciples and said, *"Receive the Holy Spirit. If you forgive anyone's sins, their sins are forgiven; if you do not forgive them, they are not forgiven"* [2]. And also, He would say such things like, *"When I sent you out without purse or sandals did you lack anything? Now I say to you sell these things and buy a Sword."* [3]

You see ... the 'first layer' are issues of the flesh, but the 'second layer' are issues of the Spirit. A transition is required. And the first layer is to do with the 'priestly' office; but after Jesus came riding on a donkey He came as King [4]. So therefore, there are the two offices of the Spirit-filled: the office of a priest and the office of a king [5]. However, Love and mercy is always the default — and so too is turning the other cheek [6]. For such is the heart of intercession: the longing and deep desire for the healing and salvation of all people.

> The **priest** intercedes ... the **king** releases the angel armies.

If you truly wish to live by the Spirit and not the flesh, then shall you begin to operate in realms of Authority and Power that shakes the world. Not in a fleshly zeal ... for that is sin [10], but in He of whom is with you. And do you recall it said, that *"During the lifetime of Samuel that the Hand of God was against the Philistines?"* I tell you ... 'prayer' is about union [8]. And to such does the Glory of the Lord come and stand in your midst. [9]

UNBELIEVING AND PERVERSE GENERATION

Scripture:
And I brought him to your disciples, and they could not cure him. Then Jesus answered and said, 'O faithless and perverse generation, how long shall I be with you? how long shall I endure

you? bring him here to me'. And Jesus rebuked the demon; and he departed out of him: and the child was cured from that very hour. Then came the disciples to Jesus apart, and said, why could not we cast him out? And Jesus said unto them, because of your unbelief: for verily I say unto you, if you have Faith as a grain of mustard seed, you shall say unto this mountain, 'remove from here to yonder place'; and it shall remove; and nothing shall be impossible unto you. But this kind goes not out but by prayer and fasting. *(Matthew 17:16-21 NKJV)*

Firstly, Jesus wasn't ridiculing this man in need, but His own Disciples. But why does He say, *"This kind goes not out but by prayer and fasting?"* The reason is, that only through a humbling [10] of heart, and hungering [11] after the Abiding Word of God; [12] that the Word and Counsel and the Authority of the Spirit comes upon you.

'Unbelief' is an issue of a **lack of union** … a lack of sitting in the realm of Rest where God fights for you [13]. For Jesus did not respond according to what He heard and saw with His eyes, but according to what the Father was saying and doing [14]. And due to His union — this Abiding under His 'Shadow' [15] — that Jesus' own shadow cast the very same Glory of the Lord [16]. Therefore, **"Be still, and know God."** [17]

Union is a choice. And it is to this very thing that the Father deeply desires to re-establish [18] you in — **union** — body, mind, soul, and spirit. God's Purpose has always been directed unto uniting you **One in Him** [8]. His hand being continually outstretched to a 'unbelieving and perverse generation'. But we are changing, aren't we? … we are learning, even for the sake of the nations.

There has never been any greater honour bestowed upon any created creature for all Eternity — on earth or in Heaven — than that of which has been presented man. And it is to this very Dream that was stolen the Father at the Fall. However now, through the Cross and gifted Spirit of God, has this opportunity now been *re-*presented this very day [19]. And how you personally choose to respond: echoes in this life … and for all Eternity.

In Christ, you are not supposed to wait until death before you participate in such things. For what has been made clear in Gospel, and through the finished work of the Cross; that Jesus Christ died for you and was raised again — so that you need not die in order to **rise up in the <u>fullness</u> of God**. For it is in Christ's Image and very Likeness that you are purposed to be conformed [20] — not unto 'death' **but <u>unto</u> Life**. Not unto a carnal *fallen* mind or reality; but unto the Mind of Christ. For truly, it is true, that Christ Jesus is ... '*but*' ... the **<u>first</u> of many born sons and daughters** of the Most High. [21]

Where God dwells, is in the Realms of Authority. Where man dwells, is in the realms of the dirt and dust. The flesh is the lowest form of man, hence what man needs, is to become **<u>Alive</u> again** unto the Spirit [22]. The Heart of Love: is God unto all man [23]. Hence, the fundamental Purpose of God always remains bent on us responding, and coming up to sit in the realms of the Rest and Power of the Lord [24], *ie;* the Garden realms, the realms of Glory and Authority, the realms of **Dining** and **Receiving** from God. And just as there is the nature of the priest, that intercedes on behalf of another. So too is there the station of a king: of whom makes 'judgements' [25] releasing the Kingdom of God.

To seek the Face of God, so shall you also get His Hand. But to seek only His Hand, you will never come to *know* Him or your true place in Him. The word 'prayer' has dual meaning: ***1.*** the asking for help in times of need. And ***2.*** the asking to meet with God; to sit with Him and *abide* in His Holy Presence [26]. For only in this Place of Meeting, of reclining in the Presence of the Most High [27], can your sonship be ever truly revealed; as one **Empowered to bring change** [28]. The Fruits of the Spirit is Life and Peace, but the fruits of *unbelief* is death and despair. The Keys of Heaven have been bestowed upon the Church: therefore, the Power of God is always in your own personal choice.

PRIESTS AND KINGS

In reading the earlier chapters of the Book of Revelation *(chapters 1 to 3 (NKJV))* we find, that by the Blood of Jesus, it is God who has **Positioned** His children with Him as 'priests' and 'kings' [29]. Even as a people who hold the very Keys of Heaven in your very hands *30*. And to such these, the gates of Hades **cannot** prevail.

Therefore, a heart that is **set unto union**, and a heart that is bent upon the Spirit and manifest Presence *31* of the Person of God; *32* here Jesus continues, and says to you, that *"You shall cast aside all opposition, every 'mountain' of opposition that comes shall you cast into the sea"* *33*. Such is the Legacy of the Son, for all the generations. All forms and works of Satan shall be cast out and torn down, even strongholds over nations. *34*

In these Seven Letters to the Churches, they also express how the early Church were facing the prospect of **losing the Glory of God** *(losing the flame, losing the Fire)*. And why was this? But because carnal thinking and deeds had begun to retake the Church. And though the Grace of God still remained, a **firm turning of heart** was required. A turning and setting of one's heart firmly in Him — again, an issue of **union**.

Carnality and self-sufficiency had started to enter the Body of Christ. Therefore, the Seven Spirits of the Lord, as represented in the '**Lampstand**' *35* — it was King Jesus that was warning of its removal. Do you recall where it was said, *"Revelation was rare in the land (visions and dreams)?"* *36* Can you imagine where this reality was totally **reversed**, where it was now abundant? Such is the Heart of the Father concerning you ... but it takes someone who is bent unto union to release it.

A CLOSING THOUGHT

To walk in the Authority of God, with angels responding and moving according to the words of your mouth, be one who abides under the Authority of God *37*. To be clothed in the Glory of God *38*, and to have the Fear of God ever upon you where the demon is terrified, be one who '**delights**' in the Fear of God. *39*

To operate in the Powers of 'Judgement' to bring lasting change *40*, be one who comes under the Judgements of God *41*. To walk where your own 'shadow' touches and heals, be one who abides under the shadow of the Almighty *42*. To operate where your 'counsel' influences God of Heaven and earth; come stand under His

Counsel [43]. What is the Throne of God? … but the realm of Power and Authority. Even then, as one who acts on behalf of the broken and the lost. [44]

A world within a world, a Kingdom within a kingdom: The world goes on and pursues the things of the world. But then there are those whose hearts are set unto God and unto the broken and the lost. To such have the Glory of God ever revealed, and the Anointing of the Lord resting mightily upon them.

If you were to condemn another, then so would you come under condemnation. But if, by your yearning desire, you chose to live under the 'Judgements' of God, then so would you be ever schooled and built up in Him. And now, when you make a 'judgement' regarding a situation … as one standing in His Holy Presence … then that of which is presented is now fully exposed before the Glory and Vengeance of God.

When you look at lands of great poverty, or lands of great demonic and spiritual strongholds, recognise that they remain because no one from within the land is coming up to speak over the land.

The same in the earlier centuries, when the demon drove out the last of the Christian Churches in the Middle East. How was this possible? But because, though they still believed and professed the Name of Jesus, their sufficiency was not in God [45]. They lived and operated religiously, and in the eyes of one another, but not in union with their Heavenly Father. They operated on the earthly plane; in their flesh and own understanding [46]. But **not in the Heavenly plane**; nor in Heavenly Places [47] in the Divine Revelation and Counsels of God. [48]

They believed in Jesus,
*but just did not live **like** Him.*

Let me share an example: For years the Christian church in Columbia has been held siege by the drug cartels. With pastor's wives being kidnapped and held for ransom. And as Christians, they felt that they must just 'turn the other cheek' … who should just love the drug lords and forgive them. But what you have here, is the demon overshadowing the Kingdom of God. Relentless evil allowed to dominate and work against the people of God.

Scripture:
Beloved, do not avenge yourselves, but rather **give place to wrath**; for it is written, "Vengeance is Mine, I will repay," says the Lord. *(Romans 12:19 NKJV)*

There are other ways to deal with these things ... other ways to deal with gross injustice and purposed evil intent in the land. The demon must be put in its place, the day of judgement must be now. The presenting of the situation before the Throne of God and call for justice.

Now, in God ... you are not called to be a people of the flesh — but a people of the Spirit. So here, in rising up with the Sword of the Spirit in your hands; the Powers and Authorities of God come and rectify the situation [49]. And now the tide truly turns.

> *"Lord, I bring these drug lords before you. And I pray that they come into the Knowledge of God. I pray that they come to know the Love and Salvation of the Lord. But if they will not turn, may these 'mountains of opposition' to the Kingdom of Heaven be cast into the sea. In Jesus Name, save them, move them ... or remove them."*

It is the same that comes against your children, against the political landscape, or against your business. You have Authorities purposed of God to **win** the nations unto Christ [50]. However, if you only want to 'play' Christianity, or refrain from looking more deeply into the perfect 'Law of Liberty' [51], then the Church, as a whole, will remain weak and frail ... a people easily blown over. However, if you were to truly respond to the Testimony of both the Word and the Spirit, then so shall you be raised a most Powerful people with far-reaching influence and power [52]. Taking land instead of losing land ... and bringing the nations unto Christ. [53]

So, you can attempt to prepare yourself when problems come, or you can otherwise live in a **state of readiness**. You can either be one always coming under things, or you can otherwise be one who rises up Above. How you **choose** to live on earth is where you dwell and abide.[54] And if you were to truly choose to abide in Him, all is now laid bare before the Glory of His Might.

*In Christ Jesus "You are the head and not the tail"[55]. It was God's Dream to bring Heaven to earth way **before** it became your dream. And a simple 'amen' to this links arms with the Son and the Prayers of the Father. In treasuring this truth deep in your soul; the free-flowing Will of the Father is released into your world.*

You are a Gateway, you are a Portal of the Most High, simply by who you are in Him. And where you walk ... so does He with you, to the blessing of the world. The Fire of God ... spot fires as 'embers' in the air ... angels moving bringing the healing and the revelation of God in the land. This beyond your conscious awareness, and far beyond any physical effort.

In reference to Isaiah chapter 11 ... do you notice how the 'Might' of the Spirit is paired with the 'Counsel' of the Spirit?[56] For they work in tandem and function together. So realise, in order to truly operate in the Powers and Authorities of God, be one who draws near to the Counsel of the Lord. To such then, when you pray, you may not even use words. But otherwise spit on the ground and make mud in your hands; and after placing that mud on the eyes of a blind man ... so shall they be healed.[57]

The Disciples were used to praying, *"Be healed, in Jesus Name"* and seeing powerful results. But then came a boy who suffered with epilepsy[58]. Where Jesus responded to them and said, *"This kind only comes out through prayer and fasting."* So the question is, what does fasting do? But that fasting is a humbling of oneself in order to hear and see ... and receive.[59]

You see ... there are times where you need to step out of just praying, *"Be healed in Jesus Name."* And step into the realms of sonship, where you draw a firm line in the sand and command[60]. This can only be given of God[61]. And though we know in principle that we are sons and daughters of God; the 'revelation' of this ... *ie;* the manifestation real and alive, is only given through tight Relationship with Him.

This is why Jesus so celebrated Peter when He said, *"Flesh and blood has not given this to you ... but was given of my Father in Heaven"* [62]. For the result of your ear that hears is: that when you stand before hardship brought on by the demon ... **God causes you to win every time** [63]. The Gates of Hades cannot prevail for you are clothed in 'Immortality' [64] ... you are clothed in Glory ... the very Everlasting Life of the Spirit of God. And this comes as you cross over from one who 'just' believes in Jesus ... to one who walks like Him.

Bless you, in Jesus Name!

Appendix:

1. Matthew 6:14, *2.* John 20:23-24, *3.* Luke 22:35-36, Revelation 3:18, *4.* Matthew 21:5, *5.* Revelation 1:5-6, 5:9-10 *NKJV*, *6.* Matthew 5:38-40, *7.* Deuteronomy 32:35, Romans 12:17-19 *NKJV*, *8.* John 17:20-24, *9.* Deuteronomy 23:13-14, Exodus 33:14-17, Luke 17:20-24, *10.* 2 Chronicles 7:14, Matthew 16:17-19, Daniel 10:12, *11.* Deuteronomy 8:3, Matthew 4:4, 6:11, 16:17, Jeremiah 23:21-22, Zechariah 3:7, Revelation 3:17-22, *12.* John 15:7, Isaiah 11:1-4, *13.* Psalm 110:1-2, 82:6-7, 2:7-8, 91:1-16, Exodus 14:14, 33:14, Isaiah 28:12, Hebrews 4:11, *14.* John 5:19, Isaiah 11:3, *15.* Psalm 91:1, *16.* Luke 4:14, Acts 5:15, *17.* Psalm 46:10, *18.* Genesis 2:17, *19.* Genesis 1:26, 3:1, 3:24, 5:3, Exodus 14:14, 33:1-23, Deuteronomy 3:22, 2 Chronicles 5:14, Ezekiel 10:18-20, Psalm 2:7-8, 110:1-2, John 1:12, 14:12, Acts 2:3, 1 Corinthians 2:16, 15:54, 2 Corinthians 3:18, Revelation 1:5-6, 3:18-21, 5:10, *20.* Romans 8:29, 12:2, 2 Corinthians 3:18, Colossians 3:10, 1 Corinthians 15:49, Ephesians 4:24, *21.* Romans 8:29, John 12:24, *22.* Genesis 2:17, *23.* 1 Timothy 2:4, *24.* Hebrews 4:11, *25.* Isaiah 11:1-4, *26.* Psalm 27:4, *27.* Isaiah 28:12, *28.* Romans 8:19, *29.* Revelation 1:5-6, 5:9-10 *NKJV*, *30.* Matthew 16:19, *31.* Exodus 14:14, 33:14, 23:28, *32.* Romans 8:1 *NKJV*, Galatians 5:16, *33.* Matthew 17:20, Mark 16:17-18, *34.* Isaiah 25:7, *35.* Revelation 2:5, *36.* 1 Samuel 3:1, *37.* Luke 7:8, John 1:51, Matthew 26:53, *38.* Luke 24:49, Genesis 3:10, Revelation 3:17-18 *(Luke 14:28-33)*, 1 Corinthians 15:53-54, 2 Corinthians 3:18, 2 Kings 2:14, 6:17, Matthew 16:17-19, Mark 16:17-19, Acts 5:15, Colossians 3:1-3, Psalm 91:1, 2:7-8, 110:1-2, 34:7, 104:2, 93:1, 84:5, John 1:51, Exodus 33:14-18, 34:29, John 17:24, Genesis 1:26, *39.* Hebrews 12:21, Exodus 20:21, Isaiah 11:3-4, 33:14b-15a, Revelation 1:10, 17, Psalm 91, *40.* Isaiah 11:1-4, *41.* Isaiah 11:3, *42.* Acts 5:15, Psalm 91, *43.* Zechariah 3:7, *44.* Luke 4:18, *45.* Revelation 3:17, 2:4-5, *46.* Genesis 2:17, Proverbs 3:5, 14:12, Romans 8:5-6, 12:2, 1 Corinthians 2:16, *47.* John 3:13 *NKJV*, Ephesians 2:6, *48.* John 5:44, *49.* 2 Corinthians 10:4, Romans 12:19, Psalm 110:2, Isaiah 11:4, Revelation 19:15, *50.* 1 Timothy 2:4 *KJV*, *51.* James 1:25, *52.* Exodus 33:16-17, 1 Samuel 7:13b, *53.* Genesis 13:17, Joshua 1:3, *54.* Colossians 3:4, *55.* Deuteronomy 28:13a, *56.* Isaiah 11:1-3, *57.* John 9:1-7, *58.* Matthew 17:14-21, *59.* 2 Chronicles 7:14, *60.* Kings 2:13-14, *61.* Revelation 2:26–27, *62.* Matthew 16:17, *63.* Isaiah 59:19 *KJV*, *64.* Mark 16:17-18

Dated: 7/8/19

AARON'S STAFF

15. Aaron's Staff (#98)
FAITH WROUGHT THROUGH ENCOUNTER

Christ Jesus is the **opened Door** unto Encounters with God. And through Divine Encounters are you ever uplifted where **Life** overshadows sin, death, and decay. It is the Faith that is 'wrought' through Divine Engagement [1] that make you a most powerful people. Natural law superseded by Higher Law. [2]

Your Saviour has made Way unto perfect union in the Father [3]. Before, you saw only through the eyes of the flesh and that of the world. But now, in Him, do you begin to operate by the **Faith OF the Son** [4]. Now when you speak, all things are brought to stand before the Throne and Glory of God; being made able to *"Rule in the midst of your enemies"* [5]. Divine Action released from within the Presence of the Lord. Before you were born of the dirt and dust [6], but now are you born of the Immortal and Eternal realms of God. [7]

Scripture:
Who hath saved us, and called us with an **holy calling**, not according to our works, but according to his own purpose and grace, which was given us in Christ Jesus before the world began, but has now been revealed by the appearing of our Savior Jesus Christ [our precedent and living example], who has abolished death and **brought life and Immortality to light** through the gospel. *(2 Timothy 1:9-10 NKJV)*

The 'Testimony' of God is not what a person has done for Him — but what **God has done** for a person [8]. Jesus stated that 'He could do nothing of Himself', that He could 'only do what He *saw* His Father doing' [9]. Therefore, let your heart and soul also always be unto **actively seeing** and hearing the Father ... just as Jesus, *ie;* unto 'Divine Encounter' [10]. And so shall your **faith become like iron** [11]. Not fleeting like a leaf in the wind [12] but as Like the Son of Man. God 'distinguishing' you from all the peoples of the earth. [13]

Oh how one's life is changed as one Encounters the Person of God. Even then as one choosing to live in a state of perpetual Encounter. Pause then for a moment and consider, what would it be like if you lived in a constant state of Encounter, Visitation, and Exchange with your Heavenly Father? How would your life be *different* ...? Just stop and ponder for a moment. And so, if this was the way Jesus Himself lived, are we not called to walk in Like as He ... with the same rights and privileges? And are we not called into His Image and His Likeness ... even to be: *"As Christ Jesus is, so are we in the world?"* [14]

Though Jesus lived in the world, He also lived fully Above the world ... Impervious, Untouchable, and a Mover of Heaven. He ate and drank like an ordinary man, but He also ate and drank of God ... and this He always preferred.

Come then and choose to settle for nothing less, but for continual Visitations and Encounters with God. *Humble* yourself to 'hear' and to 'see' [15] ... and let this become your daily norm. Put aside the 'entertainments' of this world and honour God to speak and to show; [16] for this is the Place of Power, of Glory, and of the Anointing of God [17]. Come and set your sights *wholly* upon the Throne — even here your purposed Place of Dwelling; your 'Abiding' Place [18]. For this itself always remained the sole Purpose and Drive of the Son. [19]

"I will give you every place where you set your foot" [20]

Here, faith takes on another meaning: It has nothing to do with you, but everything to do with hearing and seeing the Father; [21] as one stepping into sonship, even your rightful and designated Place in the Presence of the Person of God [22]. It is in such, that all things are brought before the Throne of God. This Place of which by choice and by will you Abide and Remain [23]. And here, as you face the genuine realities of this life; [24] so too are you made able by the Grace of God: to truly Rule in the midst of 'your enemies', *ie;* all opposition; all that comes against, all sickness and disease, and all demonic powers ... *in Jesus Name!*

Let me ask a question: As the Spirit of God rises up within you; bubbling up with 'groans' deep in your soul and you pray [25]. Does not the Spirit of the Lord respond and ride upon the words of your mouth? And are not the angels of God set to action? The Spirit of the Lord is the Chief Spirit, the Chief 'Angel': and you have He who is the God-of-the-Angel-Armies residing within you [26]. Therefore, as you speak, so does the Spirit of the Lord *'aggressively'* [27] go out before you ... *in Jesus Name!*

It is such a curious wonder: the Spirit speaking within that causes you to speak. Then in responding, He Himself moves and goes out according to your own words spoken. Such is the lifestyle of they who walk according to the Spirit of God. They live on a totally different plane and in a completely different wonder of reality as they walk this earth.

> *God is my God, not problems nor desires;*
> *therefore, am I made Powerful in Him.* [28]

Let me as a question: in Christ Jesus, where are you called to be seated? *"With Jesus at the right hand of God"*. And from this seated position, where is the Spirit of the Lord? *"Before the Throne"* [29]. And to what then is the true Dream and Heart of the Father? *"That we be with Him ... that we be **in Him** ... Like Him and in union with Him* [30] *... I in Him and He in me"*. So if it is for a Spotless Bride that the Christ has come, is not God desiring to be Four? There being no separation, but complete and perfect union in Him. To such is developed and made possible in the Presence of the Lord.

> *"Lord, I take my place in you." (B. B.)*

Theme Scripture:
But hold fast what you have till I come. And he who overcomes, and keeps My works until the end, to him I will give Power over the nations — 'He shall **rule** them with a rod of iron; they shall be dashed to pieces like the potter's vessels' — as I also have received from My Father; and I will give him the **Morning Star**. *(Revelation 2:25-28 NKJV)*

Sometimes life doesn't present very many options. And sometimes life can come at you really really rough at times. But today, here and now, each one of us have **choice** to step into the Presence of God ... just as the Son. This, at any moment and in any place. However, I tell you a little secret; as you *choose* to abide in Him, so too is that of which you are facing: also brought with you and is fully 'exposed' before the Throne of God.

You see, God's Presence can come upon you in most wonderful and marvellous ways ... and that's great. But it is your Heavenly Father's Dream and yearning Desire that you — in ***your*** presence — come up in Him [31]. You in Him and He in you. Your presence can be anywhere you wish *(your thoughts and your heart's motives)*, but by choice and by will is your presence in Him. [32]

> *'Prayer' is Presence. Prayer isn't problems, prayer is your heart set unto the Person of God. And here in Him are your prayers most Powerful.*

Did you know that you can live in a state of perpetual Encounters in God whereby **His Peace** rules your heart? [33]. And did you know that you can have Experiences whereby the burning **Love of God** continually and perpetually lifts and builds you up? And did you know that you can have Engagements in Him whereby the **Abiding Word** — His Rhema Word — speaks constantly and Alive in your soul? And did you know that the Knowledge of God, and the **Faith of the Son**, is wrought through these very same Divine Encounters? — given eyes that increasingly see and ears that increasingly hear. And this from right within His Abiding Presence. And it is in such an environment, whereby you are made able to 'hold fast' *(ie; be Victorious in every circumstance* [34]*);* and of whom are raised a most Powerful, Mighty, and Triumphant people in the Lord.

Regardless, the greatest power held within the believer's hands is your ability to praise the Name of Jesus — as one entering right into His Holy Presence — and this *regardless* of season. There is no greater prayer or purpose, than sitting at the feet of Jesus [35]. As is said, *"My Presence will go before you and I will give you* **Rest**"[36]. And as is referenced in another place, *"My Spirit will drive the Enemy from the land."* [37]

When the Gospel speaks of 'hearing and seeing' the Lord, was this only ever purposed to be metaphorical? ... or is it not otherwise purposed to be physical and ever real? And when Jesus went into the secret place, was He only *just* a man with His faith in God? ... or as Son of God, isn't the Secret Abiding Place so much more? And are believers, only ever intended to be just individual pebbles separate and devoid of any real tangible connection in God? ... or are you not **born into sonship** and into union? And when Adam walked in the Garden of Eden, was he just mortal? ... or was he not supernatural? And so, if supernatural, what are you called into? This is your Purposed direction and fundamental Calling in God.

Understand then, that praying for needs or for the sick, even for the raising of the dead; is not a 'high' prayer. But simply the function of intercession *('priest')*. **The high prayer** and calling of the Son is: that you might be with Him — where He is now — seeing Him in His Glory [38]. Ever abiding in His Holy Presence, sitting at the feet of Jesus — hearing and seeing — raised as a Lion *('king')*. The fruit of which is in likeness of Mark 16 *(vs. 17-18)* ... and extending into the Book of Acts. And in such, the world will come to **truly know** that the Father truly did send the Son. [39]

"Come up with me and I will give you the nations." [19]

Come, and gain the Mind of Christ; and so shall you become the **embodiment** of Him. The Word made flesh; [40] in mature physical Likeness of the New Adam. No longer a Fatherless generation, but **Father-full** — walking in the fullness of your sonship in Him as you walk this earth. To this, *"All creation is earnestly and eagerly waiting for the sons of God to be revealed."* [41]

John 17:20-24:
- That those given Him -
- Might be **with Him** where He is -
- And that they might **see Him** in His Glory -
- That the world may **know the Father** sent the Son -

So again, picture the scene: As a person who, by culture and deep purpose of soul, preference the seeking the Presence of God; [42] when facing problems, that of which has been hounding you is also brought to stand before the Judgement and Grace of God. However, as a son of the Living God, you go on through and step up into *Daddy's* arms. Now, that of which you face in life; lays fully exposed before the Throne of God. Hence, just as Jesus is the 'Door', so too are you called to enter and pass through [43]. Not to linger where you are, but decisively choose it in your heart to enter the Presence of God. Even to prepare and make a highway unto the Kingdom of Heaven [44]. Unto the caravans and processions of Heaven and the Spirit of Life made active in your world. As is written, *"So shall the Glory of the Lord be revealed."* [45]

It is, however, the *Enemy* — that always seeks to **disorientate** — whereby you become lost in the forest; through a nagging sense of unworthiness or disappointment, fear or concern. **But**/ ... it is the Spirit's Desire that you perpetually come up in Him and **eat liberally of the Tree of Life** ... drinking deeply of the New Wine daily [46]. For in such is unceasing Life.

As you step through into God
God steps through you into your world.

Hence in seeking **first** the Kingdom of Heaven, all these other things come under the Management, Orchestration, and Authorities of God [47]. Recognise then that the 'bread' mentioned in the Lord's Prayer is **not daily food** ... but the **Word given through Divine Encounter**. And it is to such that truly come to **truly 'live'**. As is said, *"Man does not live by bread alone but by every Word that proceeds from the mouth of God"* [48]. Hence the flip side is, that if you centralise yourself to truly dine of the Rhema and the Abiding Word; then so shall you also come to live in Divine and Active experience of Life in Him.

Before the Fall, the *dimension* of Heaven was fully integrated and intertwined in Adam ... then Adam fell. But today, in Christ Jesus ... it is the **'risen'** *(the raised and lifted up)*, that step up into that of which was lost. Even as Jesus says, *"Everything the Father has is mine. And by the Spirit, He will take what is mine and transmit, impart, and make known to you"* [49]. Such is the Presence of the Lord.

For the Curtain has been rent, now they of whom were not ever permitted: [50] enter the Holy of Holies and enjoy free and liberal access. As is said, "**Be still**, and **know** the Lord" [51]. Not just a copy or shadow built by man [52], but directly into Heaven. Right into the Presence of the Person of God: through **He who is the Door**. And what spawns from this is expressed in the life of Jesus … and in the Book of Acts. For before the Cross, Jesus had free access: going 'behind' the Curtain. However now, after the Cross: this **right of access has been gifted** and offered you. Not that of which is on earth, but the Holy of Holies that is in Heaven.

Recognise, that those who choose to come *under* the Spirit's Counsel, are also a people raised up *by* Him to sit upon the Table of His Counsel *with* Him. And here does God listen *intently* to the counsel of your mouth [53]. Not that He needs your counsel, but He honours you so much as to listen intently to the words of your mouth [53] … *and* the dreams of your heart [54]. Such is 'Anointed' prayer; that of which is spoken in Him.

It is the Legacy of the Son [55] that you may be one '**made**' able; to strike with a 'Rod of Iron' — and this given of the Lord [56]. And to such, "*Smash the mountains and make them small, and like chaff are blown away in the wind*" [57]. And where the God of Heaven and earth sets a Banqueting Table — right in the midst of your *enemies* — with Life swallowing up death, disease, and despair [58]. And the Triumphant believer ever made able to walk in the Victory of the Son. And all that of which tries to obstruct or oppose — regardless of size! — is cast into the sea.

*A side note: In Scripture, there are places where the word 'angel' and the word 'spirit' is exchanged. And in the case where Jesus said, "See to it that you do not despise the little children for their angels always see the Face of God" [59]. It's not only angels that stand in representation of you, but **your** own very spirit. And truly, "Who can come against the Lord's anointed and be guiltless?" [60] In the book of Acts Peter's 'spirit' was referred to as his 'angel' [61]. And in the case of 'the Angel of the Lord', as referenced in Zechariah 3; it is not that we are called to come under the instruction of an angel but the very Spirit of the Lord. He referred to not as 'an' angel … but 'the' Angel of the Lord.*

Jesus lived with angels actively ascending and descending upon Him as He walked the earth [62]. So too is it so, that as sons and daughters of the Living God, is this **Precedent** made firm and true for both you and I as well. The 'Example' made whereby you begin to walk in the very same. And this in ever-increasing measure ... Glory upon Glory, and unto exceedingly great Glory [63]. And to they who choose to live according to the Spirit — so shall you also walk in the **very same Power of the Spirit**.

Another side note: As represented in the Ark of the Covenant; **embodied within you** *is the Spirit of the Lord (the Gateway, the Veil rent ... the Cherubim parting* [64]*), the Law written on the* **Tablets** *of your heart* [65]*,* **Aaron's Staff** *of which has budded, and the* **Manna** *of Heaven (your 'daily bread'). And here, pictured in Aaron's Staff, is your Divine gifted ability to function, draw from, and release Heaven on earth. One made able by Him to usher forth Life in hopeless and dead situations. A dry and dead stick that sprouted, budded, blossomed, and produced ripe fruit* [66]*. And this* **fully** *outside the realms of natural law or provision.*

Theme Scripture in parallel:
He said to me, "You are my son; **today** I have become your father. **Ask me**, and I will make the nations your inheritance, the ends of the earth your possession. **You will break** them with a rod of iron; you will dash them to pieces like pottery." *(Psalm 2:7-9 NIV)*

Do you notice the request of God to '**ask me**?' So, if it was the same for the Son, then so too is it for us: the asking, the seeking, the knocking [67]. The drawing nigh unto God from within His Abiding Presence [68]. To such as these, are the nations your *inheritance* and the ends of the earth your very *possession*.

Not only so, but with a Rod of Iron: all pretences of man, all opposition, all sickness and disease, and all poverty shall be dashed to pieces; all the works of Satan, and all 'mountains' of obstruction, shall be removed and cast into the sea [69]. And the unfading glow of the Glory of God shall rest upon your life [70] ... such is the Word of the Lord. And just as King David was raised triumphant and victorious ... so shall you also, through the exact and very same **culture** of seeking His Presence [71]. And the Anointing of the Lord shall rest mightily upon you, as you too are personally raised: a warrior, a prophet, and a king.

> *The Blood has taken you out of 'Egypt'. However, it is the 'Spirit engaged' that makes you able to **possess** the Promises given.*

Recognise then, that today you too are a son of God; this gifted by the Grace of God. So what is the wording, *"**Ask** me, and I will give you the nations as your inheritance ... even the very ends of the earth your possession."* And whatever comes against you, *"You shall **dash** to pieces like pottery".* For so it is, that in such a station, such a position, all that comes **against** the Kingdom of Heaven is brought before the Throne. All disease, all poverty, all lies and deceit, and all works of the *Thief* ... are brought before the Glory of God. Even this, the very same Glory comes with you as does the 'Radiance' of the Presence of the Lord. 72

Religion by no means has any place here; neither does law or self-righteousness. For it is through the likes of '**Joshua**' that part the waters and pass through. **Moses** represented the Law, and hence by the 'command of God' you left Egypt behind. But it is only through Jesus; who is represented in the man Joshua, that you are made able to walk freely in the realms of Promise. Whereby — in Him — **everything is yes! and amen! to you** unto the Glory of God.

As is said, *"The Lord would speak to Moses face to face, as one speaks to a friend. Then Moses would return to the camp, but his young aide Joshua son of Nun **never** left the Tent of Meetings"* 73. This, then, is the Way of the Triumphant and the Mighty in the Lord: **never leave His Abiding Presence** — never leave the 'ever-present' Counsel and Presence of the Lord. And to such: strike and part the waters, leading multitudes into Life and into the Freedom of the full Promises of God. 74

Scripture:
The LORD says to my lord: "**Sit at my right hand** 75 until I make your enemies a footstool for your feet. The LORD will extend **your mighty scepter** from Zion *('rod of your strength')*, saying, "Rule in the midst of your enemies!" *(Psalm 110:1-2 NIV)*

In Christ Jesus, to where is it that you are called? ... but to sit with Jesus at the right hand of God. For they who truly believe, *decidedly* choose it within themselves: to firmly enter the Rest of the Lord [76]. And to such as these, so do they enter the 'School of Ministry' ... the personal 'Tutoring' of the Son.

In Mark chapter 3, starting from verse 13, we read of how *"Jesus ascended the mountain and **called** to Him they of whom He wanted, and they came to Him. Then He ordained twelve, that they might **be with Him**."*

You see, that is the very reason why you are here ... you *feel* called. You feel pushed out and driven, with a deep burning in your heart for the things of the Kingdom of God. And so in reading, what is it then that is your first and primary calling? But that Jesus has Ordained you ... He has Called and Ordained you to 'be with Him' where He is *(ie; never leave)*. Do you see this? And so it is, that here — with Him — He will raise you to preach, and He will give you Authority to heal the sick and drive out demons.

Therefore, in order to have Jesus with us — in His Glory — we first must go to Him. We first must seek Encounter ... seek Presence ... seek to Wait on the Lord. **We have to respond** ... we have to 'ask'. And here, God will actively fight for you. And here with Him ... *upon* the Throne ... He will raise you one able to *release* that Fight!

Mark 3:13-15:
- Jesus has ordained you -
- That you might be with Him -
- That He might send you out to preach -
- And have Power to heal the sick and drive out demons -

IN CLOSING

Picturing the **Sword** of the Spirit ... what is the purpose of the handle? But that you may 'wield' the Spirit of the Lord in your hands [77]. To bring the Presence of the Lord, to carry the Presence, and release and direct the very same Presence of the Lord. Now the following that has been written can be better understood:

The Rod of Iron:
- You 'feed them' [78] -
- You 'calm the storm' [79] -
- You 'move the mountain' [80] -
- You 'cast out', you 'heal', you 'raise the dead' [81] –
- *You 'do it' ...* -

Bless you ... in Jesus Name!

Appendix:

1. James 1:2-4, John 5:19, **2.** James 1:25, **3.** John 17:21, **4.** Galatians 2:20 *KJV*, 1 Corinthians 2:16, John 5:19, **5.** Psalm 110:1-2, **6.** Genesis 3:19, **7.** 2 Timothy 1:10, 1 Corinthians 15:53-54, 1 Thessalonians 5:5, John 1:12, **8.** Exodus 33:16, **9.** John 5:19, **10.** Psalm 27:4, 37:4, **11.** Revelation 2:27, **12.** James 1:6-7, **13.** Exodus 33:16-17, **14.** 1 John 4:17, John 14:12, **15.** 2 Chronicles 7:14, Jeremiah 23:22, Matthew 16:17, **16.** Exodus 33:3-6, John 5:20, 16:12-15, **17.** Zechariah 3:7, Psalm 27:4, **18.** Colossians 3:1-3, John 15:4-7, Hebrews 4:11, Psalm 2:7-8, 110:1-2, **19.** Psalm 110:1-2, 2:7-8, Colossians 3:1-3, Isaiah 11:3-4, Hebrews 12:21, John 17:24, Revelation 2:27-28, 3:21, Joshua 1:3, Mark 16:15-18 *(Luke 5:15-16, 22:43)*, **20.** Joshua 1:3, Genesis 13:17, **21.** Matthew 8:10, 16:17, Isaiah 11:3-4, Revelation 3:18, **22.** Zechariah 3:6-7, Revelation 2:28, **23.** John 15:4-7, **24.** John 16:33, **25.** Romans 8:26, **26.** Zechariah 3:6-7, **27.** 2 Chronicles 20:17, Exodus 23:28, Joshua 24:12, **28.** Mark 16:17-18, **29.** Revelation 4:5, **30.** Psalm 82:6, **31.** John 17:20-24, **32.** Matthew 6:21, **33.** Exodus 14:14, 33:14, Galatians 5:22-23, **34.** Revelation 2:25-26, 3:21, **35.** Matthew 23:9, **36.** Exodus 33:14, **37.** Exodus 23:28, 33:1-17, **38.** John 17:24, 15:7, 14:3, Mark 3:13, Luke 10:41-42, **39.** John 17:23, **40.** John 1:14, **41.** Romans 8:19, **42.** Psalm 27:4, **43.** John 10:9, **44.** Luke 12:49, **45.** Isaiah 40:3-5, **46.** Matthew 6:11, **47.** Matthew 6:33, **48.** Matthew 4:4, **49.** John 16:15, **50.** Genesis 3:24, **51.** Psalm 46:10, **52.** Hebrews 8:5, **53.** Psalm 116:2, **54.** Psalm 37:4, **55.** John 14:12, 2 Kings 2:13-14, **56.** Revelation 2:25-28; Psalm 2:7-9, 110:1-2, Isaiah 11:1-4, 41:14-15, Exodus 17:5, Numbers 20:11, 2 Kings 2:13-14, Revelation 1:5-6/5:9-10 *NKJV*, Romans 8:29, **57.** Isaiah 41:15-16, **58.** 1 Corinthians 15:54, Matthew

16:28, 2 Timothy 1:10, **59.** Matthew 18:10, 6:21, **60.** 1 Samuel 26:9, **61.** Acts 12:15, **62.** John 1:51, **63.** 2 Corinthians 3:18, **64.** Genesis 3:24, Revelation 2:7, 22:1-2, 22:14-15, **65.** Deuteronomy 10:2, Hebrews 10:16, 1 Corinthians 2:16, **66.** Numbers 17:8, **67.** Matthew 7:7, **68.** James 4:8, **69.** Matthew 17:20, Luke 17:6, **70.** Exodus 34:29-30, Isaiah 11:2, **71.** Psalm 27:4, **72.** Exodus 33:15-17, **73.** Exodus 33:11, **74.** 2 Kings 2:14, Joshua 3:6-7, **75.** Colossians 3:1-3, **76.** Hebrews 4:3, **77.** Isaiah 11:1-4, **78.** Matthew 14:16, **79.** Mark 4:35-41, **80.** Matthew 17:20, **81.** Matthew 10:8

Dated: 22/9/19

16. *Aaron's Staff (#99)*
AARON'S STAFF

I would like to start with something that happened a few years ago, that I think is quite meaningful …

Near my little boy's school is a small stony mountain stream. And on the way to work, after dropping him off each day, I used to go and do some laps in one of the small pools. Shallow at one end, and a waterfall at the deep end … it really is very beautiful. The water is clear and pure, like an aquarium; with fish, the occasional turtle, and the sun streaming through. It's a very special place … so regardless of season, I'd swim.

After a while, I started to bring food pellets for the fish. And sinking to the bottom, holding my breath, I'd feed them, and they'd all come around. Over time the fish really came to know me; and at the shallow end, after swimming, I would sit … and the fish would gather. It was really very special 'cause they would all come around … 50 or so in number, of all different ages and sizes. The larger were always the cautious ones and kept a distance, then there were the timid ones; and then others that would swim in and around me … between my arms and legs.

At one time, I couldn't go for three or four months. So afterwards, coming back, I really thought that they would have forgotten me. But to my surprise, they all remembered, from the smallest to the largest. However, if someone was to come with me … even my little boy, they would never come out but stayed hidden. However, if I told my little boy to stand up on a rock somewhere, out of the water, then they would come round me just as normal. Really really nice! They'd all surround me hovering and facing towards me, hoping for some food.

One particular morning, as I sat, with all these fish swimming in and around me; I said to the Lord, *"It's funny Lord, these fish never touch me, though they are so close … they are like Christians that never touch you."* It was a bit of a profound statement. But do you know what happened — the first and only time it ever happened; one fish came up and rubbed his mouth on my arm ... both sides. Like a 'holy kiss', a 'kiss' of greeting [1]. It happened only just that once, after saying this to the Lord.

Anyway, let's begin ...

Theme Scripture:
So Moses spoke to the Israelites, and their leaders gave him twelve staffs [rods], one for the leader of each of their ancestral tribes, and **Aaron's staff** was among them. Moses placed the staffs before the Lord in the tent of the covenant law. The next day Moses entered the Tent and saw that Aaron's staff, which represented the tribe of Levi, had not only sprouted but had budded, blossomed and produced [ripe] almonds. *(Numbers 17:6-8 NIV)*

To introduce this chapter: To *humble* yourself before the Lord [2] and choose to set your heart and eyes upon Him; [3] even in the realisation that you can personally meet with Him, dine with Him, walk with Him, and receive from Him each and every day ... and this as much as you desire! You open yourself to Divine Encounter. You open yourself to 'touch' God; and in affection, as deep and close dear friends — 'kiss' Him.

If you could truly come and love the Lord your God, and desire His personal Divine Presence upon your life — even more than your 'daily bread' [4]. Even more than your daily needs, cares, or desires [5]. Then you position yourself to receive Living Words from His mouth each and every day [6]. And this daily 'bread' given you of the Lord [7], will continually build you up in the Might and Strength of your Eternal origins [8]. And so too shall you begin to step into and operate in an 'Economy' of Heaven that is far Above the economy of this earth. With God *writing* Higher Laws in your heart [9] that fully supersede all natural laws of this world.

Held within each in Christ Jesus, is the Divine Capacity to bring life out of dead situations. Send and release both Life and Spirit in barren, dry, and hopeless places. Materialise food, finances, and provision where there was none. Joy, freedom, and hope where only despair was found. And where there was sickness now there is wholeness, and where there was death now there is life, and where there was failure now has become the staging place of great and incredible success. And the cracks and broken parts of your life, become lined and laced in gold; with a wholeness coming upon you that far surpasses. That of which the world perceives as 'wealth' fade as dust ... and that of which is highly honoured among men is long forgotten. For the children of God *enter* the Rest of the Lord [10] and function from the realms of Eternity ... from Everlasting to Everlasting. Such is the Grace of God for all who believe, for each and every one called by His Name.

To 'gaze upon the beauty of the Lord' is to enter His Rest [11]. To look up and beyond how you feel right now; and choose to Delight yourself in Him [12], is to *enter* His Presence. To say to the Spirit, *"You manage these issues of my life, as for me I seek the Presence of God"* [13] — to such step into the realm of Restoration ... the Restoration of all things. There is an exchange: God comes into your life, and you go up into His Life. You in Him and He in you. [14]

At the Fall ... all was lost. But in Christ Jesus so are you re-raised again in He who is Risen. Not just in ways that you can think or imagine, but in inconceivable and wonderful ways far beyond human comprehension [15]. Jesus would freely 'ascend' into Heaven as He walked this earth [16]. And as He was talking to Nicodemus, He was simultaneously functioning in Higher Places in Heaven ... far Above all things [17]. Therefore, so it is also, that as you too begin to raise your heart and eyes high in the Father [18] ... so too are you Taken. It is true, that your heart and thoughts can be anywhere, but in the Spirit can you be captured up in Him [19] ... and this right where you stand.

To govern with the Authorities of the 'Keys of Heaven', one first needs to step up into the Place of Authority. This a Place that is not on earth — but is Above all things — in Him. To seek the manifest Presence of God so are you taken. To seek His Courts so do you enter in. And to set your love and affection in Him ... so does the Love and Affection of God come upon you. To set it in your heart and deep in the vision of your soul; to sit at the right hand of God — so shall you!

> *"Oh Lord, how the believer needs to get this. Then they would truly walk in untold Wonders."*

In Christ Jesus, this very same 'Invitation' [20] has been extended to you as well ... for so too are you son of God. And how does it go, *"The Lord said unto my Lord, sit at my right hand"* ... and so, with your heart set here ... *"I shall make your enemies a footstool for your feet."* And in continuation, *"The Lord will extend **your mighty sceptre** from Zion, saying, '**Rule** in the midst of your enemies!'"* That is, rule against all opposing forces, all that comes against, and all works of the Thief. As Jesus instructs, **"*Clothe yourself in Immortality*"**.

In Gospel, it speaks of how the valiant take the Kingdom of Heaven by 'force' [21]. This is not a placid or idle statement. For truly, it takes great courage and fight to pursue the things of your Inheritance in the Kingdom of Heaven. For so too is there great resistance.

It has been the *Enemy* that has occupied your Promises since the Beginning. And though we are sons and daughters of the Most High — much in this world is at work to misdirect and distract us out of the realms of the Throne and that of the Sabbath Day of Rest *(ie; enjoying the full benefits of all God's labour and efforts)*. Fundamentally, we have not known how *not* to get mixed up in the world of which we have come from; in our thinking, in our hearts, and in our flesh. For there still is great entanglement. Therefore, here and now, **thrust out** the 'Vengeance' of the Spirit of God [22] against all forms of Death: body, mind, and soul. [23]

On this earth there is violent resistance against you ever truly walking in the revelation of your sonship [24]. And from ever truly coming to walk in the maturity of the Son [25] — as one no longer living *overshadowed* by sin, death, or the works of the *Thief* — but **presiding over all creation**. Over all powers on, below, or above the earth [26]. Satan is terrified of you ever truly coming to know who you are. For his jealous pursuits are firmly against you; not just to supplant you, but to supplant God of Heaven and earth.

To not have fallen, man would have never known these things of *frailty*. Hence, there still remains much 'doubt' and 'unbelief', for

Satan is <u>terrified</u> of you. Christ Jesus has *"Abolished death and brought Life and Immortality to light through the Gospel"* [27]. This is why we remain humble before God of Heaven and earth ... as students of Life, always learning and always growing. Students of Everlasting Life ... students of the Risen, students of Power and Glory.

In the Presence of the Lord — 'in Spirit' — gaze upon the Fire in the eyes of Jesus. As you behold Him in His Glory, as one in the Holy Presence of God, abiding under the Shadow of the Lord God Almighty, so shall your 'eyes' hold the very same Fire [28]. *Lamb and lion, priest and king; gentle and kind ... but one who roars.* [29]

I really encourage you, ponder what is meant by, *"Love the Lord God **with all your heart**, with **all** your soul, with **all** your mind, and with **all** your strength"* [30] — *ie;* 'The Focus'. For in Him, so shall you ever be strengthened, and ever built up; ministered to and raised in the fullness of your created and intended Purpose. And then, as you turn, so will you be able to love others with the same Eternal Love that comes from the only God. And in speaking to the needs before you; release both Heaven and the Will of God. [31]

Truly: seek *first* the Kingdom of Heaven as one become rightly aligned and attuned in Him. Before, your 'music' was like a piano out-of-tune; hard to hear and hard to listen to. But now, your 'melody' has become sweet and true [32]. And as a satellite 'receiver' is rightly aligned, so too can you turn to the needs before you and say, *"Come to life and be fruitful in Jesus Name."* And before, you only operated under the vision of natural law, however now — in Him — do you step into the symphony of His Presence. Being made able to function in 'law' that is far Higher and greater than all natural laws. For just as Heaven is higher, so are God's Thoughts and Ways [33]. And so too are the planes that you shall walk higher than this earth.

Picture again the scene: Love the Lord your God with all you are, and now when you turn are you made able to truly Love. It's important to see this: as you practice giving God **all your love**; *spirit, soul, mind, and strength* ... just as called; then so shall you also come to truly experience the Love of God. Now when you turn to others, you have incredible capacity of God's Love in you — to love. Does this make sense? And so also, just in the same way: as you abandon your life in Him [34], so will you start to truly experience Life. And this Love and Life will come upon you and minister and mentor you in Him. And shall raise you in both Power and Authority.

To re-emphasise: As you love the Lord ... so does the Love of God come upon you. And now when you turn, do you release both the Love and Power of the Kingdom of Heaven. This is the treasure, this is the purpose and motive of God.

Scripture:
What is man that You are mindful of him, or the son of man that You take care of him? You have made him a little lower than the angels; You have **Crowned** him with glory and honor, and set him over the works of Your hands. You have put all things in subjection under his feet. *(Hebrews 2:6-8 NKJV)*

Held in your hands is the very capacity to wield the Power and Authority of the Spirit of God. 'Satan has nothing in me' [35] for I delight in the Judgements of God [36]. And it is here in the Presence of God, under His Mighty Shadow [37], that I continuously seek and long for [38]. In Him shall I abide and shall not leave [39]. You cannot draw me out, and nor shall I step out of this Place that God Himself has Dreamed that I abide and remain. However now, in Him, all the works of the *Enemy* are exposed to the Glory of God — and are cut down. And in place of death — the Life of the Spirit shall bud forth — in Jesus precious Name.

TRIALS AND TESTING:
Do you think that God only performs miracles to show His Kindness? No, for before the Fall, Adam had full Dominion over the earth ... but then the *Liar* came. The same *Liar* that speaks lies in order to kill, steal, and destroy [40]. However now, in Christ Jesus, simply by who you are in Him do you release Life [41]. And by the words of your mouth do you release the Salvation of the Lord. Not for goodness' sake; but unto the releasing of the Kingdom of Heaven. For in your own possession is your capacity to release the Will of God. Such is the Power of your tongue. The releasing of Life and Spirit ... and to such, the same rides upon your words.

Again, I ask, if the Spirit of the Lord was speaking in your soul, with words deep in your belly and you prayed; [42] would not the same Spirit of the Lord ride upon your words? And would He not Himself respond to your very words uttered? So then, remain no longer as a leaf blown around in the wind, but a person truly in God; one deeply rooted and deeply established in Him.

It is the Faith of the Son, that is **wrought** through your own personal dialogue and Encounters in Him that is so meaningful. And this is why difficulties sometimes are allowed to remain, for just as Jesus learned 'obedience' by what He suffered; the same is for both you and I [43]. But it is for such a wonderful Eternal and Heavenly Purpose ... do you yet see?

Scripture speaks of how the Israelites of the Exodus, were sometimes made to hunger *(ie; trials and tribulations)* for one reason ... so that they might truly learn to hunger for the 'Word that proceeds from the mouth of God' [44]. So, for us also, instead of being a people who always need to be 'tested' with challenges; why not be **pre-emptive** and step over as one who instigates meetings in the Lord.

Actively and decisively **seeking** your 'Daily Bread' — in the Presence of the Lord — and this over needs, desires, or fears. And here in Him, becoming a people more rightly attuned and aligned, as a 'receiver' made able to continuously receive night and day ... even as one having the 'song' of the Lord coming upon your lips. As Scripture says, *"He put a new song in my mouth, a hymn of praise to our God ... and ... **many will see the Lord**"* [45]. Such is the power of waiting upon the Lord; the heavens rent apart and God stepping down in response of you. [46]

Truly, count it all joy when you face troubles, for in this deeply retained set vision of heart — unto the Presence of God — so shall you peer on through into the Love and Joy of the Lord. Even in moments of needing to 'exercise your faith' when seeking an answer ... so are you strengthened by the Lord.

The choosing to whistle a tune in the face of Adversity in total **defiance** against the *Enemy* — for **the Joy of the Lord is your**

Strength *47*. Now God has been given full rightful place to turn all things into your good. And right in the midst of things, teach you something powerful — raising the Standard each and every time *48*. And instead of being like clay; rigid and full of rocks, so shall you become most soft and supple; a joy unto Potter's Touch. And to such as these live lives of continual and catalystic growth ... in the 'kindling' of the Spirit ... unto the Fire of God.

Before, the link between you and the Kingdom of Heaven was like an overgrown trail. But now — **in Him***!* — is it being made as like a freeway in the Presence of the Lord. A path well-trodden that now has become as like a 'highway' of ever-increasing interaction and exchange. The mountains made low, the valleys lifted up, and the rough ground made smooth. And now shall the 'Glory of the Lord be revealed, and **all the people shall <u>see</u>**'. *49*

IN CLOSING

Scripture:
He who **dwells** in the secret place of the Most High shall remain stable and **<u>fixed</u> under the shadow** of the Almighty [whose Power no foe can withstand]. *(Psalm 91:1 AMPC)*

God has such high Dreams for you as a person. And though we all have various cares and troubles in this world; as I keep talking about these 'Dreams' of God, may you be able to raise these Dreams higher than your problems and cares. But however now, when you turn, so do you hold the Powers of God in your hand. The action of God released by the words of your mouth. *50*

God has a Dream, and that is for you to become a 'god' *untouchable*. Where God fights for you and angels guard your feet. The Blessings of God are there for all who love the Lord, but the Anointing of God is for they who lay their life down in Him: that you be not just 'mere men' that dies by the wayside. But made powerful in God, able to shift whole regions and nations. *51*

The giving of yourself:
*— the '****exchange****' —*
I in Him and He in me.

Therefore come, and continually value the Presence of God upon your life more than your prayers. The Presence of the Person of God more than your problems and cares. Come, **love the Lord God more than life**; the being with Him more than this world. Hunger and **long for your Daily Bread** — that of which is given from Above; and this even more than your daily needs or that of your daily concerns. And here — **in Him** — when you turn, so shall you walk in Authority releasing both Life and Spirit unto action. For God is about manifestation. Not about doctrine or beliefs ... but most real and manifest. God is about showing up!

— *The 'relocation'* —

Come, love the Lord with all your heart — and so too come to live in experience of His 'Anointed Love'. Come and release your life in Him, and so too shall you come to truly *find* and walk in Life. Lay your life down in the Lord and so shall you **ever** be lifted up on High. And instead of being one who 'rules' over your own life; [52] why not come now and step up to **rule in Heaven** *with* Him.

Submit your life unto the Lord and become one in Him, made able — by God — to 'rule in the midst of your enemies'. And in Him shall you cut off the head of the *Devourer*. And where there was poverty, now there are riches; and where there was sickness and death now there is life; and where there was hopelessness and despair now has come the ever-present riches of the Kingdom of Heaven.

Why not come and walk with angels and have them ascend and descend upon you and your daily life — continuously? And why not come and talk face to face with God? ... for so too have you, in Him, deep and inherent capacity to grow from Glory to Glory for all Eternity. For as a son or daughter — born from Above — so are you child of God. And in Image and Likeness as He, do you have capacity of infinite growth. There are many dreams one can have ... and **God is a fulfiller of dreams** [53] ... so what then, truly is your dream?

In your hand is given an Iron Rod — wrought through Divine Encounter. A 'Sceptre of Faith' given by Divine Authority [54]. And here in Him, shall you come to *wield* the Spirit of the Lord [55]. And with a heart bent upon the Fear of the Lord, a heart set unto the Fire, shall the 'Judgement' of the Lord be upon you [56] ... even His Glory. For presented in your hands is Authority and the Powers of the Spirit over the nations ... as one fully submitted to Him. [57]

Before you used to cry out to God for help in times of need; and in His Grace, God would always meet you where you are. But now are you being ever lifted up, as one transitioned from servant unto sonship. And in Him are you '**made**' to sit [instructed, constructed, placed and established] at the right hand of God. This, the very Dream of the Father fulfilled concerning you. His very own Dream held in His Heart from since before the founding of the earth. And in this ... are you one simply responding.

Religion is the practice of being right and accepted; but the Grace of God is that you ever be in Him [58]. Religion keeps you tethered on this earthly plane, even as one calling up to a Benevolent God. But Grace is that you might cross over [59] and come up in Him ... as one continually captured up. And now, when you turn, do you release the Authorities and Powers of God. As one coming to live in the open meaning of Aaron's Staff; in the 'Economies' and Powers of Life right from within the very realms of Everlasting Life.

> *"Make straight in the desert a highway for our God. Every valley shall be exalted and every mountain and hill brought low; The crooked places shall be made straight and the rough places smooth; the Glory of the Lord shall be revealed, and all flesh shall **see** it together."* [60]

The effort that you undertake in the 'making way' for the Person of God in your life; triggers and bears forth the Glory of God for 'all to see'. The humbling of yourself that God shall heal the nations [61]. The true giving of your life that God might truly pour out His Life ever abundantly ... *in Jesus Name.*

Appendix:

1. 2 Corinthians 13:12, ***2.*** 2 Chronicles 7:14, Daniel 10:12, ***3.*** Psalm 27:4, 37:4, ***4.*** Matthew 6:31, ***5.*** Matthew 4:4, 6:11, Luke 17:33, ***6.*** John 14:21, 15-18, ***7.*** Isaiah 25:6, 55:2, John 6:51, John 10:9, Revelation 2:17, ***8.*** Genesis 1:26, Psalm 110:1-2, Hebrews 4:11, ***9.*** Jeremiah 31:33, Acts 2:17, Hebrews 10:16, ***10.*** Hebrews 4:1-11, ***11.*** Psalm 27:4, ***12.*** Psalm 37:4, 43:5, ***13.*** Matthew 6:31-34, Joshua 24:15, Psalm 91:1-2, ***14.*** John 17:21, Isaiah 60:8, 55:12, Luke 10:19, ***15.*** 1 Corinthians 2:9, ***16.*** Luke 5:16, Genesis 5:24, ***17.*** John 3:13 *NKJV*, ***18.*** Hebrews 6:19, ***19.*** Revelation 1:10, 4:1, ***20.*** Psalm 110:1-2, 2:7-8, Colossians 3:1-3, Romans 8:17, Hebrews 4:11, Matthew 6:33, Revelation 1:5-6 *NKJV*, 3:17-22, Exodus 33:14, Genesis 1:26, ***21.*** Matthew 11:12 *NKJV*, ***22.*** Deuteronomy 32:35, Exodus 14:14, 23:28, Isaiah 11:3-4, 49:2, Revelation 2:26-27, 19:15, ***23.*** Mark 16:17-18, ***24.*** Romans 8:19, ***25.*** Ephesians 3:19, 4:13, ***26.*** Genesis 1:28, Romans 8:19, ***27.*** 2 Timothy 1:10, ***28.*** Revelation 1:10, 14b, John 17:24, Psalm 91:1, 13, Revelation 19:15, Isaiah 11:3-4, ***29.*** Isaiah 41:11-16, 11:3-4, Revelation 1:5-6, 5:9-10, Exodus 23:28, Romans 12:19, ***30.*** Matthew 22:37, Mark 12:30, Luke 10:27, Deuteronomy 6:4-5, ***31.*** Matthew 6:10, ***32.*** Psalm 40:3, ***33.*** Isaiah 55:8-9, ***34.*** Matthew 10:39, ***35.*** John 14:30, ***36.*** Isaiah 11:3, ***37.*** Psalm 91:1, ***38.*** Psalm 27:4, ***39.*** Exodus 33:11, ***40.*** John 10:10, 1 Peter 5:8, Luke 22:31, Genesis 4:7, Matthew 13:22, ***41.*** John 20:21-23, Isaiah 11:1-4, ***42.*** Romans 8:25-26, ***43.*** Hebrews 5:8, Deuteronomy 8:3, ***44.*** Deuteronomy 8:3, ***45.*** Psalm 40:3, ***46.*** Isaiah 64:1-4, Daniel 10:12, Psalm 116:2, ***47.*** Nehemiah 8:10b, ***48.*** Isaiah 59:19, ***49.*** Isaiah 40:3-5, ***50.*** Isaiah 110:1-2, ***51.*** John 10:34-36, Psalm 82:6-8, 91:11-12, Isaiah 11:1-4, Exodus 14:14, 33:14, 23:28, ***52.*** Genesis 2:17, ***53.*** Psalm 37:4, ***54.*** Revelation 2:25-29, ***55.*** Revelation 19:15, Isaiah 11:4, ***56.*** Isaiah 11:3-4, Exodus 33:18, 20:21, John 17:24, Luke 24:49, ***57.*** Matthew 8:9, Zechariah 3:7, Psalm 91:1, Revelation 3:18-21, John 14:30b, ***58.*** John 17:20-24, John 15:4-8 *NKJV*, ***59.*** Joshua 3, John 14:6, 10:9, ***60.*** Isaiah 40:3-5, *61.* 2 Chronicles 7:14, Daniel 10:12

Dated: 23/10/19

17. Aaron's Staff (#100)
DOMINION OVER THE BIRDS (Part 1)

AN INTRODUCTION

Did you know that before the Fall, Heaven and earth was perfectly intertwined as a seamless reality? That Adam *co-abided* both realms simultaneously ... then the Fall came? I'd like to encourage you, that we who have come from *fallen* man, we, who used to be *fallen* man; truly, our mindsets and concepts of what it means to be 'risen', what it truly means to be born again ... is so small. What it really means regarding our fundamental Birthright and Inheritance in God, is **so incredibly and inherently small** [1]. But then, the Person of Christ came.

Scripture:
This is the book of the generations of Adam. When God created man, he made him in the likeness of God. Male and female he created them, and he blessed them and named them Man when they were created. When Adam had lived 130 years, he fathered a son in his own **likeness, after his image**, and named him Seth. *(Genesis 5:1-3 ESV)*

Do you recall how it says in the Beginning, that man was made in the 'Image and Likeness' of God? [2] That's amazing ... that truly is amazing, isn't it*!* But did you actually then realise, that after the Fall, this of our true origins — our true origins as the human race — is actually now made in the 'image and likeness' of *fallen* man — and **not God**? [3] Hence, it is most true, that the mindsets of what we think we know what Christ has achieved for us ... is so *small*. What we think we know what the gifted Spirit has opened to us all ... is so *minuscule*. In many ways ... **it is caged**. [4]

The Grace of God, the Power of God, the Love of God, and His Gifts and Purposes — **defy** *understanding.*

But that's what we are about now, isn't it? We are about gaining the Mind of Christ [5]. **Not the mind of man** but the Mind of Christ Jesus. That we might **walk** — all the more — **in the fullness of Him on earth** *(Radiant Glory and Fire)* [6]. Even that we might continue to be 'made' [7] as a people; able to walk more fuller [8] in the very 'Likeness' and 'Image' of the Risen Christ — who is Himself God. [9]

For in the past, we had very little reference or understanding of the Glory from whence Adam fell. But now, **in the very Person of Jesus**, we now have — **perfect Picture** — of our true Destiny and Purpose. And through the Power of His shed Blood, and the Power of His Word spoken and the Spirit given ... so shall we.

*When we look intently at the Person of Jesus, we see **our** Destiny in Him, we see our **true** origins.*

Did you realise, that as Jesus came as the *second* Adam; [10] that He fundamentally came also as one — **openly demonstrating the 'picture' of our own Restoration**? Not in the ways of the world, not others, nor the spiritual forces of this Age — but in the very **Person of Jesus**. He came and lived amongst us, as one who openly engaged Heaven — seamlessly — just as in the Beginning; and He did it so in ways that — taught us — how to do the very same ... *even* unto greater works than He. [11]

Therefore, the chasm, *ie;* the divide between you and Heaven, the divide between Heaven and earth ... has now been rejoined in you. And you can begin to live in a way where the *intertwining*, the *integration* — the '*living* in the fullness of your Divine Origins' — you can start to walk it out, you can start to live in it, you can start to live in open experience just as the Son.

IN DOMINION OVER AND ABOVE

Adam was given Dominion over the 'birds of the air' and the 'fish of the sea' [12]. But even in this, our mindsets are so small as to what this really means. I know I can go fishing ... and I know I can go catch a bird ... but that is **not** dominion!

Actual and true Dominion is the capacity to oversee the realms where the birds operate. And oversee the realms where the fish of the sea operate: and have *mastery* and control; to direct, to move, and to multiply [13]. But even **more** importantly; in the area of spiritual powers and authority, to have mastery over the '**powers** of the air' and the 'powers of the sea', *ie;* that of which is above and that of which is below [14]. Now you are beginning to come into the understanding of your true intended Dominion and Authority in God: walking on water ... calming the seas ... multiplying food.

It says in Scripture, that all *"Creation waits in eager expectation for the sons of God to be revealed"* [15]. Well, that's today ... **I reveal this to you today**. That you truly may cease the 'groans' of your world. Such is your Salvation in the Lord. The true Restoration of your seated Place in Christ Jesus. [16]

Therefore I pray, that in all things, you might seek the Presence of God, that you truly may come into the Knowledge of God [17]. Seek Him not only through the written Word, for as believers we are called to 'worship' Him in both Truth as well as in Spirit [18]. That He might continue to reveal His Heart and His Mind towards you. Even that you might be one who steps all the more further into '**all the More**'. Into all that is your Birthright, into all that is your Inheritance ... to the blessing of others.

OPERATING OUT OF A HIGHER LAW

In the Exodus story, Aaron's Staff was laid before the 'Tent of the Covenant Law'. And here, as a dead stick: it budded, blossomed, and produced ripe fruit miraculously overnight. Come and understand, and take deeply to heart this picture for own life personally. For as you also choose to '**wait upon the Lord**' [19], and personally 'seek the Lord in His Holy Presence' [20], so are you also laying yourself down postured before the 'Tent of the Covenant Law' [21]. You are coming up in Heaven and laying yourself bare before the very Presence of the Person of God in Heaven [22]. And here, He will manifest Himself to you personally [23] — He will miraculously **manifest** His Life in you. And He will swiftly change you and cause you to blossom and be fruitful ... 'overnight'. [24]

We are called as a people of God ... unto kingship. And in Christ Jesus, we are fundamentally **called to Rule and Reign in Him** [25]. But however, the living reality requires deep and total submission before the Lord of Glory [26]. Even as one 'dead' before **the Spirit of Life** [27]. No longer living as a person who keeps eating of the 'tree' of their own knowledge and understanding. But deeply **choosing it within yourself to <u>eat</u> of the Tree of Life** [28]. And here, it will be God Himself who will Personally raise you to Rule in whatever you are going through: as a **converter** of death into life … just as the Son.

Coming under the Shadow and Authority of the Lord God Almighty … even that our own shadow might cast the very same Authority and Glory. [29]

The greatest honour one can ever give unto the Lord is: **become the fullness** of the 'why' Jesus faced the horrors of the Cross [30]. Even as one who walks in the full measure and stature of the Son [31]. That is, the Word made flesh, the Word made manifest and real and walking amongst us.

Oftentimes, the people of God miss this underlying goal and purpose of God … and therefore struggle. Failing in this most core Calling of the Church: the **becoming <u>Like</u> Jesus in Glory**. Praying only for needs and wants, and in reaction to what is seen around them; rather than 'praying' and yearning to see God — to hear and **<u>see</u> Him**. For the answer to life is not found in problems — **but <u>in</u> Him**. Unto the Places whereby our sonship is revealed; [14] the Resurrected Christ made manifest in us and subsequently standing tall in our world.

Not as a people yearning to leave earth; but yearning for the Kingdom of Heaven made manifest on earth. A heart that is deeply set unto *union*, unto a oneness in the Father … risen in Christ Jesus into where He is now [32]. That you and I release and set to charge the Glory of God.

To begin …

FULL CIRCLE
Theme Scripture:
And God said, let us make man in our Image, after our Likeness: and let them have Dominion over the fish of the sea, and over the fowl of the air, and over the cattle [livestock], and over all the earth, and over every creeping thing that creepeth upon the earth. So

God created man in His own Image, in the Image of God created He him; male and female created He them. *(Genesis 1:26-27 KJV)*

God deeply desires that you **return back** into the High plane of your Divine Origins [33]. In the Beginning there was the Fall. However now, in these that are Last Days; as you set your eyes 'in Spirit' unto the very Presence of God [34], so are you **re-raised in Glory** ... from Glory to Glory and unto exceedingly great Glory [35]. It is Jesus, as the New Adam — the very first of the many born of God [36] — that came in representation: demonstrating the 'picture' of your Restoration. That is, as one who walked and functioned; co-abided in the Joy and Glory of Heaven as He lived on earth ... simultaneously and seamlessly! [37]

The man Adam was made in the Image and Likeness of God. And was given Dominion over the 'birds of the air' and the 'fish of the sea'. But pause here for a moment and recognise two most important things. Firstly, a man of flesh [38] fundamentally has no true ability to have any real 'dominion' over the realms of the air *(or the sea)*. However, **a man of the Spirit does** *(ie; one who has been made Alive unto the Spirit, and walks in Heavenly Places [39])*. And secondly, in overlaying spiritual principles, the 'birds of the air' and the 'fish of the sea' represent the powers above and below the earth.

So understand then, that as one **now restored into the Image and Likeness of God** [40], through the Last Adam; [41] so then also have you fundamentally regained capacity to operate in both realms just as the Son, *ie;* in Heaven as on earth [42]. And this in ever-increasing living and dynamic experience unto the blessing of your world.

In your spirit you can be anywhere you wish [43] — just as in the Christ can you **live seated with Him** in Heavenly Places [44]. And this is the treasure found in praise: for to such look through the realities of this world unto the very Throne of God. And this is the value of seeking the Presence of the Lord ... irrespective of season! ... for such stand in **defiance** of Death and **fully embrace Life** [45]. And to such as these, so do they begin to live in open experience of the Lord. Stepping over death and despair ... entering into the **realms of Dominion**.

The basis of Power is a heart unto praise ... the laying down of oneself in death ... for to such they relocate.

God resides in a Place far above Satan and that of this physical world. And so too do they of whom rise up in Him — gain Divine capacity to live and move. Co-abide and function in Dominion and Authority in realms **fully** over Satan and that of creation. Made able to release both the Will and Kingdom of God on earth [46]. Therefore, in continuing to grow in personal relationship with your Heavenly Father — even He, your closest and dearest Friend — it is by the Spirit of God that you shall ever be led by Hand, deeper into the Wonders of your Salvation.

To touch God, to **'kiss' Him** with a holy kiss of affection — as deep and close bonded friends [47] — in great endearment, longing and love; with God as your all-consuming vision — so shall His Love consume you. And so too shall you come to know His Love and be greatly strengthened [48]. There are many things and to many people that one can turn to. However, in turning to the Lord are strong bonds of relationship developed. And in Him are you 'Transfigured' from creatures of flesh unto creatures of Light — walking in the manifestation of your sonship.

Jesus co-abided Heaven as He walked this earth. And it is to this very 'Prayer' that He seeks you do also [49]. And through your own personally developed relationship in Him, shall this reality become ever more real to you *(the 'giving of yourself')*. Now law and works have **no value here**, and by no means enables; only a *shift* unto the Heart and Mind of Christ.

It is through Grace and the finished work of the Cross, that you have now gained **perfect right** of access. And the Kingdom of Heaven, these Glorious and Eternal realms of God, are now right **'at hand'** for you to enter. For you to go in and out just as you please [50]. These realities forming ... even as an ever-broadening freeway [51] of Divine experiences, interactions, and exchange. And ever by the Grace of God and the Holy Spirit, shall you enter in and participate in this of your Divine Place of Origins.

Come, let the Peace of God rule your heart!

Scripture:
The Lord God planted a garden eastward in Eden, and there He put the man whom He had formed. And out of the ground the Lord God made every tree grow that is pleasant to the sight and good for food. The **Tree of Life** was also in the midst of the garden, and the tree of the knowledge of good and evil. *(Genesis 2:8-9 NKJV)*

A question to ask, 'The Tree of Life … was it on earth or was it in Heaven?' The truth is, of course, that it was not ever transplanted but has always been in Heaven [52]. So if, in the midst of the Garden the Tree of Life stood … **where was Eden?**

We know that there is both the Heaven-dimension and the earth-dimension *(the spiritual and the physical)*; with the earth being a lesser place confined by a three-dimensional reality. And Heaven, a far higher dimension; not in the physical sky above, but in higher realms of reality that are fully above Creation. Hence now it can be more easily understood how a 'pre-fall' Adam could walk in both. For man was made multi-dimensional … a creature of both spirit *(Spirit [53])* and body, ie; Heaven and earth.

Therefore now, with *your* spirit **made Alive again** in Christ Jesus, and also with the Curtain rent, so are you able to live in continual Divine Engagement in God — as **one re-born**. That is, your spirit has been made Alive again unto the Heavenly realms. No longer as a people born of the fallen [54] but a people **born of the Risen**. No longer orphan and alone … but in sonship. Heaven *united* with earth; the chasm closed, and the connection now firmly re-established through the giving of the Son of God. Therefore now, you are truly a 'New Creation' … **a totally new being of Divine origin**.

"Unto us a Child is given." [55]

A side note: Fallen man = a dead spirit, ie; zero Heaven connection. Risen man = a Living spirit, ie; Heaven abiding and intertwined. Born of the flesh = the carnal, the mortal, and the 'dead' [56]. *But born of the Spirit = a Living spirit (ie; your spirit now a Living Spirit in union with Jesus; Heaven and earth,*

*Spirit and flesh ... ie; your spirit indistinguishably Abiding in Him). Hence now, the Prayer of the Son is that you be unified **one** with Him.* [57]

The born again 'mirrors' this reality: Spirit and flesh / Heaven and earth. Hence now, where your treasure is, so too your spirit is actively engaged [58] *... 'Salvation' being simply the right of access. Therefore now, in the setting of your heart unto the High Places ... so are you seated. So are you now engaging and opening yourself up to all the more. Such is the gift in seeking the Presence of God; the stepping up into and functioning in these of your Divine Place of Origins. And this is where the Power lies* [59] *— union in the Person of God.*

To honour God is to face towards. To honour Him is to draw yourself unto Him. And in seeking the Presence so do you honour both the manifest realities of Heaven and the very Spirit of God. Therefore, it is true ... you have the Spirit of God, but does the Spirit of God have you?

The realms of Heaven are the realms of the Spirit. Hence therefore, with your spirit now made **Alive in Him** and the Spirit of God Alive in you; 'Heaven and earth' is indistinguishable. The Powers and realities of Heaven are made freely manifest on and in your life ... even as you walk this earth.

Scripture:
Though you were once distant from him, living in the shadows of your evil thoughts and actions, he **reconnected you back to himself**. He released his supernatural Peace to you through the sacrifice of his own body as the sin-payment on your behalf so that you would **dwell in his Presence**. And now there is nothing between you and Father God, for he **sees you as holy**, flawless, and restored. *(Colossians 1:21-22 TPT)*

There are a number of examples in Scripture, where the physical realm of this earth and the spiritual realms of Heaven were interchanged — **co-existing** — with lines of separation made less relevant. For example, Moses and the Elders **physically ate a meal in Heaven** — in their earthly bodies — on the Sea of Glass [60]. And Elijah, in **bodily form**, was taken up in a chariot into Heaven. And on the mountain, the Disciples witnessed Jesus Transfigured into light [61]. And Paul speaks of a man who went up into the Third Heaven ... *"In body or in spirit I do not know"* [62] ... for it became seamless and indistinguishable. For the truth is that they who choose to walk in Heaven — in the Glory of God — come also to **behold and <u>carry</u> the very <u>same</u> Glory** [63] as they walk this earth. Measure upon measure, Glory upon Glory … in ever-increasing Glory. [64]

As angels walk this earth, so can you also walk in the Heavenly realms in a measure **without constraint**. Even to they who choose to approach God as like a little child — in the *innocence* of their whole self — to such see God [65]. And even unto these 'little children', nothing shall be impossible for them: the casting of mountains, the walking on water, and the calming of storms … **with a <u>word</u>**! [66] And to what, as a believer, are you called? But to **become** as like little children. For it is only to such as these that actively *see* the Kingdom of Heaven [67]. And take heed, you don't want Jesus saying to you, *"I never knew you. Away from me, you evildoers"* [68]. Hence, we learn to be a people 'known' in Him … a people known and made 'Rich' in Heaven. [69]

King David is famous for longing for the Courts of God [70]. And would say of himself, *"My heart and my flesh cry out for the living God"* [71]. Now, it's important to realise, that these 'Courts of God' are not legal courts but the Garden realms … even Eden. The courtyards of the Dwelling Place of God; the pleasurable realms of delight, walking close in the intimate and hidden things of God. And David would then continue, *"The sparrow has **found a <u>home</u>**, and the swallow a nest … blessed are those who **<u>dwell</u> in your House**; they are ever praising you."* This reality being a spiritual Place of wonder … a Place of co-Abiding, a Place of co-creating and co-ruling in Him.

PREFERENCING PRESENCE

Apostle John was known as one who rested his head on Jesus' Bosom. And he also was known as one who was **captured up** in 'Spirit' on the Lord's Day [72]. And of these things, Jesus would say, *"No man has ascended up to Heaven but he that came down from Heaven — even the Son of man **who <u>IS</u> in Heaven**"* [73]. Therefore, it was Jesus Himself who openly demonstrated, by both word and deed; how you too can function, operate, and move in Heavenly Places as you live on earth … seamlessly and simultaneously. And as the Son of God, as a child of the Most High, with full rights and privileges:

has this Pattern and Precedent, this 'Image and Likeness', becomes yours to walk in this very day. However, love and intimacy is key … not law but love.

As one born anew in Christ Jesus, have you now been made able — by God — to **sit in Heavenly Places** [74] through the Power of the Blood of Jesus [75]. And it is to such as these — who 'in Spirit' — can be taken *anywhere* and at *any time* in Him. For we are not born of flesh, nor of the will of man [76], **but born of the Spirit of God**. And to they who choose to Abide and Remain in Him [77], to they bear Wondrous Fruits of Heaven; even the Everlasting and Miraculous Fruits of the Most High God. [78]

The lessons contained in the Gospel message, they are written in expression and picture of how, as a believer … you **can disconnect from earthly tethers** and constraints; and come up and break on through all the holds of sin and death. Passing through all the powers and influences of the 'air'. And in rising up above the stratosphere, even above the stars and the universe; you can live and have your being in the Eternal realms of the Glory of God. And here live and move **just as Jesus**. But not only as Jesus was … but **as Jesus IS**! … in His Glorified and Triumphant state [79]. And this over all powers, over all authorities, and over all natural law — **in Him**. Not as Adam of Old … but as Adam of New … walking in the Sevenfold blessings.

Enoch passed on through the Cherubim *(the barring of the way* [80]*)* and came to **walk** with God. He was often not found until the day he was 'found not' … for God took him [81]. And this way before the Blood shed or the Curtain rent. [82]

David walked in the realms of Wonder and saw and heard way off into the future many many things. And this way before the Spirit given. So **IF**, for you and I the Blood was shed and the Spirit given, even the Curtain rent and the Kingdom of Heaven come; do you not have **exceedingly far greater opportunity** than they? *(even to that of which is perceived before our time)* … oh, you of little faith! Pre-fall walking — but so much more! — Triumphant, Victorious, and Risen walking as you walk this earth. Resurrected post-Cross walking even in a greater restored reality and in Higher Places to that of which the *Thief* stole.

God fundamentally desires Heaven to be intertwined here on earth — and the Cross is the Bridge that has **closed** the gap. Forever now, as true sons and daughters of God, by *your* will and by *your* choice … do you open these incredible pathways. Come then and refresh your thinking in this Scripture verse: *"Wonderfully blessed are those who wash their robes white so they can access the Tree of Life **and** enter the City of Bliss by its open gates."* [83]

So regardless of your current happenings; your sin or your failures; your dreams or aspirations … let them **never** be a hindrance to you approaching the Glories of Heaven. Come, and wash your robes *(wash off your thoughts, your fears, and your sin)*, and pass on through and eat of the Tree of Life … daily. For to such position themselves and go freely into the City of the King … even the **City of Eternal Bliss**.

IN CLOSING

Let me speak a bit *harshly* for a moment, not in ridicule or condemnation, but in love and encouragement: On face value, Esau didn't despise his birthright … but in God's eyes, he did. Recognise, that a lack of interest in your Divine Origins, and that of the Purposed Destiny of God upon your life, is an expression of 'despising' your birthright. So come, let us all the more step out of this orphan state of thinking. And step into the state of living and breathing sonship.

Today, this very moment, come and give your life afresh unto the Lord. For truly, as one hungers … does one honour. And he who seeks is the one who pursues. And to the one who actively pursues the Face of God … so do you see. And not only see, but becoming one who actively lives in the open Rest and Power of His Glory. However, 'repentance' is key. But understand this word: it means the turning your heart fully unto the Lord. Not unto other things but as like a **sharp arrow**: your vision firmly pointed and directed towards the Lord of Glory.

Learn to practice 'Presence' [84], even as one would practice a musical instrument or a skill. And so will the melody flow … even with a **choir of angels**. As a musician practices his music, a dancer her dance, so does the born again believer exercise the being '**back in Divine Presence**'. And here the manifestation becomes alive and real: for first is the Word, then the Spirit and the Revelation, but now comes the '**Word made flesh**' — even the manifestation of His Glory in your person.

Recently, I was in the car, waiting for my little boy to finish his soccer training. And lying back and looking up at the evening sky; there in the dusk light I saw Jupiter and Saturn together so clear and so bright. And in my spirit the Spirit of the Lord spoke clearly to me, *"I am dancing with God."*

Do you realise, how this is the nature of God concerning you personally … and to **where He <u>dearly</u> desire to take you**? And Power comes from this Place. Such is His Love and to such is His Heart concerning each one of us, *ie;* the Strengthening and the Equipping. Come then, and deeply hunger for your 'Daily Bread', and this even more than your daily food or needs. For as one gains a heart to step in … so **shall** you be taken. And to who you are in Him, and to where you are seated, so do you draw from, and so do you feed of … bringing Heaven to this world.

In reference to the story of feeding and swimming with the fish, as shared in the previous chapter. By the Blood of Jesus, you have the capacity of a son to 'touch' God. Not only touch, but through deeply developed and close bonds of friendship; greet Him warmly with a 'kiss' of affection. A holy 'kiss' unto the Lord. [85]

Recognise, that in the pool all 'fish' are part of the Beloved … and all are in Christ Jesus. But here in this picture you have the larger fish; the mature and 'wise' ones who stay at a distance. You have others that come around close, and still others that come right in and swim in and around the Father. But then there are — but a few — who truly come and rest their head on the 'Bosom' of Jesus and of whom come and 'kiss' the Lord with tears. However still, regardless, all are dearly loved in the Lord … and all are **part** of the Beloved. But who is it that you wish to be?

The God of Heaven and earth is a Person ... just like you and I. For it is God Himself of whom you have been fashioned after, and this by His own Will and by His own very Hands. And just like any person; through relationship much is developed; and through bonds of connection much is shared. Both in the difficult times as well as the good times; the standing by Him as He stands by you. In this, much trust and closeness is developed. And to who is it that truly knows a person but one who draws close and one who spends time; even the one who stands by through the great traumas and difficulties of life that come. Long-suffering love, enduring kindness, a heart ever given over to another. Such can be your love for God ... for such is His Love for you. To he who is trustworthy **much is given**, and to he that can be trusted **much shall be entrusted**.

Do you recall how it says in Scripture, *"Eye hath not seen, nor ear heard, neither have entered into the heart of man, the things which God has* **prepared for them** *that love him?"* [86] How then, do you think it will be, when you truly begin to step into these things? How could you begin to explain or share that of which far **surpasses the imagination** of the hearer? That is why it is also said, *"We speak of what we have heard and have seen but you do not receive our testimony."* [87]

Have you also heard where it says, *"God is actively looking for those who worship Him in Spirit and in Truth?"* [88] For let us not be only unto the Word of God but unto Presence, *ie;* unto Encounter, unto Engagement, unto being Intertwined in Spirit. And so shall you come to co-function in Heaven just as the Son.

The Gospel message is not only about the 'Kingdom come', but the **going into the Kingdom of Heaven**; [89] The seeing, the being, the interacting and the hearing — to such move the Kingdom of God. Death is not your Saviour ... Christ Jesus is. So in this, realise that you need not physically die in order to enter Heaven and openly Engage. For it is the Christ of whom died and was raised again, that you need not die before you go and before you openly engage.

Closing Scripture:
Christ's resurrection is your resurrection too. This is why we are to **yearn** for all that is above, for that's where Christ sits enthroned at the place of all power, honor, and authority! Yes, **feast** on all the treasures of the heavenly realm and fill your thoughts with heavenly realities, and not with the distractions of the natural realm. *(Colossians 3:1-2 TPT)*

A side note: Did you notice in the opening Scripture the word 'cattle', or otherwise the word 'livestock'? Now, in light of what we have been discussing here; see how, that as one who operates from Presence, who functions in Heavenly realms: that you **preside** *over the realms of finances, provision, capacity, and livelihood?*

To be continued ...

Appendix:

1. 1 Corinthians 2:9-10, *2.* Genesis 1:26, *3.* Genesis 5:1-3, *4.* Genesis 2:17, Proverbs 3:5, *5.* 1 Corinthians 2:16, *6.* Ephesians 4:13, *7.* Genesis 1:26a, Isaiah 41:14-20, *8.* 2 Corinthians 3:18, *9.* John 14:9, 10:30, *10.* 1 Corinthians 15:45, *11.* John 14:12, *12.* Genesis 1:26, *13.* Matthew 14:13-21, 17:27, John 21:11 *(Matthew 14:25, Mark 4:39, John 2:7-9, 6:21)*, *14.* Matthew 16:17-19, Ephesians 2:2, *15.* Romans 8:19, *16.* Psalm 2:7-8, 110:1-2, Hebrews 4:1-11, Revelation 3:20-21, 5:9-10 *KJV*, *17.* Isaiah 11:1-4, Jeremiah 23:21-22, Zechariah 3:7, *18.* John 4:24, *19.* Isaiah 64:1-4, Psalm 116:2, Daniel 10:12, *20.* Psalm 27:4, *21.* 2 Chronicles 7:14, Daniel 10:12, *22.* Hebrews 8:5, 6:19, *23.* John 14:21, *24.* Numbers 17:7-8, *25.* 2 Timothy 2:12, Romans 8:17, 1 Peter 2:9, Colossians 3:1-3, NKJV: Revelation 1:5-6, 5:9-10, Psalm 110:1-2, *26.* Matthew 8:8-12, *27.* Matthew 10:39, Revelation 1:17, Genesis 2:17, *28.* Matthew 4:4, John 5:19, Luke 10:39, *29.* Psalm 91, Acts 5:15, Matthew 8:8-12, Zechariah 3:7, *30.* Hebrews 12:2, *31.* Ephesians 4:13, *32.* John 7:34, 10:30, 12:26, 13:36, 14:4-6, 17:21-24, 3:13 *KJV*, *33.* Luke 15:20, *34.* Revelation 1:10, Colossians 3:1, Ephesians 5:8, Galatians 5:25, *35.* 2 Corinthians 3:18, *36.* John 17:16, 12:24, *37.* NKJV: John 3:13, 17:24, 5:19, *38.* Proverbs 3:5-6, Romans 8:9, Galatians 5:16, 1 Timothy 4:7,

39. Ephesians 2:6, *40.* Genesis 1:27, 5:3, Romans 8:29, *41.* Isaiah 9:6, 1 Corinthians 15:45, *42.* NKJV: John 3:13, 17:24, 5:19, *43.* 2 Corinthians 12:2, *44.* Ephesians 2:6, *45.* Matthew 4:3-4, *46.* Matthew 6:10, *47.* Genesis 5:24 NLT, John 1:18, John 13:23, *48.* John 5:42, Ephesians 3:18, *49.* NKJV: John 3:13, 17:24, 5:19, *50.* John 10:9, John 3:3-12, *51.* Isaiah 40:3-5, *52.* Revelation 22:1-2, 2:7, 22:14-15, *53.* 1 Peter 3:18b, Ephesians 2:1-10, John 10:17 *(loves, reveals, shows),* *54.* Genesis 3:19, *55.* Isaiah 9:6, *56.* Genesis 2:17, *57.* John 17:20-24, *58.* Matthew 6:21, Matthew 5:28, *59.* Psalm 110:2, *60.* Exodus 24:9-11, *61.* Matthew 17:2, *62.* 2 Corinthians 12:2, *63.* John 17:24, 14:12, *64.* 2 Corinthians 3:18, *65.* Matthew 18:10, Acts 12:15, *66.* Matthew 14:16, 10:8, 8:8, Revelation 2:26, 19:15, Isaiah 41:15, 51:16, 2 Kings 2:13-14, *67.* Matthew 18:3, *68.* Matthew 7:21-23, *69.* Matthew 6:19-20, Revelation 3:17-18, *70.* Psalm 27:4, 84:10, *71.* Psalm 84:1-4, *72.* Revelation 1:10-18, *73.* John 3:13, *74.* Ephesians 2:6, *75.* Revelation 5:9-10 *KJV,* *76.* John 1:13, Matthew 16:17, *77.* John 15:4, 7, *78.* John 15:16, *79.* John 14:12, *80.* Genesis 3:24, *81.* Genesis 5:24, *82.* Matthew 27:51, *83.* Revelation 22:14 TPT, *84.* Exodus 33:14-18, 20:21, *85.* Romans 16:16, 2 Corinthians 13:12, *86.* 1 Corinthians 2:9, *87.* John 3:11, *88.* John 4:23-24, *89.* John 3:3, Matthew 18:3

Dated: 26/11/19

18. *Aaron's Staff (#101)*
DOMINION OVER THE BIRDS *(Part 2)*

In continuation from the previous chapter ...

Opening Scripture:
John, to the seven churches which are in Asia: **Grace** to you and **Peace** from Him who is and who was and who is to come, and from the seven Spirits who are before His throne, and from Jesus Christ, the faithful witness, the firstborn from the dead, and the ruler over the kings of the earth. To Him who loved us and washed us from our sins in His own Blood, and has **made us kings and priests** to His God and Father, to Him be glory and dominion forever and ever. Amen. *(Revelation 1:4-6 NKJV)*

God is Love ... so worship Him in Love. God is Truth ... so worship Him in Truth. And God is Spirit ... so worship Him and seek Him 'in Spirit'. God is not law but **Love, Truth ... and Spirit**. So how one truly becomes successful: is to set your heart in Him. And how you truly become one who truly knows God and walk close to Him; the **truth** of you needs to come approach the Truth of Him. Your spirit can be wherever you wish; however, as you choose to set your **spirit** unto the Spirit of Life, even here in your Divine Place of Dwelling: so is your spirit, soul, mind, and flesh **made Alive and Powerful in Him**.

By the Blood has Jesus made you kings and priests unto God, as one standing with Him in His Glory [1]. And here, with the full backing of Heaven, so shall you be Victorious and so shall you be made powerful in all things. There are many places where your **heart** can abide; therefore, in choosing to abide in Him, [2] *ie;* 'take your place in Him' [3] ... shall you come to interact in these unfathomable realms of Glory, Power and Wonder. Such is your Inheritance in the Lord. These, the very wondrous Eternal realms of the Kingdom of Heaven, are your inheritance.

*'**Grace**' = the Power to win and the Power to be successful.*
*'**Peace**' = of a nature and a premise that defies comprehension.*
*'**King**' = co-reign, co-seated; shareholders in Inheritance and Power.*

'IN THE SPIRIT'

Scripture:
"I was in the Spirit on the Lord's Day." *(Revelation 1:10 NKJV)*

How is it possible for a person to truly come to **know**, or **see**, or **walk** in Heavenly realms without God's assistance? Without God's ability to do so? Such is the Presence of the Lord ... *ie;* the being 'in the Spirit'. The things of the Kingdom of Heaven are so far outside the understanding and the imaginations of man [4]. Hence this is why you need *both* the Word and the Spirit [5]. The Truth mixed with Divine Encounters and Engagements. For truly, as your spirit is made enlivened and invigorated in Him, [6] so too do you begin to 'hear' and 'see' — as one led into '**all the More**' that God has for you. [7]

Throughout the generations, the focus of the Christian Church has only been about the Kingdom of Heaven 'come'. And though this is good and most right, the truth is that the Christian believer has remained ineffectual and powerless; due to a lack of the Kingdom of Heaven '**GO**'. That is, the 'entering into': the 'seeing' ... and the 'being **with** Jesus where he is' [8]. In this, the *Thief* has stolen and fundamentally works to keep you constrained and fearful. However now, through an ever-deepening awareness, are your **eyes** made ever open. And the Kingdom of Heaven is released because of where you are and who you are '**in Him**'.

>'**Love**' = *your love and motives set on Him.*
>'**Truth**' = *the truth of you set upon the Truth of Him.*
>'**Spirit**' = *your treasure set in the Lord as one relocated in Him.*

Since the Fall, there has been the divide between Spirit and flesh. A battle and a warring in the heart and soul of man, *ie;* flesh-dependence [9] *vs.* Spirit-dependence [10]. Flesh driven and focused *vs.* Spirit driven and focused. The 'tree' of your own knowledge and understanding *vs.* the Tree of Life. So today, as you are becoming one who truly lays your life down in Him in death, [11] so do you become increasingly united with Him 'in Spirit'. This is the victory to overcome in the seated realms ... the triumphant state where you are seated by the King **as** a king. [12]

It is through the finished work of the Cross that there is now the free right to **pass** through. The very right to step over the impassable chasm [13] that is between Heaven and earth. Free to 'go in and out' … just as you please [14]. The Gap has now been bridged; [15] and today, here and now, you can engage and enter, interact and experience, these wondrous Eternal realms of God. And in Him, as a people, being ever built up and equipped and made most Powerful. A people 'made' able to **shift** and move reality as you walk this earth. [16]

Such is the word '**Ekklesia**' … *ie;* Church Government. For the Christian Church is not contained by the 'four walls' of a building, nor that of the vision or control of man. Nor is it driven by the zeal of the flesh, or the methods or the ways of this world. For the Weapons of our warfare are not carnal but **Mighty in God** for pulling down strongholds. [17]

Throughout the generations, the Christian Church has held a 'Salvation message' that peaks at the vision of 'going into Heaven when I die'. But **death is not your saviour** — Christ Jesus is! Christ Jesus Himself is the Door. Therefore, the reality of this is found as one *willingly* lays down their life, only to here, 'pick it up again' in the realms of Everlasting Life [18]. Passing through He who is the Christ … as one *standing* [19] before the very Person of God. Even to here: 'abide' and 'remain' and 'have your being' [20]. For such never leave His Abiding Presence; and are made most Victorious, Triumphant … and **Conquerors** in the Lord. [21]

*The perfect intertwining of Heaven and earth in **he** who believes.*

Truth is, the way to bring Heaven to earth is first be one who goes into Heaven; into the Eternal realms, into the very Kingdom realms of Heaven. Even then as one 'aggressively' [22] laying hold of that of which Christ has aggressively laid hold of for you [23]. Laying hold of the Kingdom and the Promises … as one who '**thrusts**' out the Will of God on earth [24]. It is through the Blood that you have gained full right of access, and so then by the Spirit of the Lord … shall you be taken; shall you be ever captured up in Him 'in Spirit' [25]. And live your life intimately engaged in these realms of God as you still walk this earth.

The vehicle is the Spirit of God: the staging place ... the very sought after Presence of the Lord. And the destination is unto the very realms of Heaven's Wonders. The reality of these things are simply found through an open heart [26], a heart that honestly asks and truly inquires. A heart that is ever turned in affection and love in open and diligent pursuit. And through naturally developed spirit-to-Spirit connection — in the Joy and Presence of the Lord — do you 'wait' in the transit station postured to be taken [27]. Therefore, never belittle outpoured Revelations of the Lord; for Encounters of Revelation are Encounters in the very Person of God: spirit, soul, mind, and body. For all realms of the human condition are made able to engage the very Person of God ... to they who believe.

A side note: Become intimate in God. Intimacy is the root to Power and Authority. Intimacy ... to 'Know' God ... as one part of the Kingdom of Heaven. And what is built and established here steps through you to the blessing of the nations.

TO 'SEE' AND TO 'ENTER'

In the beginning of John chapter 3, we have the account of Jesus speaking to Nicodemus. He, a greatly learned man and a teacher of Israel. However, as He spoke, Jesus said things that were so far outside his 'linear' mind ... so far outside his earth-bound comprehension. Hence Jesus responded to him saying, *"How do you not understand these things?"* [28]

It was in **truth and in honesty of heart** that Nicodemus came to Jesus in the first place. Due to the undeniable signs and miracles that were shaking the nation of Israel. So he came at night, deeply stirred in heart ... and approached Jesus 'in truth'.

Jesus said to him, *"Except a man be born again, he cannot **see** the Kingdom of God"* [29]. And He continued and said, *"Except a man be born of water and of the Spirit, he cannot **enter** into the Kingdom of God"* [30]. Do you recognise Jesus' focus here? Do you yet notice just how much Jesus' Gospel — and the lifestyle He personally led — laid firm emphasis on 'entering' and 'seeing'? [31] And what does Jesus say about becoming as like a little child? ... *"Truly I tell you, unless you change and become like little children, you will never **enter** the Kingdom of Heaven"*

32. So, the basis of **walking in open demonstration** of the Glories of God, is first becoming one who walks where Jesus is now ... **in Heaven** ... and 'beholding Him in His Glory'. *33*

The early Church understood these things and were an unstoppable force through the Power of the Spirit of God. But over the years that followed: the 'love' of the many went cold *34*, and the Body of Christ shifted its focus away from the things of the Spirit ... unto that of law, works, and deeds *35*. That is, earthly flesh-dependence and self-righteousness, and to that of looking unto man; with no longer a heart set personally unto the Father *36*. Therefore ... the '**Lampstand**'; the Crowning and the Secret Naming; the Rod of Iron; and even the sitting upon the Throne of Glory *37* ... became **lost to them**.

> *'Passover' is the Blood shed unto Salvation. But the purpose is always the Spirit*[38]. *It is the Spirit that takes you into the Promises and the Power — ie; your Destiny. Through both 'water' and 'Spirit' you now have fundamental right and capacity to 'enter' and engage the Kingdom of Heaven — the Fire and the Glory — powerfully as you walk this earth.*

To this, Paul states, *"Are you so foolish? After beginning by means of the Spirit, are you now trying to finish by means of the flesh?"* [39] And he would continue elsewhere, *"Since you have been raised with Christ, set your heart on things above, where Christ is, seated at the right hand of God."* [40]

In continuing, Jesus said to Nicodemus, *"Flesh gives birth to flesh, but* **Spirit *gives birth to spirit***" [41]. Or another way of saying, *"Those born of the Spirit **is spirit**"* ... meaning, is alive in the Spirit. And to such who enter into the Mystery of the Spirit, they are **like the wind** ... *"You hear its sound, but you can't tell where it comes from or where it is going"* [42]. In truth, I tell you, *"We speak of what we know, and we testify to what we have **seen**, but still you people do not accept our testimony"* [43]. And finishing, Jesus said, *"I have spoken to you of earthly things and you do not believe; how then will you believe if **I speak of Heavenly things**?"* [44]

So then, the question is, are you yet able to see just how much God wishes to show, to tell, and to impart to you of the very Kingdom of Heaven? [45] There is the Gospel message ... yes, but **then there**

are also the <u>realms</u> of which the Gospel speaks; preparing you *able* to function and enter [46]. And the people who honestly and truly respond, come and stand here fully unified in Christ Jesus; [47] releasing the Glory, the Awe, and the Wonder of God on earth [48]. Another way to describe this is, *"Authentic Christianity"* ... the entering into the fullness of why Christ came.

Scripture:
This is what we speak, not in words taught us by human wisdom but in words **taught** by the Spirit, explaining spiritual realities with Spirit-taught words. *(1 Corinthians 2:13 NIV)*

Truth is, that there has always remained hostility against such things. And due to a lack of understanding *(destroyed by* [49]*)* the 'birds of the air' come and steal that of which was given [50]. And the *Scoffer* speaks [51] and the ridicule and persecution comes ... and many of whom have heard, quickly cast aside these precious things [52]. And in the exact same way; the cares and desires of this world creep in and choke the Living and dynamically active Life that is welling up within [53]. And here the believers remain 'unfruitful' of the very Glory of God revealed [54]. But to they who receive these things deeply to heart, to they of whom diligently treasure and pursue, so too do they reap a hundredfold — in this life and in the life to come. [55]

Then in ending the conversation, Jesus says to Nicodemus, *"No man has ascended up to Heaven, but he that came down from Heaven, even the Son of man **who is <u>IN</u> Heaven**."*

Do you yet realise, that Jesus lived and functioned, co-abiding in Heaven as He walked this earth? This, the 'walking according to the Spirit' ... with His heart bent on such [56] ... the hearing and the seeing. Therefore, there remains a great difference between walking according to the flesh to that of walking according to the Spirit [57]. For they who live according to the flesh; are flesh-motivated, flesh-dependant ... and flesh-encaged [58]. But they who live according to the Spirit sit in the realms of Life at the right hand of God — co-reigning as 'shareholders' in His Glory and Power. [59]

Such is the Power of praise ... and a lifestyle of prayer and fasting. The daily laying all things upon the Alter and passing through the Door [60]. For they who come ... eat liberally of the Tree of Life. Entering into and drawing deeply from the City of Bliss. [61]

CEASE THE SUFFERINGS
The purpose of Jesus coming to earth is to destroy the works of the *Enemy* [62]. Freeing people from suffering and setting them in the realms of the active and dynamic Salvation of the Lord. [63]

The flesh is the lowest form of man. Therefore, in taking these matters deeply to heart, so it shall be as though a veil has fallen from your eyes — as you step into a whole other world. And before, where you could see only buildings, trees, grass, and the physical world; now have you stepped through into the Eternal and Glorious realms of the Kingdom of Heaven. And here interact, function ... and have your being.

Blood to Spirit: Presence to Power.

It is Satan who constantly seeks to bring you *under* his feet. Hence the 'birds' come ... hence the 'birds' peck and pester [64]. However, in stark contrast, it is the very Person of Jesus in your life, who desires to **rise you up Above like an eagle** *(as 'kings' over the air)*. Therefore come, shake off these things of the earth; and become one who co-reigns and is co-seated with Him. In this, your Original Place of Dominion and Power [65] ... with all things under your feet [66]. Such is God's Purpose concerning all who love the Lord.

KING OF KINGS AND LORD OF LORDS
In reference to the opening Scripture, Christ Jesus is King of kings, and He rules over and above the kings of the earth. But it's most important to realise, that in Him also ... have you been given a 'Secret Name' [67] and Place in Him to function as 'king' and 'priest' as well. And this is your fundamental Birthright, and the underlying Purpose and Calling for all who are called by His Name.

Jesus has not made you a slave but has anointed you king; called **by** Him to sit 'as one' on the Throne of God with Him. No contradiction — no separation — **unified** one in Him [68]. That is His Purpose, and that is your Destiny and Calling. Now it can be all the more clearly seen, that Jesus isn't 'King of slaves', nor is He 'King of servants'… but He 'King of kings' and 'Lord of lords' [69]. Therefore come, and receive this precious Word for your own life personally, and step further into this of your Divine sonship and Inheritance [70]. And allow it to be so … ever posturing and setting yourself in His Presence … where God continually works to reveal Himself and make His Word alive in you [71]. Even here right in the midst of whatever you are facing in life.

On a side note: Many Bibles translate this word 'king' as 'kingdom' or a 'kingdom of people' [72]. *However, this might have been true in the Old Testament* [73] *… but in the New, we are not a 'kingdom of people' but part of the Kingdom of Heaven. Therefore today, as true kings — co-reigning and co-seated with Jesus — so do we also release and set to charge* [74] *this very same Kingdom on earth* [75]. *Even as 'priests', are you a gateway, or a portal of the Kingdom of God for your people. It is true that one of these visions leave the believer flesh-dependant and earth-bound. But so too is it true, that the other elevates and seats the believer rightly and correctly with Jesus at the right hand of God.*

Jesus lives in the realm of 'Prayer' … in the Wondrous and Eternal realms of God. So the truth is, in order to be truly successful in prayer, one needs also to step up and abide in these realms of Power. Therefore, if you can truly learn to treat all things rescinded compared to this of dwelling in His Holy Presence, *ie;* abandon yourself unto the Cross. Then as a 'lord' in His eyes … **so shall He be Lord in yours**.

PRAYER

For the believer … prayer, for the most part, typically has been a vision of going to God in times of need; then going back to normal life. However, this approach has always left the believer ill-equipped and behind the 'curved ball' rather than in front of it. Whilst Jesus' Prayer is always about Abiding in union one with Him where He is [76] — and living in open experience.

What is prayer? 'Ask, seek, and knock'. Prayer is in the '**asking**' … it is a lifestyle of asking [77]. Prayer is not only seeking God only when problems arise, but a lifestyle full of meaningful dialogue and exchange. Prayer is also in the '**seeking**' … the seeking the Face of God. Seeking the Presence of the Person of the Most High manifest in your life, *ie;* the realness of Him. His Presence manifest … meaning, the reality of the Kingdom of Heaven experienced and richly resting upon your person.

Prayer is not in the staying where you are, but in the stepping on through deeper into these Wonders and Eternal realms of God. Prayer is also in the '**knocking**' … the knocking on the Door. And being a people who pass on through into that of which has already been made open. So recognise, that a break in 'prayer' is a break from Bliss. A break from the wondrous ministering and Empowering Presence of God.

Scripture:
I do not **pray** for these alone, but also for those who will believe in Me through their word; [I pray] that they all may be one, as You, Father, are in Me, and I in You; that they also may be **one in Us**, that the world may believe that You sent Me. And the glory which You gave Me I have given them, that they may be one just as We are one: I in them, and You in Me; that they may be made perfect in one [**brought to complete unity in Us**], and that the world may know that You have sent Me, and have loved them as You have loved Me.
Father, I desire that they also whom You gave Me may be **with me where I am** [in Heaven], and that they may **behold** [see and experience] my Glory which You have given Me; for You loved Me before the foundation of the world. *(John 17:20-24 NKJV/NIV (John 3:13 NKJV))*

There are many different prayers that a person can have. And many of them honourable and most valuable. But unless you can come to respond to the most deepest Heart's Prayer of the Father [78] then fundamentally there is a misalignment … a misplacement. A failing to come into the Place under which the Goodness of God liberally pours. [79]

Therefore, to become one who walks in the Power and Glory of God, even as a person who 'wields' the Spirit of God in your hands. Then you need to greatly honour and give firm place for the Spirit of the Lord *(the union, the hearing and seeing, the learning and being raised)*. And when you do pray, always recognise where you are from ... and **who you are in God**.

The greatest prayer and motive of your soul needs always be unto hearing and seeing the Father ... *ie;* to be 'in Spirit'. Not just a people only talking about Him but a people living in a perpetual state of meeting [80]. Jesus abides in the realm of Prayer; therefore, to be truly effective and powerful in prayer *(ie; one who manifests the Glory of God on earth)* one needs first stand where He stands. To set your heart in Him is to stand in Him; the truth of you and the love of you — 'in Spirit' — standing and abiding with Him. For true it is, that a break in prayer is a break in God. For effectual prayer always comes from a state of abiding and remaining in Him ... just as the Son. Does this make sense?

To liberally and freely receive from the Father you first need to be with Him, not far away in your heart and thoughts, but — **in Him** — engaged. There is the prayer, *"Be healed in Jesus Name ... I bind ... I rebuke"* ... and this is a right prayer. But if you are not in an attitude of prayer, *ie;* in the 'realms' of Prayer, who are you praying to? For in the very same way that there is a word, but there also needs to be the realness of that word ... otherwise it's just 'lip service'. Anyone can say anything at any time, but whose heart is truly in the Lord?

There are those who are healed without any relationship in the Lord. But now that you have relationship — there is now the calling unto perfect union.

Do you remember the time when Jesus congratulated and celebrated Peter by saying, *"Blessed are you Peter for this was not revealed to you by flesh and blood, but by my Father in Heaven"* [81]. I tell you, in our flesh we are just foolish and frail creatures ... but, **IN the Spirit** ... not even the Gates of Hades can prevail. For so it is ... that in Christ Jesus, we have been given the very Keys of Heaven in our hands. So maybe now we have gained a more clearer picture of what it means to be 'in the Spirit'. For as Paul would say, *"We don't know how to pray but as the Spirit groans within our belly so do we speak."* [82]

Jesus never said to His Disciples that He was the Christ ... and why do you think that was? But that He wanted them to get it directly **from the Spirit of God**; even from of the very 'Word that proceed out of the mouth of God' [83]. For we are — by no means — purposed of God to remain separate to Him as orphans ... but to live unified ... live as **Child of the Most High**. [84]

The calling is always to the coming up in Him. Even to become a people who might increasingly **hear and see** the Lord. And from this Place of Presence so shall you be made a most powerful people [85]. And why do you think trials and troubles come? That we truly might learn to draw our hearts like roots ... ever deeper unto the Father. Not in places where you were from, but in **the Place where He is**. Therefore, don't wait until true hardship comes before you decisively choose to seek His Face [86]. For how will you win ... how will you learn to be Triumphant?

When you think of Life and Spirit, even the very Peace and Presence of God, do you realise that they are like a 'substances' of Heaven that you can physically pour out? [87] And so it is, that they who in themselves — choose — operate in realms of Heaven on a **whole other level**. But those who still remain flesh-driven, draw still only from human comprehension: human capacity, vision, and reserves. Truly, it is the Keys of Heaven that are Purposed of God to be in your hands. For Christ Jesus was crucified, and went unto the Father, that the very Anointing and Authority that He walked in [88] ... you may now also.

> *"Lord, I really appreciate all people, and I really appreciate leaders and teachers; the gifted and the talented, the knowledgeable and the wisdom of man. But what I really desire and long for, above all things, is to walk in these realities. Even to see the outpouring of the Spirit, the Power and Salvation of the Lord, poured out upon all the nations. Countering death and all the works of Satan."*

There are many prayers that one can hold, and God Himself is a *fulfiller* of **dreams**. However, to where your vision is directed, is where you are going. And to that of which you hold dear, is that of which you **draw close**. And if it is unto the Dreams of the Father fulfilled ... then **so it shall be**.

WORD — SPIRIT — MANIFESTATION

There is the Word of God, and then there is the Revelation that Word and the Spirit brings. However, what you want as a people, is to be **one who manifests what both the Word and the Spirit speaks**. And such are they who worship God in Spirit *and* in Truth; for here one begins to manifest on earth the very Kingdom of Heaven.

There is the Love of God, and many can quote Scriptures that speak of such things. But who truly lives in open living experience of the Love and Joy of the Lord? And that is the very purpose of faith. The **purpose** of faith is for the *manifestation* of what you are believing for. Faith is not ever purposed to be just a 'knowledge' … but an open and physical reality for **all to see**. Therefore, so it is most true, anyone can speak but who can manifest?

*Encounters come through invitation; a humble heart that **asks**. The Blood and the finished work of the Cross is God's open Invitation to you. Hence today, you are simply responding with a 'yes' and an 'amen' to the Heart and Dreams of the Father.*

Jesus is the Word made flesh, and through Him the Spirit came. Now together — by the Word **and** by the Spirit — does the Kingdom manifest. All things expressed in the Word of God are purposed for what is written in the Word to become 'flesh' and 'walk' amongst us. But how does this happen? You first go to Him … you first sit at Jesus' feet … you first seek daily Encounter. This is your first and fundamental 'Ordination' given of the Lord: that you be '**with Him**' where He is [89]. Not in other things, but here with Him.

THE EKKLESIA

Scripture:
I have not sent these prophets, yet they ran. I have not spoken to them, yet they prophesied. But if they had **stood in My counsel**, and had caused My people to hear My words, then they would have turned them from their evil way. *(Jeremiah 23:21-22 NKJV)*

Over the generations of the Church, there has always been a *dividing* line. A struggle reconciling flesh and Spirit … law and

Grace ... works and Rest. And when you think of the word 'Ekklesia' — the Church reigning, the believer's fundamental spiritual Authority — was it ever purposed to be rooted in the flesh of man ... or the Power of the Spirit? The Spirit of course.

In the same way, is the Church's Authority and Power purposed to be rooted in weapons of this earth or the Weapons of the Spirit? The answer of course is the Spirit. Even as mentioned before, *"The weapons we fight with are not the weapons of the world. On the contrary, they have divine power to demolish strongholds"* [90]. So, to be one truly successful, the answer always is the Presence of God. The answer always is His Abiding Love and the Glory of the Spirit. Ever one crossing over and walking in Heavenly Places of Glory in Him.

What does it say in Scripture? ... *"My sheep **hear** and follow my voice"* [91]. Therefore, as a king of the Great King, so are your eyes and ears firmly fixed in Him. Satan chose independence from God. But the children of God unite themselves one in Him ... spirit, soul, mind, and flesh. And as one in Him, in perfect union, so are you also then one who **releases** **the Spirit of the Lord**.

"Way maker, miracle worker, promise keeper ... Light in the darkness, my God, that is who you are."

Bless you ... in this year of 2020 vision.

Appendix:

1. Psalm 110:1-2, ***2.*** John 15:4-11, ***3.*** Zechariah 3:7, ***4.*** 1 Corinthians 2:9-10, ***5.*** John 4:23, ***6.*** Luke 12:49, ***7.*** Exodus 13:21, ***8.*** John 3:3, 3:5, 3:13 *NKJV*, 10:9, 17:24, Matthew 7:13-14, 7:21, 18:3, 19:23-26, 23:13, ***9.*** Genesis 2:17, 3:19, ***10.*** Genesis 1:26, ***11.*** Luke 9:23, John 10:17, Galatians 2:20, ***12.*** Revelation 3:17-22, ***13.*** Genesis 3:24, Revelation 2:7, 22:1-2, 22:14-15, ***14.*** John 10:27, John 10:4, John 14:3-4, John 10:9, ***15.*** John 14:6, ***16.*** Mark 4:41, Zechariah 3:7, ***17.*** 2 Corinthians 10:4, Exodus 14:14, 33:14, 23:28, ***18.*** John 10:17, Romans 8:5-9, Genesis 2:17, ***19.*** Zechariah 3:7, Jeremiah 23:21, Matthew 18:10, ***20.*** Acts 17:28, John 15:4-11, ***21.*** Revelation 3:5, 3:12, 3:21, Revelation 22:14, Joshua 10:7-

8, **22.** Matthew 11:12 *NKJV*, **23.** Philippians 3:12, 2 Corinthians 1:20, **24.** Matthew 6:10, Revelation 2:26-27, **25.** Revelation 1:10, 4:1-2, **26.** Revelation 3:20, **27.** Revelation 1:10, 4:1, 2 Corinthians 12:2, Psalm 27:4, Isaiah 64:1-4, **28.** John 3:10, **29.** John 3:3, **30.** John 3:5, **31.** John 5:19, Luke 5:16, Matthew 16:17, **32.** Matthew 18:3, **33.** John 17:24, **34.** Matthew 24:12, Revelation 2:4, 3:16, **35.** Matthew 23:13, **36.** John 5:44, **37.** Revelation 2-3, **38.** Exodus 7:16, Exodus 10:25-26, 19:1-6, **39.** Galatians 3:3, **40.** Colossians 3:1, **41.** John 3:6, **42.** John 3:8, Isaiah 60:8, 55:12, **43.** John 3:11, **44.** John 3:12, **45.** 1 Corinthians 2:7, John 16:14, 14:21, **46.** Revelation 22:14 *NKJV*, 1 Corinthians 2:13-16, Luke 16:10, **47.** John 17:20-24, **48.** Isaiah 64:1-4, 41:15, Daniel 10:12, **49.** Hosea 4:6, **50.** Matthew 13:4, **51.** Exodus 16:2, Numbers 14:1-3, **52.** Matthew 13:5-6, **53.** John 4:14, **54.** Matthew 13:7, **55.** Matthew 13:8, 19:29, **56.** Isaiah 11:3-4, Revelation 3:17-18, **57.** Galatians 5:13-25, **58.** Genesis 3:19, **59.** Genesis 1:26, **60.** John 10:9, 14:6, **61.** Revelation 22:14 TPT, Psalm 110:2, **62.** 1 John 3:8, **63.** John 17:3, Romans 10:13, Exodus 14:13-14, 33:14, Psalm 91, 62:1-2, 27:1-6, 50:23, **64.** Luke 4:13, **65.** Genesis 1:26-27, **66.** Psalm 110:1, Revelation 2:26-27, Psalm 2:7-9, **67.** Revelation 2:17, **68.** John 17:20-24, John 14:30b, **69.** Psalm 82:6, 110:1-2, Revelation 2:26-27, **70.** Romans 8:19, **71.** John 1:14, Romans 8:19, John 14:21, 15:5-7, **72.** Revelation 1:5-6, 5:9-10 *(NIV vs. KJV. A side note: the NIV translates the New Testament from a modernised Greek translation dated from the 1800s. However, the KJV translates from the ancient Greek. 'King' and 'priest' is the right wording. But a 'kingdom of people', this is an Old Testament reality and not the New Testament picture. The ruling in Heavenly Places, the co-seated as joint heirs ... not in the flesh but in the Spirit.)*, **73.** Exodus 19:6, **74.** Zechariah 3:7, **75.** Mark 1:14-16, **76.** John 17:20-24, **77.** Psalm "Ask me and I will give you the nations", **78.** Matthew 6:9-13, John 17:21, 24, **79.** John 4:14, John 7:37-39, **80.** Exodus 33:11, **81.** Matthew 16:17, **82.** Romans 8:27, **83.** Deuteronomy 8:3, **84.** John 1:12, **85.** Isaiah 41:14-16, **86.** Exodus 33:18-23, 24:9-11, 1 Kings 19:11-13, Isaiah 64:1-4, John 17:20-24, Revelation 1:10-17, 2 Chronicles 7:14, **87.** Matthew 10:13, John 6:63, John 20:22, **88.** John 14:12, **89.** Mark 3:13, Exodus 19:20, **90.** 2 Corinthians 10:4, **91.** John 10:27

Dated: 1/1/20

COMMAND A HARVEST

19. Command a Harvest (#102)
ROAR OF A LION

Several opening Scriptures:
1. **Habakkuk 2:1**: *"I will **stand** at my watch and station myself on the ramparts; I will **look** to see what He will say to me."*
2. **Zechariah 3:7**: *"Thus says the LORD of hosts: 'If you will walk in My ways, and if you will keep My command, then **you** shall also judge My house, and likewise have charge of My courts; I will give you places to walk Among these who stand here.'"*
3. **Matthew 8:9**: *"For I also am a man **under authority**, having soldiers under me. And I say to this one, 'Go,' and he goes; and to another, 'Come,' and he comes; and to my servant, 'Do this,' and he does it."*
4. **Psalm 82:6**: *I said, "**You are gods**, and all of you are children of the Most High."*
5. **Revelation 17:14**: *"He is Lord of lords and King of kings (you and I)."*
6. **Revelation 1:5-6**: *"Jesus Christ, the faithful witness, the **first born** from the dead, and the ruler over the kings of the earth. To Him who loved us and washed us from our sins in His own blood, and **has made us kings**."*

In Christ we are no longer sheep *lost* in the wilderness, for we have **found** our Lord. Now we are being **led by Him** and raised to rule [1]. Raised as lions over all powers and all authorities: on, below, or above the earth. Lamb to lion ... humble but strong, lifted up on 'wings' *(Spirit)* like eagles [2] *('kings' in the Dominion of God)*. As lords and kings over all that this world presents, and all that comes against, for we are called ... and chosen ... and faithful. [3]

Jesus is not King of slaves, nor is He Lord of servants; but King of kings and Lord of lords [4]. He is not distant from any of us, nor is He elevated so high as to be out of reach. But He is *with* you, with His hands outstretched that **you be with Him**. Unified in place and station; as a 'lord' in His eyes just as He is Lord in yours.

ROAR OF A LION
Over the last several years, the Spirit of God has been teaching me to *roar* like a lion. However, this 'roar' hasn't been given through

good times, but as I sought the Lord — all the same — through difficult and hard times. [5]

As you know, 'seeking the Presence of God' — *ie;* personal visits of the Person of God and to be captured up in Him — is central to my life. And in this 'open, set, and sole purpose of soul' do I prefer not to look at failings, problems, or desired things — but always unto Presence. Always unto the Fire and Glory of God [6]. So in this, He teaches me things that man cannot [7] — for I am by no means Fatherless [8] — but **child** of God. Hence therefore, here in Him, He Graces me able to walk through all things, even then to turn and face them and **roar like a lion**.

> *"On the Lord's Day I was **IN the Spirit**, and I heard behind me a loud voice like a trumpet blast."* [9]

God desires each one of us to walk in Places flesh cannot. Places where man cannot take you, only the Spirit of the Lord [10]. However, if your heart isn't directed 'in the Spirit' ... but always unto other things [11], how will you ever engage or be taken? How will you ever be lifted up and established?

Now it is Jesus who said, that 'true worshipers' will worship God in Truth and 'in Spirit'. Even that God Himself personally is **actively seeking out such as these** [12]. Therefore, to 'stand on the rampart' and harken earnestly unto His Voice; [13] then as the Shepherd ... shall Jesus lead you in and out finding Pasture *(ie; Divine Understanding, Strength, Provision, and Glory* [14]*)*. That is, He will lead you in and out of Places man cannot take you ... only the Person of Jesus. And this is the Invitation that has been extended to you: to *"Sit at my right hand"* [15], or in another place, *"Be diligent to enter my Rest"* [16]. For the Anointing of the Lord is given only of the Lord. [17]

To do life only with knowledge alone does not cause you to be Victorious. But, however, to worship 'in Spirit', *ie;* in Divine and Living Encounters in the Person of God [18], then so shall you also walk in things that *flesh* cannot. Even in realms of Dominion and Power unfathomable to the human mind. To this where you put down all sin and wrongdoing ... and in Delight of Him, close all doorways unto the *Evil One*. As the Lord continues to reveal Himself to you in the Holiness of His Presence. [19]

Love releases kingship ...

DOMINION OVER LIVESTOCK:

As we go through this, I would like to share a testimony of something that happened in line with the subject of this chapter. A testimony that is not only purposed for me alone ... but for the Church as a whole. And normally I wouldn't be so comfortable in sharing certain aspects, but due to the physical nature of what happened, I realise that it's purposed to be shared fully and openly.

Personally, I refer to the experience as a *"Thrusting out of the Spirit"*. But even this wording, I was not comfortable to share openly. But now I recognise and can picture it as: *"Through a word spoken from my mouth, I thrusted out the 'Sword' of the Spirit of God"* [20]. I '**roared**' the Word of God and the Spirit responded. And it is to this very thing of which the Lord is trying to lead us all into. These 'lessons' purposed to equip so as to become a people who **trigger the Outpouring**.

Theme Scripture:
Then God said, "Let Us make man in Our image, according to Our likeness; let them have dominion over the fish of the sea, over the birds of the air, and over the cattle ['**livestock**'], over all the earth and over every creeping thing that creeps on the earth." So God created man in His own image; in the image of God He created him; male and female He created them. *(Genesis 1:26-27 NKJV)*

Over the last two chapters, the focus has been on *"Dominion over the birds of the air and the fish of the sea"*. And as discussed, we noticed just how these realms of the 'air and sea' are not readily accessible by the flesh. Nor are they places able to be truly *dominated*. But they are however, 'accessible' in the Spirit, and are places *underneath* the Dominion of God ... the Dwelling Place of God. And in addition to this, not only are you set in Dominion in God over these physical realms of the 'birds of the air' and 'the fish of the sea' ... but also in **Dominion over what they spiritually represent**. That is, Dominion over all powers above, below, and on the earth.

Now, in continuing in this theme Scripture verse, do you notice the word '**cattle**', *ie;* Dominion over livestock? What then do you think livestock represents? ... but Dominion over provisions, finances, and livelihood. [21]

So in this thought, let's begin. But before we do so, recognise that the Purpose of the Blood is *sanctification*. Sanctification unto Salvation [22] ... yes, but also most significantly: **sanctification as *priests* in order to pass through** [23]. Not to stay where you are but the continually entering in. [24]

The original Temple of God is not on earth but is in Heaven [25] — with Dominion given of God [26]. Therefore, love releases kingship ... that is, a heart ever **set unto union** in Him [27]. The Word of God is the firm foundation ... however, its Purpose is always unto manifestation. Even as is the Blood of Jesus; the Purpose of the Blood is always unto the **Outpouring of the Spirit upon all flesh**. [28]

> "*I am the door. If anyone enters by Me, he will be saved ... **and** ... will go in and out and find pasture*" [29]. To **believe** is only just the start: **Victory** comes by going in and out.

TWO REALMS OF PRAYER

There are two realms of prayer: In the Presence of God ... on the floor of your own home. And the other; in the Presence of God on the floor of **His Home** ... upon the 'Sea of Sapphire'. [30]

The purpose of the Blood has **always** been unto the 'passing through'. Passing through the Veil and functioning from right within the House of God [31]. To no longer remain orphans or foreigners ... who only observes the Temple of God from outside [32]. But one **who enters**: worshipping and seeking the Lord of Glory from right within the Holy Place. This not on earth, nor a place made by human hands [33] ... but in Heaven, right in the Presence of God. And to they who live in the realms of the 'Spirit' also come to live in continual Experience of the Presence of the

Person of God in His Counsels [34] ... just as the Son. And of whom also live as a people, being continually captured up into the Mystery. [35]

The 'Holy Place' is a realm that is dwelt in as one decisively *chooses* to look through — **all things** [36] — in Christ Jesus [37]. The personally choosing to 'lay down your life' upon the Cross [38] *(and all its issues)* and continually **passing through He** — who is the Door — and entering in [39]. And the 'Holy of Holies' is a Place that is *beyond*. And they whom abide 'in the Spirit' so too are they continually taken. This Place being far beyond the definitions or the imaginations of man; [40] but are the realms of the continually hearing and seeing the Lord *(the heart-chatter)*. And it is here, in perfect union in Him [27], that you also come to **roar like a lion**. One made able to shake reality both in Heaven and on earth [41]. In the Heart of the Father: Courageous, Fearless, and Victorious ... able to release the Glory of God to action.

— *Spirit and Truth* —
— *King and Priest* —
— *Dominion and Power* —

A fundamental principle of Scripture: *God will show you secret things* [42] *as you enter the secret place. And taken by hand into Places where man cannot go* [43]. *Here, the hidden and concealed things shall be made plain and simple* [44] *as you step into a* ***whole*** *other reality as one clothed of God.* [45]

BY THE BLOOD ARE YOU MADE KING AND PRIEST

Referring to Revelation chapter one: What you see here, is how that — by the Blood — Christ Jesus **has made you king** and priest unto God [46]. It is called the 'rebirth' ... the being born again back into the **Dominion of God**. Not only being made 'Alive' again in the Spirit of God; but **re-established** in the realities of the seated, the realms of the Kingdom through the first born; He, the first 'Seed' of **many seeds** ... this by the Blood and by the Blood alone.

Then what we see, is how even in the early Church, there was a **'warring'** of flesh against the Spirit. Tares sown [47] causing shifts away from Grace back to law; the finished work of the Cross back unto one's own fleshly-capacity and comprehension [48]. And as we continue reading on into chapters two and three; we also see how their 'kingship' in God was being affected and on the edge of being *lost* to the early believers. The **Lampstand** removed from its place. [49]

Here Jesus started to use wording such as desiring to 'throw up' the people, 'vomit' them out of His belly [50]. Remove them from their Dominion in God ... the inner sanctum ... the inner Dwelling Place of Intimacy, Union, and Closeness in God. For just as was pictured in the Ark of the Covenant; the Glory of God is accessible **ONLY through the Blood** ... but the Blood was being trampled. [51]

Like in the Old Testament, the Temple of God was still the Temple of God when the Glory departed [52]. It was still the place of worship. But just not holding the Fire — the Presence of the Glory of God in their midst — retaining a far lesser version of what was destined and purposed for the nation. [53]

Today, it is the same, being 'physically' Alive in the Spirit — with the Door firmly open *welcoming* to come in — but a humbling is required, a submission — a 'first love' [54]. And this is why we need to be less interested in the structure or the appearance [55] of the 'building' ... and more interested in what is held within. [56]

In understanding this, we by **no means** wish to be a people of this vein. But a people truly embedded in the Heart and Purpose of the Father. And a people who are subsequently, truly made able — by Him — to '**Rule in the midst of our enemies**' [57]. Crossing over from the realms of 'mere mortal men' [58] unto the Immortal ... the perishing unto the Imperishable [59] ... the naked unto the being **clothed** in Glory. [45]

Revelation chapters two and three: Each of the Seven Letters to the Church present a need to '**repent**' and change. And they also contain additional layers, or facets, or attributes of the believer's 'kingship'. That is — your 'Crown', your 'Secret Name', your 'Iron Sceptre', your 'Morning Star' — and the being brought to sit upon the 'Throne'.

In the Beginning God's Word simply was: "Let Us make man in our Image." Then Satan came and spoke out his version ... his deception: "You can make yourself like God." Now, it is for us today, that God Himself is inviting you to come back, to "Come sit at my right hand". Another word for this is simply: "The Restoration." [60]

Recognise then the fundamental truth: *1.* The Blood has **birthed** you child of God. And *2.* the Blood is your **right of passage** to the pass through unto the Father [61]. Hence, you never need to *feel* worthy before you access [62]. You never need to feel righteous before you approach the Glory of God. But simply in recognition of the Power of the Blood, and choosing it in your heart — **right here, right where you are now** — to seek the personal Presence of God.

I tell you **this IS where your Strength lies** [63] and your ability to win. Not in yourself ... but **in Him**/ Even that you truly might be 'made' [64] Victorious and Triumphant in all things. As is said, *"I have swept away your offenses like the morning mist ... **return** to me for I have redeemed you"* [65]. So Power is in the returning. It is not in staying where you are, but setting your heart and purpose of soul upon the right hand of God. [66]

Now you are getting to understand a bit more about what it means to live by the **Spirit**. However, problems still remain because believers do not yet know how to '**wait**' [67] **in the Presence of the Lord** *(ie; in the 'Place of Prayer')*. Even becoming one who 'delights himself' in the Lord [68] — regardless of season. And abiding in the Counsels and the Authority of God to bring lasting change. For flesh gives birth to flesh ... **but** ... it is the Spirit that gives birth to Spirit. [69]

Come and learn to '**practice**' Presence; like a musician his music or a dancer her dance, come practice **seeking the Presence** of God. For the very moment you turn your heart unto the Lord, you are **in Him** ... you are in His Mighty Presence. So wait ... just be patient and wait ... and tell the Lord that you truly honour this Place. And long to have His manifest Presence come mightily upon you ... in Jesus Name.

— Pray the Blood —
— Release the Spirit —
— Command a blessing! —

Five Scripture verses:
1. So He drove out the man; and He placed cherubim at the east of the garden of Eden, and a flaming sword which turned every way, to **guard the way to the Tree of Life**. *(Genesis 3:24 NKJV)*
2. He who has an ear, let him hear what the Spirit says to the churches. To him who overcomes I will **give to <u>eat</u> from the Tree of Life**, which is in the midst of the Paradise of God. *(Revelation 2:7 NKJV)*
3. On either side of the river, was the Tree of Life, which bore twelve fruits, each tree yielding its fruit every month. The **leaves of the Tree were for the <u>healing</u> of the nations**. *(Revelation 22:2 NKJV)*
4. I am the door. If anyone enters by Me, he will be saved, and will **go in and out and find pasture**. *(John 10:9 NKJV)*
5. And these signs will follow those who believe: In My name they will cast out demons; they will speak with new tongues; they will take up serpents; and if they drink anything deadly, it will by no means hurt them; they will **lay hands on the sick, and they will <u>recover</u>**. *(Mark 16:17-19 NKJV)*

SWORD OF THE SPIRIT

Be no longer satisfied standing before life and its issues with just the Helmet of your Salvation [70]. Standing there as one 'naked' [71] and bare in your underwear. But instead, firmly make choice to rise up in the Power and Fire of the Spirit of God. [72]

Become a people truly '**<u>sick</u>**' of death; sick of disease and the works of the *Enemy*. And allow God to dress you in the full Armour of God [73]. Authority is given of God [74] and so too is the Mantle of your Anointing [75]. Now, where there is death, do you release the Life and Spirit of God [76] … not only to heal but to make whole [77]. God desires to give you an '**rod of iron**' to strike the land, just as Christ Jesus received; does He desire to give you Authority over the nations. [78]

Was Christ Jesus raised again Triumphant and Victorious over sin, death, and the grave; that you, as His people, might still remain crushed under Satan? No, by no means, for we identify with His death and are raised again in Power. As a people walking in the Resurrection Power of the Son over all things. [79]

Therefore, we look not unto present problems but unto the Presence of the Person of God. This being your **first and fundamental Ordination** in Christ Jesus — to be with Him — where He is [80]. The 'Iron Sceptre' of Divine Authority given only through deeply treasured and intimate relationship in the Person of God [81]. So therefore, earnestly 'repent' … and come back into that of your 'First Love'. [82]

The Ekklesia of the Church *(Divine Authority of God)* is not a people who operate out of flesh in the name of God … but a people who operate out of the Spirit. Even in 'Divine Governance' releasing Heaven and the Will of God on earth. The Rod of Iron, this Power and Authority given of Heaven, comes through ever-deepening union. Valuing union in the Father more than cares and desires; praise and worshipping Him more than fears. However now — **as one in Him** [83] — so shall you rise up speaking firmly to the 'mountains' saying, *"Be moved in Jesus Name."* [84]

The Holy Place IS the Abiding Place [85]. The being 'in the Spirit' [86] … and here *waiting* [87] in the Place of 'total acceptance' [88]. And here — in Him — living in enjoyment of the continual ministering Presence, Peace, and Joy of God. Divine Revelation, and the continued outpouring of the Wisdom and Knowledge of God [89] … even right in the face of the *Enemy* [90]. Such is the Salvation of the Lord. [91]

> **Revelation 2:26-27**: *"You shall rule them with a rod of iron."*
> **Psalm 82:6-8**: *"You are 'gods' … the nations are your inheritance."*
> **Matthew 16:18-19**: *"The gates of Hades shall not prevail against you."*

Do you realise that the Fruits of the Spirit [92] are tangible living realities of God for you to live in perpetual experience? These, the very 'residue' of being in Him … 'in Spirit'. The Love, the Joy, and the Peace of the Lord; the Forbearance, Kindness, Goodness, and

His Faithfulness ever resting upon you. And here in Him living as one postured: [93] continually being taken into the More. Into the Great Unknown behind the Curtain ... even the Holy of Holies. And these realities of God coming richly upon you as you simply express to the Lord — right where you are now — *"I seek Visitation" ... "I seek to Enter" ... "I seek Presence."*

It is such a Gift ... the Salvation of the Lord. The capacity to live in a continual state of Encounter in the Lord. Salvation isn't something of years ago ... but for today. Salvation is **now**! And the same gain a Gentleness of heart, a Self-Control, and a Knowledge of God that causes you to live your life Renewed. And to such as these, there is no law ... for you are standing in the very realms of God. [94]

So I ask, why wait for death before you enter Heaven? For the underlying Purpose of the Son is always to the walking in the Heavenly realms right now. This through the Blood and Blood alone ... through the Cross and triumphant Resurrection of the Son. And it is to this very thing that the Church has mostly forgotten *(ie; the 'misdirection')*; for Satan doesn't mind you becoming a Christian, so long as you never come to **know** who you truly are in Christ [95]. To Satan, it is okay for you to have a vision of going into Heaven when you die ... so long as you never bring Heaven to earth whilst you still live.

So in this, the *Enemy* sows misdirection; [96] in order to take your eyes off the **Glory Cloud** [97]. But so too is it most true — that now, through the shed Blood and the gifted Spirit — that you have gained full and perfect right of access to boldly approach the Presence of God. And not only stopping here but passing through the **Veil** [98]. And so truly, most very truly, the **Faith of the Son** is wrought through Divine Encounters in Him ... as one continuously lifted up in Him.

On a side note: The spirit of Religion sets the vision of the believer unto works and law [99]. *But it is the Spirit of the Lord, of whom seeks you to set your vision unto the Throne. Even unto the very Glory realms of the Person of God ... ie; the hearing and seeing. Not in presentation of a righteousness before man;* [100] *but* **as** *the Righteousness of God* [101]. *Made able to release the very same Spirit* and Salvation of the Lord for your people. For it is only by the Blood of Jesus that you are declared "The Righteous in Him", and in the Spirit made able to shift Heaven, and shake the very foundations of the earth. Therefore, strike the waters and pass on through. [102]

THE TESTIMONY

2 Kings 2:14 NKJV:
Then he took the **Mantle** of Elijah [Double Anointing] [103] that had fallen from him, and struck the water, and said, "Where is the LORD God of Elijah?" And when he also had **struck** the water, it was divided this way and that; and Elisha crossed over.

Matthew 6:32-33 NKJV
For after all these things the Gentiles seek. For your heavenly Father knows that you need all these things. But **seek first his kingdom** and his righteousness, and all these things will [shall be] be given to you as well.

Over the last several months I have been sharing photos of a tree set in a field. And through this testimony, I wish to share how the Spirit of God made this tree appear in the perfect shape of a **Dollar sign**. And it happened during a very stressful time; but there it was, after a word spoken unto the Lord ... a manifestation of God's response **both physically and spiritually**.

As I have mentioned before, trials and tribulations are sometimes allowed to remain, because God knows that **you need a fundamental core shift**. A shift whereby you might draw your roots deeper into the Tree of Life [104]. Deeper and more established able to bring the 'Healing Leaves' [105] to earth. Therefore, count them in all joy [106] ... like **Training ground for greatness**. For so shall God Himself personally lift you up raising the 'Standard' every time [107]. Not just for our lives alone, but for the nations.

Satan is in a totally defeated position, for everything that comes against is now converted Seven times restored [108]. And when he thinks he has won ... he has totally lost [109]. Therefore, let us be a people more established and more embedded in this of our Divine Place of Origins. No longer living as orphans anymore; but as true sons and daughters of the Living God [110]. For when you 'strike' the waters and pass on through, so do you bring with you and **release** the Glory of God for you and your people. [111]

Scripture:
I will stand my watch and set myself on the rampart, **and watch to see** what He will say to me, and what I will answer when I am corrected [taught, reproved, reprimanded, instructed]. *(Habakkuk 2:1 NKJV)*

The testimony: On the way to work there is a large shady tree that I like to park under and seek the Presence of the Lord each day. It is a most honoured place and time, specifically for opening myself up for Personal visits of the Person of God. And here I lean back in my seat; play some music, open my notebook and Bible, and posture myself to hear from the Lord journaling notes. I am very diligent about this, even first thing in the morning, and the Lord knows this ... so **He always comes**.

It is a very sacred and precious time for me, a deeply honoured and respectful place unto the Lord and **only** the Lord. Not for my needs, not for my cares ... but for the Lord. And here the Presence of the Lord always comes and alights my soul.

However, during this particular season of my life, I found myself being hounded by genuine fears regarding my finances, my family, and my future. For the last few years had been hard and the next years questionable. And you know, its ok to have fear in the form of careful consideration ... but not of a kind where **fear comes** as a spirit and **sits next to you.**

So I started saying to the Lord, *"You manage these issues, for I am here to seek the Presence of God."* And continuing after a while, coming each day, maybe over the next two or three weeks, this nagging fear **really persisted** ... so one day I got my back up.

As I said, sometimes there are serious and genuine issues that one can face, and serious decisions that need to be made. And at the same *('opportune' [112])* time, Satan can come and amplify them as though he is sitting right next to you. So after having enough ... I rose up in the Presence of the Lord and firmly said, *"Spirit of God* **YOU manage** *my finances,* **YOU manage** *my family, and* **YOU manage** *my future ... they are* **YOUR** *responsibility! My responsibility is to* **seek** *the Presence of God!"* [113] And you know what happened? As I looked up, I saw in the distance a tree ... a tree in the perfect shape of **a Dollar sign**. And I had to laugh! ... and said to the Holy Ghost, *"You have such a sense of humour."*

It may have always been there, I don't know. But right off in the distance there it was, this tree that perfectly represents the reply of the Lord ... in the physical form of 'Provision'.

You see, God is trying to teach me to **manifest Heaven** on earth. That is, to manifest from the realms and the 'economy' of Heaven onto this earth. Like Aaron's Staff ... *ie;* the bringing forth Life in hopeless and dead situations [114]. And it's a challenge, isn't it? It's a mind shift. The learning — in the face of genuine realities — to listen and respond to what both the Word and the Spirit is trying to teach.

What is fasting? But seeking breakthrough. It is a principle of God. A humbling of yourself that **God might heal the land** [115]. Now, you may or may not be able to fast food; but otherwise, it is a firm setting yourself apart unto the Lord. A humbling of yourself and what you know ... and giving yourself over in honour to hear, to receive, and to send out. It is a 'sacrifice', a laying down of life and its issues right before the Throne of God ... and here going through to step into the realms of Life [116]. And again, seeking breakthroughs in circumstances is not the 'pinnacle' of the vision. But always unto the **meeting of the very Person of God**.

A side note: We each have our prayers and dreams, but certainly so: God has His [117]. And in realising this ... and responding, so do you come into realms of Anointing and Authority that shake all the world [118]. God's Vision and Dreams are you Returning into [119]. Even the manifestation of your sonship [120]. And as you pursue ... oh, does God fight for you [121]. Even that you might be one who releases that fight! [122]

Personally, I do not wish to be one of whom Jesus says, *"Oh you of little faith."* But in myself, make active place ... continuously allowing God to cause shift and bring change. Even that I might be one who openly hears and sees and receives. Even raised up able to say to the storms of life that come, *"Be still"* and there be a great calm ... as the very earth itself responds to the words of your mouth. [123]

It is Satan who seeks only: to reduce you into your basic elements ... fully beneath him. But it is God who seeks to Restore you: back up into the Divine Realms of your sonship ... as Child of the Living God.

Reflect for a moment on these two Scripture verses. These two that I drew upon and intertwined when praying this prayer. The one in the book of Kings, *"Where is the Lord God of Elijah?"* And the other, *"Seek first the Kingdom of Heaven and His righteousness and all these other things will be added and given unto you as well."* [124]

There is real attitude in this prayer of Elisha. And it is to this 'attitude' that God has been gently leading me into over these last few years. However, I do keep this prayer most private 'cause of its apparent *irreverence*. But I tell you what, the very same Spirit of God that was held in the Ark of the Covenant is now in you. Therefore now, as you remain in Him [125] ... and come to **Know** Him; so do you live, and function, and have your being.

We all need a shift, and if God isn't 'God' in our life, then how will we ever learn? My 'problems' isn't my 'god' ... nor are my particular dreams or needs. But God Himself is my Vision and my exceedingly great Reward. [126]

Do you see in the second Scripture verse, how God said that He will actively manage my finances and provisions ... and all 'other things' ... if I was to truly seek Him? So in reality then, the truth is — by His own Word — **He Himself is responsible**. Hence, in the 'attitude' of Elisha I shifted full responsibility unto the Spirit of God ... I 'thrusted' out the Spirit of God.

Ponder then for a moment, if I can truly learn to love the Lord God with all my heart, and all my soul, and all my mind, and all my flesh ... I am also **releasing** all my loves fully into His care. **I step into Him** and He steps into me. There is an exchange: 'I in Him and He in me'.

There is another, a third Scripture verse that we all know. And it goes like this, *"If you hold onto your life you will lose it, but if you let go of it for me shall you find it"* [127]. Now, do you see, that in praying along these lines I gave full right and full place and authority for the Spirit of God unto action. I thrusted out the 'Sword of the Spirit' against the *Thief*, against the Devourer ... the 'creeping thing'.

In this, I also severed my own ties, my own grip and control ... as well as Satan's grip and hold. For Satan always tries to bring you under — that is always what he seeks to do [128]. But I refused and stepped up and **roared as a lion**. And the Vengeance of God went against him ... and the very earth released a blessing. [129]

This tree is amazing! And what's more, it's only visible from where I sit in the car. If I go a few metres to the left or to the right, you can't see it. And even if you were able to see it from another angle it would just appear as a regular tree. But from where I park the car, where I park each day ... there it is ... in a perfect shape of a **Dollar sign**.

So even now, over these last several months, I still park in this same place ... and sit in honour of the Lord just as before. And even now, as I write this chapter, here I am here sitting under this same shady tree. Oh ... I haven't mentioned, but do you know, that not only did this tree appear before my eyes *(in manifestation of words spoken from my mouth)* but my business came fully into alignment. And this totally contrary to both the season and the difficulties faced in my industry ... amen ... 'Aaron's Staff'.

PRAY THE BLOOD — RELEASE THE SPIRIT — COMMAND A HARVEST

The Blood sanctifies. Now as one in Him, by the Power of the Blood, are you now able to set to charge the Spirit of the Lord — and here in Him **Command a blessing**! And what is the purpose? But like Christ Jesus, you become a mountain mover, a storm breaker, and an issuer of Life — that is your **Mandate** in the Lord. And to this is what you are called, even that you be a gateway of Heaven on earth. An interceder *(priest)* who connects God to all obstructions. A king who makes decisions on behalf of the broken and the lost. [130]

Heaven and earth remain separate since the Fall. But in the believer — in you — is the potential of being perfectly intertwined!

Did you realise that **you** are the Authority of God for your world? You are now the 'Word made flesh' [131] and walking the earth for your generation. Therefore, come and pray the Blood that sanctifies — release the Spirit of God to go out — and by the very same Spirit of the Lord **command a harvest**! For just as Jesus breathed the Spirit upon His Disciples [132], so too — 'in the Spirit' — do you have Power breathe upon anything you wish; the same very Spirit of the Lord. To release the Forgiveness of God, and set the stage for the Revelation and Salvation of the Lord for your people. Even the Outpouring of the Spirit upon the nations, in Jesus Name. [133]

There is something greater than getting a job and earning money. And even greater than finding your 'task' or your special 'calling' in God. And that is to be one who walks in the realms of Glory — releasing Heaven and the Salvation of God on earth.

This is why the elderly in the Church can sometimes begin to feel useless. And the weak and the broken ... disillusioned. For the focus of the Christian Church has still remained only flesh-based, *ie;* unto works and law. Whilst the vision of the Christ has always been unto Spirit. That is, unto Visitations and Encounters in the Counsels of God; and the subsequent Power, Dominion, and Victory that comes [134]. Even the ability to rise up as a lion and roar the very same Glory of God.

Theme Scripture in closing:
"... Dominion over all the earth and over **every** creeping thing that creeps on the earth." *(Genesis 1:26-27 NKJV)*

I pray that you have been blessed by the words shared in this chapter. Many things are not walked in simply because you did not realise that you could. This Dollar Tree is for you a license — a personal present for you to realise — that you have much More in God, far More in Him than you have known. So therefore now, as you approach your Heavenly Father ... even as a little child, so also shall you step up into Glory upon Glory — and this in measure beyond measure. Before you did not have because you did not ask. But now that you **do ASK** [135] ... do you step further into the fullness of your inheritance. This Dollar Tree is a symbol and has been presented to me in such a way — as a Gift given to all who might believe. And I pray that you take this Gift deeply to heart.

To close with these following two Scripture verses: *"If anyone enters by me, he will be saved ...* **and** *... he will go in and out and find pasture (ie; in and out of Heaven)"* [136]. And the second, *"Take on the Helmet of Salvation ...* **and** *... the Sword of the Spirit."* [137]

Recognise that the Blood is your right of Salvation. However: it is the Spirit of God who leads the *willing* into the Promises, *ie;* the Spirit is purposed to Empower, Equip, and Reveal. In the Exodus, the Passover was protection ... **but** ... then came the Promised Land. Hence, for us today in Christ Jesus, there is the Cross ... **but** ... now what awaits is the Holy Spirit's Fire and Power. The way unto the Promised Land was the meeting of God at Mount Sinai *(ie; in the Holy Place / the Meeting Place)*. Now you have the answer ... if you truly wish to be successful.

Bless you, in Jesus Name!

Appendix:

1. Romans 8:14, John 10:9, Revelation 3:17-22, *2.* Psalm 84:3, Isaiah 60:8, 40:31, *3.* Revelation 17:14, *4.* Psalms 82:6, *5.* Habakkuk 2:1, Matthew 22:37, Psalm 37:4, *6.* Hebrews 12:21, Exodus 40:35, Luke 24:49, Acts 1:8, 2:1-4, 2 Kings 1:10, John 17:24, *7.* Matthew 23:8-12, Isaiah 54:13, John 6:45, *8.* Matthew 23:8-10, *9.* Revelation 1:10, 4:1, *10.* Matthew 16:17, Numbers 4:15, Hebrews 9:7, Genesis 3:24 — Matthew 27:51, Colossians 3:1-3, *11.* Matthew 6:32-33, *12.* John 4:23, *13.* John 10:27, *14.* John 10:7-10, Matthew 4:4, *15.* Psalm 110:1, *16.* Hebrews 4:11, *17.* Zechariah 3:7b, Revelation 3:21, Mark 3:13-15, Matthew 16:19, John 1:18, *18.* Galatians 5:22, Matthew 17:1-3, Luke 24:32, *19.* John 14:30, *20.* Revelation 19:15, 2:26-27, Psalm 110:1-2, Isaiah 11:1-4, 49:2, 2 Kings 2:13-14, Genesis 1:26, Matthew 6:10, Psalm 82:6, *21.* John 6:1-14, Matthew 17:27, Matthew 8:26, Psalm 67:5-6, *22.* Exodus 12:12-13, *23.* Hebrews 9:7, 10:19-20, *24.* Matthew 6:11, 4:4, Isaiah 25:6, John 10:9, *25.* Hebrews 8:5, Psalm 27:4, *26.* Matthew 16:19, Revelation 2:26-27 *(Dominion is Authority, but Dominion is also a Place ... the Place where God dwells. Which by default is over and Above all things.)*, *27.* John 17:21 *NKJV*, *28.* Joel 2:28, John 1:14, Matthew 3:11, 27:51, Luke 12:49, Acts 1:8, 6:8, *29.* John 10:9, *30.* Exodus 24:10, Revelation 15:2, *31.* Psalm 27:4, Romans 8:14, Psalm 110:2, *32.* Matthew 3:2, 23:13, John 10:9; Luke 21:5-6, *33.* Hebrews 8:5, *34.* John 15:4, Galatians 5:22-23, Isaiah 11:1-4, Zechariah 3:7, *35.* Revelation 1:10, Revelation 4:1, *36.* Hebrews 6:19, *37.* John 16:33, *38.* John 10:17, Matthew 10:39, *39.* Luke 9:23, John 10:9, *40.* Isaiah 64:4, John 3:9, 1 Corinthians 2:9, *41.* Zechariah 3:7, Matthew 16:19, Ephesians 2:6, *42.* Isaiah 52:6, John 17:6, 3:12, 2:24, *43.* Psalm 119:99, *44.* John 7:33, Matthew 5:20, John 14:5-6, Genesis 3:24, Hebrews 9:7, Jeremiah 33:3, John 14:21 AMPC, Hebrews 6:19, *45.* 1 Corinthians 15:53-54, Revelation 3:17-18 *(Luke 14:28-33)*, 2 Kings 2:13, Genesis 3:11, John 10:34, Psalm 82:6-8, Zechariah 3, *46.* Revelation 1:5-6, *47.* Matthew 13:28-29, 16:6, *48.* Galatians 3:1-5, *49.* Revelation 2:4-5, *50.* Revelation 3:16, *51.* Hebrews 10:29, *52.* Ezekiel 10:18-19, *53.* Luke 12:49, *54.* Revelation 3:14-22, *55.* John 5:37-38, 5:44, *56.* Mark 13:1-2, 1 Corinthians 3:16, Exodus 33:16 *(John **3:16**, 1 Corinthians **3:16**, Revelation **3:16**. The Love of God for all people, God dwells within you, honour His Presence ... treasure and* *nurture it.)*, **57.** Psalm 110:2, **58.** Psalm 82:6-8, **59.** 1 Corinthians 15:53-54, **60.** Isaiah 44:22, **61.** John 10:9, 15:4, **62.** Luke 5:32, Isaiah 44:22, **63.** Psalm 110:2, **64.** Genesis 1:26 *(let us 'make')*, **65.** Isaiah 44:22, Zechariah 3:2, Daniel 10:12, **66.** Colossians 3:1-3, Psalm 110:1-2, 2:7-8, 27:4, Hebrews 6:19, **67.** Isaiah 64:1-4, Daniel 10:12, **68.** Psalm 37:4, 27:4, Isaiah 11:2-3, **69.** John 3:6, **70.** Ephesians 6:17, **71.** Luke 24:49, Genesis 3:10, Revelation 3:17-18, 1 Corinthians 15:53-54, 2 Corinthians 3:18, 2 Kings 2:14, 6:17, Matthew 16:17-19, Mark 16:17-19, Acts 5:15, Colossians 3:1-3, Psalm 91:1, 2:7-8, 110:1-2, 34:7, 104:2, 93:1, 84:5, John 1:51, Exodus 33:14-18, 34:29, John 17:24, Genesis 1:26, **72.** Luke 24:49, **73.** Ephesians 6:10-18, **74.** John 3:27, 6:63, 5:19, **75.** 2 Kings 2:14, **76.** Luke 4:19, John 6:63, 10:10, Matthew 10:13, Psalm 79:11-13, **77.** Luke 17:14, 19, **78.** Revelation 2:26-27, Psalm 82:6-8, Matthew 16:18-19, **79.** Philippians 3:7-11, **80.** Mark 3:13, Exodus 19:20, **81.** John 1:18, **82.** Revelation 2:4, **83.** John 17:20-24, **84.** Matthew 17:20, **85.** John 15:4, **86.** Revelation 1:10-18, **87.** Isaiah 64:4, **88.** Isaiah 44:22, Zechariah 3:2, Daniel 10:12, **89.** Isaiah 11:1-4, **90.** Psalm 23:5, **91.** Psalm 91:16b, **92.** Galatians 5:22-23, **93.** Luke 12:49, 24:49, Revelation 1:10, **94.** Zechariah 3, **95.** Romans 8:19, **96.** Matthew 13:19, **97.** Colossians 3:1-4, Exodus 13:21, **98.** Hebrews 6:19-20, **99.** Romans 8:2, 2 Corinthians 3:6, **100.** Matthew 6:1, John 5:44, **101.** Romans 1:16-17, **102.** 2 Kings 2:14, **103.** 2 Kings 2:9-11, John 14:12, **104.** Deuteronomy 8:3, **105.** Revelation 22:2, **106.** James 1:2, **107.** Isaiah 59:19, James 1:2-4, **108.** Deuteronomy 28:7, Proverbs 6:31, **109.** 1 Corinthians 2:8, **110.** John 1:12-13, **111.** Exodus 34:29, **112.** Luke 4:13, **113.** Matthew 6:33, 2 Kings 2:14, **114.** Psalm 84:6, **115.** 2 Chronicles 7:14, Daniel 10:12, **116.** John 10:17, **117.** Genesis 1:26, **118.** Acts 10:38, Mark 1:28, 1 John 3:8, **119.** Isaiah 44:22, **120.** Romans 8:19, **121.** Exodus 14:14, 33:14, 23:28, Psalm 91, Job 1:10, Psalm 110:1, **122.** Psalm 110:2, **123.** Matthew 14:30-31, 8:26, **124.** Matthew 6:33, **125.** John 15:1-8, **126.** Genesis 15:1, **127.** Matthew 16:25, **128.** Matthew 13:22, **129.** Psalm 67:5-6, **130.** Isaiah 11:4, **131.** John 1:14, **132.** John 20:21-23, Matthew 16:17-19, **133.** Revelation 2:26-27, **134.** Psalm 110:2, Revelation 3:21, **135.** Psalm 2:7-8, Matthew 7:7, 2 Kings 2:9, **136.** John 10:9, **137.** Ephesians 6:17

Dated: 10/2/20

20. *Command a Harvest (#103)*
COMMAND A HARVEST *(Part 1)*

Opening Scripture — '2020':
[20] After he said this, he showed them his hands and side. The disciples were overjoyed when they saw the Lord. [21] So Jesus said to them again, "**Peace to you**! As the Father has sent Me, I also send you." [22] And when He had said this, He breathed on them, and said to them, "Receive the Holy Spirit. [23] **If you forgive the sins of any, they are forgiven them**; if you retain the sins of any, they are retained." *(John 20:20-23 NKJV)*

Do you realise that — 'in the Spirit' — you can pray the Blood of Jesus over a nation and release the **Forgiveness** of God? Now the nation has been made open to revelations of the Christ. For as one **holding** the Keys of Heaven … do you set the stage for the Spirit of God to move. And this prior to any repentance, any turning in the heart of the people; but involuntarily — visions and dreams — coming upon **ALL flesh**. [1]

God haters, demon worshipers, the vile and unbelieving … involuntarily! … having visions and dreams of the Person of Jesus. And in a moment of time; their lives, and all that they believe, **turned upside-down** by the Goodness of God. And the same clinging onto a believer saying, *"Tell me about Jesus."* And flow into the church … hanging on every word spoken. Such is the Outpouring of the Spirit of the Lord.

— Pray the Blood —
— Release the Spirit —
— Command a Harvest! —

Do you remember it written, *"Revelation was rare in the land?"* [2] What if this was totally **reversed** where revelation was now abundant? For it is by the Blood that you have been given **perfect right of access** unto your Heavenly Father … and this even in the midst of your brokenness and despair. But in regards the Spirit; the Spirit of the Lord only has 'right of access' to this world through the intercession ... and the words spoken from **your** mouth *(ie; via those who live in the Spirit; the 'revealed' sons of God)*.

By the Blood do you sanctify your people. Now, by the very same Blood, is the Spirit of the Lord free to outpour revelation, *ie;* visions and dreams, causing a shift within the hearts of all flesh.

So by the words of your mouth, bind the birds that peck and pester, and that try to steal away the revelations of God [3]. And by the very same words of your mouth **speak** and — in Him — **command a harvest**. And here shall the Spirit of the Lord *(and the angels assigned by your words spoken [4])* go out and speak into hearts and minds saying, *"This is the right way ... walk in it."* [5]

A PRAYER OF ASCENSION

Picture for yourself the scene: Heaven and earth separated by an impassable chasm. But there, by the Grace of God, the Cross has been set as a 'bridge' — connecting — but in watching, there are so few people passing over. With the vast majority seeing Heaven accessible only at the point of death. And these rich **Pastures** [6] of the Glory realms remaining untouched; as the congregation of believers, huddle together ... living life 'pressed against the edge'.

Through Christ Jesus, **death is not required** before you are **able** to openly engage the realms of Heaven [7]. For it is Jesus who laid down His life in order that you — need not die — before being able to fully access the realms of the Spirit. These, the very realms of the Kingdom of Heaven. Therefore, as you also truly lay your life down in Him — as a living sacrifice [8] — do you also identify with His death and resurrection and **relocate**. It is Jesus who became death so that you truly may enter Life — **Life in all its fullness** [9]. That is, physical ... experiential ... Divine Life.

At the point of Salvation, many experience wonderful Encounters with God. And some ... for days and months. And why is this? But because at that moment — in faith — they truly gave their life personally to the Person of God. However, the 'Sinners Prayer' uttered fails to include something **most important and crucial**. This, the very capacity and purpose of the Blood: to live in a state of perpetual Engagement ... just as Jesus [10]. Not only one who is saved but one continuously engaged. And how this Divine and living reality — is crucial — if you truly wish to live successful and Victorious lives in God. *11*

> *Wearing the helmet of your salvation is good, but not the standing there naked in your underwear.*

So now what has happened, in the modern contemporary Church, is that the typical response is, *"I gave my life to the Lord twenty years ago, and He is with me because the Bible tells me that 'He will never leave me or forsake me'. So why do I need to seek His Presence?"* And with this, the many simply walk away closing off the conversation.

But can you imagine, where a new believer continues into the Fire of God? He would never cease speaking nor sharing the Glory of God he walks in. For as we know, it is the spirit of Religion *12* that is intently at work to keep people caged in a box in the 'dirt' *13*. But in total stark contrast, it is the Spirit of God who seeks only to lift you up and rise you Above all things.

> *The Presence of God comes upon you wherever you are.*
> *But what is to be sought after is to be in —His Presence —*
> *where He is.* *14*

The certificate of marriage does not guarantee relationship. For though there is the legal notice that two are now 'related' — true relationship that engages body, mind, soul, and spirit — is a **<u>choice</u>**. Hence in the exact and very same way, receiving Christ Jesus at the point of Salvation is like a certificate of marriage. However, what God earnestly desires to lead you into is ever deepening relationship. Not 'law' based … but intimacy; a relationship that shares all of you body, mind, soul, and spirit. And just like in any marriage … there can be a 'distance', so too can a distance remain in your relationship with God. And subsequently, the people filling these gaps with so many other things.

What God desires, as does any believer, is a highly interactive and engaging relationship. One highly uplifting, inspiring, and strengthening — **<u>all the time</u>**! And to this is what your Heavenly

Father deeply desires also: even to restore you fully back into *your* former Glory.

For it was, that before, you were like a lost child that was found. An orphan now restored. Therefore, today, as you truly begin to engage in Divine Relationship ... **do you shift**. For so it was most true: before you were a creature of the dirt and dust, but now you are a Creature of Light. And before, you only had the mindset of *fallen* man, but now are you being renewed in the Mind of Christ. Transforming and transitioning ... being 'transfigured' from the flesh unto the Glory and Power of the Spirit.

To this is what Satan is terrified of: The **revelation of your True Sonship** ... for in this, you shall fully triumph over him. A Light that fully overwhelms all darkness. Consuming all his works and destroying all his plans. Leading the people out of darkness into the Glorious Light of the Son. [15]

Let us pray this prayer together: *"Thank you Lord, that by the Blood shed for me, that I can seek your Face. And thank you Lord that even here, right in the midst of things, I can love you and worship you with all my heart and soul. Lord, I lay down all my cares and considerations, all duties and responsibilities, all fears and desires into your hands ... and seek the Presence of the Lord. And thank you Lord, that by the Blood of Jesus I have here gained perfect right of access to enter your Holy Presence, even right in the midst of my mess. And that I can take my eyes off this life and set myself wholly in you this very day. Lord, you manage all things, I hand you **all** responsibilities, as for me I seek your Presence. And here, posture myself to be captured up again. This I pray in Jesus Name. Amen."*

Do you realise that I have just led you in a prayer of ascension? A prayer as one postured ready to be led 'in and out' finding pasture [16]. The crossing over the 'bridge' into your rightful Abiding Place [17]. The moving into the Holy Place to function as priest and king [18]. Passing through the Veil into the Concealed and the Hidden; the Fearful Place where no fear remains, nor can any demon hold grip upon you. [19]

These principles of Gospel just prayed, set the stage unto deep and personal engagement with the Person of God — *ie;* the 'dressing yourself in innocence' [20]. For the Blood sanctifies ... however, the purpose of **sanctification has <u>always</u> been for the passing through**. Not just staying where you are on this earthly plane but stepping into the Eternal realms of Heaven — these very realms of the Spirit and Everlasting Life. Too long has the believer lived with little or no dynamic engagement with the Person of God. However now, through stepping up in Him, shall you live as one who truly operate in realms of Governance and Grace.

What is being presented the believer this day, is not only the becoming one who comes under the Counsels of God [21]. But one who comes into — to **pray from within the <u>counsels</u>** — from right within the Heart and **Authorities of God** [22]. Firstly, the being shifted and changed through a lifestyle of engaging the Spirit of the Lord, just as Jesus. And then secondly, Anointed by the very same Spirit — in the Power and Fire of God.

UNIVERSITY OF HEAVEN

Spitting the dummy at God does not cause you to step into the realms of Dominion or Governance. Dominion comes through relationship; it comes through union. Spitting the dummy is speaking in truth, it's honesty and that's good ... and I recommend it. But what your Father deeply seeks and yearns for, is for you to come up in Him. To come into deepening and perfect union with Him and be with Him where He is. [23]

Both the Word and the Spirit bring constant testimony of such things ... but **so few are listening**. Hence it becomes so frustrating to God [24]. Even as Jesus says, *"How long do I have to put up with you?"* [25] The believer still living bent: as one constantly looking unto the flesh and that of man [26]. But hardly ever unto the Spirit nor the realms of which the Spirit seeks to take you.

As a people of God, we all need to — all the more — shift and posture ourselves as a people taught of God [27]. Dominion and Divine Governmental Authority comes only from abiding in His Presence, abiding in Him [28]. Never from a life independent of Him [29] ... but a life fully united and engaged. [30]

God Himself deeply desires to constantly speak into your life. Therefore, come and learn to value and treasure 'Encounters', *ie;* quiet times in the Holy Presence of God [31]. For honour greatly attracts … even as one captured up into unspeakable Places. Not just reading about Him, but meeting with Him daily; that is the very purpose of the Word, the Blood, and the Spirit given.

> *Awareness brings a heart open to God. And an open heart unto God … doorways open for Him to move. And as you are given things of God so shall you open all the more, and shall move in vast realities lost to the thought or comprehension of man.*

Moses went into deep *intensities* in God where he said, *"I am trembling with fear"* [32]. And it was said of Jesus also, that He *"Delighted in the Fear of the Lord"* [33]. Therefore, as you also come to direct your love, as like an 'arrow' targeting, so also do you touch the Heart of God. We are called sons of God for a reason, and it is to this very thing that Satan does not want you to know who you truly are; so he always fabricates misdirection. Therefore, as you traverse into God's Glory *(ie; the 'intensity' of Him)* so too do you also come to know Him — hear and see Him — as one continually built up in Glory. And now, when you turn, **are all things <u>exposed</u> to the very same Glory**.

Throughout the Exodus the people whinged and complained. None of them were forward focused. And none embraced the Dreams or Promises of God destined them. Hence just the same today, we all need to let God Himself become our — 'exceedingly great Reward' [34]. And so shall He give us the very ground of which we walk — as our possession.

Knowledge and capacities are good … skills and physical effort. But nothing compares to the Outpouring of the Spirit of God. Your heart open to God, opens as like a doorway for God to step into you. As well, step through you unto great and exceeding effect in your world.

KINGLY MINDSET GIVEN OF MY KING

Of myself I am nothing … but by the Spirit do I enter Unfathomable realms. And 'in the Spirit' into realms of Glory and

Wonder too marvellous to comprehend [35]. So by choice do I come here and in Him live and have my being.

Wisdom is not *of* me ... but as I seek the Lord does Wisdom penetrate my soul, as does the Knowledge of God — the very same that opens many many doors. And here, do I enter His Counsel, as one who desires to constantly see and hear. And when I inquire of Him, the Lord inclines His ear to me, drawing close listening intently to the words of my mouth. [36]

Hence now, as I walk this earth, does the Glory of the Lord come with me. Not because there is any good in me ... but because I abide in Him [37]. And here do I connect all obstructions; all difficulties and griefs; all problems, sickness and disease to the Glory and Judgements of God. And here the Spirit lingers and sets camp, working always to establish and bring forth the Goodness of God. Even the very Salvation of the Lord ... *aligning* all things unto the Promise.

A side note: Any reliance on anything, other than the Blood and the Spirit, leaves you vulnerable and insufficient. And any other reliance hinders your ability to transit into the Glory and Counsels of God. The Church plateaus — stuck in the understanding of man — on the 'Edge' [38]. Not open, nor giving rightful place, for the Spirit of God.

However, as we truly posture ourselves in deep honour before the Spirit and Presence of the Lord; so shall God continually speak, reveal, and lead you into Understanding [39]. Now here, under the very Instruction and Tuition of the Spirit, do you also become a people able to release the very same unto action. Even pouring out the Spirit and Glory of God by the words of your mouth.

He sets my 'light' in His Presence; even the congregation their 'candle'. [40]

In the earlier part of the Gospel Jesus states, *"If you do not forgive others their sins, then your Father will not forgive your sins"* [41]. It's incredible, but after His resurrection, He breathed the Spirit upon them and said, *"If you forgive anyone's sins, their sins are forgiven; if you do not forgive them, they are not forgiven."* For just as God sent the Christ ... now does Jesus send you [42] in the exact and very same manner. As one able to pour out Peace [43], even as a 'substance' ... the Spirit and Fire of God. But you must be rightly aligned, you must be rightly established.

Come, and let there be a shift of motive unto the Spirit, that you truly might walk in the Promises. For *love* forms union in God, and through *abiding* in union — Dominion over all things [44]. You in Him and He in you, operating and functioning in the Glory realms as you still walk this earth. Such is the basis of the Ekklesia; the basis and structure of Divine Church Governance.

Another side note: The 'stars' as expressed in Revelation chapters 1 and 2 are angels that represent each church — ie; the 'spirit'. The picture being, that as you personally engage the Presence of God, so is your candle (your 'light') set in His Presence. Even as a little child your 'angel', or let's say, "Your spirit always sees the Face of God" [45]. *Therefore, as you also humble yourself as a little child, even collectively as a church, so is your spirit, your 'angel' ... ie; the angel of the church, set before the Presence of God and never leaves.*

*Now you know the difference between an **Anointed** church (ie; one that walks in Miracles, Power, and Divine Authority) ... to that of a **'dead'** church (ie; one of which is just the structure). For though there might be a form of godliness present ... many still **deny its Power** (ie; stop it).* [46]

THE EKKLESIA

It is true that in a Spirit-filled Church; the people can still live in, and of, and by the flesh. Therefore, a good question to ask: is Peter himself the 'rock' to which Jesus spoke of? Or isn't it not personal revelation of the Christ and God's Living Word speaking alive in you [47] — **the Rock to which we are called** — even the Rock in which we stand?

An Anointing of God can freely come upon a people; imparted through an Anointing that rests upon a church. However, true Dominion and Authority only comes through firmly establishing oneself upon the Rock — just as Purposed. Not only the looking unto an Anointed person ... like Peter. But all men pointing to the Christ, and to the subsequent hearing and seeing the Father *(this is the basis of the Fire of God)*. For in such, not even the Gates of Hades can stand. And to such as these, even the very **Keys of Heaven are set in your hands** — to turn.

It is God who desires that you no longer retain an orphan mindset — but in all things — ever establish you in sonship; walking in the Knowledge and Revelation of who you are in Him. Your *candle* set in the Rightful Place, even your light and the light of the congregation — such is the Love of God [48]. And as one made ever Victorious in this area, so shall you eat freely of the Tree of Life — bringing Salvation and Healing of God to the nations. [49]

Two Scripture verses:
1. The mystery of the seven stars which you saw in My right hand, and the seven golden **Lampstands**: The seven stars are the angels of the seven churches, and the seven lampstands which you saw are the seven churches. *(Revelation 1:20 NKJV)*
2. To the angel of the church of Ephesus write, 'These things says He who holds the seven stars in His right hand, who walks in the midst of the seven golden lampstands. *(Revelation 2:1 NKJV)*

A church can carry a powerful Anointing as their '**lampstand**' has been set in the rightful Place ... and so too its members. However, what you personally want personally as individuals is to set your heart unto the Son. For it is in Him that you **need to be known** — to know Him and be known in Him. [50]

In times past powerful Anointed churches *lost* their Anointing, as the heart of the people shied away from the Power of the Blood and that of the Spirit: shifting away from Spirit to works and law. So I dearly encourage you, come and deeply honour the Presence of God, as one more acquainted to hearing and seeing ... just as Jesus. Not only a people who can recite Scripture; but one who walks in the Place where Jesus is now ... even as the very Word made *'flesh'*.

Truly, care less for problems and issues that you face ... and more for Presence. And so shall Counsel flood your soul as will the Strength of the Lord. And here shall you continue to be continually raised in the Authorities and Power of God, as one who walks in Glory ... able to pour out the very same.

Dominion is the Place where God dwells. So if you are in the Place where He dwells then you are in the realms of Dominion, Authority, and Governance.

THRUSTING THE WILL OF GOD TO EARTH

Jesus is the Lion of Judah. And if you truly are purposed to be fashioned into His Image and Likeness then so too are you purposed to roar. Life can get really intense at times, so don't wait until you face impossible situations before you truly begin to seek the Face of God. For this is why trials and tribulations are sometimes allowed, that you truly might begin to truly hunger to hear and see the Lord [51]. For it is God who always has a way through ... **always**! And through them, He deeply desires to raise the bar in you every time. [52]

So let us be then, no longer a people drawn 'under' problems. But a people who truly rise up Above becoming Mighty in God. Therefore, speak out the word "***Shift***" ... and say to the mountain, "***Be cast into the sea***" in Jesus Name.

It is only through intimacy that comes the ability to 'thrust' the Will of God to earth [53]. Only through union and intimacy [54], the very ability to release Heaven in all situations and in all places. For in your very hands do you hold the very Keys of Heaven; [55] made able — by God — to pour out the Spirit, the Peace, and Revelation of God. Pour out His Glory upon will.

As one truly born of God, be truly diligent to **enter the Rest of the Lord** [56], even then as one 'melding' back into the Glory Cloud. And here, lay down in rich Pastures, under the very Shadow of the Lord God Almighty [57] ... even He, your exceedingly great Reward. [58]

What are some characteristics of a lion? Other than a roar that sends a shiver down the spine of all who hear, for miles around ... the lion **lays down without fear**. And even to get to him, you still have to get past the lionesses *(ie; the Spirit and angels of God)*. Hence, you have — by Divine Purpose and Destiny of the Cross — great and incredible standing in Him. So come then and enter the Rest of the Lord and *cease* from striving [59]. For the Sabbath Day is a type of Rest that enters the fullness of the Promises — **the full Fruits of all God's labour**.

There is a Horror and Terror of the Lord that comes upon the *Enemy* when you, as a child, rise up in God. Not a person any longer of the flesh but a person in union with the Spirit [60] — taking your rightful Place in Him. Remember, that the purpose of the Blood is not just for the cleansing of sin, nor only for the guarding you in protection; but is the Divine right to personally approach your Heavenly Father and in Him make your dwelling.

Let this then, be your high calling, the deepest and most treasured prayer of your soul. And even in your ministry, or let's say, **especially in ministry**: look to Presence more than your calling, or the task set before you. For truly, so shall you live an Anointed life and with a word: pour out the Salvation, the Glory, and the Goodness of God.

Strike the waters and pass on through. *First*, for bringing Heaven to earth [61]. Then a *second* time, to bring the multitudes into Glory [62]. Strike the ground and command a harvest … *thirdly*, even for a 'harvest' of many peoples into Everlasting Life.

CLOSING THOUGHTS

Baptism = *forgiveness of sin.*
The Cross = *Curtain rent and Spirit released.*
Resurrection = *lifted up with Him.*
Born again = *child of God.*
Open Door = *ability to step into.*
Secret Place = *engaging Heaven.*
Upper Room = *Fire come.*
Fasting = *hungering for the Word that Proceeds.*
Gifts = *given of the Lord.*
Anointing = *Governance and Dominion.*

Jesus had the Spirit because He was born Child of God.
And He walked in Heavenly realms because He
is the Resurrection and the Life.

By the Blood do you have free *right* of access,
and by the Spirit, *able* to be captured up in Him.
And here walk in Dominion, in Power,
in Authority, and in Governance just the same.
For so too are you born child of God.

Appendix:

1. Acts 2:17, ***2.*** 1 Samuel 3:1, ***3.*** Matthew 13:19, ***4.*** Zechariah 3:6-7 MSG, ***5.*** Isaiah 30:21, ***6.*** John 10:9, ***7.*** Matthew 3:2 *KJV*, ***8.*** Galatians 5:24-25, Romans 12:1-2, 6:5-11, Colossians 2:20, Philippians 3:8, ***9.*** John 10:10, ***10.*** Revelation 5:9 *KJV*, ***11.*** Revelation 3:20-21, ***12.*** Matthew 23:13, ***13.*** Genesis 3:19, 2:17, ***14.*** John 17:20-24, Matthew 6:21, ***15.*** Romans 8:19, 1 John 3:8, 1 Peter 2:9, ***16.*** John 10:9, ***17.*** John 15:4, ***18.*** Revelation 1:5-6 *KJV*, ***19.*** Genesis 3:24, Isaiah 11:3-4 *NKJV*, Hebrews 12:21, Revelation 1:10, 17, 4:1-2, 19:15, Numbers 4:20, Psalm 91:4-7, Acts 5:1-11; 2:2-3, Exodus 33:18-23, 3:5, 1 Kings 19:11-13, 2 Chronicles 5:14; Psalm 82:6-7, 1 Corinthians 15:53-55, Revelation 3:17-22 *(Luke 14:28-33)*, ***20.*** Matthew 18:3, 10, ***21.*** Isaiah 11:1-4, ***22.*** Zechariah 3:7, ***23.*** John 17:20-24, 4:24, ***24.*** Revelation 3:16-22, ***25.*** Matthew 17:17, ***26.*** Psalm 118:8-9, John 5:44, ***27.*** Matthew 23:8-10, John 6:45a, ***28.*** John 15:5, ***29.*** Proverbs 3:5-6, Genesis 2:17, ***30.*** John 5:19, ***31.*** Psalm 46:10, ***32.*** Hebrews 12:21, ***33.*** Isaiah 11:3, ***34.*** Genesis 15:1, ***35.*** 1 Corinthians 2:9-10, ***36.*** Psalm 116:1-2, Isaiah 64:1-4, Daniel 10:12, ***37.*** John 15:5, ***38.*** Matthew 23:13, ***39.*** 1 Corinthians 2:13, Isaiah 11:1-3, ***40.*** Revelation 1:20, 2:1-7, ***41.*** Matthew 6:15, ***42.*** John 20:21, ***43.*** Matthew 10:13, ***44.*** Matthew 22:37, John 15:4-8, ***45.*** Matthew 18:3, 10, ***46.*** 2 Timothy 3:5, ***47.*** Matthew 16:17-20, Romans 8:5, 14-16, 26-27, 30, 31-32, Exodus 31:18, Deuteronomy 8:3, Hebrews 10:16, John 5:30, ***48.*** Revelation 1:20, 2:1-7, ***49.*** Revelation 22:2, 3:21, 2:26-27, 19:15, ***50.*** Matthew 7:21-23, ***51.*** Deuteronomy 8:3, ***52.*** Isaiah 59:19b *KJV*, ***53.*** John 1:18, ***54.*** John 17:20-24, ***55.*** Matthew 16:19, ***56.*** Hebrews 4:11, ***57.*** Psalm 91:1, ***58.*** Genesis 15:1, ***59.*** Hebrews 4:10, ***60.*** 1 Corinthians 6:17, ***61.*** 2 Kings 2:8, ***62.*** 2 Kings 2:13-14, Revelation 2:26-27, Exodus 17:5, Numbers 20:11

Dated: 15/3/20

21. Command a Harvest (#104)
COMMAND A HARVEST *(Part 2)*

In continuation from the previous chapter ...

Two opening Scriptures:
1. For through Him we both have **access** by one Spirit to the Father. *(Ephesians 2:18 NKJV)*
2. He who [chooses to] **unites** himself with the Lord is **one with Him** in Spirit. *(1 Corinthians 6:17 NIV)*

ACCESS TO THE FATHER

Access to the Father isn't just a right to approach God in times of need. But a right to **dwell** in Him, **move** in Him, be **equipped** and **empowered** of the Lord God Almighty. [1]

Let's start with a prayer. *"Thank you Lord, for the honour and privilege that I can praise and worship you with **all** my heart, my soul, my mind, and my flesh. And thank you Lord that I can seek your face the very same ... and **set my heart in the Lord**. And bless you Lord for the privilege, that I can lay down all things and as a little child pass on through. And here — in you — live and move and have my being. And thank you Lord, that here, as I come under the Shadow of the Lord God Almighty ... even positioned to be captured up again; that you take me again into the Mystery and the Concealed. Even the Hidden and Treasured things of God*[2]. *Blessed be the Name of Jesus."*

God is 'God' in my life ... not my problems, not my past ... but God! He Himself is **my prayer**. And in this, He continually takes me deeper into the unlimitedness of His Dreams and Purposes ... as He works and fights my battles. **This is His Prayer** [3]. The general problem with believers is that their problems are their 'god' ... their problems are their 'prayer' and not God Himself. Desires, fears, hurts and pains rule their life and their thoughts. But ... if you could truly make God — God in your life — and pursue Him in His Person, then you would return back into all that was lost.

Dominion is the Place where God dwells, and **union** with Him is the invitation [4]. Therefore, if you **abide** in the Place where He dwells, then do you **live and function** in realms of Authority and Governance … in Dominion with Him. [5]

In the beginning Heaven and earth was seamlessly intertwined. Hence as you choose to intertwine yourself with Heaven so is Heaven intertwined with 'us' [6]. Like a 'cloud' [7] … whisks of cloud … releasing 'spot-fires' of the Holy Ghost. Spontaneous and *unstoppable* Moves of God across the churches, the governments, the people, and the nations. [8]

Scripture:
"Therefore, believers, since we have confidence and full freedom to enter the **Holy Place** [the place where God dwells] by [means of] the blood of Jesus, by this new and living way which He initiated and opened for us through the Veil [as in the Holy of Holies], that is, through His flesh, and since we have a great and wonderful Priest [who rules] over the house of God, let us **approach** God with a true and sincere heart in unqualified assurance of faith …" *(Hebrews 10:19-22a AMP)*

God desires to **transition** each one of us from works and law unto Spirit and Life and Power. From human understanding and intelligence to 'Spirit Intelligence' … in the Sovereign Presence of God. The purpose of the Cross is always to the shifting of the believer — from earthly flesh-bound origins — to Heavenly Origins [9]. And even as 'earth dwellers' — returning back into our pre-fall dwellings in Heaven — the *joining* of two realms.

Such is the gift of the Cross: Both in the Blood that has Redeemed you and given perfect Entrance. And the Spirit of whom comes as a 'Transit Agent' … working always to *transition* each one of us into Heavenly Places [10]. That we each might truly live in the Presence and Glory of His Person. Bring made able — *increasingly* by Him — to bring His Presence and Glory on earth [11]. The Kingdom come, His Perfect Will being done on earth **just as it is in Heaven**. [12]

Who is God to you? One who is with you to help achieve your goals and desires? Or one who is Himself your goal and desire?

God has fundamentally positioned us able to do even greater works than that of the Son *[13]*. And how is this possible? ... but for **He is Risen**. Hence, as you also choose to rise up in Him, do you enter into the realms of Dominion and Authority where Jesus dwells *[14]*. Through His death and Resurrection ... he has 'resurrected' in us that which was lost. The mechanism and structure to walk in Glory just as He.

I so encourage you; many have never experienced the Person of God. But just one touch of His Love; even the Wonder of His Presence, His Righteousness, and His Goodness ... shall your life be forever changed.

I came across the following Scripture verse a month or so ago, whilst searching the Bible for the wording, 'Thick Darkness'. For God has been setting it before my eyes to come into the 'intense' Glory realms. And here I stumbled across verse 20, a verse that I have always seen as a 20/20 vision Scripture. But in this context, it now has taken on an even greater meaning.

Let's begin ...

THICK DARKNESS

Opening Scripture — '2020':
v20 And Moses said to the people, "Do not fear; for God has come to test you, and that His fear may be before you, so that you may not sin." *V21* So the people stood afar off, but Moses drew near the **thick darkness** [veil covering *[15]*] where God was. *(Exodus 20:20-21 NKJV)*

In relation to eyesight, '20/20 vision' speaks about perfect vision. Hence, I so encourage you, in this year of 2020 *(especially in these current times)* to sharpen your eyes. And with 20/20 clarity: **focus on the Presence of the Person of God** *(ie; continual Divine Encounters in Him; the very same that imparts and strengthens)*. Even as one choosing to peer on through **all things** right into the Glory of God *(look through the forest unto the Tree of Life [16])*. Choosing **not to fear** but sharpening your target to step into the 'Fear' of God; deeper into Intensities of God whereby your face comes to glow. Whereby your personage carries the Glory of God. *17*

Not only as one who sees Jesus in His Glory — beholding the Wonder of Him *11*. But carrying and made able to pour out the very same Glory as revealed *18* sons of God. The Church lifted up in its True and Divine *Calling;* and the Name of Jesus magnified before the eyes of all *19*. His Name honoured through the outpouring of the Spirit: His Goodness, Salvation, and Power.

Come, and look in as like a telescope, 'magnifying' the vision of Jesus in your eyes. Even whereby you might transit in Him, where God is no longer distant or small in your eyes ... but where you are captured up where He is now *20*. And as one stepping through the Veil, stepping through the 'Thick Darkness' right into the Radiance of God, so shall you go in and come out *21* to the blessing your world.

For truly, if you can make all things small in comparison to this Place; this Place where the Blood has Purposed and availed; then not only shall you activate the Spirit of God — releasing Him in all areas of concern — but shall you step into realms of Authority *predestined* you from since before the founding of the earth.

God is in the pipe cleaning business; for through you He desires to pour out the Spirit of God in measure beyond measure. 22

It is that, in Christ Jesus, God desires to step you into a Dominion not seen since the Beginning. Even — **as** Christ Jesus Himself — a Dominion greater than anything seen on earth *23*. The Dominion over all creation, over all powers above and below; over provision and livelihood, even over the very earth *24* ... in the Sovereignty of God. Speaking to the ground commanding Provision, commanding Change, and commanding Life. And the earth itself yielding up its fruits and its wealth. Heaven outpoured in response to the words of your mouth.

Scripture:
He replied, "You of little faith, why are you so afraid?" Then he got up and rebuked the winds and the waves, and it was completely calm. *(Matthew 8:26 NIV)*

I tell you that — in God — you are Destined to be mountain movers, storm calmers, and releasors of the captives unto liberty. You are Purposed and Destined of Him to heal the sick, cast out demons, and raise the dead. Therefore, as you also choose to step up and spend time with Him in His Holy Presence *(ie; the Holy Place)* ... does the power and attitude of your prayer-life shift. For here, are you simply stepping back into the Glory of your Dwellings. [25]

HISTORIC TIMES *(COVID)*

Never before in the history of man has the world paused in a near total lockdown. Personally, I'd prefer to see it as a time of 'fasting' before the Glory comes ... the cold before the dawn, the stillness before the lunge ... the Cross before He was Risen.

There are many ways that a person can choose to approach times and situations like this Coronavirus. For you can either come under *fear*, or otherwise lay fear down in the Presence of God ... and set your heart in 'prayer'. And yes, prayer means asking God for guidance and help, but as we see in the life and person of Jesus; **'prayer' also means <u>seeking</u> the Face of God**[26], *ie;* retaining a firm set attitude of heart and preference to meet directly and closely with the Lord. As one *(in 'death'* [27]*)* stepping up into the Glory realms; engaging with the very Person of God — in the Joy of Him — in Garden realms of Counsel and Presence and Anointing. [28]

Again, I emphasise and ask, when Jesus went into the secret place to 'pray', was He going to God with lists and lists of prayers and requests that took Him all night to pray? Or did He not otherwise posture Himself — in 'waiting' — to meet with God? And so, because He never left this Place *(neither coming under fear, unbelief, or the thinking of the world)*, He walked into Glory upon will ... whenever He desired. Even the very realms of 'Intensities' that neither Moses nor Elijah were permitted. [29]

It was Moses who approached the Thick Darkness where God was and said, *"I am terrified and my body shakes in fear"*[30]. But do you know what … he still purposed himself to enter. Who else do you know who mirrored this picture? … but our Lord and Saviour Christ Jesus. And what does Scripture say of Him, *"He delighted in the Fear of the Lord"*[31]. I so encourage you to set your vision higher, not only to problems or answer to prayer … but unto the very Glory realms. Even these realms of Presence where it feels that every cell in your body is being ripped apart — but at the same time; held together by the very Hand of God — as you burst into luminous beings. [32]

'SUPERMAN' IN TIGHTS

Our Lord and Saviour, Christ Jesus, delighted not in the Might or Power of God … but He delighted in the **Fear** of God [33]. He did not stand there before the people proudly, with His hands on His hips, like Superman in tights!

Nor did Jesus delight in the Wisdom or Knowledge of God … parading Himself before the intellectuals and leaders of the land. No, there was only **just <u>one</u> thing Jesus delighted in**: and that was the Fear of the Lord. He singularly delighted in the 'going in and coming out' of the realms of God's Glory. Even in Places where Moses was physically unable. [34]

Truth is, that many in Christ Jesus do not engage the gifted Holy Spirit. But have unwittingly structured their lives **<u>independent of all Consultation</u>** in the Person of God. And in the exact and very same way, the many do not actively engage the realms of Heaven; even these of the very realms that are 'right at hand'. Nor do they know how to engage or function here … or even knew they could.

Humility, honour, and an invitational heart; and not loving your life unto death. These are key to walking in the Glory of God.

However, this is not the believer's fault. For the *Enemy* works diligently to keep the believer from stepping into their Divine Purpose; or ever coming to know who they truly are in Christ Jesus.

Therefore, let us be all the more encouraged in this: That it is the Lord's deepest Desire to lead you deeper into the realms of the Spirit; these of the realms of Heaven, even these very realms of the Glory and Authority and Dominion of God. These realms of your pre-fallen dwelling, the **realms of <u>your</u> sonship** *35* ... for to this He gladly shed His Blood. *36*

You were gifted the Spirit of God when you received Jesus as your Lord and Saviour. Hence now, as one 'born again' alive in Him, are you born with the purpose of growing into maturity, *ie;* **the fullness of God** *37*. So don't let the phrase, *"I already have the Spirit of God, so why do I need to seek the Presence of God?"* ... hinder any longer.

You have a driver's license, but the purpose is **not** just to keep it in your pocket — **but drive a car!** In the same way the Spirit is the linkage *38*. For just as the Blood is the right to enter; Jesus Himself is the Door to pass through. And the Spirit of God is the Transfer Agent *39* ... making you able to go anywhere in the realms of God.

TOTAL RELEASE

Scripture:
And when I saw Him, I fell at His feet as dead. But He laid His right hand on me, saying to me, "Do not be afraid; I am the First and the Last. I am He who lives, and was dead, and behold, I am alive forevermore. Amen. And I have the keys of Hades and of Death. *(Revelation 1:17-18 NKJV)*

Picture these three steps, or stages ... as an example: In the area of forgiveness, there are two positions that you can choose to take, even a third if you want total release. *1.* Retain your unforgiveness. *2.* Make the decision to forgive. *3.* However, if you really want **<u>total</u> release** then switch it up further, and choose to pray a blessing upon your enemies. *40*

In the same way, when it comes to issues of fear: *1.* Remain gripped with fear. *2.* Entrust fears into the Hand of God. *3.* However, if you really desire to live Victorious and Triumphant lives, even as one made Powerful in God, then be as — Christ Jesus — and **<u>delight</u> in the Fear of God** *(ie; the intense Glory realms).*

Not only turning from fear and releasing everything to God; but continuing on further in ... and stepping into His Glory. For it is here where His Might and Glory ever **surrounds** you [41] and where the Vengeance of God *aggressively* guards [42] even as one **ruling** in the midst of your enemies. In the Domain of God; in Dominion and Authority, with the 'Fear of God' resting upon you, *ie;* Glory so intense where death, disease, and the demon cannot stand.

Salvation is just the beginning of what God has for you. [43]

Do you yet then realise, that it is God's Desire for you to not only come out of death and enter into Salvation ... but to continue on and fully **enter** into Life? Here, turning from sin unto Christ Jesus [44] ... but not stopping here. But choosing it in your heart to lay down your life: and pass on through [45] He who is the Door into the Eternal and Glorious realms of Heaven. The not just turning from death unto Life ... but stepping into **Victory**! Not just stepping out of the Curse into the Blessings and Promises ... but choosing to become a holder of **Life in your hands**. Able to pour out the Spirit, pour out the Glory and the Salvation of the Lord for you and your people.

Jesus desires to place in your hands a Rod of Iron [46]. *Meaning, the ability to reach into Heaven and grasp hold of the Will of God and* **strike the earth**. [47]

POWER OF THE BLOOD

It is by the Blood and the Blood alone that you have been made king and priest unto God [48]. And so too by the Blood; given perfect right of access unto the Father. Not because of any good deeds you have done, nor education or achievements ... but by the Blood and Blood alone.

Come then and set it in your heart to pass on through; and step on into the Glory realms. And so shall you come to behold ... and carry ... the very same Glory. Truly, I tell you, that the Salvation of the Lord is not the end of what Jesus has for you — but **only the beginning**!

There are Glory realms of God permissible to you, that were not available or permissible prior to the Cross. Places available to go into that were not open prior to the shedding of His Blood. And it is to this that Jesus says, *"The least in the Kingdom of God are greater than they"* [49]. And why is this? But because you have greater access, and greater Divine right to engage the very Person of God … just as the Son.

At the time of the Exodus, no animal was allowed, nor man permitted to approach the Mountain … but Moses [50]. However, to what Moses was unable to see … you will not only see, but live and have your being. For it is by the Blood and the gifted Spirit of God, that even the least in the Kingdom are greater than Moses; greater than Samuel, and greater than Elijah. For you are able to go into Places, and walk in a closeness of relationship, that they were unable, and here remain and make your dwelling [51]. And to this very reason why Jesus would say, *"You will do even greater things than these, because I go to the Father."* [52]

However, let's continue on even further than this: In God's eyes, you are fundamentally a 'god' [53]. For truly, if you are a son or daughter of God then you are a 'little' god … a 'baby' god growing in His Fullness and very Likeness.

That is **God's perspective**. It may not be the believer's perspective, but it is God's. A total paradigm shift. No longer looking for acceptance, but learning what sonship truly means and how to walk more fully in it. For though the Law acted as a 'guardian' [54] — for the immature — now shall you enter the full function of your Inheritance. The walking in Like as the Son.

David was anointed king fourteen years before he was seated. And just in the same, so have you been anointed, **birthed child of the Living God**. Now, the active work of the Spirit, is to reveal [55] to you what this truly means and how to walk more fuller in it.

Your world is different now, for you are no longer seeking acceptance but are part of the beloved. Part of the cherished in God … part of the family. And here, are you shifting from an orphan depraved mindset unto that of the Son. For so it is … that in God, you need not be asking so much ... but releasing. As co-creators, releasing Heaven to earth; releasing Life, Spirit, and Liberty.

HOSTILITY AGAINST THE GATE

Scripture:
And the dragon was enraged with the woman, and he went to make war with the rest of her **offspring**, who keep the commandments of God and have the testimony of Jesus Christ. *(Revelation 12:17 NKJV)*

In the modern-day contemporary Church, the Gospel message of Salvation has been greatly diminished and watered down. Whereby the highest vision of the Church has been entering into Heaven when you die ... instead of the **right vision**: of entering into Heaven whilst you still live. And to this is why the spirit of Religion and Legalism come so aggressively, lest as a people, you rise up — unstoppable — in the Power and Fire of the Holy Ghost.

Therefore, the people of God are left to live powerless lives ... caged, like sheep hemmed in and pressed against the Edge. And yes, the Blood redeems ... but however, the very purpose and focus of the Blood is not just for your sin, but always unto the '**passing through**' ... it is the entrance. The Blood of Jesus is the **entrance** unto the Father. The Door flung open, like the parting of the 'veil' [56], unto the very Promises and Possession of God [57]. For just as the Passover in the Exodus: God's Dream and Purpose is always unto the 'Promised Land', *ie;* the realms and the Promises to where He wishes to take you.

The Cross has been set as a bridge. But so it is, that so few believers are actively engaging these wondrous Kingdom realms. For they have never been instructed, nor have they known what **has been gifted them**, nor to that of which both the Blood and the Spirit have availed.

You have heard of the Presence of God coming upon a people. But have you ever heard of God's deepest Dream and Desire: that you, in your presence, come up in Him? You in Him ... and He in you. And what this opens up to you is like a 'dance', an exchange, a waltz between you and your Heavenly Father in the Glory realms. Where you step into His Glory, and He steps into you. The **going into** the Kingdom of Heaven **and** the Kingdom of Heaven coming here on earth ... through they of whom are His own.

The Blood is the right of Passage, and the Spirit is the Transit Agent, ie; your very ability to be 'in Him'. Your spirit now Alive unto God.

Scripture:
But woe to you, scribes and Pharisees, hypocrites! For you shut up the kingdom of heaven against men; for you **neither go in yourselves**, nor do you allow those who are entering ... to go in. *(Matthew 23:13 NKJV)*

It's most important to realise that there are spiritual forces, that since the Cross, have been actively at work to hinder the believer from going in and engaging these realms of the Kingdom of Heaven. Strong spiritual forces opposed, purposed and driven to disorientate you in your thoughts and understanding. Aggressively at work to *fog* up the Way, even to the placing of distractions hiding and obscuring the Gate. And why is this? But for the demon knows, that if you were ever to truly step into and abide and function in the Glory realms. Then would you gain Power to fully dismantle and destroy all the works and schemes and strongholds of the Devil.

In the same way that these forces came at Jesus at the Cross, so are their efforts fully thwarted! For so it was, that this place of such dishonour and disgrace, become itself ... the very place of greatest honour. Even the Cross itself becoming as a Bridge, even the very Doorway, whereby **anyone who might believe** has liberty to cross over into the realms of Glory — just as the Son. Going 'in and out' [58] — ever built up and Empowered of and by the Kingdom of Heaven. And as a people *able* to release the very same Glory and the Will of God on earth. Living their lives on earth — at the very same time in the realms of Resurrection Power. [59]

Let me ask a question, what is the purpose of fasting and waiting upon the Lord? The purpose has always been to seeking breakthrough. Hence therefore, in the area of obstructions and strongholds, as you also choose personally to take up a culture of 'prayer and fasting' *(ie; seeking the Face of God [60])*, so shall all obstructions and blockages be dismantled ... as one stepping out into the clear blue sunshine.

> *What we are about as a people, is learning how to liberally receive from the Lord. The 'pipe' has already been laid, hence today, we are about the clearing of obstructions that the 'Glory shall be revealed'.* [61]

Fundamentally, the modern 'Gospel' message taught in the contemporary Church, fails to properly introduce the believer how to go on further, *ie;* how to walk *in* the Joy and Power of the Spirit. Let alone how to pass on through the Door and **activate** these dynamic and glorious realms of the Kingdom.

In the same way, the many see Heaven only accessible when you die. However, realise and recognise most clearly, that the **purpose** of the Door wasn't only to be realised at the time of your death — for Christ Jesus died in place of you — Jesus became death in order that **you might have** Life ... and Life in all its fullness [62] *(this is so much bigger than you think!)*. For the Door has **always been purposed**, that today you might pass on through unto the Father and into these Glory realms — **today***!* Even then, that you might come out carrying the very same Glory [63] — as one who pours out the Will of God upon the earth. That is, the Kingdom of Heaven released on earth, and the Salvation of the Lord meeting people right where they are ... as birthers of Revival.

To re-emphasise: The modern-day Christian's thought is to do good in order to be 'accepted' into Heaven when you die. But the Christ perspective is that you are **already accepted** because of Jesus. Now from here, choosing it within yourself to enter in ... 'making' God your dwelling [64] ... in order to truly **Rule in life**. Made of God, **made by Him**, to be **Like Him**; Triumphant, Victorious, and Successful *('Risen', 'Resurrected' Life of Victory)*. Sin having no hold over you, the works of Death without effect, and as a holder of Life in your very hands ... releasing Life.

In this, let me express something most important. The Heart of Jesus is not directed towards the righteous, but the unrighteous.

Not towards the healthy, but the broken and the lost. Therefore, if you would truly come honestly and recognise your broken state, *ie;* **your <u>need</u> of Him** ... and humble yourself as like a little child. Then so shall you come into and experience the Lord ... even daily, as one constantly built up by Him.

> — **Praise the Lord** *(ie; turn your heart to Him)* —
> — **Worship Him** *(ie; elevate Him before your eyes)* —
> — **Enter in** *(ie; engage and meet with the Person of God)* —

2 Chronicles 7:14 modernised:
If my people who are called by my name would **<u>humble</u> themselves** and lay their life down and **<u>seek</u> my face**, I would **<u>heal</u> the land**. I would release and pour out my Spirit upon all flesh.

Let's close in prayer. *"Lord Jesus, I thank you and pray your Forgiveness over this nation. Lord, I pray the Blood of Jesus over this nation and release the Forgiveness of God* [65]. *And here, I release upon the nations the Spirit of the Lord, even the Vengeance and the Glory; the Love and the Grace. And Lord, I call upon the Winds of Change and* **<u>command</u> a Harvest** *in Jesus Name. Touch the people in their sleep, speak to them in visions and dreams, and lead them unto the Salvation of the Lord. Setting before their eyes the very Person of Christ Jesus. This I pray in Jesus Name."*

In the next chapter, I would like to lead you into the mysterious scriptural principle of 'waiting upon the Lord'. In the meantime, I hope that you have been blessed by the thoughts expressed here. I pray that regardless of this current season, that you step into the Peace and Rest of the Lord. Even the very Power and Authority that is found in His Mighty Presence.

Bless you, in Jesus Name. Amen.

Appendix:
1. Genesis 15:1, ***2.*** John 3:12, ***3.*** Exodus 6:8, 14:14, 33:14, John 17:20-24, ***4.*** John 17:20-24, Psalm 110:1-2, 2:7-8, Isaiah 44:22, Genesis 1:26, Revelation 3:17-22, ***5.*** Genesis 1:26, ***6.*** John 17:20-24, ***7.*** Isaiah 60:8, Psalm 84:3, 82:6, John 10:34-36, ***8.*** Isaiah 64:1-4, Psalm 110:1-2, 2:7-8, ***9.*** John 17:16, ***10.*** Ephesians 2:6, ***11.*** 2 Corinthians 3:18, John 17:24, Exodus 34:35, Acts 5:15, ***12.*** Matthew 6:9-13, ***13.*** John 14:12, ***14.*** Revelation 3:21, ***15.*** Exodus 33:22, 1 Kings 19:11-13, ***16.*** Revelation 22:2, ***17.*** Exodus 34:30, Hebrews 12:21, Revelation 1:17, Matthew 17:2, John 17:24, ***18.*** Romans 8:19, Zechariah 3:6-7 MSG, ***19.*** Isaiah 64:1-4, ***20.*** John 3:3, 3:5, 3:13 *NKJV,* 10:9, 17:24, Matthew 7:13-14, 7:21, 18:3, 19:23-26, 23:13, Hebrews 12:14b, ***21.*** John 10:9, ***22.*** Luke 6:38, Matthew 6:10, 2 Corinthians 1:20, 3:18, ***23.*** John 14:12, ***24.*** Genesis 1:26-27, ***25.*** John 14:1-4, 12, 18, ***26.*** Exodus 33:18-23, Luke 5:15-17, ***27.*** *(In 'death' ... not in a season alone ... but as a lifestyle: 2 Chronicles 7:14, Isaiah 64:4, Daniel 10:12),* Luke 14:33, John 10:17, Matthew 19:27-30, ***28.*** Isaiah 25:6-8, ***29.*** Matthew 11:11, Exodus 33:20-23, 1 Kings 19:11, ***30.*** Hebrews 12:21, ***31.*** Isaiah 11:3, ***32.*** Matthew 17:2, Genesis 1:26, 5:24, ***33.*** Isaiah 11:1-4, ***34.*** Exodus 33:20, ***35.*** John 1:12b, ***36.*** Hebrews 12:2, ***37.*** Ephesians 4:13, John 14:9, Genesis 1:26, ***38.*** Ephesians 2:18, ***39.*** John 16:14, ***40.*** Matthew 5:44, ***41.*** Psalm 91:1, ***42.*** Exodus 23:28, ***43.*** John 10:9, Ephesians 6:17, ***44.*** Exodus 12:12-13, ***45.*** Matthew 16:25, John 10:17, ***46.*** Revelation 2:26-27, Psalm 2:7-9, ***47.*** Matthew 6:10, 2 Kings 2:14, ***48.*** Revelation 1:4-6, 5:9-10 *KJV,* ***49.*** Matthew 11:11, ***50.*** Exodus 19, ***51.*** John 15:4, ***52.*** John 14:12, ***53.*** Psalm 82:6-8, John 10:34-36, ***54.*** Galatians 3:23-29, ***55.*** Romans 8:19, ***56.*** Hebrews 10:19-20, ***57.*** Romans 8:17, Genesis 15:1, ***58.*** John 10:9, ***59.*** Ephesians 1:19-20, ***60.*** Isaiah 64:1-4, 2 Chronicles 7:14 *(humble yourself, and seek the Face of God; and God will heal the land.),* ***61.*** Luke 3:5-6, Isaiah 40:4-5, Exodus 33:14, 23:28, ***62.*** John 10:10, ***63.*** Psalm 91, ***64.*** Psalm 91:9, ***65.*** John 20:23

Dated: 6/4/20

22. *Command a Harvest (#105)*
WAITING UPON THE LORD

Let's start with a prayer, *"Bless you Lord that I can love you and worship you with all my heart. And thank you Lord that I can seek your Presence manifest, even the very Glory of Jesus before my eyes. Lord, I cannot live, and nor do I desire to, without the realness of God tangible and burning in my life. I seek your Face ... I seek your Face ... even here to be captured up in you again [1]. Lord I pray, that the Kingdom of Heaven come, and the Dreams and Purposes of your Heart be done on earth — just as it is in Heaven. And here, I stand in the gap ... and release Heaven and the Will of God on earth. This I pray, in Jesus Name. Amen."*

Opening Scripture:
When I saw him, I fell at his feet as though dead. Then he placed his right hand on me and said: "Do not be afraid. I am the First and the Last. *(Revelation 1:17 NIV)*

In this world there are times and seasons. And just as there are times of sowing and times of harvest, there are also times and seasons in the Lord. Here, in this opening Scripture, we have Jesus who came to John in His Glory [2]. And though John was known as one deeply close to Him, Jesus came to him with an important message ... and ... in His Glory. And this 'intensity' of His Person caused John to fall as though dead on the ground ... but then, Jesus touched him.

There are times in the Lord that you can meet Him in His Love and Companionship, and full of Grace He opens the Secret and Hidden things of His Heart. Then there are times He can come in correction ... and why is this? But that He is a true Friend. Not one who just tells you what you want to hear, but as a King who wishes to lead you into greater things.

Your friendship with Jesus can be of a nature where He drops everything; and in surprise, comes by and 'cooks you breakfast' [3] *(spontaneous Visitations and Encounters)*. Where you sit together with Him, as close friends and companions, sharing one to another. But then there are seasons and times when Jesus can come as King —

in His Glory — with hot fire coals in His eyes [4]. He can come dressed to serve you a meal [5], but then He can come in a war footing ... not as Lamb but as Lion.

In this world, there are seasons that come. And as taught in Scripture, as a people, we need to be **equipped ready for war** [6]. In Christ Jesus, we have wonderful opportunity to be raised — and set in Place by the Person of Jesus — He, the lover of our souls. And though there are seasons where you can just smell the roses and enjoy the Goodness of God; there are also times to be dressed ready for battle. If not for yourself, then for those who are in need; for the lost, the broken, and the hurting.

Sometimes things that you go through are actually in preparation for an exceedingly great equipping. And other times, it is Satan recognising your destiny and trying to come against you in 'opportune times' [7]. And though the *Enemy* may rise up like a flood [8] ... as you 'preference praise', does the Lord shift all things unto a blessing ... even sevenfold what was stolen. This is why **seeking the Presence of God first** is of such value, for it is in this perpetual — 'looking-on-through-into-Him' — that you are swiftly raised up. With various times and seasons becoming as like training wheels, even 'stairs' of great increase. For through a heart of 'praise and thanksgiving' do you strip the *Enemy* bare and set the stage for a triumphant life. The Lord 'Kissing the chaos as you carry His Heart'. *(T. W.)*

> *"Lord, I value you more than the fears that I face. I value you more than any dream or any hope. And I purposely choose to **step through all things** as one who **stands** in your Presence. And thank you Lord, that here in you, you continually open your Heart and your Ways to me — revealing my sonship. And now when I turn and speak, I release the very same Spirit and Glory of the Lord."*

I pray that you are blessed by the thoughts expressed here. There are many ways that one can approach the Lord; and yes, His Grace and Mercy is ever-present. However, what Jesus deeply wants to do is, to raise you **mighty** and Powerful in God. Even then, that you truly might step into the fullness and maturity of your sonship.

Jesus desires to set you in such standing as to command armies of angels [9], with Life and Spirit pouring from your mouth [10]. Truly then, come and learn to approach the Lord in the deepest of humility, as one postured to be continually taught and raised in Might and Power. Even then, risen and raised by the Lord, in Divine Authority to Rule.

Jesus isn't about your 'nots' ... He is about your purpose and where you are going. He is **not** bothered by what you are not yet capable of ... but one-step-at-a-time ... in what you **are capable** of in Him. The 'cannots' will fall off all on their own as the Grace of God comes upon you. With your eyes not focused on failure ... but on your Destiny.

JOY AND PEACE

Scripture:
After he said this, he showed them his hands and side. The disciples were overjoyed when they saw the Lord. *(John 20:20 NIV)*

Let me share a thought before we start ...

The 'residue' of the Presence of God, of Visitations and Encountering Jesus, is the overwhelming Peace of the Lord. The very same Joy and Peace that heals and alights your soul; strengthens your bones and lifts the vision of your eyes. However, this 'Joy' is not ever purposed to be the pinnacle ... but simply **the ground of which you walk** [11]. These very same 'Fruits of the Spirit' simply residue of being in Him, *ie; "The Joy of the Lord is my Strength"* [12]. The being with Jesus now — walking in Heavenly realms — and seeing Him in His Glory.

So it is, that here in this preferred-Joy-of-the-Lord, *ie;* 'in the Spirit' ... are you one postured ready to be captured up again [13]. But it is to where you are taken, and what you are personally given in the Lord, that make you a most powerful people.

John 20:20 ... continued:
[21] Again Jesus said, "Peace be with you! **AS** the Father has sent me, **I am sending you**." [22] And with that he breathed on them and said, "Receive the Holy Spirit. If you forgive anyone's sins, their

sins are forgiven; ²³ if you do not forgive them, they are not forgiven."

Pictured in this John 20/20 Scripture is the Disciples being 'overwhelmed with Joy'. However, Jesus doesn't stop here ... this verse continues: Jesus releases **Peace**, breathed upon them the **Spirit** of God, and **Anointed** them with another layer of **Divine Authority** [14]. Again, such is the power of praise and thanksgiving, even right in the midst of trauma and distress. For truly, if you can learn to whistle a tune in the face of the *Enemy*, so too are you also able to **draw from Heaven and smack him down**.

> *The problem with miracles is always the same: a problem has to exist in the first place. But so too is the answer always the same: seek the Presence of God. For in God, you are Purposed to be a mountain mover, a storm calmer, and a releasor of Life. Anointed of God to command and bring change to the world.*

Let us together continue then to come up upon the *"Mountain of the Lord's House that is on top of the mountains"* [15]. For here, right in the Presence of the Lord, *"He shall **teach** us His Ways"* whereby His Glory flows. And so shall the *"Nations beat their weapons into ploughshares"* ... and there be *"No more war."* For in these, that are the Latter Days, so shall you stand in Places that are Higher than the high places [16]. And as a people, pour out the Spirit of the Lord ... even as one who triggers the Outpouring. [17]

> **Psalm 91** *(paraphrased):*
> "**No evil** will come near your **tent**."
> "God will **command** His angels to **guard** you in all your ways."
> ... *and who does He do that for? They who,*
> "**Come under** the Shadow of the Almighty."
> ... *who choose to,*
> "**Make God your Dwelling**."

SPIRIT OF LEGALISM AND RELIGION

"As the Father sent me, I am sending you ..."

In choosing to step into the Glory of God, even here as one who triggers Revivals; learn to **establish your faith** — and that of the Church — not on a 'Peter', but firmly on 'personal revelation of the Christ', and to the 'hearing and seeing the Father' [18]. Even here, as a tree set right-side-up *(righty established and rightly orientated)*, for so shall Jesus place in your hands a Rod of Iron. An Iron Sceptre of Divine Authority to **strike the earth**. [19]

For truly, if you want to be a people who truly release the Outpouring of the Spirit in situations you are facing; in your family, your workplace … in your city, or the nations. If you truly want to walk in the Glory realms as one who **grasps hold of Heaven** [20] and strikes the earth. Then look not to the hierarchy, honour, or promotion in man; nor to wealth or fame … but firmly unto the Person of Jesus — even He who died for you. For it is **only King Jesus** who is qualified, and only He who is able — to truly 'reveal' your sonship [21]. And it is only Jesus who can **Anoint you in Power**. [22]

The Anointing of God never comes by looking to the approval of man [23]. But only through a heart that is actively set upon the Father … and unto the Father's **own** Personal Dreams for you. Firmly unto Him and unto the broken and the lost [24], *ie;* a heart set upon 'connecting Heaven to the hurting'. As it is said, *"The Spirit of the Lord is upon me … **because** … He has Anointed me to preach good tidings to the poor."* [25]

So, in coming to understand these things, learn to not look unto the 'righteous' but unto the lost; unto the *"Healing the broken-hearted and binding up their wounds"* [26]. And so shall the Anointing of the Lord freely flow, and His Anointing ever rest powerfully upon your life. Even as one who moves the Heart of God … the Angelic Hosts, the Kingdom realms … even the very earth itself. For in Him are you rightly established. [27]

Three Scripture verses:
1. "Who may ascend the mountain of the LORD? Who may stand in his holy place? The one who has clean hands and a **pure** heart [pure intent and pure purpose] …" *(Psalm 24:3-4a NIV)*
2. "Who among us can **dwell with a consuming fire**? Who among us can dwell with ever-burning flames [the inner

realms of Glory, the inner realms of the Presence of the Person of God, *ie;* like Moses upon the Mountain]? The one who lives righteously and speaks rightly ..." *(Isaiah 33:14b-15a HCSB)*
3. Without holiness [purity] no one will see the Lord [will **see the Glory of God** or Dwell in His **Holy Fire**, *ie;* the Fear of God]. *(Hebrews 12:14)*

Times and seasons, Lamb and Lion: The very reason why we continue to seek to climb up 'Mount Sinai' [28], *ie;* **go into places** where flesh is 'not permitted' [29], is that we might remain a people who sit at the feet of Jesus and abide in His Holy Fire [30]. To this I delight [31] and pursue; [32] seeking to remain and **never** leave [33]. For I know, that from this Place ... the Glory of God shall outpour. [34]

Baptised in the Fire ... and never drifting out.

Here's a question for you, 'If you are not outpouring the Spirit of God in **small circumstances**, how can you ever outpour the Spirit in the big circumstances?' *Trials and* tribulations are simply training in Swordsmanship [35]. The releasing of Life and Spirit in difficult and challenging situations.

ANANIAS AND SAPPHIRA

As a people intent on stepping into the Glory of God, to 'dwell' [36] in the realms of the Holy Spirit's Fire ... so too, do you also become a people who carry and release the Glory of God. Who releases Fire, who releases Revival, and who releases unstoppable Moves of God.

However, it's most important to realise that the head must need remain the head and the tail must need remain the tail. The mixing — **no mixing***!* — the vision is God. The honour [37] is God and God alone ... and in this all things shall follow. For just as the tail follows the head, so shall the Glory of the Lord rest upon you. [38]

Here is another question for you, why do revivals cease? But for the shift of focus: from the Glory of God to man, from the Glory of God to money.

Personally, I do not like to speak against anyone or anything — but **I am for Jesus**. However, it is most important to understand: we must be aware of the cunning subtlety of the *Enemy;* of the spirits of Religion and Legalism, the spirit of Mammon, and the spirit of the Antichrist [39]. And again, I don't speak against anyone or any people, nor do I wish to segregate. But simply draw awareness to the 'spirits' that are active in the world in order to **bring forth a full release**. The Word speaks a very specific message for a reason, for Tares of 'misdirection' are planted by the *Enemy* with clear purpose to diminish the Church. And to keep you personally from ever walking in the Spirit and the subsequent Power and Authority to dismember him.

So I apologise in saying, but only in example: When looking at the back of the chair of the Papacy, what is it that you see? An upside-down Cross, the Cross inverted. And why is this, what does it represent? ... but the Catholic Church's own proud 'lineage' that leads right back to Apostle Peter.

So again I ask, is Peter the 'rock' of which the Church is supposed to be established? Or is it not unto the **revelation** of the Christ and the subsequent **hearing and seeing the Father**? This is a most important subject for the Church today, if we ever wish to be truly successful. If we truly wish to walk in the Power of the Christ.

This particular church is a most mature religious structure. But the truth is, that this very same spirit seeks to work and establish itself in all the churches, *ie;* the people not looking unto God but unto 'princes' of men [40]. And this spirit's purpose is to grow into maturity ... **standing in place of Christ**. And here forming deep strongholds that run totally contrary to the Holy Spirit and that of the Heart of the Father. [41]

A spiritual force that works contrary, placing the principles of the Gospel message 'upside-down'; in order that there be no Shekinah Glory in the Church [42]. Meaning, no open manifestation of '**God with us**' [43]. Structure and appearance ... yes, but not open Power. As is said, *"Having a form of godliness but **denying** its Power"* [44]. For it is only through the flow of Understanding that comes from God, that draws you able to 'come under' His Glory. Even the very

Shadow of the Almighty [45]. That you might also become a people able to cast the very same Glory, *ie;* walk in the Power, Dominion, and Authority of God.

Jesus desires and is motivated to set in your hands a Rod of Iron. An Iron Sceptre to 'smash' the nations. And just as Jesus received Authority from the Father, so is it purposed of God to be **given** you as well [46]. In Christ Jesus, you are fundamentally purposed of God to rule in the midst of your 'enemies' [47], *ie;* **all that comes against**. For it is by the Blood of Jesus that you have been made king and priest unto God; [48] as one structurally made *able* to release Heaven and the Will of God on earth. [49]

'Made' as a people connecting mankind to the Answer, all problems and issues unto the Glory of God. And here in this Place — in the Spirit and Presence of the Lord God Almighty — it is here that you hold the **Keys of Heaven**. Divine Authority given of Jesus to release the Forgiveness and Salvation of God [50]. And to they of whom live engaged in the Person of God, not even the Gates of Hades shall prevail. [51]

The account of Ananias and Sapphira: Here, the early Church was **entering into the 'All-Consuming Fire' of God**. *(the Ark-of-the Covenant type Glory ... the Glory within the Holy of Holies)*. But here it was that Ananias and Sapphira held deceit in their heart ... they lied before Fire of the Holy Spirit. The issue was money, the same that was theirs to keep or to give away. They hid and kept half of the money for themselves though saying that they gave it all. And **Peter released a very sharp response** *(as too with another man who sought to purchase the Spirit [52])*.

As is said, *"Who among us can dwell with a consuming fire? Who among us can dwell with ever-burning flames? The one who lives righteously and speaks rightly"*. The Intense Glory of God is a Most Holy Place — where flesh-driven man cannot come [36]. Only they who come **fully unto the Lord** with pure intent and purpose.

LIKE A CHILD

It is the Way of God that you become as like a little child: Stripped bare of any preconceptions or pain, but in 'innocence' *(pure and singular motive of heart*) crying out unto the Father … ***"Pick me up!"*** For it is to such that become most soft and pliable; able to truly learn, able to truly change and grow, and able to be **continually taken** into and shown new things. Even Ancient and Concealed things made alive and contemporary to you. And here shall you be built and here shall you ever be established.

The believer is like clay, with the **fundamental** Divine Purpose to be moulded and shaped to **hold** Divine Honour [53]. But so it can go, that the understanding and beliefs of the believer can 'solidify' whereby a hardness forms making one brittle and unteachable. Forming a 'pride' of knowledge as though the clay has been left uncovered for too long. Therefore, to this very reason: we choose to remain a people continually transitioning, a people set upon continually moving forward from flesh unto Spirit [54], from law and rules … unto Deep Enduring Love. That our hearts may remain always tender and pliable before the Lord of Glory; as **Holy vessels** of the Lord **set** within the **Holy of Holies**.

Hence, as we continue to prefer to come under the continual flow of the Living Word — that 'proceeds from the mouth of God' — *ie;* the Word and the dynamically active Spirit of God; [55] in deep honour and reverence, allowing His Presence to continually come upon you. So too do you remain pure and soft — **a joy to the Potter's Touch** [56]. For only in Him are you shaped and crafted by the very Hands of the Person of God, even unto exceedingly great and Eternal Divine Purpose.

The born again believer has been gifted the Holy Spirit. However, it is purposed of God also — as one born again — **to remain engaged**. Not living independent of Him as of old, but fully engaged. Even then as one coming to live in a state of perpetual Encounter **just as the Son** [57]. For only here — in Him — that you are positioned by Him — as one ready [58] — to be captured up 'in the Spirit' right into Heavenly Places [59]. Even these very realms of great Wonder whereby you are Empowered.

The carnal-minded believer cannot abide or function in the Glory realms, nor can they ever understand … only the spirit-minded believer, *ie;* they of whom have **their hearts set upon** the right hand of God [60]. And this is why we are called to choose to lay our lives down, for it is only in 'death' [61] that you are truly able to alight up into His Presence — spirit to Spirit, even as one made able by Him to strike the earth.

As a 'priest' do you — join — obstruction and brokenness to the Goodness of God. Even as a king — purposed able — to release Heaven and the Will of God on earth. And just as Jesus is the Door — so too are you also — a gateway of Heaven for you and your people.

Jesus is the Door, hence in choosing it in your heart to pursue and step through Him, so too are you 'captured' up in spirit, soul, mind … *and* flesh. And in Him, ever transformed, as one transfigured into His very Likeness [62]. It is the Divine Desire of God to lead you deeper into the Mind of Christ, even that you truly may — **know Him** — and the Power of His Resurrection [63]. That somehow you may also come to participate in His Glory — participate in His Resurrection Power. Beholding Him no longer only in 'spirit', but also in your soul, your mind, **and** your flesh. [64]

Personally, for me, I prefer to stand before the Judgements of God, His, that I also might be raised by Him in **all** Righteousness. Satan has nothing in me [65], for I delight in the Judgements, the Glory, the Fear of the Lord [66]. Even here, under His continual Tuition, His Training, and His Correction [67]. I delight in the Fear of the Lord … these very same realms of intense Glory where my flesh 'burns' before the Holiness of His Person [68]. Held together by the Hand of God, protected by Him within His Glory. However now, as one established and positioned in Him, trained personally by my King and Saviour, am I also charged by Him to make 'judgements' on earth — *"To govern His House and have charge over His Courts"* [69]. As is said in the book of Zechariah, this 'Legacy' shall be a **sign** for all who believe …even as is inscribed in stone *(with the 'Seven' Spirits)*: *"I will remove the sin of this land in a single day."* [70]

Trained by my King to be a king, in His Authority and Power.

To truly operate and function in these realms of Glory, I must needs also learn to live fully submitted to the Training and

Instruction of the Holy Ghost [71]. And just as Jesus, who sought only to hear and see the Lord [72] ... so do I. Even as one purposed to enter in, pitch my tent ... and **never leave**! [73] Independence of God is Satan — but interdependence is sonship. And as one 'revealed' in Him, so to am I also **revealed with Him** as He comes in His Glory; [74] as one ceasing the groans and sufferings of this world. [75]

Intimacy in God is the basis of Power and Authority; a heart unto God that moves the Heart of God. In union and of **one mind**; tender, knowing, strengthened. To behold His Glory so are you built up; to step into His Glory so too do you become a part ... not separate but **one with Him in Glory**.

Two Scripture verses:
1. The Lord says to my lord: "**Sit** at my right hand until I make your enemies a footstool for your feet." The Lord will extend your mighty scepter from Zion, saying, "**Rule** in the midst of your enemies! [strongholds of doubt, unbelief, sickness, and disease; opposition, hardship, storms, and mountains moved]." *(Psalm 110:1-2 NIV)*
2. The Lord said to me, "You are my son; **today** I have become your father. **ask** me, and I will make the nations your inheritance, the ends of the earth your **possession** [Promises, Plans, Purposes]. You will break them with a rod of iron; you will dash them to pieces like pottery." *(Psalm 2:7-9 NKJV)*

By the Blood of Jesus have you been born son of God, and **today He has become your Father** [76]. Therefore today, in *choosing* to set your affections in Him ... so do you relocate. Responding to His Invitation and sitting at His right hand in Heaven [77] ... as you walk this earth. *(* This is how to address all issues in this life; how you win and live triumphant. I in Him and He in me and all that I do.)*

Therefore, in your responding, does **He work** to make your 'enemies' your footstool. This is the way of the Spirit; even as one who **rules in the midst of your enemies** [78]. Everything that comes against, every plan and work of the *Thief* thwarted because you are 'seated' bent — Dreams of the Father fulfilled and alive in you — driven. Not only thwarted ... but converted, converted into sevenfold blessings. And here, something also is given from Above: an **Iron Sceptre of Divine Authority** to smash, to break down, and to destroy the works and strongholds of Satan. [79]

Through this most precious and most mysterious principle of '**waiting upon the Lord**' ... are you coming before the Lord as one who '**asks**' God [80]. And here in Him, He works to give you the 'nations' as your inheritance ... the very 'ends of the earth' your possession. Such is the power of one who waits upon the Lord. And everywhere you set your feet, and to all that you touch with your hands; even to that of which you hold dear in your heart ... now belongs to the Kingdom of God! They are the **property** of Heaven. [81]

Satan has no right ... nor give him any advantage or place. For in His Holy Presence, God will give you 'teeth' ... **teeth to tear down all obstructions** [82]. No longer as one 'gumming' at problems and impossible situations ... but one who has 'bite'. To 'make them like chaff to be **blown away** in the wind'. And all of us together we will 'rejoice in the Lord' and shall 'glory in the Holy One of Israel'. [83]

Say this prayer with me, *"Spirit of the Lord **you** fight my battles, as for me I ascend the mountain of the Lord. Holy Ghost, you go out before me, you prepare the way, you teach me and raise me in the Glory of God. And Spirit of God, reveal my sonship to me ... and in the world, as for me I pursue the Lord."* [84]

A FIVE-MINUTE PRACTICE

Throughout this chapter, I have been introducing this most mysterious and powerful principle; insight as to what it means to 'Wait upon the Lord'. This being one of the most powerful and effectual principles in Scripture, but also ... one of the least understood and almost forgotten. And after sharing a few more things here, I would like to lead you into a five minute 'practice'.

Let's begin ...

Theme Scripture:
Oh, that You would **rend the heavens**! That You would come down! That the mountains might shake at Your presence — as fire burns brushwood, as fire causes water to boil — to make Your name known to Your adversaries, that the nations may tremble at Your presence! When You did awesome things for which we did not look, You came down, the mountains [opposition] shook at Your Presence. For since the beginning of the world men have not heard nor perceived by the ear, nor has the eye seen any God besides You, **who <u>acts</u> for the one who <u>waits</u> for Him**. *(Isaiah 64:1-4 NKJV)*

God desires to pour out His Spirit upon the nations, but He can only do this through His people. Though there will come a time at the Last Day, when He takes full possession of the earth. However, until that day, Dominion is held in the '**Risen**', *ie;* they of whom are established upon the Rock. [85]

I so encourage you, learn and practice this exceedingly great principle of *waiting* upon the Lord, and so shall you set the stage ... where God 'rends the heavens' *(tearing apart all opposing spiritual powers and barriers)* and steps down on your behalf [86]. Where He makes the *Thief* — he the enemy of your soul, he who came to kill and destroy — **your <u>footstool</u>** — even the ends of the earth **your very <u>inheritance</u>**. For in your personally responding to the Invitation to 'lie down in green Pastures' [87], it is here that the very Presence of God goes out before you and fights on your behalf. [88]

Another Scripture verse:
"Fear not, you worm Jacob, you men of Israel! I will help you", says the Lord and your Redeemer, the Holy One of Israel. Behold, **I will <u>make</u> you** into a new threshing sledge **with <u>sharp</u> teeth**; **<u>you</u> shall <u>thresh</u>** the mountains and beat them small, and <u>make</u> the hills like chaff. You shall winnow them, the wind shall carry them away, and the whirlwind shall scatter them; you shall rejoice in the Lord, and glory in the Holy One of Israel.
The **poor and needy** seek water, but there is none, their tongues fail for thirst. I, the Lord, will hear them; I, the God of Israel, will **<u>not</u> forsake them**. I will open rivers in desolate heights, and fountains in the midst of the valleys; I will make the wilderness a

pool of water, and the dry land springs of water. *(Isaiah 41:14-18 NKJV)*

The **principle of waiting** upon the Lord is one of the most mysterious and least understood principles found in the Word of God. The pausing, the sitting down and doing nothing, but posturing yourself before the Lord in deep honour and quiet. Oh how the legalistic works-based believer can never understand such things ... even the self-sufficient: these things are **hidden** from their eyes. [89]

But ... if you were truly to come and humbly sit yourself before the very Presence of the Person of God — and it doesn't matter where, or in what place or situation — then in this 'posturing', in this 'humbling' of your soul, do you **position yourself for Encounter**. And I tell you what, man doesn't need more flesh ... but more Spirit! ... and greater and greater alignment and unification in Him [90]. Even then as one opened to be captured up ... swiftly taken right into the full Promises of God [91]. This very Place where your full Inheritance is laid open before you; the Promises and the Provision of Heaven, here for you to liberally engage.

*"I **know** where I come from and where I am going."* [92]

In a previous chapter *(#20)*, I led you in a 'Prayer of Ascension'. But this time I want to lead you in a practice; a practice prayer of **'rending the heavens'**. And as we read through this theme Scripture verse, God rends the heavens and steps down — on behalf of **one who waits upon the Lord** — such is the Power released. And not only does He rend the heavens, but He does crazy and wondrous things not seen before; things so far beyond the imaginations of man. And who does He do it for? ... but for a **single individual** of whom waits upon the Lord. Do you see now ... how you are a birther of Revival? You fundamentally are a triggerer of Outpourings of God on earth!

Do not underestimate or belittle this reaching out and engaging the Holy Presence of the Person of God. And do not *wait* for problems to come before you do so. For singerly this is the most powerful thing next to the Blood and the Spirit. Even the very Pathway opened for each and every believer — through the very same Blood and very same Spirit — *ie;* full engagement with the Person and Promises of God.

Now in fasting, one is typically seeking breakthrough. It is a 'waiting upon the Lord' with a firm placing of issues before Him. But **I so recommend**, that after you have done this, 'entrusting all things into His Hands', that you now set your hope and vision **beyond your needs and desires** and set them — to go into Him — right into the Glory of the Person of God. And what this opens to you is **Divine Encounter**, even a lifestyle of perpetual Encounter. For there is something greater that your prayers and that is God's Prayer fulfilled in you.

Do you recall what our Resurrected Saviour said when He departed? *"Wait in the in the upper room until you are baptised in Fire; until you are clothed in Power"* [93]. And this is what we are doing, this is what you are opening up to yourself: for the reality of God to fall upon you as your daily norm.

Scripture:
The servants who are ready and **waiting** for his return will be rewarded. I tell you the truth, he himself will seat them, put on an apron, and serve them as they sit and eat! *(Luke 12:37 NLT)*

THE PRACTICE

Before we proceed, let's go through two more pictures of Gospel to help provide a clearer framework:

1. Each of us have the capacity to be 'Good Soil', but it has nothing to do with good deeds.
2. And each of us have the capacity to enter right into the 'Holy Place', but this has nothing to with being holy.

To express this again, 'Good Soil' as mentioned in the Parable of the Sower ... has nothing to do with being good. Or let's say, Good Soil has nothing to do with good deeds, or that you have led a good life. But Good Soil is simply the choosing to pass through 'hardness of heart', pass through the 'ridicule and persecution', and pass through 'cares and desires' of this world; and in your heart, purposing yourself to seek the Glory of the Person of God. And what you open unto yourself will pour out upon the land. [94]

If you felt worthy, then you would be unworthy. However if, in your unworthiness, you truly received the Blood of Jesus to heart — then you are worthy. The Blood is the right of access, and the Cross ... the very doorway.

Again, the Holy Place, as described in the Tabernacle, is available for you to *enter*. This, not a place here on earth, but the original Temple of God that is in Heaven. And accessing the Holy Place has nothing to do with holiness in your life ... but everything to do with the Blood. And this even right in the **midst of your mess** ... all you have to do is turn to Him, *ie;* 'repent'. [95]

The Holy of Holies is the Fire of God, the Intense Glory of His Person. And it is to this we set our hearts. But it is only the Spirit of God that can take you, and only the Spirit that can clothe and transform you within and without.

Scripture:
Now it shall come to pass in the latter days that the **mountain of the LORD'S house** shall be established on the top of the mountains, and shall be exalted above the hills; and all nations shall flow to it. Many people shall come and say, "**Come, and let us go up** to the mountain of the LORD, to the house of the God of Jacob; He will teach us His ways, and we shall walk in His paths."
For **out of <u>Zion</u> shall go forth** the law, and the word of the LORD from Jerusalem. He shall judge between the nations, and rebuke many people; they shall beat their swords into plowshares, and their spears into pruning hooks; nation shall not lift up sword against nation, neither shall they learn war anymore. *(Isaiah 2:2-4 NKJV)*

On a side note: God is yearning to teach each one of us how to pour out Heaven on earth. Revivals in the past, all great moves of God, are simply introductions of what is yet to come. Therefore, in this chapter, we are simply learning how to trigger Outpourings; even as a people setting the stage for Christ's return. The Church free of 'spot or wrinkle' ... the Bride waiting in ready for the Groom.

So I invite you, whether you have been in the Lord for years, or returning, or even if this is your very first day ... I so invite you to 'come with me'. Let us together go up into the *"Mountain of the House of the Lord";* and here shall you find Peace and Joy in your heart, Strength and Vitality in your bones, and fresh Vision and Hope in your eyes. And made able by Him, to walk in His Wonders and Delight, as one postured to be captured up into the Mystery ... even the Concealed things of God; and here walk in realms of Power and Authority that **shake the world**.

> *Shifting darkness into Light, despair into everlasting Joy and Peace.*

So let's begin: As a child of God, you have accepted the Lord Jesus Christ as your Lord and Saviour ... and have 'cleaved' yourself to Him [96]. Now what I want you to do, is something that you may have not ever done since first receiving Jesus to heart ... and that is '**die**'. That is here and now relinquishing your life afresh; giving your life over to Christ Jesus in its fullness; all its issues, all its responsibilities, and all its cares. Another word for this is, *"Take up your daily cross"* [97] ... or otherwise said, *"He who lays down his life will* **find it**" [98]. Find what? ... find **Life**. Does this make sense?

> *Salvation is more than a word: God wants to* **show** *you.* [99]

Let's take a moment now, and pray this prayer together, *"Thank you Lord Jesus for the precious Blood shed for me. And thank you Lord that by* **your Blood** *I am sanctified and made perfect in your eyes. Lord, I lay down my life ... all its issues, all things from the furthest left to the furthest right. I lay down all my cares and my desires, all my fears and hurts, and all my hopes and dreams. Even all good things spoken ... just the same as all negative and hurtful words spoken against me; I lay down all things rescinded before the Presence of God. And here do I sprinkle the Blood of Jesus and sanctify all things in the Presence of the Lord* [100]. *Spirit of God, you manage all these things, in every detail and in every way ... you go out, you work in them ... as for me, I seek the Presence of God."* [101]

The Veil:
1. So He drove out the man; and He placed cherubim at the east of the garden of Eden, and a flaming sword which turned every way, to **guard** the way to the tree of life. *(Genesis 3:24 NKJV)*
2. There I will meet with you, and I will speak with you from above the mercy seat, from **between the two cherubim** which are on the ark of the Testimony. *(Exodus 25:22a NKJV)*
3. He shall take some of the blood of the bull and sprinkle it with his finger on the mercy seat on the east side; and before the **mercy seat** he shall sprinkle some of the blood with his finger seven times. *(Leviticus 16:14 NKJV)*
4. Then, behold, the **veil of the temple was torn** in two from top to bottom; and the earth quaked, and the rocks were split. *(Matthew 27:51 NKJV)*
5. This hope [this '**prayer**'] we have as an anchor of the soul, both sure and steadfast, and which **enters the Presence behind** the veil. *(Hebrews 6:19 NKJV)*
6. But you **have come to Mount Zion** and to the city of the living God, the heavenly Jerusalem, to an innumerable company of angels, to the general assembly and church of the firstborn who are registered in heaven, to God the Judge of all, to the spirits of just men made perfect, to Jesus the Mediator of the new covenant, and to the blood of sprinkling that speaks better things than that of Abel. *(Hebrews 12:22-24 NKJV)*

I want you to picture now, that in this prayer you have just prayed, you have stepped over into the Glory realms of God — 'in spirit' — in your heart. That is, the very same Place that King David preferred to be even just a *"Doorkeeper in the House of God"* ... rather than the wealth and honour of man [102]. Hence today, right at this very moment you have been renewed. Today you have come to the God of the Heavenly Lights anew and afresh as like a 'little child'. New ... brand new ... every day new and renewed. And so it is that here, shall the Lord of Glory pick you up and take you where man cannot go. Step by step, moment by moment, measure upon measure ... for you have opened the door.

When we say, 'in spirit' ... it is that your spirit-man has come before the very Face of God. As expressed in Scripture, *"Take heed that you do not despise one of these little ones, for I say to you that in Heaven their 'spirit-man' (ie; angels) always see the Face of my Father who is in Heaven."* [103]

So here, I would like you to sit ... just sit, and **"Be still, and <u>know</u> God"** [104]. And if you wish, have some music on that's ok, but just sit. Give yourself five minutes, say nothing, pray nothing ... **just sit**. You are now waiting upon the Lord. Now let this space take on a Life of its own ... for by faith, are you standing before the Presence of the Person of God right now — *engaged* — so anything can happen.

Prayer oftentimes is about what you want ... but is not a pursuit of what God wants. But so it is that — here in Him — He **desires to <u>give</u> you all things**. Much in life has been about the ground where your feet stand, the wall of which your hands touch, and the thoughts of your own mind. For prior, you were only creatures of flesh, confined by time and space and your own understanding [105]. But now you are **Alive** — and in the Spirit of God — transcend this world as a Creature of Light. With Power and Life given through the Living God. A people in the world ... yes, but just **not of the world**. [106]

Now it is, that in your Heavenly Father's own time and own way, He will engage with you. Very personally and most unique ... but in exceedingly great and in most precious ways. For your 'waiting upon the Lord' acts as an *invitation* for Him to respond. Like Moses and the burning bush, God responds to your turning aside [107]. And in this Place so shall you be Empowered and Strengthened and ever given Vision and Insight. And positioned by Him ready to be captured up again in your spirit, your soul, your mind, and your flesh ... unto Heavenly Delights.

Wait ... this is only a 'practice' of waiting. Honour the Lord at this time ... and wait for five minutes. Nothing.

Five minutes ...

THE REVEALED SONS

You have just spent a moment posturing yourself in honour before the Lord of Glory. In an expression of openness and invitation. In an expression as a clean slate to whom God can write and write. [108]

However, what if you extended this to hours or days ... or even as a lifestyle? Do you yet understand its value? Regardless of where you are or what you are doing; choosing to peer through all things right into the very Consciousness of God and the Glory of His Holy Presence — behind the Veil [109]. As one who holds Life, who holds 'Reality' in your hands, just as the Christ [110]. Bring a notepad ... bring a Bible and some worship music. Open yourself to contemplate and reflect on what God is saying. Free of preconceptions or preconditions, let the Spirit stir within; let Him lead you, and let Him 'bubble up' prayers in your soul ... **and God will speak** [111]. Journal, write, and offer up your thoughts unto God as a friend sitting right here!

Do you realise that honour attracts? You may have lived your life in honour of the Word of God and that's good. However, we are also called to honour the Spirit [112]. Hence here, as you wait upon the Lord; even right in the midst of your mess, even right in the midst of the busy-ness of daily life; if you can truly hunger for the 'Word that proceeds out from the mouth of God' [113], then so shall you begin to hear and see. And if anything, only hear and see all the **more**.

Prior to the Cross, you were taught to look up to God and pray, *"May your Kingdom come. May your Will be done on earth, just as it is in Heaven"* [114]. But now, after the Cross, as people of the Spirit; as kings and priests unto God just as **'Jesus is'**; [115] from a Heavenly standpoint, stand in the gap as Doorways and **release Heaven** and the Will of God on earth. Even the very Spirit of the Lord God Almighty ... to pour out as Rain, as Latter Day Rain upon the nations.

A shift is occurring ... before you were of the flesh, but now are you of the Spirit. It's about positioning, a firm **positioning yourself in sonship**. The here in Him, being one now

positioned by Him; and as a Sword from your mouth striking the earth ... **releasing** the Glory of God [116]. No longer praying only from the heart of man; but now — in the Spirit — praying from the Heart of God.

Closing Scripture:
For the earnest expectation of the creation eagerly waits for the **revealing** of the sons of God. *(Romans 8:19 NKJV)*

To be continued in the next chapter, *"Revivals and the Glory Come."*

Appendix:

1. Exodus 33:18, John 17:24, Revelation 1:9-18, *2.* John 17:24, *3.* Revelation 3:20, *4.* Revelation 1:13-15, *5.* Luke 12:37, *6.* Ephesians 6:10-18, *7.* Luke 4:13, *8.* Isaiah 59:19 *KJV*, *9.* Zechariah 3, Luke 2:13-14, *10.* Exodus 33:14, *11.* Hebrews 4:11, *12.* Nehemiah 8:10b, *13.* Revelation 1:10, 4:1, *14.* John 20:20-23, *15.* Isaiah 2:2-4, *16.* Zechariah 3:7, *17.* Isaiah 64:1-4, Daniel 10:12, *18.* Matthew 16:17-19, 23:8-10, *19.* Revelation 2:25-28; Psalm 2:7-9, 110:1-2, Isaiah 11:1-4, 41:14-15, Exodus 17:5, Numbers 20:11, 2 Kings 2:13-14, Revelation 1:5-6/5:9-10 *KJV*, Romans 8:29, *20.* Matthew 11:12, Philippians 3:12, *21.* Romans 8:19, *22.* Mark 3:13-15, Luke 9:1-2, Matthew 3:11, *23.* John 5:44, *24.* Luke 5:32, Mark 2:17, *25.* Isaiah 61:1, *26.* Psalm 147:3, *27.* Matthew 6:33, *28.* Psalm 24:3-5, Isaiah 33:14-16, 2:2-4, Exodus 19:16-25, Genesis 3:24, *29.* Hebrews 9:7, *30.* Luke 12:49, Isaiah 33:14b-15a, 11:3, Exodus 20:20-21, Hebrews 12:21, *31.* Psalm 37:4, 43:5, Isaiah 11:3, *32.* Psalm 27:4, *33.* John 15:4, Exodus 33:11b, *34.* Isaiah 2:1-4, 11:1-9, 40:1-5, 41:14-18, 61:1-4, 64:1-4, Psalm 110:1-4, 84:1-7, Acts 2:1-4, Colossians 3:1-4, Revelation 4:1-5, *35.* Deuteronomy 8:3, 8:16, Matthew 16:17-19, Mark 16:17-19, Psalm 16:8, Isaiah 41:13, *36.* Isaiah 33:14b-15a *HCSB*, John 15:7 *NKJV*, Psalm 24:3-4a, Hebrews 12:14, *37.* John 5:44, *38.* Psalm 91, *39.* Revelation 12:17, *40.* Psalm 118:8, 82:6-7, *41.* Matthew 23:13, *42.* 2 Chronicles 5:13-14, Ezekiel 10:18-19, Revelation 2:4-5, *43.* Exodus 33:12-17, *44.* 2 Timothy 3:5, 1 Corinthians 4:20, *45.* Psalm 91:1, *46.* John 20:21-23, Revelation

2:26-27, 19:15, Psalm 2:7-9, 110:1-2, Romans 8:29, 2 Kings 2:14, Isaiah 11:1-9, 41:14-20, 61:1-6, 64:1-4, Matthew 7:7-8, Genesis 1:26, **47.** Psalm 110:1-2, 23:5, **48.** Revelation 1:5-6, 5:9-10 *NKJV*, **49.** Matthew 16:19, **50.** John 20:21-23, **51.** Matthew 16:18, **52.** Acts 8:18-20, **53.** John 5:44, 2 Timothy 2:21, **54.** Psalm 84:5-7, 2 Corinthians 3:18, **55.** John 4:23, **56.** Matthew 13:11-12, **57.** Matthew 27:46, **58.** Luke 12:49, **59.** Revelation 1:10, 4:1-2, Matthew 18:3, Ephesians 2:6, **60.** Colossians 3:1-2, **61.** John 10:17, **62.** John 16:14-16 AMPC, **63.** Philippians 3:10-11 (D&R), **64.** 2 Corinthians 12:2, Exodus 24:9-11, **65.** John 14:30b, **66.** Isaiah 11:3-4, Hebrews 12:21, Exodus 20:21, Isaiah 33:14b-15a, **67.** Psalm 119:14-34, 62-78, 99-108, **68.** Isaiah 11:1-3, Exodus 20:20-21, Daniel 3:25, Revelation 1:17, Matthew 17:5-8, **69.** Zechariah 3:7, Isaiah 11:1-4, John 20:23-24, **70.** Zechariah 3:8-9, **71.** Zechariah 3:6-7, **72.** John 5:19, Luke 5:15-16, Isaiah 11:3, **73.** Exodus 33:11, **74.** Colossians 3:4, **75.** Romans 8 19, **76.** Psalm 2:7-9, **77.** Colossians 3:1-3, **78.** Psalm 110:1-2, 23:5, **79.** Revelation 2:27, 1 John 3:8, **80.** Psalm 2:7-9, **81.** Genesis 13:14-17, **82.** Isaiah 41:15, **83.** Isaiah 41:14-16, **84.** Matthew 6:33, 2 Kings 2:13-14, Psalm 110:1-2, Romans 8:19, **85.** Matthew 16:18-19, **86.** 2 Chronicles 7:14, **87.** Psalm 23:2, John 10:9, **88.** Exodus 33:14, Hebrews 4:10-11, John 10:9, **89.** Isaiah 28:12-13, **90.** John 17:20-24, **91.** Deuteronomy 30:5, **92.** John 8:14, **93.** Luke 24:49, **94.** 2 Chronicles 7:14, **95.** Matthew 3:2, **96.** John 3:18 AMPC, 15:4-6, Romans 8:1 *NKJV*, **97.** Luke 9:23, **98.** Matthew 16:25, **99.** Psalm 91:16, **100.** Leviticus 16:15-16, Genesis 3:24 *(the approaching of the Glory of God, the passing through via the Blood that was shed once and for all ... for all sin past and present)*, **101.** Matthew 6:33, **102.** Psalm 27:4, 84:10, **103.** Matthew 18:10, **104.** Psalm 46:10, **105.** Genesis 2:17, 3:19, Proverbs 3:5-6, John 8:24, Romans 8:13, **106.** John 17:16, **107.** Exodus 3:3, **108.** Hebrews 10:16, **109.** Hebrews 6:19-20, 12:21, Exodus 20:21, **110.** Mark 4:39, Matthew 14:18-21, 14:25-29, John 6:21, 14:12, 17:27, 8:3, Luke 24:49; Matthew 16:17-19, 18:18, John 5:26, 1 John 4:17b, **111.** 1 Samuel 3:1-10, **112.** John 4:24, **113.** Deuteronomy 8:3, **114.** Matthew 6:10, **115.** 1 John 4:17b, **116.** Revelation 19:15

Dated: 26/4/20

23. *Command a Harvest (#106)*
REVIVALS AND THE GLORY COME

When looking at the time of King Saul, do you remember how God wasn't ready to bring a king onto the scene, but did so because the people demanded it? Because the 'church' of the day, the very children of God, the Israelite nation as a whole … 'prayed' it? [1]

It is true, that sometimes when the church prays, it is not aligned or sensitive to the Will or Dreams of the Father. And many *(immature* [2]*)* not rightly orientated, nor positioned in their seeking God; with needs and desires set higher than the Dreams and Purposes and Heart of God. Personal motives and prayers set higher and more prioritised than treasuring the Person of God. Hence this is why the Power of God is 'rare in the land'. [3]

When looking at the life of King David, do you recall how God referred to him? … *"David is a man **after** my own Heart"* [4]. This is what you want, this is what you need … this is key if you ever want to live an Anointed life.

To express a little further, this means … dearly holding it tight in your heart: **set in pursuit 'after'** God's own Heart [5]. Not your 'prayers' … but His! … even He, the very fulfiller of prayers and dreams [6]. And so shall the Lord continue to work, revealing His 'Salvation' [7] to you. Actively revealing and making manifest His Dreams and Purposes in your life.

Eternal Salvation, yes … but so much more! … as one being 'transfigured' in Like as the Christ. Taking possession of the 'Promised Land'; [8] these very same realms of the Spirit, of Everlasting Life, and the Kingdom of Heaven.

> *If you are not 'Dream' driven, how will you ever **Know**? And if not God-driven, then how will you ever be Equipped? For His Dreams*
> *— deeply involve you! —*

In the Christian world, there remain three different and distinct realms: ***1.*** The *heart* of the believer set upon 'Egypt'; its wealth, its lust, and its attractiveness [9]. **2.** The *heart* of the believer caught up in the 'desert', *ie;* hard times and uncertainty, and in trials and testings that come [10]. **3.** Or the believer's *heart* firmly set upon [11] and actively in pursuit after the realms of the 'Promise' [12]. That is, the Heart, the Purpose, and the Destiny of God fulfilled in your life … for this makes you incorruptible and **invulnerable**.

This is true for two reasons: *Firstly,* it is God who has purposed it in Himself to take you out of 'Egypt' and bring you into the Promised Land. And if that is your honest and true purpose … then **He will fight for you** all the way unto full possession. And *secondly,* as a person bent unto the Fire of God [13], do you walk in realms of Glory that move Heaven and earth. In realms where the demon is terrified of you as one abiding under the Shadow of the Almighty [14]. These very same Places [15] where God fights to make your 'enemies your footstool' [16] … *ie;* all that comes against [17]. And where He diligently works to raise you strong and courageous, full of Grace and Love … as one able to **release that fight***!*

> *Lamb and Lion — Jesus is both —* and *to this very same are you also being raised — in the maturity of His Sonship.* [18]

Everything in this world is temporary, everything in this world fades and leads unto death. But in the Person of Jesus [19] are you a **holder of Life**; with Power of the Spirit in your hands. A believer ever *shifting* from mortal to the Immortal [20] … from the temporary unto the Everlasting. To these very Promises where God 'fights' for you [21], where God is actively at work to bring 'everything under your feet' [22]. Setting a Banqueting Table *('fine Wine and aged Meat'* [23]*)* right in the midst of your daily life … whereby you triumph … whereby you win*!* [24]

'REVIVALS AND THE GLORY COME'

Scripture:
You heavens above, **rain down my righteousness**; let the clouds shower it down. Let the earth open wide, let **salvation** spring up, let **righteousness** flourish with it; I, the LORD, have created it. *(Isaiah 45:8 NIV)*

As one born in Christ Jesus, are you a New Creation [25], a **totally new creature** — born of Christ-resurrected and victorious likeness. For as one who comes to yearn to hear and see God; heart-to-Heart focused in Him, do you hold Salvation in your hands [26].

The difference between Saul and David, was that David lived in open experience ... Encountering God. The result in which was an Anointed life; victorious, successful, and affecting the generations. Therefore, so it is also, but on a — **whole other level** — through your close relationship with God; unto the people of the world, do you have power to release the Forgiveness of the Lord [27]. Power to release Visions and Dreams upon all flesh. [28]

So therefore, shut the Gates of Hades and **open Heaven**. And by the Spirit of God and the Blood shed ... **release the Forgiveness** of God. Clear away the obstructions [29], whereby the Spirit of the Lord may fall upon all flesh. Pouring out as 'Rain' upon the righteous and unrighteous alike bearing forth the Salvation of the Lord. [30]

A '1-2-3 Step' Scripture:
How lovely is your dwelling place, Lord Almighty! My soul yearns, even faints, for the Courts of the Lord; my heart and my flesh cry out for the living God. Even the sparrow has **found a home**, and the swallow a nest for herself, where she may have her young—a place near your Altar, Lord Almighty, my King and my God. Blessed are those who **Dwell** in your house; they are ever praising you. Blessed are those whose strength is in you, whose hearts are set on **pilgrimage**. As they pass through the Valley of Baka, they make it a place of springs; the **autumn rains** also cover it with pools. They go from strength to strength, till each appears before God in Zion. *(Psalm 84:1-7 NIV)*

1. Blessed are they whose hearts **yearn** for the Courts of God.
2. They go from strength to **Strength**.
3. Turning hard and barren places into 'outpouring' springs; and places of '**Latter Day Rain**'.

Throughout David's own personal life, he continuously sought to 'gaze upon the beauty of the Lord' [31]. He was famous as one who yearned for the 'Courts of God' ... longing, above all things, to stand in His Holy Presence ... 'all the days of his life' [32]. **This is why he was <u>victorious</u>!** This is why he was successful.

Now, when David was referring to the 'Courts of God', do you yet realise that these are not 'legal courts' ... but the **Garden** realms? These deeply Wondrous Places; personally 'walking with God in the cool of the day'. Even as individuals; continuously being poured into and Imparted, Equipped and Empowered, and given many many things [33]. These are the very realms of God's Promise concerning you ... even the realms of the consuming Fire. [34]

When the people 'prayed' for a king, do you recall how they broke the Father's Heart? For it wasn't Samuel that they were rejecting ... but God Himself [35]. For truth is, that through all the generations since the Exodus, there was not ever a time in the people's own 'prayer-life' where they ever sought after God Himself. Nor ever truly honoured or desired *(with a lover's passion)* what God Himself Desired. God Himself being our "Exceedingly Great Reward." [36]

THE 'TENT OF MEETINGS'

The first and primary purpose of the coming 'out of Egypt', was not the Promise Land, but the **<u>meeting</u>** of the Person of God at Mount Sinai.

Now this is <u>key</u>: Now you know the Way unto the full Promises of God. The preferencing always the 'meeting with the Person of God', even more so than the Promises. The sitting at the feet of Jesus, even more than the needs that are before you. The deeply honouring the 'Honour' of God [37] resting upon your life, more than the *deception* of the wealth and the honour of man.

The Anointing of God comes by standing in the **rightful** Place [38]. 'Abiding' in the Promised Land of the Holy Spirit and the Kingdom realms [39]. Establishing yourself always in the 'Tent of Meetings' ... *behind* the Veil [40] ... and never leaving [41]. For here, within these realms of Glory, shall your face come to shine [42] in the Radiance of the Lord. [43]

True it is, if the people had simply paused, and if they had truly chosen just to sit; and wait in the Wonder of the God of Heaven and earth, as the Mountain shook under His mighty Presence. Then they would not have listened to the scoffer's voice *(the spirits of Doubt and Unbelief)* ... but instead listened **intently** to Almighty God [44]. Even as is said to us today, *"Diligently enter the Rest of the Lord"* ... *lest you fail!* [45]

MAKE YOU 'LIKE' GOD

Since the Beginning, God has sought to **'make'** you in God's Likeness [46]. That is what He is bent on ... and it's a continual process. To this is why the Psalmist would say, *"You are 'gods' but you will die like mere men"* [47]. For much is lost when other things become your dream. When other things, rather than the very Person of God, remain your soul's focus. For it is only God who can make you 'God-like' ... not other things. Only He can make you Valiant, Untouchable, and Powerful. [48]

Satan sought to *make* himself like God, as he impresses the very same upon us also ... that is why we fail. Hence, we learn not to be driven by what our flesh desires, nor the limitedness of own understanding and sight, but set our hearts unto the Spirit of God. For only in the fullness of Him are we made Powerful beyond measure ... clothed in the Glory and 'Immortality' of God. [49]

So the encouragement is — to within yourself — **make God Himself your dwelling Place** [50]. And here shall you ever free God to be active and at work in your life. Using all things unto your blessing.

REVIVALS AND THE ANOINTING

The focus of this chapter is not unto 'law' or 'works', but Revivals and the Anointing of God. The right vision, the right focus; ever prioritising the hearing and seeing the Lord over 'knowledge' [51]. With the overflow of such a lifestyle bearing great and incredible blessings to both your own personal spiritual walk as well as all earthly realities.

It can be summarised: 'God is more interested in **you as a person**, and to your **returning back** up in Him; than your sin, your wrongdoing, or your failures' [52]. For **1.** the Blood is your free right of access. **2.** The Spirit of God is the Transfer Agent. And **3.** the Presence of God is your **purposed Place of Dwelling**. Dwelling in the Place of Power and Might; of Counsel and the Knowledge of God. [53]

The greatest honour you can bring the Person of Jesus, is to **Manifest** Him [54]. And the greatest worship unto God is your **becoming Like Him**, *ie;* the 'New Adam' restored in you. Did you know that David was anointed king long before he stepped upon the Throne? Therefore once you recognise the Will of God concerning your life, then so shall there come great shifts in your faith and in what you seek and pray for.

God says that He **has** *"Wiped away your sin like the morning mist"* [55]. Therefore, your fundamental underlying focus is no longer unto sin or acceptance … but **unto Presence**, *ie;* physical, tangible, and living Presence and Engagement in the Person of God [56]. For this is the Place of Power. Even then, to be led [57], as one stepping up into this of your kingship 'revealed' [58]. A people ever rising up in God — with Satan firmly under your feet [59] — rather than always coming 'under' him. Sickness, sin, or slavery; rising up in Mastery and Dominion over all the works of Satan. [60]

It is amazing to think that David left such a mark, such a testimony. And so shall you also as you **enter into the full Purposes** of God. As one stepping into these realms of the Divine … so shall you also mark Heaven and earth. With Heaven and the earth itself, shifting and moving because of God who is within you. [61]

Did you realise that the spiritual *fruit* of David's own personal life; this, in his lifestyle of seeking the Presence of God; [62] is the Christ being called the 'Son of David' for all Eternity? And the earthly *fruit* of his life, is represented in his son Solomon … *ie;* abundant wisdom and prosperity.

Therefore, breathe Life unto the earth and release the Spirit of God unto action [63]. For to they of whom the Christ was sent [64], need not Religion … but the Love and Presence of God real and alive upon their lives. Even the Lord Himself coming and lifting them out of the miry mud and setting their feet on most solid ground [65]. Therefore, **1. pray the Blood** that sanctifies, **2. release the Spirit** unto charge, and **3. command** a harvest!

1-2-3 STEPS TO AN ANOINTED LIFE

In this chapter, I would like to introduce several key Scriptures that demonstrate a clear '**1-2-3 Step**' path to an Anointed life. Seven Scriptures that openly express a 'right-side-up' approach. Not the Cross inverted ... but rightly established. For example:

1. Earnestly **Love God** and seek His Person.
2. And God will continue to **open His Heart to you**.
3. He will **Anoint you** in the Power and Authority of a king. That you no longer remain a struggling or disorientated people ... but powerful in God. [66]

Let me share something before starting, you cannot live an Anointed life without the Rhema Word. You cannot live in Authority without the Living and Active Word beating Alive in your soul [67]. Independence of God is a type of witchcraft; [68] a seeking power without **submission** or union. As Jesus said, *"The Son can do **nothing by himself**; He can do only what He sees His Father doing"* [69]. And again, *"Jesus, in closest intimate relationship with the Father, has made Him known."* [70]

So, the focus need not be on the Promises ... but unto the Person of God, *ie;* He, the fulfiller of the Promises and His Dreams. Stepping back a little and giving honoured place for the Spirit and Presence of God to Move. Honouring the Word that 'proceeds from His mouth' more than your daily 'bread' ... *ie;* your concerns and needs [71]. Then so shall the Anointing come, as too the fullness of your Inheritance; as one being seated with Jesus at the right hand of God. No longer functioning only on this earthly plane [72] — but in Him — *if* that truly is where your heart is set. [73]

A person who holds God in their heart, enters 'into' the Heart of God. The Secret and Hidden Places of God revealed; and becoming your very Place of Dwelling.

Jesus is fully motivated to Anoint you with Power, for He fundamentally was sent to 'baptise' you in **both** Spirit and Power ... Spirit **and** Fire! [74] So enter into submission ... enter into humility before the Throne of Grace. As we know, these things regarding 'walking according to the Spirit' [75] are some of the most difficult concepts for the human mind to comprehend. For we all were once born of this fallen world [76] and its fallen influence. But now we born of God; as a people ever bowing unto the process of **Renewing**. [77]

Psalm 40:1
"I waited patiently for the Lord; and He **inclined** to me and heard my cry."

Psalm 130:6
"My soul **waits** for the Lord. More than the watchmen for the morning."

Psalm 37:9
"Evildoers will be cut off, but those who wait for the Lord, they will **inherit** the land."

Isaiah 64:4
"No eye has seen any God besides you, who **acts** on behalf of those who wait for him."

Luke 12:37
It will be good for them who wait upon the Lord. "Truly I tell you, I will **dress** [Myself] to serve, will have them recline at the table and will come and wait on them."

First was the Blood ... then, through the Blood, the Spirit came. However, the Spirit does not stop: for He is **purposed** to clothe you in Power. Even that you truly might rise up in this of your sonship 'revealed'. [78]

Now for some, they can only 'stomach' soup. Then others, salads and greens. But as you are personally 'strengthened' in the Lord, I pray that you truly might be able to eat 'meat'. For lions devour solid food ... babies throw up milk, but **lions eat meat**! [79]

THE NICODEMUS PHENOMENA

Presented each and every believer is the **opportunity** to 'shift'. For as a believer, you can choose to remain an 'earth dweller' … a regular human being with just regular carnal capacities [80]. Or otherwise, you can choose it within yourself to rise up in Christ Jesus as one who walks with Him in Glory. The carnal-minded man cannot understand such things, nor can they truly ever step into these realms of Dominion, Authority, and Power. However, the Spirit-minded are continually captured up again… and given 'Seeds of Faith' that move mountains. [81]

Second '1-2-3 Step' Scripture:
Even the youths shall faint and be weary, and the young men shall utterly fall, but those who **wait** on the LORD shall renew their strength; they shall mount up with **wings like eagles** *(kings of the air)*, they shall run and not be weary, they shall walk and not faint. *(Isaiah 40:30-31 NKJV)*

1. **Wait** upon the Lord.
2. Be **renewed** in Strength.
3. 'Fly' like **eagles** in kingly rule.

The treasure held in one who waits upon the Lord: God **Speaks**, God **Instructs**, God **Imparts**, and God **Anoints**. For such as these simply are positioned in themselves [82] *(in honour, welcome, and invitation)* as a people **continually renewed** and strengthened in the Lord. Even then, made able to rise up to soar on wings like eagles *(lightly, freely, easily, powerfully, and with sight over all things)*.

Truly, if there is anything about you that desires to know the Will of God concerning your life … **now you know**. Even placed as a people who cease the 'groans' of the world from 'High and Lofty' Places.

THE HIGH AND LOFTY ONE

Third '1-2-3 Step' Scripture:
Thus says the High and Lofty One Who inhabits Eternity, whose name is Holy: "I dwell in the High and Holy Place, **with him** who has a contrite and **humble spirit**, to revive the spirit of the

humble, and to revive the heart of the contrite ones. *(Isaiah 57:15 NKJV)*

1. **Humble** yourself deep within your spirit.
2. And be '**revived**' *(strengthened and uplifted)*.
3. For in you does the High and **Lofty One inhabit**.

God inhabits the realms of Eternity ... but so too in they of whom are humble and contrite of heart. To **work together with you**; to revive your heart and soul ... and that of the many. This is the Gospel message concerning you today [83]. But even more so, for such as these are continuously **captured** up into Lofty Places — with Him — as believers who **stand with Him in the realms of Eternity** [84]. And here, Anointed of Him in amazing Grace and amazing Power ... able to 'bend' Heaven and earth; able to shift and change reality. [85]

*A side note: The biblical meaning of the word 'contrite', is simply a deep desire to turn to God. As one teachable and one who **always** seeks to move forward in Him.*

Forth '1-2-3 Step' Scripture:
And he goeth up into a mountain, and calleth unto him whom he would: and they **came** unto him. And he **ordained** twelve, that they should be **with him**, and that he might send them forth to preach, and to **have power to heal** sicknesses, and to cast out devils. *(Mark 3:13-15 KJV)*

1. Respond and **come to Jesus**.
2. Personally choose to **be with Him**.
3. And He will give you an anointed message to preach and **Power to heal**.

Fifth '1-2-3 Step' Scripture:
Then the Angel of the LORD admonished Joshua, saying, "Thus says the LORD of hosts: 'If you will **walk in My Ways**, and if you will keep My command, then you shall also **judge** My House, and likewise have **charge** of My Courts; I will **give you Places to walk** among these who stand here [all my attendants standing here will be at your service]'. *(Zechariah 3:6-7 NKJV/MSG)*

1. Come walk according to the **Ways of the Spirit**.
2. **Keep His commands,** *ie;* what He is personally Teaching and Imparting within you.
3. Then you will come to walk in an **Authority far beyond comprehension**.

Sixth '1-2-3 Step' Scripture:
If then you were raised with Christ, **seek** [set your heart — affections, thoughts, and motives] those things which are above, where Christ is, sitting at the right hand of God. Set your mind [fill your thoughts with Heavenly realities] on things **Above**, not on things on the earth. For you died, and your life is hidden with Christ in God. When Christ who is our life appears, then you also will **appear with Him in Glory**. *(Colossians 3:1-4 NKJV)*

1. Set it in your heart; and seek things **Above** *(the realities of the Spirit)*.
2. Not on earthly things, for you '**died**' and your life is **hidden in Him**.
3. And so shall you **appear** with His Glory.

Seventh '1-2-3 Step' Scripture:
Behold, I stand at the door and knock. If anyone **hears** My voice and opens the door, I will come in to him and **dine with him**, and he with Me. To him who overcomes I will grant to sit with Me on My throne, as I also overcame and sat down with My Father on His throne. *(Revelation 3:20-21 NKJV)*

1. Open wide your heart to the Lord, and **He will share of Himself with you**.
2. And as you 'dine' together He will strengthen you and make you **Victorious in life**.
3. And as you overcome 'obstructions' to the Promises, and hold the Life of God in you, so shall you **operate in commanding realms in Glory**.

What we are talking about is **choosing a lifestyle of ever-deepening union** with Jesus [86]. Not in the world, or its issues or ways. Not in this life, or a vision without Him. But a heart fully set upon the Fire of God and His right hand in Glory. And what will birth from your life is the Grace of God and Divine Authority to bring change. That the Lord may truly be honoured and glorified through the **Works of <u>His</u> own hands**. [87]

THE MORE

Man needs something more than man. Each one of us **need** something more than our own self …

Let me ask a question, is Heaven and the **Joys of God** only able to be realised upon death? And are you only ever truly going to **rule and reign** when this life has passed? And is the Blood and the Spirit powerless to do more? Is the Kingdom of Heaven only a word for after this life? … or is it not so, that *"Life in **all** its Abundance"* [88] is available for each and every one of us today … this very day? So, the question remains … how do you engage?

Is the finished work of the Cross the finish of what God has for you? And is the Salvation of the Lord the end? … or is it not just the **beginning** of what God has in store? And are you not born again? This very word itself denotes a *beginning;* a birthing into, a start as 'sons' and 'daughters' of God. Not the end … but just the start*!*

Willingly lay down your life that you might truly find Life. [89]

Therefore, the Cross is the 'Entrance', it is simply the beginning of what Jesus desires to do for you — a stepping in. And how it is, that God deeply yearns to turn your life around. Even to turn your brokenness into platforms of **great success**. Lacing the very faults and brokenness of your life in gold … in high honour, turning all things around. Even now turning your frailties into great launching points as one who rises up to **soar** like eagles.

So this very day, this very moment, bow down on your knees and pray to the Lord a prayer of thanks … a simple **prayer of gratitude** for what He has done for you. In deep honour in your heart, say to the Lord, *"I really love you. And I'm so grateful for what you have achieved and done for me on the Cross. Please continue to lead me into the 'More' … into all that the Blood has birthed me into. For the Glory of the*

Name of Jesus. That all might turn their faith to Him and be healed. This I pray in Jesus Name, amen."

LATTER DAYS

Without any physical means, and without any goodness in you at all; the Blood of Jesus has opened you to the Touch of God. Hence now, as you truly respond and humble yourself before Him; so do you also open yourself up for Heaven to step into every part of your life. Even to where you yourself ... **move the Hand of God**.

The spirits of Works and Legalism seek always to keep the believer caged in a servant-like mindset. Whilst in contrast; it is the Spirit of Grace that always seeks to lead you deeper into 'sonship'. And what develops here, in sonship, is that you begin to grow exponentially. Walking in ever greater Anointing and Capacity to release the Will of God on earth.

For so it is, that a 'servant' comes only to stand before the Throne of God in times of need. Whilst it is a son, of whom responds to the underlying Heart of the Father, comes to sit up upon the Throne with Him [90]. In many respects, Jesus simply calls this 'faith' ... the least of which physically moves mountains. [91]

The Gospel message is simply about repositioning and relocating back in Him. Law says, *"I have arrived"* ... but love says, *"Take me further."* Law plateaus, but the Spirit of God takes you up in Him. And this never ceasing nor slowing down.

"Before I was under religion but now am I clothed in Immortality." (B. B.)

So let there come now, a shift in your 'prayer-life' ... and in how you seek God. For your focus and your prayers must needs now be set on what the Cross **has** achieved for you, *ie;* your '**post-Cross**' purpose rather than a 'pre-Cross' purpose *(ie; unto law and acceptance issues)*. For the truth is, that you will never truly rise up in a Triumphant life ... nor a Victorious one, until you do so. [92]

Much of the Church still lives so poorly rooted, and therefore fails to subsequently step into the Anointing of God; or truly step up upon the Throne of which the Blood has purposed them.

A CLOSING NOTE

Before, they who lived broken lives and in the gutter of despair; now enter into the Glory realms. And the same that before would feel so unworthy as to ever step into a church; they step into the Love and ministering Presence of God. And here are continuously lifted up in **His Heart** becoming truly mighty people in God. So therefore, breathe out Life and release the Spirit unto action; for they of whom the Christ was sent need not religion ... but the Love and Presence of God. Even that Christ Jesus might lift them out of the miry mud and set their feet on solid ground. [93]

Fundamentally, the purpose of the Word of God is for you to meet the Author. And now, as one who meets with Him, so it is that you shall be ever raised in your Destiny. For just as Mount Sinai came before the Promised Land, so needs your heart be unto personally **meeting** God ... **this is where your Power lies**. Even then remaining here in the 'Tent of Meetings' and never leave. This was the lifestyle of both Joshua and Jesus; the type of which forms the very basis to swiftly leading multitudes into the Promise. And into the Anointing and fullness of their Inheritance in God.

Your capacity to smash down the Gates of Hades; and to holding of the very Keys of Heaven in your hands, does not come from following man but openly hearing and seeing the Father. This is the 'right-side-up approach', this is the right target-set-vision. And just in the same that you don't launch a rocket upside-down, so too you can't 'ascend' up into Heaven and the realms of Divine Authority with your eyes set on earth.

Therefore, such is the honour, and such is the rightful place that must needs always be set unto the Spirit of God. Even then in honour: to long for, respect, and give rightful place for the Father to speak [94]. Otherwise, you shall miss it! ... eating only crumbs under the Table instead of wearing crowns. Drinking thimbles of water and not allowing yourself to delve in the River. And so, as I have expressed: **the Spirit will not be trampled**.

What you honour is what you both fear and love; the fear of being without and the love of being with. If it is money, then it is money. If it is respect and the honour of man, then it will be man. And if it is to this life, then so it will be only this life. But if it is the Lord, then in Him shall you abide, and function, and have your being. Not only so, but when you turn; so shall you strike the earth with a Divine and kingly Authority.

Bless you ... in Jesus Name.

Appendix:

1. 1 Samuel 8:6, 19-21, ***2.*** Hebrews 5:12, 1 Corinthians 3:2, ***3.*** 1 Samuel 3:1, ***4.*** 1 Samuel 13:14, Acts 13:22, Deuteronomy 32:10, ***5.*** Matthew 6:21, ***6.*** Psalm 20:4, 37:4, ***7.*** Psalm 91:16, Romans 8:19, ***8.*** Deuteronomy 1:8, Matthew 11:12, Joshua 24:13, Hebrews 10:12-13, Mark 16:19, ***9.*** Ephesians 2:6, ***10.*** James 1:2-4, ***11.*** Joshua 24:15b, ***12.*** Hebrews 4:11, ***13.*** Luke 12:49, ***14.*** Exodus 13:21, Numbers 9:15-23, Psalm 91, ***15.*** Ephesians 2:6, ***16.*** Exodus, 33:14, Psalm 110:1-2, Matthew 6:33, ***17.*** Psalm 91:9-12, ***18.*** Ephesians 4:13, Romans 8:17-19, ***19.*** John 1:12-13, ***20.*** 1 Corinthians 15:53-54, 2 Corinthians 3:18, Revelation 3:17-18, 2 Kings 2:14, 6:17, Matthew 16:17-19, Mark 16:17-19, Acts 5:15, Colossians 3:1-3, Psalm 91:1, 2:7-8, 110:1-2, 34:7, 104:2, 93:1, 84:5, Exodus 33:14-18, 34:29, John 1:51, 17:24, Genesis 1:26, 3:10, Luke 24:49, ***21.*** Exodus 14:14, 33:14, 23:28, Psalm 91:12, ***22.*** Genesis 1:26, ***23.*** Isaiah 25:6-9, Galatians 5:22-23, ***24.*** Psalm 23:5, 91:5-8, ***25.*** 2 Corinthians 5:17, ***26.*** Matthew 16:17-19, Mark 16:17-19 *(vs 19; the Reigning Christ is your right hand of Strength (Psalm 110:2, Luke 22:69, Matthew 28:18-20))*, ***27.*** John 20:21-23, ***28.*** Isaiah 61:1, Joel 2:28, ***29.*** Isaiah 64:1-4, ***30.*** Isaiah 45:8, Matthew 5:45, Psalm 84:6, ***31.*** Psalm 27:4, ***32.*** Psalm 27:4, 23:6, 16:11, ***33.*** Isaiah 45:3, John 14:21 AMPC, Psalm 110:1-2, ***34.*** Isaiah 33:14b-15a *HCSB*, Psalm 24:3-4a, ***35.*** 1 Samuel 8:7, ***36.*** Genesis 15:1, ***37.*** John 5:44, ***38.*** Zechariah 3:7, ***39.*** Matthew 4:17, ***40.*** Hebrews 6:19-20, 12:21-24, ***41.*** Hebrews 8:5, Exodus 33:11,15, John 15:7, ***42.*** Exodus 34:29-35, ***43.*** Psalm 91:1, Acts 5:15, ***44.*** Exodus 20:19, ***45.*** Hebrews 4:11, ***46.*** Genesis 1:26, ***47.*** Psalm 82:6-8, John 10:34, ***48.*** Mark 16:17-19, ***49.*** 1 Corinthians 15:53-54, Revelation 3:17-18 *(Luke 14:28-33)*, 2 Kings 2:13, Genesis 3:11, John 10:34, Psalm 82:6-8, Zechariah 3, ***50.*** Psalm 91:9, ***51.*** Genesis 2:17, ***52.*** Isaiah 44:22, Romans 5:8, ***53.*** Isaiah 11:1-4, John 15:4-11, ***54.***

Ephesians 4:13, 1 John 4:17b, Colossians 3:4, **55.** Isaiah 44:22, **56.** Matthew 17:2, John 17:24, Revelation 1:10-18, **57.** Psalm 143:10, Romans 8:14, Galatians 5:18, **58.** Revelation 1:5-6, 5:9-10, 3:21 *NKJV,* **59.** Psalm 110:1, **60.** Genesis 1:26, **61.** Isaiah 55:12, 64:1-4, Zechariah 3:7, Psalm 116:2, Daniel 10:12, **62.** Daniel 6:10, **63.** John 20:21-23, **64.** John 3:16, **65.** Psalm 40:1-3 *NKJV,* **66.** Revelation 3:17-22, **67.** John 15:7, Deuteronomy 8:3, Matthew 4:4, 16:17, **68.** Acts 8:9-24, Matthew 7:23, **69.** John 5:19, **70.** John 1:18, **71.** Deuteronomy 8:3, Matthew 4:4, Luke 9:23, **72.** John 3:13 *NKJV,* **73.** Matthew 6:21, **74.** Luke 3:16, 4:14, 12:49, 24:49, Acts 1:8, Acts 2:3, **75.** Romans 8:5, **76.** Genesis 2:17, 3:17, **77.** Romans 8:29, **78.** Romans 8:19, **79.** 1 Corinthians 3:1-2, **80.** John 10:34-36, Psalm 82:6-8, **81.** John 3:13 *NKJV,* Matthew 18:17-19, John 12:24-26, Matthew 18:3, Matthew 18:10, Matthew 17:20, **82.** 1 Samuel 30:6b, **83.** Luke 4:18, Matthew 18:3, **84.** John 17:20-24, Zechariah 3:7, **85.** Matthew 17:20, Mark 6:35-37, John 6:21, **86.** John 17:20-24, **87.** Luke 12:49, John 15:7-8, **88.** John 10:10, **89.** John 10:17, Matthew 16:24-25, Luke 24:49, 12:37, John 5:44. Colossians 3:1-4, Revelation 3:17-22, **90.** Isaiah 28:11-13, **91.** Matthew 17:20, **92.** Revelation 3:21, **93.** Psalm 40:1-4, **94.** Exodus 20:19

Dated: 19/6/20

MOUNT SINAI, THE WAY OF THE ANOINTED

24. Mount Sinai, the Way of the Anointed (#107)

MOUNT SINAI, THE WAY OF THE ANOINTED

A big subject for me these last few months is Mount Sinai. Do you remember how the first and primary calling of the Exodus wasn't the Promise Land but meeting God at Mount Sinai? Such is the subject of this chapter. That first and foremost — before **all** things — honour your time meeting with God.

To go on further, *"Mount Sinai is the 'portal' to the Promise"* [1]. Or otherwise said, *"Meeting with God causes you able to 'cross' over desert experiences right into the realms of Promise."* Or let's keep going, *"Deeply honouring the Fire of God* [2], *deeply honouring 'ascending'* [3] *into the realms of Glory, crosses you over difficulties and hardships right into the realms of Power and Life."* Crosses you over, right into the realms of your Inheritance … even these, the very realms of Everlasting Life and Dominion in God. To engage and draw from … making real and manifest on earth. [4]

Jesus fundamentally came as a Life-Giving-Spirit [5]. Therefore, as one born of Christ Jesus are you **born the very same** [6]. Sometimes the Spirit falls as rain, other times … like a river, and still yet other times He comes like a flood. Hence therefore, as a 'Life-Giving-Spirit' you have **Power to birth Revivals**. You have Power to release the Spirit of God in all things. First in things 'small' and close in your own personal life, then in things broad and wide. Then also for the nations … sweeping uncontrollably across the land. For you are born in 'Like' as the Son; even He who sits at the right hand of God. He being your very **right-hand-of-Strength**. [7]

A side note: The reason why 'revivals' are rare in Western nations is the corruption in the heart of man. Adultery, coveting, pride, religion, and mammon … and not knowing the Love of God. Then in other lands, where they have only known the demon; the darkness, the witchcraft, and the cursing. The contrast of Christ brings a full embrace. But still … darkness tries to rise.

EGYPT, THE DESERT, AND THE PROMISE

I really encourage you, first and foremost, honour the Presence of God. Honour meeting with — He [8] — of whom the Blood has so richly availed. And this more treasured ... and more greatly sought after ... than answers to your own problems and needs.

Nothing expresses this better than the Exodus account. I really encourage you, hunger and thirst for the Voice of God burning Alive in your heart [9]. Even this, the Living Water from the Tree of Life that Jesus Himself personally gives [10] ... and the continually being lifted up in Him [11]. And just as in the Exodus *('die'* [12]): put aside your past, put aside your future, and put aside the 'scoffing unbelieving' voices and troubles at hand ... and exercise the Blood. That is, exercise your own fundamental right to sit in the Place of High Honour in the Glory of God [13]. With 'Life-Giving-Power' over all problems you face and all future days before you. [14]

Come, open yourself to a culture of meeting with Jesus [15] ... and be no longer *lost* in the 'desert'. But continuously responding to the Call as one **walking** in the realms of 'Promise'. Stepping over into realms of your Inheritance; even into these of the Glory and Anointing of the Lord — which is your Birthright. [16]

Here, by the Power of the Blood of Jesus, decisively step over all 'realities of this life' ... into the realms of the Spirit. That you be continually Led and Empowered from within the Presence of God [17]. As one taken continually deeper into the great unknown 'lands' of the Kingdom of Heaven; [18] even these very same Places and Promises stolen man since the Beginning.

Before it was, that the people of Israel, were transitioning into a land that was promised them. Taking **possession** of physical 'Promised' lands as their inheritance. However today, the very **Call** of the Son is for you to transition into the very realms of Heaven ... taking possession of 'Dominion in Him' over Heaven and earth — and over all spiritual powers and authorities — from within the Sovereignty of God. [19]

It was Satan who was jealous of the love — God held — for this *creature* called 'man'. And iniquity was found in him who *was* the

Morning Star; [20] as God poured out of Himself and formed child of God. Man is not an 'angel' but is a **child of Light** — uniquely purposed '**made**' [21] to be fashioned into God's very Image and God's very Likeness. So before going on further ... always **recognise who you are** and where you are from.

Throughout the hundreds of generations prior to us, the *Liar* has stolen and worked to withhold from you your true Origins. Aggressively and tenaciously at work to misdirect, distract, and push against. Therefore, no longer retain the 'mind of this Age' ... but diligently work it within yourself to gain the Mind of Christ. He of whom was crucified that you too might **walk reborn** as son of God. [22]

So when you pray, first recognise where you are from: as one standing [23], praying from within the realms of Dominion. And just as Jesus breathed out Life over you [24], so too do you also ... upon all that you face and all that is before you. Breathe out Life and Spirit, Power and Presence ... to go out before you to aggressively 'fight' on your behalf [25]. Be not of mixed seed but wholly unto the Lord ... and let your mouth bear forth Life. [26]

PRE-DESTINED DOMINION

*"Let us **make** man like one of us, let us make man in our Image and our Likeness. And let us give him Dominion."* [27]

In this subject of 'Divine interaction' in the Kingdom of Heaven, your openness to meet with the Person of God *was* ... **is** the Way of the Son. Therefore, recognise always, that the first and underlying desire and purpose of the Spirit of God — *since the Beginning* — is to continue to 'fashion' you into the Image and Likeness of God [28]. Therefore, the retained earnest desire to meet with the Lord opens you to 'transfiguration'. And like a chrysalis, continually opening yourself up to your Divine and fundamental Destiny.

Now, it is through retaining an ever-treasured honour for the Fire and Presence of God, that softens and prepares you for the 'touch' of the Potter's hand. Even He who diligently works to take you from the dirt and dust [29] and 'make' you a child of Light [30] ...

make you **Like one of Him** *31*. This is your Divine Calling in the Lord; the fundamental underlying Purpose of God concerning you! And it's never to be forgotten ... and never to be misplaced or mislaid; for **all** efforts of God are centred unto this very thing. *9*

Through the finished work of the Cross, you have been *"Seated in Heavenly Places"* *32*. And *"In God's House there are many rooms and many mansions"* ... where Jesus will take you ... *"To be **with** Him where He is"* *33*. Therefore, the answer is always unto the humbling of yourself *34*, whereby you may continue to be led into the '**all** of which has been laid up in store' ... to participate in and eat of this very day. As one raised and seated with Him at the right hand of God Almighty upon the Throne of Glory.

The very word 'Anointing' means to be endowed with Authority, Power, and Dominion by the King *35*. This Dominion of God cannot be given you of any man, nor can it of any fleshly endeavour or zeal. But only as you personally humble yourself before He — the very Person of Jesus.

I so deeply encourage you, learn to whistle a tune in the face of Satan ... and continually praise the Name of Jesus. For you need not *live* 'under' trials or tribulations any longer ... you need not *live* in the 'desert'. But by choice, rise up to come under the Divine Authority God *36*. So in this we firmly say, *"Satan, beware! Go back to the pit of which you belong. I command Life, I command Prosperity, I command Restoration ... and I command the Fire and Glory of God in Jesus Name."* *37*

EGYPT — THE DESERT — OR THE PROMISED LAND

As believers, the heart of the Church can, at times, become despondent. For though believing in the Lord Jesus Christ; not really ever seeing the Power of God active. For so it is, that the Church has not understood the difference between the three distinct realms where your soul can be directed *(mind, will, and emotions)*. Your spirit may be 'Alive' unto God ... Alive in the Spirit and the Kingdom realm. But the **motive of your soul**, *ie;* the thoughts held within and the place where your love truly lies ... can be totally somewhere else.

Three distinct 'heart-locations': **1.** If you can be one who truly turns away from the world and its enticements *('Egypt')*. **2.** If you can truly turn your heart beyond problems and difficulties *('desert')*. **3.** And truly look beyond unto the Promises and the Dreams of God for your life *('Promised Land')*. Then you would become an **unstoppable** force. For just as in the Exodus, God would personally fight for you, He would personally **war on your behalf** ... for the 'story' remains the same.

It was God who was bent on taking the people into the Promised Land. And just in the same way: He is **bent on establishing you** in your Inheritance today. As in the Exodus, God will make you successful, He will **fight** your battles, He will **drive** the *Enemy* from the land, and He will make it so that your 'sandals' never wear out. And this *angelic* reality, this walking like the Son ... as a child of the Most High, so far surpasses all that the world has to offer.

However, even more so ... and even more incredibly; these very Promised realms destined and purposed for the believer, are themselves the very realms of Power, Authority, and Anointing. Where **you make choice** [38], where you release Heaven and the Will of God on earth. For in truly surrendering your life unto God's Dreams — He will clothe you with Himself — He will clothe you with Power [39]. For your heart is set upon the Place where God Himself is working to take you.

It is most important for the Christian Church — to know and understand — the plans God has *('Promised Land')* for the Born Again. Even these very things of His very Purpose and earnest intent. For what Christ has Promised and intended for you far *surpasses* in both this life and the life to come. Even so that you be a releasor of Life ... a releasor of Spirit.

Come, and let's pray this powerful prayer, *"Spirit of the Living God, you manage my concerns in life, you manage my finances and my ability to provide, you oversee and manage my family ... these are your responsibility* [40]. *As for me I earnestly seek and go after the Fire of God."*

Scripture:
So it is written, "The first man Adam became a living being." The last Adam became [31b] a life-giving Spirit. *(1 Corinthians 15:45 NKJV)*

Christ Jesus came as a **life-giving Spirit**. Therefore, as one born of the Christ so are you born of the very same ... hence, we lay our life down in order to pursue Life. And this is why our Father pours out His Love so generously towards us — and reveals of Himself so richly — for we willingly lay down our life down in death **only to pick it up again in Life** [41]. The shifting our hearts away from a 'flesh-driven motive' unto a 'Spirit-driven motive'; [42] our hearts set upon Heaven and the right hand of God *(ie; the 'Fire'* [43]*)*, that we might walk in the fullness and of the Glory of God. [44]

Authority in God is the ability to **release** the Spirit of God; and Dominion, is standing in a Place Above all things; and Anointing given, is Power to rule and govern ... for just as Revival starts first as rain, then forms into streams and rivers ... so too does the Outpouring of the Spirit come as a flood that totally overwhelms. Therefore, **release the Spirit** of God in all things! Do not come under, do not tolerate ... but rise up Above in Christ Jesus and pour out the Glory of God.

Revivals start in your own day-to-day life; the releasing of the Spirit of God in what you speak, in how you act, and in all your daily issues. For if you cannot command Life in your own personal day-to-day goings, then how then could you ever for the nations? The **Outpouring of the Spirit starts with you** [45] ... even unto your family that needs you. The pouring out of both Life and Spirit [46] unto the flesh, the minds, and the hearts of those around you. Then so too upon the nations: shall you release a 'flood' of the Revival of God. Ever the Sovereignty and Holiness of the Lord standing in our midst [47] where all must bow; both believing and unbelieving alike. For who can stand before the Holiness of our God?

Five Scripture verses: *(Tree of Life)*
1. So He drove out the man; and He placed cherubim at the east of the garden of Eden, and a flaming sword which turned every way, to **guard the way** to the Tree of Life. *(Genesis 3:24 NKJV)*

2. And there I will meet with you, and I will speak with you from above the mercy seat, from **between the two cherubim** which are on the ark of the Testimony. *(Exodus 25:22 NKJV (Leviticus 16:2))*
3. He who has an ear, let him hear what the Spirit says to the churches. To him who overcomes I will **give to eat** from the Tree of Life, which is in the midst of the Paradise of God. *(Revelation 2:7 NKJV)*
4. On each side of the river stood the Tree of Life, bearing twelve crops of fruit, yielding its fruit every month. And the leaves of the tree are for the **healing** of the nations. *(Revelation 22:2 NIV)*
5. I have swept away your offenses like a cloud, your sins like the morning mist. **Return to me**, for I have redeemed you. *(Isaiah 44:22 NIV)*

To the *fallen*, God has shut the way to the Tree of Life; with Cherubim set to guard the way with flaming flashing swords. To *Moses*, God appeared and spoke from between the Cherubim that are upon the Ark of the Covenant. To the *Risen*, upon the same Mercy Seat, has the Blood of Jesus been sprinkled. For the Blood-bought redeemed have now been given right to pass through into realms not permitted man.

To eat of the Tree of Life **brings healing** into your being. And to eat and dine liberally of the Tree of Life brings healing to the nations. To 'overcome' is to choose to live with a heart fully unto God … and though we live in the world, our hearts are not set in it. Hence Jesus gives us right to eat, and to be healed … and to bring Healing to the nations.

God isn't interested in your sin or wrongdoing; He has wiped them from your life. To whom He is interested in, and drawn to, are they whose desire is to move forward. You have already been redeemed through the finished work of the Cross … so **return**! Return where? … but back unto the Garden realms. The very same realms of Glory where the Tree of Life stands.

Appendix:

1. Genesis 3:24, Exodus 25:20-22, Leviticus 16:2, Luke 12:49, 24:49, Revelation 2:5, 3:17-22, 22:2, *2.* Luke 12:49, 24:49, *3.* Isaiah 2:2-5, Exodus 24:9-18, Mark 3:13-15, 2 Corinthians 3:18, *4.* Matthew 6:10, *5.* 1 Corinthians 15:45, *6.* John 20:21-22, *7.* Matthew 16:17-19, Mark 16:17-19, Psalm 110:2, Isaiah 41:10, *8.* Genesis 15:1, Psalm 16:5 *NKJV*, Romans 8:17, *9.* Deuteronomy 8:3, John 15:7, Luke 24:32, *10.* Isaiah 44:3-4, 48:18, John 4:14, 7:37-39, Revelation 22:1-2, *11.* Exodus 33:14-15, Psalm 40:2, *12.* Matthew 16:24-25, John 10:17, *13.* Exodus 20:21, *14.* Deuteronomy 31:8, *15.* Revelation 3:20, *16.* Genesis 25:34, *17.* Exodus 13:21, 33:14, Romans 8:14, *18.* 1 Corinthians 2:9, *19.* Colossians 3:1-3, Revelation 3:21, Zechariah 3:7, Genesis 1:26, *20.* Isaiah 14:12, Ezekiel 28:15, *21.* Genesis 1:26, Romans 8:29 *(Psalm 91:9)*, *22.* John 12:36, *23.* Zechariah 3:7, *24.* John 20:22, 6:63, *25.* Exodus 14:14, 33:14, 23:28, Psalm 110:1-2, *26.* Matthew 13:24-30, James 3:8-12, *27.* Genesis 1:26, *28.* Genesis 1:26, 5:3, Romans 8:29-30, 12:2, 2 Corinthians 3:18, Ephesians 4:13, *29.* Genesis 3:19, 1 Corinthians 15:49, *30.* Ephesians 5:8, *31.* John 10:30, *32.* Ephesians 2:6, *33.* John 14:1-3, *34.* Isaiah 57:15, Matthew 18:3, 18:10, Luke 14:10, *35.* Revelation 2:7, 17, 26-28, 3:12, 19-22, *36.* Psalm 91:1, Acts 5:15, *37.* Genesis 1:26, *38.* Matthew 16:19, John 20:21-23, Revelation 2:26-27, 19:15, Psalm 2:7-9, 110:1-2, Romans 8:29, 2 Kings 2:14, Isaiah 11:1-9, 41:14-20, 61:1-6, 64:1-4, Genesis 1:26, *39.* Luke 24:49, Genesis 3:10, Revelation 3:17-18, 1 Corinthians 15:53-54, 2 Corinthians 3:18, 2 Kings 2:14, 6:17, Matthew 16:17-19, Mark 16:17-19, Acts 5:15, Colossians 3:1-3, Psalm 91:1, 2:7-8, 110:1-2, 34:7, 104:2, 93:1, 84:5, John 1:51, Exodus 33:14-18, 34:29, John 17:24, Genesis 1:26, *40.* Matthew 6:33, 2 Kings 2:14, *41.* John 10:17, *42.* Galatians 5:19-26, *43.* Exodus 24:17, Isaiah 33:14b-15a *HCSB*, Psalm 24:3-4a, Luke 12:49, *44.* Colossians 3:1-4, *45.* Matthew 13:11-12, *46.* John 6:63, *47.* Psalm 84:6

Dated: 19/9/20

25. Mount Sinai, the Way of the Anointed (#108)
TRAINING FOR KINGSHIP

*"Without a king-focus, offers nothing beyond your ministry or beyond your problems. But **with** a king focus, you have Power to move reality."*

Opening Scripture:
"Behold, I send an Angel before you to keep you in the way and to bring you into the place which I have 'prepared' [the '**seated realms**' [1]]." *(Exodus 23:20 NKJV)*

I personally need the Presence of God for my sanity and wellbeing. Christianity isn't about dressing right or being perfect in the eyes of others, but about connecting problems to the Glory and Power of God. [2]

But how can I ever do that if I am still 'Egypt' focused? And the same, how can I if I am still 'Desert' focused? But … if I am '**Promise**' focused, all problems are simply obstacles in my way to be moved [3] For it's not mine to come under fear but under the Power of God … even to abide here in the All-Consuming-Fire. [4]

'Authority to Birth Revival' is simply Authority to pour out the Spirit of God; Authority to trigger and initiate [5] Moves of the Most High God *(starting with my own life and my own soul)*. And unto the Promised Rest of which I am called; [6] is simply the coming into and 'sitting' [7] at the right hand of God. These wondrous Garden realms of Grace and Unceasing Power as one being 'raised' [8] in Likeness of God. This is my Father's very own personal Dream since the Beginning … as is said, *"Let us make man in our Image and in our Likeness, and let us give him Dominion."* [9]

Hence now, if you were to truly come and make God's own Personal Dream **your own personal dream**. And if you were to truly come and make God's Personal Prayer your own personal prayer. Then as like in the 'Exodus-story-of-Promise' God would **fight** for you [10]. And not only fight and go out before you but establish you Untouchable [11]. For your Destiny is not just a land flowing with 'milk and honey' [12] … but a 'land' flowing with Life and Spirit. Your fundamental Destiny is the realms of Power and Glory as co-heirs *(ie; a reality shifter)*. Therefore, speak to your mountains [13] ... *"Move!"* And to sicknesses, finances and fear, and to all the works of the *Enemy* ... *"Be moved in Jesus Name!"*

Scripture:
"Cease striving and **know** that I am God; I will be exalted among the nations, I will be exalted in the earth." *(Psalm 46:10 NASB)*

GOD HAS A DREAM

God has a Dream; God has His own Personal Prayers. Therefore, in unifying [14] your dreams with His Dreams, your soul-prayer unto His very own 'soul' Prayer ... then you are unstoppable [15] ... incorruptible [16] ... and untouchable. [11]

God's Promises have a Purpose. His Dream, to restore man back into his 'pre-fallen' state. Satan was jealous and indignant, and war started in Heaven [17] for he saw God's vulnerability; His 'weeping' Heart fully exposed towards this creature called 'man'.

Now today, God is in the Restoration business. He is fully bent on leading the **willing** [18] back into the 'former' Glory. Therefore, be diligent to take Egypt out of your heart ... and firmly set your eyes beyond the 'desert'. The **way** to the Promised Land flowing with 'Life and Spirit' — is Mount Sinai. The **sitting at the feet of Jesus** and continually gazing upon the Wonder of Him [19]. And so shall His Presence be with you [20] and so shall He openly fight on your behalf. [21]

*"Be still, and **know** God"* [22]. *Be still, and **know** the Salvation of the Lord* [23]. *It is dangerous for that of which comes against, for all must deal with the Vengeance of God.*

Let your soul be in hot pursuit [24] after [25] God's own Dreams and Prayers. And so shall your own 'prayers' be rightly aligned; your prayers be Anointed with Power. Therefore, say to any problem that you face, *"Holy Ghost, I lay down all things and openly pursue the Fire of God. Holy Ghost ... you fight!"*

Mount Sinai:
Presence is the way to the Promises. The choosing to 'climb up' [26] into the Place where flesh cannot go [27]. To this we say to obstructions, *"Get out of my way!"* And to sickness and disease, *"Be healed in Jesus Name!"* And even further, *"Spirit of the Lord I release the Vengeance and Glory of the Lord."* [28]

Upon the Mountain of God:
It is in the Presence of the Lord that God writes His 'laws' upon your heart. Even here, right in the midst of your brokenness and sin. For all have fallen short of His Glory. The Blood sanctifies … however, it is the Spirit of the Lord that transforms.

LIFE-GIVING SPIRIT

Scripture:
And so it is written, "The first man Adam became a living being." The last Adam became a life-giving spirit. *(1 Corinthians 15:45 NKJV)*

The word 'born again' means, repositioned back into your original Place of Origins; restored, re-risen, and re-established. It means 'Revived', re-'Spirited', and re-'Seated'. Recognise, that this is not a 'dead' origin left to us by Adam, but one full of Life and full of Spirit inherent in you. Life and Spirit is **in** you: as one made in the Image and Likeness of God. Not so much about asking; but pouring out … releasing … and ushering forth.

— Pray the Blood —
— Release the Spirit —
— Command a Harvest! —

The Blood **sanctifies** all things; all you hold close to heart, and all you present before God. Now **release the Spirit**, and in this **command** fruit, command healing, command restoration. God is not interested in where you are from … but inherently and intimately in where you are going [29]. Therefore, outpour the Spirit of God and command Revival!

'1-2-3 Steps' continued …

Scripture: *(Egypt — Desert — Promises)*
1. Those whom I love I rebuke and discipline. So be **earnest** and 'repent' *(ie; turn from 'Egypt', turn from the ways and desires of the world. And allow yourself to become pliable and teachable ... as one desiring to move forward)*.
2. Here I am! I stand at the door and knock. If anyone hears my voice and **opens** the door, I will come in and eat with that person, and they with me *('desert': walking together in life's challenges. Sharing one to another and growing. Imparting and sharing with you what is in His Heart ... and **taking** you where He is, ie; the Garden realms, the realms of Dominion)*.
3. To the one who is victorious, I will give the right to sit with me on my throne, just as I was victorious and sat down with my Father on his throne *('Promises': Jesus Imparts and Empowers you by His Spirit, to walk **beyond** sin and death, and sit in realms of Authority where **you move Heaven**)*.
* Whoever has ears, let them **listen** *(intently)* to what the Spirit says to the churches *(listen intently and pay heed, look closely into and respond)*. *(Revelation 3:19-22 NIV)*

Listen! ... Jesus is calling you unto kingship so respond. By the precious shed Blood of Jesus, He has *fundamentally* Anointed you king and priest unto God [30]. But just as David was anointed king, it was fourteen years until he was seated *(with a lot of opposing forces)*. Hence, in the same way, we also are Purposed of God to 'diligently enter that Rest' [31]. This is the believer's Promised 'land' to enter ... the very Calling of the Most High God. Therefore, **humble** yourself, and allow your King to continue to **raise you as king** ... for He is Lord of 'lords' [32]. Angels are servants, but sons are co-heirs. Jesus is Lord of lords and King of kings ... **this is you**!

Let there be a shift: Slave mentality to Israelite mentality. Pre-Cross mentality ... to Risen; Resurrected, Triumphant, and Powerful.

LOOK BEYOND
Scripture:
Since, then, you have been raised with Christ, set your hearts [affections, thoughts, and motives] on things Above, where Christ is, seated at the right hand of God. Set your minds on things above,

not on earthly things. For you died, and your life is now hidden with Christ in God. *(Colossians 3:1-3 NIV)*

In accordance to your own life: It is your Saviour King that is asking — that you truly turn to Him — in all things! *33* As one continuously open, welcoming Jesus to sit and dine with you *34*. You with Him and He with you ... ever 'walking in the Garden realms with God in cool of the day'.

Jesus uses such definitive words as 'die' ... die in order that you truly might find Life *35*. Life, as 'External Input' pouring into your being; continual Divine interaction and Input pouring into your life from the Person of God. Life and Spirit flowing; as one participating in the realms of Everlasting Life. These very realms of the Kingdom of Heaven, these very same realms of Life from which Adam fell. And this very Life and Presence shall fight for you making you Untouchable *36*. Abundant Life held within that totally overwhelms sin, death, and the grave. *37*

Jesus would talk about *"Living Water welling up from within"* *38*. And He would speak of, *"Feeding on Him so that you Live"* *39*. The very Fruits of the Spirit are wondrous realities purposed to abundantly Grace your life. With the 'Breath of Life' in you, that you yourself breathe out. *40*

Continuing in this truth: It is from this precious Place that you shall be raised most Victorious, Triumphant, and Mighty in the Lord. For it is your Saviour King of whom has purposed it in Himself; *41* that you come to sit upon the Throne of Glory. Even as a people who release both Life and Spirit into the world of which we live ... that is, the Salvation of the Lord. *42*

The believer can come under many things ... depression, fear, or lust. But it is your Father who is calling you today to come up Above in Him ... even then to Rule in the midst of your enemies. The opportunity to come up in God is presented to all who believe through the precious Blood of the Lamb. Therefore come, and step back a little, and give full honoured place for the Lord of Glory to work. Come now and enter right into His ministering Grace. Learning this today before you have to tackle truly impossible situations. Train yourself like a soldier; make active steps to train yourself this very day.

Now I have taught you the right Way, that your cup may truly overflow [43]. Even then as one who sits upon the Throne of God making 'judgement' ... releasing the Goodness of God. [44]

But the people make excuses, *"I have just bought a field, and I must go and see it. Please excuse me."* And to another, *"I have just bought five yoke of oxen, and I'm on my way to try them out"* [45]. Therefore, true it is, that we all can still be so caught up in our life and the things that we deem important. But then it is God who says, *"Go out to the roads and country lanes and compel them to come in, so that my house will be full. I tell you, not one of those who were invited will get a taste of my Banquet."* [46]

So I **compel** you today ... in Jesus Name, to deeply value 'dining in the Lord' [47]. This meeting and sitting with Him daily — of uttermost priority. That, as a person, you truly might experience the Lord, as you face the realities of this world. As is said, *"He sets a Banqueting Table right in the midst of my enemies"* [48]. Walking in the fullness of your Divine Inheritance as one being raised a most powerful force.

MEETING WITH GOD MAKES YOU A FORCE OF RECKONING

Scripture:
Grace and peace be multiplied to you in the Knowledge of God and of Jesus our Lord, as His Divine Power has given to us all things that pertain to life and godliness, through the Knowledge of Him who called us by glory and virtue. By which have been given to us exceedingly great and precious Promises, that through these you may be **partakers** of the Divine Nature [participators], having escaped the corruption that is in the world through lust. *(2 Peter 1:2-4 NKJV/NIV)*

The Purpose of the Blood is your underlying capacity to meet with God. Even then to meet with Him to the measure of your own heart's desire. Nothing represents this picture better than the Mount Sinai account. I really encourage you, let us no longer be a people who only gather around the Mountain ... but a people who

'Ascend' [49]. A people truly open to come 'up' to truly hear and to truly see the Lord [50]. Even that we, as a people, might be led further into Places where flesh is not permitted. [51]

God's Word that speaks is full of Life and full of Spirit.

Through the Cross, you have incredible and inherent capacity to go into God in widths and depths that was not possible even for Moses [52]. I so encourage you — **step into 'the More'**. Prioritise the stepping into all of which has already been freely given. Come, put aside all things — even through a culture of prayer and fasting. For Meeting with God is the Way of the Son. Meeting with God is the Way of the Anointed.

The Blood — right now — has 'seated you in Heavenly Places'. So come then and be seated! Especially here and now in the midst of whatever you are facing. The Anointing and Glory of God rests upon they of whom choose it within themselves to sit and abide — regardless; [53] and this in Measure upon Measure; Glory upon Glory; [54] Place upon Place; and Anointing upon Anointing. And so it is that you shall be led continually deeper into that of which is already yours. Authority upon Authority, Dominion upon Dominion, and Power upon Power. And this pressed down shaken together and running over. [55]

Jesus asks, *"How can you believe since you accept glory from one another but do not seek the Glory that comes from the only God?"* [56] For the kind of 'belief' that truly moves mountains, is derived only from 'seeking the Glory that comes from the only God'. The receiving 'Seeds of Faith' planted by the Spirit of God. And these things have nothing to do with someone else … but are given you personally of the Person of God.

Now here, are you entering into the 'Faith' realms. Entering into the realms of 'Prayer' … deep in Him. And as you continue to humbly come and sit before the Lord of Glory, just in honour of Him and His Word and Love ever resting upon your life; [57] then so does God Himself — respond with Honour — and lift you up like nothing else. God Himself gracing your life with incredible and Divine *'External Input'*. The same integration of Heaven active Alive in your life that Adam himself lived in prior to the Fall [58]. The deep flow of Everlasting Life in you ... and into your world. Like a gateway — a portal — for you and your people.

I really encourage you in this; depression, hopelessness and despair is removed by a single Touch. But don't stop there! ... make it by choice **your Place of Dwelling**. Now it can be more easily understood, how you can step into greater realms of Anointing, Power, and Glory. For in Him shall you live and move and have your being [59]. And so too, in the continual meeting, are you made an unstoppable force ... walking in the Divine.

1 Corinthians 2:9-13 *(paraphrased):*
No human mind has conceived the things God has prepared for those who love Him. Come, let's go together and meet with God, so that we truly may know Him and step into all that God has freely given us. Even these very things that cannot be expressed by human wisdom, but are revealed through **Spirit-taught words** in the Presence of the Lord.

So again, I say, the Purpose of the Blood is your ability to meet with God. And so can you meet with Him to the measure of that of which you yourself believe. And so it is, that as you meet with the Person of God; does the width and depth of your belief and faith ever increase. Your tent pegs expanding and expanding [60] by the Hand of God. Here, ever opening you up to greater and greater capacity to 'participate in His Divine Nature' [61]. That of which is inconceivable to the human mind ... freely stepped into, engaged, and drawn out in casual ease.

'Darkness' [62] remains due to a lack of Knowledge. And this kind of Knowledge that heals the soul and empowers you; is given up upon Mount Sinai.

True, we can all still be operating out of various forms of religious practices. Setting up structures according to what we ourselves believe. But what God wants for each one of us, is that we be ever open to the Spirit — and to what He Himself believes. The shift from a human perspective unto God's Vision of why He spilt the Blood of His Son. The shift from our limited human vision to God's Vision that far exceeds!

HOLY OF HOLIES

Scripture:
Moses approached the thick darkness where God was. *(Exodus 20:21b NIV)*.

This account of meeting God at Mount Sinai was for Moses a 'Holy of Holies' experience — the All-Consuming Fire of God. The Glory realms, the intense Presence, earthquakes and lightning — fearful and terrible. Moses trembled and feared as he entered; but it is to this very place where Jesus Himself delighted in. Hence, I too also delight ... pursue ... and long for. [63]

The Place of the Fear of God whereby you have nothing to fear.

At first it was only Moses who was permitted to approach the Mountain. No other person *(or animal)* was allowed even to come near; but all stood at a distance. And this very same picture remained true all the way until the Cross, with only the Divinely appointed given right of access. However now, it is the Blood of Jesus that has — 'Divinely appointed' you — not only to observe at a distance, but to fully enter in. And this is the Purpose of God concerning you this very day — such is the Way of an Anointed life — such is the Way of they who choose to walk according to the Spirit of God. [64]

Most believers have been so set upon the question, *"What is my calling?"* ... *"What is my purpose as I walk earth?"* Without ever recognising the true and full **Purpose of the Blood** and subsequently engaging. First, there was the Inner Court where the people gathered ... however, **your purpose is to ascend** [65]. Then there is the Holy Place, but do not forget or despise the Holy of Holies ... this the all-consuming Glory of God behind the Veil. As a king and a priest unto God: here you have incredible opportunity to pitch your tent and never leave! And Jesus simply calls this ... 'Abide' and 'Remain'. [66]

There is the Outer Court of which is the world, then the Inner Court that is for the citizens of Heaven. But then there is the Holy Place and the Holy of Holies. Therefore, do not despise your birthright ... like Esau did. Do not despise the Presence of God.

Scripture:
And Jacob gave Esau bread and stew of lentils; then he ate and drank, arose, and went his way. Thus Esau **despised** his birthright. *(Genesis 25:34 NKJV)*

Let's close with this prayer, *"Thank you Lord, that we can honour you and love you with all our hearts. And thank you Lord, that by the Blood of Jesus we can **meet** freely with our Heavenly Father ... daily. Even then to truly leave Egypt behind and ascend up into the 'Mountain of the House of the Lord that is Above the mountains'. And thank you Lord that here you continue to lead us into all that you have prepared and made ready for each one of us. Even to step into all that is Promised; into all of our Inheritance, and into all that is far beyond human comprehension. Therefore today, I sanctify myself in your Presence* [67] *and step up in you in Jesus Name. Amen."*

Appendix:

1. John 14:1-3, *2.* 1 Corinthians 4:20, 2 Timothy 3:5, *3.* Deuteronomy 8:3, Matthew 4:4, *4.* Psalm 91:1, Acts 5:15, Exodus 34:30, John 17:24, Isaiah 11:1-4, 33:14b-15a *HCSB*, 64:1-4, Matthew 8:26, 17:17, 20, Mark 16:17-19, *5.* Matthew 16:19, *6.* Hebrews 4:11, *7.* Isaiah 28:12, Psalm 110:1-2, *8.* Revelation 3:19-22, *9.* Genesis 1:26, Psalm 110:1-2, *10.* Exodus 11:1-2 // Matthew 26:28, 27:51, Hebrews 9:22), 14:21-31, 14:14, 33:14, 23:28, Joshua 24:12, *11.* Psalm 91:9-16, Matthew 16:17-19, Mark 16:17-19, *12.* Exodus 3:17, Numbers 14:8, Deuteronomy 28:1-14, *13.* Romans 8:17-19, *14.* John 17:21, *15.* Exodus 14:14, 33:14, 23:28, *16.* John 10:17, 14:30b, Isaiah 33:14b-15a *HCSB*, *17.* Revelation 12:7–10, *18.* Revelation 22:11. *19.* Psalm 27:4, John 17:24, Numbers 21:9, Hebrews 8:5, *20.* Exodus 33:14-18, *21.* Exodus 14:14, 33:14, Joshua 24:12, *22.* Psalm 46:10, *23.* Psalm 91:16, *24.* Revelation 2:4, Luke 24:49, *25.* Acts 13:22b, *26.* Colossians 3:1-4, Isaiah 2:1-4, *27.* Exodus 20:19, John 5:19, 10:17, Matthew 18:3, 10:39, *28.* 2 Kings 2:14, Proverbs 6:31, Deuteronomy 28:7, 7:20, Isaiah 54:13-17, Revelation 2:26-27, 19:15, *29.* Isaiah 44:22, *30.* Revelation 1:5-6, 5:9-10 *NKJV*, *31.* Hebrews 4:11, Isaiah 28:12, *32.* Psalm 110:1-2, *33.* John 16:33, *34.* Matthew 6:11, Psalm 23:5, Isaiah 25:6-8, Revelation 3:20, *35.* Matthew 16:24, 10:39, *36.* Psalm 82:6, *37.* 1 Corinthians 15:53-55, *38.* John 4:14, *39.* John 6:57, *40.* John 20:22, *41.* Luke 12:49, Matthew 3:11, Acts 1:4-5, *42.* Romans 8:19, *43.* Psalm 23:5, *44.* Psalm 110:1-2, Isaiah 11:3-4, 61:1, John 20:21-23, Matthew 16:19, Revelation 2:26-27, *45.* Luke 14:15-24, *46.* Luke 14:15-24, *47.* Isaiah 2:2-4, *48.* Psalm 23:5, *49.* Isaiah 2:2, *50.* Exodus 20:19, *51.* Exodus 19:12, *52.* Exodus 33:18, *53.* Hebrews 4:11, *54.* 2 Corinthians 3:18, *55.* Luke 6:37-38, *56.* John 5:44, 17:22, 17:24, *57.* John 5:37-38, 42, *58.* Matthew 6:11, Deuteronomy 8:3, *59.* Acts 17:28, *60.* Isaiah 54:2, *61.* 2 Peter 1:4, *62.* Psalm 82:5-6, *63.* Isaiah 11:3, Hebrews 12:21, Exodus 20:21, Isaiah 33:14b-15a, *64.* Galatians 5:16, 25, Ephesians 5:8, *65.* Mark 3:13-15, *66.* Exodus 33:11, John 15:4, *67.* Joshua 3:5, Romans 12:1-2

Dated: 19/9/20

26. *Mount Sinai, the Way of the Anointed (#109)*
REALMS OF DOMINION AND ANOINTING

As a Church we have not known ... nor understood ... nor necessarily believed in an Anointed Power-filled life. That truly, as a person today, one can live life 'Empowered' of God. Jesus came to baptise you in Power; He came to baptise you in Fire *[1]* ... that is what 'rebirth' means. That is what being born again means: one *'re-seated'* ... one *'re-clothed'* in Glory. *[2]*

God has a Dream ... did you know, that as a born again believer, you are the Temple of God? That you are a living walking 'Temple of God' made flesh and walking amongst us? But what's more, you are Purposed of God to be as the 'Ark of the Covenant' with the Fire and Glory of God resting upon your life. The 'Spirit' ... as the Awe of God upon you; 'Gold' ... as the Glory covering you; and the 'Cherubim' ... as an everlasting gateway into the deep and Hidden things of God *[3]*. And held within you is 'God's Law', being written on the 'Tablets' of your heart by the Finger of God *[4]*. Heaven's Divine 'Manna' ... as a Banquet for your soul *[5]*. And 'Aaron's Staff' budding forth leaves *[6]* and ripe fruit.

God fights for you! But not only fights but seeks to clothe you in Glory and Grace where you release that fight. 'Aaron's Staff' represents drawing from the Economy of Heaven onto this earth. It represents the bearing forth of Life in barren and hopeless places. Blossoming and bearing forth fruit 'overnight' ... as a sure sign to the nations. The Economy of Heaven, the realms of Everlasting Life ... the Resurrection Power of God bearing Living testimony in your midst.

Therefore, as you personally set the core root of your heart, set your soul 'possession' in the Presence of the Person of God ... the Awe of the Lord comes upon you birthing forth Revival. First budding, then flowering, then unto manifestation of ripe fruit for all the peoples.

The encouragement of these chapters is God's continual desire to lead you deeper in the reality of how you, as a believer, can step into an Anointed life. Even into greater levels of Anointing and Dominion whereby God shows you what is already yours. These of the realms of the Promises, these of the realms of your Inheritance; even that today, you may all the more liberally access ... bringing Heaven to earth. For as is the Lord's own Prayer being made now manifest, *"Your Kingdom come, your perfect Will being done on earth just as it is in Heaven."* [7]

It is my opinion, that accessing the 'Promised Land' is not through the *desert* but via 'Mount Sinai'. Mount Sinai is the portal. For it is through a heart ever set to **meet with God** — as the first and foremost — that swiftly brings you over into the realms of Promise. Not the desert but the meeting ... not the voices or opinion of man, but the Voice of God that causes man to 'shake and tremble' in the Holiness of God. [8]

The underlying purpose of struggles is that you might learn how to walk in the **fullness of your Calling**. The purpose of difficulties is like 'bench-press' ... the exercising your kingship and your swordsmanship. The purpose of barren times is that you might learn to hunger for the 'Word that proceeds from the mouth of God' [9]. Hence truly, if your heart already hungers and yearns, even more than your daily bread and needs, then why would you 'need' desert experiences?

In reference to the Ark of the Covenant: The Cherubim guard the way unto the Glory realms. The Mercy Seat was the second 'alter' where the Blood was placed. God 'speaks' from between the two Cherubim, from the other side, from realms of Everlasting Life. Hence, a heart that seeks to meet the Lord of Glory; humbles himself and **passes through**. To eat of the Tree of Life brings Life into your bones and healing into the depths of your soul. And as you dine so do you release the Healing unto the nations. [10]

The truth is, that we have very little real imagination of what God has truly opened to us all. And even if we were all to sit together collectively for a year imagining what the Promises of God entail; these, the realms of which have been given and laid before us ...

we would utterly fail. And what it means to be made in the 'Likeness of God', and this, the 'participating in His Divine Nature' … we would utterly fall short. Hence, therefore, as you honestly seek the Presence of God so are you clothed of Glory.

Again, this is why 'Meeting' is so important, not independence but interdependence; in ever-deepening union. Not flesh … but Spirit. Not worldly desire … but earnestly desiring the Glory realms of the Kingdom of Heaven. The intimate and vulnerable places of your heart, meeting with the **intimate and vulnerable** places of the Heart of God. For in this is revealed, through the Spirit of the Lord God Almighty; through both sight and hearing, even through the Word that Proceeds out from the mouth of God. In these of your personal closed sessions with the Lord … is that of which was already given, made known and made freely accessible.

So the question remains, if you as a believer — born of Water, born of Blood, and born of Spirit — have been presented the realms of Promise; these, the very realms of Power and Anointing. How is it, that today you can step in? How is it, that today you gain access to that of which is already yours in Heaven and bring it Alive and Real into your reality? Not ever in the notion that Heaven is accessible only through death. But that Christ Jesus *became* death that today you may truly function in Life.

EVERLASTING LIFE

Nowadays, I would refer to the Eternal realms, these wondrous realms of Heaven and the Spirit of God; I would refer to them as the realms of Eternal Life … the realms of Everlasting Life. And that today we can all access and all the more engage … bringing and making real and manifest on earth.

That of which was lost and separated at the Fall, now physically being plugged into and engaged … that you may be **full of Life** … that you may be full of Spirit. And as the Lord comes and anoints your head with oil and your 'cup' [11] begins to truly overflow, so does the oil of anointing overflow into this world … and sweep across the nations. These realms of Life, these the very realms of Everlasting Life … touching the earth. That of which was lost at the Fall; made real and contemporary this very day.

It is good to read about Jesus, and about your Heavenly Father ... **but**/ ... your purpose is to meet. For just as the purpose of marriage is not to only read and study about your wife, but to meet with her and draw her close. So it is the exact and very same regards our Heavenly Father; our Saviour Christ Jesus, the Holy Ghost, and the Kingdom realms.

In the same way, it is good to receive a prophetic word; and it's good to receive counsel and encouragement for your soul. But what you and I both greatly need is dynamic interaction in the Person of God. And so it is, that to this very thing, the *Thief* has been at work to steal since the Beginning ... lest you become a powerful force of reckoning.

Theme Scripture:
However, as it is written: "What no eye has seen, what no ear has heard, and what no human mind has conceived" — the things God has prepared for those who love him — these are the things God has **revealed** to us by his Spirit.
The Spirit searches all things, even the deep things of God. For who knows a person's thoughts except their own spirit within them? In the same way no one knows the thoughts of God except the Spirit of God.
What we have received is not the spirit of the world, but the Spirit who is from God, so that we may understand what God has freely given us. This is what we speak, not in words taught us by human wisdom but in words taught by the Spirit, explaining spiritual realities with **Spirit-taught** words. *(1 Corinthians 2:9-13 NIV)*

There is only one subject that I only ever wish to talk about, and that is the Presence and Fire of God. And I know I drive people crazy, but truth is, this very same subject is expressed all throughout Scripture. So the question remains, if the Promises and your Inheritance in the Lord; even the Anointing of God to make lasting change is right 'at hand', then how do we access? ... how do we engage?

In this theme Scripture verse, it firmly demonstrates how the vastness of what we have in God, even the vastness of who we are in Him, is so great that we don't even know what to ask or look for.

And so it is then, that this is why Presence *(and Fire focus)* is so valuable, *ie;* personal meetings in the Person of God. For how dangerous it is for the Devil when one meets with God ... for what can stand against such as these? Even they who are revealed sons.

As expressed here, the Way of the Anointed is to love God. For without love you would not even seek His Person. But now, with your heart's affections set and directed unto the Spirit [12] in honour, so is the Mind and Hidden things of God ever made known to you. Even that we, as a people, may continue to step further into that of which has already been freely given *('Seeds of Faith' given in the Lord)*. Now you know the right way ... how you, as a believer, can step into the realms of Anointing. Even then, that you may truly bring everlasting change to the world of which you live. And in most manifest form ... outpour Heaven in all situations.

In this subject, I wish to continue to speak about how, just as was in the Exodus account there was — the Promised Land; that how, for each and every one of us today in Christ Jesus — there are now the **inexpressible Promises**, the incomprehensible Inheritances, and inconceivable Treasures of the Kingdom realm laid here before you. And how, as a believer, you can go in and freely access today as you still live here on earth. And this in measure upon measure, Glory upon Glory, and in ways unfathomable to the human mind.

I call this section of chapters, *"Mount Sinai, the Way of the Anointed"*. Or another way of saying, *"Mount Sinai, the Way **unto** an Anointed life."* For the answer always remains the same: the meeting with God, *ie;* seek '**first**' the Kingdom of Heaven ... or another way of saying, *"Seek first the manifest Presence of God alive and active in your world."*

Come and say this prayer with me, *"Lord Jesus, I deeply desire to step into all that you have laid up in store for me. Please forgive me for being so caught up in the needs and desires of this life. I lay all things in you here and now; and diligently seek the Presence of God.*

Lord, please take my hand ... I humble myself deeply in your Holy Presence, please continue to lead me ever forward in you. Please draw me ever close, even lift me up into where you are now. I desire to go deeper into your Promises, and into my Inheritance. This in honour of the Son, and unto the outpouring of the Spirit of God in the land. Bless you, in Jesus Name."

God has a Dream, and if you could truly make God's Dream — your dream — **He will fight for you**. God shall fight for you! Not only fight but clothe you in Glory and **Grace to release that fight**." [13]

It is our Abba Father who has invited each one of us to come sit up at the right hand of God ... but so few are responding. This being our underlying calling; this being our fundamental goal ... the 'peak' of the mountain. Our 'pilgrimage walk', our objective and lens by which we live; as we face and deal with all that comes against ... from Glory to Glory [14]. All that we love and fear, and all ministerial gifts and callings and responsibilities, unto exceedingly great Glory.

It is that 'out of Zion' our Anointing comes, even as an Iron Sceptre of Divine Authority to strike the earth. Not only in the fact that our Saviour sat down at the right hand of God above all authorities [15] ... but that **we too have chosen to sit down**. The responding to the Call to enter the Rest of the Lord. For the war is not ours, nor is it our battle to fight the demon. But to release the Spirit and Glory of our God. The All-Consuming Fire [16] ... even the same that I delight to be baptised in and fully submersed. [17]

There is much that comes against this vision of the Lord. Even the congregations that still is huddling together *'around the mountain'* in various doctrines. But the Gospel of the Lord is, that the Church may walk as a '**mature man**', to the measure of the stature of the fullness of Christ. [18]

IN CLOSING

Truly, there is something that the Lord is leading us all into ... a better way to fight. A better vision ... a better 'root' of Anointing. For the war and the battle is not ours.

The 'prayer' is not in answers to our ministry, but that our cup be filled. The 'prayer' is not only in what we see, but God's Dreams and — our Destiny in Him — fulfilled. For at the right hand of God are the Gardens realms, the Place where your mouth is constantly filled.

The battle is not yours ... nor is your ministry, your gifts, or your calling. They are the Lord's. And here, in the Gardens realms, shall you have Visions and Dreams; and the Revelation of the Lord shall flood your soul. His Love, His Grace, and His Power ... unceasing Energies, unceasing Life, unceasing Provisions. This is the way to do the **work of God**, for the world does not need you running on an empty cup, but the Glory of God. Now turn to the opposition that tries to come against and say, *"Be thou cast into the Sea!"*

If it was the Lord's fundamental calling to 'sit at the right hand of God'. If that was God's vision for the Christ, then how much so is it not ours as well? For if we are called into perfect union, how can we truly be unified in two different places? Of course not, that is called a broken marriage. And are we not the Body of Christ? Therefore, the Destiny is: **co-habitation**, co-seated, and co-ruling. And this is what the demon is scared of, lest you triumph over him in the state of a 'Revealed' son. [19]

Today, have you been reborn. A weight has been removed from your shoulders and a strength has entered your soul. A single vision has been set before your eyes that no one can remove. However, from this Place does the Glory of God outpour in your life. Glory upon Glory ... unto exceedingly great and inconceivable Glory.

So then, there is truly a vision other than the Presence of God ... and that is the Fire and Glory. The Place where your flesh trembles in the Holiness of His Presence. The same Place where the Hand of God shielded Moses from, and the cleft of the rock shielded Elijah. Layer upon layer, level upon level — let your heart always be set unto **beholding Jesus in His Glory** [20]. This is our modern-day Pillar of Fire at night.

Bless you ...

Appendix:

1. Luke 3:16, 4:14, 12:49, 24:49, Acts 1:8, Acts 2:3, *2.* Romans 8:19, *3.* Genesis 3:24, *4.* Hebrews 10:16, 2 Corinthians 3:3, Ezekiel 11:19, *5.* Psalm 23:5, *6.* Revelation 22:2b, *7.* Matthew 6:10, *8.* Exodus 20:18-19, *9.* Deuteronomy 8:3, Matthew 4:4, *10.* Genesis 3:24, Exodus 25:22, Revelation 2:7, 22:2, Isaiah 44:22, *11.* Psalm 23:5, *12.* Matthew 22:37, Colossians 3:1-3, *13.* Psalm 110:1-2, Exodus 14:14, 33:14, Hebrews 4:11, Genesis 1:26, Revelation 3:16-21, *14.* 2 Corinthians 3:18, *15.* Ephesians 1:20-21, *16.* Isaiah 33:14b-15a, *17.* Matthew 3:11, *'Baptism' in Greek simply means to 'dip' or 'immerse',* *18.* Ephesians 4:13, *19.* Romans 8:19, *20.* John 17:20-24

Dated: 19/9/20

27. *Mount Sinai, the Way of the Anointed (#110)*
MEET WITH GOD

PSALM CHAPTER #110 VERSE 1 & 2

The Lord said to 'my Lord',
1. "**Sit** at my right hand, till I make your enemies your footstool."
2. The Lord shall send the rod of **your** Strength out of Zion. **Rule** in the midst of your enemies!

Let's say this again ...

The Lord said to '**my sons and daughters**',
1. "Come **sit** at my right hand ... in the Presence of the Lord, and I will fight for you." [1]
2. The Lord shall heal you and Anoint you strong, with the full **backing** of Heaven.

Once more ...

The Lord said to '**my child**',
1. "Come sit here next to me, and I will fight your battles." [1]
2. Learn from me and let your mouth be filled. And I will teach you how to release that fight.

This is part of the revelation of your sonship. The *revealing* [2] of who you are '**in**' Christ Jesus. For Victory comes from the realms of the right hand of God ... *ie;* the Garden realms. The realms of the Sabbath Day of Rest ... walking in the **full** fruits of all God's labours and purposes. [3]

The central message to the Christ, was to come sit at the Father's right hand. And just like in the Exodus story ... 'God fought for Him' ... for His Father was with Him [4] to **fulfil** the Promises of God in Him. Today, by the Blood of Jesus and the gifted Holy Spirit, have you exactly the same Invited Calling. However, just as the Christ, your 'Promised Land' is not a physical Land flowing with 'milk and honey' ... but the Seated realms flowing with 'Life and Spirit'.

King David was an Old Testament picture of your new life in Christ Jesus. And the victory he walked in was achieved by where he fixed his vision. As he said, *"One thing I ask from the Lord, this only do I seek: that I may dwell in the house of the Lord all the days of my life, to gaze on the beauty of the Lord and to seek him in his Temple"* [5]. However, this vision had nothing to do with an earthly reality, for as Christ Himself ascended ... so did He also **co-abide** [6]. The Temple David's soul yearned for was not on earth but in Zion. [7]

1. The Christian believer is more than a man.
2. The Christian Church is more than a people.

God has a Dream! ... to **Empower His people**. God has a Dream; to give Power and Glory to His people. As Jesus said, *"I came to Baptise you in Power"*. And again, as He says, *"I have come to pour out Fire upon the earth and how I wish you were already kindled"*. Meaning, *"How I wish you were in **hot** pursuit ... ready to be ignited."* [8]

1. The Exodus Story was a Land flowing with *milk and honey*.
2. The Christ Story is a Land flowing with Life and Spirit.

1. The Exodus Story was a Land of *wealth and provision*.
2. The Christ Story is a Land of Glory and Grace.

But unlike the Exodus, your objective in Christ Jesus is not earthly wealth, but to be clothed with Power [9] ... Power of which manifests God [10]. It is God who has a Dream: to clothe you in Power and Grace. To baptise you with Fire, which is the Glory of God. Therefore, come up into the High Places. [11]

I tell you a trick unto an Anointed life: It's not about seeking answer to your prayers — but seeking answer to His. Let me say that again, It's not so much about seeking answer to your prayers — but yearning and seeking for His Prayers to be answered in you. And this Dream that we are speaking of, was God's Dream way before it became yours.

Satan freaks out when your prayer is God Himself [12], for nothing can stand against such as these. Your sharp singular eye, your sharp and incorruptible [13] purpose ... bringing a sharp response.

1. The 'Exodus Story' is where **God fights** for you.
2. The 'Christ Story' is where God **Anoints** your mouth to **release** that 'fight'.

Seek 'first' the manifest Kingdom of Heaven. Seek first the manifest Presence of His Person [14], *ie;* your 'Destiny' *(your Destination, Purpose, and Promise* [15]*),* and God will take care of everything else. God will fight for you [1], not only fight; but Anoint and Clothe you to release the Glory and Fire of God.

God has a Dream ... *(Genesis 1:26)*
1. "Let us **make** man in our Image and our Likeness.
2. And let us give him Dominion."

So again, let's paraphrase this opening Scripture verse ...

The Lord said to '**my Church**',
1. "Enter the **Rest** of the Lord [16] as one 'seated' in the Holy Presence of God *(the Sabbath Day Rest, operating in the fullness of the fruits of all God's efforts and labour).* And I will deal with what you are facing."
2. And out of the Presence of the Glory of God shall your Anointing come [17], saying, "Rule in the midst of all that comes against. Against all sicknesses and disease, all works of the demon, whereby death is swallowed up by Life." [18]

One vision. One focus. One drive: a sharp eye makes you 'dangerous'.

MEET WITH GOD

Verse 20, 1 Corinthians chapter 4:
The Kingdom of God is not about word alone, but open demonstration of Power and the Person of God.

It is good to know the Word of God, and subsequently being a people blessed in life because of that Word. However, the Bible clearly speaks of **manifestation** [19]. There is 'Jesus in the Word', but then there is 'Jesus in the flesh' [20]. Great blessings come into your life because of the Word ... **but**/ ... the answer to your life is sitting at the feet of Jesus. Where He Empowers you, where He

Anoints your words to 'preach', and where He gives you Authority to cast out devils. [21]

When you pray, you connect problems to the Power of God. Concerns and issues and weakness; to the Guidance, the Involvement, and the Glory of the Christ. However also — we must remember — that it is **the Spirit's Mission to impart**; [22] that we each might continue to transition into the full Likeness of the Christ [23]. Then as one whom speaks Life; outpours Heaven on earth — the Sovereignty, the Grace, and the Power. For the fundamental Purpose of God, is that you might walk '**as**' the Son on earth — as *co-heirs* of His Glory.

So far, your highest prayer may have been to heal illnesses or to help you in your ministry. But God's Prayer is that you might "Become mature, **attaining to the whole measure** and stature of the fullness of Christ." [24]

... Elevate Jesus ...
... Worship the Son ...
... Pass through Him [25] *...*
... and be Empowered ...

Scripture:
Then they said to Moses, "You speak with us, and we will listen; but let not God speak with us, lest we die." *(Exodus 20:19 NKJV* [26]*)*

So to continue in this subject, let me share a radical statement: *"The Exodus account that we all have known and read about for these last three and a half thousand years, is wrong! ... is totally wrong. And so too then ... all subsequent recorded history is askew."*

For the truth is, that all events that followed after exiting Egypt is based on a *stubborn* people, is based on an 'unbelieving and perverse generation' [27]. And not based on a people of whom simply desired to turn their heart unto God ... even then in truth to meet Him. A people treasuring the sitting in His Presence: desiring to hear and to see the Lord. [28]

The Passover ... the Meeting ... the Promises.

However, the complete opposite is true! Mount Sinai, this — the **meeting personally** with God — is the 'portal' to entering the 'Promise Land'. It is the doorway unto all the Promise of God, ie; the Way of the Spirit. Even this, the very Purpose of the Blood: your capacity to meet with the God of Heaven and earth ... and subsequently, been given Power to release Him. [29]

Scripture:
Man shall not [cannot] live by bread alone, but by every word that proceeds from the mouth of God [even as one engaging the realms of Everlasting Life]. *(Matthew 4:4, Deuteronomy 8:3)*

THE 'CASTRATION' OF THE CHURCH

As is the main heading of this section of chapters ... "The Way of the Anointed", is not achieved through the following of rules or hand-me-downs. But through personal, and deeply retained respect and honour — to hear and see the Lord [30]. And just the same as He of whom was the 'Word made flesh', so shall it be that His Living-speaking-Word shall ever abide in you and become manifest. For as Jesus says, *"If you abide in me, and my words abide in you, ask whatever you desire, and it shall be done for you."* [31]

Egypt ... Mount Sinai ... the fullness of God.

Scripture:
No one has ascended to heaven but He who came down from heaven, that is, the Son of Man who **is** in heaven [co-abiding]. *(John 3:13 NKJV)*

A side note: Co-abiding, co-seating, cohabitating in Heaven as one walks this earth. Seated in Heavenly Places over and above Satan and his works. Not only looking up to Jesus in times of need — but Dwelling in [32] Him where He is now — as one who sits with Him upon the Throne. In Genesis, Satan is but a snake on the ground, but in Revelations, Satan is a dragon. I tell you; success comes by where you position yourself. And it is through Christ Jesus, He is the Door ... He is the Way! [33]

Verily I say, it is to this very approach that is the launching point, even the very *access* to coming to walk more liberally in the realms of Promise. God's Living and active Word ever Abiding in you and 'walking amongst us'. Even as one raised triumphant and mighty in the Lord [34] ... taking 'Possession of the Land' *(Heavenly Places)* [35]. For such wonder is held in they of whom truly leave Egypt behind, of whom truly set their heart unto the realms of the Spirit [36]. Even desiring nothing else but to sit at the feet of Jesus [37]. For to such these, walk with God in the Garden realms, being ever established and built up in the Presence of His Person ... in the Presence of His Glory.

The way to face any 'desert' experience is through a heart set upon meeting ... a heart set upon Presence. And it will be He who Anoints you with Power to pass through. Being strengthened in the trial ... even then to Rule! This is the basis of any miracle: the releasing forth the Glory of God.

In this account of meeting with God at Mount Sinai, if the people had simply honoured the 'pause' ... simply honoured the 'waiting upon the Lord'; just loving the 'hearing and the seeing' ... then they would have swiftly passed through any 'desert experience' [38]. And instead of living 'outside' the Promises; becoming a people **full of Promise**. Such is the fundamental Dream and Purpose of the Father concerning you.

You see, the answer to the human condition ... **is** ... a heart set upon hearing and seeing the Person of God. This very same reality that was stolen man in the Beginning [39]. Where the people became *separate* ... and subsequently marooned in the confined limitedness of their own flesh and understanding. However, don't get 'spooky' ... for you may or may not hear or see anything, but are left with a 'Knowing' that deeply moves you.

It is Jesus who came to restore and reunite. But this very reality itself has to be treasured and pursued. For since the Genesis, you have only ever known the 'sweat' of your own labour and that of your own 'knowledge' [40] ... **but**! ... that is not where you are originally from.

Egypt ... Presence ... Authority.

As we know, the core motive of many believers today is still money [41] ... or otherwise, their position in the eyes of man. But as Jesus says, *"I see that you have not the Love of God in you. For how can you **believe** if you seek the honour of man, but do not **seek the honour** that comes from the only God?"* [42] Truly, the Church is made weak; the Church is made powerless when we make 'kings' of man. When we set rulers over us to tell us what to do [43] ... without a heart set and personal driven upon God Himself.

Power only comes from sitting at the feet of Jesus. Even then — just as He — as one coming up upon the Mountain of God; deep into the Holiness of His Person [44]. Power comes from God, not from man but from God. And Fire is poured upon they of whose hearts remain in hot pursuit.

> *Honour the Presence ... honour the Meeting ... enter the Rest of the Lord that releases the fight of God.* [45]

The desert is not the Way to the Promises ... but meeting personally with the God of Heaven and earth. Hence here, in this Exodus story, we had the people who did not want to hear God themselves. I tell you, that was their point of failure!

There is in God, a Place called — "The Place of Repose" [46]. It is a Place where you constantly receive from the Lord [47] ... and are constantly built up. However, Scripture speaks of how people refuse to enter. So the Word of the Lord — to them — becomes 'rules upon rules', statutes upon statutes, till they fall back and are ensnared.

Scripture:
Then the LORD said to Moses: "How long will these people reject Me? And how long will they not believe Me, with all the signs which I have performed among them? *(Numbers 14:11 NKJV)*

At the time of Samuel, the people demanded a king [48]. Not God Himself as the king ... but a mere man [49]. And so too in the Gospels came the warning of Jesus; recognise that there is only **one** Father and **one** Christ and **one** Teacher — all must come to Him. But again, the people refuse ... even to this very day!

So I say, **elevate** Jesus that **you be saved**. Worship Him that you be focused ... with eyes on. And pass through Him as called, that you may truly be Empowered and Equipped of God. Ever 'clothed' in ever-increasing Glory from on High. [50]

> *God has a Dream ... that you live no longer in the desert. But live full of Promise, full of Glory, and full in the Light of Life."*

The word 'Castration' is a strong word, and I apologise for using it. But in relation to the work of Satan — his efforts are continuously at work to undermine the Power of God active in your life. His drive and all his efforts is to strip you bare: making the Church impotent, powerless, and ineffectual. A church in 'appearance' ... yes, he is fine with that ... but just no Shekinah Glory![51] No demonstrable Power.

Man needs more than man ... man needs more than knowledge; man **needs** the Fire of God. So then, come and put your life aside, and pursue God ... in order to behold Him in His Glory [52]. And here, in His Glory, be given Authority and Power *('Fire'* [53]*)* to strike the earth. Whereby God makes His Name known in the nations. [54]

Do you see ... pictured in Jesus' own life, that He was the Word made flesh? Moses carried the Law and presented it to the people. But Jesus, He was the very embodiment of the Word of God on earth. Therefore, it is most true: Jesus has taught and made possible — through the spoken Gospel message and His own shed Blood — your very own capacity to have the same Word active and Alive in you; being made manifest and walking amongst us.

Scripture:
The one who loves me will be loved by my Father, and I too will love them and show myself to them [reveal, impart, transmit]. *(John 14:21b NIV)*

The Anointing of God that you seek, the Power and the Glory, it comes only through deeply held and treasured relationship with your Heavenly Father. This, the very thing of which the Blood itself has purposed and made possible ... even *intimacy*. [55]

Not just a Grace message that makes you feel good about yourself ... but a Grace Message that Empowers and takes you into the realms of Glory; that takes you into the realms of Power and Dominion. This, the Place where God continually shows and reveals Himself to you ... and Himself, **is** made manifest.

Now it can be more easily understood when Jesus says, *"My sheep follow me ... and where I am so shall my sheep also be"* [56]. For this, by no means is just an earthly vision or reality ... but the very same Heavenly reality that Jesus Himself walked in — the being with Him where He is. [57]

Here and now, you are truly beginning to respond to this: the elementary Calling of God [58] ... as a follower of Jesus. As is said in the opening Scripture, *"Come sit at my right hand, and I will fight your battles. Come learn from me and let your mouth be filled, and I will teach you how to release that fight."* [59]

Two Scripture verses:
1. And He went up on the mountain and called to Him those He Himself wanted. And they came to Him. Then He **ordained** twelve, that they might be **with Him** and that **He might send** *(anoint)* them out to preach, and to have power to heal sicknesses and to cast out demons. *(Mark 3:13-15 NKJV)*
2. Jesus answered and said to him, "Blessed are you, Simon Bar-Jonah, for **flesh** and blood **has not revealed this** to you, but My Father who is in heaven. And I also say to you that you are Peter, and upon **this rock** I will build My church, and the gates of Hades shall not prevail against it. And I will give you the **keys of the kingdom of heaven**, and whatever you bind on earth will be bound in heaven, and whatever you loose on earth will be loosed in heaven." *(Matthew 16:17-19 NKJV)*

ENTERING THE REALMS OF EVERLASTING LIFE

When you say to the Lord, *"I love you Lord and seek your Face"* ... your spirit-man is relocated and *sees* the Face of God [60] And when you give your life fully over to the Lord, so are you making full connection. Entering into Life; even these of the Eternal realms of God [61]. And though this world may still creep in and come around you at times: in the Presence of the Lord do you step into realms of His Counsel, His Might, and His Wonder in ever-increasing measure! [62]

> *God fights for you, as you enter the Rest of the Lord.* [1]

So now, when you turn and face the realities of this world; do you do so from within the realms of the Spirit. From within the very realms of Glory and Dominion. As is said in Scripture, *"He who clings onto his own life shall never **find** Life"*, *ie;* this Life that Jesus speaks of. *"But He who abandons himself unto the Cross, passes through and engages the realms of Life as a holder of Life."* [63]

Scripture:
"This is Eternal Life: that they **KNOW you**, the only true God, and Jesus Christ, whom you have sent." *(John 17:3 NKJV)*

Here, it can be more easily recognised the value found in treasuring the Presence of God [64]. For truly, in this space, do you truly come to know Him … and so too come to know **who** you are in Him, *ie;* your sonship revealed [65]. As one ever preferencing Presence over problems, preferencing Presence over plans and personal purposes, and Presence over any fear or any dread; and in this Place shall you step out from whatever you are under and step into the 'all of which is yours'. Coming ever more to walk in the Likeness **as** the Son.

It is true, that each one of us have capacity to read and study the Word of God. But so too is it also true, that as you engage the very Person of God … do you enter into open living experience of the Word. Eternal Life, even these of the very realms of the Kingdom of Heaven … becoming real and alive to you.

There is always so much more for each and every believer than what is currently known or experienced. Even as Jesus would say, *"Whoever drinks the water I give them will never thirst. Indeed, the water I give them will become in them a spring of water welling up to Eternal Life"* [66]. Recognise then, that as you personally choose to meet with Jesus … does He **give you** Living Water [67]. And it is this Living Water that truly begins to rise up within, lifting you up into the realms of the Everlasting. That today, you may freely live in *experience* of Life.

Truly live drawing from Eternity; these of the realms of Everlasting Life ... unto this world.

Man must clothe himself with Immortality. [68]

Have you ever felt a dryness of soul? ... now you know the answer. The very Fruits of the Spirit such as Love, Joy, and Peace ... even Faith, Hope, and Love [69] ... these realities are simply trace residue of where the Spirit-rooted believer now abides. These, in ever-flowing and ever-increasing manifestation of the Presence of God.

The title of this chapter is 'Meet with God'. And how it is, that through this simple lifestyle of purposed-meeting: that you open yourself up, and swiftly cross over, into the realms of Inheritance and Promise.

*"I will **show** you my Salvation."* [70]

It is true, that long has the Christian believer lived defeated lives. But now, in this making decisive choice to *dwell* in the Tent of Meetings [71], even right here in the midst of the realities and challenges of life, that you are raised most Triumphant and Victorious in and by the Lord. And like King David — but now in the Kingdom realms — are you given right to sit upon the Throne of Glory [72]. This very same Throne of Grace and Authority, whereby you say, *"Spirit of the Lord, I release you into this situation. You manage, you make right, you restore."*

This lifestyle of laying yourself bare before the Lord of Glory; [73] this, of ever opening yourself up to **meet** with Him daily, are you also continuously given Living Water. And it is this Water that begins also to rise up in you as like a fountain ... lifting you up into the realms of Everlasting Life. Even then, as like a geyser, shooting you up right upon the Sea of Sapphire [74]. And as you continue to walk in these realms of the Spirit, making it here your **Place of Dwelling**, do you also come to live most Victorious lives ... personally Empowered of the Person of God. And so too shall you step into realms of Anointing and Authority that blow your mind. [75]

I so very much encourage you: Be diligent to enter the Counsel of God ... and centralise it in your vision to **abide** here. Truly become one who approaches all life's issues from this Place of Honour [76]. **Pause**, be **still**, and **know God**. And it will be God who will tell you things such as, *"Pray like this and see how I move"*, or *"Do that and see how Heaven works."* And here you will be constantly given Wisdom and Understanding and Grace to ever be successful. And shall you also begin to step into Places as one who pours out Heaven on earth.

Profound shifts to the reality of people's lives, where even the very ground rises up more productive; sicknesses falling away, and the prosperity of the people expanding and expanding ... body, mind, soul, and spirit. Everlasting and profound shifts as Heaven rests upon the people. I tell you, even in your own life; such a measure of the Love of God shall rest upon you. Such a measure of Grace to do life well; even as one who rises up and overcomes for the nations.

So to conclude: To operate in these realms of Anointing ... there is the right way going about it. For example, do you recall how Jesus speaks of sitting in the place of humility? How does it go, *"Take the lowest place, so that when your host comes, he will say to you, 'Friend, **move up** to a better place.'"* [77]

So it is the same, that if you truly wish to live an Anointed life, then I have just told you the right way [78]. This, the approaching the Father as like a little child. For without such an approach you will never enter or ever truly engage these Eternal realms of the Kingdom of Heaven. Nor ever truly participate in this Everlasting Life that God has Destined and Purposed for you as you still live and walk this earth. [79]

Let me close with a prayer ...

"I call over you this day ... the Meeting of the Person of God. I set before you a life of Divine Encounter. I do not care what state you are in, nor where you are with God; I pour and release over you His Spirit, His Strength, and His Goodness [80]. *It is by the Blood that you are sanctified in the Presence of the*

Lord. Now by this prayer spoken is the Spirit ever released to minister richly into your life ... even to bring mighty change."

IN REFERENCE TO PSALM #110
and the fruits of engaging the meeting with God:

*"Come sit at my right hand, and I will fight your battles. Come learn from me for I am gentle and kind ... and let your mouth be filled. And I will Raise and **teach** you how to release that fight."*

Scripture always speaks in this vein; for if this word was central to the very Person of Christ Jesus, then so too is it also central for the Christian Church. Entering into the Garden realms, into the Heavenly realms ... entering Zion as you walk this earth and co-functioning. This is the basis of the revelation of your sonship, and who you are in Him. And it is the basis of living whole and Victorious lives.

Bless you, in Jesus Name ...

Appendix:

1. Exodus 14:14, 33:14-18, Joshua 24:12, **2.** Romans 8:19, **3.** Hebrews 4:10-11, **4.** Exodus 33:3, 14-17, John 1:18, 5:19, Luke 4:14, 5:17, **5.** Psalm 27:4, 37:4, 43:5, 84:1-7, Colossians 3:1-3, **6.** John 3:13 *NKJV*, **7.** Hebrews 8:5, John 3:13 *NKJV*, **8.** Luke 3:16, 4:14, 12:49, 24:49, Acts 1:8, Acts 2:3, **9.** Luke 24:49, Genesis 3:10, Revelation 3:17-18, 1 Corinthians 15:53-54, 2 Corinthians 3:18, 2 Kings 2:14, 6:17, Matthew 16:17-19, Mark 16:17-19, Acts 5:15, Colossians 3:1-3, Psalm 91:1, 2:7-8, 110:1-2, 34:7, 104:2, 93:1, 84:5, John 1:51, Exodus 33:14-18, 34:29, John 17:24, Genesis 1:26, **10.** Matthew 6:10, **11.** Isaiah 2:1-4, 33:14b-15a *HCSB*, Psalm 24:3-4a *NIV*, 27:4, Exodus 24:17, 33:11-14, Mark 3:13-15, Zechariah 3:7, Psalm 110:1-2, Matthew 17:1-3, Acts 1:13, 2:1-4, Colossians 3:1-4, Revelation 1:10-18, Genesis 3:24, **12.** Genesis 15:1, Psalm 91:1, **13.** John 14:30, Isaiah 33:14b-15a *HCSB*, Psalm 24:3-4a *NIV*, **14.** Exodus 33:14-23, John 17:20-24, **15.** Genesis 1:26, Psalm 110:1-2, Revelation 3:17-22, **16.** Hebrews 4:11, **17.** Psalm 2:7-8, 2 Kings 2:9-14, Revelation 2:26-27, **18.** 1

Corinthians 15:54-55, **19.** 1 Corinthians 4:20, 2 Timothy 3:5, **20.** John 1:14, **21.** Mark 3:13-15, Zechariah 3:7, Psalm 110:1-2, Exodus 33:11-14, **22.** John 16:14-15, **23.** John 16:14, Genesis 1:26, **24.** Ephesians 4:13, 2 Corinthians 3:18, John 14:12, **25.** 1 Peter 3:18a, **26.** 1 Samuel 8:7, **27.** Matthew 17:17, Romans 6:14, **28.** John 17:24, 5:19, 30, **29.** Zechariah 3:7, Exodus 33:12-18, **30.** Matthew 23:8-13, **31.** John 15:7, Matthew 16:19, **32.** John 17:20-24, 15:4, Psalm 110:1-2, **33.** John 14:1-12, **34.** John 14:30b, **35.** Revelation 3:20-21, Psalm 110:1-2, Hebrews 4:11, **36.** Revelation 2:4-5, **37.** Luke 5:15, Matthew 14:15, **38.** Deuteronomy 8:3, **39.** Genesis 2:17, **40.** Genesis 3:19, 5:3, Proverbs 3:5-6, **41.** Mark 4:19, **42.** John 5:41-44, **43.** Exodus 20:19, 1 Samuel 8:7, Matthew 23:8-9, **44.** Isaiah 11:3, **45.** Exodus 14:14, **46.** Isaiah 28:12-13, **47.** John 7:38, **48.** 1 Samuel 8:6-7, **49.** Psalm 118:8, **50.** Luke 24:49, **51.** Exodus 40:34-38, 34:35, 33:9-11, 24:16-18, 19:10-20, 13:21-22, 3:1-6, 2 Chronicles 5:13-14, 7:1, Numbers 9:15-23, Leviticus 16:2, Ezekiel 10:18-19, Joshua 3:14-17, Matthew 17:1-2, Luke 4:1-2, 14 *(first bind the strongman)*, Luke 1:35, 12:49, 24:49, Acts 1:4-5, 2:1-4, 2 Corinthians 3:18, Revelation 2:4-5, Genesis 3:24, **52.** John 17:20-24, Exodus 33:18-23, **53.** 1 Kings 18:24, **54.** Isaiah 64:1-4, **55.** John 1:18, **56.** John 10:27, 12:26, **57.** John 17:24, **58.** Mark 3:13-15 *(in spirit, in Heavenly Places)*, **59.** Psalm 110:1-2, Isaiah 10:27, **60.** Matthew 18:10, Acts 12:15, **61.** John 4:14, 17:3, Ephesians 3:20, **62.** 2 Corinthians 3:18, **63.** Matthew 10:39, **64.** John 5:19, **65.** Romans 8:19, **66.** John 4:14, **67.** Revelation 3:20, 22:1, Luke 12:37, **68.** 1 Corinthians 15:53-54, **69.** Galatians 5:22-23, 1 Corinthians 13:13, **70.** Psalm 91:16, **71.** Exodus 33:11, **72.** Revelation 3:21, Zechariah 3:7, **73.** Matthew 18:3, **74.** Exodus 24:10, Revelation 15:2, **75.** Genesis 1:26, **76.** Zechariah 3:7, John 5:44, **77.** Luke 14:10, **78.** John 12:43, 5:41-44, **79.** Matthew 18:3, John 9:41, **80.** John 20:21-23, Matthew 16:19

Dated: 19/9/20

28. *Mount Sinai, the Way of the Anointed (#111)*
WAY MAKER

In continuation from the previous chapter ...

Ephesians 4:13:
"Until we become mature, attaining to the whole measure and stature of the fullness of Christ."

I really encourage, you are called of God not only to believe in Jesus ... but to **become** Him! The calling of the Church is not only to call upon the Name of the Lord in times of need ... but to **walk as He**. The underlying Dream of the Father is that you might grow into the full Image — attaining to the whole measure of the Resurrected Christ.

God has a Dream! ... and that is to cast Fire upon the earth. God has a Dream, to deeply enrich and **Empower** His people. That you might walk in the Power of the Son for you and your people. The Church is more than a building, the Christian more than a people; so too as a believer are you more than a man. You are a child of the Most High God; **co-heirs** of the Glory of Heaven as you walk this earth. One who 'stands in the gap' to direct and outpour the Spirit of God. [2]

> *"It only takes one to change the world."* [1]

One touch of the Presence of God **surpasses** the brokenness of man. Surpasses their ignorance, their indifference, and their sin ... and **presents to them God!** And the same grow; being openly demonstrated the gift of the Holy Spirit, of whom they too pour out the Spirit of God. First there was Egypt ... then the Promised Land; but now has come the Christ; the veil rent, that you too can participate in the fullness of God.

INTIMACY BIRTHS REVIVAL [3]

Regardless of the evil in the land, it only takes one who **knows** their sonship to change the world [1]. One who knows who they are in Christ Jesus. The Blood has re-purchased the world; [4] therefore, pray the Spirit … pray the Knowledge of God upon all flesh [5]. Come, rest your head in the Father's Bosom [6] and call what is not into being [7]. Prosperity of soul is yours … success in all your goings: health, vitality, and hope. So settle for nothing less!

"You are my son, today I have become your Father. **Ask** *me and I will give you the nations, the ends of the earth your inheritance"* [8]. What this means is, that you don't have to ask permission; Satan does not own anything … he has no rights. So move Death and establish Life; set in place the 'Aggression' of the Lord to deal with all obstructions [9]. For as opposition does come, they themselves become avenues of incredible change — for God demands sevenfold retribution. [10]

Theme Scripture:
I looked for someone among them who would build up the wall and **stand** before me in the gap on behalf of the land [so I could heal it], but **I found no one**. *(Ezekiel 22:30 NIV)*

A question to ask, 'Are you one of whom God can find?'

God is openly **looking** for people who might stand in the gap for the nations. Who might stand in the gap for the people … that God might '**heal the land**' [11]. A heart to bind up the wounds of the people, to heal the brokenhearted, and release the Glory of God upon all flesh. [12]

In Christ Jesus, the believer is destined of God to be a 'Way Maker'. And by the Power of God … build up the 'walls' of the local Church; build up the heart and strength of the people [13]. And as one 'found' in Him … one known of God; the very Person of God shall **step through you** unto the blessing of the world. [14]

Long has the Church functioned without of the Power of God [15]. Devoid of any open manifest Presence … *ie;* the Shekinah Glory that rests upon His 'Holy Temple' [16]. Walls and 'structure' [17] … yes, all the 'appearance' of a church, but no Holy Spirit's Fire!

This is what we seek … underlying all things and all purposes, we seek the manifest Presence of God. Come, and honour the Glory of His Person come: *"Raise up the valleys, knock down the mountains, and clear the way for the Glory of the Lord to be 'revealed'. And all flesh shall see it together, for the Word of the Lord has spoken."* [18]

There is the Old and then there is the New. The Old had its purpose unto the birthing of the Christ. However now, **in the very Person of the Christ**, are you Destined to hold the very Power of God in your hands [19]. And just as in the Old: first there was Abraham ... and then unto Egypt, then came the Promised Land. However now, in the Christ, you are Purposed of God — Divinely Destined in Him — to be clothed in Glory. [20]

As exampled in the Exodus, God said, *"I will send my Angel before you, to drive out the enemy from before you. Go up to a land flowing with milk and honey."* But then He said, *"I will not go up with you, lest I destroy you on the way ... for you are a stiff-necked people."* [21]

Another question to ask, 'What if you weren't a still-necked people? ... what reality would you walk in?' The same Glory that destroyed the *demons* of Egypt [22] and went out way before the people leading them into Glory.

To live with the Presence of the Most High God upon your life, the Holiness of His Person ... what is more precious? [23] And truly what could ever come against such as they? The 'Glory of the Lord revealed' [24] — the Shekinah Glory — open manifestation — and death utterly destroyed by Life, *ie;* the Living God [25]. For God **has re-purchased** the world through the Blood of His Son. Therefore, the only thing hindering the Outpouring of the Holy Spirit's Fire ... is the *indifference* of His people. [26]

There is only one prayer worth to be had: To make way for the 'Glory of the Lord to be revealed'. **One prayer** that brings answer to **all prayers** ... the Presence of the Most High God in His Majesty. Even this, the very Purpose of the 'why' God sent His Son. For Jesus' own personal Prayer concerning you this very day: is that you might *"See Him in His Glory."* [27]

Scripture:
"I have come to cast Fire upon the earth; and how I wish it were already kindled!" *(Luke 12:49 NASB)*

By the Blood are you priest unto God, purposed as one '**standing** before God' **in the gap**. Joining the Spirit to the people, the Power of God unto problems, and the Glory of God unto the very earth. [28]

Also as king, **purposed of God to direct** and release the very same Presence of the Lord, according to what you 'see' [29]. Your 'lampstand' firmly set in the Presence of God [30], your flame burning bright in His Holy Temple, and the 'flame' of His Person standing amongst you and upon you [31] unto the glory of God. [32]

So again I say, *"Come Rest your head upon the Father's Bosom and call what is not into being".* For to be with Jesus *"Where He is"* … as one *"Seeing Him in His Glory"* [27]… causes you able to carry and release that very same Glory. [33]

IMPARTED BY THE SPIRIT

Through the Power of the Spirit are the people touched of God. With great Moves of the Spirit that deeply mark the heart and soul of man. When you release the Presence of God … when you pray the Spirit over people, it is the Spirit of God of whom Imparts of Himself with a **Knowing** that surpasses understanding. [34]

There is knowledge that comes through the Word of God … yes, but then there is **Knowledge that is imparted** by the Spirit that deeply Strengthens [35]. Deep impressions 'Given' in the soul of man [36], 'Seeds of Faith' [37] that grow into Oaks of Righteousness [38], and a 'Flame' set that rips across the land [39]. And this is what you want.

The Mission of the Spirit is to take of the very Person of the Christ and impart and install into your person [40]. Transference and Impartation … Knowledge and Capacity that comes not from intellect, but from 'Hearing' [41]. The Word made 'flesh' in you … and identity in Him revealed; even this, your sonship revealed on earth as one ceasing the groans and suffering of creation. [42]

This is the pathway of Knowledge: [43] True knowledge of who you are as a son, who you are as a child of God; comes only through a heart that yearns for the 'Fire'. [44]

Truly ... it takes humility to sit upon the Throne of Grace at the right hand of God [45]. It takes true honesty of soul to abide [46] and *function* here in the Fire of His Glory [47]. And it takes integrity to stand before the Holiness of His Person; even as one who 'pitches' your tent and never leaves. But to this is what we are called [48] ... and truly, who can come against the Lord's Anointed? [49]

The Christian believer is the entrance point for God to heal the land [50]. Therefore, through opening your heart [51] unto Him in welcome ... so are you also extending 'invitation' for God to strengthen and build you up. Even so, for God to 'construct' you able to hold His very Glory upon your person [52]. And as one choosing in all things to sit at Jesus' feet [53] ... listening attentively to Him, does He lead you into the fullness of the Promises making you a force unstoppable; revealing and making real unto you that of your full Inheritance.

But of course, these things don't stop here. Your 'cup' overflows unto the nations. Spot Fires of the Spirit of God springing up all over the land as God heals and restores; setting Life where there was none, Hope when none could be found, and Liberty when only desolation was found.

> *The Purpose of the Blood is the Spirit. And the Purpose of the Spirit is the Fire of God ... as one able to 'cast Fire upon the earth', ie; open manifestation of His Glory.*

INVITATION TO ASCEND

I deeply encourage you to go wait upon the Lord. Even 'ascend up' into the High Places to meet with Him daily. Setting yourself simply as one humbling yourself again to be captured up in Him [54]. For here are you ever transformed, ever 'Transfigured' in the Holiness of His Presence ... unto exceedingly great exploits. [55]

First it was Moses who went up upon Mount Sinai to Meet with God. Then later ... Moses, Aaron, and seventy elders also went up. However, this time ... they were taken right into the Heavenly realms and saw God, and ate a meal in the Presence of God before on the 'Pavement of Sapphire'. [56]

There is God's Presence that comes upon you and the congregation that is most valuable. But then ... there is a 'dining' in the Lord in **His Place of Dwelling**. There is your own strength and understanding, but then there is the Strength and Understanding that comes from Above [57]. And though there were incredible Places that Moses and the Greats of Old entered; they themselves are simply picture and precedence for us also ... for **all who believe** [58]. Even to go into Places man is not permitted.

First was Mount Sinai, then the Tabernacle ... then came the Temple of God. However now, the Veil has been rent both on earth [59] as well as in Heaven [60], whereby the honest [61] and the innocent; [62] they of whom *purely* seek to enter in ... shall do so. Not on this earthly plane but in Heaven [63]. And to such are increasingly clothed in Power. [64]

Today, I set before you an invitation, that in these that are the 'last days' ... God is inviting you to come up into the Mountain of the House of the Lord that is Above the mountains [65] ... and it will be the Lord of whom shall give you of His Heavenly Delights. And if you can set His Fire before you, shall He raise you in all holiness; with Divine Gifted Authority to move Heaven and earth. [66]

ORDINATION AS KING
Ordination as King [67] ... "The University of Heaven."

I deeply welcome you to the **School of Ministry**. I deeply welcome you to the School of the Anointed ... Heaven-based Training for the Blood-bought Righteous.

I welcome you to the Tutorship of the King. Apprenticeship in this of your Divinely Ordained Kingship [68]. Come then and submit yourself to the training of the Holy Ghost. Continually learning to look through all things unto the very Presence of God. Be singularly motivated and envisioned ... and it will be God Himself who will raise you Triumphant.

God will fight for you [69]. He will go out before you and bring everything under your feet [70]. And here He will Anoint and gift you Place to Stand amongst those that are here [71], over Heaven and earth: as one seated in Him … to bring Everlasting change to you and your people.

In the Book of Isaiah, it speaks of how in the Last Days, that there will be people who will invite you to come up into *"The Mountain of the Lord's House that is on the top of the mountains"* [72]. Therefore, I deeply encourage you — in this Season — to '**come up with me**'.

Just as the seventy of the elders of Israel came up with Moses … I invite you to come up with me. And it will be the Lord who will *"Teach us His ways"* **whereby Revival comes**.

Flesh and blood cannot teach you [73]. But in the honoured Presence of the Lord … such abundance is given you of the Lord [74]. Even as one who chooses to come before the Lord in the Tent of Meetings … and never leave! [75] The Blood is purposed to sanctify … but the Spirit is purposed to Empower, even then to Transfigure and Translate you in a moment of time. As children of Light, not of darkness … but Luminous beings.

The answer isn't man, the answer is the Glory of God.

Chapter 3 of the Book of Zechariah, speaks in incredible *example* of how the men referenced, are simply picture and precedence for the New Testament believer today. And how, if you were also … to truly humble yourself and set yourself to learn from the Spirit; you would be given Authority and 'Charge' over Heaven and earth. And this man Joshua, who was brought right up into the Presence of God; the Angel of the Lord called for the '**Clothing of Honour**' to be placed upon him [76]. This is the inherent Calling of the Church, the Destined Purpose of each and every believer.

Then in the Psalms we read, *"Come, sit at My right hand, till I make your enemies your footstool. The Lord shall send the rod of your Strength* **out of Zion**" [77]. You see, the strength to win does not come from you, nor does it come from man … but from God. It comes from the Heavenly Jerusalem … the City of the King. Even with the 'kingly' Anointing of the Christ to strike the earth [78] … that the Church might rule in the midst of your enemies!

In the life of Daniel, God prophesied the total abolishment of sin. Then in the life of Jesus, God spoke of the casting of Fire on the earth. But now, here in the Everlasting Life of God, He is calling you to come sit at His right hand — where you move Heaven and earth. Jesus 'birthed' the Spirit into earth, hence as one found in Him — do you also direct and release and outpour.

Scripture:
At the time of the banquet he sent his servant to tell those who had been invited, '**Come, for everything is now ready**.' But they all alike began to make excuses. The first said, 'I have just bought a field, and I must go and see it. Please excuse me.' Another said, 'I have just bought five yoke of oxen, and I'm on my way to try them out. Please excuse me.' Still another said, 'I just got married, so I can't come.' *(Luke 14:17-20 NIV)*

Up upon the Banqueting Table in Heaven, the truth is the many are just **too busy to partake**. Too concerned, too caught up with life to ever come here [79]. That is why the many are weak and failing. However today, as you are becoming aware, I deeply invite you to 'come up' with me. That you also might eat and drink deeply of the New Wine. Whereby your bones may be strengthened, your soul uplifted, and your eyes made clear. [80]

A side note: If you want to be on a war footing, you have to be on a Heaven footing. The Testimony of both the Spirit and the Blood shed for you ... is the Fire of God. The royal 'Glory of God' whereby angels themselves are the train of your gown. You can't win, you can't be successful as an earth-dweller. You must needs gain a Lofty vision and dwell in Lofty Places. [47]

You can't be successful without an orientation unto a Heavenly dwelling. As Jesus said, "Abide in me and I will abide in you." And where is our Resurrected Christ now ... not was, but is now? At the right hand of God in Glory. Nothing can stand against such as these; they who have made their 'nests in the clouds'. [104]

A WAY MAKER

Now, as one walking with God in the 'Garden realms', are you constantly given 'Seeds of Faith' that move mountains [81]. Given the Anointing of God to make way **establishing** Heaven on earth. [82]

In Christ Jesus — **you***!* — are a Way Maker. One who clears away obstructions and opposition [83] through the Faith of the Son in you [84]. The same move mountains ... build up and restore, making way for the Kingdom of Heaven made manifest on earth. [85]

For where your Strength comes from — **IS** — the Presence of God. Therefore, honour and give place for the Presence of His Person active in your life ... *ie;* **ask***!* [86] Fill the valleys, tear down the mountains; put aside hindrances and sin [87] ... for the Person of God Himself is your exceedingly great reward [88]. Come, walk with God 'in the cool of the day', for the right hand of God is the Garden realms. The Place of *exceedingly* great Joy and Delight ... where your right hand is God Himself*!*

Though, believing in Christ Jesus, many still walk **according** to the flesh. But then, there are those, who have purposed it within themselves to truly turn their heart unto God. It is true, that one can study the Word, even as one would study biology or a history subject. But then there is the meeting with God ... even He the very — Author — of the Word.

Now here, as one continuously being captured up into His Love, into His very Presence and Goodness ... not only turning to the Lord, but 'returning' [89]. Do you also continue to step *'back'* into the fullness of your Inheritance, into the Possession and the Promise. And as you continue to rise up in Him, as a people *re-risen* ... are you also availing yourself to this Wondrous process of being *'made'* into the Likeness of the Christ.

The Fall brought an impassable separation [90]. However now, it is the Holy Spirit who is at work, to refashion you into the Image and very Likeness of God. As is said, *"Let us make man in our Image and our Likeness, and let us give him Dominion"* [91]. Hence, in this restored Dominion so are you **seated**; whereby Life and Spirit; even the very realms of Heaven, are released and set to action through the words of your mouth.

The Dominion that was lost now re-stepped into: Such is the treasure found in meeting with the Person of God [92]. Christ Jesus is called and referred to as the 'Way' ... but what is He the Way to? Unto the Father of course. Even then as one who chooses to make your Dwelling in His Holy Presence; [93] to abide in these — Divine realms of Encounter — and never leave*!*

Now, when you speak over your family, when you speak over your future and your finances, and the people in your care, do you do so from within the realms of Dominion and Life. Not separate from Him but united body, mind, soul, and spirit; bringing everlasting change to all that you set your heart to. Heaven responding to the words of your mouth, and your hidden dreams read ... and God responding to them. [94]

STEPPING INTO THE REALMS OF THE SPIRIT

Adam walked with God in the cool of the day, and here God shared and imparted of His very self ...

Now you can more easily understand how true it is, that as you personally avail yourself, desiring and hungering after the Lord [95], so shall you be with Him '**where He is**' [96]. And together, just as Adam of Old, shall you 'co-labour' ... looking out over all creation. Bringing all things under the Goodness and Purposes of God. Even His Kingdom come, and His perfect Will being done on earth, just as it is in Heaven.

Scripture:
For [even the whole] creation waits expectantly and longs earnestly for God's sons to be made known [waits for the revealing, the disclosing of their sonship]. *(Romans 8:19 AMPC)*

Moses spoke face to face with God ... as friends. However, it was **Joshua** *(who led the people into the Promises)* who was also known as one who never left the Presence of God [97]. So it is then, that through the precious Blood shed ... you now have exact same right to enter into the Glory realms, and meet with God in the 'Tabernacle of God' — just as they — and **never leave**. But even more so, for by the Blood, have you also been *gifted* the Spirit of God. [98]

Therefore, if there is anything about you that desires to see change ... seek the manifest Presence of God. Seek to continually meet with Him as your fundament and first root motive of soul. For our walk with God is purposed to be an experiential one ... just as Jesus. A highly experiential one ... such is the lifestyle of a 'Joshua', even they who come to walk as the Son. So therefore, in this incredible Place of **Standing** in the Presence of God [99], shall you also 'part the waters' ... leading the multitudes into Life. And as a people like the 'Wind' [100] — Untouchable — releasing Heaven and the Will of God on earth.

UNTOUCHABLE [101]

Scripture:
Now it shall come to pass in the latter days that the Mountain of the LORD's house shall be established on the top of the mountains, and shall be exalted above the hills; and all nations shall flow to it. Many people shall come and say, "Come, and let us go up to the mountain of the LORD, to the house of the God of Jacob; **HE will teach us His ways**, and we shall walk in His paths." For out of Zion shall go forth the law, and the word of the LORD from Jerusalem. *(Isaiah 2:2-3 NKJV)*

... and the verse continues, 'Nation shall not lift up sword against nation, neither shall they learn war anymore' [102]. **The outworking of such a lifestyle is Revival** ... the Outpouring of the Spirit in these that are the Last Days.

Jesus lives in the realm of 'Prayer', in the Eternal and Wondrous realms of God. So, if you truly wish to be successful in prayer, then respond and come step up into and abide in these realms of Power. For to truly treat all things rescinded in face of His Presence, *ie;* abandon yourself unto the Cross [103], then **as a 'lord' in His eyes** ... shall He be Lord in yours.

God's vision of you far surpasses. Jesus is 'King of kings' and 'Lord of lords' — **this is you**! Even as God is 'God of Heavenly lights' — so are you light. You are 'children of light', meaning ... a people *re*-risen, *re*-positioned, *ie;* the **returned ones** in Him. A people who have made their dwelling amongst the 'clouds', who have made their dwelling in the Most High God [104]. People who walk as His Children manifest on earth. [105]

In the past, the Temple of God was on earth … and people from far and wide came to it. However, the Temple was simply a replica … a 'shadow' of the original one that is in Heaven.

However now, in these that are the 'Latter Days' — people like you and I shall come up into the original Temple of God that is in Heaven — through the gifted Spirit of God. And here, out of this 'Place of Dwelling', shall you lead a most Powerful, Anointed, and Unlimited lives. A people triumphant over all things: over all powers and all authorities … birthing Life in hopeless places. God placing everything under your feet … and setting before you a Banqueting Table that never ceases to give. [106]

The Blood comes before the Law … even today the Meeting the very Person of God *before* you have done anything right. Now you can more easily understand how the drunken — even they in the gutter of hopelessness and despair — can meet the Lord of Glory. And this even before they have ceased wrongdoing … or their life of depravity. For the Blood comes before the Law as too the meeting the Holiness of God. [107]

Now it can more easily be recognised, that connection and Divine Interaction with the Person of God has nothing to do with right doing or righteous deeds. But everything about rightly receiving the Blood of Jesus upon your life. Even here and now; purposing it within your soul to *return* to God — even this, your original Place of Dwelling!

Ah, how … when one meets with God … he is Renewed. Even he who chooses it within himself to continually meet with Him — as a lifestyle — is **made Victorious** and most Powerful. There are many places that you can be … but in God, can you step into realms unfathomable to the human mind. Even here, right from within your brokenness and hopelessness. And it is unto they who prefer to 'love on God' — even right in the midst of despair — that God Himself takes you out of the gutter of your situation and places you where He is. And here, He shifts your thinking as He clothes you in Honour, taking off your filthy clothes and dressing you in Glory. [108]

Before the Throne of God are the Spirits of the Lord [109]. And before the Spirits of God ... innumerable hosts of angels. Therefore, to continue to choose to *remain* here; the God-of-the-Angel-Armies shall remain diligently at work to establish you in this of your blood-bought Dominion. Re-positioning you back as one sitting upon the Throne of Authority and Grace ... the Throne of Judgement and Absolute Power [110]. Whereby **you** make judgement [111] on behalf of the needy; releasing the Goodness of God on behalf of the broken and the lost. [112]

*The Blood of Jesus has made you both king and priest unto God. **Priest**, as one standing in the gap joining Heaven to the hurting [112]. And **king**, as one releasing and pouring out Heaven and the Will of God on earth. [113]*

Scripture:
"I have wiped away your sins [and wrongdoings] like the morning mist, **return** to me for I have redeemed you." *(Isaiah 44:22)*

Your Purpose in God is always unto 'returning'. Not just turning ... but stepping back up **into** the Place where Adam fell. For it is not ever enough that you know about God, but that you **know Him**. And this comes only through the Blood and honouring the Spirit. Deeply honouring your closed sessions in the Lord ... meeting personally with the Glory of God and Him showing up.

The Spirit is fundamentally tasked to 'make' you into the Image and Likeness of God [114]. And this *reality* being so far beyond what you can imagine or ever comprehend. However, through your honest and continued availing of yourself ... do you step continually further in.

Scripture:
Woe to you, teachers of the law and Pharisees, you hypocrites! You **shut** the door of the kingdom of heaven in people's faces. You yourselves do not enter, nor will you let those enter who are trying to. *(Matthew 23:13 NIV)*

One of the last 'obstacles' facing the Christian believer are the religious and legalistic spirits. They are the '**leaven**' that influences and affects the whole Church. And these religious unbelieving spirits are constantly at work against the 'revelation' of your sonship and your rich heritage in the Lord [115]. However, as you continue to seek the Face of God, seeking the Lord and the Lord alone; it is here in His Presence that He continues to reveal and open His Heart to your understanding. That you truly may step deeper into this of your *predestined* Dominion.

By the Blood of Jesus ... the Spirit and Life of God is inherent in you. Being — purposed made — in the Image and Likeness of God; re-raised in your true Place of Origins.

Much of the Christian world has come under *misinformation*. The very same of which caused Adam to Fall in the Beginning. Hence, I shall always encourage you in this fundamental truth, *"The Kingdom of Heaven is at hand"* ... therefore, never cease from entering in. For the Purpose of the Blood is the entrance unto these Glorious realms. The realms of the Kingdom of Heaven, the Spirit and of Everlasting Life, and that of the Outpouring of the Fire of God on earth*!*

ONE CLOSING THOUGHT

Do you still have but only the vision of man? Or do you not yet have the Love and Vision of God upon your life? What I mean is, the Love that comes from God, the Love that is poured out liberally deep in your soul [116]. This is part of 'Ascension'.

For it is not just the trying to see through the eyes of Jesus that is meaningful. But the being 'translated' into His Eyes ... spirit, soul, mind, and flesh. Into the Eyes ... into the Mind ... and into the very co-seated realms of the Christ. To see, to walk, to receive, and to speak from this place. No longer just an earth-based love or knowledge of God ... but Heaven-based. The Love and Faith of Jesus [117] coming upon you. **This is totally different** ... so very different.

So right where you are, bow down on your knees and pray with me this short prayer, *"Blessed be the Name of the Lord, you are beautiful in my eyes. I seek you Face, I seek your Face ... I seek the Presence of the Lord."*

ISAIAH 61:1-4 NIV

v1 The Spirit of the Sovereign Lord is on me,
because the Lord has anointed me
to proclaim good news to the poor.
He has sent me to bind up the brokenhearted,
to proclaim freedom for the captives
and release from darkness for the prisoners,
v2 to proclaim the year of the Lord's favor
and the day of vengeance of our God,
to comfort all who mourn,
v3 and provide for those who grieve in Zion—
to bestow on them a crown of beauty
instead of ashes,
the oil of joy
instead of mourning,
and a garment of praise
instead of a spirit of despair.
They will be called oaks of righteousness,
a planting of the Lord
for the display of his splendor.
v4 They will rebuild the ancient ruins
and restore the places long devastated;
they will renew the ruined cities
that have been devastated for generations.

BIBLICAL MECHANISMS
"Simple Biblical Mechanics to an Anointed life. A life full of the Power of the Holy Ghost."

Simply 'Love on God'.
'Enter the Gates with thanksgiving, enter the Courts with praise'.
'Delight yourself in the Lord'.
'Seek first the Kingdom of God'.
'Praise and worship'.
'Prayer and fasting'.
Enter into the 'secret place'.
Abide 'under the Shadow of the Lord'.
'Sit at the feet of Jesus'.
'Enter the Rest' of the Lord.
'Be still and know the Lord'.
'Meditate day and night on His Word'.
'Wait upon the Lord'.
'Repent' *ie;* turn your affections and thoughts unto the Lord.
'Open the door' so you can eat and drink in Him.
'Seek the Face of God'; manifest.
'Go in and out and find pasture'.
'Drink deeply of the New Wine'.
'Feast of the fatness of your house'.
'Like infants at the breast, drink deep of God's pure kindness'.

Appendix:

1. Isaiah 64:4, *2.* Matthew 16:18-19, John 20:21-23, Revelation 2:26-27, *3.* John 1:18, *4.* Daniel 9:24, 12:11, Isaiah 44:22, Psalm 2:7-8, Genesis 1:26, 2 Kings 2:9, *5.* Isaiah 11:1-4, Acts 2:17, *6.* NKJV: John 1:18, 13:23, 16:14-15, Psalm 110:1-2, 2:7-8, *7.* Romans 4:17, Hebrews 11:1, *8.* Psalm 2:7-8, Genesis 1:26, *9.* Exodus 14:14, 33:14, 23:28, Joshua 24:12, Psalm 91:12, *10.* Deuteronomy 28:7, Proverbs 6:31, Revelations 5:6, *11.* 2 Chronicles 7:14, Joel 2:28, *12.* Isaiah 2:1-4, 11:1-9, 40:1-5, 41:14-18, 61:1-4, 64:1-4, Psalm 110:1-4, 84:1-7, Acts 2:1-4, Colossians 3:1-4, Revelation 4:1-5, *13.* Isaiah 61:1-4, Ephesians 4:12-13, *14.* Isaiah 64:1-4, Zechariah 3:7, Nehemiah 4:17, Romans 8:19, *15.* 2 Timothy 3:5, 1 Corinthians 4:20, Revelation 2:5, 3:16-18, John 17:24, Zechariah 4:6, *16.* Exodus 40:34-38, 34:35, 33:9-11, 24:16-18, 19:10-20, 13:21-22, 3:1-6, 2 Chronicles 5:13-14, 7:1, Numbers 9:15-23, Leviticus 16:2, Ezekiel 10:18-19, Joshua 3:14-17, Matthew 17:1-2, Luke 4:1-2, 14 *(first bind the strongman)*, Luke 1:35, 12:49, 24:49, Acts 1:4-5, 2:1-4, 2 Corinthians 3:18, Revelation 2:4-5, Genesis 3:24, *17.* Ezekiel 10:18-19, Revelation 2:4-5, *18.* Isaiah 40:4-5, *19.* Matthew 16:19, John 20:21-23, *20.* Luke 24:49, Revelation 3:17-18, Psalm 110:1-2, 2:7-8, *21.* Exodus 33:2-3 *NKJV*, *22.* Exodus 12:12b, *23.* Genesis 15:1, *24.* Isaiah 40:4-5, *25.* 1 Corinthians 15:26, 54-55, *26.* Exodus 20:19, 1 Samuel 8:7, Luke 21:34, *27.* John 17:24, *28.* Matthew 6:10, Hebrews 7:17, *29.* John 5:19, 20:21-23, Isaiah 11:3-4, Exodus 33:14, Psalm 82:6-8, Zechariah 3:7, Revelation 2:26-27, *30.* Revelation 2:5, *31.* Exodus 13:21-22, Colossians 3:4, *32.* John 14:13, 15:7-8, John 6:40, *33.* Psalm 91:1, Acts 5:15, *34.* Philippians 4:7, Exodus 33:14, *35.* John 14:21-23, 5:19-20, Matthew 4:4, Revelation 3:20, Psalm 110:2, *36.* Luke 24:32, *37.* Matthew 17:20, *38.* Isaiah 61:3, *39.* Luke 12:49, Acts 2:17, *40.* John 16:14, *41.* Deuteronomy 8:3, Matthew 4:4, 16:17-19, John 5:19, *42.* Romans 8:19, *43.* Proverbs 9:10, *44.* Hebrews 12:21, Exodus 20:21, Isaiah 11:3-4, Psalm 27:4, Acts 2:2-3; Exodus 33:18, 24:10-11, 20:19-21, Revelation 1:10/17, *45.* Psalm 110:1-2, Matthew 18:2-4, *46.* John 15:5-8, *47.* Isaiah 33:14b-15a *HCSB*, Psalm 24:3-10, Exodus 33:18-23, *48.* Hebrews 12:14, *49.* 1 Samuel 26:9, *50.* 1 Chronicles 7:14, *51.* Revelation 3:20, *52.* 2 Timothy 2:21, Acts 9:15, John 15:16, 2 Kings 25:14, *53.* Luke 10:41-42, *54.* Revelation 1:10/17, 4:1, Exodus 33:18,

John 17:24, **55.** Exodus 20:21, 24:9-11, 24:12, 33:18-23, Psalm 24:3, Isaiah 2:2-3, Mark 3:13, Revelation 1:10 // Matthew 17:1-3, Psalm 2:6-9, Revelation 1:5-6 // Isaiah 64:1-4, 41:15, Matthew 17:20, Revelation 2:25-28 // Daniel 11:32 *NKJV,* **56.** Exodus 24:9-11, Revelation 4:6, **57.** Psalm 110:2, **58.** Psalm 27:4, Isaiah 2:1-4, Matthew 17:1-3, Acts 1:13, 2:1-4, **59.** Matthew 27:51, **60.** Genesis 3:24, **61.** John 4:24, **62.** Matthew 18:3-4, **63.** Psalm 27:4, Isaiah 2:2-4, Hebrews 8:5, Matthew 4:11, John 3:13, 17:21-24, **64.** Luke 24:49, Revelation 3:18-21, 2 Corinthians 3:18, **65.** Isaiah 2:2-4, **66.** Zechariah 3:7, Matthew 16:17-19, Mark 16:17-19, **67.** 1 Samuel 16:12-13, **68.** Revelation 1:5-6, 5:9-10 *NKJV,* **69.** Exodus 14:14, **70.** Exodus 6:6-8, Psalm 110:1-2, 23:5, **71.** Zechariah 3:7, **72.** Isaiah 2:2-4, **73.** Matthew 23:10, **74.** Luke 6:38, Psalm 23:5, **75.** Exodus 33:11, John 13:23 (KJV), 17:24, 1:18, Acts 13:22, **76.** Luke 24:49, Genesis 3:10, Revelation 3:17-18, 1 Corinthians 15:53-54, 2 Corinthians 3:18, 2 Kings 2:14, 6:17, Matthew 16:17-19, Mark 16:17-19, Acts 5:15, Colossians 3:1-3, Psalm 91:1, 2:7-8, 110:1-2, 34:7, 104:2, 93:1, 84:5, John 1:51, Exodus 33:14-18, 34:29, John 17:24, Genesis 1:26, **77.** Psalm 110:1-2, **78.** Revelation 2:26-27, **79.** Luke 14:15-24, 21:34, **80.** Revelation 3:18, **81.** Matthew 17:20, 4:4, 16:17-19, **82.** Matthew 6:10, **83.** Isaiah 59:19 *NKJV,* **84.** Galatians 2:20 *NKJV,* **85.** Isaiah 40:1-5, **86.** Psalm 2:7, **87.** Isaiah 40:3-5, **88.** Genesis 15:1, **89.** Isaiah 44:22, **90.** Genesis 3:24, **91.** Genesis 1:26-27, 5:3, Romans 8:29-30, 2 Corinthians 3:18, **92.** Romans 8:29, Psalm 24:9, **93.** Psalm 91:9, **94.** Psalm 37:4, **95.** Matthew 4:4, Luke 10:41-42, **96.** John 17:24, 3:13, **97.** Exodus 33:11, **98.** John 16:14-15, 14:12, Matthew 11:11, 2 Corinthians 1:20, Exodus 33:22, **99.** 2 Kings 2:14, Hebrews 4:16, **100.** John 3:8, Isaiah 60:8, **101.** John 3:8, Matthew 14:25, John 6:21, Luke 4:30, John 14:12, Isaiah 60:8, Isaiah 55:12, **102.** Isaiah 2:4, **103.** Luke 17:33, **104.** Isaiah 60:8, Psalm 84:3, 91, **105.** John 1:12-13, **106.** Exodus 24:9-11, Psalm 23:5, **107.** Zechariah 3:1-2, **108.** Zechariah 3, **109.** Revelation 4:5, **110.** Genesis 1:26, Revelation 1:5-6, 5:9-10 *NKJV,* 3:21, Zechariah 3:7, Ephesians 2:6, Colossians 3:1-3 // 1 Samuel 16:13, 2 Samuel 5:4, **111.** John 20:21-23, **112.** Isaiah 11:3-4, **113.** Matthew 6:10, **114.** Genesis 1:26, **115.** Revelation 12:17, **116.** Romans 5:5, **117.** Galatians 2:20 KJV

Dated: 19/9/20

29. Mount Sinai, the Way of the Anointed (#112)
BANQUETING TABLE *(Part 1)*

Verse 1-2, Psalm 84:
How lovely is your dwelling place, Lord Almighty! My soul **yearns**, even faints, for the courts of the Lord; my heart and my flesh **cry out** for the living God.

The theme of these last several chapters has been the meeting with God at 'Mount Sinai'. And how Mount Sinai, this 'meeting with God' ... is the path to **fully stepping into** the Promises of God. Not the desert but the meeting.

So in this, what is something that you remember about the people in the Exodus? They were always so fixated on the past, so fixated on the future or problems at hand ... **rather** than on that of which God **had for them**. Hence therefore, God would allow 'desert' and 'wilderness' experiences to occur for this single reason: to teach and reaffirm one thing, *"Man cannot live on bread alone but every word that proceeds from the mouth of God."* [1]

Hence the truth is then, that the very opposite is most very true: that '**Life**' and the Promises of God, *ie;* the 'Promised Land', are swiftly entered into, lived in, and expanded in you ... through treasuring the 'Presence of God'. That is, ever **valuing meeting** with the Person of God — and 'hearing' Him — today! And allow these meetings with Him to become more treasured and more sought after than answer to hardships, unknown futures, or past issues.

For in this choosing to — look beyond — the realities of this life, and coming to deeply value and treasure the hearing and the seeing *(even the Fire and Glory of God)*, does God set a Banqueting Table right in the midst of your 'enemies'. With such Grace and such a measure of Heaven coming upon you that causes you to rule in the midst of difficulties, hardships, and impossibilities. Even then, becoming one who **conquers** ... always taking new ground with relative ease. [2]

Verse 3-4, Psalm 84:
Even the sparrow has **found a home**, and the swallow a nest for herself, where she may have her young — a place near your altar, LORD Almighty, my King and my God. Blessed are those who dwell in your house; they are ever praising you.

A few points to touch on here: If the **Dwelling Place** of God was on earth, and was a place where all the people could come, then it would be very crowded. And if all the people made it their 'nest' ... their *place of dwelling* ... then there would be no place to sit or lay your head. Ask yourself, **where is the House of God**? Where was the Temple of God where David's soul constantly longed for? Now you know where your Strength lies.

Now, what happens in the 'Dwelling Place' is that you go from strength to strength. What happens is that you go from being a little 'ruddy kid' to a **king**. And what happens is that you become inspired ... *'in-Spirit-ed'*... poetic, prophetic, and a musician of praise. And what happens, is that you become one established and seated as a 'king' ... touching Heaven for all Eternity.

Problems become places of praise ... *difficulties,* opportunity to love on God. Hardships and unknown times; simply another day to seek the Face of God. And here are you one who creates springs in barren places, Life and Spirit in hopeless situations. And with God watching you ... in His delight He responds and outpours Heaven. Meaning, outpours **'rain'** of Divine activity in and all around your life, in Jesus Name.

Another subject that we have been talking about, is how Adam fell out of the realms of Life ... into death. And how, ever since then, for all these eons and generations, man has only **known these realms of death** and mortality ... and not Life. Therefore, so it is, that man has very little imagination or reference of what the Promises really mean ... for they are fundamentally foreign to us.

A side note: Think of it for a second, Adam lived for 900 years. But the reality was, that if he didn't 'fall' then he would never have died. For us, when we think of 'dying and going to Heaven' ... this too Adam would never have thought of. For prior to the Fall there was no separation.

The 'death' God was warning about was **separation** *to Life, ie; the realms of Everlasting Life ... the realms of Heaven. In Christ Jesus, simply He is providing opportunity for you and I to return back into what was lost (the Immortal realms, the realms of the Untouchable ... the Unlimited nes whereby nothing is impossible). And what is most meaningful concerning your loved ones?* **Don't wait** *until death before you walk here.*

In the Exodus, the people were given physical lands flowing with 'milk and honey' ... with homes, vineyards, and cities. And as they moved forward so did they also step all the more further in, taking possession of what was already theirs. And so it is the exact and very same for us as well, but instead of physical lands, we have been given lands flowing with 'Life and Spirit' ... gifted even the very realms of Heaven as our Inheritance.

However now, this world of 'Inheritance', is not a waiting until you die before you gain access. But that Christ Jesus died — in place of us — that you and I might have '**Life** and Life in its fullness' [3] — today! Let me rephrase that, 'Life ... **Everlasting Life** ... in all its fullness in us now, here and today'. Therefore, because of what Christ Jesus — has already — achieved for you, every Promise is made 'yes', and every Promise 'amen' for us, to the glory of God. [4]

Truth is, that our 'Promise Land' — this, the Salvation and realms of Life gifted us through the Son — is so far beyond what we can imagine or comprehend. For as God says, *"My thoughts are not your thoughts. As the heavens are higher than the earth, so are my thoughts higher than your thoughts"* [5]. And in another place, *"No eye has seen, nor ear heard, nor has it entered into the heart of man all the things which God has prepared for those who love Him."* [6]

So now, it can be more easily recognised, just how much we need the God of the Promise — to **take** us into the Promises. Just how much we need the Spirit of God to take us deeper into the realms of the Spirit. Even into the mysteries of God; into the open Wonders of the Kingdom realms. For just as God reveals so does He impart ... so does He Empower.

PRINCIPLES OF THE PROMISE

"My Presence will go with you, and I will give you **Rest**." [7]

"The Lord will **fight** for you; you need only to be still." [8]

"If your Presence does not go with us, **do not send** us up from here." [9]

Truly, the believer has very little reference or imagination of what their Inheritance truly entails; nor how to access, engage, or make manifest on earth. For as far as death is to Life, so is the Spirit of the Lord.

Hence therefore, as Jesus 'stands at your door and knocks' [10] so does He also seek to sit down together with you and share as close trusted friends [11]. That you might be shown and revealed to, and taken into experience; even that you might be healed, might be raised up and strengthened, and might be ever filled with the Might of the Lord. Becoming one ever established in the Love and the Authority of the Son. [12]

Three Scripture verses:
1. If anyone serves Me, let him **follow** Me; and where I am, there My servant will be also [in Risen Glory]. If anyone serves Me, him My Father will honor [Clothe in Glory]. *(John 12:26 NKJV)*
2. My sheep hear My voice, and I **know** them, and they follow Me. *(John 10:27 NKJV)*
3. I am the door. If anyone enters by Me, he will be saved, and will **go in and out** and find pasture. *(John 10:9 NKJV)*

There are always two paths: The knowing of a thing and living in experience. One who only *observes* as like an 'astronomer', or one who is like an astronaut. The fundamental **purpose of the Blood** and the Spirit is to come into a living experience of the Goodness and reality of God ... not just knowing about it. An astronomer is proud of his studies, but an astronaut goes into and travels the stars.

In a spiritual sense ... Moses fundamentally represented Law, which is why he could not have *entered* the Promised Land. The Hebrew name for Jesus is Yeshua, meaning to 'rescue' or to 'deliver' ... and another way to pronounce is 'Joshua'. Therefore, in this picture of Joshua in the Exodus, it is **only through the Grace** of God, and not obedience to Law, that are you Purposed of God to enter the full Promises of God. [13]

Do you remember how Jesus would often say to the Pharisees, *"It says in **your** Law?"* [14] ... because Law was not Him. And what was Joshua famous for ... as was Jesus? He never left the Tent of Meetings [15] ... such is the Secret Place. Hence now you know the pathway unto the **full manifestation** of the Promises of God for you and your people.

Today, in Christ Jesus, God has set before you an invitation: to dine with Him upon His Banqueting Table. For just as the Psalmist expressed, *"They shall feast on the abundance of your house; you give them drink from your River of Delights. For with you is the Fountain of Life;* **in your light we see Light**.*"* [16]

The fundamental truth, however remains ... that the believer is just too busy. Always so mentally and physically caught up with one thing or another. So God keeps looking out for someone who might respond [17]. And to he who honestly responds, to the one who truly opens his heart, does God take you by hand deeper into the realms of Life. These, the very same realms of Life that Adam himself fell from. [18]

Verse 5-7, Psalm 84:
Blessed are those whose strength is in you, whose **hearts are set on pilgrimage**. As they pass through the Valley of Baka, they make it a place of springs; the autumn rains also cover it with pools. They go from strength to Strength, till each appears before God in Zion.

So now, in this *preferencing* the Presence of the Lord, and the richness of His Word alive in you, do you enter into experience of the 'River of Delight'. Your life with God forming as like a fountain ... a geyser ... a river of Living Water welling up within [19]. Or another way of saying, does the Water of Life continue to lift you up into the realms of Eternity ... the realms of Everlasting Life. These, the very same realms of the Spirit that are yours: the

Kingdom realms, the Glory realms, the Place of God's dwelling. To live in experience of, to be raised and re-established in, the very realms of Inheritance and Dominion that is yours. [20]

Therefore, to the one who values the *pause*, to he who simply treasures sitting before the 'Mountain of God' ... even then to ascend, [21] do you continually open yourself to **receive**. And things that you didn't even know to ask for, according to your new found faith ... so are you **now given** [22]. And it is here, in the 'Place of Dwelling' [23], that the Lord your God extends His Hand saying, *"Come up here with me."* [24]

PSALM 84
"They make it a place of springs; the autumn rains also cover it with pools. They go from strength to Strength, till each appears before God in Zion."
(Verse 6)

Scattered throughout this chapter are verses from Psalm 84; that each culminates in something most powerful. This example in verse 6 ... speaks of how, through the setting your heart on 'pilgrimage', that when you come to a 'Valley of Baka', *ie;* a place of weeping, a desert place, a place of trials and tribulations — do you make it a place of springs, through the Power of the Spirit of God in you.

This inherent nature in you of 'digging' for the Presence of God — **irrespective of season** — and coming always into experience of Him. And through this fervent and diligent approach unto the — 'Dwelling' of the Lord — does God of Heaven and earth look down upon you, and in His own delight ... pours out the Autumn Rains.

This biblical term 'Autumn Rains' has great spiritual significance. Another word for it is the 'Latter Rains', or better said, the 'Outpouring of the Spirit in these that are the Last Days'. So it is then, that through a heart that ever 'yearns' to dwell in the House of God, so are you also one who triggers the Outpouring of the Spirit.

Verse 8-10:
Hear my prayer, Lord God Almighty; listen to me, God of Jacob. Look on our shield, O God; look with favor on your anointed one. **Better is one day** in your courts than a thousand elsewhere; I would rather be a doorkeeper in the House of my God than dwell in the tents of the wicked.

So in these thoughts, let's begin. But before we do so, it's really most important to realise just how pivotal this current moment of time is for you. For just as the people in the Exodus said to Moses, *"Speak to us yourself and we will listen. But do not have God speak to us or we will die"* [25]. So too do you have opportunity to give **great honoured place for God to speak**.

Today you have a choice, to either stay the same as you are, or otherwise make it by choice to open your heart wide unto meeting with your Heavenly Father. For God always has something greater than what you are currently believing for. And that is to the giving you greater **possession** of what is **already yours**. For by the Purpose of God are you a Way Maker [26] … God stepping through you into your world.

Remember that sometimes, this is the very reason why wilderness experiences are allowed to occur at times. That personally, you truly might come into Personal Divine Engagement. And here, continue to be transitioned from an earthly fleshly vision and standpoint unto a Heavenly one, *ie;* coming 'to sit at the right hand of God'. [27]

"Clothing for righteousness … Clothing for Glory."

Jesus says to you today, *"I counsel you to **buy** from me gold refined in the fire … white **clothes** to wear … and salve to put on your eyes, so you can see."* [28]

God clearly is about leading you back deeper into what is already yours … the *'pilgrimage'*. This is His Prayer; this is His Vision concerning you today.

But in many ways, the believer remains so indifferent. However, if you truly could come to understand these things a bit more and respond, then you would continually step into greater Authority and Anointing to deal with all that is in front of you.

The way of the world is very different, the *fashioning* everything according to one's own 'tree of understanding' [29]. But God is about relationship, and this is the **basis** of Salvation. And through relationship, fashion you into the Image of the Risen Son. However, as with the people in the Exodus, it was they who didn't want to hear God themselves; they who only looked unto the *instruction* of man ... that is why they failed*!* Or let's say, that is the very reason why they never stepped into or experienced the Promises ... nor that of which God had purposed for them.

I really pray you are most blessed by the thoughts expressed in this chapter. Let's begin ...

THE BANQUETING TABLE

To they who set their hearts firmly upon the Lord, eat richly of His Banqueting Table. And what is given [30] nourishes the soul, the mind ... and your very bones. And regardless of what this life is presenting, it is the Lord your God that has you recline in His Presence dining [31] that you be **full of Life** and **full of Spirit** [32]. And it is here, in this Place of 'Dining', that the Lord your God shall cause you to rise up in the midst of any trial or any difficulty — Mighty and Triumphant in the Lord [33] — even as one who truly 'rules in the midst of your enemies'. [34]

Now it is the Lord your God whom desires to set in your hands a Rod of Iron [35]. To smash down mountains and make them as *"Chaff to be blown away in the wind"* [36]. Even then, as one who clears obstructions and opposition ... *"Casting them into the sea."* Making way for the Glory of the Lord to be revealed ... unto the healing of the nations. [37]

God has set an Invitation and calls each one of us to dine upon His Banqueting Table [38]. But the truth is, the many are too busy ... are just too caught up with this life and its issues. With hearts ever drawn between the hurts and needs of this world ... or its desires

39. But to one who values the *'pause'*, to he who truly honours the meeting God at 'Mount Sinai', do you continually open yourself up to He who knocks. *40* Open yourself up to the **realms of Life** and to the Tutorship of the Son. *41*

Ah, there is nothing more precious than this. This, the very thing of which was lost man in the Beginning ... walking with God in the *Garden* realms. And even now, as one who *dwells* in His House and never leaves. For to such as these that hunger, to he who deeply values and treasures the Meeting *42*, are you simply opening your mouth to Life and the Spirit of God. And this, the very same, being poured into every part of you. Life and Spirit pouring in building you up in every way. And as Life and Spirit continue to rise up within you, do you simply continue to find yourself passing from the realms of death into the realms of Life. *43*

No longer a 'worm' in the dirt under Satan's grip and purpose. But rising up on wings like eagles and striking from High and Lofty Places *44*.

The butterfly eats differently from a grub ... the eagle different to the worm. But to he who receives from the Lord, so are you ever transformed in His Presence.

THE BIG PICTURE

In the Beginning, Adam lived in the realms of Life as he lived and walked the earth. For at his time, Heaven and earth were perfectly united and intertwined ... but then the Fall came. And Adam 'fell' out of the realms of 'Life and Spirit' into *death* *45*, *ie;* Heaven, the very source of Life ... was made separate to man.

Then God set the Cherubim to bar the way to these realms where the Tree of Life stands. And this creature of *Divine Purpose* called 'man', was no longer able to go back into that of which was lost. The way was firmly closed. And this 'guarding' was both ways: Man, no longer able to engage the realms of Life and Spirit. But also, Life and Spirit unable to engage these of the realms of man ... without the express interest of God. Whereby God raised men like Enoch, Noah, Abraham, and Moses.

Then the Lord called for the making of the Ark of the Covenant and the Tabernacle of God. This, the very **first** 'footprint' of the Spirit of God on earth. And as the people moved ... the Spirit of God moved with them. And no one ever dared touch or look inside the Ark, for the Glory of God too intense for the unredeemed. The very same Cherubim guarding with flashing flaming swords. [46]

Verse 1-2, Isaiah 11:
There shall come forth a Rod from the stem of Jesse, and a Branch shall grow out of his roots. The Spirit of the Lord shall rest upon Him, the Spirit of wisdom and understanding, the Spirit of counsel and might, the Spirit of knowledge and of the fear of the Lord.

So here, the story continues in the Person of Christ Jesus. He the First Seed, the first of many ... He the very Tabernacle of God in this 'tent' called man. The Son of God, not 'son of Adam' ... but Son of Man. He, of whom lived in perfect union just as in the Beginning — 'Heaven in Man' perfectly intertwined.

Now, what is most important to know, is that because of what Christ Jesus has achieved for you on the Cross: this very same picture **is now Template** and the Purpose of God concerning you and I, *ie;* the 'Promise'. And in choosing to believe in Jesus ... here it is, that the Father truly weeps with joy [47]. For you are simply responding to His own Eternal Dream. And as we continue to avail the Spirit to fill and ever expand you, so are you transformed into this 'Picture' of the Man Christ Jesus. Heaven and earth perfectly intertwined in this — New Creation — of which is **you**!

Today, in Christ Jesus, **you are the Tabernacle of God** in the flesh, as the Shekinah Glory fills the Temple [48]. You are a 'portal' of Heaven with angels ascending and descending upon you [49]. You are a 'seed' birthed out of the First Seed; [50] you are grafted into the same Branch. Planted in the same 'sap' of the River of Life ... unto the Glory of God. [51]

A Temple made by the Hand of God ... not by man, but God Himself. And so is your heart ever purposed unto praise. Not as a Temple full of 'merchandise' [52] ... that is, a heart set upon the desires of this world. But ever unto the Presence of God; unto the very Glory of God. With the Sovereign Presence of God — in His Person — ever resting upon you.

The angel of God came to the mother of Jesus saying, *"The Holy Spirit will come upon you, and the power of the Most High will overshadow you; and for that reason, the holy Child shall be called the Son of God."* [53]

Today, this very same word is declared over you — this very moment. The Spirit of the Lord says most firmly, that in Christ Jesus you are born not of flesh but of the Spirit and Will of God [54]. Therefore here, in the allowing of the Spirit of the Lord to 'overshadow' you, so are you too 'holy child of God'. And in the Presence of the Lord, so are you called 'son of the Most High'.

This is **His Vision** concerning you ... therefore, become increasingly Christ-centred [55]. For this is His Purpose and Prayer since the Beginning. Even for you to go into Places in God of such intrigue that angels can only dream [56]. So here and now — **today** — allow the Spirit of God to overshadow you, in the Holiness of His Presence. That you might be made a most different creature [57]. For as one who receives from the Lord, so have you also been given *right* to become son of God. [58]

Verse 3-4, Isaiah 11:
His delight is in the fear of the Lord, and He shall not judge by the sight of His eyes, nor decide by the hearing of His ears; but with righteousness He shall **judge** the poor, and decide with equity for the meek of the earth; He shall strike the earth with the rod of His mouth, and with the breath of His lips He shall slay the wicked.

So then, now, where Life and Spirit were held back from God's creation, the Spirit of the Lord is now outpoured through the shedding of the Blood. This same Blood that was shed upon the Mercy Seat; the very same that was sprinkled upon the Ark of the Covenant where the Cherubim guard the way [59]. Therefore, as one redeemed through the Blood of the Lamb, and of whose heart is ever set unto Jesus and the realms of the Spirit, so are you now free to pass in and out of Heaven just as you please [60]. Releasing the very same Spirit of God on earth ... opening Heaven to touch the many. [61]

> *"By your precious Blood, Lord, have you purchased the earth and the souls of man. Satan has no right ... nor any possession. Therefore, I make 'judgement', and release the Life and Salvation of the Lord. Unto the broken and the lost ... I release the Spirit of God. However, unto the practisers of witchcraft, and practitioners [62] of evil I say 'repent', for the day of Vengeance is at hand."*

You are a triggerer of the Outpouring of the Spirit for your world. You are a living, breathing, Tabernacle of God in the flesh [63] — Baptised with Fire, with incredible doors of profound opportunity — *if* that is truly where your delight lies [64]. And with Life and Spirit in your hands, and as a Sword from your mouth, so shall you *strike* the earth. Therefore, pray the Blood that sanctifies all things, release the Spirit of God to touch and to heal ... and command a harvest, *ie;* **"Take up your mat and walk*!"* [65]

All of Heaven has been presented before the believer. But as an heir, are you still subject to the 'trustees' appointed. That in time, under the Tuition and Instruction of the Spirit of God ... *in perfect union* ... shall you be given full right over the whole 'Estate'. [66]

The Father has been yearning for you to return. But there is a right way, and His Name is Christ Jesus ... the Branch [67]. That through ever 'Abiding' in the Son [68] so shall the Spirit of God ride upon your words. For simply, are you returning back into the Dominion predestined you from since before the founding of the earth [69]. This is the Divine Created Purpose concerning all who truly love and follow the Lord. As Jesus says, *"If anyone serves me, let him follow me; and **where I am**, there my servant **will be also**."* [70]

Verse 5-6, Isaiah 11: *(Revival)*
Righteousness shall be the belt of His loins, and faithfulness the belt of His waist. "The wolf also shall dwell with the lamb, the leopard shall lie down with the young goat, the calf and the young lion and the fatling together; and a little child shall lead them."

> *The Temple is the Place of the Holy Spirit, not a place for 'merchandise' ... but the Fire of God.*

Moses went into Places where man was not permitted. Glory so intense whereby he said, *"I am trembling with fear"* [71]. In Christ Jesus the same opportunity is presented each and every believer, hence we seek the Lord. He of whom has given us all things ... ever held in the Bosom of the Father.

The Cherubim: It is said of Jesus that He *"Delighted in the Fear of the Lord."* Hence, if your heart is truly set in the exact same likeness as the Christ, then so shall He take you into Places where 'flesh and blood' cannot go [72]. And as the Glory of the Lord comes and overshadows you, so shall you be raised up as one who makes 'judgements' on behalf of the broken and the lost. Meaning, one with Authority, who raises your hand ... and releases the Spirit of God to action through the Keys of Heaven given you.

Then such a Peace shall come upon the nations that they will put down their weapons of war. The 'leopard' shall lie down with the 'goat', the 'calf' with the 'lion' ... that is, great rifts in society, enmity and broken relationships amongst the people, shall be touched and healed. As the Spirit of the Lord is poured out upon the land.

"Lord, this Fear of the Lord that you are leading me in ... Lord, it removes all fear in my life. The Terror of the Lord keeps the demon far from my life. And this same 'Fear' of the Lord takes me into intimacy, and deep places in the Father where He fights for me. And as I draw near does a Fire come upon me; a Glory and Authority that goes out far and wide and rips the Demon — and all his works — asunder."

So I say, don't delay ... time is short! Come up into the Glory that is yours. Don't wait until hardship comes before you truly seek the Lord. Don't wait until calamity comes ... but rise up ... rise up ... and say to the storms of life, *"Be still in Jesus Name."* And there be great calm. Authority is yours, therefore come up into this Place predestined and purposed you from since before the founding of the world.

On a side note: In the past, the Israelites of old battled enemies with sword and shield. However now, through Christ Jesus, God has transitioned us from a nation of people ... unto **citizens** *of the Kingdom realms. Therefore, we battle* *not flesh and blood, but spiritual authorities that have held captive the nations. These very same spiritual forces that have stood in place of the Divine in man ... to such, we smash them down.* [73]

Have you ever pondered what it would be like to have been with Moses as he climbed up the Mountain of the Lord? This very same Mountain that shook with fire and earthquake as the Presence of the Lord descended upon it? You can be anywhere you like, but Power and Authority comes by going into Holy Places in God. Deep into the awesome Holiness and Glory that totally *burns* the flesh. But as one who allows yourself to be ever held in the 'Intimate Love and Presence of God' — in the cup of His Hands — so are you taken Places man has no comprehension.

First theme Scripture:
You prepare a Table before me in the presence of my enemies; you anoint my head with oil; **my cup runs over**. Surely goodness and mercy shall follow me all the days of my life; and I will dwell in the House of the Lord Forever. *(Psalm 23:5-6 NKJV)*

Recognise, that you cannot become one who **rules** ... without first becoming one who dines in the Lord — **Dining is Key**.

THE HIGH CALLING

Second theme Scripture:
The LORD said to my Lord, "**Sit at My right hand**, till I make your enemies Your footstool." The Lord shall send the rod of **your Strength out of Zion**. Rule in the midst of your enemies! *(Psalm 110:1-2 NKJV)*

As a son of the Living God, redeemed through the precious Blood of Jesus, this **Invitation is picture** and type for all in Christ Jesus.

In Christ Jesus, you are Purposed and Destined of God to be a 'living embodiment' of the Son on earth. You are a seed of the First Seed; you are grafted in the Branch and birthed of the very same Spirit of God — purposed unto the very same Glory and Fire of God. Therefore, come then, and drink deeply of the Water of Life — then in Likeness so shall you be formed. And as you eat liberally and drink deeply, so shall you ever be crafted into the very Image of the Son. **This is your High Calling**; this is the first and fundamental Calling and Purpose of the Father concerning you this very day.

Verse 2-3a, Isaiah 2:
Now it shall come to pass in the latter days that the Mountain of the Lord's House shall be established on the top of the mountains, and shall be exalted above the hills; and all nations shall flow to it. Many people shall come and say, "Come, and let us go up to the mountain of the LORD, To the house of the God of Jacob; He will teach us His ways, and we shall walk in His paths.

I so encourage you to **pause** in all things [74] ... *selah*. Truly, there is something more powerful, and much more precious for each one of us in God, than what we are currently thinking, believing, or asking for. For most true it is, that the many are just too busy, just too caught up with this life and its issues ... always prioritising problems or desires over the Presence and seeking the Face of God.

But if you could truly embrace the 'pause'. If you could truly decide [75] it deep in your heart to treasure and value sitting quietly before the Lord ... and *wait* upon Him. Then He would build you up in every area of your life. In your marriage and family life; finances and friendships; ministry, giftings, and callings. Even then, unto mighty and powerful exploits in the Lord [76]. Again, I am sharing with you what is key: so that the Lord your God might go out before you and fight on your behalf. For His Presence *transcends* all things!

> *"To he who has an ear, let him listen **intently** to what the Spirit is saying to the churches."*

The believer prays earnestly for what is current on his mind. But is there anything about you that desires to gain the Mind of Christ? You have an ear *gifted* of the Spirit of God, but it is as though what you have to say is always more important. Like a stereo turned up too loud ... that you cannot hear anything else.

Two callings: There is your earthy task and calling, and then there is your Heavenly and Divine Calling in Him. But if you could truly come and respond to God's first and fundamental Calling, then you would be most successful in the 'why' God planted you on earth at this season of time.

*A side note: If you are a missionary and go out far and wide ... when facing trouble who do you turn to? If you are a preacher or an evangelist, do you just group together with other preachers and evangelists to get support and guidance? Who do you **ultimately** turn to? ... but God of course. Only He has the real answer, it is 'He who is your Strength' and works to equip. So, when speaking of these things regarding the Spirit, if I speak in an 'urgency' to meet with God ... why should this ever be last when it should be first? And if this is how Jesus Himself lived, why would we not ourselves centralise this motive and vision in our own soul? And I tell you, this is so much bigger than you think!*

As you simply treasure the 'personal meetings' with the Person of God — just quietly honouring His Presence with your mouth ever open; will God of Heaven and earth continually pour into you, into every spectrum of your being. And so He will take you Places — in Him — that man cannot go. He will take you Places where the understanding and imaginations of man have no vision even to ask. And the overflow of your intimate Relationship with the Lord God Almighty will touch all you say and all you do. [77]

Therefore learn, then, to put aside your fleshly zeal ... and ever open yourself up to the Spirit and Fire of God. For there is always something far greater that God has for you than what you are praying or believing for. And so it will be, that as He opens your eyes [78] ... so will you weep. So will you be overwhelmed by the Goodness of God, and to the Heavenly Places that He continually takes you.

Verse 3b-4, Isaiah 2:
For out of Zion shall go forth the law, and the word of the Lord from Jerusalem. He shall judge between the nations, and rebuke many people; They shall beat their swords into plowshares, and their spears into pruning hooks; nation shall not lift up sword against nation, neither shall they learn war anymore.

In retaining a deep hunger for the Meeting [79], so shall Life and Spirit liberally pour into your soul ... effervescently rising up from deep within [80]. And this same Life, this very same Spirit of God, shall build you up most Triumphant and most Powerful in God.

For as Life and Spirit continually rise up within you, do you simply find yourself passing from death into Life [81]. Do you ever find yourself simply passing from these realms of 'death', these the realms that we have only ever known [82] ... right into the Unknown and Mysterious realms of Everlasting Life [83]. With all of Heaven laid open before you ... coming deeper into *Knowledge* of your sonship. Deeper into the *Revelation* of who you truly are as one who releases *Unfathomable* Glory. Confronting the Devil, whom has held the world captive, and casting him down. For since the Beginning, all creation has groaned in tribulation, in earnest wait for the sons of God to be revealed [84]. This is you and I.

To be continued ...

May this new year of 2021 ... and beyond, be a New Year of **receiving** like never before. A shift in season of continually and ever receiving from the Lord. Even then, a people coming to see a greater and greater measure of God's Glory [85]. So therefore, I 'breathe' upon you the Spirit of the Lord.

Closing Scripture:
For since the beginning of the world man have not heard nor perceived by the ear, nor has the eye seen any God besides You, Who **acts for the one** who *waits* for Him. *(Isaiah 64:4 NKJV)*

Appendix:

1. Deuteronomy 8:3, Matthew 4:4, *2.* Exodus 14:14, *3.* John 10:10, *4.* 2 Corinthians 1:20, Matthew 11:11, Isaiah 9:6, *5.* Isaiah 55:8-9, *6.* 1 Corinthians 2:9, *7.* Exodus 33:14, *8.* Exodus 14:14, *9.* Exodus 33:15, *10.* Revelation 3:20, *11.* John 1:18, 13:23, Luke 12:37, Revelation 3:20, Isaiah 28:12, *12.* Revelation 3:21, *13.* Hebrews 4:11, *14.* John 10:34, *15.* Exodus 33:11, *16.* Psalm 36:8-9, *17.* Luke 14:15-24, Matthew 13:1-23, John 4:23-24, *18.* John

14:21, Matthew 13:16, **19.** John 4:14, **20.** Revelation 3:15-22, **21.** Exodus 24:18, 24:9-11, Isaiah 2:2-3, **22.** Matthew 9:29, James 4:2b, Romans 8:26, **23.** John 15:7, **24.** Revelation 4:1, **25.** Exodus 20:19, **26.** Genesis 1:26, **27.** Psalm 110:1-2, **28.** Revelation 3:18, **29.** Genesis 2:17, **30.** Matthew 6:11, **31.** Luke 12:37, Revelation 3:20, Hebrews 4:3, Exodus 14:14, 33:14, 23:28, Isaiah 28:11-12, **32.** John 17:24, 11:25, 14:12, 7:38, Matthew 16:18-19, **33.** Isaiah 40:31, Revelation 3:19-21, Mark 4:35-41, **34.** Psalm 23:5, 110:2, **35.** NKJV: Isaiah 11:1, 11:4-9, Psalm 2:9, Revelation 2:27, 19:15, **36.** Isaiah 41:15-18, Psalm 35:5, 83:13-16, **37.** Matthew 17:20, Mark 4:35-41, Isaiah 41:15, 40:3-5, 35:8, 11:6, 2:4, Revelation 22:2, 22:14, **38.** Luke 14:15-24, **39.** Matthew 13:36-43, Luke 5:15-17, **40.** Revelation 3:20, Exodus 24:10, **41.** John 14:21, **42.** Exodus 24:9-11, 33:11, Daniel 6:10, Luke 5:16, **43.** John 4:14, 5:24, 1 John 3:14, 1 Corinthians 15:53, **44.** Isaiah 57:15, 41:13-18, 40:31, Genesis 1:26, **45.** Genesis 2:17, **46.** Genesis 3:24, **47.** Luke 15:10, **48.** Exodus 40:34-38, 34:35, 33:9-11, 24:16-18, 19:10-20, 13:21-22, 3:1-6, 2 Chronicles 5:13-14, 7:1, Numbers 9:15-23, Leviticus 16:2, Ezekiel 10:18-19, Joshua 3:14-17, Matthew 17:1-2, Luke 4:1-2, 14 *(first bind the strongman)*, Luke 1:35, 12:49, 24:49, Acts 1:4-5, 2:1-4, 2 Corinthians 3:18, Revelation 2:4-5, Genesis 3:24, **49.** John 1:51, **50.** John 12:24, **51.** Jeremiah 17:8, **52.** John 2:17, **53.** Luke 1:35, **54.** John 17:16, **55.** John 14:1-7, **56.** 1 Peter 1:12, Revelation 3:21, **57.** 2 Corinthians 5:17, **58.** John 1:12, **59.** Genesis 3:24, **60.** John 10:9, **61.** Isaiah 64:1-4, **62.** Romans 1:32, Galatians 5:19-21 *NKJV*, 1 John 3:4-10, **63.** John 1:14, **64.** Leviticus 16:2, Isaiah 11:3, **65.** John 5:8, **66.** Galatians 4:1-2, Zechariah 3:6-7, Revelation 3:18-21, Isaiah 11:1-4, **67.** Isaiah 11:1-4, Zechariah 3, John 15:7, **68.** John 15:7, **69.** Genesis 1:26, **70.** John 12:26, **71.** Hebrews 12:21, Exodus 33:22, **72.** Matthew 16:17-19, Exodus 19:12, 33:22, **73.** Isaiah 41:13-16, Matthew 17:20, **74.** Isaiah 64:1-4, Psalm 116:2, Daniel 10:12, **75.** Psalm 37:4m, **76.** Daniel 11:32, **77.** John 1:18, **78.** Revelation 3:18, 2 Kings 6:17, **79.** Exodus 24:9-11, 33:11, Daniel 6:10, Luke 5:16, **80.** John 4:14, **81.** John 4:14, 5:24, 1 John 3:14, **82.** Genesis 2:17, **83.** 1 Corinthians 2:9, **84.** Romans 8:19, **85.** Exodus 20:21, John 20:21-23

Dated: 4/1/21

30. *Mount Sinai, the Way of the Anointed (#113)*
BANQUETING TABLE *(Part 2)*

Jesus' Prayer is to bring Heaven and the Will of God on earth [1]. Hence, as you also choose to personally make God's Prayer and Dream *your* prayer and dream ... do you become as like a Portal ... a Gateway of Heaven on earth.

Jesus came as a living 'Tent of Meetings' in the flesh. He was the very first Tabernacle of God in this 'tent' called man. And in drawing aside He continually met with God; and as He walked the earth ... Heaven was upon Him with angels ascending and descending upon the Son of Man.

Through the Blood the way has been opened; that by the Spirit you are called to live exactly as Christ Jesus. To this, we say 'amen' to the Glory of God [2]. There are many places the believer can be ... but as you ascend, do you have perfect opportunity to be with Him where He is. As Jesus says, *"You know the way to the place I am going."* [3]

In ever-expanding measure shall you pour out the Spirit of the Living God on earth. Knowingly or unknowingly; even unto the furthest reaches of the land [4]. Come, then, and displace the works of the *Enemy* with the Works of God [5] ... for in this the believer is key.

The prophet Elijah ascended up into Heaven before his disciple Elisha ... as did the Jesus before His Disciples. Hence, the very same Mantle of the Lord has been passed onto you to do — even greater works than He [6]. For until the Christ returns, the Keys of Heaven are in the believer's hands [7] ... therefore, go take **possession** of the nations. [8]

IN GOD'S 'LIKENESS'

Satan is a fallen angel and holds no authority except that of which you give him. Satan is not of the — **'God' class** — of created beings, **but <u>man</u> is**. This is why Jesus came as the 'Word made flesh' ... so to fully countermand the lie. He came as the very — Open Demonstration — and Example of the Renewed Man.

The Heart of the Father is Purposed that each one of us be fashioned into the Image and very **Likeness** of the Son. From Glory to Glory and unto exceedingly great Glory [9]. Therefore, **learn to look past sin** and death [10] and seek the Lord. [11]

It is through the Christ, that your Heavenly Father has presented this opportunity to return back into the pre-fallen state. This is why He sent His Son — that you might be fully reunited — in the Father through the Spirit of God [12]. Step by step, Glory unto Glory.

Do you know that when you **approach** your Heavenly Father, He sees His Son? You are the embodiment of the Christ, the very extension of Jesus as a member of His Person [13]. Therefore, 'in' Christ Jesus, God is extending His hand ... and with an open heart, inviting you to *"Sit at His right hand until He makes your enemies your footstool'* [14]. Hence, as this was for Jesus, this too remains now our core and fundamental Calling — the sitting in the Place of the Risen Man.

Such is the mystery found in walking according to the Spirit and not the flesh. The coming in and entering into the Place where Jesus went before us ... **and** has openly shown the way. And that from this Place, it is God who shall go out before you and fight on your behalf [15]. As Jesus said, *"The Father who dwells in me does the works."* [16]

With this underlying motive, we 'continually sanctify ourselves in His Holy Presence. Ever bowing unto this wonderful process of 'renewing'. And as we liberally receive from the Lord, so are we also raised up by Him to Rule!

In God's opinion... He thinks of us as 'gods' [17], with the full backing of Heaven, the angels, and of the Spirit of God. Therefore, I personally continually choose to live as I am Destined and Purposed ... and no longer as a 'mere mortal man'. You are born of Royal Blood — you are sons of the Most High — born not of defeat but Victory. Even then to 'lord' over and Above death, disease, and despair.

God is greater than the problems we face. Not just in His capacity to deal with them ... *but* ... **who He is in our eyes**. True, we have our prayers and needs ... but if God Himself could become our 'prayer', then so shall we be lifted up to tower over all things. Come, and learn to be one able to — 'sleep in the back of the boat' — in the midst of the storms of life. That we all might walk truly with Jesus in the realness of His Glory and His Delight.

In all things, truly make the active choice — to cross over — and live in the House of the Lord [18]. For it is from this 'Place of Prayer', this Place of the 'Ministering Presence of the Lord', that we truly are able to turn to the storms and say, *"Cease and be still"* ... and there be great calm. [19]

You are Purposed of God to be a portal of Heaven, a living breathing gateway of the Kingdom realms [20]. You are purposed of God to be a 'god' as you walk this life — ruling and reigning over all creation [21]. So come then and break free of the persistent diminishing lies and lures of this world ... and come back up into your true and rightful Place of Dwelling. Now, when you pray, shall you release the Spirit of the Lord unto charge. Hence, therefore, remain fully submitted to the Spirit of God ... that we truly might be raised a king. [22]

The Tabernacle of God held the Holy of Holies ... and within the Holy of Holies held the Ark of the Covenant. This same truth remains for all who *"Contemplate the Lord's Glory"* [23], that there is another 'room' ... another layer of God's Glory presented to each and every one of us. Even this very Place where the Cherubim part way [24] as you enter into the Ancient Places of Man.

So I, in the security of my salvation, 'repent' before the Lord of Glory. And through the Spirit go back into the time of the Beginning. And as I stand here, I fully reject the fruit of the Tree of *(my own)* Knowledge of Good and Evil, and I spew out of my mouth the Lie. Then, in embracing my Heavenly Father I ask, *"Let me eat of the Tree of Life that I might dwell in your Presence forever."* [25]

The 'Tabernacle' represents your ability to meet with God. And the Holy of Holies — His Glorious and Abiding Presence. This same Presence that you honour as you actively seek the Lord. And it is here, in this Place of Glory and Honour, that what is given you of God is most precious. And as you are ever transformed in His Presence [26] ... so do you go into things; [27] the hearing, the seeing, the receiving; that of which is far beyond the comprehension or imaginations of man. [28]

Scripture:
Jesus said to them again, "Peace to you! As the Father has sent Me, I also send you. *(John 20:21 NKJV)*

Here and today, God is reigniting the function of your Divine Origins. The ancient 'motors' and functions that have laid dormant since the Fall ... are being made re-enlivened *(on a cellular, mental, and spiritual level)*. Now, as you continually allow yourself to re-engage, in this of your pre-fallen state, *ie;* your union in the Father that was broken but now restored — do you step into the Divine Origins of who you are as a son of the Living God.

Identity is key: Satan sits in the atmosphere 'over' the hearts and minds of man. Speaking a greatly diminished vision that you might be *less* than who you are. However, as you choose to turn to the Lord, and praise His Holy Name, do you punch through right into the Presence of God. And what He gives you in this Place is like a fine meal — establishing and building you up. Ever feeding you [29] ... and ever revealing who you are in Him, layer upon layer. That you might come into the fullness of Christ Jesus as you walk this world [30]. With Authority and Dominion to bring lasting change.

Up until now, the Christian believer has been asking; asking and waiting for God to answer prayer. But it has been God — all this time — that has been waiting for you to answer His. This, the stepping into the very reason why He sent the Son. Standing in position where very earth responds to the words of your mouth.

Humble yourself then, in the Presence of God, and confess your 'blindness' ... that God might give you eyes that truly see [31]. For they who openly hear and see the Lord are an Unstoppable force; [32] Untouchable and Powerful in God.

Jesus would say to His Disciples, *"You feed them"* ... and in other places, *"You heal the sick and raise the dead"*. And Peter, as he walked on water ... was a practice and an invitation of Jesus to walk — just like Him. You see, Jesus taught both who His Father is ... that you too might see. And as well, He taught to live like the Son — in the fullness of Him — as a son, just like He.

Bless you.

To continue in the following chapter ...

Appendix:

1. Matthew 6:10, ***2.*** 2 Corinthians 1:20, Luke 1:38, ***3.*** John 14:4, ***4.*** Isaiah 2:2-4, 11:1-8, 41:13-18, Psalm 84:1-10, ***5.*** 1 John 3:8, ***6.*** John 14:12, 20:21-23, 2 Kings 2:11-3, Genesis 32:24, Matthew 11:12, ***7.*** Matthew 16:19, ***8.*** Matthew 28:19-20, ***9.*** 2 Corinthians 3:18, ***10.*** Isaiah 44:22, ***11.*** Matthew 18:10, ***12.*** 1 Corinthians 15:45, ***13.*** Ephesians 5:30, ***14.*** Psalm 110:1, Revelation 1:5-6, 3:21, Psalm 82:6, Hebrews 4:11, ***15.*** Exodus 33:14, 14:14, 33:15, ***16.*** John 14:10, 5:30, 5:19, ***17.*** John 10:34, Psalm 82:7, ***18.*** Isaiah 2:2-4, ***19.*** Mark 4:35-41, 11:23, ***20.*** Romans 8:19, *21.* Genesis 1:26, ***22.*** Revelation 3:18-21, Zechariah 3, Isaiah 11:1-4, 1 Samuel 16:1-13, ***23.*** 2 Corinthians 3:18, ***24.*** Genesis 3:24, ***25.*** Genesis 3:22-24, ***26.*** Matthew 17:2, ***27.*** John 3:12, ***28.*** 1 Corinthians 2:9, John 3:12, John 14:15-16, 14:21, ***29.*** 1 Peter 3:18, John 6:35, ***30.*** Matthew 4:3, Romans 8:19, ***31.*** John 9:41, *32.* Psalm 82:6-8, 91:10-13

Dated: 3/3/21

31. *Mount Sinai, the Way of the Anointed (#114)*
BANQUETING TABLE *(Part 3)*

Opening Scripture:
So He humbled you, allowed you to hunger, and fed you with manna which neither you nor your ancestors had known, to **teach** you that man does not live on bread alone but on every word that proceeds from the mouth of the LORD. *(Deuteronomy 8:3, Matthew 4:4 NIV/NKJV)*

Prayers can often be delayed. Sometimes God allows 'desert' experiences in the hope and 'prayer' that you truly might come to **hunger** for and seek after — give honour and respect for, pursue and diligently go after — the 'Word that proceeds from the mouth of God' *¹*. For the believer can never come into experience, nor ever truly walk liberally in the realms of Promise, without God's Active and Living 'spoken' Word abiding in you. *²*

However, so the complete opposite is also true. That Life is swiftly entered into, lived in and experienced, through ever valuing the Presence of God. That is, allow your meetings with God — and His Glory ever coming upon you — to become more treasured and sought after than current realities, unknown futures, or worldly issues *³*. For the type of faith that moves mountains is heavily rooted in the **Witness** of the Spirit speaking alive in you. *⁴*

Now as one here, in truly coming to value and treasure the hearing and the seeing; even then as one who openly and liberally receives from the Lord, does God set a Banqueting Table right in the 'midst of your enemies'. With such Grace and such a measure of Heaven coming upon you that causes you to rule in the midst of difficulties, opposition, and hardship — as one Mighty and Powerful in God. Even then as one who conquers; continually taking ground with relative ease.

A GREATER 'TEMPTATION'
To seek the Presence of the Person of God manifest personally upon your life — is to open yourself to the healing and blessings of the Lord. Long has the believer sought Jesus at the Cross, but the

Cross isn't the 'destination' ... it is a *Gateway*. Again, I say, long has the Christian Church worshipped at the Cross ... and that's fine. But the Cross isn't the vision ... it is a *Doorway* [5]. The fundamental Calling and Purpose of God is to come into the Place of ruling and reigning; as 'heirs of God', and 'co-heirs with Christ Jesus' [6] ... and not stay outside.

To *behold* the Glory of God so shall you *carry* ... and so shall you release and pour out the very same Glory. Even as one who outpours Heaven and the undeniable realities of the Person of God [7]. The world has only known the works of Death and does not understand. But to he who *knows* Christ Jesus [8], is transformed into a holder of Life. Even as one who pours out the very same upon the nations.

This ancient phrase ... *"Seek the Face of God"* ... is pictured in the purposed-held desire and intent; to meet, to sit with, and to come openly see the Glory of God. This phrase comes out of the time when Moses asked God to see His Face *(His Glory)* upon the mountain. And in a way he did; God protecting him in the cleft of a rock by His hand as He passed by. [9]

In the book of Hebrews, it speaks of how Moses *"Trembled with fear"* as he approached the place where God was [10]. However, still he went in. And in the book of Isaiah, Jesus is expressed as *"Delighting in the Fear of the Lord"* ... are you yet coming to see and understand?

There is a realm of Glory that both Moses and Jesus exampled, that by the Blood you yourself can pursue and ask God for [11]. Even here, to set your tent and never leave. Everything is rooted here: Knowledge, Counsel, Wisdom, and Might **<u>starts</u> with the Fear of the Lord** [12]. Even then to go into Places flesh cannot go [13] ... and these Places far exceed that of which the world has to offer. And here, in these Glory realms of the Most High, shall you come to command earth and the very Heavens. Ever clothed in *Immortality* where death has totally lost its grip! [14]

The world needs a greater 'lure', a greater offering or 'temptation' than what the world has to offer. And in this, the believer holds Key! [15] Moses said to God, *"Do not send us out without your Presence with us."* And he continued, *"What else will distinguish me and your people from all the other people on the face of the earth?"* [16]

I tell you, purpose it in yourself unto the Glory realms, and so shall the Glory of the Lord rest richly upon you. The Presence of God upon you; not in word alone, but in open demonstration for all eyes to see. And this is what is meaningful. This is what your world needs ... and the kings of the earth shall quake and quiver. [17]

The world doesn't need you telling them what they should do. Nor listing out instructions; or though logic and reason alone. But introducing the very Person of God and one's place in Him.

TWO REALMS OF PRESENCE

There are two 'realms' of Presence: One where the Presence of God comes upon you and the congregation. And the other is to where both the Cross and the Spirit point and bears continual testimony [18] ... and that is the **Abiding Place**. The Dwelling Place of the Most High God, the realms of Rest ... the Place of continually Receiving that is Above all things!

And it is Jesus' own personal prayer concerning you, *"Father, I desire they whom you have given me may be with me where I am"* [19]. This is not, by any means an earthly vision ... but a Divine one. A deep yearning of the Son, that you come right up into the Glory realms ... where He is. And here, Abide and Remain and have your being [20] in the Dominion of God.

The picture of the Lord's Presence coming upon you is not **ruling**. But the picture of going into God's Presence is to come into the Place of Ruling, of Dominion, the realms Above all things [21]. And here it is, that as you speak ... Heaven listens, because of where you stand. Then Jesus continues in this verse and prays, *"May these that you have given me, behold my Glory which you have given me."* [22]

Again, I say, to approach the Cross is not ruling. But to pass on through and be one raised by the Father, is to enter into Dominion over all things [23]. And that is what we want, to join Heaven to earth: Heaven to the situations, the Spirit unto problems, and Life liberally poured out. And the undeniable realities of God flooding the land as the waters cover the sea. [24]

People think of 'Heaven experiences' only as a spiritual vision or visitation. But in Moses' day he, and the elders of Israel — in human bodily form — ate a meal on the Pavement of Sapphire in God's Presence [25]. I tell you ... seek the Presence of God! Not *only* in the vision of His Presence coming upon you, but ever more importantly ... in the vision of **going up** into His Presence. Now you have the right 'prayer'. That you, in your person, go right in before the open Glory and Wonder of God and never leave [26] — ever 'held' in His Hand by the Person of God.

BE TAUGHT BY GOD

Three Scripture verses:
1. I will **lead** the blind by ways they have not known, along **unfamiliar paths** I will guide them; I will **turn the darkness** into light before them and make the rough places smooth. These are the things I will do; I will not forsake them. *(Isaiah 42:16 NIV)*
2. All your children shall be **taught** by the Lord, and great shall be the **peace** of your children. *(Isaiah 54:13 NKJV)*
3. But you are not to be called 'Rabbi,' for you have **one Teacher**, and you are all brothers. *(Matthew 23:8 NIV)*

Long has man only followed man. However, to be a 'prophet' of God is to be raised personally **by God**. Better still *as* a son, as child of the Most High God, the Father Himself raising you to walk openly in the realms of your inheritance as co-heirs with Jesus.

How is it possible to rule and reign on earth, if you do not walk in the realms where God walks? Learn then, to treat all problems simply as a practice ground in kingship and release the Glory of the Lord unto charge. If you truly have compassion for the broken and the lost [27] seek the Glory of God, for so it shall be — that held in your very hands — shall you pour out the very same Glory. Releasing Heaven and setting charge both Spirit and Life [28], such are the children of God.

Truly, long has the believer only ever come to the Cross in times of need, or ... to find forgiveness for sins. But then going back to normal life not understanding that there is more. However, recognise, that the Cross is not only your Salvation and Redemption ... **but** ... the very Doorway unto the Father and the realms of the Spirit. [29]

The religious cannot come here, nor the legalistic; they becoming even hostile against any who try [30]. But to they of whom choose to truly *follow* the Son, so are they captured up and taken into the Place where He is. Even then to openly 'see' Him in His Glory [31]. Walking with Him in the 'cool of the Morning' [32]... not according to the flesh but the Spirit of God.

PRIVATE MEETINGS IS THE MINIMUM OFFERING OF THE HOLY GHOST

Two High Prayers of Heaven: First is the Lord's Prayer that we know, *"May your Kingdom come and your Will be done on earth just as it is in Heaven"* [33]. **This is His Purpose**. And then there is God's 'Prayer' concerning you personally, that you might be — with Him — ruling and reigning in Heavenly Places [34], *ie;* the 'Returning' [35]. The returning back into that of which Adam fell ... the *flesh* being the lowest form of man.

Christ Jesus is the very open Invitation for you to walk just as Him. He, the living Example of what it means to be a son. God sits in the Place above Heaven and earth ... *and* ... is His Dream and Invitation that you do also.

Jesus came in open demonstration of the Renewed Man, as living Example; the **first** 'Seed' of many seeds [36]. So come then, and truly walk in His footsteps — and here also in His Likeness — as child of God. [37]

There are two accounts in the biblical text where disciples openly witnessed their masters going up into Heaven. And do you realise, that in both accounts; including our Lord Jesus Christ, a Mantle fell to the earth for you to pick up? And when we say 'Mantle', it is the very same Anointing that rested upon our Saviour that is available for you [38]. Even the passing on their Anointing to 'finish' what they themselves were assigned to do. Even then, unto greater works than He. [39]

Both Elijah and Elisha were 'power' prophets. Meaning, they didn't just speak a prophetic word about the future but were powerful in the words they spoke. Multiplying food, parting rivers, pouring out fire, and raising the dead. Now it can be more easily understood just how much hearing and seeing God is most central to living Powerful and Victorious lives in God. For it is through your own personal Heaven Engagements that you are made most Powerful in Him; ever seated in Divine Authority of the Son. [40]

TO BE "WHERE I AM"

Scripture:
I have swept away your offenses like a cloud, your sins like the morning mist. **Return** to me, for I have redeemed you. *(Isaiah 44:22 NKJV)*

The Way of Jesus is to be 'where he is' … ever walking with God in the Glory realms. *Co-habiting* Heaven as you go about regular earthly life. Jesus was a Portal; an open Gateway of Heaven wherever He went. He did not come only to save us from sin, but also, as living and open demonstration of what it **means** to be a child of God. Therefore, be ever transformed and transfigured into His very Image and Likeness. As is said, *"We with unveiled faces contemplate the Lord's Glory, are being **transformed** into His Image with ever-increasing Glory."* [41]

As a people born of the Spirit, we are no longer born of the 'Abrahamic line' … but the line of Melchizedek [42]. Abraham believed, and it was credited to him as righteous … but he did not 'see' the Promise. However, we are different, we are a people born into the Promise. A people born not of flesh but of the Spirit of God … born not of the line of Abraham that is preached, but a people of the Fulfilment. A people of a different line … *"A priest forever, in the order of Melchizedek."* [43]

Do you recall in John chapter 7, where Jesus was speaking to the Pharisees and said, *"You will seek me and not find me, and where I am you cannot come?"* For these … the realms of Heaven, remain elusive and completely foreign to they who seek God only through religion and law. [44]

However, to they who personally receive the Blood to heart, and personally follow the Person of Jesus [45], so shall you ever open yourself to Heaven realities. As Jesus says, *"If anyone serves me, let him follow me; and where I am, there my servant will be also"* [46]. And what does this mean ... *"Where I am?"* But as Jesus said elsewhere, *"No one has ascended to Heaven but He who came down from Heaven, that is, the Son of Man who is in Heaven"* [47]. This, He said, as He was talking with Nicodemus ... the religious leader of the day, of whom had no idea or comprehension of what Jesus was talking about.

Truly, long has it been the believer's highest worship: the worshipping Jesus at the Cross. But the Cross was never intended or purposed to be the destination — the Cross itself is the Gateway! The religious declare that they have already been to the Cross ... *yesteryear*. And the sinner comes only for forgiveness of sin. Truly, long has the Church only approached the Cross in time of need, but **who** truly is passing through?

BUY 'GOLD' THAT YOU MIGHT BE 'RICH'

Scripture:
I counsel you to **buy** from Me gold refined in the fire, that you may be rich; and white garments, that you may be clothed, that the shame of your nakedness may not be revealed; and anoint your eyes with eye salve, that **you may see**. *(Revelation 3:18-19 NKJV)*

Have you yet come to realise that the realms of Heaven; these, the very realms of God, of Jesus, and of the angels are Purposed for you to see? Not only to know or read about ... but in ever-increasing measure: to walk in, to live in, and to openly engage? For this is the very purpose of the Blood; this, the Kingdom of Heaven being **right at hand**. [48]

Throughout the Old Testament, particular people were called up ... like Moses. However now, in the New ... all are called, and all are invited [49]. And it is through this chosen *lifestyle* that you are made most powerful in God. And these lifestyle experiences, becoming an exceedingly great wealth for you and your people.

Pictured here in this Scripture, is Jesus placing emphasis on 'purchasing' gold ... representing in the 'purchasing' of the very Glory of God. The Religious don't come here, the legalist is oblivious and even hostile. But to they of whom truly humble themselves before God ... 'as like a little child' [50] ... pass through and are taken by the Spirit into Unspeakable things. [51]

The purpose of 'seeing' in the Spirit is that you may **also see** 'in the flesh'. Just as faith is first 'unseen' *(ie; in the 'spirit')* ... the **purpose** is that what you are believing for is made manifest before your eyes. Jesus is the Word made flesh ... that is, Heaven was manifest before our eyes, *ie;* the revelation and manifestation of God and Heaven on earth. Therefore, a heart purposed unto the manifestation of Heaven, just as Jesus ... **sees** both God work, and His Spirit outpoured.

Many believers, in many different walks of life ... plateau and pause, and do not move on with God. They become comfortable in where they are at, even in the 'charity' that they give. But God wants to raise you as a people who shift both Heaven and earth. Even to raise the dead, heal the sick, and cast out demons. But how can it be, that you can ever do this if you have found a place of comfort, where you are no longer *challenged* or raised by God?

Hence problems of the world remain because people are not coming up into the Presence of God. Nor, as a people, entering into the Rest of the Lord. Being then, made able — by God — to release the very same Presence of the Lord. [52]

To be continued in the next chapter ...

Appendix:

1. Revelation 2:29, John 8:28, Exodus 33:11-13, *2.* John 5:19, 15:7, Hebrews 4:11-12, Zechariah 3:7, *3.* John 2:15-17, *4.* Matthew 16:16-19, 17:20, *5.* John 14:6, *6.* Romans 8:17, *7.* Isaiah 64:1-4, *8.* Exodus 33:13, John 14:21, *9.* Exodus 33:12-23, *10.* Hebrews 12:21, *11.* Matthew 7:7-8, *12.* Proverbs 9:10, Isaiah 11:2-4, *13.* Exodus 33:21-23, John 3:13, Revelation 3:14, John 5:26, Genesis 3:24, Revelation 2:7, *14.* 1 Corinthians 15:53-54, *15.* Matthew 16:19, *16.* Exodus 33:15:16, *17.* Isaiah 64:1-4, Joshua 24:12, *18.* Revelation 2:29, *19.* John 17:24, *20.* John 15:4, 7, *21.* Colossians 3:1, *22.* John 17:20-24, *23.* Matthew 18:3, 23:9, Isaiah 54:13, Revelation 3:21, *24.* Habakkuk 2:14, *25.* Exodus 24:9-11, *26.* Exodus 33:11, *27.* Luke 4:18, *28.* John 6:63, 11:25, *29.* John 14:6, *30.* Matthew 23:13,15, *31.* John 12:26, 7:34, 14:4, 17:24, 3:13 *NKJV*, *32.* Revelation 22:16, 2:28, 2 Peter 1:19, *33.* Matthew 6:10, *34.* Romans 5:17, *35.* Isaiah 44:22, *36.* John 12:24, *37.* John 12:26, *38.* 2 Kings 2:9-13, 1 Kings 19:16-17, John 14:12, *39.* John 14:12, *40.* Revelation 3:22, *41.* 2 Corinthians 3:18, *42.* Psalm 110, *43.* Psalm 110:4, Revelation 1:5-6 *NKJV*, *44.* Isaiah 28:11-13, *45.* 1 Kings 19:19-21, *46.* John 12:26, 7:34, *47.* John 3:13, *48.* Mark 1:15, *49.* Isaiah 2:2-4, *50.* Matthew 18:3-5, *51.* Matthew 18:3, *52.* Exodus 14:13-14, 33:14, 23:28

Dated: 24/5/21

32. Mount Sinai, the Way of the Anointed (#115)
BANQUETING TABLE *(Part 4)*

God presents an unconditional environment where He fights for you. Hence, in seeking the Face of God ... so do you release!

In God you are called to come into a 'stillness' where God fights for you [1]. But even more so — in the New Covenant — to enter into the 'seated' realms where you command [2]. Whereby you make 'judgements' according to what you 'see' [3] — as one releasing Life and Presence from within the Glory of God.

Dominion in the Lord is a realm ... it is a Place where God has always yearned to lead His people [4]. Even in mirror of the Son, where God Himself works to make your enemies your footstool [5]. The realness of this comes from union, not from religion or obedience to law, but deeply treasured intimacy in the Person of God [6]. Therefore, in insistently and persistently set your heart unto God's Divine and Living Presence *(behind the 'cloud'* [7]*)*, and so shall it be God Himself who rends the heavens and steps down because of you. [8]

I so very much encourage you ... intimacy is key. Not answer to prayer or needs, but a deep *yearning* for the Person of God; with a mouth wide open to receive what He desires to give. What He desires to fill you to overflow. 'Things' ... or 'answer to prayer' are outside of this ... for if God is your God, then He fights for you. If the fullness of His Dreams fulfilled in you is **your** dream ... is your 'prayer' ... then God is aggressively for you.

Intimacy trumps needs: A preference for being tight together with God — irrespective of the happenings of life — irrespective! The natural 'run to' point ... the preferred place to go. God ... of whose I am, of whose I belong ... and of whom is **always** with me. God is a protector and a fighter for you; even then that you be raised to release that 'Fight'.

Let me ask a question: If death came into the world because of the sin of the one man named Adam. **How much more**! ... are you Purposed of God to Rule and Reign in life through the one man Christ Jesus? [9]

Hence, each one of us are presented choice of where to direct our hearts; either in the Victory that God has purchased for each one of us ... or the struggles of sin, death, and decay [10]. The problem with miracles is always the same — **problems have to exist in the first place**. But so too is the answer — seek the manifest Presence of the Person of God. For as you enter into a heart of praise, as you truly choose to move deeper into a state of Intimacy; of humility, revelation, and righteousness; so do you also enter into the realms where God is. Where Death is swallowed up by Life. [11]

God dwells in me for I *choose* to dwell in Him. And here there is an exchange, 'I in Him' ... and ... 'He in me'. And through this exchange; as I enter into Him, it is the Lord God Almighty who goes out and does the work [12]. He Delights my soul [13], continuously pouring into me of His very self ... as He goes out before me and fights my battles [14]. I in Him ... and He in place of me.

In reference to Isaiah 25: *"By will and by choice do I clothe myself in the 'Imperishable'. And by will and by choice do I come up into the Presence of the Lord* [15]. *Regardless of season .... even up upon the Mountain of God* [16]. *And here, it is the Lord who continuously gives me 'aged' meats* [17] *and the 'finest of wine', removing the 'shroud' that has enveloped my life ... as He 'wipes away my tears'. And so does He come, and so does He stand firmly in my midst: removing the 'disgrace of His people from all the earth.'"* [18]

In the Word, there are phenomenal visions, and God continually works to unlock your heart to incredible opportunity. And as you seek the Lord ... He opens your eyes to see, and to see all the more. For without vision 'the people perish' [19] ... but the Vision that the Lord gives, causes deep yearning in your heart to move ever forward. And here, He converts your past sin and pain into the very soil of which your tree flourishes.

If you don't yet know how to 'command' Spirit ... if you can't command Presence, then who are you? But just a man. However, you are not Destined to be just a man ... but child of the Most High God.

Scripture:
The perishable must clothe itself with the imperishable, and the mortal with Immortality. When the perishable has been **clothed** with the imperishable, and the mortal with immortality, then the saying that is written will come true: "Death has been swallowed up in victory." *(1 Corinthians 15:53-54 NIV)*

The subject of this chapter is Jesus' own personal calling for you to buy from Him gold that you might be 'rich'. White clothes to cover your 'nakedness', and salve for your eyes that you might 'see'. [20]

Now, in this, Jesus is not speaking to the unbelieving but to the Church. He is not speaking to the world but to you. For this picture of 'white clothing' is not the clothing of your salvation or acceptance ... but something else. Something of which the Cross and the Spirit has Divinely opened unto you. Jesus is speaking of 'purchasing' the Honour that comes from the only God [21]. Mortal man being clothed in Immortality whereby Death is destroyed. Where Death ... and all its fruits ... is swallowed up by Life. [22]

As a believer of the Lord Jesus Christ, you have your faith in God. However now, it is God Himself who seeks that you might gain the faith 'of' the Son [23]. Not a faith according to your vision or understanding, but a Faith according to His. According to His Resurrected Glory and to where He is now standing.

This is the delightful transition: the being clothed and imparted to of the very Person of Jesus [24]. And this is opened to you as you continue to humble yourself and **dine** at His feet. As one preferencing seeking the Face of God [25] over problems ... ever Trained by Him from within the Divine realms of God; in the realms of the Victorious ... that **you too might Rule**.

"Who are these that fly along like clouds, like doves to their nests?" [26] *It is the Christian Church that has been operating in a fraction of what has been given. The Christian Church has been operating at a minuscule level of Power compared to what has been ordained. However, this is changing ...*

Scripture:
They feast on the abundance of your house; you give them drink from your river of delights. *(Psalm 36:8 NIV)*

Feasting is part of this — 'buying salve for your eyes that you might see'. The seeing and receiving in the realms of God ... just as the Son. And these Wondrous realms of Heaven becoming more real to you; more tangible and more dynamically real than that of this world. For here, in this state of constantly receiving, *ie;* dining upon His 'Banqueting Table', shall you truly come to walk in Like as the Son [27]. For this is the underlying Calling, this is your Divine Destiny in God.

Come then, and truly give your life unto Jesus. Not in word alone, but in firmly drawing a line in the sand — in defiance of Death! — as one fully embracing Life. And through this 'turning' — as one standing in the realms 'where He is' [28] — so are you also able to release and pour out the very same Life and Spirit on earth. [29]

The Way of God is for Him to go out before you. Jesus came in open demonstration of what it means to be a child of God: He became the 'victim' that you truly might become the Victory [30] ... so go to Him. For so it is, that through the Spirit of God, He has Imparted unto you the very same that He spoke of Himself, *"As the Father has Life in Himself, so has He granted the sons and daughters of God to have Life in themselves."* [31]

So therefore, continually humble yourself unto the Fire of the Holy Ghost [32]. That you truly might be raised as one who pours out the Holy Spirit's Fire on earth. Pouring out the Spirit, the Power, and the Revival of God upon the nations *(starting with your own life)*. For just as Jesus has given you the right to become son of God [33], so has He also placed in your hands the very Keys of Heaven: that **you** might make choice, that **you** decide [34] ... releasing Heaven on earth. And to such as these even the gates of Hades cannot prevail against them [35], in Jesus Name.

First, the 'Word made flesh' came and walked amongst us ... then after, through the Blood that was shed, the Door opened that you truly might step into Life. Now, through the gifted Spirit of God, the Holy Spirit leads you in all things that are now yours [36]. And here with your heart ever set on the Beyond, ever set Above, even unto these of the Glory realms of God [37], *ie;* your 'Promised Land', so too do you naturally become an ever-expanding portal of the Kingdom of Heaven in this world [38]. And even though your thinking may yet be so small and carnal; it is the Spirit Himself who captures you up in the Father ... even here into all that is yours. [39]

A side note: To say that we 'command' the Outpouring of the Holy Ghost is not prideful ... it is the Heart of God. For through the deepest of humility and submission are you given charge over and above [40]. Here, the sitting in the place of a priest in the 'Holy Place': even now as a king, as one who decides and makes decisions.

Submission is key, *ie;* the 'purchasing of gold', that you truly might come to walk in the fullness of the Son [41]. Even then as one standing in Vengeance against the works of the *Enemy* [42]. Therefore, honour not the problems that you face, but **He** who fights for you. [43]

The most powerful thing that you can do, is 'Be **still**, and **know God**'. The entering into the Presence of God, and here giving full rightful place for His Presence and Fire to come upon you. And subsequently then, for His Presence and Glory to go out before you in **all** that you do. [44]

God says, "*Vengeance is mine and I will repay*" [45]. Hence, it is much more dangerous for opposition that you face that you step back a little. For so it is that — in Him — all things are exposed before the Glory of God. Now you can understand a bit more what Faith truly means: 'Divine interaction with your Heavenly Father' [46]. For it is through your own death *47*, *ie;* what is released unto Him, that make you a most powerful force of reckoning ... *Untouchable!*

In the book of Isaiah, it expresses how Jesus delighted in the Fear of the Lord *48*. Even these, of the 'intense' realms of God's Glory. And continues saying that Jesus did not live based on what He heard with His ears or saw with His eyes; but from within the 'realms' of Righteousness *49* ... did He make 'judgement' on behalf of the broken and the lost. That is, in the Presence of His Father, here in the realms of the 'Hearing and Seeing', did He make choice and decision ... releasing both Life and the Spirit of God.

Hence then, so it is also, by where **you choose** to 'delight in', even here under the continual Tuition and Fire of the Holy Ghost *50*, that Heaven is released and set to charge by the words of *your* mouth. That is, as one who follows Jesus, as one who chooses to walk in His very 'footsteps' ... even these, the very 'stepping stones' of His Truth and Living Example ... do you also come to walk in Likeness of the Son. *51*

For this is the fulfilment of trials and tribulations: That you might truly learn to hunger the 'Hearing and Seeing' God. Honouring the Lord come ... honouring the Lord continually taking you and capturing you up. For if you are truly 'Promised Land' focused — so are you also free from 'correction' — so are you made Victorious in Him *52*. For the depths of your heart seeks that of which the Father desires. Not honour before man ... but the Honour of God that comes upon you *53*. Divine Glory upon your life; bearing forth great Glory through the open demonstration of the Fire and Power of God.

To be a billionaire is a form of great poverty. For even the wealthy die and come to nothing. But to be a son of God, does Heaven and earth respond to you ... as one returning back into your Eternal Place of Dwelling. For he who clings onto his life dies. But to he who gives it up for Jesus, *ie;* releases their life unto God ... **lives***!* ... becoming themselves releasers of Life.

Today, it is Christ Jesus who is calling you to buy from Him gold. In order that you truly might step into the Wealth that is yours. One transitioning from flesh unto the Heavenly realms. Transfigured ever into the Image and Likeness of the Son ... as children of Light. [54]

It is God who is seeking to lift you up into the realms of the Untouchable and the Invulnerable [55]. Just as in the Exodus ... where the nations of the earth shake and quiver. Here, even right in the midst of all that life presents — it is God Himself who sets a **Banqueting Table** before you — as one who continuously Receives [56]. A people ever walking in the realms of His Delight; with all things being brought under your feet. [57]

The realms of Heaven are far far higher than the realms of Satan or that of this earth. Even as the Morning Star [58] is higher than the earth, so too is your Heavenly Calling and Dwelling [59] far above all realities ... and all that is presented in this life [60]. Therefore, ever set yourself to transitioning from the mortal to the Immortal. Ever availing yourself in the Presence of the Lord, whereby you are constantly taken [61]. For the Joy that was the Lord's, as He faced the horrors of the Cross, is that He **foresaw His <u>Glory</u> in you**!

Living in a Place beyond matter ... beyond time and space.

God's vision and purpose for you is that you might enter into the Glory of God today. That is, return back into ... *here* to 'Abide' [62] and have your being. And it is God's own vision, for He Himself to go out before you, 'taking possession of the land' and 'warring' on your behalf. And just as Death came into the world through the sin of one man ... now, through the Triumphant, Victorious Christ Jesus alive in you, do you enter into Life as a people who pour out Life. As ever-expanding portals of Heaven ... Death itself being swallowed up by Life. As is said, *"I and my Father are one."*

Theme Scripture, Revelation 3:18-22:

Verse 18: *(first step)*
v18 I counsel you to buy from me **gold** refined in the fire, that you may be rich; and white garments, that you may be **clothed**, that the shame of your nakedness may not be revealed; and anoint your eyes with eye salve, that you **may see**.

Verse 19-20: *(second step)*
v19 As many as I love, I rebuke and chasten [Train and Instruct]. Therefore be zealous and repent [self-motivated]. *v20* Behold, I stand at the door and knock. If anyone hears My voice and opens the door, I will come in to him and dine with him, and he with Me [open discussion, openly fed].

Verse 21-22: *(third step)*
v21 To him who overcomes [made incorruptible: singularly visioned and motivated] I will grant to sit with me on My throne, as I also overcame and sat down with My Father on His throne. *v22* "He who has an ear, let him hear [listen intently to] what the Spirit says to the churches.

Throughout the Gospel message, Jesus continuously spoke of 'earthly things' … ever with the *desire* to show and speak to you of 'Heavenly things'. Even these very things of which the religious and the legalistic do not understand [63]. Even they, of whom themselves become hostile and aggressive against you ever pursuing.

The 'gold' mentioned represents the Glory of God. God's Glory ever resting upon you; the Shekinah Glory, the Fire of God, the realms beyond the Cherubim [64]. And 'white garments' represent the Honour of God [65]. And as mentioned, this is not to be confused with the purity of your Salvation bought through the precious Blood. The clothing here is the 'radiance' of the Lord. Just as Jesus says elsewhere, *"Anyone who serves me, him my Father will Honour."* [66]

Then continuing, 'anoint your eyes with eye salve' that you truly might see [67]. That is, become one who truly sees and hears in the realms of Heaven — just as Jesus. Jesus Himself being the

Template and living Example for all who believe. And just as the stars are far above the earth ... so are these realms far above all things. And are far more real and powerful than that of both the first and second heaven. For which came first ... Heaven or earth?

It has always been God's fundamental Dream that you return back into this of which was lost. To here, live and move and have your being. Even as a people who truly come to live; operating out of Heavenly Places, rather than the confines of your own understanding and strength ... or that of which the demon is trying to impress upon you. For here and now, are you simply beginning to step back up into the realms of the New Adam; that is, the Last Adam, *ie;* Jesus who went before you; has made and has demonstrated for you the Way.

This Scripture verse continues and speaks of a 'training ground'. That one coming here is taught and learns directly from King Jesus. For as He says, to whom *"As many as I love, I rebuke and chasten."*

> *Witchcraft is hostile to you ever walking in the fullness of Christ Jesus. Hence, they scoff and scorn and berate. Recognise then ... where their words come from. There is no love or life in them, only hatred and lies.*

Your Saviour has been pursuing you, and has been trying to keep you moving forward in the right direction. However, the Christian has been stubborn like a goat ... and not like a lamb that is led. But ... if you would truly be willing, then so would you also be positioned as one personally **Tutored** by the King. Hence submission and humility is key, not a 'righteousness' like the Pharisees; but honest, with honest intent and purpose ... as one raised and taught and positioned by your Saviour [68]. For who truly is your 'Rabbi' ... who too truly is your Master?

The wording used is *"Be zealous and repent"*. That is, to be really really keen to move continually forward into the **all** that God has for you. A willingness, an eagerness, to ever learn and be ever change. And so it shall be, that Jesus doesn't have to use an Iron Sceptre to 'strike the earth' in your life ... but 'a rod' with subtle and gentle touches on your shoulder saying, *"This is the right way walk in it."*

This is why, in all things, I say ... 'Seek first the tangible manifest Presence of God'. For it is unto this — the High Calling of God — that you need to set your vision. That 'in Him' you might ever be trained and truly raised by Him most triumphant in all things. As one being led *by* the King ... and **seated <u>as</u> a king**.

The Presence of God is far more important than your ministry or that of the responsibilities of your life; the being 'covered', the being 'led' and 'empowered' in all things [69]. Even then as one set in 'charge' over and above [70], able to release the very same Presence of God.

Truly, as you come into the Love of God, and are continuously ministered to in His Love; then so too are you also able to truly love ... even as one able to pour out the very Love of God. In the same way, as you come into the Presence of God, so are you ministered to and healed; and here, from this state of the 'healed' are you made strong for others ... even then 'Anointed' to heal. And to come into the Glory and Intensities of God — even the Fear of the Lord — so does His Glory ever rest upon you. Even then as one who pours out the Holy Spirit's Fire ... consuming the nations.

Continuing in Revelation 3 ...

Jesus speaks of 'knocking on your door' that **you might open** it up. Whereby, He might sit with you, and share one to another as close trusted friends. And in parallel to the passage in Psalms, it is Jesus who comes and sets a 'Banqueting Table' in your midst ... that is, right 'in the midst' of all that you face. With such a Peace, and such a state of continual Receiving from the Lord; such Presence, and such Grace ever coming upon you ... that makes you most Powerful and Unstoppable. And this even right in the midst of hopeless and impossible situations [71] ... here being made Powerful and Invulnerable in God. [72]

Learn to enter the Presence of God. Learn to seek His manifest Presence in the midst of all things. And here, enjoy His Presence ever upon you. And so it shall be also; that all that is before you is now fully exposed to His Holy and Glorious Presence.

THE 'OVERCOMER'

In mirror of the man King David, here you are also being raised and trained to reign as king. For by the Blood have you been anointed king ... just as David [73]. And just as he, so too is there a training and a testing ground [74], that you might live truly Victorious and Triumphant in Him [75]. Not in yourself, like Saul ... but in like as the Christ.

Therefore, in this life we learn ever to set our 'vision' of soul into the Beyond [76], that we truly might become a 'commander' of Life [77]. Ever unto the leading of the Spirit of God ... of whom *carries* us ... and *leads* us ... even unto the very Throne realms of Glory [78]. That we might *sit* [79] down ... and truly be seated ... as one holding the Glory of God in your hands.

Listen and pay attention then to what the 'Spirit is saying' to you this day. Sharpen your ears, and the vision of your soul: firmly set unto the things that your Saviour has purposed you. Be no longer a people denying [80] or hindering the Spirit's Power; no longer like they in the Exodus of whom were left wandering in the desert ... or like Esau who despised his birthright [81]. But come up into a state of ruling as called, whereby the nations of the world are brought into their Salvation. Not by human strength, nor by human might, but by the Spirit of God. [82]

Closing Scripture verse:
Unto us a Child is born, unto us a Son is **given**; and the government will be upon His shoulder. And His name will be called Wonderful, Counselor, Mighty God, Everlasting Father, Prince of Peace. *(Isaiah 9:6 NKJV)*

To seek to enter the Presence of God, to choose to turn your heart in Him, so do you ever have the Prince of Peace with you. This not of yourself, nor is it self-contrived ... but here Peace rules your heart, Counsel speaks in your soul; the Might of God rises up in your countenance as He takes and leads you personally by hand into Unknown Splendours. That as a son, you too may carry Peace like a liquid to pour out ... carry the Wonder and the Might of the Lord to direct and release. And so shall He counsel you in all your goings, and counsel you in the how's and the when's, ever giving you ever deepening Revelation and Awareness. And 'He' is Mighty ... and so shall **you do Mighty things** for Christ.

Hence here, so too do you, by the way you *choose* to live — ever submitted to the Lord of lords — do you live open unto the 'gifted' Child. The *Child* ... '**unto you**' ... of whom has been given.

Bless you, in Jesus Name. Amen.

Appendix:

1. Exodus 14:14, Psalm 110:1, 82:6-7, Isaiah 28:12, *2.* Romans 5:17, Revelation 1.6 *NKJV,* 2:26-27, John 14:10-14, John 15:7, Psalm 110:2, *3.* Isaiah 11:1-4, John 5:19-23, 26-27, 30, 14:12, 20:21-23, Matthew 16:19, Revelation 2:5, 2:26-27, *4.* Genesis 1:26, Joshua 21:43–45, John 15:7, Psalm 110:1-2, Revelation 1:5-6, 5:9-10 *NKJV,* *5.* Psalm 110:1-2, Genesis 12:1-3, *6.* John 1:18, John 15:4-11, 17:21-24, *7.* Exodus 20:18/21, 1 Kings 19:11-12, *8.* Isaiah 64:1-4, Psalm 116:2, Daniel 10:12, *9.* Romans 5:17, *10.* Deuteronomy 30:19, Revelation 2:7, *11.* 1 Corinthians 15:54, *12.* Philippians 2:13, John 5:19, 30, Isaiah 44:22, *13.* Psalm 36:8, *14.* Psalm 23:5, Luke 12:37, Revelation 3:20, Exodus 24:9-11, *15.* John 17:24, *16.* Isaiah 2:2-3, Exodus 24:10, *17.* Psalm 24:9-10, Jeremiah 33:2-3, *18.* Isaiah 25:6-8, Exodus 33:14-18, 1 Corinthians 15:53-54, Revelation 3:20, 2 Chronicles 7:14, *19.* Proverbs 29:18, *20.* Revelation 3:18, *21.* Zechariah 3:7, John 5:44, 12:26b, *22.* Mark 16:17-19, *23.* Galatians 2:20 *KJV,* *24.* John 14:21, *25.* Psalm 37:4, *26.* Isaiah 60:8, Psalm 84:3, *27.* 2 Corinthians 3:18, *28.* John 12:24-26, *29.* John 5:26-27, 20:21-23, *30.* Revelation 3:21, *31.* John 5:26, 20:21-23, *32.* Genesis 3:24, Exodus 3:2, 19:18, 1 Kings 18:37-39, Isaiah 11:3, 33:14b-15a,

Matthew 3:11, Luke 12:49, 24:49, Acts 2:3, 5:9, Hebrews 12:21, 12:28-29, Revelation 1:10-14, **33.** John 1:12, **34.** Isaiah 11:3-4, **35.** Matthew 16:18-19, **36.** Isaiah 11:1-4, **37.** Exodus 33:18, **38.** Genesis 28:16-17, John 1:51, **39.** 2 Corinthians 1:20, **40.** Zechariah 3:7, **41.** Ephesians 4:13, **42.** 1 John 3:8, **43.** Exodus 14:14, 33:14, 23:28, **44.** Psalm 46:10a, Exodus 3:5, Luke 24:49, Exodus 33:14. 14:14, 23:28, 1 Kings 18:38, 2 Kings 1:10, **45.** Romans 12:19, **46.** Matthew 16:16-19, **47.** Matthew 10:39, **48.** Isaiah 11:3-4, **49.** John 5:19, 26-27, 30, **50.** Hebrews 12, 5:8, Zechariah 3:7, **51.** 1 Corinthians 2:16, 2 Corinthians 3:18, **52.** Romans 8:1 *NKJV*, **53.** John 5:42, 44, **54.** Luke 16:8, Ephesians 5:8, John 1:12, **55.** Psalm 82:6-8, 91:10, **56.** Psalm 23:5, Revelation 3:20, Isaiah 28:12, **57.** Psalm 110:1-2, Matthew 5:5, **58.** 2 Peter 1:19, Revelation 22:16, 2:26-29, **59.** John 3:13 *NKJV*, **60.** Ephesians 2:6, John 15:7, **61.** Genesis 5:24, Exodus 24:9-11, Psalm 27:4, Matthew 17:2-3, Luke 5:15-17, Revelation 1:10, 12, 17, **62.** John 15:5-8, **63.** John 3:12, 9-10, Matthew 23:13, **64.** Genesis 3:24, Exodus 25:22, Revelation 2:7, 22:2, **65.** John 5:44, **66.** John 12:26, **67.** John 5:19, 2 Kings 6:17, **68.** Matthew 23:8-12, **69.** Exodus 33:12-18, 13:21, Joshua 24:12, **70.** Zechariah 3:7, **71.** Isaiah 40:30-31, **72.** Luke 5:15-17, **73.** Revelation 1:5-6 *KJV*, 1 Samuel 16:12, **74.** Revelation 3:19, **75.** 1 Samuel 23:14, **76.** Exodus 24:9-11, **77.** John 5:21, 26-27, Isaiah 11:1-4, **78.** Colossians 3:1-2, **79.** Psalm 110:1-2, **80.** 2 Timothy 3:5, **81.** Genesis 25:29-34, **82.** Zechariah 4:6

Dated: 17/7/21

33. *Mount Sinai, the Way of the Anointed (#116)*
RELATIONSHIP: 'BORN TO RULE'

The 'worship' of the Lord ... is not to elevate Him out of reach. But to worship Him ever in the inspiration: *"To be **taken** with Him where He is."*

People fail in Christ Jesus because they live according to lists of rules and regulations; but they **win** if they become 'Christ-focused' ... *meaning,* walking in the same intimate relationship with God as He. Same **elevated** realms, same **experience** of Love and Glory and Revelation. Same Spirit and Host of Angels, same holiness and righteousness and character. And same **seated** realms of Power: this is the Kingdom of Heaven.

For if you can't put to the forefront of your life — what Jesus did — in **clear picture** that you are purposed to do the same. Then your 'gospel' is not the Gospel of the Lord Jesus Christ, but someone else's. For He said, *"**You do it**!"* ... *"You heal the sick"* ... *"You feed them"* ... *"You walk on water"* ... *"You move mountains"* ... *"You cast out the demon"* ... *"You raise the dead."*

Jesus lived in a way — like a parent to their young — saying, *"**This is how you do it**."* With clear intent and purpose that you walk just like Him — this was His 'joy' as He faced the Cross. Not separate, but with Him; not apart but unified and close. Not in separate places, but in Him ... if that *truly* is where your heart lies *(rests)*.

This walking 'like' Jesus, is more than just in 'appearance' of the Man ... but in the same Likeness as Him. And just as Jesus was called to be seated in Heavenly Places ... **so are we**! Man cannot do this for you, this is up to you to respond. For by intimacy are your taken. And by the Power of the Blood are you positioned. For by the work of the Spirit are you raised Triumphant and Victorious. And by the Living Word spoken Alive in you so are you seated with Him — born to rule.

Theme Scripture:
You say, 'I am rich; I have acquired wealth and do not need a thing.' But you do not realize that you are wretched, pitiful, poor, **blind and <u>naked</u>**. I counsel you to buy from me **gold** [Glory] refined in the fire, so you can **become rich**; and white **clothes** to wear, so you can cover your shameful nakedness [mere mortal state]; and salve to put on your eyes, **so you can <u>see</u>**.
Those whom I love I rebuke and discipline. So be earnest and **repent** [turn to the Lord]. Here I am! I stand at the door and knock. If anyone hears my voice and **<u>opens</u> the door**, I will come in and **<u>eat</u> with that person**, and they with me.
To the one who is victorious, I will give the right to **<u>sit with me</u>** on my throne, just as I was victorious and sat down with my Father on his throne. **Whoever has ears**, let them hear [listen intently] what the Spirit says to the churches." *(Revelation 3:17-22 NIV)*

This subject links together: Divine intimate relationship, and Power and Authority with God. They work together. Satan is separate, a god unto himself. However, through Christ Jesus, are you unified one ... a 'god' in the Father, untouchable.

You are called to be as a 'mini-god', with a singular **purpose** to grow in ever-increasing Glory. But intimacy and deeply unified oneness in the Father is Key — body, mind, soul, and spirit — as Jesus said, *"I and the Father are One."* You are a child of God ... meaning, that you are born of the same Spirit to dwell in the **same** Heavenly Places as sons and daughters of the Most High. Therefore, we remain not a people of the flesh, but increasingly a people of the Spirit.

Let me ask then, *"Who is Jesus to you?"* Is He one who walks with you to help you in your life? Or is not Jesus Himself — your Lord of whom you follow; as co-rulers, co-heirs of God — just as He. And are you not then called to **follow** Him in order to be with Him where He is? To be surrounded as He, and to walk just as He on this earth ... is that not who your Jesus is?

A 'STUDY'
Work to build a tight relationship with God, and He will work in all your relationships.

An opening line to introduce this study:
Rest [1] your head on the Bosom of the Father [2]. *Enter* realms of Ruling, Power, and Authority through intimate relationship with the Person of God. *Value* what God seeks, *dream* what God Dreams ... and it will be God Himself who goes out and *fights* before you [3]. And here, in Him, it will be God Himself who will *clothe* you with Power from on High. [4]

The **purpose** of the Cross is to pass through unto the Father. Not to stay where you are, but to go on through in Him. It is to where God takes you that makes you *untouchable*. And it is what He gives you, and what He reveals, that makes your life in Him so special and so meaningful. Even to gift the very same unto the many.

Seven theme study points:
1. Be still, and know I am God.
2. The invitation of the Third Person.
3. Mind Poo. [5]
4. On the way to Damascus.
5. The Warrior's Pose.
6. Praise brings down the walls of Jericho.
7. The Secret Place.

1.
"BE STILL, AND KNOW I AM GOD"

Scripture:
Be still, and know I am God. *(Psalm 46:10a)*

In this short and most precious Scripture verse, do you notice the comma? ... do you notice the pause? This comma represents the **whole answer for your whole life** right there: *'pause'* ... and **know** God [6]. Anyone can know about God ... as one would the sciences or history, but who knows God? [7]

Let me start with a question ...
God, is He a person or is He God? God, to you personally, is He a person or is He God?

The opportunity of intimate relationship with the Person of God is so much bigger than you think. And how you personally come to see Him in your personal life makes such a **huge difference**. And it is in this *difference,* that opens up vast doors of unfathomable wonder; both to you as a person and to the world at large. So then, to you personally ... do you see God as a 'person', or do you see Him as God?

> *Passover — Mount Sinai — the Promised Land.*
> *Alter — Meeting Place — the Holy of Holies.*
> *Blood — Secret Place — the Fire of God.*

To continue this question ...
If you were born into the royal family, is the Queen your mum ... or is she queen? Well, she is both isn't she ... but to you personally, she is mum.

Do you realise, that in Christ Jesus, you are born of God and of the very realms of Heaven? Therefore, the greatest thing that you can ever bring to your relationships — **is your relationship** with God. Because now, as a person — you are **more** than who you are. I really encourage you, above all things, **build** a tight relationship **with God first**. For this opens Him able to work in all your relationships ... and in all your dealings.

It is through **embracing** the Spirit of God, that enables you also able to **release the Spirit of God**. For unity brings you into the seated realms [8]. Here, through ever-deepening relationship, is union built: '**threads of closeness**' uniting you one; body, mind, soul, and spirit. Ever reclining in the Bosom of God — over Heaven, and over all creation — flesh being the lowest form of man.

So to continue this question ...
If in the Castle you were raised a servant, then there would be no relationship with the King. However, if you were raised a son ... then you were born to rule.

I so very much encourage you in this, if you truly wish to serve God, then learn to approach God as a son or a daughter. For as Jesus says, *"A servant doesn't know the Father's business"* ... but a son does. What are we talking about? But a greater manifestation of the Person of God in your midst. What are we talking about? Greater manifestation of the Goodness of God, and His manifest Glory sweeping over your whole life; touching the world just as the Son. For as God says, *"The Kingdom of God is not a matter of talk but of Power"* [9]. Not of word alone, but God manifest in the 'flesh'. [10]

*— The Blood birthed your **relations** to God —*
— Meeting with Him imparts Seeds of Faith planted in you —
— And God continually taking you Places flesh is not permitted —

1b.
JESUS WAS THE GREATEST EVANGELIST THAT EVER WALKED THE EARTH.

Scripture:
No one has ever seen God, but the one and only Son, who is himself God and is in *closest* relationship with the Father [the 'Bosom' of the Father], has made him known. *(John 1:18 NIV)*

There you go, now you **know** the path of total ministerial success. It is through intimate and closest of relationship with your Heavenly Father ... then you will make Him known on earth.

Close relationship with the Person of God is the root of success, in all walks of ministry and in all areas of life. For what you have is the Person of God with you for you are choosing to be with Him.

Today, I am telling you things most encouraging. There are many things; when you go to the supermarket, lots of things on the shelf. But what I am telling you is about what you should get ... what you should buy and where you should put more of a focus on. For the *Enemy* always tries to drag you down and head you into different directions. But it is the Lord Himself, who is saying to you today, *"This is the right path ... walk in it!"*

As we see, represented in Jesus' own personal life: intimacy in the Person of God is the single greatest Evangelical tool to bring everlasting change to this dying world. God first working powerfully in your own personal life ... then subsequently, powerfully **through** your life, as ever-expanding gateways of

Heaven. 'Ladders' unto whom angels ascend and descend upon you before the eyes of all. [11]

"If your Presence does not go with us, do not send us up from here." [12]

Above all cares and all considerations, learn to **seek** the Presence of the Person of **God manifest** ... *ie;* 'with you'. Ever humbling yourself before Him where He lifts you up [13]. Better still, how about you go and be 'with Him' where He is. For this is the deepest Heart's Prayer and motive of the Son concerning you this very day [14]. The Spirit of the Lord taking you by hand into the Hidden and the Concealed.

The greatest mystery and wonder in the Exodus story, is the Person of God — 'with them' — in **His Person** [15]. However today, you and I have — in addition to this — unique and incredible opportunity to be with God where He is — with Him in **your person** [16]. And this is what you personally need. And this is what brings the Kingdom of Heaven actively manifest on earth.

In Christ Jesus, you no longer have to live confined to this earthly plane; for your spirit has been made Alive in Him [17]. Therefore, you have unique and special opportunity to live now in a whole other realm of Joy, of Meaning, and of Power.

For what occurred at the Fall is *separation*. However, what occurred at the Cross is perfect opportunity of *union* in the Godhead. To retain relationship with God most treasured and dear ... this knits you close in the Person of God. Not He in the earthquakes, nor He in the storm or the lightning, but He in the 'still small voice' [18]. And where God is — so are you also — for **unity brings you part** of the realms of 'seeing God' [19]. The seated realms, with Power and Authority over all things.

Scripture: *(full scripture)*
Be still, and **know** that I am God; I will be exalted among the nations, I will be exalted in the earth! *(Psalm 46:10 NKJV)*

Now you know how, through *stillness* ... through the 'pause' ... are you truly able to come into intimate Knowledge of the Person of

God [20]. And here, God Himself stepping through your life in such manifest ways ... that He shall be exalted.

So in answer to the opening question ...
God needs to be Person first, then God. He needs to be Father ... then Lord God Almighty [21]. For 'ruling' comes through close and intimate personal relationship.

*On a side note: When referring to cattle, there is the cow and the bull. But as we know ... there is a third, and it is called a 'steer'. And also, as we know, the steer is the bull castrated; becoming fat and docile and is ultimately devoured. Hence I say most clearly, you are **not purposed** to be a steer. You are, however, Divinely Purposed of God to 'Rule in the midst of your enemies'.* [22]

*Satan has worked with **firm** intent to steal away your true identity. He works always in the purposed intent to keep the Church impotent and ineffectual. For so it is, that in the Person of Christ Jesus are you gifted the Morning Star;* [23] *Purposed and Destined of God to abide Powerful in the realms of influence.* [24]

2.
THE INVITATION OF THE THIRD PERSON

When typing, has it happened to you ... where your fingers miss the keys and you accidentally type something else? For example, when typing the word 'name', when typing fast I sometimes accidentally type the word 'amen' instead.

The other day, when typing the word 'son', for some reason I kept hitting the letter 'i' instead of the letter 'o'. So instead of the word 'son' ... I kept typing 'sin'. Then after a while, I realised that it was God who was wanting to show me something: the close approximation of 'sin' *vs.* the dynamic and undeniable nature of 'sonship'.

Let me explain, the letter 'I' denotes *independence*. That is, 'I by myself' ... 'I of myself'. Hence, the true meaning of sin is *separation, ie;* independent of God ... 'I by myself independent of Him'. And this is what the world has only ever known since the Beginning, but in this, God clearly says, *"You shall surely die."* [25]

However, in contrast to this, the letter 'o' speaks of 'our' ... or 'us together', *ie; relationship*. Relationship of which ultimately leads to ever-deepening knowledge of your sonship. Therefore, true success can only ever be found in truly bonding, not in independence of God ... but ever in the desire to draw close, *ie; intimacy*. [26]

The involvement of the Third Person: Recently someone asked me for advice; should they see a secular counsellor or a Christian one?' So I thought for a moment and said, *"Definitely a Christian one, 'cause it won't be their wisdom and education alone, but the rich involvement of the Person of God"* ... and this is what you want.

That is, bringing the 'Third Person' into the picture, to work in the background; to bless, to heal, and to minister into your life. For we know, what is impossible for man is possible for God.

2b.
GOD SEEKS RELATIONSHIP, AND MAN NEEDS RELATIONSHIP

I personally love 'God-conspiracies'. Not conspiracies about God, but God actively *conspiring* on our behalf. I really love and welcome my Heavenly Father orchestrating things, and He working always in the background. Therefore, I give Him **full** rights ... I give Him full place. I invite Him, and as a lifestyle; I deeply deeply welcome Him.

So another word for this could be, 'I love the blessings of God'. And I love the Mysteries of God been ever laid out before my eyes, and the continually being led deeper and deeper in.

For true, isn't it? ... that just as in the Exodus story; we always **need** God 'navigating' our lives; God raising, training, and continually leading us forward. And we always need God's Love continually coming upon each one of us and His Love ever filling our lives. And so too also, what we need — we really need the Might of the Living God upon us each day — to bring shift and great change. For the answer to the human condition **is not man** ... but Heaven on earth.

So to emphasise: Relationship with God, even tightly bonded personal relationship with Him, brings about powerful *involvement* of the very Person of God. The 'invited' [27] and welcomed place where God Himself comes and stands with you in all your doings and in all your relationships. Establishing health in your bones, sanity in your mind, and the original Purpose of God's Plan for man ... being fulfilled in your life. [28]

A side note ... the 'Morning Star': Just as the Exodus story represented the coming into the 'Promised Land'. Today, this also is God's Dream and very Purpose concerning both you and I. However, so it is today, that our Promises are so much greater than you think, **so** *far greater than you can comprehend or imagine.* [29]

For just as there is always a resistance to the taking 'possession' of the Land; the dispossessing the Enemy of whom has established himself in the very Place of Destiny. So is there also, the retaining of a God-centric — 'Glory' vision — whereby it is God Himself who fights and wars for you as a people clothed and covered by the Prince of Peace.

Satan was in Creation in the Beginning ... the 'crafty one' ... and so he schemes and plots. Satan works ever with the same intent that he held since the Beginning: the **dispossession** *of your Identity, the dispossession of your true self. But however, so it is also, that in the Person of God ... He takes you personally by hand into Places man is not permitted.* [30]

3.
'MIND POO'

I personally really value the Exodus story. I really love how God desires to continually lead us forward into wonderful and powerful and as yet unknown things. Deeper into the realms of Promise ... into unspeakable and inconceivable things [31] beyond the confines of 'death'. [32]

And here, in the area of God fighting for us, there is *this* hidden gem that expresses so much. How God, in His Person, dearly desires to stand with you — Holy and Powerful in His Person [33] — but how it is that your thought-life can 'defile' you. Defile, not on a Salvation level, but in the area of His Glory and Power actively working on your behalf.

In reference to the following Scripture:
"As part of your equipment have something to **dig** with, and when you relieve yourself, dig a hole and cover up your excrement. For the LORD your God **moves about in your camp** *(ie; the very singular Man of the Person of Jesus)* to protect you and to deliver your enemies to you. Your camp must be holy [34], so that he will not see among you anything indecent and turn away from you." *(Deuteronomy 23:13-14 NIV)*

Here, as the Israelites were moving deeper into what the Lord had for them; the very — **singular Man** — of the Person of God was with them — **in Person** — to guide and to lead them forward. He, not in a lofty vision 'up there' somewhere, but physically walking amongst the camp.

1. The Person of God with you.
2. To fight and protect you.
3. Your 'camp' must be holy.

Do you yet see just how close and intimate God desires to be in relation to you as an individual — to you as a person? And do you see just how much He desires to walk closely with you: walking in and amongst your life in most powerful and most manifest ways? Even how He deeply wants to lead you forward and fight for you ... however, your 'thought-life' defiles you.

It is God who wants to come really close to you and walk and lead you in most wondrous realities ... but your heart-life defiles you. Hence, God says, *"Dig a hole and bury it."* Truly, die to things that grip you so that you truly might walk in the realms of Life. 'Your camp must be holy' ... that He will not see anything indecent in you and His Glory turn away from you.

In this most central area of our lives ... we must needs learn to keep a close check on what we cling onto in our hearts; and what we hold in our thought-life and in the hidden chambers and motives of our soul [35]. For this is most crucial in your ability to draw richly from the Kingdom realms, or ever truly be led into the Glory realms — as one standing over the nations [36]. Standing in Dominion over the powers of sin [37], death [38], and the grave. [39]

Therefore, as mentioned before ... 'pause' before you say something. 'Be still' before you feel something ... and '**know**' God. That is, let the **Knowledge and Love of God** [40] come upon you and Grace your life. It is not enough to know about God, or just believe in Him — for you are called to become Jesus. And so it shall be that His Presence and His Kindness shall ever change and empower you as He shows you His Glory [41]. Such is the treasure found in a heart ever bent on seeking the manifest, tangible, and divine nature of His Presence.

In God, you hold the nations in your hands. Therefore, as a people in God, we need to learn to treat all things regarding the heart and mind with far greater care than the people of the world. Not that we are 'different' from them, for we used to be ... we *were* them. But now, for the Glory and Grace of God to rest upon our lives; there must be a purity of soul that surpasses. A holiness that is not of the world but is of God. [42]

> *The Grace of God is always there for us. But what we want is the Glory and Power of God to rest richly upon us.*

A side note: '**Wrestling**' *with the Person of Jesus ...* '**Ladders**' *appearing where angels ascend and descend upon you. Jesus has a much higher vision for you than what you currently know:* '**Glory-of-God-upon-your-life**' *kind of vision that totally transcends. The Gospel* **is** *Life ... therefore, as you are honest and truly 'wrestle' the Word; leads you able to function in the realms of Everlasting Life. Come, know the Word, and wrestle with God and say, "Do not go until you bless me!"* [43]

Two Scripture verses:
1. So He drove out the man; and He placed cherubim at the east of the garden of Eden, and a flaming sword which turned every way, to guard the way to the tree of life. *(Genesis 3:24 NKJV)*
2. And there I will meet with you, and I will speak with you from above the mercy seat, from between the two cherubim which are on the ark of the Testimony. *(Exodus 25:22 NKJV)*

You do not know the awesomeness that is inside you: The Ark of the Covenant was the very first stepping of the Spirit of God in the world for a thousand years. Never since the Fall had the Glory of God appeared before man till that day.

God 'spoke' from between the wings of the Cherubim — from the Eternal realms of Heaven. And sacrificial blood was sprinkled before the Mercy Seat in atonement for the sins of the people. However today, in Christ, His own Blood has redeemed man once and for all. Not only for the forgiveness of sin, but for whomsoever might believe — may pass through into that of which was forbidden man. That of which was closed off and guarded by the very same Cherubim … with *flaming* swords.

The Ark itself was a Gateway unto the Glory of God. But now — in Christ Jesus — you have the exact same *Gateway* held within you; to hear and to see … and to carry the very same Glory of God.

The Spirit of the Lord is upon me — *because* — He has Anointed me to build up and elevate the broken and the lost. Build up the saints unto to the **whole measure and stature** of the fullness of Christ. The Spirit of the Lord is not upon me to seek approval of man … but to the lifting and building up the Church. Hence, as I eat of the Tree of Life, so do I release the 'Healing of the Nations'. [44]

The Garden realms are the realms of Dominion, where God feeds and liberally pours into your soul. It is a Place full of the Love and full of the Grace of God [45]. Victory is in the Spirit; of whom the very same goes out before you in the Holy Spirit's Fire.

3b.
KEEP A TENDER HEART UNTO GOD.

Two Scripture verses:
1. But the things that come out of a person's mouth come from the heart, and these **defile them**. *(Matthew 15:18 NIV)*
2. See to it that no one falls short of the Grace of God and that no bitter root grows up to cause trouble and **defile many**. *(Hebrews 12:15 NIV)*

I so very much encourage you, be not shy, but **invite God to help**. Pause, and give place for God to enter into all that you are dealing with. Success comes through invitation ... it is the Person of God who transforms.

An example of things that defile. We all struggle at times in the area of unforgiveness. We all at times struggle with offence, pride, and hatred. Bitterness towards someone that runs deep and does not let go; and if not dealt with, this bitterness can defile you. God's heart and hand remain outstretched to you, but in 'grieving the Spirit' ... a distance is formed. [46]

The Nature of God is that He desires to fight for you. Therefore, as you personally continue to choose to clothe yourself in Immortality; [47] everything you touch belongs to the Kingdom of God. Vengeance is the Lord's, and He will repay and defend for He is a Righteous God. But to pick up an unloving heart is totally contrary to the Heart of God. So how can He fight for you for you are no different to the world?

The wondrous reality of God upon your life, brings a 'distinction' between you and all the peoples of the world. The manifestation of His Power, His Person, and His Love ever richly upon you [48]. So today, in firm security of your relationship with God, **ask Him** to come upon your life. Put aside all forms of hatred, put aside all forms of bitterness and ill-will; and all kinds of resentment, selfish desires, and lust. For how you treat and consider your brother ... is how God treats and considers you [49]. Be encouraged, God is a gracious God ... and He is a firm converter of pain and trauma into Life and Liberty. So lift up your face unto God.

Always involve the Lord. Ask Him to work with you ... that is what relationship is all about! You are not supposed to be living and doing things alone. Even better, ask God for the Love of God to come upon you ... for His Love and Goodness surpasses all things. Be still, and **know** God.

This is why the Pharisees could never come into the 'Knowledge of God', even though they could quote every Scripture. For it is only through deeply honouring close relationship that draws Him.

And here, the Lord shall freely reveal to you that of which cannot be given of man.

*On a side note: The Exodus story represents the Church as an **unstoppable** force. God seeking the fulfilment of His Promises concerning you personally and for the nations at large. Therefore, let us continue to work to keep our hearts ever pure unto Him. And let us also learn to carry a 'shovel' and clean up our mess and our ways. Even making a whip to drive the evil from the 'temple' of our hearts [50]. In quick response — in **diligent** honour — in respecting the very Person of God with you. For as is said, "Be holy as I am Holy."* [51]

4.
ON THE WAY TO DAMASCUS

Let me say this, if Paul can change overnight … you can change! But let's go further, if Paul can change overnight so can your husband change. And let's go even further still, if Paul can change overnight so can the one hostile against you change.

Scripture:
Meanwhile, Saul was still breathing out murderous threats against the Lord's disciples. He went to the high priest and asked him for letters to the synagogues in Damascus, so that if he found any there who belonged to the Way, whether men or women, he might take them as prisoners to Jerusalem. As he neared Damascus on his journey, suddenly a light from heaven flashed around him. He fell to the ground and heard a voice say to him, "Saul, Saul, why do you persecute me?" *(Acts 9:1-4 NIV)*

Truth is, as one close, and of whom lives in tight relationship with the Person of God; can you seriously — 'in the Spirit' — **firmly present someone before the Lord**. Do you think it possible, in the time when Saul was terrorising the Church, that there was not someone out there praying, *"Lord, please intervene?"*

The picture of the calling of Apostle Paul speaks volumes, this is the Way of God: His fundamental desire to turn a problem into a blessing. The converting of that of which is against you … converting it into avenues of great support and strength. Even unto the calling someone into Salvation. And as exampled in Saul's case,

God going against someone hostile, who morally desires to kill you … and turning them into beacons of Light.

Hence, the striking Saul off 'his horse', and Jesus saying to him, *"Why are you persecuting me?"* This is the way of God in response to one who prays. Someone who prays as a person — bond tied — in Him. One who does not take matters into their own hands … but one who releases God. [52]

As we know, the way of the world is *"One step forward, two steps back"* … life's a struggle [53]. But that's not God's Way; His way is "One step back, seven steps forward" … life's a blessing.

'One step back': You might be pushed back, or you might even choose to step back a little, *ie;* the pause … *"I will step back from these circumstances and situations, and I will release God into them."* And so it is, the result of this lifestyle is one of continual catalystic growth.

So again, I will not take matters into my own hands, I will step back and embrace the Lord. I will come and enter into the place of 'knowing' Him. And I will release this person; these circumstances and the issues before me unto the Lord. Saying, *"Spirit of the Living God, I command a seven-fold return on this situation. Convert all griefs and sorrows into platforms of great success, in Jesus Name."*

Now you know God's Way. God wants to lead you into realms, that when you speak, you release something. That when you speak you release something that bypasses unbelief, bypasses unrighteousness, bypasses religion or hostility; and outpours the open demonstration of the Power, the Love, and the Goodness of God. Totally bypass … releasing and outpouring the Spirit and Fire of God on earth.

It's all 'relationship' isn't it … someone coming against you? Injustice, lying, cheating; they who seek to do you harm. But your heart is full of love … hence the underlying desire is to see them saved, to see them blessed. So here, the 'Lord of Glory' … the **Lord as <u>Lion</u>** … shall go out and intervene on your behalf. That is His Way.

However, you can't release the Glory of God if your heart-life is no different to theirs. This is also why we work to clean our heart and though-life. Then again, sometimes the Way of Salvation is different ... God removing that person from your life; or removing them completely.

5.
THE WARRIOR'S POSE

I was sharing with someone this wording, I never had used it before ... but I was sharing with him, *"In your walk with the Lord, take on a Warrior's Pose"*. And recently I coined the phrase: *"Embrace the Lamb that you might be **raised** a Lion."* For as we know, when referring to the Lamb, we are speaking of Jesus.

So I say ...

> *Embrace the Lamb in all child-like tenderness.*
> *Embrace the Lamb ... He your Rock and sure foundation.*
> *Embrace the Lamb in your hour of need.*
> *Embrace He ... the Lover of your soul.*
> *Embrace the Lamb who is gentle and kind.*
> *Embracing He ... who only has your best in mind.*

Two kinds of Christians: One who believes *and* one who becomes. Over the generations, Christians have come to the Lord seeking refuge. And as believers, we have come to the Lord seeking forgiveness and Grace. And to He who is the Christ we have come finding strength in our hour of need. But what I would like to so encourage you, is now let's together [54] come and seek the Lord to meet Him as Lion.

The Blood ... the Spirit ... the Fire!

Jesus is referred to as both Lamb and Lion. And so far we have only been coming to Him as Lamb. So I say ... we already know that we dwell in the realms of the Beloved. We already know that we are part of the family and the cherished. For by the Lamb have we come into relationship ... even here, our Eternal Place of Dwelling.

We no longer are servants but sons. We no longer live lost in the 'forest' but live in the Castle. We are part of the Family of God ... we know this, we are certain of this. So now, what is also deeply desired, is to go meet Jesus as Lion. Love Him as Lamb ... yes! But come also to love Him as Lion ... even as a people raised by Him to Rule. One personally tutored and trained by Lord of Glory ... full of the Holy Spirit's Fire! [55]

It is the Blood that leads to the Spirit ... but it is the Spirit that leads to the Power and Fire of God. For just as there is the Temple, the building and the Alter; there is also the very Meeting Place of God ... the 'Holy Place' destined for each and for all.

The Holy of Holies: It is God who is bent on Empowering His people. His Dream being to Personally restore you back [56] into your *former* Glory within the Bright Morning Star [57]. So love Jesus as Lamb ... *yes* ... but also love and approach Him as the Lion of Judah [58]. As one passing through the flaming flashing sword right into the quiet still voice. [59]

Jesus is Lamb but He is also Lion. And you can come to Him at any time as Lamb in all confidence ... to be nurtured and healed. But now set the vision of your soul to approach Him as Lion [60]. The Blood has purposed you to stand in a whole other realm ... that you stand in a whole other Place of opportunity. Therefore, learn to look through all things ... that the Lion may stand in the midst of all you face. Even then becoming a people raised by Him to Roar! [61]

I so encourage you to clear up the vision of your eyes; [62] setting the — purpose of your soul — more firmly unto the Person of Jesus. Even your heart sharply directed unto the Glory of the Person of God [63]. In every way: no longer live in *question* ... but be certain of your salvation. Then now from here, **in the <u>certainty</u> of God**, let us now seek the Lord to raise us as kings. [64]

There are three realms: First, the dirt and dust that we have known ... 'striving to make a living by the sweat of our brow' [65]. Then there is the spiritual. The spiritual forces that have occupied the land since the Fall. All cultures and all peoples have been influenced and have lived under this reality for all generations. Witchcraft and sorcery; idol worship, control and suppression ... come from this realm.

But then there is the Kingdom of Heaven [66]. That through the Name of Jesus we enter and call upon, wherever we are and in whatever we are facing. Intelligence comes from here, Knowledge and Understanding, so does the Love and Power and Grace of God [67]. And here we can abide, and by the Blood pass through and live and have our being. Even then to bring the Love and Liberty of God into our world; Everlasting Life, into these realms that have only known death and decay ... as a people clothed in Glory from on High.

*Problems are a part of life. But **winning** is your Destiny.*

Taking on a warrior's pose: So if you were to stumble, trip over or fall; then simply dust yourself off quickly and get up again and set your heart back unto the 'High Vision'. Don't wait until you have a track record of being 'good' ... that is never going to happen. But here, right here and now ... right where you are ... set it in your heart to Meet the very Person of God in His Glory [68]. It is the Blood that is your 'birthright' of passage [69], but it is the Spirit of whom 'transfigures' you into creatures of Light. Satan comes to separate, but it is the Blood that is the 'joiner' ... and the very Person of God of whom makes you an unstoppable force. [70]

So it is true, that for far too long the Christian believer has viewed their walk; only in the hope that one day they might enter Eternal Life when they die. **But**! ... the encouragement is today ... that your world needs you walking in Eternal Life, **in the realms of Everlasting Life**, whilst you yet still live. What you and your world needs is the Person of God with you in 'Shekinah' manifest form [71]. Even that you might live strong and most powerful lives ... gifting the same unto the many.

This is Key ... 'the Alter': The laying your life down and its issues, only then to pick it up again in Life [72]. Laying down of your own life as though dead ... and *passing* through ... only then to pick it up again in the realms of Everlasting Life. The Cross is the

Doorway, the Blood powerful and the Name of Jesus unstoppable — but **Glory** comes from Abiding [73]. The looking right through the 'forest' unto the Tree of Life [74]. The preference of going in and out finding 'pastures' ... just as you please. [75]

> *Jesus is the Way, the Truth, and the Life.*
> *But what is He the Way to? ...*

Problems come to all who walk this world. But the answer isn't found in the problems themselves but in the Person of Jesus [76]. By the Power of the Spirit — Jesus desires to lead you into a **whole other realm**. Into a Place of Dominion over all things. You might have *your* prayers ... but so does God! For the very Purpose of the Cross and the shed Blood is — **to relocate you**. Whereby you heal, you move mountains, you heal the sick, and you outpour the Spirit of God. The toddler raised to be a man ... an orphan unto a very **child** of God.

So come, pray this prayer with me, *"Lord, I forsake all things unto the Glory of God ... even for the **sake** of all things. Bless you Lord. Even for all that I love and all that I care for ... I forsake all things, that the Glory of the Lord may come upon all peoples. I lay down my life even that I may be led into the realms of Life; to pour out the Love and Grace and Power of God in my world."*

So referring to the Cherubim, the same that closed and barred the way. Through the Blood sprinkled on the Mercy Seat — have you now right to pass through. Not only in the forgiveness of your sin, but your ability to eat liberally of the Tree of Life. The opening up of the way, that by default — what is released — is Healing for the nations. This, outside of your consciousness or awareness: the Glory of God released in response to you. [77]

6.
PRAISE BRINGS DOWN THE WALLS OF JERICHO

Now, I have shown and taught you how to take on a war footing: **1.** problems, **2.** 'pause', **3.** know God. Problems ... *pause* ... **know God**. For everything that you want to achieve in life, and in everything that you face, is summarised right here. The very birthing place of the Knowledge and Might of God. [78]

And it's not as though you have to travel the seas far and wide to find, no ... the 'Word' is in your heart, and in your mouth to speak [79]. It is not 'over there' hidden ... but inside you. And even though I want to have my 'million dollars' I am not holding onto it. I will go the other way ... I will put a *'pause on this'* ... and here I will come into the 'Knowledge' of the Lord. And it will be the Lord who opens doors ... *"It will be the Lord who 'projects' His Glory upon the 'galaxies' of my life as the Bright Morning Star"*. (E. P.)

When facing issues, the answer is not in the issues themselves ... but in God Himself. The answer is not in problems or obstructions ... but in praising the Name of Jesus. And it will be He who takes you into the realms of Knowledge; [80] and it will be He who knocks down the walls and tears down the obstructions; and He who releases action and brings great change! [81]

The basis of a miracle-filled life is a heart of praise. The always-preferencing and the 'always-looking-past-problems' and praising the Name of Jesus instead. And really, the most powerful thing you can thank Him for is the Blood ... thank Him for the Blood and the Spirit.

Praise brings down strongholds of sin. Praise 'relocates' you and centres your heart in Him. Or let's say ... praise centres your spirit-man right into the realms before the Glory and Intensities of God. And in these very realms do you release the Spirit of God into your family life, into your thought life, and into your finance life. Therefore, we face not the problems of life head on, but face and orientate ourselves unto the Lord ... ever releasing Him unto problems.

The Alter is the place for leaving prayers. Now, it is our 'praise' that is bent on going in ... on passing through. The Holy Place is the 'transit lounge' ... waiting to be captured up. And where He takes you ... that is the Power point. The realms to be hungered for more than our 'daily bread'. Even the very Word that proceeds out of the very mouth of God [82]. That is the basis of a miracle-filled life — be still, and **know** God.

Psalm 110:1-2: *(Ric's version)*
Our '**job**' is to sit down at the right hand of God. And God's '**job**' is to fight for us. Not only fight for us, but to Anoint our hands to release that 'fight'.

Each one of us can remain creatures of flesh ... however, this is the lowest form of man. We can be creatures of the mind and soul, or otherwise, creatures of the Spirit. All four levels of the human condition are ours to pick and choose. However, here and now, it is '**in**' the Spirit that you are taken Places that man cannot go. Even these very things far beyond imagination or comprehension.

*On a side note: In looking at the Exodus story. God did **all** the work in taking them out of Egypt. Then there was the meeting of God at Mount Sinai. Then God continued to **work**; leading them into all that was Promised. However, it was they who had to enter in ... it was they who had to **take** possession.*

*Therefore, the answer is always the Tent of Meetings; the meeting and sitting down with God. The '**pause**', the honoured inquiry ... waiting on God. **But!** ... it was always then God who went out and **fought** on their behalf.*

God has you very much in mind. As well as fulfilling His Promises in you and His Heart unto the nations. Therefore, His thinking is different; His thoughts are higher. And He is also about trying to train you that you might grow all the more into the knowledge of your sonship; even as one stepping further into 'manhood'.

So, a heart unto God is always key: And this even more prioritised than the very Promises themselves ... or problems that lay before you ... just as in the Exodus story. A heart unto God is key. For just as the Ark of the Covenant went into the water first — then the river Jordan was parted — so it is first for us as well. Be, then, one who cherishes the 'Ark' gifted within you. If not even more so, become the very embodiment of the Ark for your world — parting the way for your people.

7.
SECRET PLACE

Jesus so very much demonstrated the Secret Place in His Person. By the way He lived and approached His ministry [83]. Therefore, if you also truly want to walk in the path of great success, then ... *'Be still 'comma' ... and 'know' God."*

I so encourage you ... *in everything!* ... to open up the secret places of your heart and make yourself **vulnerable** before the very Person of God. Even then, that He might take you into the Secret Places of His own Heart ... into the Places that He Himself is vulnerable. The Bible refers to this as the Hidden and Concealed.

This is why 'time away' in the Lord is of such value to you personally — just as it was with Jesus. The 'Holy Place' of meeting, of sitting ... being quiet and receiving. Times of worship and praise, even fasting and seeking the 'Face' of God ... is of such incredible value to you. For in the — being 'captured up' — so are you Enlightened in your spirit, your soul and mind ... *and* ... in your flesh. 'Mustard Seeds' of Faith planted deep in your very being that move mountains. And themselves grow into great Trees of Righteousness.

I tell you, we all need that ... times of being captured up in Him. And I so encourage you ... don't wait until calamity comes before you do so; for **Power comes by where you live**. Where you Dwell and Remain; [84] where you live and have your being. Do you see how this is 'dangerous' for anything that you might be facing? Dangerous for the *Enemy!* Not that I feel bad for him, but he really is in a losing battle. And now you know the way to make this so.

Everything that Satan comes against you with; you, as a person, have the capacity to peer right on through. To 'pause', and praise the Name of Jesus, and come into 'Knowledge' of Him. And the more that you live in experience of the Lord — *in the pause* — the more that rich pathways are made. And so too, the more that you are able to draw from these linkages and connections ... and **demand** a shift*!* Faith comes by what you know ... God never leaves us ... we leave Him. Power comes from a rich and most sure foundation.

Everything! ... that tries to come against is converted into sevenfold blessings. 'Land' taken as you continue to move forward into the Promised realms ... into what has been Promised.

For 'answers-to-problems' ... isn't your Destiny, but the Seated realms. The right hand of God, the realms of Grace and Glory ... this is your Destiny and High Calling. The Morning Star 'next to' the Bright Morning Star. For here have you Authority over the nations, even as an Iron Sceptre to strike the ground [85]. An Authority standing over all that you love and all whom you hold dear. And God shall bring a beautiful answer to trauma that you might have faced ... to bring wonderful results.

So in closing ... to 'Rule in God', this comes by where the 'secret' places of your heart truly abides. And so too, to the Places God Himself takes you. *Amen?*

> *Problems ... pause ... know God.*
> *Desires ... pause ... know God.*
> *Ministry ... pause ... know God.*
> *Success ... pause ... know God.*
> *Fear ... pause ... know God.*

I pray that this has been a blessing. Bless you, in Jesus Name.

TO CLOSE WITH ONE MORE THOUGHT

If you would wish to just sit in God's Holy Presence, and to hear Him and see Him, then you would become like 'gods' [86] *unstoppable!* [87] Just like the Israelites at Mount Sinai; if they had just 'delighted' [88] to sit in the intensities of God's Presence and to hear His Voice without telling God to be quiet [89], then they would have blasted through any desert experience and any opposition that came.

I have heard of simple farming folk in the juggles of Mexico, who can't even write their name. That have shrouds of light coming around them as Jesus appears ... right in the middle of the cornfield ... and personally, teaches them the Gospel and Power of God. And this, not about their being specially called ... it's about a heart and a vision. I pray now you have both.

Appendix:

1. Isaiah 28:12, Psalm 110:1-2, 82:6-7, Hebrews 4:11, *2.* John 1:18, *3.* Exodus 14:14, 33:14, 23:28, Isaiah 64:1-4, *4.* Luke 24:49, *5.* Deuteronomy 23:13-14, *6.* John 5:42, Ephesians 3:18-19, *7.* John 1:18, 13:23, Acts 13:22, *8.* John 17:20-24, *9.* 1 Corinthians 4:20, *10.* John 1:14, *11.* John 1:51, *12.* Exodus 33:14-18, *13.* Luke 14:10, *14.* John 17:20-24, Mark 3:13-15, *15.* Exodus 33:1-3/15-17, *16.* John 12:26, 7:34, 14:4, 17:24, 3:13 *NKJV*, *17.* Genesis 2:17, Ephesians 2:4-5, *18.* 1 Kings 19:11-13, *19.* John 1:18, 5:19, *20.* Isaiah 11:1-4, *21.* Isaiah 44:22, *22.* Psalm 110:1-2, *23.* Isaiah 14:12, Job 38:7, 2 Peter 1:19, Revelation 22:16, 2:26-29, *24.* Zechariah 3:7, *25.* Genesis 2:17, *26.* James 4:8, John 1:18, *27.* Psalm 2:7-8, 110:1-2, 2 Kings 2:9, *28.* Luke 19:42, *29.* 1 Corinthians 2:9-10, *30.* Genesis 3:24, *31.* 1 Corinthians 2:9-10, *32.* 1 Corinthians 15:53-54, Mark 16:17-19, *33.* Exodus 33:2-3, 13-23, *34.* Hebrews 12:14, *35.* Matthew 5:27-30, *36.* Zechariah 3:7, Revelation 2:27-28, *37.* Genesis 4:7, 1 Peter 5:8, *38.* John 10:10, *39.* 1 Corinthians 15:54, *40.* John 5:42, Philippians 4:7, *41.* John 17:24, *42.* Hebrews 12:14-15, *43.* Genesis 32:22-32, John 1:51, *44.* Isaiah 61:1-6, Ephesians 4:13, John 5:42-44, Revelation 2:7, 22:2, *45.* Psalm 27:4, Galatians 5:22-23, *46.* Ephesians 4:30, James 4:8, *47.* 1 Corinthians 15:53-54, Revelation 3:17-18 *(Luke 14:28-33)*, 2 Kings 2:13, Genesis 3:11, Mark 16:17-19, John 10:34, Psalm 82:6-8, Zechariah 3, *48.* Exodus 33:14-18, *49.* Matthew 7:2, *50.* John 2:15, *51.* 1 Peter 1:16, *52.* Deuteronomy 32:35, *53.* Genesis 3:19, *54.* Isaiah 2:1-4, *55.* Luke 4:14, 5:17b, *56.* Isaiah 44:22, *57.* Revelation 22:16, 2:26-29, *58.* Revelation 5:5, *59.* Genesis 3:24, Hebrews 12:21, Exodus 19:16, 2 Chronicles 5:13-14, 1 Kings 19:11-12, Acts 2:2-3, Revelation 1:10-18, 2:5, Isaiah 11:3, 37:16, Ezekiel 10:1, *60.* Revelation 5:5, Genesis 3:24, Hebrews 12:21, Exodus 19:16, 2 Chronicles 5:13-14, 1 Kings 19:11-12, Acts 2:2-3, Revelation 1:10-18, 2:5, Isaiah 11:3, 33:14b-15a, 37:16, Ezekiel 10:1, *61.* Psalm 110:1-2, Revelation 3:18-21, Genesis 1:26, *62.* Revelation 3:18, *63.* Colossians 3:1-3, *64.* Revelation 1:5-6, 5:9-10, 3:17-22 *NKJV,* John 10:34, *65.* Genesis 3:19, *66.* 2 Corinthians 12:2, *67.* Psalm 27:4, 110:2, Isaiah 11:1-4, *68.* Exodus 33:18, 1 Kings 19:11-13, John 17:20-24, Revelation 1:10-18, *69.* John 10:9, *70.* Psalm 110:1-2, *71.* Exodus 40:34-38,

34:35, 33:9-11, 24:16-18, 19:10-20, 13:21-22, 3:1-6, 2 Chronicles 5:13-14, 7:1, Numbers 9:15-23, Leviticus 16:2, Ezekiel 10:18-19, Joshua 3:14-17, Matthew 17:1-2, Luke 4:1-2, 14 *(first bind the strongman)*, Luke 1:35, 12:49, 24:49, Acts 1:4-5, 2:1-4, 2 Corinthians 3:18, Revelation 2:4-5, Genesis 3:24, **72.** John 10:17 *NIV,* **73.** John 15:7, **74.** Revelation 22:2, Genesis 3:24, **75.** John 10:9, **76.** John 16:33, **77.** Isaiah 64:4, **78.** Isaiah 11:1-4, John 5:42, **79.** Deuteronomy 30:11-14, **80.** Isaiah 11:1-4, **81.** Isaiah 64:1-4, **82.** Deuteronomy 8:3, Matthew 4:4, **83.** Luke 5:15-17, **84.** John 15:4-9, **85.** Revelation 2:26-29, **86.** Psalm 82:6-8, **87.** Mark 16:17-19, Isaiah 60:8, Revelation 5:9-10 *NKJV,* **88.** Isaiah 11:3-4, Revelation 1:17, Exodus 33:22, Hebrews 12:21, **89.** Exodus 20:19

Dated: 15/8/21

THE PERSON OF GOD WITH US

34. *The Person of God with us (#117)*
EVOLUTIONAL LEAP

Let me start this chapter with a question: *"Who is God to you? One who is with you to help achieve your goals and desires? Or one who is Himself your goal and desire?"*

Over the following next few chapters, I want to express further, this picture of God **physically** being with us in His Person. God in His Glory upon us individually ... that's for certain! ... as well as upon His Church as a whole. Not just as a church 'building' of bricks and mortar ... but **filled with the Shekinah Glory** of God [1]. Not just in a knowledge about Him, but in most manifest ways that shake the earth [2]. To this we honour, and to this we give rightful and full honoured place.

It is God's desire to fight for us and **Himself** go out before each one of us personally in our lives; aggressively and most actively [3]. Even as a people clothed with Glory from on High ... **clothed** with 'Immortality' [4]. With a *"Pillar of Cloud by day and a pillar of Fire by night"* [5] ... as a people passing through into the fullness of Him. For God Himself is our Promised Land ... God Himself is our 'exceedingly great reward'. [6]

But how much this is rooted in a heart that is fully bent unto Him as a Person. Regardless of where you are, regardless of what you are doing ... for in this God works [7]. For here, in the choosing to 'lay your life down in death' *(all you know and all you hope for)* do you also come into Authority over it [8] *(all life's issues and all that is presented)*. For the 'prayer' isn't only just a focus on salvation, but the firmly — passing through — into the full reason **why** Jesus went upon the Cross [9]. Just as in the Temple, it is the passing through, as one being led into the Untouchable realms [10] — the Unapproachable realms of the Most High God — that brings a blessing to the world [11]. And just as in the Exodus, the celebration isn't only in the fact that you have been *liberated* from Egypt; but that you are **coming into and entering** the full Promises of God! [12]

Jesus said of Himself, *"The reason my Father loves me is that I willingly lay down my life — only to take it up again"* [13]. I want you to get this ... I really want you to understand this, it's most important.

There is a Love in God [14] ... where **He becomes vulnerable**. Where He shares deeply of Himself ... Secret things of His Heart and precious Gifts. In Christ Jesus, it's my job to come here; [15] for to he who truly lays his life down in death — as God Himself is our Eternal vision and 'prayer' — also comes to pick it up in the realms of Life.

A heart bent on His Person — to such as these pass through. It is God Himself who imparts; and to such are made Invulnerable — are made Impervious and Untouchable. As Jesus says, *"And these signs will accompany those who believe: In my name they will drive out demons; they will speak in new tongues; they will pick up snakes with their hands; and when they drink deadly poison, it will not hurt them at all; they will place their hands on sick people, and they will get well."* [16]

Egypt is not your 'promised land' *(the world or its desires)* ... nor is the 'desert' *(problems, sickness, or despair)* your dwelling place. But the ascending into the High Places where man is not permitted [17]. People are not your instructors, nor is the Law *(a temporary 'custodian')* ... but the mouth of God [18]. For what flows from Him shall cause your face to shine and your eyes not to go dim. And the very Person of God — with you — causing a 'differential' between you and all who walk the earth. [19]

Now, not only shall you lead multitudes into the Promises ... *like Joshua*. But so shall you bring the **Promises** and Glory of God to earth ... *just as Jesus*. Shall you bring Heaven and the Will of God to this world. For — **first!** — are you called to sit at the right hand of God [20]. Then now — **as one 'with Him' seated** [21] — are you here raised with an Iron Sceptre in your hands to 'strike' the earth [22]. For it is purposed of God, that the 'rod' of **your** strength shall come out of Zion saying, *"Rule in the midst of your enemies."* [23]

Right now, the Spirit of God is here in the room with us. He is gentle and He is quiet; [24] He will not impose ... but He definitely has things to say. His Words may not be words, but He has healing in His wings. Honesty draws Him ... as does an invitational heart. He may not speak, but as you enter in; Waterfalls of rejuvenating Life wash over you. The right hand of God are the Garden realms, the Place of Ministering Grace. But it also is the Equipping Zone where Anointing and Authority is realised [25]. Sometimes doors may open unto Visions and Dreams; [26] even as one captured up into untold Wonders. Hence the 'prayer' is the Lord Himself ... not grief or sorrow ... for God is a consuming Fire!

So again I ask, *"Who is God to you? One who is with you to help achieve your goals and desires? Or one who Himself — **is** — your goal and desire?"*

WE ALL NEED THE FIRE OF GOD

The Cross is only the **beginning** of what God desires to do for you. Just as in the Exodus ... the 'Passover' wasn't the end but just the **start**. God wants to fight your battles; God wants to lead you in lost and barren places; and God wants to take you into mysteries untold. And as one — in Him — does God desire to Anoint and clothe you with Power. [27]

He will heal your body ... *and* ... put **healing in your hands**. He will fight your battles, but as well: Anoint your hand to **release that Fight**! He will lead you into places flowing with milk and honey ... the very essence and cream of the Land. But most importantly, He will lead you into the fullness of Himself; the fullness of the Christ ... where you walk *as* the Son.

For what the world is coming into; it's not going to be enough just to *believe* in Jesus ... for fundamentally, we have always been called to — become — Christ Jesus [28]. This then, is why there can be failure; for way too long, the prayer of the believer has only been set on needs and desires [29]. But how we come — to truly win — is for the Glory of God Himself to be our prayer [30]. As Jesus said, *"I came to baptise you in the Fire of the Holy Spirit (the Glory and the Power), and how **I yearn** that you were kindled ready"* [31]. Water Baptism is for the cleansing of sin, **but now comes the Fire** ... now comes the Glory [32]. The entering into the Likeness of God; [33] the very realms of which He sits.

*"This is my dream ... to **meet** with the Lord. But so too in the knowledge that it is the Strengthening place; the Place of Anointing and Grace.* [34]

The Passing through — and as like in a capsule — being captured up again and taken [35]. *All other things pale in comparison ... as well, all things are dealt with by the Lord.* [36]

To serve is the nature of God [37]. *But so too is it to* ***receive*** [38]. *For how can I give out of an empty cup?* [39] *The tree bears fruit from an abundant heart. So much fruit that it does not care where the fruit falls. But soon, there is a forest of trees."* [40]

AN INTRODUCTION

All throughout biblical history, we see that there were times and seasons that bought great change. Pivotal times in history that brought fundamental change to the people of the day. But also in the world: 'next level' steps necessary in the fulfilment of God's Plans in the salvation of man. Recently, I have come to call these events ... *"Evolutional Leaps."*

In the time of Jesus, they sought to stone Him for alluding that He was Son of God. However today, this language has become the norm ... do you see how much things have changed? But now, as we look throughout the world, it seems that we are coming into yet another season of change ... *even* the 'Last Days'. And though we may have had 'sonship' as a word; it is God Himself who earnestly seeks to cause our 'sonship' to be made manifest on earth. As is said, *"All creation waits in eager expectation for the children of God to be revealed"* [41] ... **this is you**! ... this is you and I.

In Scripture, we see how God allowed periods of great turmoil and upheaval. But as we read, we also see that in these times there were people, truly honest people [42], of whom truly — inclined — their heart unto the Lord [43]. Even of whom truly humbled themselves to truly seek out the Heart of God [44]. And instead of focusing on grief and sorrow; they went into the — 'Secret Place' — and were ministered to and raised of God. And here, through their own personal engagements; God brought about deep and great shifts within their own lives personally. As well as 'next level' evolutional leaps in the consciousness of the people of the day. And further ...

subsequent, next level steps necessary in God's Plans and Purposes for mankind.

It's funny, but over the last few months, I happened to stumble across movies of which all somehow climaxed: in the grandeur of mankind's supposed 'next step' in the evolution of the human species. There were a few of them: *"Lucy"*, *"The 100"*, *"Transcendence"*, and *"Interstellar."*

Of course, each film was heavily rooted in the modern atheistic vision of man … of which I personally find nauseating: Darwinism, Trans-humanism, Eugenics.

However, in relation to the Christ, it's most important to realise just how much God holds deep Personal vision for you personally. How He dearly desires to draw each one of us close to Himself and transform us. Even 'transfigure' us into creatures of Light … in a moment of time. [45]

That is … transform both you and I into '**manifest**' sons of God: [46] Walking on water, healing the sick … and being translated to different places. Raising the dead, calming storms, casting out devils … and being captured up in Heavenly wonders. Even as a people who 'cease the groans and suffering in the world' [47] … bringing people into the Knowledge of God. And so shall there never, in all the history of man, be a time of such an Outpouring of the Spirit than these that are the last days.

Today, it is our Heavenly Father, through the finished work of the Cross and gifted Spirit of God; whom causes transformational 'leaps' within each one of us personally. In our consciousness and awareness — mentally, spiritually, and physically — whereby we truly walk in Like as the Son [48]. Not only like of Adam of Old … but Adam of New; in Like as the Resurrected Christ walking the earth. No just in word alone, but in the 'Victory' … in open manifestation of Heaven on earth. That is, the Word made flesh and walking amongst us — this is His Prayer.

"The wonder of the realms of Heaven transferred through physical man. The realms of Life and Spirit passing through us like a portal into this broken

> *physical world. The flesh is the lowest form of man ... but so too is it the* **connection** *point between Heaven and earth. Those who have gone before us have passed, but you remain ... you are here!*
>
> *Therefore, as you continue to humble yourself, and truly allow your soul to ascend; does your spirit-man abide before the Throne of Grace* [49]. *Even as one 'returning';* [50] *being led as one to sit at the right hand of God* [51]. *This was His Dream and Purpose since the beginning ... even for they who truly love the Lord.*
>
> *Therefore, speak into the issues you face, speak to the concerns in your heart ... and* **release** *Life. Release the Spirit and Power of God to go before you (the Might and the Aggression* [52]*) ... for so too are you son of God. So too are you an Unstoppable force."*

It is Love [53] that leads you here ... not the paths of legalism or religion; but honour, invitation, and a heart open to receive. The 'spirit' of the Pharisees is hostile to such things, as too lust and pride that preoccupies. The Devil is terrified of the Fire of God, for God's Radiance consumes all things. Consumes all sickness, all disease, and all the works of Satan. Therefore, as you personally choose to enter into the realms of Life, as one passing through the Fire [54], all doubt and unbelief is washed away — and here, are you clothed with Power from on High.

To me now, problems and difficulties are simply training ground in — the Victory — that is mine. The practice and pathways unto manifestation. And opposition is simply 'bench press' as one who walks in Glory. It is God Himself who trains you in the Presence of the Lord; in all things and through all that one might face. That you personally might experience the win and be built up greatly in your faith.

> *First there is the Word, then the Blood and Spirit, now comes the Fire and Glory of God!*

It is through both the Blood and the Testimony that you are saved [55]. Via He, the Son, of whom desires to lead you in your sonship ... that is, deeper in the revelation of your sonship ... that your sonship may be ever more 'realised'. Firstly, that your sonship may be revealed in you ... as well as then made increasingly manifest in the world. Death cannot stand in the realms of Life; Glory shines and darkness is totally consumed.

BIBLICAL HISTORY

There were pivotal seasons recorded in the Bible that could **not** be changed. Set in place regardless; irrespective of individual preferences, prayers, or desires. For example: Noah's Flood, the Exodus, and 70AD Israel.

Pillar of Cloud by day and Fire by night: [56] And in these various seasons that came, the only thing left available to them was to be Empowered in God [57]. But that has always been the Heart of God through the sending of the Son: that you be Powered by Him [58]. Like Elijah who was made not only able to navigate these times; but was made impervious and untouchable *(Elijah himself being an Old Testament example of your new life in Christ)*. As he lived surrounded by the Lord, where God 'clothed' him in the Power of the Spirit to stand for others.

In the Old Covenant there were those who were chosen; but here in the New Covenant ... all are chosen.

Hence, the Bible has these accounts recorded for a reason ... a very specific reason: that you too might learn, through the lives of those who went before us; how you personally can walk and **grow** in the Power of God. This, the very value of the biblical text: your own capacity — through the Power of the Spirit — to walk in anything that they walked in. Even to the whole measure and stature of the fullness of Christ. [59]

So, as we look through these biblical accounts, we see that these seasons brought about great change. Great change in man's overall awareness towards God, of which only shifted and grew. As well as next level steps completed in God's Plans and Purposes for mankind. And they were completed according to the times set by God before the founding of the earth.

Here, as we go through this chapter, I would like to centre around the following four biblical accounts:

1. Joseph in Egypt.
2. Daniel in Babylon.
3. Elijah in fallen Israel.
4. Jesus in Roman-occupied Israel.

To emphasise firstly ... these four men, each of them were prophets of God. And I think it's really important to talk about it here; and bring a shift in the perceived meaning of this word 'prophet'. Bringing this reality into far greater relevance and far greater personal meaning for us today.

For in the past, there were 'special' people who were called. But however, today ... so it is, that each one of us are called in Christ to be prophets of God [60] ... even *priests* and *kings*. 'Priest' ... meaning, to stand in the gap for another as one who hears and sees and intercedes. And 'king' ... meaning, Anointed in Authority to direct and release the Power of God.

A definition of a prophet: One 'called of God'; [61] one who hears God [62], one who sees God [63], one who has visions and dreams [64] ... and one who is given Grace to endure [65]. Even then: one who bonds with God, one who speaks the Word of God, one who moves the Hand of God ... and one who 'transcends' in Him. That is, 'transfigured' as one who affects and brings change to the world.

So, as we read through these instrumental seasons of change, we see that all had calamity, and all had 'global' hardship. But as we also read, all these men looked 'beyond' in God; of which caused great shift in their own lives personally ... and subsequently, following; 'global' shifts in the nations. Here, God fulfilling yet another level in the consciousness of man as a whole, as well as next level, or layers, fulfilled in God's plan on earth. Hence, I have come to phrase this term as ... 'Evolutional Leap'.

But before we go on ... let's consider something most significant: Jesus walked 'oblivious' to His surroundings. And yet ... He brought something that smashed the reality of the world. It says in the book of Isaiah, *"Jesus did not live by what He saw with His eyes, or heard with His ears, but from (within the realms of) righteousness did He make judgement on behalf of the broken and the lost."* And the verse continues,

"With the Rod of His mouth He **struck** *the earth; and with the breath of his lips he will slay the wicked."* [66]

I really want to encourage you in this, that we — as children of God — are **born of the very <u>same</u> Root**. Are born of the very same 'Branch'. We, in Christ Jesus, are born of the very same Spirit and of the very same Kingdom as He. Subsequently then, Purposed and Called by Him to be seated as He. Therefore, if we truly can come — to continually choose — to bow down in all humility and honour; then so too shall we be also continually led and raised. For we are all fundamentally called to be **one in Him**; Purposed born of the very same Likeness and seated with Him in the very same Heavenly Places … if that truly is your personal dream and heart's desire.

The office of the Priest is right there … just as is the Office of the King; but for the believer … it is fully up to us to come here, God cannot make us. He has prepared and made the Way through the shed Blood of His Son; the realms of Everlasting Life are ours for today and evermore. So, as sons of God … it is **our job** to get off the 'street' in our thinking and into the Inheritance that is ours. For the world needs something more than you and I — the world needs God! — He our very 'Inheritance', who is in us. The world dearly needs Heaven, for so it is true that Satan has had enough at diminishing man, **<u>now</u> is time for firm change**!

Tell him, the *Liar* and the *Thief*, the one who hates and kills and sows deceit; tell him, *"Come into the Terror and Fear of the Lord with me, the very Glory of God that I love and long for. I don't think you will like it here, for so shall you be totally consumed. As for me, I delight in the Fear of the Lord."* [67]

I believe that this subject is most relevant for us all today … the *rising* Glory. Especially in these times and seasons that the world is coming into globally. And I pray that this message comes as a deep encouragement and blessing for you personally; truly … for you and the world of which you live.

On a side note: It would be good to talk further about the subject of Eugenics. However, I really encourage you to look it up. Eugenics was a concept developed by Charles Darwin's cousin Francis Galton (though originally from Plato). And where Darwin's Theory of Evolution spoke of the spontaneous natural development of life without God. Eugenics is different: it is the manipulation of genetics and the development of technology to produce a superior race. And really, this is what drove the Nazis during the Second World War; just as is driving much of the darkness that that we see happening in the world today. As well, of course, the rising up of Baal and the worship of ancient demons in order to gain control and power.

DEEPENING ROOTS

Hard times either kills the plant *(shallow root)* or otherwise cause its roots to draw down deeper; the plant made stronger and even more well-grounded. Recognise, that God makes a way through every difficulty and every temptation that comes your way ... every one of them! [68] So the answer isn't found in what you are dealing with ... but **always** in Him. He, of whom you draw near; He, of whom deeply desires to draw near to you and Personally fight your battles.

So, as you continue to humble yourself, ever drawing your heart unto the Secret Place, *ie;* the Meeting Place ... the Holy Place. As you continually choose to come under the Shadow of the Almighty ... to be ministered to, to seek His Face, and hear His voice ... so are you continually given Grace to win. Are you continuously given a Joy and a Peace that feeds and nourishes your soul. And this Grace causing your heart to go ever deep into the things of God: deeper into all that of which the Blood has already purchased and availed. And these 'deepening' Living and Divine experiences, causing great and everlasting 'evolutional leaps' within you personally; causing you to transcend all things. For first are you called to sit at the feet of Jesus, and here it will be He who gives you the 'words' to speak *(new tongues)* ... and Power and Authority over all works of the demon. [69]

This is why hardship can come, sometimes pain is required; a season of dryness, a shaking of things ... lest you never change. Grapes made sweeter, fruit more abundant ... and Joy more plentiful. Bless you, in Jesus Name.

'JOSEPH' IN EGYPT

Joseph was a son of the man named Israel. One of twelve boys who made up the Twelve Tribes of the Nation of Israel. He was a prophet of whom had visions of God, and such Grace was upon his life that caused him to endure things far beyond what man could normally. He endured the dungeon, he stayed faithful when his master's wife came to him, and he kept his sanity even though his brothers betrayed and sold him into slavery.

However, in his retained tenderness unto God, Joseph had powerful visions and dreams that caused him to transcend. This, as a blessing for himself personally, as well as for his family that were all saved. But also, the very outworking of his own personal and close relationship with God *(his 'tenderness');* paved the way for the **next** step in God's Plan of Salvation for the nations.

A side note: At many times, when the world is going through massive events, the focus is on the issues rather than on the likes of Joseph and Daniel. Just like in the times that we are in today, with major global power moves, the answer isn't in them but in your relationship with the Father ... that brings the Lord of Glory to bear.

I really encourage you in this, the Presence of God — visions and dreams in Him — **are the most precious thing**. And are always laced with Hope and Peace and Love; they being the very nature ... the *'aroma'* of Encounters. As David says, *"In your Presence is fullness of joy; at your right hand are pleasures forevermore"* [70]. And in another place, *"The fruit of the Spirit is Love, Joy, Peace, Longsuffering, Kindness, Goodness, Faithfulness ... against such things there is no Law."* [71]

Truth is, that knowledge and self-discipline is **not ever enough**. But otherwise building ever deepening and enduring personal relationship with the Person of God. And it is to this that **makes you powerful**, and this that makes you able to win. And what shall outpour from your life, is God Himself ... the very Hand of the Lord with you.

It is God who fundamentally *seeks* relationship, and Jesus Himself — is God's very *Invitation Card*. For this is why He sent His Son: not to judge nor condemn, but *free* the way unto perfect unity. And to this is what He seeks and yearns for; right living and right actions ... they come later. For truly, righteousness can only be birthed out of the 'Love of God' that liberally outpours in your soul. As the Bible says of Jesus, *"Through the closest of relationship with the Father, Jesus has made Him known."* [72]

Do you remember the story of Joseph? Joseph was sold into slavery ... however, God's blessings were upon him. He found favour in his master's eyes ... but then found himself in the dungeon, but in the end God elevated him to be in charge of all of Egypt. And as a result, the whole family of Israel were saved, and they themselves became a nation of people in the midst of the Nation of Egypt. For so it was, that through their own difficulties it formed their unity — as well as their identity. They not being just another family or tribe of people, but as is said, a 'kingdom of priests'. [73]

To summarise then, they didn't just blend in but were outcasts. But so it was, that through their difficulties they were birthed a nation. And the favour of God was so greatly upon them ... in open demonstration ... to the blessing of the whole world.

'DANIEL' IN BABYLON

The story of Daniel came at a time when Israel was taken into captivity. They went into Babylonian captivity through Israel's prolonged and persistent sin. However, here, in this time of exceedingly great difficulty ... brought to Daniel a heart that truly sought to know the Heart of God.

So again ... **the word 'prophet'**: One who **hears** God, one who **sees** God, one who **receives** Grace and Strength from God, and one who has **visions and dreams**. [74]

Through Daniel's own personal struggle, and otherwise continuously *choosing* to come before God; that God Himself stepped mightily through him. Capturing the heart of the king and changing the Nation of Babylon. **Just one man!** Shifting the consciousness of the people and the nation as a whole. Subsequently, bringing about next steps in God's Plan: the rebuilding of the Nation of Israel — it itself being the very birthing 'canal' for the Christ to come.

'ELIJAH' IN FALLEN ISRAEL

I speak of Elijah for two reasons; not only was he a prophet like Joseph and Daniel, but both he and Elisha were 'Power' prophets. That is, prophets of whom not only heard from the Lord, but of whom themselves openly demonstrated the Power of God before all people *(pre-examples of the New Testament believer)*.

There are a number of overlays here for us in Christ:
1. The miracles demonstrated by both Elijah and Elisha mirror the famous miracles of our Lord Jesus Christ.
2. The disciple-like relationship Elisha had with Elijah resulted in Elijah's Anointing being passed onto him.
3. Both Elijah and Jesus ascended up into Heaven before the eyes of their disciples. Passing on an even greater Anointing to do 'greater works' than they; to 'finish' and complete their calling on earth.
4. This demonstrates for us all, that each one of us, are called to walk in the same Power and Authority of Elijah ... even to that of the Christ.

Therefore, the restriction is not God ... **it is us**! The restriction is not ever God ... **it is the believer**. The believer who becomes 'shipwrecked' in their faith; [75] coming under all kinds of teachings, distractions, concerns, and lures. But however, so is the Word most clear: all Promises are 'yes' and all Promises are 'amen' for us unto the glory of God. [76]

A side note: The 'glory' of God vs. the 'Glory' of God; the 'honour' of God vs. the 'Honour' of God ... there are two. First is the glory and honour unto God, and second is the Glory and Honour of God resting upon you. The latter brings great glory and honour unto Jesus and the Father.

So in this understanding, we each deeply need to recognise this next necessary 'evolution leap' that is pre-purposed and pre-destined for each one of us — *ie; the shift*. And how this shift can never come through pride; but through a heart ever truly humbled and truly set upon the Heart of the Father. Not unto the world, nor its concerns ... but unto the very Person of God. One to one, in perfect unity one in the Father; of whose we are and to whom we belong and live and have our being. As is said, *"I in Him and He in me."* [77]

Elijah demonstrates an Old Testament parallel in the miracles of Jesus. The multiplication of food, the healing of the sick, the raising of the dead, and the outpouring of the 'Fire' of God. And this very same — vision — acts as an Old Testament 'prophecy' for both you and I to walk in. Therefore, in this, I deeply deeply encourage you: *"To **he** who has an ear — **listen**! — listen **intently** to what the Spirit is **saying** to the Churches."*

Sometimes I hear Christians say, *"God has the Power why doesn't He just fix everything? ... He has the Power why hasn't He healed, or helped, or provided?"* But I most very much encourage you in this: God is not Power ... 'God is Love'. [78]

God is not Power He is Love ... and He is firmly about raising us in Love. We are sons and we are daughters; we are children of Glory. Hence the fundamental objective of God is always about raising **you** to rule. Raising you as kings, and raising you to be God-like. Therefore, there is always something more than Power, and always something more than answer to prayer. So let's together — **come to listen** — and pay more attention to what the Spirit is trying to lead us in; His direction and His motives.

Again, I so encourage you, that out of the 'revelation' of your sonship', out of deep shifts in your awareness — this, that God is intently at work for you to realise and be renewed — does Power flow. Power that shifts and changes the world. Therefore, God is about **raising us** in Love, raising us in Grace and Union ... *and* ... He is about raising us in Power.

'JESUS' IN ROMAN-OCCUPIED ISRAEL

Lastly, I want to speak of Jesus. And unlike any of those who came before it is Jesus who **has given** us — both rights and capacity — in measure far surpassing all the prophets of Old. Even then to say, that all the prophets that came before, are themselves picture and precedent for each one of us to walk in today. Every one of them*!*

So again, to emphasise, Jesus has raised us not only to be prophets but priests. But then also ... not only to be priests but kings. However — even more so — not only to be a king but sons and daughters of the Most High. Born from Above, not from below ... born not of flesh, but of the Will and Spirit of God — just as the Christ. Therefore, so it is also most true — you are born an entirely different creature. [79]

It is the devil who works to bind and blind ... however, in firm stark contrast, it is the Spirit who seeks to give you eyes that see and ears that hear. Understanding and Wisdom, Knowledge and Counsel, Might and Power that wildly surpasses; as one seated in Heavenly Places far above all things. This by *your* choice and by *your* will. For first the Blood has led you unto Salvation. Now here, by the very same Blood ... and by the same gifted Spirit of God ... are you being led into Victory.

Jesus was born in turmoil. He was raised in the midst of pagan Roman-occupied Israel. But just to reflect upon, there was not ever anything in His language that spoke of hardships; that spoke of conspiracies, or confusion, or of the fear that was prevalent in His day. But through Him, and through the life that He led, He demonstrated a deep relationship in God ... and also Faith and Love and Power in the Spirit. And He Himself opened up richly to each one of us personally ... a completely 'other-level' evolutional leap in consciousness. As well as in a — living reality — for each one of us to walk in.

Israel had been marked for destruction, from all the way back to the time of Daniel. As Jesus warned, *"When you see the 'abomination of desolation' (spoken of by Daniel the prophet), standing in the holy place (whoever reads, let him understand), then let those who are in Judea flee to the mountains"* [80]. This marked the 'final' chapter of Israel as a nation. And it would come about **regardless** of prayer, regardless of the heart or desire of the people. This time of change was set in stone.

Therefore today, we are reminded of the essentials: That each of us have unique opportunity to **hear and see** God. That we all have unique opportunity to **receive Grace**, and all have the same capacity to be built up and **strengthened** in the Lord. But so too also, we all have capacity to enter into evolutional leaps of awareness; evolutional leaps of understanding; evolutional leaps of monumental change; and evolutional leaps of Power, of Glory, and of Love.

IN CLOSING

There is so much rising fear in the world, and so much controversy and evil. And our land is being overrun by carnal thinking and demonic ways. Fear of what is to come; unrest and natural disasters … all of which has been long warned about in Scripture [81]. And in addition, the conspiracies of men of whom only seek to dominate … just as in all the ages.

Today, in these that are that Last Days, Satan is rising up seeking to bring everything unto himself. For the time is coming near when he is no more; for all creation shall be rolled up like a scroll [82]. Satan's days are numbered … and he knows it.

Eugenics and Darwinism: It is the demon-inspired-man who seeks to control the 'evolution' of man. A darkness at work to manipulate the human condition. The creation of a 'superior' race; the manipulation of the gene pool; the experimentation of gender transition; and the bypassing of morality for the 'higher' good. And this, all being done fully outside any acknowledgement of God … but all unto death.

The 'queen of heaven' and New Age: Though in wording, this speaks of a 'New Age' coming … but in reality, it is a rising up of the old demons, and the old spiritual practices that used to be in the land prior to the Christian faith. The darkness that is *behind* the darkness, a darkness behind the scenes … hidden behind and out of sight. They operate in darkness; both in 'good' and in 'evil', presenting an 'enlightenment' that leads nowhere. Promises like a carrot whereby you never arrive. Black and white magic; various spiritual and religious practices; as well as for some, the seeking of more power that results in the greatest of dark and evil acts. Even themselves, not believing that there is any such thing as evil … *"For who is to say that Satan is evil"* they have been instructed … *"For all return back to the 'one'"*.

Like an aerial, the New Age movement reach out to the spiritual. And though many are seeking good and spiritual enlightenment, their seeking also attracts the evil *(for they are of the same realm)*. For the realms of the spiritual are not the realms of God, but the realms of the fallen. The *encaged* realms of the second heaven by which mankind has only ever known. And for many, as they pursue New Age, they actually think that they are pursuing God ... but they have been *duped* and conned. For the God of Heaven and earth is unique to the Bible. For there is nowhere in history, nor in any lands or nations of people, that He has ever been known ... except by the Word of God.

Jesus is the way to God, and only through the Christ can we know Him [83]. When spiritualism reaches out to 'God' ... they are actually reaching out to 'gods' *(the gods, plural)*. Satan creates nothing ... he does, however, masquerade as an angel of light [84]. He is a counterfeit, a corrupter and twister of truth, where 'lying' is his native tongue [85]. Presenting himself always in replacement of 'God' ... and true it is, he is the god of this age. [86]

However now, the complete opposite is true: There is the singular God of Heaven and earth, who resides in the third Heaven. He, who has been continually at work [87] in the effort to restore man ... to restore the *willing*. And He has been diligently at work throughout the ages, to bring shifts in the consciousness and awareness of mankind. Always in the underlying vision unto the restoration of that of which was lost; and all with the Hope, and all in the Love and Grace and Delight of the Lord. And this 'path of Life' is full of Love and full of Light ... and full of the Glory and Blessings of God.

A side note: Those in the New Age can be very knowledgeable of the Bible. Though but, at the same time, refusing to submit to the Christ. Like in Hinduism, of which is open to studying all spiritual texts; or ancient Rome that welcomed all gods ... so long as you worshipped theirs. So, in taking a liking to various aspects of the Bible, selecting various truths and sowing them into their 'knowledge' (living by the own understanding, a god unto themselves) ... they, at the same time, fully reject the Power of the Blood. And fully reject the Cross and the Power of the Name of Christ.

Held within the Christian believer is the Power to bring great change through the Christ of whom is in you. Even to where the Lord of Glory desires to lead you, and of whom also earnestly dreams that you might be: **"With Him where He is"** [88]. Becoming ever-expanding bridges of Life to the hopeless; bridges of the Spirit to this dying world. For truly, we are in the Last Days … but also most true, so shall the 'Latter Day Rains' pour out in a measure like never before. For the Grace of God triumphs over sin and death; [89] the Grace and Love that transcends all human comprehension.

Hence, as believers, we always have a choice. We can allow ourselves to be caught up in it all. We can allow ourselves to be carried off with the crowd. Or otherwise, we can do as Jesus and the prophets of Old always did, and that is come before God and humble ourselves and seek His Face. Not like a reed in the wind [90] … but with a deeply prioritised heart unto the Heart of God. A heart to hear God; a heart to see God; and a heart unto His Grace, His Power, and His Might. And allowing ourselves to be continually captured up in His Delight — captured up in His Spirit and His Presence. Even that the Presence of His very Person might come stand Mightily in our midst. [91]

Further then also — that we might 'transcend'. And in doing so, allow God to all the more step through our lives. That He might truly fulfil the next step in His Plans and Purposes. Unto the capturing of the nations unto Christ; the pouring out of His Spirit upon all flesh; and the Bride made Spotless unto Christ's Return.

A closing Scripture to finish that I pray is a great blessing. Perhaps we could all begin to treat this Scripture as our own personal 'prayer' … the '**making**' of God our dwelling.

PSALM 91:1-12 NKJV

*"He who **dwells** in the secret place of the Most High shall **abide** under the shadow of the Almighty. I will say of the Lord, "He is my refuge and my fortress; My God, in Him I will trust."*

Surely He shall deliver you from the snare of the fowler and from the perilous pestilence. He shall cover you with His feathers, and under His wings you shall take refuge; His truth shall be your shield and buckler. You shall not be afraid of the terror by night, nor of the arrow that flies by day, nor of the pestilence that walks in darkness, nor of the destruction that lays waste at noonday. A thousand may fall at your side, and ten thousand at your Right Hand; but it shall not come near you. Only with your eyes shall you look, and see the reward of the wicked.

Because you have made the Lord, who is my refuge, even the Most High, your dwelling place, no evil shall befall you, nor shall any plague come near your dwelling; for He shall give His angels charge over you, to keep you in all your ways. In their hands they shall bear you up, lest you dash your foot against a stone."

One last thought …

There are two layers in Gospel, just as there are two layers in the Spirit and Grace of God [92]. Jesus Himself *delighted* in the Fear of the Lord [93], *ie;* He delighted in the Glory and Fire of God; the 'Untouchable' … that one be clothed Untouchable. The Cross is your salvation, but so too is it also a **doorway**; to enter into the Glory of God … even as one being clothed in Glory. And this is our **high** Calling in Christ Jesus.

These times and seasons we are coming into require something more than believing … you must *become* Christ … He is your Standard. To survive, one must needs be clothed with Power from on High [94] just as called. And to he who has an ear, let him **listen intently** now to what the Spirit is saying to the churches [95]. Pride has no place here, nor does sin or selfish ambition … to such the Veil remains closed, the Veil itself remains hidden.

But if you were to truly humble yourself and pray, and seek the Face of God *(seek His Glory and Fire)*, then so **shall He come** and heal the land. [96]

Bless you, in Jesus Name.

Appendix:

1. Exodus 40:34-38, 34:35, 33:9-11, 24:16-18, 19:10-20, 13:21-22, 3:1-6, 2 Chronicles 5:13-14, 7:1, Numbers 9:15-23, Leviticus 16:2, Ezekiel 10:18-19, Joshua 3:14-17, Matthew 17:1-2, Luke 4:1-2, 14 *(first bind the strongman)*, Luke 1:35, 12:49, 24:49, Acts 1:4-5, 2:1-4, 2 Corinthians 3:18, Revelation 2:4-5, Genesis 3:24, *2.* Isaiah 64:1-4, *3.* Exodus 33, 14:14, 23:28, 33:14, Deuteronomy 32:35, *4.* 1 Corinthians 15:53-54, Revelation 3:17-18 *(Luke 14:28-33)*, 2 Kings 2:13, Genesis 3:11, Mark 16:17-19, John 10:34, Psalm 82:6-8, Zechariah 3, *5.* Exodus 13:21, *6.* Genesis 15:1, *7.* Luke 12:37, Exodus 14:14, *8.* John 10:17, Mark 10:29-30, Matthew 6:33, *9.* Hebrews 12:2, Matthew 3:11, *10.* Psalm 82:6-8, 91:10-13, *11.* Genesis 3:24, Exodus 19:12, Numbers 4:15, John 17:24, *12.* Ephesians 4:13, Exodus 23:20-30, *13.* John 10:17, *14.* John 5:42, *15.* Psalm 110:1-2, *16.* Mark 16:17-19, John 14:30-31, Psalm 91:10-13, 82:6-7, *17.* Genesis 3:24, Exodus 19:24, Hebrews 9:7, 12:18-24, Isaiah 2:1-4, Zechariah 3, Revelation 1:10-18, *18.* Galatians 4:1-7, Deuteronomy 8:3, Matthew 4:4, 16:17-19, 23:9-10, Revelation 3:22, Exodus 20:18-19, *19.* Exodus 33:14-18, Deuteronomy 23:13-14, Mark 4:41, James 4:8, *20.* Hebrews 4:11, *21.* John 15:7, Mark 3:13, *22.* Revelation 3:17-22, 2:25-28, 2 Kings 2:13-14, Mark 3:14-15, *23.* Psalm 110:1-2, *24.* 1 Kings 19:12, *25.* Romans 8:19, *26.* Revelation 1:10-18, *27.* Luke 24:49, Genesis 3:10, Revelation 3:17-18 *(Luke 14:28-33)*, 1 Corinthians 15:53-54, 2 Corinthians 3:18, 2 Kings 2:14, 6:17, Matthew 16:17-19, Mark 16:17-19, Acts 5:15, Colossians 3:1-3, Psalm 91:1, 2:7-8, 110:1-2, 34:7, 104:2, 93:1, 84:5, John 1:51, Exodus 33:14-18, 34:29, John 17:24, Genesis 1:26, *28.* Luke 9:13, Matthew 10:8, 16:19, *29.* 1 Corinthians 13:11-12, *30.* John 17:20-24, *31.* Luke 12:49, 24:49, *32.* Acts 2:2-3, *33.* Genesis 1:26, *34.* Luke 24:49, Acts 1, 2, *35.* Hebrews 11:5, *36.* 1 Samuel 26:9, Matthew 6:33, Psalm 110:1, *37.* Matthew 20:28, Isaiah 9:6, *38.* Luke 12:37, *39.* Psalm 23:5, *40.* Mark 3:13-15, *41.* Romans 8:19, Colossians 3:4, Ephesians 5:27, *42.* 2 Chronicles 7:14, Daniel 10:12, *43.* 2 Corinthians 6:2, 2 Chronicles 7:14, Daniel 1:8, *44.* Matthew 4:4, Deuteronomy 8:3, *45.* 2 Corinthians 5:17, *46.* John 1:12-13, *47.* Romans 8:19, *48.* Ephesians 4:13, *49.* Revelation 3:21a, *50.* Luke 15:20-23, *51.* Revelation 3:21b, *52.* Exodus 14:14, 33:14, 23:28,

53. John 5:42, ***54.*** Genesis 5:24, Hebrews 12:18-24, ***55.*** Revelation 12:11, ***56.*** Romans 8:14, ***57.*** Judges 6:11-12, ***58.*** Deuteronomy 8:3, 1 Corinthians 4:20, Matthew 3:11, Luke 24:49, Zechariah 4:6, ***59.*** John 14:12, Ephesians 4:13, ***60.*** 1 Corinthians 14:1-5, ***61.*** Mark 3:13-15, ***62.*** Revelation 3:22, ***63.*** Matthew 16:17, 18:10, ***64.*** Acts 2:17, Revelation 1:10, ***65.*** Galatians 5:22-23, ***66.*** Isaiah 11:1-4, ***67.*** Isaiah 11:3, ***68.*** 1 Corinthians 10:13, ***69.*** Mark 3:13-15, ***70.*** Psalm 16:11, ***71.*** Galatians 5:22-23, ***72.*** John 1:18, ***73.*** Exodus 19:6, ***74.*** Acts 2:17, ***75.*** 1 Timothy 1:19, ***76.*** 2 Corinthians 1:20, ***77.*** John 17:20-24, ***78.*** 1 John 4:8, 16, ***79.*** 2 Corinthians 5:17, ***80.*** Matthew 24:15-16, ***81.*** Revelation 3:10, ***82.*** Isaiah 34:4, 51:6, Luke 21:33, Revelation 6:14, 21:1, ***83.*** John 14:6, ***84.*** 2 Corinthians 11:14, ***85.*** John 8:44, ***86.*** 2 Corinthians 4:3-4, ***87.*** John 5:17, ***88.*** Hebrews 4:11, Mark 3:13-15 *NKJV,* John 17:20-24, 8:14, 14:5-6, 7:34, 14:1-3, 10:27, 12:26, ***89.*** Romans 5:20-21, ***90.*** Isaiah 58:5, 2 Chronicles 7:14, Daniel 10:12, ***91.*** Isaiah 64:1-4, ***92.*** Luke 22:35-36, John 20:19-23, ***93.*** Isaiah 11:1-4, ***94.*** Luke 24:49, ***95.*** Revelation 2:29, ***96.*** 2 Chronicles 7:14

Dated: 25/8/21

35. *The Person of God with us (#118)*
BLUEPRINTS FROM HEAVEN

In continuation from the previous chapter ...

I have a strange question that I would like to ask: *1.* As a Christian, are you still in Noah's time? *2.* As a Christian, are you still in the Exodus? ... I mean in your thinking. *3.* Or are you still, in your thinking, in Israel at the time of Jesus? *4.* Or otherwise, as a Christian, are you yet living in the Victory? Living in the Resurrection Power of the Book of Acts ... *ever* held in the Mind of the Christ? [1]

In our current generation, the Christian Church has generally been so focused on being — 'good little Christians'. Whilst it's the Father who has been focused on **raising** you in Power [2]. Is driven in His own Purpose of raising you in **your Destiny** — raising you in your **sonship made manifest on earth**. That is, as 'little gods' [3]. Not 'sons' or 'daughters' in word alone ... but **manifest**, *ie;* made flesh and living amongst us [4]. Hence being 'good' is not your destination, but is something you 'do' on the way ... however, walking in the Glory of God is.

Acts 10:38 *(NKJV)*
God anointed Jesus of Nazareth with the Holy Spirit and with Power, who went about **doing good** and healing all who were oppressed by the devil, for God [the Glory of God] was with Him.

1. God anointed Jesus of Nazareth with the Holy Spirit ... and with Power.
2. Who went about doing good.
3. And healing all who were oppressed by the devil.
4. For the Glory of God was with Him.

First came the 'Invitation' of the Christ ... through the finished work of the Cross, now one can liberally engage the Person of God in Glory. Engage, regarding all issues of life and all that life presents ... *releasing* Him forward. And so, as you go on in life, it is God Himself whom shall continue to raise you — '**attaining** to the

whole measure of the **fullness** of Christ'. [5] For this is the fundamental Purpose of the biblical text, and the purpose of all the testimonies of all who went before us. And is God's Dream at work — in you [6] — through the Power of the Spirit of God.

So I say to you, **welcome** to the University of Heaven! Welcome to the personal Tutorship of the Son — walking in the Glory of God made manifest on earth. In Glory and ever-increasing Glory [7]. Just as this opening Scripture verse says, not only 'doing good' ... but coming to '**walk in the Power of God because God with us**'.

The theme of this chapter is how Moses ascended the Mountain of the Lord, and received blueprints and plans for what God had for him and his people. And how God brought a Light to 'glow' on his face that was not from this earth but came from standing in the Glory of God [8]. For fundamentally, there are always the two purposes to Encounter: **1.** Grace, Wisdom, and Knowledge for current situations, and **2.** Divine 'Countenance of God'. Meaning, the Person of God with you — in Person — wherever you go in undeniable reality. [9]

I often say that Mount Sinai was the unspoken *first* Temple of God. Not made by human hands ... but was untouched by man. And just as with the Temple of Solomon; there was the 'Inner Court' by where the Church came and congregated. However **today**, in Christ, it is Jesus Himself who has availed perfect opportunity to come up upon His Holy Mountain; or, as in regards the Temple ... perfect opportunity to enter the Holy Place. That is, enter into the quiet ministering Presence, in the Delight of the Lord, to **receive directly** from Him. But what is also truly magnificent to realise ... is the Holy of Holies. This, the Hidden and Secret Place of the Most High ... the dwelling in the 'All-Consuming Fire' [10] whereby God imparts Hidden and Secret things of Glory. [8]

Then here, situated in the Holy of Holies was the Ark of the Covenant. The Ark whereby the Cherubim were set in physical representation of true and as very real spiritual guards [11]. This is why death and awe always surrounded the Ark, for man was by no means permitted to pass through. [12]

Hence now, through your own heart of 'invitation' — *ie;* in your humility and honour; through a heart of whom freely lays their life down in death — only to freely pick it up again in the realms of Life [13] — does one pass through. Jesus is both the Resurrection and the Life, I tell you, this is so much bigger than you think. And it is to this that you have been called: not unto the things that have passed but unto the **Newness** of Life. The very focus being now — **beyond the Cross** [14] — unto Resurrection Life and Power.

— Noah's flood —
— the Exodus —
— the time of Christ —
— and the Resurrected Life —

And so it is, that unto a right heart *(I really want you to get this!)* and only unto a right heart do you pass through [10]. For believing is not enough. The Word connecting to reality — the Word walking amongst us — you, yourself, becoming the **embodiment** of the Christ.

For it is through *inviting* Jesus … preciously, ever inviting and asking the Holy Spirit and the Father — welcoming Him, loving and honouring Him — and not loving your life unto death [15] — does God personally lead you into realms unspeakable. This, for the blessing of your own life, but also unto the exceedingly great blessing to the world. The Glory and Power of God stepping through you unto the honour of the Son.

This was the 'Way of the Son', even the very 'summation' of the Word of God. The underlying purpose of the Cross and gifted Spirit of God: that we too might walk in *like* [16] — **AS the Son** on earth. He, our Saviour, even our very Living personal Picture and Example … He our trailblazer.

Theme Scripture:
v10-11 Then the LORD said to Moses, "Go to the people and consecrate them today and tomorrow, and let them **wash** their clothes. And let them be ready for the **third day** [17] For on the third day the LORD will come down upon Mount Sinai in the **sight** of all the people.

ᵛ¹⁷ And Moses brought the people out of the camp to meet with God, and they stood at the foot of the mountain.
ᵛ²⁰ Then the LORD came down upon Mount Sinai, on the top of the mountain. And the LORD called Moses to the top of the mountain, and **Moses <u>went up</u>**. *(Exodus 19:10-11, 17, 20 NKJV)*

This particular account of the Exodus story is powerful and a most relevant picture for you and I today in our current and everyday life. In the problems you face, in the sanity of your soul, and your ministry and calling on earth.

The here, learning to 'Walk according to the Spirit' where His Grace and Power lays richly upon your life. The Presence of the Person of God with you; and here, being brought up to stand in the realms of Counsel, Understanding, and Might [18]. These, your friends and companions; ever surrounded by the Spirits of God.

However, the truth is, that you can never truly step into these areas of rich engagement, without truly giving your life over to the Lord [19]. And this 'giving of yourself' can be often tested. Meaning, **1.** Satan never wants you returning into these realms of Glory, lest you tower over him. And **2.** God has intent and purpose that you connect deeper in Him [20]. That all things be converted into a blessing [21] — as one being established and made stronger and ever more powerful in Him.

For it is only through trials and 'testing' that gold is made pure; able to reflect more the Glory of God. Your roots growing more established ever deeper in the fullness of God ... where it is said, *"Nothing shall be impossible for you"* [22]. Self-pity and fear, lust and desires; these are all of the old ways ... and the answer is not found in them. But only in the Presence of God.

This chapter is centred around the Exodus story, where God would give Moses blueprints and plans for the times and seasons they were in. And how Moses was personally led by God, and where the Presence of the Person of God was most Powerfully with him — as one *untouchable*. And how God purposed it in Himself to bless the nation, leading them ever further into a greater 'possessing of the land'. These 'unknown lands' that are to us flowing with great 'riches' and wonder. [23]

It is most important for us to realise, that all Promises and Purposes of God are 'yes' and 'amen' [24] for us who are called by His Name. But even more so, whereby the very Person of God Himself comes and walks Powerfully with you — in His Person — and wars against everything that comes against. And how, as a people, you are Destined to become an unstoppable force; a powerful force of reckoning in the world [25]. With Lord Himself carrying you as like a lamb clutched in His arms [26]. But at the same time, working to **raise** you as a **lion that roars**; as an eagle that rules in high and lofty places. [27]

This very same is purposed for all in Christ Jesus, today ... this very day. And if you are really serious about life, if you are really serious about the things of God: how by the Blood of Jesus, you have this exact same opportunity in God — if not *greater* — than that of Moses and all the Greats of Old [28]. But it is a choice, isn't it? It is a decided decision made within you personally to step into ... no one can make you. The here, continually opening yourself up to the Power and Fire of the Holy Ghost. [29]

But again, it is true isn't it? ... that **humility** is key. For if you really truly want to be healed and made strong, even then as one who releases the very Healing and Strength of God; then we must needs learn to submit and humble ourselves ... and **seek His Face**. [30]

For so it is, that in our current present age, the believer has forgotten God. And when I say 'forgotten' ... one may know His Name and can quote Scripture; but as a people, you have forgotten how to walk in the Spirit — powerful as in the Book of Acts [31]. And when the believer does choose to seek the Lord, the 'humbling of oneself' can be more like that of a 'reed bowing in the wind' [32] ... and that is why Christians fail.

These pursuits of God that we are speaking of, are serious pursuits for serious and committed people. And just as does these very same *pursuits* bring about very serious results. Even then, as one who is continually taken Places in God that man has no comprehension or idea [33]. For such are brought into the 'Knowledge' of God — hearing and seeing Him — with God bearing great testimony of His Goodness through their lives [34] ... through great signs and wonders. [35]

To begin ...

In this chapter, I'd like to focus on these three main points, as referenced in the opening theme Scripture:
   1. 'Consecrate' yourself.
   2. Stand at the foot of 'the Mountain'.
   3. Respond to the invitation and 'come up' upon the Mountain of God.

Let's modernise these Old Testament references in Christ Jesus:
   1. Set yourself apart unto Christ.
   2. Sit at the feet of Jesus. [36]
   3. Respond to the invitation and come up in Him right where you are. [37]

Just as in the Exodus, the Blood of the Lamb *(ie; the 'Passover')*; the shed Blood of Jesus, has firmly set you apart and birthed you as a People of God. And water Baptism *(ie; the Red Sea)* has set Egypt *(the world)* behind you and placed you on the path of the Promise. And just the same as in the Exodus, how you personally choose to move forward is totally up to you. For the answer is not found in the old ways but the New ... following Jesus; walking with He who is the 'Light of Life'. [38]

Now, this picture of 'consecration' is always about the clear and purposed intent: to meet, to hear, and to see God [39]. It's not about seeking acceptance or approval, for you are already part of the Beloved. Consecration and sanctification remain this: the single-eyed heart's desire and set purpose ... an expression of preparedness to receive; to go somewhere or to meet someone of great importance. And so it is with God, and in this are you simply following the Way of the Christ; [40] meeting with 'His God and Father'.

***So hence**,*
The coming up upon the 'mountain' — *ie;* the Holy Place — and meeting with the Person of God, is the Way of inner healing and restoration. The Way of being made whole, and the Way of Empowerment and the Anointing of God. [41]

***Even then in God**,*
Entering into 'Places' where you are continually being captured up in Him — into things and places man cannot take you — only the Lord. Ever positioning yourself as one being ever transformed; as one 'transfigured' into Creatures of Light. [42]

***As pictured with Moses**,*
It's most important to realise just how much God desires to give you blueprints and plans … *meaning,* imparted Counsel and Knowledge and Strength regarding your life in Him; as well as all the needs before you and all that will ever face. And how He also wants to guide you in the midst of all things, even as one personally standing with you: to fight and war on your behalf. And just as with the people in the Exodus: the Kingdom of God is about taking possession of the 'Promises' *(the Promised Land),* as is said, *"All the nations of the earth will be blessed."* [43]

***However, this picture continues on further**,*
For by the Holy Spirit — held and deeply cherished within you — God seeks to raise you further in your sonship. Not as servants, but as children in Heavenly Places of Divine Authority and Standing [44], to speak over life and death; moving both Heaven and earth as one in Him. Sanctification therefore means — no separation, no distinction — but perfect union [45]. You in Him and He in you — seamless — that the 'world may know that the Father sent the Son'.

Picture then yourself as one in the Exodus … and here, who would you wish or desire to be? Today, in Christ Jesus you can be anyone: **1.** A whiner and a complainer. **2.** One who remains 'standing at a distance'. **3.** Otherwise, a 'Moses' of whom goes up upon the Mountain. **4.** Better still, a 'Joshua' who never leaves this tent of 'meetings' [46]. As one living in continual dialogue — in perpetual Encounter — in the Lord. Who went on to lead the people into the 'Promised Land'. Leading the people through all that came against them in the Might and Power of God. This is your Destiny in Christ Jesus.

In this chapter, we are focusing on the time in the Exodus where God led the people to meet with Him at Mount Sinai. And just to say again, Mount Sinai was the *first* Tabernacle of God. It was the very first Meeting Place of the Person of God for all the people. Not a tent or a temple made by human hands, but made by the Hand of God. Then afterwards, the Tabernacle was made, which was known as the 'Tent of Meetings'. Then years later, we know, the Temple was built, the Temple that King Solomon made of stone.

The importance of what I am trying to raise here, is that as believers — as disciples of our Lord Jesus Christ — you and I have something far greater than these 'old' physical places of meeting. That through the Blood of Jesus, you and I have right of passage to pass on through into the original Temple of God that is in Heaven. That within yourself, the Temple of God is now held within you … even as a Gateway unto Zion. A very Gateway unto the Original Temple that is in Heaven; destined and purposed for all who love the Lord.

Hence, this is why the New Covenant is so far superior than the Old. For you are now able to engage with the very Person of God Himself — with Him where He is — in Heavenly Places [47]. Not a 'copy' or a 'shadow' thereof, but behind the Curtain … right behind the 'veil' that separates. [48]

But love is key … not law, a 'hope' that goes behind the Curtain seeking the very Lord Himself. And in this, everything shall follow.

On a side note: If one cannot receive what I'm sharing here, how can they ever step into an unlimited life? How can they ever step into the Glory realms where you are unlimitedly provided and unlimitedly made successful? Your destiny is not to remain under but raise above … not to be the tail but the head. Hence, the way this is achieved is to become like David, who sought only to 'gaze upon the beauty of the Lord'. [49]

For so much in 'prayer' has been only the seeking answer to needs and wants. When true breakthrough comes by seeking God. Not denying praying for needs — but the true 'prayer of the Lord' is unto the Garden realms; the realms of meeting, dining, and being relocated in Him. Transformation, as from a practical 'task-based' believer ... unto the 'fullness' of the Mind of Christ.

The 'Jericho' moment, was not the praying down of the walls of Jericho ... but worshipping and seeking God. And what was released was the 'Outpouring' of the Spirit. What am I saying? Fair enough, pray for needs ... but move on from there unto seeking Him. With the vision and the prayer unto the fullness of His Destiny fulfilled in you.

People know how to 'do' ... but not how to 'be'. But it's this 'being' that triggers Moves of God. God is more interested in transforming you and rooting you centred; that from here, He might step out through you in Glory. He will work in your 'doings' — to bless it — He will 'fight' your battles. But what He seeks is you to — be seated — in the Place He has made for you [50]. For from here, so shall you release that Fight. The Glory of God flowing liberally like 'water' ... as like a waterfall pouring out from your 'faucet'.

Hence, with this vision of soul ... your 'measure' or reference, is Christ Himself. Not people, nor success or failure; not church size, or the respect of others; not problems or issues ... but the Presence of God. For from here, God works and does His Will; and from here, the Spirit of God is outpoured; and from here, God Anoints you in Power and Authority ... extending your arm out of Zion, saying, "Rule in the midst of your enemies".

LATENT MINDSETS

In the modern contemporary Church ... the problem remains, that many in the 'Christian faith' have still been walking in the mindset of an 'Old Testament' believer. Even with *latent* or residual thinking of that of an 'Israelite' ... rather than that of embracing the Mind and Risen state of the Christ — alive in you. And 'going about doing good' [51] as good faithful Christians ... but forgetting about the Resurrection Power. Even the fact that Christ Jesus is the Victory in us; and focusing on where **He personally desires** to take you. [51]

For just as the Apostles of old, you are not called only to 'admire' the Temple from the outside ... but to pass on through and enter in. Just as Jesus said, *"Each and every stone shall be torn down"* [52]. Therefore, so it is the same for us, that in all things, our old human mindsets must be torn down — 'every single stone'. And here, in the Person of the Lord, so shall you be continually raised and so shall you be continually built up in your thinking — in perspective and in station — unto the very Likeness of the Christ. [53]

So again, the importance of the picture of Mount Sinai: is the meeting with the Person of God. For these things cannot be given of man. For though we can teach one another, and we can encourage and impart to a degree; these things of Glory can only be given of He to whom you point [54]. The only Answer and the only Doorway is — the Person of Christ Jesus.

> *Sanctification isn't about being squeaky clean. It is about the giving of ourselves more complete and more fully unto God.*

Therefore, here and now, let us continue to choose to sanctify ourselves **in His Holy Presence** *(the realms of deep Acceptance and Love)*. Setting ourselves ever more firmly apart in 'death', that we truly might be made 'Alive' in God. Even then ... being made able by Him ... to truly **participate** in His Glory. As a people ever responding to the Call: the clothing of ourselves with the Immortality, the clothing of ourselves with Glory and the Power of the Most High God *(the 'child-of-God' reality)* [55]. As Jesus says, *"If anyone desires to come after me, let him deny himself, and take up his cross daily and follow me ... and **where I am my servant will be also** ... and him my Father will **honour**."* [56]

Did you know, that the Tabernacle of Old was made according to very specific and precise measurements: to that of the actual Temple of God that is in Heaven? [57] And so it is, that to this very Place ... it is God Himself that is inviting you in. Not on the earthly plain ... but in Heaven.

In today's contemporary Church, we've generally had this concept of the Presence of God 'in the building'. The Presence of God coming in and descending upon a meeting ... perhaps in worship, or in a particularly anointed gathering. But what God is talking about here, is you being with Him 'where He is' — **in His**

Presence — Above all things in Heavenly Places [58], and meeting Him here. [59]

It is true, that these things have been so missed over the generations. Hence a blindness has remained, a 'forgetfulness' [60] ... therefore also, a weakness. For Power and Authority is given only of God; not to live any longer as a fallen man but as He who is risen.

The modern-day believer has only recognised the Blood as for the remission of sin. But it is so much more than that; the Blood is itself the very Key that re-opens up the Way between you and the Glory realms; the realms of the Kingdom of God, the realms of Heaven, the wondrous realms of God's Presence and Power and Dominion. For so upon the Mercy Seat has the Blood been poured out and the Cherubim part way [61]. Therefore, the Cross was never intended to be the 'final destination', but the very Doorway that you pass through. The *"Going in and out"* just as you please ... and *"Finding pasture"* [62]. This, not unto a physical place made by human hands, but right into the Eternal realms of the Most High God ... the Place 'where He is'. [63]

So here — from the other side of the Curtain — Jesus Himself is saying, *"Even the least of the Kingdom is greater than they"* [65]. Or in another place, *"You will do even greater works than I, for I go unto the Father"* [66]. For the opportunity afforded you by the Blood today, is so far superior than anything that came before. And therefore also, so far superior to anything that you might face in life, or any offering or lure presented to you in this world.

So the awareness now, is on the importance of consecration, *ie;* 'cleaning your clothes'. For you have already been made clean and set apart by the Blood. But, however, the focus of your mind and your heart's 'thought-life' can remain unclean and misdirected. As Jesus says, *"Your thought-life defiles you."* [67]

Hence, in the exact same way as the 'serving priests' of the Temple of God, so are you also called to sanctify yourself. The humbling of yourself, and putting aside unholy things; with the clear intent and purpose of — entering into the Holy Place — to meet, to sit, and to see God. And this regardless of where you are.

On a side note: I tell you a most important trick in regards sanctification and holiness. It is God who is fundamentally about meeting you where you are at. A heart that is honest and true ... God is drawn to. As is said, "He heard my cry, and stepped off His throne and inclined his ear to me." [68]

It doesn't matter where you are or what you have just been involved with; a true reaching out to God — a true 'cry' — a true calling out to the Lord, deeply draws God. Even from the gutter of your drunkenness and sin, as is said, "I have wiped away your sins like the morning mist, **return** *to me for I have redeemed you"* [69]. *Hence the focus is never where you have been ... but where God is taking you. Strength and Power to win — Grace and a renewed Vision — comes from Him.*

Therefore, make it ever the **root culture of your soul** *to seek the Face of God ... and enjoy the Presence and Divine Visitations of the Lord. Why then not prioritise it? For the inherent structure and mechanism has always been within you ... but now is being re-enlivened. The Joy of the Lord is just the 'scent' of Him, the feeling stronger. But what we seek is the volume to be turned up and up and up ... until we each burst into luminous beings.*

The Blood of Jesus is singularly the most powerful thing in the universe, next to the Name of Jesus and the Spirit of God. It is singularly the very reason why you are who you are: you are part of the Redeemed, you are part of the Beloved and Cherished, as too have you been made king and priest unto God.

But in thinking of the Temple of God; the mindset of the believer is much still in the vision of seeking acceptance ... even though you are already accepted. Your person **has** *crossed over into the station of a 'priest' who seeks God, instead of one who seeks forgiveness. Jesus came to bring both Spirit and Fire, you already dwell in the realms of the Spirit; therefore, the 'Upper Room' reality, the 'Holy Place' dwelling ... commands you to go into the untold Glory.*

Perhaps we can all understand a bit more where it is said, *"Without holiness no one will see the Lord"* [70]. Or in other places, *"Whoever looks at a woman to lust for her has already committed adultery with her in his heart"* [71]. And again, *"Unless you humble yourself as like a little child you will never* **see** *the Kingdom of Heaven"* [72]. For these things speak of your inner-man — with regards your own personal engagement with the Person of God. Pride of knowledge won't cut it; righteous deeds doesn't make you right. But truth to Truth, spirit to Spirit [73] ... from here within the Temple of God in Heaven. For today your spirit **has been made Alive** in Him.

So another way to express it would be, that as living, walking, temples of the Most High God ... you have the Holy of Holies within you. You yourself are the Holy Place of God, made by the very Hand and Will of God. But so it is, that here, even right in the very midst of the 'Holy Place' within you — these same places destined and purposed only for God, *ie;* your heart — one can be holding things that are unholy.

As the Temple of God, you already have been cleansed and consecrated set apart unto God. However, in your 'Holy Place' one can still hold hatred, lusts, and all kinds of wicked motives and desires.

Do you see then ... do you yet understand, just how much your heart-life is one of the most important areas in your life to manage? For out of your heart *"Springs the issues of life"* [74]. And do you also see, how this very same 'inner-man', also is the very connection point between earth and the Kingdom of Heaven? As Jesus said, *"Out of your heart the mouth speaks"* [75]. Or in another place, *"Where your treasure is there your heart is also"* [76]. For your heart truly is the 'Gateway' to God. For in truly loving God, then you would also truly pursue Him. Not wisdoms or ideas of man about God — but God Himself! And therefore, just as a 'little child', so shall your spirit-man continuously **see** the Face of God. [77]

A few chapters ago *(#33)*, I used the wording ... 'mind poo'. And for me it is a most incredible picture that primarily expresses just how much the Person of God wants to walk in and around your life ... in His Person. But how, the problem remains, that your heart-life defiles you.

What this means is, that of which you hold in your heart and thought-life, turns away the manifestation of the very physical Person of God from standing right next to you [78]. And how, in these same Scriptures referred, they are about just how much God desires to walk with you personally; to fight for you, to protect and to go out before you ... therefore, *"Your camp must be holy."*

So, as we know, our minds can be often drawn off to various things. And so too our hearts drawn off to various regrets, thoughts, or desires in ways that are unholy. And even so, our minds and our hearts can be sometimes so overwhelmed by lusts, fears, or past pains. Therefore, in this picture of Divine pursuit, *ie;* the choosing to open ourselves up ever to the Dreams and Purposes and Promises of God fulfilled and active in our lives; how we must needs learn to practice the laying down of all things down in 'death' at the feet of Jesus. That we truly might continue to open ourselves to greater and ever more deeper engagement with the Person of God.

The here, choosing to sanctify ourselves from right within the tangible Delight of the Presence of God, even unto a greater vision! This most incredible vision of having the Person of God — physically manifest — in our lives as we go about normal and regular life. As one being ministered to and taught ... and personally continually raised in the Heavenly realms. Even as a people captured up in Him unto untold Splendours.

Hence, now you know the Source of the Strength Christ Jesus lived in [79]. The very same of which He openly demonstrated in His life ... and through the Gospel He taught. For so has He opened up the Way for us also, the very same reality — to live and do just as He — through His own death and Resurrection. But so is it most true ... that so few are entering in. [80]

Humility and honour, invitation and the laying your life down as though in death; this is what opens you up to liberally receive. Pride and dishonour, indifference and holding on; these are the things that keep the Door closed ... and these are the things that cause deception to rule.

Let's imagine the scene again, as expressed in Exodus chapter 19 ...

Scripture says, that *"Three months to-the-day"* after leaving Egypt, the people came and *"Encamped at the Mountain of the Lord"*. And how the people were called to sanctify themselves ready ... ready to meet the very Person of God at Mount Sinai. And as we know the people were not permitted to come near the Mountain; God did not let them — opportunity came only by invitation.

So, as the story goes, anyone who tried to force their way through ... *died*. The Glory of God was — not permitted man — except through invitation [81]. Hence, it's most important and most valuable today for us to realise; that now in Christ Jesus, this *same* invitation that was presented Moses, has now been presented the believer.

So to conclude: Sanctification means, 'a heart firmly set apart unto God'. The here, retaining always a clear and firm intent and purpose to meet, to engage, to hear, and to see Him ... and allow the Glory of God to pour out [82]. As is said, *"I have* **come** *to pour out* **Fire on the earth** *and how I wish it was already kindled"* [83]. And what is this? The Glory of the Lord poured out, the Will of God done on earth just as liberally and as freely as it is in Heaven; the Spirit of the Lord moving, the Angels of God going out far and wide, and the *"The earth filled with the knowledge of the Glory of the LORD, as the waters cover the sea."* [84]

It is not about seeking approval or acceptance, but about the gaining of greater security and strength and revelation — as you sit with Him. As a people continually being built up by the Person of God in your sonship. Meaning, deepening personal revelation of who God is ... who you are ... and who you are in Him. And how this opens you continually, to being perpetually poured into from the realms of the Glory of God. This for the blessing of your own life ... and to that of your people.

Perhaps now you are coming to understand the meaning of the 'Upper Room' experiences a bit more [85]. For so it is, that the believer is called of God to be a Portal, a 'Ladder' — an open Gateway of the Kingdom and Glory realms of God on earth — and this in ever-expanding measure. Such is the Power of the Spirit. Such is the Power of the Fire of God that Jesus **commanded His Disciples to <u>wait</u> for**.

So hence then, this Scripture shall become true for you also, you shall go out into the world as true 'witnesses' unto the Lord — in **open demonstrable Power** — as in the Book of Acts. For as Jesus says, *"You shall receive power when the Holy Spirit has come upon you; and you shall be witnesses to Me in Jerusalem, and in all Judea and Samaria, and to the end of the earth."* [86]

IN CLOSING

To the people in the Exodus, God clearly stated that they were not permitted to come up upon the Mountain. However, today, it is Jesus Himself who is asking, who is inviting you to be like *Moses* ... and freely come up upon the Mountain of the Lord [87]. But even more so — be taken into Places where man is not permitted.

Another name for this Place would be the 'Equipping Zone' [88] or the 'Garden realms' ... the eating of the Tree of Life [89] and here 'gazing on the beauty of the Lord' [90]. Meaning, one-to-one walking with the Person of God; receiving Counsel and Wisdom, Might and Power [91] for the seasons that are before you. Blueprints and plans directly from the Person of God ... continuously! Even then, in Christ Jesus — being converted by Him — **into Him**. Into Him as a Person, in Likeness; and into Him where He is now. Ultimately then to **win**! As one laying captive and taking [92] 'possession' of the land to the blessings of it ... and for you and your people. [93]

So just to repeat, the invitation has been offered ... but it is **up to you to enter**, it is up to you to draw close [94]. The Word of God speaks of it as, *"Strive to enter the Rest of the Lord"* [95]. Work and 'strive' to enter the Place *where* you constantly receive and are constantly nourished. Striving always to enter the Place of 'Repose' [96] ... where you are given continually of the Lord.

A side note ... the 'Place of Repose': It is always a battle to enter the Rest of the Lord; the Abiding Place, the realms of God's Love, Peace, and Surety [97]. *This Place where we hear and see the Lord ... the 'remaining' in His Counsel and Might. For everything Satan is about is to draw you out of these realms of Receiving* [98]. *For as you are poured into from God, with your mouth ever open, so are you terrifying to the demon. Hence we seek the 'Presence of God' ... we seek the Face of God as a firm culture of soul; do we peer through all things unto the Glory and Fire of God. For such who live like this also release and pour out the very same.*

But as we know, as demonstrated by the people in the Exodus story; the hearts of the people were always 'back on Egypt'. Always set upon worldly affairs, concerns, and desires. Therefore, so it is just the same today, the many fail to enter into the More that God has for each of us ... hence the world suffers. [99]

So in this we make firm change ... we are **not** like them*!* For we personally make a choice to draw our hearts firmly unto God in all things, especially in testing times *('Desert' trials)*. And here, learn and are encouraged to sanctify ourselves; setting our hearts firmly in Him, rather than to the realities of this life. As King David would say, *"Delight yourself in the Lord, and He will give you the desires of your heart."* [100]

I so encourage you to *sanctify* yourself before God. And give Him greater place to 'walk amongst' you. Drawing your heart ever to Him ... 'entering the Place of Rest' ... that God may continue to take you into the realms of the 'Untouchable'. Into the realms of the 'Blessed and Anointed'. For God deeply desires to raise you as one who Conquers and takes possession. Takes possession of this 'Land flowing with Milk and Honey'. Even these, the Heavenly 'Lands' of endless Supply and Wonder.

Therefore, meeting with God is key. Not man, not your own understanding or that of others; but always coming to God Himself and building tighter bonds of relationship with Him personally ... as He with you. As Jesus says, *"Very truly I tell you, the Son can do nothing by Himself; He can do only what He sees his Father doing"* [101]. And so it is then, that this 'level' of engagement allows you to walk in ever greater measure in Likeness of the Son ... just as we are called.

Again, another way to say it, sanctification means the laying down of your dreams ... only then to pick up the Dreams of God. Even He who is the fulfiller of dreams. The dispossessing of your own life for His — and in this all Heaven becoming yours. That is, all that belongs to Jesus now belongs to you as well. [102]

Do you remember how Jesus says, *"Wherever your treasure is your heart is also?"* [103] Here and now, you are simply positioning yourself — by where you set your heart upon. Make sense? Do you understand yet, that where your heart truly is ... so too your inner-man is also? This is why trials and tribulations are of such value, for your roots become more deeply established in Him; tried, tested, and true. And this is why we consider it all joy in the midst of hardships. For either the plant fails or is made stronger ... as we respond and learn to 'seek the 'Face of God.' [104]

For the result of seasons of 'drought' *(ie; hard times)* is that your roots may go down deep in God. Even then being made able to draw ever deeper from Him regardless and irrespective of the season. [105]

So the moral of the story is, that if you can truly make the Person of God your treasure; then like a true trusted foundation, can God truly begin to build Himself up powerfully upon your life. For as we read in Scripture, *"Jesus would not entrust himself to them for He knew what was in their heart"* [106]. Hence today, God knows your heart and responds ... drawing nearer and dearer.

As Moses was invited to come up upon the Mountain of God, he was not only led upon the Mountain where God was — but into Places and realms of intensities where Moses became afraid [107]. As we also read, the Glory of God was so intense that he 'trembled with fear.' [108]

However now, in Christ Jesus, as one responding to the invitation of God; so are you coming up into the realms *"Above the mountains"* to Mount Zion [109]. Into the New City ... the Heavenly Jerusalem, *"With thousands upon thousands of angels in joyful assembly."* [110]

So as the story goes, Moses asked God to see His Glory, but was told that it was not permitted. And as we know, God hid him in a cleft of a rock to protect him, shielding Moses by His own hand as he went by [111]. However today, you and I have something different ... we are entering into the *"Church of the firstborn"*; the very Church of those born Alive in Him, here right before the Glory of God. Hence the Places we are called to go into are realms greater than Moses was permitted.

A side note: Did you know that Moses and Aaron and the Seventy Elders were, at one time, invited and brought up in their human bodily form right up upon the Sea of Glass? And here ate a meal with God with all of creation under their feet? [112]

It really is important for you to recognise; just how much God wants to make you more than who you are. But this does not come from our own capacities or understanding but from where God Himself takes you. Therefore, recognise most truly, that as we continue to humble ourselves before God ... does He set us in Places of High Honour. It's very precious.

Perhaps you can understand this phrase a bit more, 'Seek the Face of God'. For in this, do we delight in the cleansing of our heart and thought-life, and all inner motives and desires — with firm intent to 'see' God, *ie;* engage with God manifest and most real.

For we know that the finished work of the Cross has cleansed us from all wrongdoing. And so it is that here, from right within the Presence of God, from right within the Place of Acceptance and Divine engagements, that we pull out of our hearts all unholy lusts and desires ... that we might truly continually go on further in [113] ... fully unhindered.

Are you now coming into understanding the New Testament meaning of, *"Walk according to the Spirit?"* [114] The things I am talking about here are not about being 'flesh' focused ... but Spirit focus. And how, by these very same things, shall you become a powerful force of reckoning in the world.

So, as I would say, if it was right for Moses to ask God to see Him in His Glory, then it is right for you to do as well. Not only so, but Jesus Himself exampled this very reality by the very same lifestyle, *ie;* by the way He lived.

So I deeply encourage you, if you truly have compassion for the world ... if you truly wish to help people, even that of your loved ones; the answer is not in yourself, but in He of whom you position yourself. Even in these very same Places where you see God in His Glory [115]. Regardless of season ... let this remain the root and core motive and prayer of your soul. For where your treasure truly is, there your heart is also.

In all things … and through all things; in worship and in praise; when reading the word or listening to a message; in good times and bad times; in all seasons … for truly, as a 'lord' in Jesus's eyes, so is Jesus Lord in your eyes. And to such so does He respond.

Scripture:
Then the LORD said to Moses, "Leave this place, you and the people you brought up out of Egypt, and go up to the land I promised on oath to Abraham, Isaac and Jacob, saying, 'I will give it to your descendants.' I will **send an <u>angel</u> before you** and drive out the Canaanites, Amorites, Hittites, Perizzites, Hivites and Jebusites. Go up to the land flowing with milk and honey. But **I will <u>not</u> go with you**, because you are a stiff-necked people and I might destroy you on the way." *(Exodus 33:1-2 NKJV)*

The Power and Wonder of having God with us — in Person. Today, God is saying to you, "***<u>Leave this place</u>*** *and go on*". This story is very much the same for us as well, so let's do that*!* I so encourage you, leave your thinking, and the ways that you have known behind, and continue to go on deeper into the Promises. It is God who has 'promised on oath' — to lead the church forward — through the finished work of the Cross. But just as God said, He wants to personally walk with you in Fire and Power … ***but*** … *"You are a stiff-necked people."*

In closing, I want to emphasise again this word 'gateway'. That in the Person of Christ Jesus, you are a 'portal' destined and purposed of God, for Him to step through you … but are you willing? Is this truly something that you desire?

Closing Scripture:
The Father **loves** the Son, and **shows Him all things** that He Himself does; and He will show Him greater works than these, that you may marvel. *(John 14:12 NKJV)*

I speak this over your life this day, *"The Father **loves** you."* And He deeply desires to **show** you all that He does, and even greater works than these ... that **all may marvel**.

So again, I ask, if you really want to be powerful and effective. If you really want to **win** and live life Victorious and Triumphant. If you really want God with you powerfully working in every part of your life. And if you really want to be given strategies and plans; blueprints from Heaven for what is in front of you. Then you need to come up where Moses himself went. And even more so, where Jesus went before us and **has made the Way**.

So to finish then, reflecting on this precious Scripture in Exodus, we are also called to '**leave this place**'; that is, we are called to 'move on with God' ... and not 'stay where we are'. For it is God who wants to continue to **lead us all** further into all the Promises of God. Lead each of us deeper into all that is ours. So you can't stay any longer where you are; in your thinking, in your attitudes, or in your ways ... but move on from here in God, amen?

Let's pray, *"Lord, I desire to humble myself before you Lord, I deeply desire to give my life more fully into your hands. I desire to give my cares and desires, give my fears and dreams. Lord, I give you my life, please lead me in the fullness of your Heart and Dreams. Lord, I receive the Blood of Jesus upon my life, and sanctify my heart anew this day. Please lead me to come up upon the Mountain of the Lord, that I might be ministered to personally by God Almighty ... in all things ... just as the Christ. This I pray in Jesus Name, amen."*

Appendix:

1. 1 Corinthians 2:16, Colossians 3:3, *2.* Acts 10:38, *3.* Psalm 82:6-8, John 10:34-36, 1:12-13, 20:19-23, Matthew 16:17-19, Mark 16:17-19, *4.* John 1:14, *5.* Ephesians 4:13, John 17:21, *6.* John 17:21, *7.* 2 Corinthians 3:18, *8.* Exodus 34:34-35, John 20:24, *9.* Exodus 33:1-3, 13-18, *10.* Isaiah 33:14b-15a *HCSB*, Psalm 24:3-4a, *11.* Genesis 3:24, *12.* Revelation 2:7, *13.* John 10:17, *14.* Colossians 3:1, *15.* Revelation 12:11, *16.* Genesis 1:26, 5:1-3, 1 Corinthians 15:45, Romans 5:17, 2 Corinthians 3:18, *17.* Acts 10:40, *18.* Isaiah 11:2-3, Zechariah 3:7, John 17:24, 12:26, 8:12,

19. John 12:24, *20.* Deuteronomy 8:3,16-18, *21.* Romans 8:28, *22.* Matthew 17:20, 2 Corinthians 12:9-11, 2 Corinthians 3:18, *23.* Deuteronomy 26:9, *24.* 2 Corinthians 1:20, *25.* Exodus 14:14, Psalm 82:6-8, Matthew 16:18, Romans 8:31, *26.* Isaiah 40:11, *27.* Isaiah 40:31, Zechariah 3:7, Isaiah 33:14b-15a *HCSB,* Psalm 24:3-4a, *28.* Matthew 11:11, *29.* Acts 1:8, Mark 16:17-18, John 5:36-37, *30.* 2 Chronicles 7:14-15, Daniel 10:12, *31.* Deuteronomy 6:10-12, *32.* Isaiah 58:5, *33.* 1 Corinthians 2:9-10, John 8:21, 14:4-6, Exodus 19:23, Genesis 3:24, Isaiah 2:2-5, Zechariah 3, Luke 10:21, Matthew 17:1-2, Exodus 24:9-11, John 10:9, Revelation 4:1, *34.* Isaiah 53:1, John 3:11, *35.* John 5:36-37, 5:44, Mark 16:17-18, Matthew 11:21, *36.* Mark 3:13-15, *37.* Isaiah 2:1-4, *38.* John 8:12, Exodus 13:21, *39.* John 5:19, *40.* Luke 5:15-17, *41.* Revelation 1-3, *42.* 2 Corinthians 5:17, 1 Thessalonians 5:5, Isaiah 40:31, *43.* Genesis 22:17-18, *44.* Zechariah 3:7, *45.* John 17:20-24, *46.* Exodus 33:11, *47.* Hebrews 12:18-24, *48.* Hebrews 6:19, Genesis 3:24, *49.* Psalm 27:4, *50.* John 14:2-6, *51.* Acts 10:38, *52.* Mark 13:1-2, *53.* Luke 6:40, *54.* Matthew 23:8-12, 1 Corinthians 2:9-10, John 3:14-15, *55.* 1 Corinthians 15:53, Luke 24:49, Revelation 3:17-18 *(Luke 14:28-33),* *56.* Luke 9:23, John 12:26, 5:44, *57.* Hebrews 8:5, *58.* Mark 3:13-15, John 3:13, 14:3-6, 17:24, 5:19, 13:3, 33, 36, *59.* Exodus 24:9-11, *60.* Deuteronomy 6:10-12, *61.* Genesis 3:24, Exodus 25:17-22, Hebrews 9:5, 12, Revelation 2:7, 22:1-2, *62.* John 10:9, 14:6, *63.* Mark 3:13-15, John 3:13, 14:3-6, 17:24, 5:19, 13:3, 33, 36, *65.* Matthew 11:11, *66.* John 14:12, *67.* Matthew 15:11, *68.* Psalm 116:1-2, *69.* Isaiah 44:22, Psalm 18:6, 40:2, Romans 10:13, *70.* Hebrews 12:14, *71.* Matthew 5:28, *72.* Matthew 18:3, *73.* John 4:23-24, *74.* Proverbs 4:23, *75.* Luke 6:45, *76.* Matthew 6:21, *77.* Matthew 18:10, *78.* Deuteronomy 23:13-14, Exodus 33:1-3, Matthew 15:11, *79.* John 5:19, *80.* Matthew 7:14, *81.* Genesis 3:24, Numbers 4:15, Hebrews 9:7, *82.* Isaiah 40:3-5, Colossians 3:1-4, John 17:24, Revelation 1:10, 17, Psalm 91, Exodus 33, Acts 5:15, *83.* Luke 3:16, 12:49, 24:49, *84.* Habakkuk 2:14, Joel 2:28, Acts 2:17, Matthew 6:9-10, *85.* Luke 24:49, *86.* Acts 1:8, *87.* Isaiah 2:1-4, *88.* Revelation 3:17-22, Psalm 110:2, *89.* Genesis 3:24, Revelation 2:7, *90.* Psalm 27:4, John 17:24, *91.* Jeremiah 23:22, Isaiah 11:1-4, 92. Matthew 11:12, *93.* Genesis 1:26, *94.* James 4:8, *95.* Hebrews 4:11, *96.* Isaiah 28:12, *97.* Exodus 14:14, 33:13, John

15:16, 5:42, 10:17, 2:24, Hebrews 4:11, Isaiah 11:1-4, **98.** Matthew 16:25, John 7:38, Romans 8:1, Revelation 1:10, Psalm 27:4, 37:4, Jeremiah 23:22, **99.** Romans 8:19, **100.** Psalm 37:4, Matthew 6:33, **101.** John 5:19, **102.** Romans 8:17, **103.** Matthew 6:21, **104.** 2 Chronicles 7:14, Daniel 10:12, **105.** Psalm 1:3, **106.** John 2:24, **107.** Exodus 20:21, **108.** Hebrews 12:21, **109.** Isaiah 2:3, **110.** Hebrews 12:18-22, **111.** Exodus 33:18-23, **112.** Exodus 24:9-11, Revelation 4:6, 15:2, **113.** Matthew 5:28, **114.** Galatians 5:16, **115.** John 17:20-24, Revelation 1:10-17

Dated: 22/1/22

36. *The Person of God with us (#119)*
SHEKINAH GLORY

Revivals of God, Outpourings of the Spirit; these of the Latter Day type 'rains' [1], are themselves an unstoppable force. Nothing can stand against them … but wash openly across the land. The Goodness and Salvation of the Lord touching and changing lives; even the unprepared and unexpecting. The hostile and the broken, God-haters and sinful, even in their deep-rooted unbelief coming into the Knowledge of God. And when I say 'knowledge', it's not the type of knowing Scriptures about God, but a Knowledge of God [2] that heals the soul and sets the people on the path of earnestly seeking Him.

The Shekinah Glory was a physical cloud … an open visual experience of the Presence of the Person of God descending upon a place or a people. In Scripture, there are four main accounts recorded that I would like to focus on. However, why I speak of such things is that the principle remains: how God desires to come — in His Person — in such intensity and wonder that rips across the land. Healing and touching and restoring; destroying all the works of the demon. And in your hand you hold key.

The way in Noah's time was the **flood**. The way of the Exodus was the **sword** and the spear. And the way of Israel was **rules** and regulations. However today, the way of the Resurrected Christ is the **<u>Outpouring of the Spirit</u>**. The liberal flow of the Spirit of God of whom touches and heals the souls of man; birthing Joy and Hope and the Righteousness of God from deep within the heart of man. And the Holiness of God standing in our midst … the Light of God … the Joyful assembly of angels [3] … the Kingdom of Heaven here with us in great manifest signs and wonders.

Nations saved in a day. Strongholds and principalities torn down. And the Knowledge and Salvation of the Lord setting Liberty and Love in the hearts of man through the manifest Presence and Power of the Holy Spirit. The Bride made spotless … ready for the Day of the Lord. The Glory of God shining as Christ is revealed in throughout the world.

I tell you the truth, that today ... these that are the Last Days, are the 'summation' of the Word of God. And what do I mean by that? But that every story, and every event in Scripture; all the men and women who worked powerful deeds in God ... these are all set as **precedent** and picture for you this very day.

So I say, **live in it**, walk in it — even in the fullness of the Resurrected Christ inherent and alive in you. In the *fullness* of the **finished** work of the Cross. Live *beyond* the Blood, *ie;* the 'Passover' Lamb, for the Blood now is for the *serving* God as priest ... serving God as kings. Co-reigning with Christ Jesus in Heavenly Places in Dominion — *with* Him — over all the creation. [4]

Not pre-Cross living ... but *post-Cross* living; in the Victory and Triumphant reality of the Resurrected Christ. For as God says to you today, *"I have swept away your sins like the morning mist. **Return to me**, for I have redeemed you"* [5]. Therefore now, the focus is not on seeking acceptance, for you are accepted. The focus now is returning back into the **fullness** of the Christ ... *ie;* the *pre-fallen* state. Not as Adam of old ... but the New Adam ... in Dominion, walking as He to the glory of the Father. [6]

Diligently enter into the realms of the '**All-Consuming Fire**' [7], even then as one who releases very same Fire of God on earth. Practice dying that truly you might be raised in the realms of Life. For if you haven't died, how can you ever truly walk in *Resurrection* Power? [8] And how can you ever truly be lifted [9] and captured up in the seated realms with Jesus at the right hand of God? For this is the Victory [10]. It is unto Union [11] that is our driving force: made one in Him to be with Him where He is. Abiding [12] in the Dominion of God over and above all powers, and all authorities, with your heel crushing the head of the serpent. *Unapologetically* destroying **all** the works of Satan. [13]

> *"Holy Ghost, what capacity and what vision can truly stand against the evil in the land ... and the horrific evil practices of witchcraft and demonic powers? Holy Ghost ... the **Outpouring** of the Fire of God."*

THE BLOOD PRELUDES THE SPIRIT

The Blood is powerful. The finished work of the Cross is most powerful. And unlike anything that we read of in the Old Testament ... as carriers of the Holy Spirit, it fully abolishes the sin of the land. Cleansing the hearts and ways of man before God. Therefore, the very same Blood of Jesus — when prayed — sets the stage for the Spirit to outpour 'upon all flesh'. [14]

There are a number of prophetic Scriptures that speak of such things, expressing realities that totally transform. And the following two are most prominent: Isaiah 2 states, *"Nation shall not lift up sword against nation, neither shall they learn war anymore."* And Isaiah 11, *"The wolf shall dwell with the lamb, the leopard shall lie down with the young goat, the calf and the young lion and the fatling together; and a little child shall lead them"*. And then continues ... *"The earth shall be full of the knowledge of the Lord as the waters cover the sea."*

Seven Scripture verses:
1. He who has an ear, let him **hear** what the Spirit says to the churches. To him who overcomes I will give to **eat** from the Tree of Life, which is in the midst of the Paradise of God. [15]
2. So He drove out the man; and He placed **cherubim** at the east of the garden of Eden, and a flaming sword which turned every way, to **guard** the way to the Tree of Life. [16]
3. He shall take some of the blood of the bull and sprinkle it with his finger on the **mercy seat** on the east side; and before the mercy seat he shall sprinkle some of the blood with his finger seven times. [17]
4. And there I will meet with you, and I will speak with you from above the mercy seat, from **between** the two cherubim which are on the ark of the Testimony, about everything which I will give you in commandment to the children of Israel. [18]
5. Above the ark were the cherubim of the **Glory**, overshadowing the atonement cover. But we cannot discuss these things in detail now. [19]
6. He is the **atoning** sacrifice for our sins, and not only for ours but also for the sins of the whole world. [20]
7. In the middle of its street, and on either side of the river, was the **Tree of Life**, which bore twelve fruits, each tree yielding

its fruit every month. The leaves of the tree were for the **healing** of the nations. *21*

As one in Christ Jesus, as a 'priest' called to stand in the gap *22*, so are you also called one able to **set yourself fully apart** unto God ... body, mind, soul, and spirit. This for the sake of your loved ones, for the sake of all that you treasure and hold dear ... even unto the very nations. *23*

Even then like a *Moses* who 'comes up' in Him *24* ... entering into intensities of His Holy Presence that totally transform *25*. No longer just a people marvelling at God at a distance *26* ... but a people coming and entering in. And here, in the fullness of God; the Outpouring that you trigger is of an 'Exodus' type manifestation that nothing can stand in the way *27*. The Salvation and the Healing of the land *28* so complete that *"The earth shall be full of the knowledge of the Lord as the waters cover the sea."* *29*

A side note ... the 'Mercy Seat': Within the Holy of Holies was the Ark of the Covenant. And upon the top of the Ark was the Mercy Seat, with the Wings of the Cherubim arching and spreading over 30. The significance of this is most wonderful and incredible. For it is by the Blood of Jesus, that — through your own purposed will — you can go into Places where the high priests of Old could not go. And here draw out from and pour out upon the nations 31. Such is the station of the Church.

The Old Covenant was about finding acceptance. But the New Covenant is that now you are accepted: part of the Beloved, part of the Cherished people of God. Hence today, it's about what God **has for you** that is most meaningful, even as one born in the realms of the Child. As God said, *"I have swept away your offences like the morning mist ... return to me"* *32*. And in another place, *"I will remove the iniquity of that land in one day"*. Therefore, entering into the living Example that is yours. *33*

Scripture:
And they sang a new song, saying: "You are worthy to take the scroll, and to open its seals; For You were slain, and have redeemed us to God by Your blood out of every tribe and tongue and people

and nation, and **have made us kings** and priests to our God; and we shall **reign** on the earth." *(Revelation 5:9-10 NKJV)*

As introduced in this incredible Scripture — that girds and underlies — our full Calling in Christ Jesus. The continuing Purpose of the Blood: is to serve God as priest, even then as one raised by the King — as a king *(ie; the returning back into the 'forgotten things'* [34]*)* — that you truly may 'reign' on earth [35]. Becoming a people made impervious and untouchable; [36] ever clothed in the Immortality of God [37]. Not only in a vision for when you die for what value is that to the world? No, these realms of Everlasting Life are purposed for us to **engage today**; let no one — or no thing — take your crown, nor the Lampstand from its place. [38]

I am saved — now I am raised.

It is true, that much of the Church around the world has only known the 'standing at a distance' [39]. Serving God only through the vision of man [40] or that of their own understanding. And that is why there has been little basis of Power to truly transform or bring change. For until now, the Christian believer has only known the 'walking according to the flesh', rather than that of truly coming to 'walk in the Power of the Spirit'. For in Christ Jesus, Scripture always speaks of these two distinct realities. [41]

Scripture:
For as many as are led by the Spirit of God, these are **sons** of God. *(Romans 8:14 NKJV*[42]*)*

The book of Acts demonstrates a 'Shekinah Glory' of the physical Presence of God descending upon the disciples in tongues of Fire; upon each of whom responded to the Word of Jesus of which clearly stated, *"Wait in the city until you have been **clothed** with Power from on high"* [43]. And this today is the same; that you are called of God also to — **embrace the 'Upper Room'** — as a living Experience [44]. For here, it shall be, that the Glory that comes upon your life shall 'radiate' [45] the Power of the Spirit for all the nations.

A side note ... for they who intercede: The demon sits in the 'atmosphere' over the hearts and minds of man. Spirits of doubt and unbelief speaking lusts, greed, and fear. However, when the Spirit of the Lord is outpoured, so are all hindrances removed. And in place of the demon the Lord stands. The 'heavens' rent and God stepping down because of a single man or peoples whom 'wait' upon the Lord [46]. Therefore now, as one who intercedes: pray the Blood that sanctifies, release the Spirit unto charge, and in striking the ground … command a harvest! [47]

IN SIGHT OF ALL THE PEOPLE

Theme Scripture:
[v10-11] Then the LORD said to Moses, "Go to the people and consecrate them today and tomorrow, and let them wash their clothes. And let them be ready for the third day *(resurrection day)*. For on the third day the Lord will come down upon Mount Sinai in the **sight** of all the people.
[v17] And Moses brought the people out of the camp to meet with God, and they stood at the foot of the mountain ['waiting' on the Lord [48]].
[v20] Then the LORD came down upon Mount Sinai, on the top of the mountain. And the LORD called Moses to the top of the mountain, and Moses went up. *(Exodus 19:10-11, 17, 20 NKJV)*

The focus of this chapter is in this wording, *"In sight of all the people."* And the best definition to express or describe this phenomenon is *"Shekinah Glory"*. Throughout biblical history, there are four main accounts that I would like to refer to where this Shekinah Glory came in open visual experience before all the people. A 'Cloud' of the Presence of the Person of God openly descending in sight of all.

But before we start, I want to emphasise two main key points of this chapter:

1. God is calling you to come into these realms of Glory *(ie; coming up the Mountain and 'beyond')*.
2. As one choosing to come up here *(even 'pitching your tent' and never leaving* [49]*)* so are you one who releases. [50]

* It's most important for you to realise … and I know it's hard to imagine how, but as ordinary human beings: you and I are triggerers of the outpouring of the Spirit of God. I know it's unfathomable to think, but as simple plain and ordinary Christians, you and I are able to participate in God in realms where such Glory ... such *Fire* ... falls upon the nations.

* But that is how it works. Man has firm part to play in how God operates. **God stepping through you** as a Spirit-filled believer — as children of the Most High God — us, as believers fashioned by the very Hand and Will and Purpose of God. He steps through His 'vessels' of whom He Himself fashioned and of whom He Himself abides. For this is the very purpose of the Spirit: that you might be living walking Temples of the Most High God on earth; each with our own tongues of Fire upon our heads. [51]

SHEKINAH GLORY

Scripture:
The sun shall no longer be your light by day, nor for brightness shall the moon give light to you; But the LORD will be to you an everlasting light, and your God your glory. *(Isaiah 60:19 NKJV)*

In Hebrew, the word Shekinah means 'Dwelling' or 'Presence'. And as seen throughout Scripture, there are such wonderful and powerful accounts where God came openly and visibly.

* However, before we continue, I need to bring this reality to earth. Bring this 'Heavenly reality' into a practical sense for each one of us today: As you personally step into the Glory so do you become one who carries.

Four key times in history where the Shekinah Glory came in the visual 'consecration' of the 'Temple':

1. Mount Sinai ... *(Exodus 19:16-18)*.
2. The Tabernacle ... *(Exodus 40:34-38)*.
3. The Temple of Solomon ... *(2 Chronicles 7:1)*.
4. The Upper Room ... *(Acts 2:3)*. [52] *

* *"For I, says the Lord, will be a **wall of fire** all around her, and I will be the Glory in her midst"* [52]. Recognise, that this is the **reality** that is now ours. For all in Christ Jesus, for all who *choose* to live according to the Spirit and not the flesh.

There are a few other examples in Scripture, where the Glory of God came in open visual form ... can you remember some?

1. During the Exodus, the Israelite nation was led by a 'pillar of fire' by night and a 'pillar of cloud' by day. [53]
2. And another is where God came and spoke with Moses in the burning bush. [54]
3. And at the birth of Jesus, *"An angel of the Lord stood before them, and the Glory of the Lord shone around them, and they were **greatly afraid**"* [55]. * The physical radiance of the Glory of God came and lit up the room.

Now, there is something really special in this wording, *"They were greatly afraid"* ... it's so very precious and very dear. Do you recall how Moses was greatly afraid as he approached the thick Cloud where God was? [56] Well, in Christ Jesus, there is a very precious overlaying picture that is most key for us today ... *if* we truly wish to walk in these realms of Glory.

Do you recall in Isaiah where it speaks of how Jesus *"Delighted in the Fear of the Lord?"* [57] Well, the truth is, to enter the realms of God's Glory is a fearful and terrible thing [58] ... but **Jesus loved it**! And Isaiah speaks of abiding in the *"All-Consuming Fire"*. And who can truly come here? ... *"He who walks righteously and speaks uprightly."* [7]

I mention this as key. For truly, it is the pathway of absolute and total success; as a people who walk in these realms of the Untouchable ... so are you made Untouchable [59]. For just as Moses went up upon the Mountain ... when he returned, so did his face glow [60] ... no one could touch him, nothing could harm him. And in the exact same way, Jesus said of Himself, *"No one can take my life, but I lay it down willingly."* [61]

Why do you whinge ... when you can command?

In the Gospels, Jesus speaks openly that you shall walk in an 'untouchable' nature [62]. But it doesn't stop here, for so shall Power come from your hand to heal. And if we were to continue reading where Jesus 'delighted in the Fear of God' *(Isaiah 11 verse 1 to 6)*, it speaks that the fruit of this lifestyle is the very 'Outpouring of the Spirit' … where Peace rules the land.

In Corinthians, Paul speaks of how *"God's Glory was displayed in the face of Jesus"* [63]. This, the very same Glory that was witnessed by the Disciples when Jesus was Transfigured before them … *"Shining bright like the sun"* [64]. And when Moses approached Mount Sinai, Scripture speaks of how Moses went behind the dark Cloud where God was; or let's rephrase that, *"The thick darkness that 'veiled' like a curtain the very Glory of God; of which no one was able or permitted to see."* [65]

You see, the Glory of God was not ever permissible for man except **by invitation** [66]. However, today in Christ Jesus it is most different for the 'veil' has now been rent [67]. Therefore the 'Invitation' has been firmly set for you: **inviting you to come in**. And why is this so important? But just as the Temple of old was only just a building without the Glory of God within [68], so too is the believer just a man [69]. For in order to walk with the Glory of God upon your life, means that you have to first walk in the Glory.

It is the very *Calling* of the Christ, the very *Invitation* of the Blood spilt and the Spirit given; that you *come* be 'with Him where He is' [70]. For so it is true, that as a Temple of God, so are you an entirely different 'model' [71]. Not an earth-based Temple, but a Heaven-based Temple … fashioned by God's own hand. Therefore, so too then also, that Power only comes from where you are rooted and from where you abide [72]. No longer only 'calling up to God' in times of need, but one with Him … where He is. [73]

YOU ARE A PORTAL, A GATEWAY

This subject is a most important message for us to understand. That in Christ Jesus, you have been brought into greater wonders than you can possibly comprehend. And the fundamental outworking of these wonders is that we all might become a people — who move — and walk — and do — just as Jesus. Coming into the *"**Unity of the Knowledge** of the Son, to the measure of the stature of the fullness of Christ Jesus."* [74]

Even as one who plays an active part in the Outpouring of the Spirit ... in these of the Last Days. Not only so, but becoming even greater Equipped, gaining greater Revelation and Anointing; as a people who trigger Revivals, spontaneous Fires, and 'Latter day rain' upon the land.

> *Knowledge and awareness bring a desire to pursue; and a heart that pursues opens many many doors.*

In the Book of Ezekiel, prophet Jeremiah writes how he witnessed the Glory of God depart the Temple ... ascending up and leaving the Temple [75]. And as I have mentioned, the Temple still remained — the Temple of God by name — however, the Glory of very Person of God was no longer there.

Then in parallel to this, in Revelations chapter 1, John is openly speaking of the believer's kingship. But then straight after, in chapters 2 and 3, Jesus ... speaking from Heaven, warns that this Glory of God is about to be **removed** due to the *indifference* of the people. Hence, these things that we are discussing here in this chapter; these things of great Authority, Glory, and Kingship; I have come to call them ... the *"Forgotten things."* For though by the Blood, Christ Jesus **has** made us priest and kings to rule on earth; this 'throning' of God, became forgotten and lost in later generations ... hence also, in our own.

The truth is, that the modern-day contemporary Church has very little knowledge of such things; let alone the Shekinah-*type* Glory of God being made manifest in our midst. Even this, of which was meant for unto the greatest of honour for the Son ... bringing Salvation to the nations. Therefore, it has been, that in many ways, the Church has been operating in an 'outward' appearance of Christ Jesus [76] but with a great 'substance' missing. The 'building' ... yes, however, the outward appearance being far less important compared to what is purposed within. As Paul says, *"Having a form of godliness, but denying its Power."* [77]

It's important here to understand a few things in Gospel: Jesus spoke how the Temple of God was going to be torn down ... **"*Every stone*"**. And why was this? But that the Spirit of God was moving and shifting from a place made by human hands, into places made by the Hand of God — this being you and I. And also, in continuing with this story, as the *"Disciples were marvelling at the Temple's construction"*, the **purpose is** for the sons and daughters of God — to remain no longer 'outside' — but **enter in**. Not into a place made by human hands, but through the Blood and the Spirit — into the original one that is in Heaven [78]. The exact and very same that the Tabernacle *itself* was made but as a 'shadow' — a 'replica' [79]. This is the Calling of the Son for all who believe.

Shekinah Glory = *"Deep Counsel"*
— *"Deep Presence"* —
— *"Deep Experience"* —
— *"Deep Empowerment"* —
— *"Deep Anointing"* —

Scripture:
For God, who said, "Let light shine out of darkness," made his light shine in our hearts to give us the light of the knowledge of God's glory displayed in the face of Christ. *(2 Corinthians 4:6 NIV)*

There are so many accounts and examples in Scripture regarding this subject of *Shekinah Glory*. I hope this is bringing a bit more insight.

IN HEBREW, THE NUMBER FOUR REPRESENTS 'COMPLETION'

I let you in on a little secret, God is a Trinity but He seeks to be four. The Father, the Son, the Holy Spirit, and the fourth … the *Bride of Christ*. No other creature or angel, nor any ancient spiritual being of nobility has been presented such wonder as has the Church.

So now we can all the more recognise why Satan was so jealous and vengeful … he who *was* called the Morning Star. Seeing the vulnerability held in God's own Heart in relation to this creature called 'man'. And so too, is it good for you and I to understand — in greater measure — your Divine Calling and Destiny in Christ Jesus, for all who love the Lord.

The number 'four': In the theme of this chapter, there are four primary Shekinah Glory events recorded in the Bible associated with this subject of the Temple of God:

1. The Mount Sinai experience.
2. The Tabernacle.
3. The consecration of the Temple.
4. The 'Upper Room', with tongues of Fire resting upon each individual consecrated temple.

Mount Sinai demonstrated the unspoken *first* Temple of God on earth. But what is most valuable for us in Christ Jesus, is that you and I can go into Places Moses could not [80]. Even as a people, able to pour out into the world [81]. Such is the meaning of 'walking according to the Spirit' ... ever surrounded and covered by the Counsels and Might of God. [82]

When Christ was crucified and the Curtain rent, it itself means that not only has the Spirit of God been released and poured out — but also, that you and I are freely able to go and enter in. And as one going in, so are you also able to release the Spirit of God unto all that is before you. This being the very picture of 'kingship'. The very picture of the Sword of the Spirit and your Authority in God. Authority ... meaning, your ability to 'author' and rewrite reality that is before you.

The Sword of the Spirit has a handle for a very specific reason; that you may take hold of and thrust out! This being the nature of a warrior and a king ... and of which was exemplified in the life of a young boy David who became king. The same whom which for all Eternity ... the Christ shall be called, *"Son of David."*

Moses was the first 'priest' of God. And as we know initially, it was only he who was permitted to come up upon the Mountain, with everyone else directed to stay at a distance. However, as I have said ... now, in the New Testament it is a most very different reality. For all in Christ Jesus, God is calling His people to come up. For it is God who **has called** you 'priest' like Aaron of old ... however, a priest of an entirely different order [83]. For not only have you been ordained and consecrated of God as priests to serve; but ordained by the King — as a king — with destiny and purpose of God to Rule and Command. [84]

Scripture:
The LORD has sworn and will not change his mind: "You are a priest forever, in the order of Melchizedek." *(Psalm 110:4 NIV)*

The Temple of God has four parts:
1. The Outer Court, an area set aside for 'foreigners' *(ie; the tourist)*.
2. The Inner Court, the area for the People of God *(ie; the Israelite nationals)*.
3. The Holy Place, the area designated for the priest to meet and serve God.
4. The Holy of Holies, the sacred area where the Ark of the Covenant was held. And that no one was permitted except the high priest once a year ... *and never without blood.*

Can you see the similarity in the Exodus story:
1. Egypt; the thinking and ways of the world *(the 'unsaved')*.
2. Passover; they who 'crossed over' via the blood on the doorposts and the Red Sea *(ie; the 'people of God' permitted to come around the Mountain)*.
3. First priest; Moses who went up upon the Mountain *(as 'priest')*.
4. Glory of God; the Place Moses himself was not able to fully engage.

There is a most very important picture here for us to understand. A most meaningful and relevant picture for you and I this very day. Let's overlay this Exodus picture to our contemporary Church:

1. The people of the world *(ie; 'Egypt')*.
2. The people 'saved' *(ie; the Blood bought and redeemed)*.
3. Baptism in Spirit.
4. Baptism in Power and Fire.

*On a side note: Another picture of 'four' relating to the Temple of God: **1.** The believer as body. **2.** The believer as mind. **3.** The believer as soul. **4.** and the believer as Spirit, ie; 'Living' Spirit; spirit made Alive unto God.*

To re-emphasise, at the consecration of each of these pivotal points in biblical history, there was always the **open demonstration** of the Shekinah Glory descending upon the Temple. Just as expressed in the theme Scripture, *"In the **sight** of all the people."*

I really encourage you, that *this* is such a treasure for you to understand, and to lay hold of personally in your life today. No one can do this for you ... *only you*. Even to personally prioritise in your prayer-life, the opportunity in God to see Him in His Glory [85]. And within yourself ever coming under His great Counsels and Might as your singular root-motive of soul ... as one made able to Release. And the type of Glory that shall *descend* upon your life is of such a nature that sweeps across the land — as an unstoppable 'flood' — as an unquenchable Fire.

In repeat ... four Shekinah Glory events: *1.* Mount Sinai, when God came as a cloud and fire upon the mountain. *2.* The Tabernacle when it was consecrated. *3.* The Temple of Solomon in open demonstration. *4.* The early Church through Wind and Fire. Therefore then, in likeness for each of one of us personally, there is: *1.* The world, *2.* the church congregation, *3.* they who personally meet with God, and *4.* they who walk in the Fire and Power of God. To which is it that you prefer?

GOD'S LOVE HAS NO DISTINCTION

You know, God loves each and every one of us *unfathomably*, and in Him there is absolutely no distinction. And in just the same way, it is to here, unto this very Place, that God Himself is calling each one of us to move further into. However, as I have said before, there are so very few responding.

There is a River, a flow in God for you to step into. But the truth is, people are either interested in it or they are not. And this River is like the 'Place of Meeting', that once you step into — the same where Jesus Himself continually went — then so too will you be continually led into Untold Wonders. But it is a choice, isn't it? Not God's ... but yours! With Jesus' very own Blood ... the Invitation, and the Spirit ... the very Hand that Guides.

The Blood is the right, the Blood is the basis:
— The Grace of God to Save —

The Spirit is the 'conduit', the Spirit is the means:
— the Grace of God to Empower —

So it is true, one can remain just a people of the crowd; or otherwise, you can choose it in your heart to be one who comes up. The 'crowd' being not Egypt ... the people of the world, the crowd is the Church, *ie;* the congregation that lingers around the Mountain [86]. But the vision of God is even so much bigger still: that in Christ Jesus, you are no longer of the Abrahamic line, but of the line of Melchizedek [87]. Therefore, for us in Christ, there is always the repositioning ... always the *shift*.

What this fundamentally means is, that you are no longer purposed to remain just an 'Israelite' *(a People of God)*. And so too, by rights and by destiny, you are no longer purposed to remain under old Israelite mindsets or limitations [88]. But by choice: you are a son of the Most High God ... just like Christ Jesus ... therefore, come up and **live like Him**. [89]

For just as Jesus *learned* from the Father [90] — as you also come up in Him, are you also constantly trained and made whole. Even as one healed and ever Strengthened and Empowered in the Presence of the Most High God [91] — made Victorious and Triumphant in Him [92]. Even then Anointed by the Lord unto great deeds and mighty exploits. [93]

Scripture:
What I am saying is that as long as an heir is underage, he is no different from a slave, although he owns the whole estate. The heir is subject to guardians and trustees until the time set by his father. So also, when we were **underage**, we were in slavery under the elemental spiritual forces of the world. But when the set time had fully come, God sent his Son, born of a woman, born under the law, to redeem those under the law, that we might receive **adoption to sonship**.
Because you are his sons, God sent the Spirit of his Son into our hearts, the Spirit who calls out, "Abba, Father." So you are no

longer a slave, but God's child; and since you are his child, God has made you **also an heir**. *(Galatians 4:1-4 NIV)*

What I am emphasising here is that it's a choice, for this is how both King Jesus and King David lived. As is said, *"One thing I ask from the LORD, this **only do I seek**: that I may dwell in the house of the LORD all the days of my life, to gaze on the beauty of the LORD and to seek him in his temple"*. [94]

Therefore, personally also, come make it by choice to go after and no longer stay where you are [95]. For everything is *'yes'* and *'amen'* for you unto the Glory of God. For as we increasingly come to realise … the things of God are purposed for **you to ask** for, and for **you to seek** after, and for **you to knock** and go pursue: [96]

1. The Power of the Blood *(Passover)*.
2. The Power of water Baptism *(Red Sea)*.
3. The Power of Encountering and meeting God *(Mount Sinai)*.
4. The Power of the Holy Spirit's Fire *(see God's Glory [97])*.

Let's overlay the Temple of God *model* over that of the modern-day Church. Firstly, the typical vision of the believer has been living as though a people '**congregating**' within the Inner Courts *(ie; at the base of the Mountain)*. Discussing their knowledge and their opinions of God, but never truly **going further in**. Perhaps not ever realising that there was more [98] … nor that it was possible, or even what it means to 'climb up the Mountain' or 'wait upon the Lord'. In any case, never coming to — **enter the Holy Place**.

— Abide in Him —
— Be with Him where He is —
— Behold His Glory —
— Co-reign, co-seated —

Hence, this is what has generally remained in the Church: Modern-day believers have remained a people addressing the problems of the world, only through the collective's own strength and understanding. Calling up to God … as though a people separate to Him. Where, it is God's first and fundamental Calling that you personally also **come up** into 'unity' *99* — and enter and dwell in these realms of Authority. As Jesus said, *"I can do nothing of myself, only what I **see** my Father doing" 100*. Or as Paul says, *"Seek those things which are above, where Christ is, sitting at the right hand of God. For you died (have you yet?), and your life is hidden with Christ in God." 101*

Two distinct paths: The Father dwells in the realms of Wonder ... and marvels to Himself, *"Why are my people not laying attentive to the gentle whispers of my Spirit?" 102* The definitive words of Scripture that expresses, *"The Spirit gives life; the flesh counts for nothing" 103*. That is, *"The flesh profits you nothing at all, only a heart unto the Spirit of God."*

Therefore, as one treasuring always the inherent desire to be 'Spirit led' and 'Spirit attentive'. That is: 'Presence focused', 'Right-Hand of God focused', 'Shekinah Glory focused'; even that we might truly become 'Holders of the Glory and Fire of God' — just as Christ Jesus. For as is said, *"All your children shall be **taught** by the Lord, and **great** will be their peace" 104*. And in another place, *"You will do greater works than I because I go to the Father." 105*

AN UNFATHOMABLE BIRTHING

A few days ago I was cleaning up around the kitchen, and my wife had bought a large tray of eggs; and in putting them away in the fridge, for some reason, she had left one still in the tray. So as I was making coffee and preparing for my morning ... I became so captivated looking at this egg. And starring and marvelling at it, I pondered and thought, *"The hen, each day, lays one of these ... the complexity of this little thing!"*

The 'egg' ... there is the shell and the complexity of its construction. Then there is the thin fine membrane just underneath *(this is where we get the word 'osmosis' from)*. And then, within, there are the precious contents and the life that comes forth. So then, I started thinking, *"The hen, she has no idea how she does it ... her little pee-sized brain has no idea."* And even if she did come to really think about it, there would be nothing that she could do that in any way could make any change.

The reason I make mention of this, is that you and I also ... we have no idea. We have no measure of understanding how to make one of these eggs either. And even if we did have high-end quantum AI computers ... no one is able, nor knows in any way how. But there it is each day ... this little hen, her body produces this incredible marvel without her knowledge.

So the point I want to raise here is, that this is exactly the same with you and I in regards the Spirit. What you trigger in the Spirit as you personally choose to come up here, and in Him feed of these realms of Wonder; [106] what is naturally produced is of such an incredible marvel, that will cause the world to stop in awe![107] And so it will be also, that such a wonder shall come upon the hearts and minds of man, that the many will give their lives freely unto Liberty.

Truly then, the honour that you personally express to the Lord ... opens such incredible Glory that totally defies your 'pee-sized' brain. And even if you had all knowledge, even such a super brain like an AI computer linked to everything; you have no idea how to birth an egg. And in the exact same way, you have no way of understanding what God has prepared and made ready for those who love and earnestly seek Him [108]. Nor that of which you will birth forth from your life as one richly rooted and continuously drawing from His Glory.

So in this simple 'egg picture': As you truly come to Him, as you personally choose to truly respond and come up in Him where He is; the triggering of the Spirit of God that you produce is so far outside what you can imagine. And so too then also, so far outside what the world can stand against *(as the "Autumn Rains cover it with pools"* [109]*)*. The Spirit of the Lord being **poured out upon all flesh**, whereby the world has no ability or capacity to resist or stand against.

Scripture:
Since the beginning of the world Men have not heard nor perceived by the ear, nor has the eye seen any God besides You, who **acts for the one who <u>waits</u> for Him**. *(Isaiah 64:4 NIV)*

TWO DISTINCT PATHS

Today, as a priest who 'serves the Lord', what you and I are doing is passing on through *(the Cross)* into the Holy Place to serve Him here. Not into a 'copy' thereof ... or a 'shadow' *110* ... but in Heaven itself. And the way you do this is by laying your life down upon the Alter *(ie; all you know and all life's issues; all responsibilities and cares)* and in 'death' enter in *111*. Even here, in the Presence of the Lord, responding to the very Invitation of the Spirit and going behind the Curtain; serving the Lord God from within the realms of the Hidden and Concealed. And from this Place, from these realms of Authority and Bliss speaking into your life and situations; **declaring change**, declaring blessing, declaring outpourings and moves of the Spirit.

Jesus said, *"I go to **prepare** a place for you. And if I go and prepare a place for you, I will come again and **receive** you to myself; that **where I am**, there you may be also. And where I go you know, and the **way** you know."* *112*

I so encourage you; Jesus **has not left** you orphans, and so He comes and receives you where He is. It is so important to realise, just as Jesus said that 'He could do nothing on His own' ... nor can you! But He also says concerning both you and I, that we shall do '**greater works**' than He. Therefore realise, that it is truly about following the 'Way' *(the ways and pre-trodden footsteps)* and coming into the Place Christ **Jesus has prepared for you**. Glory comes from the Lord and so shall He also clothe you in Glory and Power.

Two defining Scriptures, between the Old and the New Covenants ...

The Old way, 2 Chronicles 23:6: *113*
"No one is to enter the temple of the Lord except the priests and Levites on duty; they may enter because they are consecrated *(ie; set apart)*. But all the others are to observe the Lord's command **not to enter**."

The New way, Revelation 1:4-6: *114*
"Grace to you and peace from Him who is and who was and who is to come, and from the seven Spirits who are before His throne, and from Jesus Christ, the faithful witness, the firstborn from the

dead, and the ruler over the kings of the earth. To Him who loved us and washed us from our sins in His own blood, and has made us kings and **priests to His God** and Father, to Him be glory and dominion forever and ever. Amen."

A side note: This testimony in the book of Revelation, expressed by Apostle John, was recorded before he entered into 'Heavenly Encounter'. Then later repeated again, in a second account (in Heavenly Encounter) — as 'prayers of the saints' in Heaven [114]. Therefore, it is most clear that this is both your present-day Destiny as well as your future-day Destiny. Even this, the very heart's cry of your Saviour — before He faced the Cross — that you truly might 'be with Him where He is'. [115]

Now, it is most easy for us to recognise the superior nature of the New Covenant. This, for each one born not of the flesh, nor the will of man, but the Will of God. Consecrated and made whole in Him, set apart — as we embrace — Christ Jesus' shed Blood Invitation.

Today, if you truly wish to be effective and bring Everlasting Life to this dying and suffering world, you must first respond and come up just as Jesus. Putting aside all fleshly pride and vision [116], ever humbling yourself before the Most High God in the Heavenly realms. Each and every day actively responding ... and purposing yourself to seek the Face of God [117]. And so it shall be that the Lord your God will heal the scars of your soul and mind ... as He openly pours out His healing and saving Grace upon the 'land'.

Closing Scripture:
The Lord said to Moses, "I am going to come to you in a dense cloud, so that the people will hear me speaking with you and will always put their trust in you." *(Exodus 19:9 NIV)*

To conclude then, God is calling you as a people to *sanctify* yourself ready *(be set apart)*. Ready to meet with the Person of God at Mount Sinai *(ie; a heart set ever upon the 'Upper Room')*. Entering into these very same realms where opportunity came only by invitation. But that is the point isn't it: the **Blood is the invitation** unto all who believe in His Name. [118]

God Himself sent His Son as a — personal Living Invitation [119] — to you [120]. Whereby you yourself may come up into the very realms where the 'people' were not permitted. The old Temple has gone, for now — **you are the Temple of God on earth** [121] — purposed and destined to cohabitate [122] in the Temple in Heaven as 'holy' living portals [123]. And here, so shall you be given Power to overcome and ever be victorious — in all things — with Power to win in God [120]. Given blueprints and plans for every season, even then raised as seated kings, with an Iron Sceptre of Governmental Authority to strike the nations. [124]

The picture of the man Elisha, I call *'Second Level Anointing"* ... where **you** say, *"Enough!"* As Elisha said when facing the Jordan, *"Where is the God of Elijah!"* ... as he struck the water, and it parted way [125]. However, this most powerful 'Anointing' doesn't come from an *indifferent* lifestyle, nor one whom only observes God 'at a distance'. But ever through a heart purposed and driven in Him to come up ... *ie;* the 'singular vision'. [126]

The 'Prayer of the Anointed':
1. **One thing** I ask from the Lord, this **only do I seek**:
2. that I may **dwell in the house** of the Lord all the days of my life,
3. to [behold] **gaze on the beauty** of the Lord and to
4. **Seek him** in his temple. *(Psalm 27:4 NKJV)*

I really encourage you, through the words of this Scripture, this is the **pathway of a king** unto a 'kingly' Authority. The word 'Anointing' means; given an Authority to rule in a particular area. But today, in Christ Jesus, through His shed Blood — you have been Anointed both priest and king [97]. Therefore, as you are seated [127], so do you have Authority in all things — purposed of God to Rule!

A side note ... 'juggling life': Be Heaven and Glory of God — 'soul' envisioned — both in prayer and in purpose. And when facing pressing problems, concerns, and issues ... simply say to the Holy Ghost, "You deal with it" [128]. *Elisha demonstrated a man who laid down his life to follow his master. He burned his past ... for his 'prayer' was God and a Double Anointing.*

It was he ...and not the other prophets, who witnessed the ascension of Elijah. And as a result, God granted him his prayer. And this is what Jesus means when He says, "Lay down your life ... 'sell everything' ... and follow me". For the heart pursuit unto the 'Glory of God manifest on earth' [129] *opens you to walk in such things. The Resurrected Christ is your Double Anointing — but it is God who responds to such who worships Him in "Truth and in Spirit". For it is they of whom He is actively on the lookout and is deeply drawn to.* [130]

Bless you ...

Appendix:

1. Psalm 84:5-6, Joel 2:23, ***2.*** Isaiah 11:9, ***3.*** Hebrews 12:22-24, ***4.*** Revelation 5:9-10, 2 Timothy 2:12, Genesis 1:26, ***5.*** Isaiah 44:22, Revelation 3:19-22, ***6.*** John 15:5-8, ***7.*** Isaiah 33:14b-15a *HCSB*, Hebrews 4:9-11, ***8.*** John 10:17, ***9.*** 2 Kings 2:11, Acts 1:9, Colossians 3:1, ***10.*** Revelation 3:21 *(3:17-22)*, ***11.*** John 17:20-24, ***12.*** John 15:7 *NKJV*, 5:19, 5:42-44, Deuteronomy 8:3, Matthew 16:17-19, ***13.*** 1 John 3:8, ***14.*** Joel 2:28-29, Acts 2:17, ***15.*** Revelation 2:7 *NKJV*, ***16.*** Genesis 3:24 *NKJV*, ***17.*** Leviticus 16:14 *NKJV*, ***18.*** Exodus 25:22 *NKJV*, ***19.*** Hebrews 9:5 *NIV*, ***20.*** 1 John 2:2 *NKJV*, ***21.*** Revelation 22:2 *NKJV*, ***22.*** 2 Chronicles 23:6, Revelation 5:9-10, 1:5-6, Zechariah 6:11, ***23.*** Hebrews 9:7, ***24.*** Exodus 19:10, Isaiah 2:2-3, Mark 3:13, ***25.*** Hebrews 12:21, Exodus 33:22, 34:29-35, Matthew 17:1-2, Isaiah 33:14b-15a *HCSB*, ***26.*** Mark 13:1-2, ***27.*** Mark 3:13-15, Matthew 16:17-19, ***28.*** 2 Chronicles 7:14, Revelation 22:2, ***29.*** Isaiah 11:9, Habakkuk 2:14, ***30.*** Genesis 3:24, ***31.*** Revelation 22:2, ***32.*** Isaiah 44:22, ***33.*** Zechariah 3, ***34.*** Revelation 2-3, Psalm 82:6-8, ***35.*** Genesis 1:26, ***36.*** Mark 16:17-19, Luke 10:19, ***37.*** 1 Corinthians 15:53-54, ***38.*** Revelation 2, 3, ***39.*** Exodus 19:23, ***40.*** Exodus 20:19, ***41.*** John 6:63, 2 Timothy 3:5, 1 Corinthians 4:20, Matthew 23:11, ***42.*** John 1:12, Luke 6:35, ***43.*** Luke 24:49, ***44.*** Hebrews 12:22-24, ***45.*** Exodus 34:29, ***46.*** Isaiah 64:1-4, Psalm 116:2, Daniel 10:12, ***47.*** Isaiah 11:4b, 2 Kings 2:14, ***48.*** Isaiah 40:31 *NKJV*, Acts 1:12-13, ***49.*** Exodus 33:11, ***50.*** Zechariah 3:6-7, 2 Kings 2:14, ***51.*** Acts 2:3, Luke 3:16, Revelation 2:5, ***52.*** 'Fire': Exodus 3:2, Zechariah 2:5, ***53.*** Exodus 13:21-22, ***54.*** Exodus 3, ***55.*** Luke 2:9, ***56.*** Exodus 20:21, Hebrews 12:21, ***57.*** Isaiah 11:1-4, ***58.*** Hebrews 12:21,

Matthew 18:3, **59.** 1 Corinthians 15:53, **60.** Exodus 34:29-30, **61.** John 10:18, **62.** Luke 10:19, Mark 16:17-18, **63.** 2 Corinthians 4:6, **64.** Matthew 17:2, **65.** Exodus 20:21, **66.** Exodus 33:20, Genesis 3:24, **67.** Matthew 27:51, **68.** Ezekiel 10:18, **69.** Revelation 2:5, Psalm 82:6-8, Isaiah 28:12-13, Romans 8:14, **70.** John 12:26, 7:34, 14:4, 17:24, 3:13, **71.** Hebrews 7:17, 2 Corinthians 5:17, **72.** John 15:7, **73.** Mark 3:13-15, John 3:13, 14:3-6, 17:24, 5:19, 13:3, 33, 36, **74.** Ephesians 4:13, **75.** Ezekiel 10:18, Revelation 2:5, **76.** Mark 13:1, **77.** 2 Timothy 3:5, **78.** Mark 3:13-15, John 3:13, 14:3-6, 17:24, 5:19, 13:3, 33, 36, **79.** Hebrews 8:5, **80.** Revelation 2:7, 22:2, **81.** Matthew 16:19, **82.** Isaiah 11:1-4, **83.** Revelation 1:4-6, 5:9-10, Psalm 110:4, Hebrews 7:17, **84.** Psalm 110:1, **85.** John 17:20-24, Psalm 27:4, 2 Chronicles 7:14, Isaiah 64:4, **86.** Exodus 17:3, 32:7, Numbers 14:2-3, Matthew 17:17, **87.** Psalm 110:4, Hebrews 7:17-21, Revelation 1:5-6, 5:9-10 *NKJV,* **88.** John 3:8-12, **89.** John 3:13 *NKJV,* **90.** John 15:15, Galatians 4:1-7, **91.** Psalm 110:2, **92.** Revelation 3:21, **93.** Daniel 11:32 *NKJV,* **94.** Psalm 27:4, **95.** Exodus 13:21, **96.** Matthew 7:7, **97.** Exodus 33:19-23, 1 Kings 19:11-12, John 17:20-24, **98.** Matthew 23:13, **99.** John 17:20-24, **100.** John 5:19, **101.** Colossians 3:1-2, **102.** Revelation 3:22, 1 Kings 19:12, **103.** John 6:63, **104.** Isaiah 54:13, **105.** John 14:12, **106.** John 10:9, **107.** Habakkuk 1:5, John 5:20, **108.** 1 Corinthians 2:9, Isaiah 64:4, *109.* Psalm 84:6, **110.** Hebrews 8:5, **111.** Matthew 16:25, John 12:24, **112.** John 14:1-3, **113.** Exodus 19:23, **114.** Revelation 1:5-6, 5:9-10 *NKJV,* **115.** John 17:24, **116.** Philippians 3:8, **117.** 2 Chronicles 7:14, Psalm 27:4, Daniel 10:12, **118.** Mark 3:13-15, **119.** Isaiah 9:6, **120.** Revelation 3:20-21, **121.** *Mark 13:1-2,* **122.** John 3:13 *NKJV,* **123.** 2 Timothy 2:20-21, Isaiah 41:15, **124.** Isaiah 11:1-4, **125.** 2 Kings 2:14, **126.** Matthew 19:21, Colossians 3:1-3, 1 Corinthians 15:53, Psalm 110:1-2, Hebrews 4:10-11, **127.** Psalm 2:7-8, 110:1-2, Hebrews 4:8-10, Matthew 14:31, 16:17-19, 17:20, John 17:20-21, **128.** Matthew 6:33, **129.** Matthew 6:10, **130.** John 4:23–24

Dated: 23/3/22

AUTHORITY TO BIRTH REVIVAL

37. *Authority to Birth Revival (#120)*
AUTHORITY TO BIRTH REVIVAL

This chapter is part of a section that I would have liked to have called, *"Learning How to Pray, Learning How to Stand, and Learning How to Advance."* And as I say, it's really important to have people pray and stand with you during difficult times. But if you truly want to live 'victorious' and 'triumphant' **you need to know** how to pray. **You need to know** how to stand. And **you need to know** how God desires to fight for you whereby advancing becomes easy. As God says, *"My Presence will go out before you and I will give you rest."* [1]

Now part of this 'learning' is rooted in knowing who you are, *ie;* what Christ Jesus has achieved for you — and — where God has now positioned you in Him. And here 'in Him' *(intimate nurturing 'bosom'* [2]*)* gaining greater and ever greater revelation of your sonship [3]. So the focus of this particular chapter is in the emphasis: that you yourself, as a child of the Living God — by Birthright — are a '**triggerer**' of Revival.

The next chapter, following this one, is titled *"Manifesting Sonship."* And these two subjects combined are most powerful. For just as Jesus came and lived amongst us, so did He also come in real and open 'Testimony' of **your new life in God**. Christ Jesus Himself came — as a demonstrable living Picture — of who you are born and Destined to be. Hence our personal path of revelation is rooted in the fact that *"All creation is waiting in eager expectation for the sons of God to be revealed"* [4]. This is you and I.

So I really encourage you — picture the Person of Jesus — look intently at how He walked, what He did, and His relationship with God. That is your **reference** point, and that is your vision and goal. Not the world, nor the vision of others, but the — **fullness of God** — resting upon your life. This, for your own blessing, for the blessing of your loved ones, and for the blessing of the whole world. And it is to this very thing that the *Enemy* is terrified that you ever come to walk in.

As a church, oftentimes we are so 'practicality' focused, so works focused and achievement focused. But there is such a higher *calling* unto God, and that is unto relationship; intimate, close, and intertwining relationship in the Bosom of the Father. This is the **root reality** of how Jesus Himself lived, as too where His Power was from; again — in open demonstration — of the right way to live. Relationship focused ... then the practical; in this shall you be successful in all things.

So in these thoughts, let's begin ...

REVIVAL STARTS WITH YOU

The first miracle of Jesus, the very beginning of His ministry, started within the needs of His own family. The mother of Jesus, knowing the Power of her Son ... told the servants, *"Do whatever He tells you."* [5]

Jesus's mother Mary knew the Power of God that was at work in her son's life. She saw it even way before the day of His birth. And she saw His Power develop as He grew being evident in their day-to-day life. Jesus was more than the 'Word' ... He was the Word 'made flesh' on earth. He manifested Heaven on earth; the 'Word' being the very Power of Creation. This, for all the generations ... this, as a child of God, **is your Destiny**!

What I am saying is, that you can't effectively pray for the 'multiplication of food' in the public arena, if you still live anxious and strained not knowing how to pray multiplication in your own home. And in the same way, you can't effectively pray for Moves and Outpourings of the Spirit of God in the nations, if you still don't know how to pray and release the Life of the Spirit of God in your own family; in your own work life, in the various difficulties and issues that come ... and see the Spirit move.

What you and your world needs is the **Power** of the Spirit 'aggressively' at work in your life [6] ... even then, as one becoming totally *unsatisfied* with anything else [7]. Hence this, the Outpouring of the Spirit 'ministry', starts within your own life. 'Revival' **starts with you** personally, and in what lies before you ... as one who fundamentally is a converter of 'death' into Life. And that's who you are ... one made able *('make' you able [43])* to **materialise** possibilities in impossible situations.

Therefore, the centre-most prayer of life always remains the same, *"I seek the manifest Presence of God real, alive, and unceasing."* For you can only release from God what you yourself freely walk in ... in what you have freely received.

Jesus always walked in the Presence of God ... let that be your own personal vision; He lived openly hearing and seeing God ... perpetually *'encountering'*. Hence therefore, **intimacy** is so very important: one-to-one with — His Person — just as Jesus. For it is only God who can set you in these realms of great Hope and Glory; the very kind of which revolutionises the world. Therefore, I deeply encourage you — earnestly shift — and put yourself in an environment conducive of maturity [8]. And from here, as you Encounter the Holy Fire of God [9] ... so too are you able to *release*.

Scripture:
He who unites himself with the Lord is one with Him in Spirit. *(1 Corinthians 6:17 NIV)*

I so encourage you, recognise your sonship and pray from union. **Unite yourself** with God and pray from a place of rich acceptance and belonging. You already have the fullness of the Power of the Spirit of God residing at work within you. So, it's not a matter of getting more of the Holy Spirit ... but allowing the Holy Spirit to get more of you*!*

Surrender plays a big part. The ever-increasing Power of God is found as you *yield* to the Holy Spirit. Allowing yourself to become increasingly unified one with the Father, the Son, and the Holy Spirit [10] ... *absorbed* in union. Not separate but one. Now from here, when you pray, do you release the Eternal realms of God into creation. Do you release the very Prayers *promised* of God, ie; that of which has already been declared in Heaven ... into this earth. [11]

For everything is 'yes' to you ... every Promise is 'amen' to the Glory of God [12]. Therefore, I so very much encourage you, make the seeking of the tangible manifest Presence of God central to your life. For in Him all things are possible. Why struggle, why be in angst ... for fear and dread is not who you are, but Liberty and Life in the Joy and Power of the Lord. [13]

> *"The Kingdom of God is not a matter of eating and drinking, but of righteousness, peace and joy in the Holy Spirit."* [14]

> *"The Kingdom of God is not a matter of talk but Power."* [15]

I tell you a little secret, *"The Joy of the Lord is your strength"* [16] ... amen? But so too also, is the Peace and Joy of God a *doorway*. Have you ever experienced, in times of prayer, a peace coming upon you? **Peace is Presence**. Hence ... I so encourage you, after praying for your needs and wants, set your heart in honour for the *Peace* of the Presence of God. For the Peace of God itself is a doorway; it is a **floodgate of openings**. For it is what God *has* for you that is so very precious. Even in the realms He takes you and what is imparted to you here. Therefore, there is always something far greater than answer to prayer and that is the *meeting* with the Person of God.

It is a crucial realm for the believer ... this 'walking' **in** the Spirit. It is the realm of being 'Seated' in God; a Place of Rest where you constantly Receive. This very Place is called the *"Right hand of God"*, it is called the *"Abiding Place"* ... the *"Remain in my Love."* And this Place is the realms of Counsel and Might ... the realms of Glory and Fire. It is also an Authoritative Place of great Fellowship, Grace and Peace; a Place where you also come to Rule.

There are many things that you can dream for, but Scripture calls you to *dream* for this Place; to pursue, to go after, and to honour [17]. Flesh profits you nothing at all ... what counts is the Spirit [18]. Everything else degrades, everything else decays and is no more. But the things of the Spirit are like gold that enriches and endures [19]. And from this Place what you release is the Might of God. What you release is the Counsel and Knowledge of God flooding the earth. And what you release is Glory and the Holy Spirit's Fire. [20]

The very meaning of the word 'prayer' is ask, seek, and knock [21]. For whatever you believe you go after, and whatever you love you will pursue, and whatever you treasure so shall you establish and make your dwelling. If you believe you will ask … you will seek … and you will diligently lay hold of that of which Christ has *already* laid hold of for you. [22]

Scripture:
That the God of our Lord Jesus Christ, the Father of Glory, may give unto you the Spirit of Wisdom and **Revelation** in the Knowledge of Him: the eyes of your understanding being Enlightened; that ye may know what is the hope of **His calling**, and what the riches of the Glory of His inheritance in the saints, and what is the exceeding **greatness of His Power** to us-ward who believe. *(Ephesians 1:17-19 KJV)*

TO DISPEL ANY DOUBT

"I will bring you up out of your misery into a land flowing with milk and honey." [23]

Up until now, the Christian believer has been going about their walk the best way they know how. But it is the Spirit of God that has a whole other means that is so far greater … that so far surpasses. And it is based on the 'Outpouring of the Spirit' and 'Revivals of God'.

As we go through this last section, I will be introducing several key Scriptures that I like to refer to as *"Recipes for Revival."* But before we start, I feel it most important to first dispel any doubt of who you are in Christ Jesus. Or let's say, remove any 'spell' that Satan has cast over the hearts and minds of man. As Paul says, *"Who has bewitched you?"* [24]

A key first point to begin with is in the recognition that — in God's eyes — you are the same as Jesus. That in God's eyes, you are fundamentally structured and birthed exactly the same as Jesus — as a 'God' class of being. What this means is, that through the precious shed Blood of the Lamb, when God looks at you … He sees Jesus. God sees His 'Child' — a precious and treasured 'seedling' of His Son; with inherent capacity to grow and walk in the fullness and whole measure of the Christ. [25]

Therefore, just as Jesus came carrying the Spirit — so do you also. And not only did He carry, but as He chose to 'lay down His life' [26] did He 'release'. Christ Jesus Himself came and 'triggered' the Outpouring of the Spirit of God on the earth.

What this means is, that you have the exact and very same capacity to trigger 'Moves' of the Spirit of God ... just as Jesus. And even more so expressed, it is Jesus who has presented to you the very Keys of Heaven that **you** yourself might turn [27]. As Elisha of old, the Mantle of the Christ has now fallen to you, that you might pick it up and walk in the **fullness** of the Son [28]. Hence, therefore, as you also choose to lay your life down 'in death' [29] so too do you **release** and set to charge the Spirit of the Lord.

It is the Christ who became 'death' [30] ... so that you do not need to. That today you can walk in Resurrection Life and Power on earth — in the Triumphant Living state — without physically needing to die first. So I say, *"Let God be God!"* and not your own vision of life or what is before you. For it is so, that God's centremost Prayer concerning both you and I has always been the same. That you truly might respond and come *"Sit at His right hand ... where the Person of God goes out before you and 'wars' on your behalf, to the blessing of the nations"* [31]. Even then, that you might continue to be raised; and in maturity, be established in Divine kingly Authority.

God prepares a 'Banqueting Table'.

Faith is ... when you trust, do you sit down; when you trust and feel safe ... **do you recline**. And when you truly 'enter' Rest, do you find yourself free and able to eat and drink in the Presence of the Lord. Even in the 'wilderness'; knowing full well that God has gone out before you and is clearing the land before you arrive.

Scripture:
Until we all reach unity in the faith and in the knowledge of the Son of God and become mature, **attaining** to the whole measure of the fullness of Christ. *(Ephesians 4:13 NKJV)*

Jesus seeks that you 'be' Jesus, not just one who only believes in Him. And God has greater plans and purposes for your life than only blessing it. For the Holy Spirit is tasked that you too might come to **walk** in 'Like' as the Son ... doing just as He [32]. Even as one who moves and 'wields' Life and Spirit in your very hands. Before, you were a lost sheep that was found, but now as one — 'found' in Him — it is God who is raising you to Roar!

Christ Jesus came as a Lamb for the slaughter, but now He is *Risen* and is a Lion that roars. And so it is for us, we who are risen in Him; the Authority and 'Aggression' of the Lord is upon you to bring great change. Therefore, shift out of the way the 'works of Satan' [33] and set in place the Glory and Intensities of God. **Roar!** ... be unsatisfied ... and command change! For you are no longer a sheep that is lost in the desert but part of He who is Victorious.

It is my job to receive, and it is God's 'job' to work [34]. *It is God's job to work, and my job to enter the Rest of the Lord* [35]. *To push through and come sit at the right hand of God — in all things!* [27]

The Christ was sent by God to — **relocate you!** — to restore and re-position you back in Him. The Christ came as a Living 'Picture': as the Living 'Example' of your true and original Destiny and Purpose. Even in the very Calling of God to **become just as He**. And so it is the same, as one in Him — part of His very Body — has the Invitation of God been extended to you as well: *"Come, sit at my right hand, till I make your enemies your footstool"* [36]. For — **in Christ** — there is **no separation**.

The Purpose of the Christ coming is so far more than just taking you out of 'Egypt'. For it is the Person of God who **seeks also** to bring you up into the 'Land' — flowing with milk and honey. And though before, this land was a physical place on earth ... now it is unto the Heavenly Jerusalem, the City of Zion, the City of Bliss ... the City of the King that is in Heaven. And until you recognise this fundamental Calling of the Lord, you will always remain as though one 'wandering' in the wilderness. Therefore come, and grasp hold of this higher vision and look past the world and your current situation. For God is Transformational by nature — God is Relocational — and He is personally bent on Restoring you in Him. As is also said, *"The LORD will extend **your mighty scepter** from Zion, saying, "Rule in the midst of your enemies!"*

Scripture:
On this mountain the LORD Almighty will prepare a feast of rich food for all peoples, a banquet of aged wine — the best of meats and the finest of wines. *(Isaiah 25:6 NIV)*

So today I *invite* you into the Presence of God, here into the realms of the ministering Presence of the Lord; a Place where you **constantly Receive**. And I so very much encourage you in this — prioritise this Place **over all things** — and all that you face. And what you shall come into experience of, as you behold the 'beauty of His Face' [37] — as you behold His Glory [38] — so shall you release.

In the flesh, very little is possible ... but in the Spirit, do you enter into realms without limit. Till now you have been striving in your own efforts becoming tired and discouraged. Therefore, here and now do I 'breathe' [39] upon you a **fresh Vision** ... even the Presence of God. May you ever be strengthened and ever be lifted up in the Lord. Entering in behind closed doors as one **dining in the Gathering** [40]. And what shall pour out from your life will 'flood' the land to the blessing of your loved ones and that of the nations.

Truly, if you really want to be successful ... come and **appropriate the office** that the Blood has bought. The 'Office of a Priest' as one who serves God in **His Holy Presence** [41]. It is *not* about you, but where God has brought you as His Beloved child. Even then, as one who connects the realities of the world unto the Power and Goodness of God.

In the Old Testament, believers could only view the Dwelling Place of the Lord from outside the walls. But now, in the New

Testament — Christ Jesus is inviting you — to pass through into very realms where man is not permitted. Even unto the original Temple of God that is in Heaven. [42]

You are born of the Spirit, so come walk in the Spirit. There are many places you can be, but what you and your world needs is the liberal Outpouring of the Spirit of God. So far, the Christian believer has only known the 'clinging' onto this world in all that they do; with the hope of getting into Heaven when they die. But this is the wrong focus point. For if you were truly able to lay your life down in Christ Jesus, so would you also come to — walk and dine — upon the 'Sea of Sapphire' [43]. These very realms of close and intimate relationship with God Almighty mingled in Fire. [44]

I hope that these introductory words have been encouraging. There is so much more that I can talk about here … and in following chapters we will go further. But in the meantime, let's start with the first of the 'Revival' Scriptures.

'BIRTHING A REVIVAL'

First 'Birthing Revival' Scripture:
Now it shall come to pass in the latter days that the mountain of the LORD's house shall be established on the top of the mountains, and shall be exalted above the hills; and all nations shall flow to it. Many people shall come and say, "Come, and **let us go up** to the mountain of the LORD, to the house of the God of Jacob; He will teach us His ways, and we shall walk in His paths." For out of Zion shall go forth the law, and the word of the LORD from Jerusalem. He shall judge between the nations, and rebuke many people; they shall beat their swords into plowshares, and their spears into pruning hooks; nation shall not lift up sword against nation, neither shall they learn war anymore.
O house of Jacob, come and **let us walk in the light** of the LORD. *(Isaiah 2:2-5 NKJV)*

Oh, how precious this is. And as we go through these Revival Scriptures … the picture will become clearer. But firstly, if you can visualise:

1. God is **inviting** His people up upon the Mountain ... just as Moses went up and met with God. But this Invitation goes further; the *"Mountain of the House of the Lord that is **Above** the mountains."*
2. Into Places where you are **taught** and raised in the Presence and Glory of God. [45]
3. Then from here — in the 'Abiding Place' — God is triggered and responds, **going out before you**.
4. The Fire of God poured out where whole regions and nations are changed. And where there was great enmity and division, God shifts and causes deep bonds of friendship. 'Spears into pruning hooks' ... as the Knowledge of God floods the earth.

Today, in light of the Gospel message, Christ Jesus is inviting you into these precious **realms of Receiving**. Deeply humbling realms in the Fire of God where you recline and dine [46]. Like the Elders of Old who were brought up upon the 'Sea of Sapphire' and ate a meal in the Presence of God [47]. For here, so are you Equipped. And here, so are you Imparted of Divine Glory. [48]

In the Gospels, Jesus spoke of what He called 'earthly things' ... however now, in this area of believing, does He dearly desire to teach and show 'Heavenly things' [49]. For it is to where God desires to take you that is of great value and importance. Not to where you have been ... but to where He desires to lead you in Him. Therefore, come lay your life down, and yield yourself to the work of the Spirit. For this is what you want — walking with God in Glory — as you still walk this earth [50]. The continual shift ... the relocation and expansion; ever abiding in the realms of His Love. [51]

As we know, we have *our* faith in God ... and that is good and that is right. However now, it is God who is imparting to you the **Faith of His Son** [52]. You may know the word 'love', and it is a word that you can reflect upon and contemplate and study. But until you have been *gripped* and taken over by love you have no idea what it is. So too are these realms of the Spirit; hence until you fully yield and lay your life down in Christ Jesus ... even as one dead, you will never live in open experience of the Life and Power of the Spirit of God.

For this is the very *purpose* of trials and testings; that you truly might **Transcend**. Therefore, in choosing to be pliable ... so are you also teachable ... and therefore in Him, made **indestructible** [53]. God converting all difficulties into constructive blessings, as you live in open experience of the Father and His Hand upon your life. Satan tests with lures to disorientate and ensnare. But God 'tests' in order that your roots may go down deeper into His Love. Deeper into Trusting and Knowing, and deeper into seeking His Mighty Presence that causes great breakthrough.

A side note: "God's Presence sought — the seeking of the manifest Presence of the Lord God Almighty — brings His Presence. And this Presence 'sought' is sensed wherever I go ... and I don't want anything messing with that; for God is my Dream ... not the cares or issues of this life. Therefore, He navigates my life giving me Counsel in my day-to-day, and Graces me where I am energised and greatly inspired. If I sense a 'withdrawing' then I pause; if there are unknown things, then I wait; but if I am to go forward then it is by the Power of the Spirit that I breakthrough. God is my God, not this life ... therefore, I am Guided by Him in His Love, and His Presence and Power never leaves me."

In this world, there is only death and decay; but in the Spirit of God, there is Life Everlasting. Testings are purposed for the developing of your 'roots' as a strong and established tree. Therefore, set yourself — regardless of season — to be proactive in the seeking of the Presence of God. And so will you bear forth of these Eternal realms manifest on earth — irrespective of season [54]. This is the basis of the Outpouring of the Spirit and a life full of miracles. A life of walking in the Promises rather than wandering in the Wilderness.

Do you recall the story of Aaron's Staff? The account where Aaron's walking stick turned into a blossoming and fruitful branch overnight? So it is the same, God seeks that you might — **bridge** the Eternal realms of Life — to this world of which we live. Do you yet understand that? Not just to be good little Christians looking forward to going to Heaven when you die. But walking in the 'pre-fallen' state as a New Adam restored. In Christ Jesus ... as 'Adam' who **oversees all creation**. [55]

Truly, if you can make the Lord ... 'Lord' in your life, He will continue to draw you into a whole other reality. Praise is key ... for praise is **relocational** by nature ... through the Power of the Blood. Your heart set in higher things in Him and being **Translated**. For as you elevate Christ Jesus in your eyes so are you **Elevated**. The very word 'faith' meaning, a belief and a trust and a preference ... for He who is greater than you, and who is greater than the problems you face. Therefore, in such, shall God become most **real** to you. And so does He come, and so does He stand powerful in **place of all that you face**.

In closing ...

Did you know that the very first prayer uttered is God's own personal Prayer? And it went like this, *"Let us make man in our own Image and Likeness"* [55]. So, therefore, practice when you pray ... let yourself **pray as one in His Person**. Pray as one part of '**us**' ... part of the Trinity of God, within His Person. Not separated but unified through the Power of the Blood. For as Jesus continues, *"As You, Father, are in Me, and I in You; may they also be **one** in Us."* [56]

Prayer itself is a most holy calling ... for it is purposed to release both Heaven and the Will of God on earth. I so very much encourage you, **be more interested** in the Divine Presence of God upon your life than what you are believing for. However now, when you speak, turn to the needs before you and have 'Dominion' over them. For no longer are you one looking up to God for help, but one who is responding and have **entered into His Prayer**. Now as one — in Him — are you also one addressing the needs before you from a **commanding** position. A position of sonship and of royalty ... as one who Rules.

Creation is in your mouth: Just as Jesus was the Word made flesh, and the Power of Creation was in Him — this reality is now inherently in you as well. Keep a close check on what you say — be not of mixed seed. **Have one Lord** and therefore **'lord'** over

all things. Do not come under the deception of this Age but rise up in the Light of Life.

Scripture:
And He went up on the mountain and **called** to Him those He Himself wanted. And they came to Him. Then He appointed [**ordained**] twelve, that they might **be with Him** and that He might send them out to preach, and to have **power to heal** sicknesses and to cast out demons. *(Mark 3:13-15 NKJV)*

Again, here in this *Mountain* picture ... Jesus is calling His Disciples. Can you see now — that the crucial part of a 'miracle-filled' lifestyle — is rooted in these words, *"That they might be with Him"*. So the focus is not in your ministry, it isn't healing or the casting out of demons; for the first and primary calling and root purpose of your soul is to ***"Be with Him"*** ... do you see that? As He says elsewhere, *"Abide in my Love"* ... and *"Remain in Me"* [57]. Until you get this, you will always struggle and be tossed around. Until you get this, frailty will remain in you.

The right hand of God is a Place of richly receiving. It is a Place of great Companionship and Counsel — ever **dining** in the Lord — in the Wonder and Delight of His Presence. And ever surrounded by the Father, the Son, the Holy Spirit, and the Cloud of Witnesses ... in the Joy of the Lord.

Truly, it is an incredible treasure to be one who holds Life in your hands ... one who moves both Heaven and earth ... nothing else compares. And this reality ever expanding and expanding; there is no greater wealth, no greater vision — **all else pales**. Therefore, come and deny yourself ... and follow Jesus; and allow the Spirit of the Lord to come richly upon you. We can't still love the world for there is no Life in it only depravity and decay. For on this earth, Satan is earnestly at work to keep you under his feet. But '**in**' Christ Jesus, it is God of whom is earnestly **at work to rise you up** where you walk in the Light of Life.

"Be thou ever transformed by the renewing of your mind." [58]

To be continued in the following chapter ... *"Manifesting Sonship"*.

Appendix:

1. Exodus 33:14, 14:14, *2.* John 1:18, 15:4, 9, 13:23, Isaiah 66:11, 25:6, *3.* Romans 8, Revelation 2-3, *4.* Romans 8:19, *5.* John 2:1-11, *6.* Exodus 33:1-3, Isaiah 64:1-4, Acts 5:15, *7.* Exodus 33:15-18, *8.* John 3:13, 1 Corinthians 3:2, Hebrews 5:12, *9.* Isaiah 33:14b-15a *HCSB*, Psalm 91:1, Acts 5:15, *10.* John 17:20-24, *11.* Matthew 6:9-10, *12.* 2 Corinthians 1:20, *13.* John 15:7-11, *14.* Romans 14:17, *15.* 1 Corinthians 4:20, *16.* Nehemiah 8:10, *17.* Colossians 3:1-3, John 17:24, *18.* John 6:63, *19.* Revelation 3:17-18, 1 Corinthians 3:12-13, *20.* Habakkuk 2:14, Isaiah 11:9, 59:19 *NIV,* *21.* Matthew 7:7, *22.* Philippians 3:12, *23.* Exodus 3:17, *24.* Galatians 3:1, *25.* John 12:24, *26.* John 10:17-18, *27.* Matthew 16:17-19, *28.* 2 Kings 2:9-14, John 14:12, Ephesians 4:13, Luke 6:40, *29.* 1 Kings 19:21, Matthew 16:24, 18:3, John 12:24-26, 10:17, *30.* Genesis 2:17, Hebrews 2:14, Romans 14:9, 2 Corinthians 5:15, Matthew 10:39, John 12:24-25, John 10:17, 11:25, Romans 8:13, *31.* Isaiah 28:11-12, Psalm 23:5, 110:1-2, Exodus 14:14, 33:14, Genesis 1:26, *32.* John 16:12, 14:12, Luke 6:40, *33.* 1 John 3:8, Hebrews 2:14-15, *34.* Psalm 23:5, John 20:22, Exodus 14:14, 20:2, 33:14, *35.* Hebrews 4:10-11, *36.* Psalm 110:1-2, *37.* Psalm 27:4, Song of Solomon 8:5a, *38.* John 17:24, *39.* John 20:22, *40.* Exodus 24:9-11, Zechariah 3:6, *41.* Revelation 1:5-6 *NKJV,* *42.* Hebrews 8:5, Psalm 27:4, *43.* Exodus 24:9-12, Revelation 4:6, 15:2 *44.* Isaiah 33:14b-15a *HCSB,* Revelation 1:12-17, Exodus 3:2, Luke 12:49, *45.* Revelation 3:20, 1 John 2:27, Hebrews 10:16, Exodus 24:12, *46.* Isaiah 28:12, *47.* Exodus 24:9-12, *48.* Revelation 3:21, *49.* John 3:12, *50.* John 3:13 *NKJV,* *51.* John 15:9, *52.* Galatians 2:20 *KJV,* *53.* Mark 16:17-19, *54.* Jeremiah 17:8, *55.* Genesis 1:26, Romans 8:29, 1 Corinthians 15:45, 2 Corinthians 3:18, Matthew 14:31, *56.* John 17:21, *57.* John 15:1-9, *58.* Romans 12:2

Dated: 14/7/22

38. *Authority to Birth Revival (#121)*
MANIFESTING SONSHIP *(Part 1)*

Opening Scripture:
For the earnest expectation of the creation eagerly waits for the revealing of the sons of God. *(Romans 8:19 NKJV)*

The vision and the focus *is* the Presence of God. And the here being captured up in Him. Let that be your 'soul' pursuit [1]. For in this Place it is God who works, it is God who fights [2]. The Love of God is a realm, the Strength and Spirit of God the Abiding Place. And as you respond and come up in Him, it is He who **comes** in place of you.

The Power of God is yours. The Glory of God your very 'Covering' [3]. And the ends of the earth your Possession [4]. In the flesh, the believer seeks to honour God through the works of their own hands. But in the Spirit, it is God who seeks to honour both He — and you — by the works of **His hands**. The vision is the Son, and the Honour is His. But His focus is in the *re*-establishing you in the Glory He Himself dwells and walks in.

The subject of this chapter is about *who* you are in God's eyes. And the crucial part you play in God's Purposes being fulfilled on earth. In the future, when the Christ comes ... all will know God. But that is the time of Judgement, when creation is rolled up like a scroll [5]. Until that time, the Keys of Heaven have been set in *your* hands. And with these Keys given — Heaven can remain closed to you and your people — or otherwise, Heaven can be opened. Revival birthed by who you are in Him.

Anointing means that *you* have Authority to Bless — you choose! All things have been placed under your feet. All Heaven and earth are yours. Therefore, as you humble yourself in the Presence of God so are you Honoured [6], are you lifted up in Place of Honour [7]. And through submission are you elevated and made whole — ever strengthened in His Love, ever built up in the Presence of God — unto exceedingly great exploits. [8]

Who walks in the Power of God? Sonship is about taking *ownership;* it's about knowing who you are in Him. Not in word alone but as a living reality.

Jesus is about revealing Himself to you, revealing the Father unto greater manifestation. We all come from an orphan state, with deep-seeded *fallen* mindsets. But in Christ are we of royalty. Today, we are His children purposed to grow in the Mind of Christ and the fullness of Him. The *Invitation* has been presented, it's now up to you to enter … it is up to us to 'ask'.

TODAY, GOD HAS BECOME YOUR FATHER

Scripture:
I will proclaim the LORD's decree: He said to me, "You are my son; today I have *become* your Father. Ask me, and I will make the nations your inheritance, the ends of the earth your possession." *(Psalm 2:7-8 NIV)*

In Christ Jesus you are the embodiment of the Son on earth. With rights of the Son to walk in 'Like' as Him. The Possessions of the Son are yours. What is Promised Him, now has been Promised you … as *co-heirs* of His Glory. It is God who is in the 'Restoration' business; diligently at work to bring man back into his 'former' Glory. The continuing in the Dream that was lost Him at the Fall … the *making* you 'like one of us'. [9]

The Invitation of your Father is most clear. This *decree* of the Lord is directed to us as well: the walking on the Path in 'Like as the Son'. Come then and place it in your heart to — **'ask'** Him! — ask, seek, knock … and pursue [10]. Truly, unite yourself unto God's Dream and Prayer, and so too shall you engage in participation with Him. In a waltz … a dance … the joining and pursuing what God is pursuing. And in this, so shall God **fight** for you … and so shall you be led and step into realms of the 'Authority of the Son'. The Resurrected Triumphant Authority … to 'author' and rewrite the destiny of many.

This Dwelling Place of God is yours. The very same where God imparts of the Mind of Christ. Where you gain His Vision and His

Eyes; not that of fallen man ... but He who is Risen.

A side note: Held within the word 'authority' is a hidden gem ... the word 'author'. What this means is, that in Christ Jesus, you have Authority in Him to author change. As is said, the 'ends of the earth' are before you; to re-write your destiny and that of others [11]. To initiate, trigger, and birth 'Revival' — ie; great 'Moves' of God. In the details of your own life, in the hope and future for your family and loved ones; and in the 'Outpouring' of the Spirit of God upon the nations.

Now ... just as in the life of David, so were you anointed king years before you were seated. And just as David went through difficulties ... so have you, though God has been with you all the time. There are many things that vie for your attention, but as you keep on moving forward it will be God who shall raise you to Rule.

THE 'EXAMPLE' OF THE SON

Jesus said that *"It is good that I go"* [12] ... for He, in His Person, continually pointed to the Spirit of which His Blood ushers forth. Jesus came as 'Picture'... demonstrating what it means to be a son of God. For by the Power of the Blood have you been *birthed* unto the Spirit; now by the Power of the Spirit are you able to **'Transcend'**. Are you able to be risen up Above, deeper into the Revelation of your sonship. Even this, your sonship made manifest on earth ... as is said, *"All creation waits in eager expectation for the sons of God to be revealed."* [13]

John the Baptised pointed to Jesus,
Jesus pointed to the Spirit,
and the Spirit points to the Fire and
Glory of the Father.

The Blood has opened you to the Power of the Spirit of God [14]. However, it is only through the welcomed 'kindling' of the Spirit that opens you to the Fire of God [15]. The **Blood is the Power of Revival**, for it sanctifies both the hostile and unbelieving unto the Touch of God [16]. But the very — Purpose of the Spirit — is to pour out Fire on earth. Even this the intense Glory of God that shuts the mouth of the Devourer and tramples the snake underfoot. [17]

A side note: This is why I can't help but always speak of 'seeking' the Presence of God. To let it become your soul's — sole — pursuit. The prayer beneath your prayers, your underlying pursuit under all pursuits. Like the 'mantle' just underneath the earth's crust ... let the Living Word burn in your soul. And just behind the lens of your eye; let your singular sole pursuit and drive be unto the open manifestation of the Fire of God.

The underlying drive of the Spirit is the Fire of God. And if you are not yet driven unto the Fire of God for you and your people ... then there is still a misalignment. Shekinah Glory, and the Authoritative Power of the Son; is the Destiny of the Children of God. It is the 'Promised Land' of the Kingdom of Heaven. And unless you knit this into your personal mission then you are operating outside of the definitive Guidance and Fight of God.

The Root of Strength is the Lord [18]. Something beyond you, something apart ... but held deep within [19]. And this is what you want. Not religion or indifference [20] but deep enduring relationship within the Person of God [21]. In the Old Testament, King David was called from his youth. But today — in Christ Jesus [22] — all are called [23]. Heaven opened and through the Power of the Spirit — the fullness of God. Here to sit as a king with King Jesus ... with all things *brought* under your feet; [24] a priest together with the High Priest of God.

Think for a moment and picture the scene. If Satan was removed from the earth, and the Spirit of God outpoured ... what would you have? Heaven on earth. Hence, this is the basis of Revival: the removal of the demon through the Power of the Blood, and the Spirit poured out ... birthing Life in place of death.

The Power of the Blood is in your own very hands. And the Spirit of God is in your mouth to pour out and release. You have fundamental and inherent Power to convert death into life. Hopeless situations into realms of great opportunity. Abiding in the realms of Everlasting Life; pouring out Spirit and Life as you walk on earth. Co-abiding, co-seated ... people in the world but not of the world; aliens, foreigners, 'angels' ... sons of God in human bodily form.

'Abiding' in the realms of Everlasting Life:

— Pouring out Spirit and Life on earth —

If you can truly come to make God's Dream, *your* dream. Then when facing problems, as one Heaven envisioned; then so are you a most powerful creature. Satan fully exposed to the Intensity and Fire of the Glory and Radiance of God in you. For it is by God's Dream that you are seated … and as you sit, so do you release. Ever Abiding in the Place of Rest; the Place of Peace … the Place of Power and deep Companionship.

Moses went up upon the Mountain, into the Place where man was not permitted; and God wrote His 'Word' on tablets of stone. However here, in the Presence of God, Moses sought more *(the 'Fire')* asking, **"Show me your Glory"**. You see, as you also personally love and seek the Presence of God manifest, so shall He continually *write* His Wonder on your heart. And as you continue to ask and seek, does He impart of His very Glory. Taking you into Places where your face glows the Radiance of the Lord.

This is God's Divine motivation:
To return man back into the Creative realms
— The realms of Origins —

'Legalism' is rooted in the Tree of your own Knowledge of Good and Evil. 'Liberty' is rooted in the Spirit. And Power is released as you liberally eat of the Tree of Life [25]. However, humility is most crucial … as is said, **"The meek shall inherit"**. The doorway unto Heaven-activity is humility and submission … for pride *never* comes here. And so too, is the Presence of God itself deeply humbling; for the Heart and Intent of the Father always Elevates.

The 'God'-like state:
— "Let us make man in our Likeness." —

WINNING COMES THROUGH 'CO-HABITATION'

Theme Scripture:
One thing I ask from the Lord, this only do I seek: that I may **dwell** in the House of the Lord all the days of my life, to gaze on the

beauty of the Lord and to **seek Him** in His Temple. *(Psalm 27:4 NIV)*

Oh, the Wonder and Splendour found in treasuring the Lord! [26] Have you yet come to realise, that as Christ Jesus came and lived on earth ... *ie;* 'in creation', that He also fully lived **Above creation**? And as Jesus walked the earth, so did He also live fully outside all natural restrictions and limitations. So what is most important to realise is: that this very same *fundamental* reality remains true for both you and I as well ... if that truly is where your dreams truly lie.

— *The revealed son* —

Jesus walked and operated out of Heaven as He walked this world [27]. Now and today, by the Power of the Blood and the gifted Holy Spirit has this same *reality* been presented you as well. Do you remember how King David would say, *"The Lord is my Strength?"* I so encourage you ... this is **so much more** than a faith statement.

— *Manifest sonship* —

There is a Strength available in the Lord that is Greater than you. A Strength and a Love far greater than knowledge; that fully comes from outside of you. In the Old Testament, there were people who *were* chosen. However today, in Christ Jesus, *all* are chosen [28]. For unto the willing: Heaven is opened ... and through the Power of the Spirit; the very Possessions of Heaven.

Hidden within the Gospel message is a most precious and treasured 'Prayer'. A Prayer most treasured and tender to the Lord. And if you could quieten yourself down ... and pause. And here in the Presence of the Lord, make Jesus' personal Prayer your own personal heart's prayer as well. Then this would cause incredible shift ... and open you to such incredible Wonder. [29]

The Lord's Prayer:
Father, I [pray] desire that they also whom You gave Me may be with me where I am [in Heaven], and that they may behold my Glory. *(John 17:24a (John 3:13 NKJV))*

This, the personal Heart's cry of the Lord, presents to you an incredible 'Invitation'. And if you wish to, respond and join and unite yourself with. Making this — His Prayer — your soul's sole pursuit as well ... *ie;* 'ask'. For here, are you simply *uniting* yourself with the 'Yes' and the 'Amen'. [30]

The realms of Heaven <u>are</u> your possession. The Power and the Strength ... and the inexpressible Joy and Peace; your very dwelling Place. Therefore, as you also come and 'behold' the Glory of the Lord so shall you also carry.

Jesus beheld the Glory of God night and day. This is why He only did what He 'heard' and 'saw'. And this is why He Himself walked in the Glory of God ... for as He said most firmly, *"The Son can do nothing of Himself."* [31]

Hence, this also provides incredible insight concerning our personal walk with God. And it provides incredible encouragement. The Blood is the Invitation, and the Spirit the vehicle and the guide; but Prayer itself is rooted in 'asking'. Asking for what is already yours ... *ie; ask, seek, and knock.*

> *"You are my **son**;*
> *today I have **become** your Father.*
> ***<u>Ask</u> me!** ..."*

Pray you have been blessed.

To be continued in the following chapter ...

Appendix:

1. Psalm 27:4, Colossians 3:1-4, *2.* Matthew 6:33, Psalm 110:1, Exodus 33:14, *3.* Genesis 3:10, 1 Corinthians 15:54, Revelation 3:18 *(Luke 14:28-33)*, Psalm 104:2, 110:1, *4.* Psalm 2:7-8, Matthew 5:5, Genesis 3:19-reversed, *5.* Isaiah 34:4, *6.* Luke 14:10, *7.* John 5:44, Zechariah 3:7, *8.* Daniel 11:32, *9.* Genesis 1:26, John 17:21, *10.* Matthew 7:7-8, *11.* John 15:7, *12.* John 16:7-8, *13.* Romans 8:19, *14.* Matthew 12:28, Luke 5:17, 4:14, *15.* Luke 12:49, 24:49, Matthew 4:2-3, Isaiah 64:1-4, *16.* John 16:8, *17.* Genesis 1:26, 3:1, 3:24, Exodus 14:14, 33:14, Deuteronomy 3:22, Ezekiel 10:18-20, Psalm 110:1-2, Isaiah 40:5, John 14:12, 1 Corinthians 15:54, Revelation 3:17-18 *(Luke 14:28-33)*, *18.* John 5:19, Isaiah 11:1-2, *19.* John 3:13 *NKJV*, *20.* Matthew 22:29, Luke 21:34, *21.* John 17:3, Exodus 33:11, 18, John 1:18, *22.* John 15:7, *23.* Revelation 5:9-10, *24.* Galatians 3:28, John 17:16, Psalm 110:1-2, Matthew 16:17-19, Revelation 1:5-6 *NKJV*, *25.* Revelation 22:2, *26.* Matthew 6:21, *27.* John 3:13 *NKJV*, 17:20-24, 13:33, 36, 5:19, *28.* Revelation 5:9-10 *NKJV*, *29.* Psalm 46:10a, Revelation 1:10, 17, *30.* 2 Corinthians 1:20, *31.* John 5:19

Dated: 26/11/22

39. *Authority to Birth Revival (#122)*
MANIFESTING SONSHIP *(Part 2)*

Scripture:
Father, I [pray] desire that they also whom You gave Me may be with me where I am [in Heaven], and that they may behold my Glory. *(John 17:24a (John 3:13 NKJV))*

GOD 'RENDS' THE HEAVENS

Beholding the Glory of God opens you to manifestation. The Presence of the Person of God sought, opens you to the Real and the Tangible. Even unto the very same whereby Jesus exclaimed to Peter, *"The Gates of Hades cannot prevail"* [1]. To hear and to receive from God, even as small 'Mustard Seeds of Faith' planted in your soul ... moves mountains [2]. Such is the power of 'waiting upon the Lord'. Such is the Power opened and released ... the *Unexpected* and the *Wonderful*. Moves of Glory where God makes Himself **known**.

The Gates of Hades cannot prevail against *such* who hear and see God. So then come and let this become your soul's sole pursuit. The Middle East was entirely Christian, then it was totally overrun. Hence, religion will not save you, nor will belief alone, only Divine interaction from in the Person of God ... just as the Son.

Do you recall in Scripture, where God speaks about 'rending the heavens?' This an incredible picture where God comes and steps down and does amazing and crazy things, as seen across the nations [3]. And do you realise that this 'rending', this 'tearing away' of opposition, this personally 'making way' by the Person of God — is triggered by a *single* man or peoples [4] — who wait upon the Lord? Of whose heart within is deeply purposed to engage with the very Person of God.

Now, we all have our prayers and needs ... but Authority doesn't come by obsessing over them. Authority comes by joining with the Father's own central Dream of Restoration, *ie;* the 'asking'. His very Prayer of restoring you back into the *former* things from whence man fell. The very same Glory where you walk in 'Dominion' *(Governmental Authority)* over all things [5]. Hence, therefore, your heart fixed on the Presence of the Glory of God — irrespective! — such is *faith*. Such is the firm connection whereby nothing is impossible for you, nor can anything stand in your way.

To such as these, God Himself 'rends' apart, pushing everything aside ... even the very 'heavens' [6]. Meaning, all powers and established authorities; all resistance and hindrances. God Himself firmly going out and acting firmly on your behalf. This has always been the way of the Father.

A side note: To the establishing of deep roots are you made unshakeable. The problem is ... the being 'pushed off', that is the issue. When you cling onto your life; there are so many things that vie for your attention, that can corrupt and manipulate. But when it is the Lord, it is the Lord God Himself who responds to you ... for it is He who truly is God in your life.

The Spirit of the Lord is He of whom is *freely* given. But it is the Glory of God that **costs your whole heart**. Itself then ... becoming your very 'Clothing'. As is said, *"They shall take up serpents; and if they drink any deadly thing, it shall not hurt them; they shall lay hands on the sick, and they shall recover."* [7]

Scripture:
My Father's house has many rooms; if that were not so, would I have told you that I am going there to **prepare a place for you**? And if I go and prepare a place for you, I will come back and take you to be with me that you also **may be where I am**. You know **the way to the place** where I am going. *(John 14:2-4 NIV)*

Your home is Heaven. Your home is right within the Divine realms of Power and Grace. Jesus departed for a most important purpose: to make a Place for you. But it is also most important to realise — that it doesn't take Jesus 2000 years to complete!

Jesus didn't leave His Disciples orphans [8] — He is true to His word — He didn't abandon them! ... but even continues, *"You know the way to the place where I am going"*. And so we do. Your home and Place of Dwelling is **today** waiting for you to enter and **take** your place. God is waiting, the Spirit is yearning, and the Blood is bearing a greater 'testimony' ... a greater *Calling* than we have known. And that is to '**be <u>with</u> Him where He is**'. *9*

Therefore, truly learn to look past the 'forests' of issues ... always unto the Tree of Life. For in this you will never fail. Don't wait for overwhelming concerns to come, it may be too late. But learn and practice ... and become **accustomed** to the Presence of God gracing your life. For just as a soldier trains, and a musician practices ... so does a Warrior of Power.

> *"If I go and prepare a place for you, I will come back and take you to be with me that you also may be where I am."*

BE WITH ME 'WHERE I AM'

At the time of Jesus ... there were many disciples. Many of whom believed in the Person of Jesus. But then, there were those who responded to His 'Call' and came to Him. As He asked ... that they might 'be with Him'. *10*

There is a Place in the Lord that the intelligence of 'Nicodemus' cannot comprehend *11*. A Place where in the Spirit ... you are 'like the wind' *12*. And here, in this Place, it is Jesus who Anoints you with a message to 'preach'. And it is He who gives you Power and Authority over **all** the works of the demon. *13*

It is Jesus who seeks that you become Jesus ... not just one who believes in Him. To say that again, Jesus seeks that you walk as Him on earth, not only one who holds a belief. Jesus said of Himself, that He is the 'Gate' through which the sheep of whom — 'hear the master's voice' *14* — 'go in and out' finding Pasture *15*. Go in and out of where? But Heaven of course. To believe is not enough, but to *enter* in ... that is the path of a **miraculous life**!

The Pastures of the Lord are the Garden realms. The rich Place of continually Receiving. The realms of the Banqueting Table where you live in constant and Divine Fellowship in God. These realms of God's Love; the Ministering realms, the Imparting realms ... where you live being ever transformed in '**Likeness**' of God. *16*

Christ Jesus, through the gentleness [17] and kindness of His own heart — in His own quietness, humility, and meekness — it is He who *gives* you Power and Authority over all things. It is Jesus who Anoints, and it is He who clothes you in High Honour in the Presence of the Lord [18]. No one can bring you here and no one can take you away. But to here, each one of us is called to point [19] ... not to one another but to this Place of Power.

In the forest there are many trees ... just as in the Garden, there is the Tree of Life [20]. Truly, if you can learn to look through, and see past all the 'trees' of this life, and actively pursue after the Glory of God [21]. Then, you will never get lost in the forest [22]. The root of your soul would never get disoriented, nor overwhelmed in the responsibilities of ministry and life; but in all things be made stronger in the Presence of God — and openly see His hand at work.

It is God who is in the Restoration business. The restoring you back into the Original Glory that is yours. And if you cannot grasp this then you will always struggle. However, if you can truly come and lay hold of these things ... as like in the targeting of an arrow; then you would grow exponentially. And would swiftly come out of hopelessness and frailty ... into the realms of Dominion, Grace, and Power.

LIVING IN A STATE OF PERPETUAL ENCOUNTER

Let's break this theme Scripture down:

1. One thing I **ask**, this only I will seek,
2. That I **dwell** in the House of the Lord ... all the days of my life.
3. To **gaze** upon the Beauty of the Lord.
4. And **seek** Him in His Temple.

Since David was a young boy, he lived in Encounter of God *('kindling' is the basis of Revival* [23]*)*. When fighting the lion and the bear, his Strength and Confidence came from Above. And when confronting Goliath, his Courage and Capacity came from He to whom his heart 'Abided' [24]. Let me then reveal a little secret: the

'House of the Lord' that David's soul yearned and cried out for ... was not on earth.

David was a warrior and a king. He was a most practical man to whom the many looked to. So the question would be, was the 'House of the Lord' that David's soul longed to dwell in 'all the days of his life' ... was it on earth or was it in Heaven?

Further, in regards the 'Temple', as we know ... David did not build the Temple of God. His son Solomon did after he was gone. So, to which Temple then ... was David referring to?

Let me share another mystery; 'Zion' is not the earthly Jerusalem, but the Heavenly Jerusalem [25]. The very same Place where *your* Strength comes from. As is said, *"The Lord shall send the rod of your strength out of Zion, saying, 'Rule in the midst of Your enemies!'"* [26]

Did you know that the Tabernacle, the 'Tent of Meetings', was made after the original Temple of God that is in Heaven? Scripture refers to the Tabernacle as but a 'shadow' and a 'copy' [27]. Therefore, in the practicality of life ... your own heart set in quiet to meet with the Person of God ... engages the realms of the Divine. Engages the realms of Heaven, Glory, and Power.

Today, it is Jesus who is openly Inviting you here. For His Blood speaks of greater things than the betrayal of this world [28]. So cry out then ... with a true humble heart unto God. And with a tender ear say to Him, *"Speak for your servant is listening"* [29]. For from this Place, so shall a Strength flow upon you [30] ... something that is not of you but rising up within, that you might truly Rule over all that comes against.

Mount Sinai was the first 'Temple' of God on earth. The very first 'Meeting Place' of the Most High God for the people. Then later came the Tent of Meetings ... 'Mount Sinai' portable in a tent.

However today, we know, that we ourselves are the Temple of God; [31] made by the Hand and Will of God ... and within, do you *carry* this 'Place of Meeting'. Hence truly, your heart is a Gateway. Your 'affections unto God' the very doorway unto the Heart of the

Father; and the Glory held within ... *ie;* the Power and the Strength of God to win. [32]

The Holy of Holies within you joining the Holy of Holies in Heaven.

Therefore truly, where your treasure truly lies so your *heart* does also. Even this very day, as one who stands before the Glory of God [33]. And here, your words become most powerful, and your dreams begin to unfold before your eyes. As is said, *"Delight yourself in the Lord, and He will fulfil the desires of your heart"* [34]. The Lord Himself working to bring all things under your feet. Removing the tears from your eyes. Bringing you out of darkness into His marvellous Light.

'David is a man after my own Heart' ... oh, how this is relevant to us today. If ever there is a day that you would truly desire to pursue after God's Heart and Dreams; then you would be a most unstoppable force.

HE WHO LAYS DOWN HIS LIFE FINDS IT
David was a man before his time. His life pre-exampled that of our own 'ruling life' in Christ Jesus. Meaning, both Anointed Royalty and the Divine Purposes of God actively at work in our own lives. For so too ... are you of the 'kingly line'; pre-destined in Him to rule in Heavenly Places ... as *seeds* of the Living Christ.

However, these things do not come automatically ... deep personal *relationship* is key. Here, by choice and by will: choosing to walk in deep personal experience in the Person of God — just as David — and so too — the Christ [35]. And here, in Him, allowing your sonship to become ever more known to you. And hence, therefore, ever made more manifest on earth. But in this — surrender is most key.

Scripture:
Very truly I tell you, unless a kernel of wheat falls to the ground and dies, it remains only a single seed. But if it dies, it produces many seeds. *(John 12:24 NIV)*

In the Kingdom, the Promises of God are not automatic. And how one comes to unlock the — Unfathomableness of God — in your life, *ie;* the Catalytic growth, the Miraculous Hand of God continually at work, your Royal seated station in Him actively functioning — is through surrender. The laying down of your life in 'death'; only then to pick it up again in the realms of Life. [36]

God, by nature, rarely pushes. He isn't rude or forceful ... but is gentile, kind, and patient. Jesus spoke in Gospel how the *"Meek shall inherit the earth"*[37]. So what is most important for us to realise is, that God doesn't ask anything of you that He Himself isn't willing to give. Jesus speaks so clearly of such things for — His very own nature is **meek** — His own nature is *"Lowly and humble of heart."* [38]

The underlying culture of Heaven is rooted and based rich in Honour — rich in love, in care, and in humility. Hence, you can't retain a heart of Satan and expect to live in the Authority of God. True 'possession' of the Kingdom only comes through the laying yourself down and allowing God Himself to Personally lift you up and position you [39]. Authority comes by the giving of your 'prayers' unto God ... laying them down, even as though in death. For only then — 'in the realms of Everlasting Life' — can you truly breathe Life and Spirit into them.

Like 'fishing' ... catch and release. Catching your cares and your fears ... and releasing them unto the Spirit of God to manage. For it is the Spirit of God of whom is so much more Creative than you, and so much more Capable. And He never works alone ... nor in just a singular vision. But with a great host of angels in 'conspiracy' for your whole good. And He isn't only interested in the healing of your singular prayer, but in the healing and restoration of many things all at once.

Humility mixed with a heart of honest pursuit; these very things are so highly valued in God. Even here, right in the midst of your broken state. Not a prideful Pharisaic attitude in approaching God, but the true laying yourself down 'broken' before Him. Even as Paul himself ... of whom, *"Considered everything refuse compared to the Wondrous things God is leading me in"* [40]. To such the Lord comes, and to such the Lord is called and drawn unto. Not to the 'righteous' ... but to the broken and the lost. *41*

The very first message of Jesus, the message that initiated the very start of His Ministry, went like this, *"The Spirit of the Lord is upon me, because He has Anointed me to preach the Gospel to the poor; He has sent me to heal the brokenhearted."* *42*

So therefore, what is most important to recognise is, that Power and Glory comes not because of pride — but because you have a heart for the hurting. Not unto the looking 'up' to leaders for approval but 'down' unto the lowly ... to lift them up and *establish* them on solid ground. And God comes not because you yourself are something — but because you recognise that you are not. For it is to such as these that He comes; and it is to such these you are called. Not to appease the prideful but to strengthen the weak through the Power of the Spirit. Amen?

Did you know, that in the Exodus account, that there were people who physically went up and ate and drank a physical meal in the Presence of God in Heaven? *43* Let me share then another secret with you — if it was OK for these men in the Old Covenant — **how much more** is it right for you today in Christ Jesus? And what do you think 'holiness' in the Lord really means? But a *whole* purpose, a *singular* objective and drive; one who is *incorruptible* by nature ... as Jesus Himself said, *"Satan has nothing in me."* *44*

The Kingdom of Heaven is right 'at hand' — meaning, that the Kingdom of Heaven is purposed to be fully **engaged** ... that is how you win*!*

For as a people, you are not called to be a 'kingdom' unto yourselves — but part of the Kingdom of God in Heaven *45*. Therefore, as you also choose to *remain* Heaven focused, not only in the mindset for when you die ... **but today whilst you still live**. Then so shall you come to walk in Heaven — and the delights thereof *46* as you still walk this earth — just as the Son. *47*

'GAZE' UPON YOUR BEAUTY:

Scripture:

The LORD said to my Lord, "**Sit** at My right hand, till I make your enemies Your footstool. The Lord shall send the rod of your **strength** out of Zion. **Rule** in the midst of Your enemies!" *(Psalm 110:1-2 NKJV)*

This prophetic word spoken by David, was itself a most evident reality in David's own life as well. And though it was a word spoken of the Christ to come — it's most important to realise — that as one in Christ Jesus, one unified in the Lord; body, mind, soul, and spirit; that this is God's Vision and **underlying Purpose** concerning the Church as well.

For as one in Christ Jesus — 'co-heirs' with Him — so are we Purposed and Called of God to *co-reign* and be *co-seated* with Him where He is. As brothers and sisters of our Lord Jesus Christ — fellow children of the Most High God — it is here, that God is Inviting each one of us personally; to respond and sit with Him at the Father's right hand. Hence, as is purposed, you have the capacity and the right to be Heaven focused. [48]

Fundamentally you have the right to personally choose it within yourself, to respond to the Invitation of God; and sit here in the realms where God Himself dwells. And just like in the life of David, so shall it be God who shall **raise** you in the Victory of the Son. Not in an Old Testament vision, nor even just of the New ... but in the Triumphant Victorious Glory state of the Risen Resurrected Christ.

The Blood is pointing to the Spirit ... however, where is it that the Spirit is pointed to? But to the Fire and Glory of the Father. His Glory so intense that not even Moses could see the Face of God ... and it is to this that Jesus Himself 'delighted' in. The Blood is within your grasp ... it is in your very hand's reach. It is in your heart to receive, and in your mouth to speak. It is both your 'covering' to **protect** ... but also the Power to release the Aggression of God.

"As the Father taught me I speak these things." [49]

These things I am speaking of, are they easy to understand? Can you ... *are* you able to receive it? Maybe not in our fallen carnal vision or opinion, nor in a legalistic religion mindset ... but in the Mind of Christ. In a humble heart ... ever before the Lord of Glory. As Mary said, *"If it be thy Will make it so."* [50]

To emphasise then, when you look at Adam and where he fell from — these are the very same Places Christ Jesus came, and was crucified and raised again — that you too may be Restored. However, it is a challenge ... isn't it? For this 'walking in Glory'; there is so much for us to untangle ourselves from. But don't worry, you have the Presence of the Father at work in you ... **if** truly it is His Presence that you seek and yearn for.

Christ Jesus' personal Dream and Prayer for you this day, is that you truly might also be here with Him where He is. Not just in the life to come, but today here and now. This, for your own life personally ... for your ministry, and for the sake of your people. For this sums up the Gospel message, and all the efforts of God since the Beginning. Till we also come into the 'Sabbath Day of Rest' as called [51] ... *just as did Jesus*. Entering into the fulfilment of our Destiny revealed and made manifest on earth.

What was one of the three 'temptations' Satan came at Jesus with, in the wilderness ... do you remember? Satan attacked His identity saying, *"If You are the Son of God, throw Yourself down"* [52]. And this is who this devil is; he is so godless and so God hating ... and he hates you. And he has been actively coming against your **true identity** in God since the Beginning. However, if you truly would welcome the Presence of God to come upon you, then He would continue to lift you up and break the Lie. As one stepping out into the Light, even that of your true sonship and true station in the Lord.

THE INCONCEIVABLE LOVE OF GOD

Consider the love of Jesus towards you personally. For it is Jesus who is looking most intently at you today, and with deep Love in His eyes saying, *"Come sit with me at the right hand of God. And it will be God who works to bring everything under your feet"* — ie; the focus — the very focus and target point of the complete Gospel message.

The right hand of God is the Place of Rest. It is the 'Place of Repose' [53] — where you also come to walk in a 'god' like force — as one unstoppable in Him [54]. And it is to here, that the Spirit of the Lord is yearning for each one of His people to come [55] — into this Place of 'Knowing'. This Place of Love and Joy unspeakable; the Place of Instruction and Counsel, and the Place of Power and Divine Wonder. No one can bring you here, though each one of us can point and encourage [56] ... **only you can give your heart** unto God.

Scripture:
"I and My Father are one." *(John 10:30 NKJV)*

There are many many voices in the world ... so many. But to whose voice do you truly wish to adhere to? As a king **you possess** the Kingdom of God [57] ... it is yours! And so too, as a cherished child, are the very Keys of Heaven. The difference between the Blessed and the Anointed is most clear: not only are the Anointed blessed, but they themselves **Command** a blessing! By choice and by will **do you direct and release**.

Let me ask a question, why do you think the Sword has a handle? That you, as a child of the Living God, might lay hold of the very Spirit of God ... and 'thrust out'.

It is only through the deepest of humility and unto full submission in the Holy Ghost that you can release [58]. And as one who bows in the Holy Presence of God's Divine Counsel, so are you presented by Him ... able to rule. Tutored and Instructed, and given Authority through ever-deepening bonded relationship.

The Sword has many purposes: It is for defence and to deflect, to sever and to cut off. And when taking a stand, it is to draw a line in the sand and say, *"No more!"* But most importantly, it is to point and direct; to 'thrust out' the Activity, the Life, and the Authority of the Spirit. The no longer clinging onto fear but the releasing of Power with a word. And the 'word spoken' *(ie; out of your mouth* [59]*, a Spirit-Word ... a 'Sword')* setting firm place for the Spirit of the Lord to go out and take charge.

It is true ... how far man has fallen [60]. But it is also true, how much the Father seeks to Restore.

'NEXT LEVEL' ANOINTING

Scripture:
The reason my Father loves me is that I [willingly] lay down my life — only to take it up again. *(John 10:17 NIV)*

When Jesus was about to be crucified, He asked His Disciples this, *"When I sent you out without a purse did you lack anything? And they said 'no'. But then He said, now 'sell' your cloak and 'buy a sword.'"* [61]

What this means is that as a disciple of the Lord Jesus Christ, as a child of the Most High God, you have the right to willingly lay down your life in *death* — only then — to **pick it up** again **in Life**. Meaning, pick it up in the realms of Everlasting Life; in the realms of Authority — in 'death' — picking up as like a 'Sword' the very Anointing of God.

There is a realm of God's Love that **only surrender can access**. A realm of the Love of God that only they who *willingly* lay down their life find. A realm even — where the words of your mouth — become as like a 'Sword', and where Life and Power liberally flow. Hence therefore, as you also choose to deeply humble yourself, and in the Presence of God lay your life down in Him *(responsibilities, duties, fears, and betrayals);* [62] then so too are you able to truly pick it up again in the realms of Authority, Power, and Glory.

The Sword represents the Spirit of God; all Seven attributes. The Spirit of the Lord, the Spirit of Wisdom and Understanding, the Spirit of Counsel and Might, and the Spirit of the Knowledge and of the Fear of the Lord [63]. What this means is, that as the Spirit of God is cherished and held most dear ... deep within you, so too are you able to release.

> *One is only able to release God in a measure that they have laid their life down.*

The handle of the Sword represents the Anointing of God. The Authority given of the Son to 'wield' in your hands the Life and the Spirit of the Lord. To direct and release the Salvation and Judgement of the Lord with a — Spirit-unified — 'word'. [64]

The outworking of this is, that as 'one in Christ', as one united and bonded with Him, that out of your mouth shall come a 'Sword to strike the nations' [65]. Meaning, out of your mouth shall you **birth Revival** [66]. Birth moves of the Spirit; birth moves of the Knowledge and the Understanding of God ... and birth moves of the Might and Fear of the Lord *(His Power and His Fire)*. As a child of God, shall you trigger 'Outpourings' of the Spirit of the Lord unto the nations. This, for your loved ones and for your people, for the broken and the lost, and unto the hostile and the godless.

*A side note: To make 'Judgements' on the Throne of Grace is one's established right — **in** — Christ Jesus. Not to condemn people ... but in Life; to proclaim, to declare, and to decree over situations and health matters. As well as in defence of the Kingdom, and the domains of God that He has given you; the Hand of God to guard and protect, and to go out before you and respond against that of which is coming in opposition to you (see Isaiah 11 verse 3 to 4).*

Say this short prayer with me, *"Heavenly Father, I willingly lay down my life in its entirety. Only then to pick it up in the **fullness** of you."*

BE CLOTHED IN GLORY

Scripture:
Because you say, 'I am rich, have become wealthy, and have need of nothing'— and do not know that you are wretched, miserable, poor, blind, and naked. *(Revelation 3:17 NKJV)*

Jesus here speaking to the Church, continues on further saying, *"I counsel you to **buy** from me Gold that you might be rich"* [67]. And to this, what does 'gold' represent? But to 'buy' of Jesus the Glory of God.

In the Beginning, at the Fall ... Adam and Eve were found 'naked' [68]. It's a mystery, but what do you think this mean? But that Adam and Eve were found without the very 'Clothing' of God's Glory. The very same to which they were created wearing.

Scripture:
The perishable must **clothe** itself with the imperishable, and the mortal with immortality. When the perishable has been clothed with the imperishable, and the mortal with immortality, then the saying that is written will come true: "**Death has been swallowed up in victory**." *(1 Corinthians 15:53-54 NIV)*

The people of God are *Called* to go on further in Christ Jesus … as rightful heirs of Glory: to lay down what is temporal and fleeting and **clothe** yourself with ever-increasing Glory *('turning to the Lord, and with 'unveiled faced' contemplate His Glory [80])*. This, the laying down in 'death' — that **in this life** — you might truly pick up the **Life of God**. And these realms of Glory; this being 'Clothed' of the Most High God — leading you in as one entering into the realms of the 'Untouchable' — as is said, *"Death, where is your sting?"* [69]

Scripture:
I have swept away your offences like the morning mist. Return to me, for I have redeemed you." *(Isaiah 44:22)*

It is Jesus who has paid the ultimate price for you. **However**, if you truly want to walk in the fullness of what He has purchased … **you have to pay the price**!

The Mantle of God doesn't cost anything … except your *whole* self. The relocation from this carnal life, with its fears and desires, into our New Life in Christ Jesus. Out of this world of depravity and decay … *into* the 'world' of Immortality, Power, and Possession *(the 'Exodus')*. For as you truly **choose to give your life** to Jesus … and the issues of it, then so too are you truly able to Command. That is, walk on water, calm storms … trans-relocate, and take gold out of mouths of fishes. Heal the sick, raise the dead, and cast out demons. Cleanse the land and open up the way for the Fire of God to fall.

It is true, that so much in life … the believer has been clinging onto but *trinkets*. When it is God Himself who **has given us the whole world**. And so too, much in our 'prayer life' has been misaligned to the very times and seasons that we are in. For we are not purposed to remain 'Old Testament' believers … *only* going to God asking. For it is God Himself who has **already** given you everything and all things *(Heaven and earth ... but are you trustworthy?).*

God has worked and planned since the Beginning, with firm and clear Purpose to the *"**Making** man into His Image and Likeness".* God Himself working to establish and give you 'Dominion' over the whole earth. Dominion over 'livestock' *(income, provision, and finances),* Dominion over powers both above and below, and Dominion over 'every creeping thing' [70]. And it is to this Place of Dominion that the Father seeks to lead all His people ... this Place of Restoration. The walking in the *former* Glory as like Adam; but better still, today, in Likeness of the Glory of the Risen Son.

Authority to birth Revival starts with you. It starts within your own heart and thought life and wellbeing. For you yourself have the *right* to release the Life and Joy of the Lord ... Revelations, Visions, and Dreams. Revival and Moves of God in your finances, in your health, and in your work life. Revival and Outpourings of the Spirit in your children, in someone in need; in the fearful, the broken, and the lost. Revivals in the Church, great Moves of God in the governments, Latter Day Rains in the 'barrenness' of the land where sin and death has only gripped.

Elisha — who burnt his past — left everything in *celebration* to follow his master. And as he lived in witness of his master rising up he received a double portion. This, I call 'Next Level Anointing'. For in Christ Jesus, we too are called to lay down all things and follow Him. Even — to 'burn' our past — that we too might truly walk in the Anointing of God; in the Anointing of the Son to do even greater works than He. The secret then is, that in the Presence of God, do we each live in witness of the Resurrected Christ.

THE MEEK SHALL INHERIT THE EARTH

Choosing to 'suffer' in order to do what's right. Paying the price — the 'cost' of walking in what God desires — instead of what is common and desirable in the world. So too, indeed, shall you walk in a greater 'revealed' Glory as you walk this earth [71]. The Path of Glory costs, for you can't still live a life of depravity, you have to make a stand!

Here Jesus continues further in this verse in Revelations, and says, *"Buy from me eye salve that you **might see**."*

Oh, the Wonders of God ... truly, that you might be one who openly hears and sees just as the Son [72]. Anyone can read, anyone can quote knowledge. But who truly *knows* how to receive from God?

Now Elisha, the very moment that he 'picked up' the Anointing that was his, the very first prayer he uttered was, *"Where is the God of Elijah?"* Or another way of saying, *"Where is the Power of God to act?"* Such is the attitude of the Anointed. Not one who still lives under the vision of a fallen mindset ... *asking*, but under the Living and Active Word of God. And as he said this, he struck the River Jordan and it parted to the left and to the right so that Elisha could pass through.

I so encourage you ... we all need to step further into, and grow more fuller in, the maturity that is ours. We all need to come out of 'nappies' in our thinking — into the maturity of the Son — even that of the maturity of a king. We need to stop drinking only milk but eat solid food. For lambs drink milk, but lions eat meat.

Truly, our children need something more than us ... more than our strength and knowledge. They need the miracle Life of God resting upon them. Christ Jesus has clearly made the way: not only in personally demonstrating and picturing that of our true and purposed Destiny. But that you too may come to do even greater works than He. [73]

A side note: Three times the River Jordon was parted. And for us, in Christ Jesus, this parting of the river 'picture' has great spiritual significance. Firstly, at the time of the Exodus, it represented the physical crossing over into the Promised Land. Then secondly, for us in the New Testament, it now represents the birthing of the Spirit; the parting of the veil, and here coming into the realms of Promise; the new birth into the Spirit as cherished children of God. However now, in this third 'parting' concerning Revivals, it represents the 'Third Day' [74]*. The Anointing to strike the waters ... where all the spiritual opposition, all indifference and godlessness, part way for the Fire of God. Part way for the Outpouring of the 'Latter Day Rains' unto the nations.*

There comes a time when something rises up within you to say, "**No more!**" Where you personally come to strike the ground in the attitude and Authority of the Son and command change. In times of injustice or unfruitfulness, in sickness or disease; in dry, barren, or hard seasons ... where you say, "***Enough is enough!***"

For today, in Christ Jesus, you now are fundamentally also in the 'Restoration' business. Therefore, come and assume the attitude of the King. For here, it is Jesus who shall give you an Iron Sceptre — to 'strike the nations'. [75]

Scripture:
The Spirit of the Lord is upon me [the Power of God], because He has Anointed me to proclaim good news to the poor. *(Luke 4:18)*

The River Jordan was parted three times in biblical history. And the third time — through the double Anointing of Elisha — unto a mission for the nation.

Today, we are under this '**Third Day**' Anointing of the Resurrected Christ; that you too may strike the 'waters' for you and your people ... *birthing* Revival. For if your heart is truly set unto the restoring of Life in place of Death — then you also have both the Power and the Authority — you have the Anointing given of God... in **ever-increasing** measure.

However, very truly I tell you, *"Be so careful and aware of the yeast of the Pharisees"* [76]. For **your calling is never** unto the seeking of the approval of leadership or the voices or opinion of men. But always unto the yearning and seeking of the Approval and Honour that comes from the only God. As is clearly said, *"How can you believe if you seek honour of one another but seek not the honour that comes from the one and only God?"* [77]

For the Anointing of God does not come, nor does the Revelation of Heaven ... through the seeking of the praise or acceptance of man — that's totally contrary. It doesn't come through looking 'up' but looking 'down'; unto the broken and the lost, the orphan and the widow [78]. The Power and Glory of God is unto the **lifting** up of another that all might be healed and made strong in the Lord.

That the Body of the Christ may become mature, lacking no good thing ... *"Unto the whole measure of the stature of the fullness of Christ".* [79]

Fundamentally, the way of the 'Pharisees' is cyclic and closed. Progressively becoming more closed and more caged. But the Way of the Son is Liberty and Love ... becoming a people full of the Power of Holy Ghost. [80]

To be continued in the following chapter ...

Appendix:

1. Matthew 16:17-19, *2.* Matthew 17:20, *3.* Isaiah 64:1-4, *4.* 2 Chronicles 7:14, Daniel 10:12, *5.* Genesis 1:26, *6.* Exodus 14:14, 33:14, 3, 15, *7.* Mark 16:18, *8.* John 14:18, *9.* John 14, *10.* Mark 3:13-15, Luke 24:49; John 14:1-6, 13:33, 36, 7:34,10:27, 12:26, *11.* John 3:9, *12.* John 3:8, Isaiah 60:8, Psalm 84:3, *13.* Matthew 16:17-19, Mark 16:17-19, *14.* John 10:27, *15.* John 10:9, 6:51, *16.* Genesis 1:26, 2 Corinthians 3:18, *17.* Matthew 11:29, Revelation 3:20-21, *18.* Zechariah 3:5-7, Revelation 3:18, *19.* Isaiah 2:2-3, *20.* Genesis 2:9, 3:22, Revelation 2:7, 22:2, *21.* Exodus 33:18, 24:10-11, 20:21, 20:19, Hebrews 12:21, Isaiah 11:3, Revelation 1:17, *22.* Matthew 10:39, 6:33, *23.* Luke 12:49, *24.* John 15:4, *25.* Revelation 3:12, *26.* Psalm 110:2, *27.* Hebrews 8:5, *28.* Hebrews 12:24, *29.* 1 Samuel 3:9, *30.* Isaiah 40:30-31, *31.* John 14:23, 28, *32.* Colossians 3:1-3, 1 Corinthians 15:53-55, Mark 16:17-18, *33.* Exodus 33:18, *34.* Psalm 37:4, *35.* John 1:18, Psalm 37:4, 27:4, Exodus 33:2-3, 15-16, Matthew 16:17-19, *36.* John 10:17, *37.* Matthew 5:5, *38.* Matthew 11:29, *39.* Luke 14:10, *40.* Philippians 3:8, *41.* Luke 4:17-19, Mark 2:17, *42.* Luke 4:18, *43.* Exodus 24:9-11, *44.* John 14:30, *45.* Revelation 1:5-6 *NIV vs. NKJV*, *46.* Galatians 5:22-23, Psalm 23:5, *47.* John 3:13 *NKJV*, *48.* Colossians 3:1-2, *49.* John 8:28, *50.* Luke 1:38, *51.* Hebrews 4:10, *52.* Matthew 4:6, *53.* Isaiah 28:12, *54.* Exodus 33:14, Psalm 82:6-8, John 10:34, Mark 16:17-19, *55.* Hebrews 4:11, *56.* Isaiah 2:2-3, *57.* Matthew 25:34, Luke 12:32, Ephesians 1:18, 2:6-7, Romans 8:17, Galatians 4:7, *58.* Zechariah 3:7, *59.* Revelation 19:15, *60.* Romans 3:23, *61.* Luke 22:36, *62.* Luke 5:15-17 *NIV*, Matthew 10:38, 16:24, Mark 8:34, Luke 9:23, 14:27, *63.* Isaiah 11:2, *64.* John 20:19-23 *(for they who live by the Spirit, not the flesh but the Spirit. Lest the judgements of God fall on you)*, *65.* Revelation 19:15, 2:26-29, *66.* Acts 2:37-39, *67.* Revelation 3:18, *68.* Genesis 3:10, *69.* Exodus 14:14, 33:14, Mark 16:17-18, 1 Corinthians 15:55, *70.* Genesis 1:26, *71.* Romans 8:18, 2 Corinthians 3:18, Colossians 3:4, *72.* 2 Kings 6:17, *73.* John 14:12, *74.* 1 Corinthians 15:4, *75.* Revelation 2:25-28, *76.* Matthew 16:6, *77.* John 5:44, *78.* James 1:27, *79.* Ephesians 4:13, *80.* 2 Corinthians 3:16-18

Dated: 26/11/22

40. *Authority to Birth Revival (#123)*
MANIFESTING SONSHIP *(Part 3)*

Jesus came as the Word made flesh, then as purposed ... He shed His Blood and released Life in the Spirit of God. Hence, therefore, much of what we have been discussing in these last chapters has been laying foundation in preparation for a great Outpouring.

Again, first came the Word in the form of the Son of Man. Then through the shedding of His Blood did He release the Spirit. But so it is now, that these three Witnesses: the Word, the Blood, and the Spirit ... they continue, they all point to the Fire of God [1]. The Fire and the Glory of the Father standing in our midst and going out in the nations.

Oh, the Power and Authority inherent in all who believe. The inherent Power and Authority to heal and release the Salvation and Grace of the Lord. For truly there comes a time, that the only way you can win is to *become* Jesus. Meaning, not only one believing in His Name but picking up the Anointing He left in His Resurrection ... and 'striking' the ground. [2]

ELIJAH AND ELISHA / JESUS AND HIS DISCIPLES
There were two times in biblical history when disciples witnessed their master going up into Heaven. And in both cases, their masters left their Mantle; their own Anointing to do even greater works than they. The first time was Elisha and the second time was the Apostles. [3]

I so deeply encourage you, above all else ... in all, with all, and through all ... seek the **manifest** Presence of God. Even as the underlying prayer of your life — *ie;* your *'soul'* pursuit. As like a sharp arrow, targeting right up upon the right hand of God. [4]

Today, this very day, your Heavenly Father is saying to you, *"You **are** my son, today I have **become** your Father. **Ask** me, and I will make the nations your inheritance, the ends of the earth your possession"* [5]. And in the same way, Jesus is saying to you this day, *"Stay in the city until you have been **clothed** with Power from on High."* [6]

There is the 'Invitation' of the Lord that as — one — in Christ Jesus you can '**ask**' ... so ask. Ask, seek, and knock [7]. Come, wait upon the Lord ... and go after. Pursue and ask and go after. For truly, there are things most important to learn and be equipped in; and come into greater understanding and living awareness. And also, there are things within your own character and fortitude that need shifting. This is why humility is of such importance. For so are you teachable and so are you made sensitive unto the Holy Spirit's quiet still voice. [8]

The primary reason why God sent His Son upon the Cross, is to restore you back into the Place where Adam fell. With outstretched hands and deep love in His eyes; that you truly might respond as one being *re*-seated in your Destiny. Re-seated in Dominion ... re-seated in the Glory of God. This, for the sake of your own wellbeing, for the sake of your loved ones and 'neighbours', and for the sake of the world [9]. The Spirit cries and yearns for you, but in truth ... so very few are listening. [10]

In 'carnal' contemplations, the believer has been accustomed to listening to Satan's vision for the human race. When it is otherwise the Christ, who has yearned for you to **lay attentive** ... even clean out your ears; and in the midst of all the noise, '**Listen intently** to what God is saying to the Churches' [11]. For you have both the testimony of the Blood and the Word; you have the Spirit and the Calling; and you have your Destiny in the Father speaking in 'Prayer' for you this very day.

Second 'Birthing Revival' Scripture:
There shall come forth a Rod from the stem of Jesse, and a Branch shall grow out of his roots. The Spirit of the Lord shall rest upon Him, The Spirit of wisdom and understanding, The Spirit of counsel and might, The Spirit of knowledge and of the fear of the Lord.
His delight is in the fear of the Lord, and He shall not judge by the sight of His eyes, Nor decide by the hearing of His ears; But with righteousness, He shall judge the poor, and decide with equity for the meek of the earth; He shall strike the earth with the rod of His mouth, and with the breath of His lips He shall slay the wicked.

Righteousness shall be the belt of His loins, and faithfulness the belt of His waist.
The wolf also shall dwell with the lamb, The leopard shall lie down with the young goat, The calf and the young lion and the fatling together; and a little child shall lead them. The cow and the bear shall graze; Their young ones shall lie down together; and the lion shall eat straw like the ox. The nursing child shall play by the cobra's hole, and the weaned child [Mark 16:17-19] shall put his hand in the viper's den. They shall not hurt nor destroy in all My holy mountain, For the earth shall be full of the knowledge of the Lord As the waters cover the sea. *(Isaiah 11:1-9 NKJV)*

In the Old Testament, Jesus was referred to as the Branch [12]. However now, in the New Testament, we all are called the 'branch'. A branch of whom draws out of the very Spirit of God just as the Son. Today, Jesus is referred to as the Vine. Hence, therefore, out of the Vine we all are *equally* destined to bear forth the Divine reality of the Spirit … just as Jesus.

Jesus is the Vine and we — as the 'branches' — are in Him. Jesus is the Victorious King, and through the Power of the Blood are we joined *united* in Him. Ordained equally and individually as 'priests' and 'kings' to rule … *ie;* **walk in the Victory of the Son** [13]. And we also are called and ordained in Christ Jesus, under an entirely different priestly order. As is said, *"You are a Priest forever, in the order of Melchizedek."* [14]

Third 'Birthing Revival' Scripture:
The Lord says to my lord: "Sit at my right hand until I make your enemies a footstool for your feet." The Lord will extend your mighty scepter from Zion, saying, "Rule in the midst of your enemies!"
Your troops [kings and priests] will be willing on your day of battle. Arrayed in **holy splendor** [Glory and Fire], your young men will come to you like dew from the **morning's womb** [powerful workers clothed of the Morning Star]. The Lord has sworn and will not change his mind: "You are a Priest forever, in the order of **Melchizedek**." *(Psalm 110:1-4 NIV)*

The Inheritance is yours … **this Promise**. But it's up to each one of us personally — to respond and enter in — through a heart of submission. For in order for us to walk in Authority, we all need to come *under* the Authority of God [15]. Your 'Guardian' is the Holy Spirit; [16] He is your Counsellor, your Tutor, and your very Covering. But so too is He … of whom rides upon your words. [17]

A side note: There are many voices; but it is the Spirit's Voice you want to harken to. There are the opinions of others, there are leaders and elders … but then there is the Christ. You are called to have one Master and one Father; hence by the Spirit of God so shall you be raised in Glory.

The '**sap**' of Life is in you. However, it doesn't just stop there; Life and Spirit comes out of your life *producing* Life … that Spirit and Life might freely flow. You are a Portal of the Living God. You are a Gateway of Heaven whereby the Spirit moves. The Keys are in your hands for this very purpose: that you yourself might turn.

Jesus is the Vine, and we are the branches. Meaning, the very same Spirit of the Lord that was in Jesus … is **now in you**. Hence, in choosing to 'remain' in the Vine — and it is a choice — the Spirit of the Lord shall actively flow through you just as in Jesus. What this means is, the same Authority of the Son is now in us to make 'judgements' [18]. Judgements to release the Glory and Healing of God on behalf of the broken and the lost.

As instructed and demonstrated in the Person of Jesus [19] — as a people co-reigning with Him — we too also choose to not live by what we see with our eyes, or hear with our ears; but in righteousness, make 'judgements' on behalf of the poor. We release the Outpouring of the Spirit, we release the Revival of the Lord; the very same 'Peace of God' that causes the *"Wolf to dwell with the lamb"* and the *"Leopard to lie down with the young goat"*. So what are we talking about here? That you and I fundamentally are releasors of Revival. Releasors of the Healing, the Restoration, and the Salvation of God unto the nations.

There is also something else *hidden* here that is most special, and that is the *"Spirit of the Fear of the Lord"*. And this picture is so very dear and most precious to my heart, as is said … Jesus personally

"Delighted in the Fear of the Lord". This very same 'Fear' that is the Fire and Glory of the Lord. The same intensity, the same radiance, the same 'terror' that Moses felt as he passed through the 'dark cloud' to meet the Person of God [20]. Hence also, this has become so precious that I too delight and yearn for.

We find this also in John's vision on the Island of Patmos. When, 'on the Lord's Day' ... he was 'in the Spirit' *(in the manifest Presence of God)*, and heard the sound of a 'loud voice'. And when looking behind him, he saw the Resurrected Christ standing in His Glory. And the sight was so *awesome* and so terrifying that he fell to the ground as though dead. [21]

This same Fear of the Lord is also represented in the Shekinah Glory [22]. The same, where the priests on duty in the Temple could not stay ... but had to leave. Even the same, as the Fire that came upon the Disciple's heads in the Upper Room ... in a 'violent wind'. [23]

The Fear of the Lord is represented also in the Exodus, at the time when God spoke upon the Mountain. The very same, when the people cried out to Moses saying, *"Speak to us yourself and we will listen. But do not have God speak to us or we will die"* [24]. The sight and the sound so awesome and terrible. However, but in saying that, if the people had truly persisted ... even treasured this very Place of Glory, then they would have been as like 'gods' [25]. They would have lived as an unstoppable and incorruptible force.

The basis of faith = the hearing and seeing God. [26]

Trials and testings come for a purpose, or they are allowed in order to truly test and secure this very reality: the Presence and the Glory of God resting powerfully upon your life *(test, prove, ensure, make trustworthy)*. That neither 'sin' or the grips of 'Egypt' ... nor the *Enemy* or any lure can retain any hold over you. Even as this next Scripture describes, *"I have come to test you that you do not sin."* [27]

Scripture:
When the people saw the thunder and lightning and heard the trumpet and saw the Mountain in smoke, they **trembled with**

fear. They stayed at a distance and said to Moses, "Speak to us yourself and we will listen. But do not have God speak to us or we will die."
Moses said to the people, "Do not be afraid. God has come to test you, so that the fear of God will be with you to **keep you from sinning**."
The people remained at a distance, while Moses approached the thick darkness [**the veil**] where God was [Fire, Glory, Intensity, Fear]. *(Exodus 20:18-21 NIV)*

* To reemphasise: If you could make it within yourself — by choice — to **whole** heartedly seek after the Presence of God, then there would be no reason to be tested [28]. And when difficulties do come, then it would be God Himself who 'fights for you'. As is said, *"You do not have to pick up a weapon"* [29]. For the 'Fear' of the Lord — the very Glory of God upon you — shall actively and *aggressively* be at work against the *Thief* and the *Liar* … and against all the works of the *Enemy*.

There is an 'Intensity' in the Lord that my heart and soul longs for. An intensity and a 'Fear' that I deeply cherish as my singular root core prayer and drive. This, the very same yearning that Jesus Himself held dear and close to His own heart. Therefore, I very much encourage you in this, all **capacity to win** resides in the Presence of God — *ie;* the Jericho principle. The coming under, the coming into, the coming up into the Presence of the Most High. For *"**Fear is the beginning of Wisdom**"* [30]. It is the entrance point, the opening, the very basis to the Glory of God made manifest on earth. And another word for 'Fear' is Fire … the All-Consuming Fire of God's Holy Presence. [31]

This is also why *submission* to God is so important … *ie;* humility. For how can pride ever compare to the Radiance of God's Glory? And how can arrogance ever think to stand here and expect to survive? But so it shall be, that the Spirit of the Lord shall take you personally by hand; and as a little child … lead you personally behind the veil into the fullness of God.

The Blood has given you the right, and is itself your covering and very access. But it is only by the Spirit of the Lord who is able to take you in. It is the Spirit of God that comes and takes the willing; and sets you in a Place where man cannot go. Nor where words can explain, or the imagination of man can comprehend [32]. Taking you further and deeper in … from Glory to Glory, unto exceedingly great Glory. [33]

The Blood is the most **powerful** thing in the universe … for what it gains you access to. The Blood is in your reach to cleanse and make pure; as well as to mark the ground in protection. But it is also in your hands to gain access and give entrance. As one could never approach the intensity of the sun, so it is the same with the Glory of God. However, by the Blood and Blood alone, opens and clears the way … and the Spirit is your 'Transit Agent' that takes and leads you in.

Think of it for a moment, the right hand of God is more than a chair … or chairs. The right hand of God that the Word, the Blood, and the Spirit has called you into — is a realm. It is the Garden realms … yes, a Place of intimacy, and of receiving, and the being poured into. But it is also a Place of Glory; impossible to enter except by the Spirit of the Lord. And another wording for this is, *"Wait in the City until you have been clothed with Fire."* [34]

A side note: Recognise, that we can't walk in the Glory of God with sin still treasured in our hearts. For so it is that the more that we are risen in the Glory of God … the more the 'moths' are drawn to the Light. Hence, God works to protect you on two fronts; and to he who is trustworthy with little much is given.

> *The Word spoken,*
> *The Blood shed,*
> *The Spirit given,*
> *and the Fire and Glory*
> *of the Father outpoured.*

Scripture:
But we all, with unveiled face, **beholding** [John 17:24, Psalm 27:4] as in a mirror the glory of the Lord, are being transformed into the same image from glory to glory, just as by the Spirit of the Lord. *(2 Corinthians 3:18 NIV)*

As you come and respond, and truly begin to enter into the maturity of your sonship, so shall a Mantle come upon you [35] to make decisions [36]. And here, the very same Spirit of the Lord shall respond and ride upon the words of your mouth just as Jesus [37]. And as one who comes to 'embody' the very Person of the Christ [38], even He the very 'Word made flesh' in you, so shall your words also carry both Life and Power. And what will birth from this … Jesus Himself exampled. For in the very same way, God will clothe you in Glory and Honour; [39] even for the honour of His own Name. [40]

*"Hold on to what you have, so that **no one** will take your crown."* [41]

Another very special Scripture verse is found in Zechariah chapter three. And it speaks of how the Spirit of God will take off your dirty clothes, and that of your carnal mindsets … and **clothe you in Honour**. And if you could truly submit and truly turn your heart to harken to Him; then it would be He who would give you the right to **stand in these realms of Dominion**. With Authority *given* to 'govern' His House and have 'charge' over His Courts. As one 'standing' in realms of Authority in Heaven over all the earth. And what's more, this verse continues … and is most **very specific**: the Spirit of God states how these very things are exampled for us today, in the New Testament believer.

The fundamental outworking of your New Life in Christ Jesus is Revival. And not in ways that you necessarily understand or can be controlled. But in great Wonder … whereby all shall gasp in awe. And the nations shall 'lay down their weapons of war', the 'lamb will lay down with the lion' as the Peace of the Lord covers the land. And as the Healing comes, the *"Knowledge of God shall cover the earth as the waters cover the sea."* [42]

Forth 'Birthing Revival' Scripture:
If My people who are called by My name will humble themselves, and pray and seek My face, and turn from their wicked ways, then I will hear from heaven, and will forgive their sin and heal their land. *(2 Chronicles 7:14 NKJV)*

Oh, the beauty of humility and submission in the Holy Ghost — and what this opens to you. In many ways, as human beings, we tend to remain in the 'box' of our own Tree of Knowledge. And in standing tall in our pride — we become total blockheads; unreachable, unteachable, obstinate, and scorners of all the new things God is trying to lead us into … just like the people in the Exodus. However, if you could truly lay your life down in the Lord in all humility, then it would be Jesus Himself who would give you of the Tree of Life. Even of the Leaves that heal the nations … and the River of Life that makes you whole.

It is submission to the Lord that opens you to the Revelation and manifestation of the Lord God Almighty 'aggressively' active in your life. Or another way to say this, He will clothe you with Glory … even the Glory of His very own Countenance.

As believers, we are called to action, as the people of God we are called … for we hold the very 'Keys' to manifestation. The world doesn't need more opinions or voices, what the people need is God manifest in our midst. We need God's Presence, we need God's Grace, and we need God Healing the nations. And we all need God to continue what He has started; to be free to liberally work in the Restoring us back into the fullness of Himself. For truly the very earth groans in tribulation, waiting for us … waiting for the 'sons of God' to be revealed. [43]

Jesus is fundamentally about **manifestation**. He is not about talk alone, but open Moves of God's Power [44]. Therefore if, as a people, you could truly humble yourself — not temporarily like reed in the wind [45], but as a lifestyle — then as a people we would initiate the 'Healing of God' upon the land. Both you and I in ourselves, we would initiate Revival.

The very Keys of Heaven have been given each believer, unto each of us … with the purpose to operate just as Jesus. Hence, in truly humbling yourself and truly seeking the Lord, so shall you release.

Fasting has become an incredible gift to me. The capacity to willingly humble myself before the Lord. The laying down of my life ... in what I know and understand. And in a 'physical' form of prayer ... earnestly seek the Face of God.

Oh, the wonder that this has opened to me is indescribable. My heart — in all earnestness for God to speak — and His Dreams to be fulfilled. And I know that the outflowing of such a lifestyle births Revival in me personally. But it also triggers something much further, something **far beyond me** ... the reality of God at work in the land.

A side note: It's most important to realise, that this bowing before the Lord is not just a momentary thing. It's not just a 'Let's give it a try'. It is a serious devotion with a serious motive to seek the Lord, ie; 'death' to find Life. Scripture speaks of the people 'Bowing like a reed in the wind' [45]*. It is not enough! Make God* — *'God' in your life* — *and it will be He who breaks forth.*

Because of you, because of me ... because of we as a people; [46] it is God who 'rends the heavens' and steps down and does crazy and wonderful things. This for our own personal blessing, and to the blessing of our loved ones; but also, God stepping through us unto the blessing of the nations. Truly, it is unfathomable to think, but to us who 'wait upon the Lord' ... we *unconsciously* release unstoppable moves of the Spirit.

Fifth 'Birthing Revival' Scripture:
Oh, that You would rend the heavens! That You would come down! That the mountains might shake at Your **presence**— as fire burns brushwood, as fire causes water to boil— To make Your name **known to Your adversaries**, that the nations may tremble at Your presence! When You did awesome things for which we did not look, You came down, The mountains shook at Your presence. For since the beginning of the world men have not heard nor perceived by the ear, nor has the eye seen any God besides You, **who acts for the one who waits for Him.** *(Isaiah 64:1-4 NKJV)*

To him who waits. To he who honours. To the one who seeks the manifest Presence of God — alive — active — and real. To such as these, God 'rends' the heavens *(ie; all spiritual opposition, strongholds, or attacks)*. And for he who seeks to meet with God — to he who sits with Him; to walk with Him and learn from Him; to such as these, God tears away the obstructions. He moves the demon hordes of opposition and pours out the manifestation of His Person. And as He comes — He stands in your midst — and His Holiness consumes the hearts and thoughts of man.

If you can for a moment picture the *structure* of the 'heavens'. There is the earth ... that is referred to as the *1st* **heaven**. Then the realms of the demon, that is referred to as the *2nd* **heaven**. And then there is the *3rd* **heaven**, of which is God's own dwelling place. Therefore, as seen here, between you and the manifestation of God, has **always** been the *Thief*. The very same, of whom came in the Beginning — the 'cunning' one [47] — the one whose word by nature deceives and lies *(the fog of the demonic, the hindrance, the atmosphere over)*. He who seeks always to **stand in place** of God; your Destiny, and your Divine right in Him. He always works to stand between you and — all the Promises of God — **so move him**! Forbid him to speak, and place your heel firmly on his head; have nothing to do with him ... for he is *beneath* you.

Through the Blood, you have stepped over into the *realms* of your Salvation. You have — stepped over — the 'powers of the air' into the ruling realms of the King. But still, the demon always tries to stand between.

As a snake he has occupied your Promises, and that of the people, since the Fall. Hence this is why we 'pray' the Blood; for it is the Blood that is the most powerful thing in the universe. For it strips away the power of the demon making him null and void. And it releases the Spirit of God of whom heals and restores and establishes Life [48]. The Blood itself piercing through any opposition unto the Throne room of God.

Sixth 'Birthing Revival' Scripture:
How lovely is your dwelling place, Lord Almighty! **My soul yearns**, even faints, for the Courts of the Lord; my heart and my flesh cry out for the living God. Even the sparrow has **found a home**, and the swallow a nest for herself, where she may have her young—a place near your Altar, Lord Almighty, my King and my

God. Blessed are those who **Dwell in your house**; they are ever praising you.

Blessed are those whose strength is in you, whose hearts are set on pilgrimage. As they pass through the Valley of Baka, they **make it a place of springs**; the autumn rains [Latter Day Rains] also cover it with pools. They go from **strength to strength**, till each appears before God in Zion. *(Psalm 84:1-7 NIV)*

This Scripture is a personal favourite; for in its wording, it expresses so much of the way God has been actively at work in my life these past years. And in the same manner, its language openly speaking of Revival and God Outpouring.

Let's open this Scripture up further: Right in the midst of difficult and barren places; as you personally choose to love and seek the Presence of God ... do you find 'water'. Clear and refreshing water for your soul and personal wellbeing. But however, not only do you find moisture and water ... but God, in His own delight, in *response* to your heart seeking; pours out the 'Autumn Rains'.

Another word for Autumn Rains is 'Latter Day Rain'. The liberal pouring out and the free flowing of the Spirit ... in these that are the Last Days. Hence, as you also continue, as you also diligently pursue and go after the Presence of God alive and active in your life. As you continue to seek His Face regardless of circumstances, or various seasons that you might find yourself in ... you initiate and trigger something. Without realising, you trigger Moves of the Spirit of God.

Now healing is simply the removal of the demon, and Life springing forth where death once was. This is the basis of Revival ... this is the basis of faith; the clearing of the 'cloud' of the demonic and in its place Salvation flowing. The preference for Presence over problems. The preference for the manifest Presence over blockages or difficulties that may be before you — and God aggressively responding. Responding, not only with a heart to heal, but **a heart to restore**. Or in these words of Revival; touching you ... and subsequently touching the nations.

So now, as you continue seeking the Presence of God; from here, in the Presence of God [49] ... full of the Joy of the Lord, still 'digging'. This water that you have found only continues to rise. Rising up like a 'spring' that never ceases. A spring of perpetual Water from the River of God ever increasing and ever flowing ... just as Promised you of the Lord. [50]

But it doesn't stop here, for in God's own personal delight towards you personally. Seeing you — in your own personal delight towards Him — He opens up Heaven and pours out the Rain. Uncontainable, unstoppable, unceasing Rain: great Moves and Touches of God in your own personal life; Encounters and Visitations, and the being continuously captured up in Him. And in this wondrous realm of Perpetual Interaction ... you, as a person begin to be replaced by the Person of God. As is said, *"I am in Him and He is in me"*, or in another place, *"I and the Father are one."* [51]

God wipes away our tears as we enter into these most precious things. And because of you, God Himself wipes away the tears of the generations.

IN CLOSING

Revivals trigger 'Engagements' in God. Moves of the Spirit; deep Touches and Experiences in the Person of God that are life changing [52]. And it is to these very things that open up a person to an Everlasting Vision; even to such of your sonship and rich Place in Him. Here far Above all this life presents and all that comes against — all strongholds and powers of this world. Therefore, so it is true that faith statements alone are not ever enough; but life in Living Experience of the Living God just as the Son.

zzzzzz

This Door has been opened; however, spirits of Religion and Legalism work to obscure and hide the Door from your eyes [53]. Just as there are many trees in the forest; there is just one that you **need** ... and that is the Tree of Life. So today, even here and right now, give your life afresh unto the Lord, ie; *"Be still ... and know God"*. For your focus is no longer purposed unto the sin of which you have come from ... but **the Returning**. Do you yet see that? The returning back into the fullness of God of which the Blood has bought. Stepping through the Door unto the Pastures beyond. Not unto a life of self-righteous perfection; but entering here into your rightful Place Above: in Dominion over all things, that you might truly bring Life to the world.

So be refreshed, Scripture is calling you today to **choose Life** [54] — so choose Life. Just as the Lord is saying to you today, *"I have swept away your offences like the morning mist. Return to me, for I have redeemed you."* [55]

So, when there are worries and concerns, submit them to God and release the Spirit. Like training in Swordsmanship: submit your fears and struggles and 'thrust out' the Spirit of God. Like in a dance of movement — *'in the Spirit'* — exercise your faith and breathe out Life [56]. For truly, as you set your heart 'first' unto the seeking of the Kingdom of God, so do you also open yourself to the — 'all things being taken care of'. [57]

In Christ, you are no longer weak but Powerful in God. Though you may have come out of great brokenness and pain ... you are no longer alone. You are more than a man, you are more than flesh and blood, but sons and daughters of the Kingdom. Hence here — are you Purposed in God — whereby nothing shall triumph over you.

Come then, and diligently lay hold of that of which Christ Jesus has already laid hold of for you. Even the Promises and the Resurrected Power of the Son dynamically alive and active in your life [58]. For these realities — all of them today — **are your birthright**!

Treasure the Lord and seek Him alone: the Word, the Spirit, and the Fire. Meditate upon Him and draw Him close. And call things as they should be; not how you yet see them now, but what you want. If it is sickness — speak Life! If it is brokenness or financial hardship — speak the very Spirit of God. And if in a spirit of heaviness or despair — speak the Glory and Aggression of God. And it will be the Radiance of the Lord that shall go out before you clearing the atmosphere and setting the Spirit to move

Speak to the very earth, *"Yield your increase!"* Speak to your body, *"Be whole!"* Speak to your bank account, *"Multiply!"* ... *in Jesus*

Name. Don't wait*!* For it is God who has placed in *your* hands the very Keys of Heaven [59]. Not that you are purposed to worry, but that you turn and release the very Kingdom of Heaven to action.

Belief is not enough! ... but become.

At one time man was fallen, but now are you *re*-Risen in Christ Jesus [60]. In God's eyes, He considers His people ... as 'gods' [61]. Therefore, shift and be no longer one who walks in the mindset of 'mere' men. But a people who rises up in the Power of the Holy Ghost.

Your own personal Experiences in the Person of God, regardless of 'size' ... are most Powerful [62]. Faith rooted in the *"Word that proceeds out of the mouth of God"* [63]. As one coming ever into deeper personal knowledge of His Goodness; because you meet with Him continuously. Even right in the midst of struggles that come. [64]

But also, because you see change; and are 'trained' and raised in them — and by them. Just like King David, who from his youth *knew* God [65]. It was God who established him firmly upon the throne. And though he was anointed king as a young man, it was only through the 'Guardianship' of the Presence of God at work in his life ... that he was seated.

To finish then, the word 'Revival' fundamentally means: the demon removed from your finances, your health, and your heart. And in place of the *Thief* ... the Life of the Spirit made active. This in your family life, your town, and your nation. The demon removed by the Hand of God; and in place of him, the Life and Salvation of the Lord poured out.

The singular greatest thing lost man at the Fall was the Glory of God. And the greatest thing lost God ... was man in His Glory.

* The word 'Kingship' means, in a Heavenly sense, your *pre-fall* Adamic Dominion. The word 'Sonship' is your fundamental *rebirth* back as Adam restored. The word 'Promise' means, that *all* is yours; God Himself being your very **Inheritance**.

* The word 'Ask' is a pursuit, an interest in *receiving* from God. The word 'Manifesting Sonship' is, the coming out of immature fallen thinking, into the Mind of Jesus, *ie;* the Word **made flesh** in you and walking amongst us.

* The word 'Authority' means, the ability 'author'; to *rewrite* or *initiate* your destiny and that of others, *ie;* initiate moves of the Spirit. And the word 'Resurrected' means, not of the old but of the *Risen*. The being with Him where He is now … **Risen and Resurrected** as you still walk this earth.

Truly, the vision we have of what our Salvation really means is so very small compared to God's vision. And our vision of what God thinks our sonship is — is so much less than His. And in the same way, our vision of what 'Revival' means, is so far short in both imagination and comprehension.

Much in life we have only been asking God for *trinkets*. When it is God Himself who is offering you the whole world … and Heaven itself. And much in our prayer life has been obsessed over what we are fearful of or are wanting. But if you could truly come to respond to God's Dream, then you would have the Joy of His Dreams fulfilled in you … as well as all you ever hoped for.

God seeks that you might 'be seated' — that is His Dream. The restoring you back in the realms He dwells. Authority does not come just because you believe in Jesus, but in *responding* to where Jesus' own life points. The Authority of God comes by — joining — with His Dream. And it is though humility that you come to possess, as is said, *"The meek **shall** inherit the world."*

Sometimes, what we are *asking* for … can be so much greater, and so much more important in our eyes; than what the Dreams are, that the Father has for us. Hence, when it comes to Authority — fundamentally, there is a misalignment. For when you pray, are you praying from afar — or are you praying from in Him?

But, if you were to truly lay down your life, then so too would you pass through … entering deeply into His Rest. And now, when looking back at problems; then you are doing so from a totally different realm. Praying from within Him, in the very Heart and Authority of God; Above in Heaven, and Above all the earth. Over all powers and authorities, and over all natural laws and realities. For it has always been God's Dream — first and foremost— that you come to live and walk in 'Likeness' of the Son.

I pray that you have been blessed by the thoughts expressed in this book. This, the incredible opportunity of living in a state of 'Perpetual Encounter' ... just as did Jesus. And the powerful outworkings of such a lifestyle. Even how this opens and sets the stage ... preparing the ground for the Revival of God upon the nations. The Outpouring of the Latter Day Rains in preparation for the Christ's Return. A bountiful harvest in these that are the Last Days. Even the Church of the Lord Jesus Christ presented Pure as a Spotless Bride for Him to receive.

Bless you, in Jesus Name ...

Closing Scripture:
But you have come to Mount Zion and to the city of the living God, the heavenly Jerusalem, to an innumerable company of angels, to the general assembly and church of the firstborn who are registered in Heaven, to God the Judge of all, to the spirits of just men made perfect, to Jesus the Mediator of the new covenant, and to the Blood of sprinkling that speaks **better** things than that of Abel. *(Hebrews 12:22)*

A COLLECTION OF 'BIRTHING REVIVAL' SCRIPTURES
*Isaiah 2:1-4, Isaiah 11:1-9, Isaiah 40:1-5,
Isaiah 41:14-18, Isaiah 61:1-4, Isaiah 64:1-4,
Psalm 110:1-4, Psalm 84:1-7,
Acts 2:1-4, Colossians 3:1-4,
Revelation 4:1-5*

Appendix:

1. Luke 3:16, 4:14, 12:49, 24:49, Acts 1:8, 2:3, Isaiah 64:1-4, Exodus 33:15-17, ***2.*** John 14:12, 16:7, 2 Kings 2:14, Psalm 110:2, 2:6-9, Revelation 2:26-27, 19:15, Genesis 1:26, ***3.*** 2 Kings 2:11, Acts 1:9, ***4.*** Psalm 110:1-2, 27:4, Colossians 3:2-3, *(2 Kings 13:18-19)*, ***5.*** Psalm 2:7-8, ***6.*** Luke 24:49, Exodus 33:15-16, ***7.*** Matthew 7:7, ***8.*** 1 Kings 19:12, ***9.*** Romans 8:19, ***10.*** Revelation 1-3, ***11.*** James 1:25, Revelation 2:29, ***12.*** Isaiah 11:1-2, ***13.*** Revelation 1:5-6, 5:9-10 *NKJV*, ***14.*** Psalm 110:1-4, ***15.*** Matthew 8:5-13, ***16.*** Galatians 4:2, ***17.*** Zechariah 3:7, John 6:63, ***18.*** Isaiah 11:3, ***19.*** Isaiah 11:2, ***20.*** Exodus 20:21, ***21.*** Revelation 1:10, 17, ***22.*** Exodus 40:34, 2 Chronicles 5:14, ***23.*** Acts 2:2-4, ***24.*** Exodus 20:19, ***25.*** Psalm 82:6-8, ***26.*** *Matthew 17:20, 4:4, John 5:19, 5:44, Romans 10:17 KJV*, ***27.*** Exodus 20:20, ***28.*** Deuteronomy 8:3, ***29.*** Joshua 24:12, 1:5, Exodus 14:14, 33:14, ***30.*** Proverbs 9:10, ***31.*** Isaiah 33:14b-15a *HCSB*, ***32.*** Zechariah 3:7, 1 Corinthians 2:9-10, ***33.*** Philippians 3:12, 2 Corinthians 3:18, ***34.*** Luke 24:49, ***35.*** Acts 2:3, Revelation 3:11, ***36.*** Isaiah 11:4, ***37.*** John 6:63, ***38.*** John 1:14, ***39.*** John 5:44, ***40.*** Acts 5:15, ***41.*** Revelation 3:11, ***42.*** Isaiah 11:1-9, ***43.*** Romans 8:19, ***44.*** 1 Corinthians 4:20, ***45.*** Isaiah 58:5, ***46.*** Revelation 5:10 *NKJV*, ***47.*** Genesis 3:1, ***48.*** Luke 5:17, Matthew 12:28, ***49.*** Revelation 1:10, 4:1, ***50.*** John 4:14, Isaiah 58:8, 40:31, ***51.*** John 14:20, 10:30, 17:23, ***52.*** Matthew 16:17, ***53.*** Matthew 23:13, Luke 11:52, ***54.*** Deuteronomy 30:19, ***55.*** Isaiah 44:22, ***56.*** John 20:22, ***57.*** 2 Kings 2:14, Matthew 6:33, ***58.*** Philippians 3:12, 8, ***59.*** Matthew 16:19, John 16:23, ***60.*** 1 Corinthians 15:45, 55, ***61.*** Exodus 14:14, Joshua 1:5, 24:12, Isaiah 28:12, Psalm 82:6-8, Mark 16:17-18, John 10:34-36, ***62.*** Matthew 17:20, ***63.*** Matthew 4:4, 16:17, Romans 10:17, ***64.*** Psalm 23:5, ***65.*** 1 Samuel 17:34-36

Dated: 26/11/22

*"In these that are the Last Days, there will be those who come into the **Knowledge** of their sonship. And cease the groans and sufferings in the world."*

Romans 8:19

*"It only takes one who **knows** who they are in God ... to change the world."*

"Faith is never
a matter
of size,
but *is* a matter
of how big
God is
in your eyes".

www.ingramcontent.com/pod-product-compliance
Lightning Source LLC
Chambersburg PA
CBHW031358290426
44110CB00011B/201